中山大学资讯管理丛书
中山大学资讯管理学院35周年院庆纪念特辑

资讯管理研究文集

本书编委会◆编

中山大學出版社
SUN YAT-SEN UNIVERSITY PRESS
·广州·

图书在版编目（CIP）数据

资讯管理研究文集：汉、英/本书编委会编. —广州：中山大学出版社，2015.11
ISBN 978-7-306-05508-8

Ⅰ.①资… Ⅱ.①本… Ⅲ.①信息管理—文集—汉、英 Ⅳ.①G203-53

中国版本图书馆CIP数据核字（2015）第258918号

出版人：徐　劲
策划编辑：李海东
责任编辑：李海东
封面设计：曾　斌
责任校对：何　凡
责任技编：黄少伟
出版发行：中山大学出版社
电　　话：编辑部 020-84111996，84113349，84111997，84110779
　　　　　发行部 020-84111998，84111981，84111160
地　　址：广州市新港西路135号
邮　　编：510275　　传真：020-84036565
网　　址：http://www.zsup.com.cn　E-mail：zdcbs@mail.sysu.edu.cn
印 刷 者：佛山市浩文彩色印刷有限公司
规　　格：787mm×1092mm　1/16　30印张　760千字
版次印次：2015年11月第1版　2015年11月第1次印刷
定　　价：100.00元

总　序

从1980年到2015年，这三十五年，在历史长河中只是弹指一瞬。然而，这三十五年，对中山大学资讯管理学院来说，是从诞生到壮大的三十五年；这三十五年，对图书情报与档案管理学科来说，是发展变化最快的三十五年。

三十五年来，我们从图书馆学专修科、图书馆学系、图书情报学系到信息管理系、资讯管理系、资讯管理学院，从单一的图书馆学到图书馆学、情报学、档案学、信息管理与信息系统、保密管理等多学科融合发展，从专科生培养到本科生、硕士生、博士生完整的人才培养层次，伴随着国家的长治久安、经济的高速增长，赶上了高等教育的空前繁荣，顺应了学科发展的内在要求。我们以学科建设为龙头，以人才培养为根本，依靠全体师生的努力，借助国内外同行的支持，在不断探索中进步，在持续变革中壮大。

三十五年来，如果要问哪些学科面临的环境变化最剧烈，图书情报与档案管理学科肯定是其中之一。从信息爆炸、信息技术革命，到信息化、网络化、数字化，从互联网到移动互联网、物联网，从数字地球到智慧城市，从电子商务、电子政务到互联网+，从云计算到大数据，导致了信息的无处不在和多元异构、信息需求的广泛多样、信息资源的价值凸显、资讯管理的泛化复杂。这些对图书情报与档案管理学科提出了崭新的要求，包括我院师生在内的图书情报与档案管理学人展开了积极的回应，图书情报与档案管理学科发生了全面和深刻的变化。同时，如果要说将传统与现代兼顾得最好、将人文与技术融合得最佳的学科，图书情报与档案管理学科也会是其中之一。这些特点既体现在图书情报与档案管理学科的研究领域、研究方法和研究成果中，也体现在图书情报与档案管理学科的人才培养目标和教学内容之中。

为了鞭策我们自己，为了向同道汇报，我们在几年之前就开始编辑出版“中山大学资讯管理丛书”。值三十五周年院庆之际，学院决定继续编辑出版这套丛书，既是院庆献礼，更为就教于同仁。

陈定权教授、张靖副院长承担了本文集的文稿征集和编辑工作。博士生苏日娜，硕士生黄梦琪、赵越、龚萍萍等人参与了文集的排版和校对。在此一并表示感谢。

中山大学资讯管理学院院长　曹树金

二〇一五年十月

目　录

权利的觉醒与庶民的胜利——图书馆权利思潮十年回顾与展望 ……………… 程焕文（1）
图书馆数字化服务发展的新趋势 ……………………………………… 黄晓斌（22）
The Propagation of the Library Rights Ideology in Mainland China: A Case Study
…………………………………………………………………… Yantao Pan（30）
图书馆在关联数据运动中的角色解析 ……………………………… 陈定权　卢玉红（49）
An Empirical Study of Everyday Life Information Seeking Behavior of Urban Low-Income Residents in the Haizhu District of Guangzhou ………… Yongying Xiao, Lanman He（58）
广东省图书馆权利状况调查 …………………… 张　靖　苏日娜　何靖怡　梁丹妮（74）
采用因子分析法构建数字资源选择标准体系的研究 ………………………… 唐　琼（92）
岭南大学图书馆中文善本书研究 ………………………………………… 周　旖（105）
大型文献数字化项目元数据互操作的调查与启示 ………………… 宋琳琳　李海涛（125）

我国图书情报领域研究者对网络信息资源的利用分析 …………… 曹树金　李洁娜（139）
Non-Topical Attributes of Academic Papers and Implications to Information Retrieval
…………………………………………………………………… Yongli Zou（158）
基于复杂网络演化模型的三元闭环合著网络研究 ………………… 张　洋　麦江萌（175）
多因素影响的特征选择方法 ………………………………………… 路永和　李焰锋（195）
客户信息保护认知模型构建及保护措施探讨 ……………………………… 马芝蓓（206）
Textual Characteristics Based High Quality Online Reviews Evaluation and Detection
…………………………………………………………………… Hui Nie（214）
低被引期刊论文学术价值的评价方法研究 ………………………… 杨利军　万小渝（227）
基于多种测度的术语相似度集成计算研究 ……………………………… 徐　健（239）
开放数据驱动城市创新——以 Smart Disclosure 为例 ……………… 武　琳　伍诗瑜（256）
基于 AHP 的社区空间犯罪热点预测研究 ………………………………… 曹效阳（265）
网络舆情视角下中国政府形象评价指标体系之构建 …… 郑　重　张　星　聂　冰（276）
现代信息服务业区域发展模式的识别与优化 ………………………… 丁玲华　张倩男（284）
学术虚拟社区用户持续知识共享的意愿研究 ……………………………… 陈明红（293）

Additive Noise Detection and Its Application to Audio Forensics …………… Rui Yang（307）
学术博客的概念、类型与功能 ……………………………………… 甘春梅　王伟军（319）
Adaptation of Cultural Norms after Merger and Acquisition Based on Heterogeneous Agent-Based Relative-Agreement Model ……… Hou Zhu，Bin Hu，Jiang Wu，Xiaolin Hu（327）

政府信息资源趋利性整合共享及其应对策略 ……………………… 陈永生　聂二辉（351）
档案保护信息整合的认识与实践 ………………………… 黄广琴　瞿楠香　颜川梅（359）
论个人信息的非技术性保护 ……………………………………… 张锡田　范晓蔚（366）
论《汉书》载文述史的史纂范式 ……………………………………………… 陈　方（374）
民生档案远程协同服务机制研究——以上海市为例 ……………… 聂勇浩　郭煜晗（380）
工程项目电子文件接收规范研究 ……………… 李海涛　宋琳琳　高　晶　赖莉蓉（392）

中美 LIS 学院课程设置比较研究 ………………………… 韦景竹　何燕华　刘颉颃（405）
构建高校"程序设计基础"微课程的探索 …………………………………… 王乐球（416）
椭圆曲线离散对数的不动点 ……………………………………… 杜育松　张方国（424）
Differential Evolution With Two-Level Parameter Adaptation ……… Weijie Yu，Meie Shen，Weineng Chen，Zhihui Zhan，Yuejiao Gong，Ying Lin，Ou Liu，Jun Zhang（434）

教师简介：

程焕文，男，武汉大学文学学士、管理学硕士，中山大学历史学博士。1986 年起任教于中山大学。现任中山大学资讯管理学院教授（二级、图书馆学专业博士生导师、（历史系）历史文献学专业博士生导师），校长助理（2015 年至今）、图书馆馆长（1998 年至今），图书馆与资讯科学研究所所长。历任中山大学信息管理系副主任（1994—1996 年）、信息管理系主任（1996—1998 年，第二任系主任）、信息科学与技术学院副院长（1997—1999 年）、网络教育学院院长（2000—2003 年）、信息与网络中心主任（2003—2005 年）、资讯管理系主任（2005—2007 年）、传播与设计学院院长（2007—2010 年）、总务处处长（2011—2012 年）、校长助理（2011—2012 年）。主讲“图书馆学基础”、“信息资源共享”、“图书与图书馆史”等本科生课程，“图书馆学专题研究”、“图书馆学原理”、“图书情报基础与研究方法”等研究生课程。研究方向包括信息资源管理、图书和图书馆史、图书馆学史、图书馆权利与道德、图书馆学基础理论、历史文献学、目录学。出版学术专著20 余部，专业学术丛书 3 种，大型学术丛书 4 种；在国内外学术刊物及学术会议上发表学术论文 200 余篇；获得各级教学和科研奖励 30 余项。美国加州大学洛杉矶分校、美国伊利诺大学、美国哈佛大学哈佛燕京图书馆和哈佛燕京学社访问学者。兼任国务院学位委员会全国图书情报专业学位研究生教育指导委员会委员，教育部高等学校图书馆学学科教学指导委员会副主任委员，教育部高等学校图书情报工作指导委员会副主任委员，广东省高等学校图书情报工作委员会主任委员，中国图书馆学会副理事长，广东图书馆学会名誉理事长。兼任《中山大学学报》（人文社会科学版）、《中国图书馆学报》、《大学图书馆学报》、《图书情报工作》、《图书馆杂志》、《图书情报知识》、《图书馆建设》、美国 *Library Quarterly*、英国 *Library Management*（中国版）、美国 *Preservation*，*Digital Technology & Culture* 等 10 余种专业学术期刊编委。联系方式：huanwen@ mail. sysu. edu. cn。

所选论文《权利的觉醒与庶民的胜利——图书馆权利思潮十年回顾与展望》原载于《图书馆建设》2015 年第 1 期

权利的觉醒与庶民的胜利

——图书馆权利思潮十年回顾与展望[①]

程焕文

摘　要：论文分图书馆权利思潮的酝酿（2003—2004 年）、图书馆权利思潮的兴起（2005—2007 年）、

① 本论文系国家社会科学基金重点研究项目“中国图书馆学史专题研究：中国现当代图书馆学史研究”（项目编号：13AZD066）的研究成果之一。

图书馆权利思潮的高涨（2008—2010 年）和图书馆权利思潮的盛行（2011—2014 年）四个阶段，梳理新世纪以来以平等权利和自由权利为中心的图书馆权利思潮在中国的发展变化，认为图书馆权利的研究方兴未艾，图书馆权利的实践困难重重，图书馆权利的传播任重道远。
关键词：图书馆权利；平等权利；自由权利；公共图书馆；核心价值观

Ten Year Progress and Prospect of the Ideological Trend of the Library Rights in China in the 21st Century

Huanwen Cheng

Abstract: This article describes the progress of the ideological trend of the library rights—the rights of equal access to public library and freedom of information—in China in the 21st century, which include the brewing phrase (2003-2004), the rising phrase (2005-2007), the upsurge phrase (2008-2010), and the prevai-ling phrase (2011-2014), and concludes that it is essential to promote the study, dissemination and practice of the library rights in China in the future.
Keywords: Library rights; Equal access; Information freedom; Public library; Core values

当历史迈入 21 世纪的门槛后，遮天蔽日的数字化丛林掩盖着中国图书馆学研究的园地，无远弗届的网络化海洋淹没了中国图书馆学研究的根基。图书馆权利犹如茂密森林中的星星之火迅速燎燃，焚化中国图书馆发展的“整体非理性”；恰似浩瀚海洋中的明亮灯塔闪现在天际线，指引中国图书馆学思想航船的前进方向。以 2005 年图书馆学界率先发出“走向权利时代”的呐喊为时间节点，图书馆权利的理论研究与实践探索已经迈过了十年。十年弹指一挥间，中国的图书馆理念与实践悄然发生了脱胎换骨的根本性转变，进入了一个崭新的图书馆权利时代。这十年是图书馆权利思潮兴起发展的十年，更是中国图书馆价值观更新重建和公共图书馆前所未有繁荣发展的十年。

梁启超曾精辟地论道：“今之恒言，曰‘时代思潮’。此其语最妙于形容。凡文化发展之国，其国民于一时期中，因环境之变迁，与夫心理之感召，不期而思想之进路，同趋于一方向，于是相与呼应汹涌，如潮然。始焉其势甚微，几莫之觉；寖假而涨——涨——涨，而达于满度；过时焉则落，以渐至于衰熄。凡‘思’非皆能成‘潮’，能成‘潮’者，则其‘思’必有相当之价值，而又适合于其时代之要求者也。凡‘时代’非皆有‘思潮’；有思潮之时代，必文化昂进之时代也。”又言：“凡时代思潮，无不由‘继续的群众运动’而成。所谓运动者，非必有意识、有计划、有组织，不能分为谁主动、谁被动。其参加运动之人员，每各不相谋，各不相知。其从事运动时所任之职役，各各不同，所采之手段亦互异。于同一运动之下，往往分无数小支派，甚且相嫉视相排击。虽然，其中必有一种或数种之共通观念焉，同根据之为思想之出发点。此种观念之势力，初时本甚微弱，愈运动则愈扩大，久之则成为一种权威。此观念者，在其时代中，俨然现‘宗教之色彩’。一部分人，以宣传捍卫为己任，常以极纯洁之牺牲的精神赴之。及其权威渐立，则在社会上成为一种共公之好尚。忘其所以然，而共以此为嗜，若此者，今之译语，谓之‘流行’；古之成语，则曰‘风气’。风气者，一时的信仰也，人鲜敢婴之，亦不乐婴之，其性质几比宗教矣。一思潮播为风气，则其成熟之时也。”[1]

近十年的图书馆权利思潮正是梁启超所言的真实写照，已在中国图书馆界呈现“宗教之色彩”，成为一种价值观、一种权威和一种信仰；在全社会“播为风气”，广为流行，成为一种“共公之好尚”。

1　图书馆权利思潮的酝酿（2003—2004 年）

进入新世纪以后，在数字化与网络化的迷雾中，多种学术因素开始集聚，悄然发酵，酝酿中国图书馆学研究方向的重大转变。

1.1　中国图书馆学会发起“百年图书馆精神”研究

2003 年 11 月 17 日，中国图书馆学会发布以“回顾与展望——中国图书馆事业百年”为主题的《中国图书馆学会 2004 年年会征文通知》，将“百年图书馆精神”列为首要研讨的主题。[2]

2004 年 7 月，中国图书馆学会 2004 年年会暨学会成立 25 周年纪念大会论文集《中国图书馆事业百年》正式出版，其中将“百年图书馆精神”列为首要标题，收录了 7 篇相关学术论文。[3]中国图书馆学会主编的《中国图书馆百年系列丛书》之《百年大势——历久弥新》、《百年情怀——天堂，图书馆的模样》、《百年文萃——空谷余音》、《百年建筑——天人合一馆人合一》陆续由科学出版社、中国城市出版社出版发行，旨在“从历史的、人文的，以及学术研究、建筑文化等各个层面对中国图书馆事业的百年历程作一个完整而深入的诠释和展示，借以传承‘智慧与服务’的行业精神，彰显前贤，激励后学。同时，以此祝贺中国图书馆学会成立 25 周年”[4]。

2004 年 7 月 23—26 日，“中国图书馆学会 2004 年年会暨学会成立 25 周年纪念大会”在江苏省苏州市隆重举行。7 月 24 日上午，中国图书馆学会 2004 年年会暨学会成立 25 周年纪念大会举行开幕式和年会主旨报告。程焕文做题为《百年沧桑，世纪华章——20 世纪中国图书馆事业回顾与展望》的年会主旨报告。“在展望 21 世纪图书馆发展前景时，他指出应日益重视人文精神、读者自由获取知识的权利、图书馆职业道德、人性化服务、社区图书馆服务以及弱势群体图书馆服务等几个方面。”[5]

7 月 25 日，中国图书馆学会 2004 年年会暨学会成立 25 周年纪念大会第一分会场举行以“百年图书馆精神的魅力”为主题的专题讨论。范并思教授做题为《中国图书馆精神的百年历程》的主旨演讲，李明华研究馆员做题为《从浙江人物看百年中国图书馆精神》的发言。[6]第三分会场举行以“国际视野下的图书馆员职业伦理与知识产权保护”为主题的“第二届图书馆法与知识产权论坛”专题论坛。中国图书馆学会图书馆法与知识产权研究专业委员会主任委员程焕文做开坛致辞，副主任委员李国新等 7 位海内外学者做主旨演讲或主题发言。[7]

1.2　程焕文首倡“图书馆权利”研究

在中国图书馆学会 2004 年年会暨学会成立 25 周年纪念大会期间，中国图书馆学会秘书长汤更生向学术研究委员会副主任委员程焕文征询有关中国图书馆学会2005年学术年会主题的意见，程焕文提出：鉴于图书馆职业道德已在全国广泛宣传推广，研讨“图书馆权利”的时机已经成熟，必须列入年会主题。其时，中国图书馆学界对“图书馆权利”十分陌生，疑窦丛生。

2004年12月9日，中国图书馆学会发布以“以人为本　服务创新”为主题的《中国图书馆学会2005年年会征文通知》，正式将“图书馆权利”列为年会分主题。程焕文为“图书馆权利”做了专门的“分主题注释”：“平等利用图书馆的权利，自由利用图书馆的权利，免费图书馆服务，弱势群体图书馆服务。”[8]第一次在中国图书馆学界正式提出和通俗地解释了“图书馆权利”。

与此同时，应中国图书馆学会的邀请，程焕文于2004年11月22日在海南省琼海市举行的中国科协2004年学术年会中国图书馆学会分会场上做了题为《权利与道德——关于公共图书馆精神的阐释》的主旨报告[9]，于2004年11月24日在海南省海口市举行的中国图书馆学会图书馆服务研讨班上做了题为《图书馆精神——体系结构与基本内容》的专题报告[10]，对“图书馆权利”做了进一步的阐释和宣传。

1.3　中国图书馆学会将“图书馆权利”列为新年峰会议题

在“图书馆权利”已经列入中国图书馆学会2005年学术年会分主题之后，2004年下半年，国内图书馆界相继出现了所谓的“国图事件”[11]、“信阳事件”[12]等图书馆公共危机。鉴于这些事件在媒体上的相继曝光，以及其他迫切需要研究对策的现实问题，中国图书馆学会理事长詹福瑞召集相关学者于2005年1月8日在哈尔滨市黑龙江大学举行“中国图书馆学会2005年峰会”，是为中国图书馆学会首次峰会。“与会的20多名代表各抒己见，共同探讨了图书馆权利、著作权在图书馆的合理使用、图书馆行业荣誉体系的构建与维护、中国图书馆立法：现状与任务、图书馆与社会阅读等5个议题。”“‘图书馆权利’，是本次峰会讨论最为热烈的议题”。黑龙江大学信息资源管理研究中心的蒋永福教授简明扼要地从三个方面对所要讨论的问题进行了议题的说明。“与会代表对‘图书馆权利’内涵的界定发表了两种不同看法。一种观点认为，‘图书馆权利’应以‘读者权利’为核心，即读者平等、自由地利用图书馆的权利。以中山大学信息管理系程焕文教授为代表。另一种观点则认为，‘图书馆权利’必须要兼顾图书馆的生存、发展权利，保障图书馆拥有实现读者权利的实施手段和基础条件，否则，自由、平等利用文献信息只能是一种‘理想’。强调在理想与现实的博弈中协调发展图书馆事业，对图书馆深层机制中存在的问题进行理性思考，而不能简单地批评实践界缺乏自由与平等意识。以首都图书馆副馆长周心慧、湖南图书馆常务副馆长张勇为代表。中山大学信息管理系程焕文教授指出：这几年来，中国图书馆学会图书馆法与知识产权研究专业委员会，一直致力于图书馆职业伦理道德及图书馆权利的宣传，然而推广起来很困难。虽然如此，程教授依然抱乐观态度，认为‘只要坚持做下去，总会有效果的’。他认为，近20年来，中国图书馆事业的发展整体上是非理性的，‘有偿服务’等有悖于图书馆公益性的思想与实践都在向非理性的方向引导图书馆的发展。启动《图书馆服务权利宣言》是非常必要的，但一定把它放在图书馆基本价值层面来思考；图书馆是无国界的，应借鉴世界各国的相关做法，制定出让全世界同行都能理解的《宣言》，而不是以‘中国特色’为由拿出一个和世界上任何国家都不同的《宣言》，那就不可思议了。总之，只有平等、自由地利用图书馆这一理念得到共识并根植在图书馆实践活动当中，中国图书馆事业才会进入真正的发展时期。詹福瑞教授认为，谈图书馆权利应该对以下几个问题予以关注：一是法律的缺失。这是导致目前图书馆行业面临困难状况的最根本原因。没有《图书馆法》，图书馆自身以及读者权利的定性都无法解决。要根本解决‘图书馆权利’问题，首先要解决立法问题。二是投入不足。不是图书馆本身缺乏权利意识，而是保障权利的运行经费严重不足。三是有关图书馆权利方面的教育太少，对读者自由、平等利用图书馆的权利缺乏理性认识。”[13]

2　图书馆权利思潮的兴起（2005—2007 年）

2004 年中国图书馆学会相继将“图书馆权利”列入中国图书馆学会 2005 年学术年会的分主题和“新年峰会”议题以后，“图书馆权利”忽如一夜春风来，千树万树梨花开，于 2005 年迅速演变成为席卷整个中国图书馆学界的研究热潮。

2.1　图书馆学专业期刊的倡导

“中国图书馆学会 2005 年峰会”之后，黑龙江图书馆学会《图书馆建设》自 2005 年第 1 期起率先开设“走向权利时代”专栏，提出：“‘走向权利时代’，是我们为所有拥有正义感的图书馆人（包括关心图书馆事业或公民信息权利的其他人士）提供的专题性论坛。凡是有关图书馆保障公民的信息自由、信息平等、信息权利方面的法律、政策、制度、伦理及实践性的论文，皆为欢迎之列。”[14]

与此同时，湖南省图书馆学会《图书馆》自 2005 年第 1 期起开设“21 世纪新图书馆运动论坛”专栏，提出：“‘21 世纪新图书馆运动’旨在以人为本，弘扬公共图书馆精神，倡导图书馆走进平民，关心弱者，平等服务，缩小数字鸿沟，建立一个信息公平和信息保障的制度。”[15]

武汉大学信息管理学院《图书情报知识》自 2005 年第 1 期起亦开设“弱势群体与知识公平”专栏，探讨“图书馆权利”的一些相关问题。

《图书馆建设》、《图书馆》和《图书情报知识》三种专业期刊，不约而同地“三箭齐发”，共同指向“图书馆权利”，组织学人撰写专文，研讨“图书馆权利”的相关问题，使“图书馆权利”迅速成为席卷全国的图书馆学思潮。

《图书馆建设》的“走向权利时代”栏目持续了两年之久，在推动“图书馆权利”研究上贡献良多。蒋永福曾总结道：“两年来，该专栏共发表‘图书馆权利’专题论文 43 篇，成为这一时期发表该专题论文最集中、最多的专业刊物。陈传夫、李国新、范并思、程焕文、王世伟、肖燕、张久珍、张勇、王惠君等 56 位作者，奋笔疾书，就‘图书馆权利’问题激情诠释、呐喊、献策。”“《走向权利时代》专栏结束了，但走向权利时代的思考和步伐不应该停止！”[16]

《图书馆》的“21 世纪新图书馆运动论坛”专栏，借鉴 20 世纪初的“新图书馆运动”概念，以唤醒公共、公开、平等、共享的公共图书馆理念，但是，因为“运动”一词不受待见，颇有异议。2005年4月，李爽在《图书情报知识》上发表《“新图书馆运动”质疑》一文，对湖南《图书馆》发起的“21世纪新图书馆运动”提出了诸多质疑。[17]又因为专栏文章的个性比较张扬，引发了不少相关争论。[18-20]即使如此，《图书馆》在宣传公共图书馆理念、精神等诸方面做出了重要的贡献。[21-22]

2.2 “图书馆权利”主题论坛的召开

2005年7月，中国图书馆学会2005年年会在广西桂林召开，图书馆法与知识产权研究专业委员会于7月22日主办以“图书馆权利”为主题的“第三届图书馆法与知识产权论坛”。李国新主持论坛，程焕文做开坛致辞：“回顾了该委员会成立四年以来走过的历程，讨论过的话题以及取得的成就，……认为该委员会四年的作为在中国图书馆界产生了重要和深远的影响，将会在中国图书馆事业发展的历史上‘留下痕迹’。”上午，蒋永福讲《图书馆权利：内涵与实现机制》，卢海燕讲《国际图联关于著作权问题的立场及著作权与其他法律问题委员会2004—2005战略发展计划》，肯尼亚国家图书馆阿部讲《肯尼亚图书馆服务与图书馆权利》。下午，程焕文、陈传夫和李国新教授共同主持“公开讨论：图书馆权利的迷失与复归——由事例说权利”。“在公开讨论之先，程焕文教授先对图书馆权利作了一点说明，强调图书馆权利的内涵乃是民众的图书馆权利，不可以望文生义认为是图书馆自身的权利。之所以使用这样的叫法，是沿用了国际惯例。程教授以PPT形式提供了几个在我国图书馆服务中普遍存在的事例，讨论以这些事例为‘靶子’展开。”[23]

2.3 “图书馆精神”与“图书馆权利”的争鸣

2004年7月，程焕文、潘燕桃主编的《信息资源共享》正式出版。程焕文在这部教育部“高等教育面向21世纪课程教材”中提出了“信息资源共享四定理”：“一切信息资源都是有用的”，“一切信息资源都是为了用的”，“人人享有自由平等利用信息资源的权利”，“用户永远都是正确的”。其中定理三“人人享有自由平等利用信息资源的权利”下有三条基本阐释：“平等利用信息资源是用户的基本权利”，“自由利用信息资源是用户的基本权利”，“免费服务是自由平等利用的保障”。是为我国在图书馆学教科书中第一次从信息资源共享的角度正式阐述“图书馆权利”的思想。[24]

围绕着程焕文提出的“图书馆精神”与“图书馆权利”及其相关理论，图书馆学界展开了激烈的争论。

（1）关于“图书馆精神”的争论。关于图书馆精神的争论颇为广泛，其中以程焕文与黄俊贵之间的“程黄之争”最为激烈、最为感性，可谓新世纪中国图书馆学术争鸣的一个奇观。“程黄之争”起于有关“丑陋的图书馆学”的争论[25-32]，而纠结于有关“图书馆精神”的争论。

2005年，黄俊贵率先发起与程焕文的“图书馆精神”论战，其后程焕文开始与黄俊贵展开直接的和间接的争论，其间亦有部分学人卷入讨论。[33-39]争论的主题是“图书馆精神”，焦点是与图书馆权利直接相关的“公共图书馆精神”，特别是有偿服务与免费服务之争，黄俊贵竭力为公共图书馆有偿服务辩护，程焕文则以“汉奸论”痛斥公共图书馆有偿服务的“整体非理性”，被学界视为“不理性”。

2006 年，《国家“十一五”时期文化发展规划纲要》发布，从国家层面确认公共图书馆是公共文化服务的重要组成部分。程焕文发表个人博文，坦言：“高潮来了，整体非理性的时代结束了，公共图书馆精神获得了胜利，淘汰了有偿服务。公共图书馆没有再一次倒在有偿服务的愚昧无知面前！……这个《纲要》是一个绝对理论上的绝杀，绝对的英明。公共图书馆进入了高潮！”[40]从此，“程黄之争”偃旗息鼓，有关公共图书馆有偿服务的一切主张开始成为历史的垃圾。

（2）关于“图书馆权利”的争论。2005 年 6 月 1 日，程焕文申报的“图书馆权利研究”被列入 2005 年度国家社科基金年度项目，是为我国第一个国家立项的图书馆权利研究项目。[41]然而，图书馆学界对程焕文创造的“图书馆权利”一词，从术语的选用是否“正宗”，到对含义的界定是否科学，均颇有争议。[42]18-24

2007 年，程焕文相继出版《图书馆精神》和《图书馆权利与道德》两本著作[43-44]，有关图书馆权利术语与概念的争论逐渐平息，图书馆学界开始转入图书馆权利的深入研究。

（3）关于“用户永远都是正确的”的争论。2004 年 7 月，程焕文、潘燕桃主编的《信息资源共享》正式出版后，图书馆学界对程焕文提出的“用户永远都是正确的”展开了从大众网络到专业期刊，乃至课堂的专门讨论，使该图书馆理念得到了十分广泛的传播。[45]

2.4 “百县馆长论坛”与“图书馆权利”思想的传播

2005 年，中央发布《关于进一步加强农村文化建设的意见》后，为适应建设社会主义新农村的需要，推动和发展我国县级公共图书馆事业，发挥其在城镇、农村基层文化事业中的积极作用，促进和谐社会的构建，在李国新、范并思、汤更生等同仁的倡导和推动下，中国图书馆学会于 2005 年 6 月 9 日发布以“中国县级图书馆的生存与发展”为主题的首届“百县馆长论坛”征文通知。[46]

2005 年 10 月 31 日至 11 月 2 日，以“中国县级图书馆的生存与发展”为主题的全国首届“百县馆长论坛”在河南省林州市召开。首届“百县馆长论坛”的重要成果是通过了《林州共识》，其中第一条共识为：“公共图书馆是政府公共服务的重要组成部分，它的存在是使公民享有最基本的文化信息权利与受教育权利的重要条件，是实现面向大众的文化关怀、文化享有、文化提高、文化创造的重要方式。”[47]

2007 年 11 月 1 日，在常熟举行的第二届“百县馆长论坛”通过了《常熟共识》：“呼吁各级政府进一步重视公共图书馆建设，加大基层公共图书馆投入，支持公共图书馆服务体系建设”；“为实现普遍均等、惠及全民的公共文化服务目标，必须充分发挥县级图书馆在社区乡镇图书馆建设中的核心作用，改革县（区）乡镇（社区）图书馆管理体制，重新界定县级图书馆在公共图书馆服务体系中的基本职能”。[48]

其后，中国图书馆学会又相继举行了两届百县馆长论坛，形成了《江阴共识》[49]、

《神木共识》[50]。

百县馆长论坛的四个共识，比较真实地反映了基层图书馆界对公共图书馆精神和图书馆权利认识的逐步深化和升华。

2.5 “志愿者行动”与“图书馆权利”思想的普及

2005年7月，北京大学信息研究所与湖南图书馆、衡阳市图书馆组成联合调查组，对衡阳地区11个市县基层图书馆进行了详细调研，调研成果引起社会各界的广泛关注。2005年10月，李国新在首届“百县馆长论坛”主旨报告中提出：“有必要实施全国县级图书馆馆长的培训计划，培养出一批深刻理解和谐社会的内涵、深刻理解现代图书馆的理念和实现方式、有一定专业水平和管理能力的职业图书馆馆长。”[51]

2006年初，中国图书馆学会2006新年峰会将开展基层图书馆馆长培训列入学会工作。3月8日，中国图书馆学会在网上发布了“基层图书馆培训”志愿者行动招募公告，在全国范围内招募担任基层图书馆馆长培训班主讲人的志愿者。经过公开招募，最终确定陈力、王余光、杨沛超、李国新、毕红秋、范并思、富平、郭斌、金武刚、李超平、刘小云、邱冠华、师丽梅、唐承秀、陶青、王涛、王惠君、王世伟、王学春、徐建华、杨玉麟、叶新明、尤敬党、于爱君、于良芝、郑玲26人入选“基层图书馆培训志愿者”。[52]

7月25日，中国图书馆学会在2006年年会闭幕式上举行了“志愿者行动”启动仪式。志愿者分三组，分别在湖南衡阳、陕西榆林、黑龙江牡丹江开展为期5天的培训行动，讲授五个专题：①社会主义新农村建设中的图书馆（主要讲授现代图书馆理念、精神，中国图书馆事业的现状与未来，基层图书馆的功能、定位等）；②基层图书馆馆长实务；③基层图书馆的资源建设与服务；④基层图书馆的自动化网络化建设；⑤宣传推介图书馆示范讲座。[53]

志愿者行动通过对基层图书馆工作者的专业培训，不仅提高了基层图书馆工作者的业务工作能力，而且普及了图书馆权利理念，特别是公共图书馆的理念，同时也加深了志愿者对基层图书馆的认识和了解。[51]

志愿者行动自2006年起至2011年，历时6年，足迹遍及全国各地，可谓是20世纪以来最大规模的公共图书馆理念与图书馆权利理念的宣传与普及，为基层公共图书馆的发展奠定了理论与思想基础。

2.6 国家政策的改变与“图书馆权利”国家意识

2006年9月，政府发布《国家“十一五”时期文化发展规划纲要》，制定了“坚持以人为本，保障和实现人民群众的基本文化权益，使广大人民群众共享文化发展成果”，“坚持把社会效益放在首位，实现社会效益和经济效益的统一，最大限度地发挥文化引导社会、教育人民、推动发展的功能”等方针原则，明确提出了“保障和实现人民群众的基本文化权益”的理念。《国家“十一五”时期文化发展规划纲要》将文化事业明确地区分为公共文化服务事业和文化产业两个部分，第一次明确图书馆为公共文化服务事业，要求“完善公共文化服务网络。积极推进政府职能转变，实行政企分开、政事分开、政资分开和管办分离，切实把政府的职能由主要办文化转到社会管理和公共服务上来。要从现阶段经济社会发展水平出发，以实现和保障公民基本文化权益、满足广大人民群众基本文化需求为目标，坚持公共服务普遍均等原则，兼顾城乡之间、地区之间的协调发展，统筹规划，合理安排，形成实用、便捷、高效的公共文化服务网络”。“公共文化服务”、“实现和保障公民基本文化权益”、“坚持公共服务普遍均等原则”等国家文化治理理念的确立从根本上否定了20世纪80年代以后，公共图书馆“以文养文”、“以文补文”有偿服务的“整体非理性”，重新确立了公共图书馆公共、公开、平等、免费、共享的基本理念和正确发展方向。[54]

国家文化政策的改变和“实现和保障公民基本文化权益”观念的确立，是中国社会发展的必然结果，由此亦导致了一系列有关文化工程性质国家观念的改变。例如2002年启动的“全国文化信息资源共享工程”，最初的主旨为：贯彻落实“三个代表”重要思想，抵制西方文化渗透，以德治国，科技创新。[55] 2007年其主旨则重新定位为：“是公共文化体系的基础工程，是政府提供公共文化服务的重要手段，是实现广大人民群众基本文化权益的重要途径，是改善城乡基层群众文化服务的创新工程。”[56]

2.7 《国家“十一五”时期文化发展规划纲要》专家笔谈

《国家“十一五”时期文化发展规划纲要》的发布，确立了公共图书馆为“公共文化服务”机构的公益性质和“实现和保障公民基本文化权益”、“坚持公共服务普遍均等原则”的国家政策，从此，图书馆权利思潮开始从图书馆学人的理念演变为国家意识。

2007年，甘肃图书馆学会《图书与情报》组织发起“《国家“十一五”时期文化发展规划纲要》专家笔谈”，全面阐述“图书馆权利”的国家观念。李国新、范并思的《迎接图书馆事业的大发展大繁荣——纪念〈国家“十一五”时期文化发展规划纲要〉发表一周年》，范并思的《政府公共图书馆服务理念的根本性转变》，程焕文的《普遍均等 惠及全民——关于公共服务普遍均等原则的阐释》，邱冠华的《解读〈国家“十一五”时期文化发展规划纲要〉的服务网络》，李国新的《立法保障是最根本的保障》，白雪华的《切实履行政府职责 保障公民基本文化权益》，蒋永福的《发展图书馆事业必须纳入政府议事日程——“五个纳入”随想》，崔建飞的《共享工程在公共文化服务体系中的地位和特点》，褚树青的《城乡共享生活品质》，王素芳的《弱势群体文化权益保障的国家战略视野——基于〈国家“十一五”时期文化发展规划纲要〉的解读》，于良芝的《建立覆盖全社会的公共图书馆服务体系》，全面阐释了《国家“十一五”时期文化发展规划纲要》的公共图书馆发展理念和图书馆权利思想。[57-67]

2.8 公共图书馆“岭南模式”的崛起

在图书馆权利思潮兴起的同时，广东图书馆界率先开始了图书馆权利的全面实践探索。2003年9月，深圳市开始启动《深圳市建设图书馆之城（2003—2005年）三年实施方案》，2005年11月，东莞市开始启动《东莞市建设图书馆之城实施方案》，广州、佛山等地亦先后启动了一系列公共图书馆发展计划，形成了广东省立中山图书馆的“流动图书馆”模式、深圳图书馆的“图书馆之城”模式、东莞图书馆的“集成图书馆”模式、广州图书馆的“政府主导”模式和佛山图书馆的“联合图书馆”模式。这些公共图书馆的发展模式均产生在《国家十一五时期文化发展纲要》发布之前，成为新世纪公共图书馆理念和图书馆权利思想全面实践的先导，并因此成为新世纪中国公共图书馆发展的典范，被全国各地公共图书馆竞相学习、模仿和复制。2007 年，程焕文在《中国图书馆学报》上发表《岭南模式：崛起的广东公共图书馆事业》一文，全面阐述公共图书馆发展的“岭南模式”。[68]从此，总结各地公共图书馆的发展模式开始成为学界的时尚。

3　图书馆权利思潮的高涨（2008—2010 年）

2008 年，中国图书馆学会《图书馆服务宣言》的诞生，标志着新世纪的图书馆权利思潮达到高潮。从此，中国图书馆界开始从图书馆权利的理论探索转向图书馆权利的全面实践。

3.1　《图书馆服务宣言》的颁布

中国图书馆学会《图书馆服务宣言》的制定始于 2006 年 12 月中国图书馆学会在苏州召开“2007 新年峰会”的提议。2007 年 3 月，中国图书馆学会正式启动并资助“中国图书馆的核心价值与《图书馆服务宣言》研究”课题，范并思和倪晓建担任课题负责人。经过一年的起草、征求意见和修改，2008 年 3 月，中国图书馆学会七届四次理事会原则通过《图书馆服务宣言》。2008 年 10 月，《图书馆服务宣言》在重庆召开的中国图书馆学会年会上正式发布。是为中国图书馆界的第一个行业宣言，标志着中国图书馆界核心价值观的重建，标志着中国图书馆界步入了行业自觉的新时代。[69]

《图书馆服务宣言》宣称：“现代图书馆秉承对全社会开放的理念，承担实现和保障公民文化权利，缩小社会信息鸿沟的使命。中国图书馆人经过不懈的追求与努力，逐步确立了对社会普遍开放、平等服务、以人为本的基本原则。”提出了图书馆服务的七个目标，特别强调：①“图书馆以公益性服务为基本原则，以实现和保障公民基本阅读权利为天职，以读者需求为一切工作的出发点”；②“图书馆向读者提供平等服务。各级各类图书馆共同构成图书馆体系，保障全体社会成员普遍均等地享有图书馆服务”；③“图书馆在服务与管理中体现人文关怀。图书馆致力于消除弱势群体利用图书馆的困难，为全体读者提供人性化、便利化的服务”。[70]《图书馆服务宣言》的发布标志着图书馆权利思潮所宣扬的平等、公共、公益等图书馆理念已经成为中国图书馆界的普遍共识和核心价值。

3.2　《公共图书馆建设用地指标》的施行

2008 年 5 月，住房和城乡建设部、国土资源部、文化部批准发布《公共图书馆建设用地指标》（2008 年 6 月 1 日起施行）。这是新中国成立以来首个文化设施建设国家标准，其颁布实施意味着国家对公共图书馆无偿划拨土地、无偿使用土地有了政策依据，也使我国公共图书馆建设进一步走向统一规划、合理布局、因地制宜、配套建设。

《公共图书馆建设用地指标》充分吸收了图书馆权利思潮中所涌现的公共图书馆理念，使用了服务人口、服务半径、公共图书馆体系等公共图书馆服务普遍均等的新术语。《公共图书馆建设用地指标》规定：公共图书馆根据服务人口数量分为大型馆、中型馆和小型馆；公共图书馆建设用地主要包括公共图书馆建筑用地、集散场地、绿化用地及停车场地；公共图书馆的设置原则应符合《公共图书馆建设用地指标》的要求，逐步发展成为公共图书馆体系；公共图书馆的选址应在人口集中、公交便利、环境良好、相对安静的地区，同时满足各类公共图书馆合理服务半径的要求。

《公共图书馆建设用地指标》明确提出，用地指标的设立要综合考虑所在城市的人口规模和结构、社会经济发展状况、人文和自然环境条件等特点，特别提出要考虑公共图书馆的服务人口、服务半径，合理确定建设用地规划布局和用地规模，而不是按照行政级别确定图书馆的基本规模。这是时代的进步。

3.3 《公共图书馆建设标准》的实施

继2008年6月1日起正式施行《公共图书馆建设用地指标》之后，国家又正式发布由文化部主编、住房和城乡建设部与国家发展和改革委员会批准的《公共图书馆建设标准》（建标108—2008），并自2008年11月1日起正式施行。这是我国又一个规范公共图书馆建设的全国统一性标准，是公共图书馆建设逐步走向科学化、法制化、规范化的重要步骤，也是新世纪我国图书馆事业法制建设取得的一项标志性成果。

2005年5月，文化部委托中国图书馆学会组织图书馆界、建筑界的专家开始《公共图书馆建设标准》编制工作的前期准备，9月，由李国新、汤更生等人主要参与的编制工作正式启动。在编制过程中，编制组先后实地调研了国内外80多所公共图书馆，搜集和研究了50多个国家和地区的相关标准和规范，普查、测算与分析了国内外大样本的统计数据，召开了近30次专题研讨会，对近400条来自各方面的意见或建议进行了汇总分析，逐一处理，历时三年多才完成编制工作。

《公共图书馆建设标准》确定了公共图书馆建设项目的规模分级和项目构成，制定了公共图书馆的总建筑面积和分项面积控制指标，提出了公共图书馆建设选址、总体布局的原则要求，明确了公共图书馆建设项目实施过程中的基本要求。其主要突破表现在以下四个方面：第一，确立了以服务人口为主要依据确定公共图书馆建设规模的原则。以服务人口为主要依据确定公共图书馆建设规模，是公共文化服务"以人为本"、"普遍均等，惠及全民"原则在公共图书馆设施建设上的具体体现，符合图书馆事业的发展规律，也符合国际惯例，为构建覆盖全社会的普遍均等的图书馆服务体系奠定坚实的基础。第二，形成了比较系统的基于公共图书馆建设现实水平且具有一定前瞻性的控制指标体系。以服务人口为主要依据确定公共图书馆的建设规模，需要通过一系列具体的控制指标来实现。该标准在广泛调研、国内外比较、海量数据分析概括的基础上，第一次明确提出了未来5～10年我国公共图书馆建设规模控制的主要指标，不仅使"以服务人口为主要依据"的原则得以具体化，使公共图书馆建设的规模控制有据可依，有规可寻，可操作性强，而且对未来公共图书馆的服务、评价、发展目标具有指导意义。第三，提出了体现现代图书馆理念、与现代图书馆服务方式相适应的公共图书馆布局与建设要求，使建筑和设施能够适应现代图书馆服务方式变革和创新的要求，使公共建筑“功能优先、经济适用”的方针落到实处。第四，重视公共图书馆的环境建设。在公共图书馆建设中主体建筑与馆区建设并重，并与城市建设有效衔接，有利于公共图书馆充分发挥知识信息传播、文化活动阵地、休闲交流场所等整体效能。[71]

《公共图书馆建设标准》的实施，标志着我国公共图书馆设施建设由此进入了一个新的发展阶段。

3.4 深圳市在全国率先推行公共图书馆免费服务

深圳市委、市政府高度重视公共文化服务体系建设，注重发挥美术馆、公共图书馆、文化馆（站）在实现市民文化权利方面的重要作用，在全国开公共图书馆免费服务的风气之先，堪称地方政府的典范。

2003 年，深圳全市各级公共图书馆除了复印等个别项目外，全部取消收费项目。2007 年 3 月 1 日，深圳市在全国率先推出包括图书馆、博物馆、美术馆、群艺馆等市属公益性文化场馆的免费开放服务，使深圳市的公益文化场馆公共服务正式进入“零门槛”时代。

2008 年 7 月 15 日，深圳市文体旅游局为进一步完善全市公共文化服务体系，丰富市民文化生活，保障市民文化权利，落实市委市政府“实施深圳市民生净福利指标体系”的精神，专门下发了《关于加强基层公共文化场馆管理的通知》（深文〔2008〕191 号），对基层公益文化场馆的免费开放作了更加明确、细致的规定，免费开放范围延伸到深圳各区属公共文化场馆。该通知强调“基层文化场馆免费开放工作是保障市民基本文化权益的一项重要举措”，要求下属各单位：①坚持公益性，搭建实施公共文化服务的基层平台；②突出服务性，积极开展免费服务工作；③保证开放时间，保障群众基本的文化权益；④规范管理，不断提高服务水平；⑤加强业务指导。“从构建公共文化服务体系、建设和谐文化和培育城市人文精神的高度提高对该项工作重要性的认识，加强领导，认真部署，将免费开放服务作为本单位重点工作，采取切实可行的措施，落实到位。”[72]

3.5 深圳全面推行“城市街区 24 小时自助图书馆”

“城市街区 24 小时自助图书馆系统”是深圳市建设图书馆之城（2006—2010 年）五年规划的重点建设项目，也是一项由政府出资承办的社会公益事业。

2008 年 4 月 7 日，深圳图书馆“城市街区 24 小时自助图书馆系统”项目通过阶段成果技术验收，10 月，已有 10 台“城市街区 24 小时自助图书馆”在深圳市各个居民小区投入使用。2009 年 10 月，“城市街区 24 小时自助图书馆”项目获文化部第三届“文化创新奖”，并列入国家文化创新工程；2010 年 5 月，获文化部第十五届“群星奖”。其后，开始在深圳市广泛布点设立，形成星罗棋布的街区公共图书馆服务网络。

“城市街区 24 小时自助图书馆”集数字化、人性化、智能化为一体，具备自助借书、自助还书、申办新证、预借服务、查询服务等图书馆的基本服务功能，突破了传统图书馆的时空限制，将高新技术和图书馆延伸服务有机结合，开创了中国公共图书馆管理、服务和发展的新模式，是实现和保障民众公共图书馆权利的重大创新和实践，对构建公共文化服务体系具有积极意义。

2010年以后，上海、北京、西安、合肥、长春、郑州、马鞍山、广州等城市相继引进“城市街区24小时自助图书馆”，“城市街区24小时自助图书馆”迅速成为全国各大城市街区公共图书馆服务的靓丽风景。

4 图书馆权利思潮的盛行（2011—2014年）

2011年1月26日，文化部、财政部发布《关于推进全国美术馆、公共图书馆、文化馆（站）免费开放工作的意见》，杭州图书馆“乞丐进图书馆”成为网络热点，标志着图书馆权利思潮从理论传播、制度建设开始全面转向图书馆权利的实践——公共图书馆服务。

4.1 公共图书馆免费开放国家政策的施行

自2006年国家发布《国家“十一五”时期文化发展规划纲要》和2008年中国图书馆学会发布《图书馆服务宣言》以后，虽然公共图书馆为公共文化服务机构的性质和必须坚持公益性服务已经成为国家意志和图书馆界的共识，但是，在实践中，公共图书馆有偿服务的现状并没有从根本上转变，公共图书馆界不再有为有偿服务辩护的声音，但是，公共图书馆有偿服务根深蒂固，各地公共图书馆顽固地坚持有偿服务的现象十分普遍。

2011年1月26日，文化部、财政部发布《关于推进全国美术馆、公共图书馆、文化馆（站）免费开放工作的意见》，指出公共图书馆免费开放“是实现和保障人民群众基本文化权益的积极行动”，确立了“全面推开，逐步完善”，“坚持公益，保障基本”的公共图书馆免费开放工作原则，要求公共空间设施场地免费开放、基本公共文化服务项目免费服务。[73]

2011年3月7日，财政部发布《关于加强美术馆、公共图书馆、文化馆（站）免费开放经费保障工作的通知》，提出公共图书馆免费开放经费保障的分担原则和补助标准，开展基本公共文化服务项目支出由中央和地方财政共同负担。规定：自2011年起，地级市图书馆的补助经费为每馆每年50万元，县级图书馆为每馆每年20万元，乡镇综合文化站为每站每年5万元。为公共图书馆的免费开放提供了基本的经费保障。[74]

2011年5月26日，文化部、财政部发布《关于实施“数字图书馆推广工程”的通知》，要求“切实保障数字化、信息化、网络化环境下公共文化服务的公益性、基本性、均等性、便利性”[75]。

在国家明确要求公共图书馆免费开放，并且制定了提供切实的免费开放经费保障的情况下，虽然各地公共图书馆免费开放已经蔚然成风，但是，不少公共图书馆都是迫不得已，其实施的效果并不尽人意，普遍存在“免费开放相关制度设计需要加强”，“免费开放业务人才需要补充"，"免费开放服务内容形式需要创新"，"基层公共文化服务设施设备情况需要改善"，"免费开放服务经费保障能力需要提高" 等问题与困难。[76-77]

4.2 "乞丐进图书馆" 成为社会关注热点

2011 年 1 月中旬，全国各地遭遇罕见冰雪，天寒地冻，交通阻塞，返乡过春节的人们苦不堪言；河南林州为节能减排而停止供暖，民众哆嗦着抱团取暖，敢怒不敢言。恰在此时，杭州市图书馆馆长褚树青多年前有关"乞丐进图书馆" 的一句话"我无权拒绝他们入内读书，但您有权选择离开"，出现在刚刚兴起的微博上，并迅速广为传播，让寒冷的中国社会霎时"有温度"，使杭州图书馆顿时成为"史上最温暖的图书馆"，使褚树青一夜之间成为网络红人。[78]

杭州图书馆的"乞丐入馆案" 肇始于微博，迅速漫延至博客，成为网络的热门话题，然后从网络媒体转向平面媒体，各地报纸纷纷发表专文，最后上升到电视媒体，形成了全媒体"热炒" 的局面。《新华每日电讯》、《人民日报》、《工人日报》、《广州日报》、《浙江日报》、《中国文化报》的记者专稿和中央电视台、浙江电视台等电视台的专题节目，使民众利用图书馆的平等权利思想迅速在全社会传播，成为民众普遍赞誉的图书馆权利实践美谈。[79-86] 虽然社会上，特别是图书馆界，仍然有人不完全理解和认同褚树青的作为，不完全明了图书馆平等权利的价值，但是，"这必将记入中国图书馆的发展历史，特别是公共图书馆的发展历史，因为它开启了全社会传播图书馆权利思想的新时代，是图书馆权利思想从图书馆学人在中国图书馆界业内的传播正式转向民众和媒体自觉向全社会传播的里程碑"，"是中国图书馆权利思想传播的一个里程碑，是新世纪第二个十年图书馆权利思想传播新起点的标志"。[87]

4.3 《公共图书馆服务规范》的颁布实施

2011 年 12 月 30 日，国家质量监督检验检疫总局、国家标准化管理委员会批准发布《公共图书馆服务规范（GB/T 28220—2011）》（2012 年 5 月 1 日起实施）。《公共图书馆服务规范》是国家质量监督检验检疫总局、国家标准化管理委员会批准发布的第一个规范公共文化服务的国家级标准，是我国图书馆标准规范体系中的首个服务类标准，填补了我国图书馆规范体系中服务类标准规范的空白。《公共图书馆服务规范》与《公共图书馆建设用地指标》、《公共图书馆建设标准》等共同构成了我国公共图书馆标准规范体系的基础，是新世纪图书馆权利思潮影响下产生的最为重要的成就与成果。[88]

《公共图书馆服务规范》规定了图书馆服务资源、服务效能、服务宣传、服务监督与反馈等内容，适用于县（市）级以上公共图书馆，街道、乡镇级公共图书馆，以及社区、乡村和社会力量办的各类公共图书馆基层服务点，是文化行政部门推进图书馆事业发展的指南，是公共图书馆实现服务立馆、促进科学发展的实践纲领，对于保障公共图书馆事业发展，推进公共文化服务标准化、规范化建设，进一步完善覆盖城乡的公共文化服务体系，有效保障社会公众的基本文化权益方面，具有积极的推动作用和重要的指导意义。

4.4 《全国公共图书馆事业发展“十二五”规划》的实施

2013年1月30日，文化部印发《全国公共图书馆事业发展“十二五”规划》。《全国公共图书馆事业发展“十二五”规划》将公共图书馆定位为“是保障人民基本文化权益的重要阵地，是开展社会教育活动的终身课堂，是国家公共文化服务体系的重要组成部分，是城市文明进步的标志”；确立了全面系统的公共图书馆发展指导思想：“坚持以中国特色社会主义理论为指导，深入贯彻落实科学发展观，以建设社会主义核心价值体系为根本任务，以丰富人民精神文化生活、保障人民群众基本文化权益、满足人民群众基本文化需求为出发点和落脚点，按照体现公益性、基本性、均等性、便利性的要求，坚持政府主导，依循‘保基本、强基层、建机制、重实效’的基本思路，以城乡基层建设为重点，以基础设施建设为依托，以技术创新为动力，以机制体制建设为保障，努力构建普遍均等、惠及全民的公共图书馆服务网络，全面提升各级公共图书馆的服务能力、服务水平和服务效益，最大限度地发挥公共图书馆在保护文献典籍、传承中华文化、建设学习型社会、培养公民高度的文化自觉和文化自信、提高全民族文明素质、建设社会主义文化强国等方面的重要作用，推动公共图书馆事业更好更快地发展”。《全国公共图书馆事业发展“十二五”规划》明确提出：“政府主导，社会参与；强化基础，注重创新；统筹兼顾，分类指导；以人为本，提升服务”的基本原则；确立了“逐步建立覆盖城乡、结构合理、功能健全、实用高效的服务网络，进一步增强活力，提高效能，服务能力、服务水平与服务效益明显提升，部分地区图书馆接近或达到国际先进水平”的“十二五”公共图书馆发展目标。[89]

《全国公共图书馆事业发展“十二五”规划》的制定和颁布几乎融合了此前图书馆权利思潮所产生的有关公共图书馆的全部理念。

4.5 “人有好恶　书无好坏”专家笔谈

2013年3月21日《光明日报》发表孟其真的《图书馆，请择善而藏》一文，对首都图书馆近年来藏书布局的变化进行了批评，旁征博引，一针见血。针对“择善而藏”的思想观念，程焕文于3月22日和23日在个人博客上连续发表了题为《人有好恶　书无好坏》和《勿左勿右　客观中立》的两篇博文，阐述图书馆权利的核心理念——“自由收藏与自由阅读”。[90-91]博文发表以后立即在网上引起热议，支持者与反对者彼此论战，而更多的是不能理解。

有鉴于此，黑龙江图书馆学会《图书馆建设》邀请潘燕桃组织“人有好恶　书无好坏”笔谈。2013年，《图书馆建设》第9期刊发了潘燕桃、程焕文、吴晞、李超平、蒋永福、褚树青、刘洪辉、俞传正、宋显彪等学人撰写的笔谈专文。[92-102]是为新世纪以来图书馆权利思潮发展中有关“自由权利”的第一次学术讨论。

4.6 《广州市公共图书馆条例》呼之欲出

早在2006年，广州市委宣传部就已将“《广州市图书馆条例》立法研究”列入广州市哲学社会科学发展“十一五”规划重点课题，委托中山大学程焕文和潘燕桃负责前期调研和草案的起草工作。在刘洪辉、方家忠、吴晞、李东来等广东图书馆界同仁的共同参与下，经过八年的反复调研和征求意见，2014 年 10 月 28 日，广州市十四届人大常委会第三十四次会议对《广州市公共图书馆条例（草案修改稿）》进行了第三次审议，三审通过后已报广东省人大常委会，即将在 2015 年初正式颁布。《广州市公共图书馆条例》的问世将是继《深圳经济特区公共图书馆条例（试行）》（1997 年）、《内蒙古自治区公共图书馆管理条例》（2000 年）、《湖北省公共图书馆条例》（2001 年）、《北京市图书馆条例》（2002 年）之后，我国颁布的第五部地方性公共图书馆法规，也将是图书馆权利思潮兴起后我国颁布的第一部地方性图书馆法规，将会成为中国公共图书馆法的先导。事实上，在《广州市公共图书馆条例》的制定过程中，其有关服务人口等关键理念已经被国内的相关标准和规范所借鉴。

5 图书馆权利思潮的未来展望

图书馆权利思潮酝酿于2004 年，兴起于 2005 年，高涨于 2008 年，盛行于 2011 年，十年间经历了四个飞跃阶段。从历史的角度来看，20 世纪初的新图书馆运动促使公共图书馆观念在中国的广泛传播和公共图书馆的普遍建立；21 世纪初的图书馆权利思潮则促使图书馆权利观念在中国的广泛传播和覆盖城乡的公共图书馆服务体系的建立，二者具有惊人的相似性。在表面上看，图书馆权利思潮不过是新图书馆运动的复兴；但是，在本质上，图书馆权利思潮的发展比新图书馆运动的开展更加艰难困苦。20 世纪初新图书馆运动兴起时，公共、公开、平等、共享、免费等欧美公共图书馆思想是新生事物和新潮流，受到社会各界的普遍欢迎；21 世纪初图书馆权利思潮兴起时，虽然传播的公共图书馆理念大同小异，但是，因为20 世纪 80 年代以后市场经济的冲击使中国原有的公共图书馆价值观几乎荡然无存，取而代之的是普遍的有偿服务和广泛的对民众图书馆权利的漠视。这种整体非理性犹如枷锁和牢笼禁锢着图书馆界的世界观和价值观，而世界观与价值观的改变是最为艰巨的工作。在被市场经济扭曲的“中国特色”公共图书馆价值观与被图书馆权利思潮推出的“世界公认”公共图书馆价值观剧烈冲突的时刻，因为图书馆权利国家意志的确立，特别是社会主义核心价值观的确立，世界公认的公共图书馆核心价值观才在中国得以重新全面确立。这是图书馆权利思潮的胜利，更是庶民的胜利，是构建覆盖城乡的公共图书馆服务体系，实现和保障民众基本公共图书馆权利的胜利。

在十年图书馆权利思潮中，程焕文倡导的图书馆权利研究，吴晞、程亚男等导演的深圳图书馆之城建设，李国新、汤更生等发起的“百县图书馆论坛”和“志愿者行动”，以及《公共图书馆建设标准》和《公共图书馆服务规范》的调研与编制，范并思、倪晓建负责起草的《图书馆服务宣言》，褚树青执掌的杭州图书馆允许乞丐进图书馆，李东来主导的东莞“集成图书馆”，王惠君、屈义华独创的佛山“联合图书馆”，以及中国图书馆学会的图书馆权利相关学术会议，《图书馆建设》、《图书馆》、《图书情报知识》、《图书与情报》等专业期刊的专栏与笔谈，……诸此种种都已成为图书馆权利思潮的美好记忆。

十年图书馆权利思潮不是图书馆权利思潮的终结，而是图书馆权利思潮正能量的积累。在未来十年，图书馆权利思潮将会继续荡涤中国图书馆理念与实践的尘埃，进一步推进民众图书馆权利的实现和保障。

5.1 图书馆权利的研究方兴未艾

十年来，有关图书馆权利的研究成果层出不穷。程焕文著《图书馆精神》（北京图书馆出版社，2007 年），程焕文、张靖编译《图书馆权利与道德》（上、下）（广西师范大学出版社，2007 年），程焕文、潘燕桃、张靖著《图书馆权利研究》（《国家哲学社会科学成果文库》，学习出版社，2011 年），潘燕桃著《近 60 年来中国公共图书馆思想研究（1949—2009）》（中山大学出版社，2011 年），程焕文著《图书馆的价值与使命》（上海科学技术文献出版社，2014 年）；王世伟主编《世界著名城市图书馆述略》（上海科学技术文献出版社，2006 年），王世伟著《国际大都市城市图书馆指标体系研究》（上海科学技术文献出版社，2009 年）；蒋永福著《信息自由及其限度研究》（社会科学文献出版社，2007 年），蒋永福著《现代公共图书馆制度研究》（知识产权出版社，2010 年）；范并思著《20 世纪西方与中国的图书馆学：基于德尔斐法测评的理论史纲》（北京图书馆出版社，2004 年），范并思编《百年文萃：空谷余音》（中国城市出版社，2005 年），范并思著《图书馆学理论变革：观念与思潮》（北京图书馆出版社，2007 年），范并思著《图书馆资源公平利用》（北京图书馆出版社，2011 年），范并思编《公共图书馆未成年人服务》（北京师范大学出版社，2012 年）；于良芝、李晓新、王德恒著《拓展社会的公共信息空间：21 世纪中国公共图书馆可持续发展模式》（科学出版社，2004 年），邱冠华、于良芝、许晓霞著《覆盖全社会的公共图书馆服务体系：模式技术支撑与方案》（北京图书馆出版社，2008 年），于良芝、邱冠华、李超平、王素芳著《公共图书馆建设主体研究：全覆盖目标下的选择》（国家图书馆出版社，2012 年），于良芝、许晓霞、张广钦著《公共图书馆基本原理》（北京师范大学出版社，2012 年）；汪东波主编《公共图书馆概论》（国家图书馆出版社，2012 年）；李国新、段明莲等著《国外公共图书馆法研究》（国家图书馆出版社，2013 年）：诸此种种，各有千秋，各有建树。但是，总的来说，我国的图书馆权利研究仍处在初级阶段，尚有许多理论和实践问题需要深入研究。

5.2 图书馆权利的实现困难重重

虽然《全国公共图书馆事业发展“十二五”规划》确立了“逐步建立覆盖城乡、结构合理、功能健全、实用高效的服务网络，进一步增强活力，提高效能，服务能力、服务水平与服务效益明显提升，部分地区图书馆接近或达到国际先进水平”的公共图书馆发展目标，但是，要实现这个目标仍然困难重重：政府主导目前仍然停留在国家文化治理理念层面，各级政府、各地政府履行公共图书馆的责任十分不平衡；财政“分灶吃饭”的体制和公共图书馆经费短缺的现状并没有根本改变；县级以下基层公共图书馆的建设仍然十分落后，远远不能满足民众的基本文化需求。要克服其中的困难，解决个中的问题，绝非一朝一日可以完成，也许还要十年、二十年，甚至更长时间。

5.3 图书馆权利的传播任重道远

"图书馆权利是指民众利用图书馆的平等和自由。"[41]36 "平等权利"和"自由权利"是图书馆权利不可分割的两个组成部分。十年图书馆权利思潮主要集中在"平等权利"的传播和实践上，"自由权利"的研究、传播和实践只是偶有涉及。公共图书馆免费服务的推行困难重重且不尽如民意，说明"平等权利"观念和价值观并没有在政府层面和公共图书馆界完全树立。中国图书馆学会颁布的《图书馆服务宣言》刻意回避民众的"自由权利"，反映了中国图书馆界的普遍心态。"自由权利"是《中华人民共和国宪法》赋予中国公民的普遍权利。党的十八大提出24字社会主义核心价值观：富强、民主、文明、和谐是国家层面的价值目标，自由、平等、公正、法治是社会层面的价值取向，爱国、敬业、诚信、友善是公民个人层面的价值准则。自由、平等、公正、法治作为社会层面的价值取向，完全应该成为图书馆的核心价值，予以深入研究、广泛传播和积极实践。

十年图书馆权利思潮是中国图书馆界的权利觉醒，这种觉醒是一场图书馆核心价值观的集体洗礼。十年图书馆权利思潮更是基本公共文化权益的庶民胜利，这种胜利是一场构建和谐社会的权利实现。然而，这场集体洗礼并没有完成，这场权利实现还只是刚刚开始，任重而道远，决不可半途而废。中国图书馆的未来十年仍将是惠及全民的图书馆权利时代。

参考文献

[1] 梁启超. 清代学术概论［M］. 桂林：广西师范大学出版社，2010：1-2.

[2] 中国图书馆学会. 中国图书馆学会2004年年会征文通知［EB/OL］.［2014-12-05］. http://www.csls.org.cn/academic/yearmeet2.html.

[3] 中国图书馆学会. 中国图书馆事业百年［M］. 北京：北京图书馆出版社，2004.

[4] 周和平.《中国图书馆百年系列丛书》序言［M］//中国图书馆学会. 百年情怀——天堂，图书馆的模样. 北京：科学出版社，2004：7.

[5] 中国图书馆学会. 中国图书馆学会2004年年会暨学会成立25周年纪念大会隆重举行［EB/OL］.［2014-12-05］. http://www.csls.org.cn/academic/yearmeet6.html.

[6] 中国图书馆学会. "第一分会场：百年图书馆精神的魅力"会议总结［EB/OL］.［2014-12-05］. http://www.csls.org.cn/academic/2004yearmeet1.html.

[7] 中国图书馆学会. "第二届图书馆法与知识产权论坛"小结［EB/OL］.［2014-12-05］. http://www.csls.org.cn/academic/2004yearmeet3.html.

[8] 中国图书馆学会. 中国图书馆学会2005年年会征文通知［EB/OL］.［2014-12-05］. http://www.csls.org.cn/academic/2005yearmeet1.html.

[9] 程焕文，周旭毓. 权利与道德——关于公共图书馆精神的阐释［J］. 图书馆建设，2005（4）：1-4，42.

[10] 程焕文，周旭毓. 图书馆精神——体系结构与基本内容［J］. 图书馆，2005（2）：3-9.

[11] 周继武. 国家图书馆借书记［N］. 南方周末，2004-10-14.

[12] 何正权. 大学图书馆向学生"卖"座位事发　信阳师范学院学生投诉其乱收费　馆长称收取的是管理费［N］. 大河报，2004-12-11（8）.

[13] 毕红秋. 权利正觉醒　激情在燃放——中国图书馆学会2005年峰会综述［J］. 图书馆建设，2005（1）：12-14，29.

[14] 蒋永福，毕红秋. 走向权利时代——献给2005年新创专栏［J］. 图书馆建设，2004（6）：封二.

[15] 南山图书馆，等. 以人为本弘扬图书馆精神——本刊与南山图书馆、湖南大学信息研究所共倡“21 世纪新图书馆运动”[J]. 图书馆，2005（1）：1.
[16] 蒋永福. 激情燃放之后话别——《走向权利时代》专栏结束语［J]. 图书馆建设，2006（6）：16.
[17] 李爽. “新图书馆运动”质疑［J]. 图书情报知识，2005（2）：90－92.
[18] 崔红娟. 论范并思的公共图书馆原理思想［J]. 图书馆，2005（1）：13－17.
[19] 赵燕群. 中国图书馆学没有大家吗？[J]. 图书馆，2006（2）：105－107，113.
[20] 谭祥金. 为公共图书馆辩护——“21 世纪新图书馆运动论坛”之我见［J]. 中国图书馆学报，2006（2）：19－24.
[21] 谢树芳，等. 一曲图书馆人文精神的交响——“21 世纪新图书馆运动论坛”书评（上）［J]. 图书馆，2007（1）：45－51.
[22] 陈文，沈占云，刘恋，等. 一曲图书馆人文精神的交响：“21 世纪新图书馆运动论坛”书评（下）［J]. 图书馆，2007（2）：37－42.
[23] 中国图书馆学会. 中国图书馆学会 2005 年年会第二分会场总结［EB/OL]. [2014－12－10]. http://www.csls.org.cn/academic/2005yearmeet6.html.
[24] 程焕文，潘燕桃. 信息资源共享（教育部“高等教育面向 21 世纪课程教材”）［M]. 北京：高等教育出版社，2004.
[25] 黄俊贵. 丑陋的图书馆学——“实话实说”访谈录［J]. 图书与情报，2000（2）：37－42.
[26] 程焕文. 丑陋的《丑陋的图书馆学》——致《图书与情报》的信［J]. 图书与情报，2001（1）：49－50.
[27] 邱蔚晴，等. 图书馆学“丑陋”？——中山大学信管系 99 级部分研究生座谈录［J]. 图书与情报，2001（1）：50－52.
[28] 黄俊贵. 图书馆学需要哲学——从《丑陋的图书馆学》引发的思考［J]. 图书与情报，2001（2）：64－67.
[29] 鲍振西. 尽淘污浊始见金——就《丑陋的图书馆学》致《图书与情报》编辑部的信［J]. 图书与情报，2001（2）：68.
[30] 罗德运. 除却丑陋繁荣学术［J]. 图书与情报，2002（2）：16－20，24.
[31] 郁青. 关于《丑陋的图书馆学——“实话实说”访谈录》的一些看法［J]. 图书馆界，2001（2）：56，60.
[32] 梅雪. 浅说《丑陋的图书馆学——“实话实说”访谈录》[J]. 图书情报论坛，2001（4）：35－37.
[33] 黄俊贵. 看图书馆现状要客观　讲图书馆精神要科学——对《图书馆精神——体系结构与基本内容》一文的商榷［J]. 图书情报知识，2005（6）：36－39.
[34] 程焕文. 图书馆精神始终是最重要的——答黄俊贵先生［J]. 图书情报知识，2006（3）：35－36，48.
[35] 黄俊贵. 学术批评需要理智——兼对《图书馆精神——体系结构与基本内容》再商榷［J]. 图书情报知识，2006（4）：38－42.
[36] 黄俊贵. 公共图书馆的服务原则及其实践［J]. 中国图书馆学报，2006（6）：5－11.
[37] 程焕文. 实在的图书馆精神与图书馆精神的实在［J]. 大学图书馆学报，2006（4）：2－14.
[38] 陈记建. 再论图书馆学理论研究与构建的方法论问题——对我国“图书馆精神”研究与争鸣的反思［J]. 图书馆建设，2007（4）：22－27.
[39] 张金国，王梅. “图书馆精神”仍然是最重要的——为“图书馆精神”辩护之一［J]. 图书馆建设. 2007（3）：33－37.
[40] 程焕文.《国家“十一五”时期文化发展规划纲要》激情解说［EB/OL]. [2014－12－11]. http://blog.sina.com.cn/s/blog_4978019f0100051f.html.
[41] 全国哲学社会科学规划办公室网站. 2005 年度国家社科基金年度项目评审结果揭晓［EB/OL]. [2014－12－05]. http://www.npopss-cn.gov.cn/planning/xm2005/tsqb.html.
[42] 程焕文，潘燕桃，张靖. 图书馆权利研究（《国家哲学社会科学成果文库》）［M]. 北京：学习出版社，2011：18－24.
[43] 程焕文. 图书馆精神［M]. 北京：北京图书馆出版社，2007.
[44] 程焕文，张靖. 图书馆权利与道德（上、下）［M]. 桂林：广西师范大学出版社，2007.
[45] 程焕文，王蕾. 竹帛斋图书馆学论剑：用户永远都是正确的［M]. 广州：广东人民出版社，2008.
[46] 中国图书馆学会. 首届“百县馆长论坛”征文通知［EB/OL]. [2014－12－02]. http://www.lsc.org.cn/c/cn/

news/2006 - 04/03/news_208. html.

[47] “百县馆长论坛”林州共识 [EB/OL]. [2014 - 12 - 02]. http://www. lsc. org. cn/c/cn/news/2006 - 04/03/news_210. html.

[48] 常熟共识 [EB/OL]. [2014 - 12 - 02]. http://www. lsc. org. cn/c/cn/news/2007 - 11/01/news_1587. html.

[49] 中国图书馆学会第三届百县馆长论坛江阴共识 [EB/OL]. [2014 - 12 - 02]. http://www. lsc. org. cn/c/cn/news/2010 - 05/21/news_4518. html.

[50] 中国图书馆学会第四届百县馆长论坛神木共识 [EB/OL]. [2014 - 12 - 02]. http://www. lsc. org. cn/c/cn/news/2012 - 07/16/news_6081. html.

[51] 托起中国图书馆事业的希望：记中国图书馆学会首次志愿者行动 [EB/OL]. (2006 - 09 - 26) [2014 - 12 - 02]. http://www. lsc. org. cn/c/cn/news/2006 - 09/26/news_994. html.

[52] 基层图书馆培训志愿者名单 [EB/OL]. [2014 - 12 - 02]. http://www. lsc. org. cn/c/cn/news/2006 - 05/26/news_624. html.

[53] 基层图书馆培训志愿者行动招募公告 [EB/OL]. [2014 - 12 - 02]. http://www. lsc. org. cn/c/cn/news/2006 - 05/26/news_632. html.

[54] 中办国办印发《国家“十一五”时期文化发展规划纲要》 [EB/OL]. [2014 - 12 - 02]. http://news. xinhuanet. com/politics/2006 - 09/13/content_5086965. html.

[55] 文化部、财政部关于实施全国文化信息资源共享工程的通知（2002 年 4 月 17 日文社图发〔2002〕14 号）[G] //国家图书馆研究院. 我国图书馆事业发展政策文件选编（1949—2012）. 北京：国家图书馆出版社，2014：169 - 181.

[56] 文化部、财政部关于进一步推进全国文化信息资源共享工程的实施意见（2007 年 4 月 3 日文社图发〔2007〕14 号）[G] //国家图书馆研究院. 我国图书馆事业发展政策文件选编（1949—2012）. 北京：国家图书馆出版社，2014：218 - 223.

[57] 李国新，范并思. 迎接图书馆事业的大发展大繁荣——纪念《国家“十一五”时期文化发展纲要》发表一周年 [J]. 图书与情报，2007（5）：1.

[58] 范并思. 政府公共图书馆服务理念的根本性转变 [J]. 图书与情报，2007（5）：2 - 3.

[59] 程焕文. 普遍均等 惠及全民——关于公共服务普遍均等原则的阐释 [J]. 图书与情报，2007（5）：4 - 7.

[60] 邱冠华. 解读《国家“十一五”时期文化发展规划纲要》的服务网络 [J]. 图书与情报，2007（5）：8 - 9.

[61] 李国新. 立法保障是最根本的保障 [J]. 图书与情报，2007（5）：10 - 11.

[62] 白雪华. 切实履行政府职责 保障公民基本文化权益 [J]. 图书与情报，2007（5）：12 - 13.

[63] 蒋永福. 发展图书馆事业必须纳入政府议事日程——“五个纳入”随想 [J]. 图书与情报，2007（5）：14 - 15.

[64] 崔建飞. 共享工程在公共文化服务体系中的地位和特点 [J]. 图书与情报，2007（5）：16 - 17.

[65] 褚树青. 城乡共享生活品质 [J]. 图书与情报，2007（5）：18 - 19.

[66] 王素芳. 弱势群体文化权益保障的国家战略视野——基于《国家“十一五”时期文化发展纲要》的解读 [J]. 图书与情报，2007（5）：20 - 22.

[67] 于良芝. 建立覆盖全社会的公共图书馆服务体系 [J]. 图书与情报，2007（5）：23 - 24.

[68] 程焕文. 岭南模式：崛起的广东公共图书馆事业 [J]. 中国图书馆学报，2007（3）：15 - 25.

[69] 践行《图书馆服务宣言》推动图书馆事业发展 [EB/OL]. [2014 - 12 - 02]. http://www. lsc. org. cn/c/cn/news/2009 - 01/05/news_2771. html.

[70] 中国图书馆学会. 图书馆服务宣言 [EB/OL]. [2014 - 12 - 02]. http://www. lsc. org. cn/c/cn/news/2008 - 10/28/news_2579. html.

[71]《公共图书馆建设标准》答记者问 [EB/OL]. [2014 - 12 - 02]. http://59. 252. 212. 6/auto255/200811/t20081119_13029. html? Keywords：=公共图书馆建设标准.

[72] 深圳市文体旅游局. 关于加强基层公共文化场馆管理的通知 [EB/OL]. [2014 - 12 - 02]. http://www. sz. gov. cn/whj/zcfggfxwj/wtys/200909/t20090904_1173518. html.

[73] 文化部、财政部关于推进全国美术馆、公共图书馆、文化馆（站）免费开放工作的意见（2011 年 1 月 26 日文财务发〔2011〕5 号）[G] //国家图书馆研究院. 我国图书馆事业发展政策文件选编（1949—2012）. 北京：

国家图书馆出版社，2014，10：258－261.
［74］财政部关于加强美术馆、公共图书馆、文化馆（站）免费开放经费保障工作的通知（2011 年 3 月 7 日财教〔2011〕31 号）［G］//国家图书馆研究院．我国图书馆事业发展政策文件选编（1949—2012）．北京：国家图书馆出版社，2014，10：61－262.
［75］文化部、财政部关于实施“数字图书馆推广工程”的通知（2011 年 5 月 26 日文社文发〔2011〕27 号）［G］//国家图书馆研究院．我国图书馆事业发展政策文件选编（1949—2012）．北京：国家图书馆出版社，2014，10：265－269.
［76］文化部关于三馆一站免费开放督查工作情况的通报（2012 年 9 月 27 日文财务发〔2012〕37 号）［G］//国家图书馆研究院．我国图书馆事业发展政策文件选编（1949—2012）．北京：国家图书馆出版社，2014，10：298－303.
［77］程焕文．庶民的胜利：全国公共图书馆免费开放［EB/OL］．［2014－12－03］．http://blog.sina.com.cn/s/blog_4978019f01017h7d.html.
［78］程焕文．答网友：乞丐进图书馆取暖是乞丐的基本文化权利［EB/OL］．［2014－12－02］．http://blog.sina.com.cn/s/blog_4978019f01017gkw.html.
［79］冯原．读书且取暖，请到“最温暖图书馆”［N］．新华每日电讯，2011－01－21（2）.
［80］冯原．一扇门为乞丐而开才叫“天堂”［N］．工人日报，2011－01－22（5）.
［81］冯原，顺春．杭州图书馆，零门槛“最温暖”［N］．人民日报，2011－01－21（12）.
［82］何涛．“史上最温暖图书馆”追踪：小偷也有进图书馆的权利——“公共图书馆岭南派”领先全国专家提议建澡堂给乞丐［N］．广州日报，2011－01－24（18）.
［83］曹小芹．图书馆不禁乞丐不能一概而论［N］．中国经济导报，2011－01－27（B6）.
［84］汪成明．冬天里的一把火［N］．浙江日报，2011－01－27（20）.
［85］李超平．大写的图书馆职业理念［N］．中国文化报，2011－02－10（7）.
［86］段菁菁．“温暖图书馆”里的拾荒者——杭州图书馆“平等免费无障碍”理念吸引了很多拾荒者阅读，为他们提供平等的人文关怀［N］．新华每日电讯，2014，11，27（5）.
［87］程焕文．“乞丐入馆案”是图书馆权利思想传播的里程碑［EB/OL］．［2014－12－02］．http://blog.sina.com.cn/s/blog_4978019f01017gp5.html.
［88］《文化部关于做好〈公共图书馆服务规范〉宣传贯彻工作的通知》［G］//国家图书馆研究院．我国图书馆事业发展政策文件选编（1949—2012）．北京：国家图书馆出版社，2014：305－307.
［89］《文化部关于印发〈全国公共图书馆事业发展“十二五”规划〉的通知》［G］//国家图书馆研究院．我国图书馆事业发展政策文件选编（1949—2012）．北京：国家图书馆出版社，2014：316－327.
［90］程焕文．人有好恶　书无好坏［EB/OL］．［2014－12－02］．http://blog.sina.com.cn/s/blog_4978019f0102e2d7.html.
［91］程焕文．勿左勿右　客观中立［EB/OL］．［2014－12－02］．http://blog.sina.com.cn/s/blog_4978019f0102e2dy.html.
［92］潘燕桃．图书馆专业主义的涟漪——关于“人有好恶　书无好坏”笔谈［J］．图书馆建设，2013（9）：1－2，6.
［93］程焕文．人有好恶　书无好坏［J］．图书馆建设，2013（9）：3.
［94］程焕文．勿左勿右　客观中立［J］．图书馆建设，2013（9）：4.
［95］吴晞．三个故事　一条宗旨——阅读自由随笔［J］．图书馆建设，2013（9）：5－6.
［96］李超平．书有好坏　自由阅读　好书推荐［J］．图书馆建设，2013（9）：7－8.
［97］蒋永福．继续推进图书馆观念的与时俱进——读程焕文两篇博客文章有感［J］．图书馆建设，2013（9）：8－10.
［98］褚树青．择善之辩［J］．图书馆建设，2013（9）：11.
［99］刘洪辉．图书馆阅读自由杂谈［J］．图书馆建设，2013（9）：12－13.
［100］俞传正．“书无好坏”引发的中立性价值的思考［J］．图书馆建设，2013（9）：14－15.
［101］宋显彪．“人有好恶，书无好坏”论争评述［J］．图书馆建设，2013（9）：15－17.
［102］张彬．“书无好坏”争论反思［J］．图书馆建设，2014（3）：92－94.

教师简介：

黄晓斌，男，中山大学理学硕士，武汉大学管理学博士。现任中山大学资讯管理学院教授，博士生导师。主讲“竞争情报研究/企业竞争情报”、“情报学理论与方法”、“数字图书馆学研究/建设”、“竞争情报研究/竞争情报”、“情报分析与研究”等课程。主要研究方向为数字图书馆、网络信息开发与利用、竞争情报等。主持科研项目10余项，发表论文100余篇，出版著作8部。1995—1996年任美国伯克利加州大学访问学者，2000—2001年任美国佛罗里达州立大学访问研究员。兼任中山大学信息经济与政策研究中心研究员、中国科学评价中心兼职研究员、中国科学技术情报学会专业委员、中国竞争情报学会会员、广东省社会科学情报学会常务理事。联系方式：isshxb@ mail. sysu. edu. cn。

图书馆数字化服务发展的新趋势

黄晓斌

摘　要：数字技术为图书馆服务注入新的活力，促使图书馆通过各种新的方式，让读者享有更多优质、高效、专业的知识与信息服务。本文从数字资源的集成服务、基于内容与知识服务、主动提醒服务、个性化推荐服务、Web 2.0 环境下的服务、虚拟社区服务、移动服务等方面介绍了图书馆数字化服务的一些新近进展，并指出图书馆数字化服务的发展趋势与方向。

关键词：图书馆；数字化服务；发展趋势

The New Development Trends in Library Digital Service

Xiaobin Huang

Abstract：Digital technologies，is an active force for library services，enabling various new services，so that users can have high-quality，efficient and professional knowledge and information. This paper elaborates on current developments of digital technologies and services in terms of integration service，content and knowledge service，alert service，individualized service，recommendation，web 2. 0 and mobile service，and also points out the developing direction of library service.

Keywords：Libraries；Digital services；New development trends

中国图书馆学会发布的《图书馆服务宣言》中提到：“图书馆充分利用现代信息技术，提高数字资源提供能力和使用效率，以服务创新应对信息时代的挑战。”[1] 目前，许多图书馆收藏了数字化资源，为读者利用图书馆提供了极大的便利。数字化技术可以使图书馆提供更多更快的新型服务方式，并使工作人员从繁忙的事务性工作中解脱出来，为读者提供优质、高效、专业的知识与信息服务。本文从数字资源的集成服务、基于内容与知识服务、主动提醒服务、个性化推荐服务、Web 2.0 环境下的服务、虚拟社区服务、移动服务等方面对数字技术及图书馆数字化服务的新近进展进行介绍。

1 数字资源的集成服务

集成，亦称整合、融合。数字资源集成是指将分散在不同地点、不同类型的文献资源汇集为一个有机整体，方便用户查找和利用。数字资源开发商在建设数据库时，大多是依据自己的标准，如使用不同的操作系统和管理软件，用户需要分别熟悉每个数据库的内容和要求才能进行利用。而集成能够将异构数据库用统一的格式予以融合、类聚和重组，形成一个效能更好、效率更高的资源体系。[2]随着学科的分化与融合，用户的需求也呈现出了多元化的特点，即使是专业性较强的研究课题，在很多情况下都需要得到多学科理论方法的支持，而分散化的资源只能解决某些方面的问题，只有将这些资源联系起来，形成一个有机整体，才能充分满足用户的需求，发挥更大的效益。

信息资源的集成模式可以分为两类：虚拟法和实体法。虚拟法集成是通过中间件等技术将用户的查询请求转换为相应信息系统的查询语言和检索方法。虚拟法的适用对象为独立性强、更新比较频繁、数据量大的数据库。其不足是在检索利用时，由于要分别调用不同来源的数据，因此耗时较长。实体法集成需要建立独立的数据仓库，要把不同来源、不同结构的数据导入库中，以主题或时间等方式并用统一的规范将这些数据组织起来，用户直接从数据仓库中进行检索。实体法的优点是检索效率较高，格式较为规范；缺点是更新不够及时，建库需要耗费较大的人力和物力。

为了给读者提供多样化的资源，目前许多图书馆都购买了多种文献数据库。不同数据库的资源各有倚重，同时又存在着一定的重复。一些大型数据库的子库往往处于“不可见”状态。为了避免读者重复检索，充分揭示各类资源，图书馆有必要建立跨库检索系统，为读者提供统一的获取入口。不同数据库拥有不同的检索规范，通过系统在后台做出相应配置，使其得到统一；采用并发检索方式，即把用户的提问分别提交给不同的数据库，然后对检索结果进行去重，以统一的格式显示。跨库检索的不足是响应时间比较长，一些个性化的检索方式，如利用化学的分子式检索，经过格式统一后很可能会被屏蔽掉。

链接是通过超文本传输协议将网页中的知识点如概念、文字、照片、音频、视频联系起来，形成立体化的资源组织模式。根据链接的建构方式，可以划分为静态链接与动态链接两种。动态链接并非专门指向某一链宿，可以由用户根据需要进行选择，或根据用户的意图如点击率自动生成。动态链接可对用户链接前刚出现的链接对象或位置予以链接，也可在链接计算规则中嵌入选择机制实现选择性链接。在动态链接中，用户可以管理链接内容，克服死链的现象。目前，开放式动态链接技术已经出现了一些标准，如“OpenURL（开放链接）”，是一个开放的信息资源与查询服务之间的通信协议标准，是开放、动态、上下文相关的链接框架。[3]开放链接需要设置一个链接资源库，用户在点击时不是指向链宿，而是指向该库的服务器，服务器则向用户提供一个链接的表单，由用户从中选择。目前许多图书馆集成系统都引入该标准，如 ExLibris 公司推出的网络电子资源链接融合软件系统“SFX（Special Effects 的缩写）”即采用了该标准，它可以深入到文献的内容当中提供服务，每当有新的资源更新，系统就会自动更改链接信息，使读者第一时间获取和利用，可以把论文、网上资源、全文资源、机构库以及一些服务方式如馆际互借等通过链接整合起来。南京师范大学图书馆引进 MetaLib/SFX 学术资源整合门户，应用在馆藏目录、搜索引擎、自建数据库、服务集成等方面，还将图书馆资源与服务嵌入各类应用平台，如集成 CALIS 馆际互借系统以及 CASHL 文献传递系统，取得较好的效果。[4]北京师范大学图书馆曾经在其学术资源门户中使用了 SFX 链接，方便读者获取多种扩展性服务，如参考咨询、馆际互借、引文分析及网上书店提供的信息和服务。[5]除上述之外，数字资源集成在其他领域也发挥着重要作用，如图书馆的 OPAC 跨资源检索、数字资源导航、元数据采集与增值服务等。

2 基于内容与知识的服务

传统的文献检索由于受技术限制，大都属于元数据查询，不能深入到文献的内容当中去。随着数字化技术的发展，深入到文献内容的全文检索已成为现实。根据检索的媒体类型，内容检索可以分为文本内容检索与多媒体内容检索两类。

文本内容检索是以文本型文献如图书、期刊等为检索对象，对其内容进行知识元查询、挖掘分析、知识发现和情报研究。目前超星公司的读秀电子书库可以深入到某些图书章节内容中进行检索。美国情报学家 Don R. Swanson 在阅读有关鱼油和雷诺氏病的文献时，发现鱼油对雷诺氏病具有较好的疗效，于是得出结论：一些表面上看似不相关的医学文献实际上存在着一定的联系，通过发现这种联系就可以找到治疗疾病的药物。基于这一假设，他提出了一种新的知识发现方法——基于非相关文献的知识发现法。为此，他获得美国情报科技学会的最高科学成就奖。Swanson 还开发了一种称为 Arrowsmith 的工具，用以进行文献主题匹配，运用全文检索技术对内容进行相关分析，找到多种治疗疾病的药物。[6]可见，内容分析具有广阔的应用前景。

多媒体内容检索的对象包括图像、音频、视频等媒体资源。如在图像检索中，可以通过颜色、形状、纹理、质感、轮廓等提问。多媒体内容检索主要是从媒体里面提取特征，检索不是一个精确匹配的过程，而是一种近似匹配，需要不断进行调整。多媒体的内容检索可以采用样例提问方式，用户可以选择系统提供的样例，也可以自己画一个。以图像检索为例，用户可以运用色彩进行检索，通过颜色之间的组配提问，还可以利用颜色比例法，借助调色板，使用鼠标拖动颜色的滑杆确定色彩比例进行检索。把多种检索方式综合起来就称为多特征检索，如把颜色、纹理、轮廓和关键词组配起来进行查询，就可以深入到检索对象各方面的特征，提高命中率。目前国外已有一些多特征检索系统，如 IBM 的 QBIC 邮票与博物馆图片检索系统、哥伦比亚大学的 Visual Seek 系统、密歇根大学和 MIT 多媒体实验室的 Virage 系统。美国数字图书馆项目中就有多项有关内容检索的研究，如伯克利加州大学数字图书馆计划将加州水资源和其他自然资源图片进行数字化处理，建成一个多特征数据库，可以检索照片上的对象，也可以用颜色斑点或颜色比例检索。为了把内容更清晰地展现出来，一些系统采用可视化方法协助用户检索或显示检索结果。可在检索前对内容做可视化说明，方便用户对有关检索提问方式的理解，或在检索中以可视化方式帮助用户调整检索要求，将检索词与数据库的匹配流程动态显示出来。并以可视化图表显示检索结果。有些大学图书馆为了方便用户从分类角度查找图书，把检索界面设计成一个书架，用户只要点击相关类目，就如同在实体图书馆中找书一样查阅资料。

知识服务通过知识组织处理技术，实现信息查询语义化、智能化，向用户提供满意度较高的服务。知识检索能够利用信息的语义知识，理解用户的检索需求，通过知识学习、分析理解和推理归纳来实现检索的智能化，能帮助用户快速定位、获取所需信息，使得用户获得充分的语义信息，提高检索效率、精确性和智能性。武汉大学信息资源管理研究中心开发的“第二次国共合作历史数字图书馆（GGHZ - DL）”是以历史事件为研究领域的本体数字图书馆，实现本体基本功能（本体建库、本体检索、本体推理、本体可视化）的跨领域知识检索平台。[7]

3 主动提醒服务

提醒服务也称主动服务，指根据用户的需要，动态监测环境与资源，运用主动推送技术，由服务方把有关信息定期推送到用户桌面。提醒服务以定制为主，由用户根据自己的需要主动定制有关栏目，定制方式主要有 RSS、电子邮件、网页订制、专用软件、移动订阅等。[8]用户除需要确定定制的主题和方式外，还可以确定推送频率，如一个月一次或一个星期一次。中国期刊网 CNKI 提供了 RSS 订阅服务，订阅方式包括期刊订阅、关键词订阅与主题订阅。如果以电子邮件进行订阅，用户需要将自己的电邮地址告诉系统，系统通过电邮向用户发送最新资源和服务信息，如 Springer Link 等许多数据库的提醒服务就采用了这种方式。网页定制指用户在网站提供的信息和服务栏目中做出选择，如内容、风格、发送形式等，由网站根据用户的要求定期更新相关栏目，或将有关内容以用户确认的方式发送给用户。Science Direct 数据库收录了 2000 多种电子期刊的全文和文摘，向用户提供期刊的引用推送和检索策略推送。服务商通过对用户的订制需求进行分析，可以监测用户的需求动态，为主动服务打下基础。一些数据库还提供了专门的推送软件，如 Dialog 开发了一个推送插件，类似聊天软件的客户端，用户下载并安装后，系统就可以与用户互动并及时推送信息。移动定制指用户运用移动设备订制数据库的资源和服务信息，当前使用较多的是手机短信订制，用户将自己的号码告诉系统，系统通过群发机制向用户传送信息。一些搜索引擎利用订制服务帮助用户监控网上动态，如 Google Alert。当用户希望知道竞争对手的最新情报，如新产品、人才招聘，或希望了解某方面的行业进展时，都可以通过搜索引擎的订制服务跟踪和了解。用户可以了解特定关键词的搜索结果或某些类型资料如新闻、博客等的更新。百度、MSN 等也提供了类似的新闻订制功能。由于各种网络数据库尤其是学术资源类数据库的内容并非每天都更新的，用户通常不会每天去浏览相关数据库。网络数据库可以根据数据库的内容变化作为提示内容，当用户关心的任何网站在内容方面发生变化时，网络数据库便会主动地把相关的最新消息送至用户。提醒服务的主要优点是：及时性好，针对性较强，应用面广，对用户没有技术上的特别要求。

4 个性化推荐服务

个性化服务是指针对用户的个性特点，如知识结构、需求、心理和行为方式等，为用户量身定制提供相关服务和资源。个性化服务的方式很多，在图书馆界运用比较普遍的是“我的图书馆”（My Library）。“我的图书馆”可以协助图书馆区分不同用户的需求，个性化服务以用户为中心，让用户充分表达自己的需求意愿，提高服务质量。读者通过“我的图书馆”，能了解自己借阅图书的情况，办理续借手续，并订阅资源和服务，它是联系图书馆与读者的桥梁。“我的图书馆”一般包括“我的门户、我的链接、我的更新、我的储存、我的信使”等功能模块，还可以提供一些扩展功能，如利用 Web 2.0 技术建立用户空间，形成一些共同兴趣读者的虚拟社区。美国的康奈尔大学图书馆较早开通了“我的图书馆”服务，中国科学院国家科学图书馆与浙江大学图书馆则是国内较早提供这一服务的单位。“我的图书馆”近年来出现了一些新的研究课题，如保护用户隐私、用户偏好和行为研究等。在个性化信息服务中，一个重要环节就是系统主动发现用户需要的信息并推送到用户桌面，即“为人找书，为书找人”的数字化推荐服务。推荐服务涉及用户需求信息的搜集、分析和文献内容特征的揭示，推荐方法包括基于内容的推荐、协同过滤推荐、基于用户统计信息的推荐等多种方式。[9]

基于内容的推荐指系统根据文献内容特征和用户兴趣的匹配度，主动向用户推送有关资源的过程。系统通过跟踪用户查阅文献和利用服务的历史，运用数据挖掘等技术手段对用户兴趣建模，作为为用户推荐文献与资料的依据。系统对用户需求与兴趣的了解程度越深，推荐结果的准确率就越高。

协同过滤推荐依据用户之间的兴趣关联进行推荐，其假设是如果用户在某些兴趣点上相似，他们在其他兴趣点上相似的可能也较大。协同过滤推荐的优点是不用揭示文献的内容特征，只需要依据用户之间的关联度进行彼此推荐，对推荐对象没有特殊要求。网络书签（或称社会书签）是协同过滤推荐的一种，它提供一个公共平台，由用户根据自己的意愿共享信息。在使用网络书签时，用户不需要掌握太多的专业知识，使用的是自然语言，标签组织方便，共享灵活，可以不受地域限制，不与特定机器关联。通过网络书签，用户可以建立一个信息共享兴趣小组，成立虚拟社区。亚马逊书店成功地将协同过滤推荐嵌入系统，可以根据用户的评级和推荐介绍图书，它的推荐内容丰富，自动化程度高，具有良好的推荐成功率。协同过滤算法也得到了图书馆界的关注，许多图书馆将其引入数字化服务领域。例如，美国 Oregon 州立大学图书馆开发了一个图书馆协同过滤推荐系统，通过读者的使用数据互相推荐；中国人民大学数字图书馆个性化推荐系统也采用了协同过滤算法，读者借还书时被要求对图书打分，并用简单的文字提供评语，其他读者可以根据这些评价信息决定是否借阅这本书。

基于用户统计信息的推荐指根据对用户信息的统计结果向用户推荐符合其需要的资料。多数数据库都建立了日志文件，用户查找数据或点击网页，日志文件都会留存相关记录，如访问 IP、访问时间、逗留时间、访问顺序等，利用这些日志文件就可以分析出用户的关注点。传统图书馆的业务统计比较粗糙，准确性低，数字图书馆可以实现精准统计，统计结果和分析结论可以作为服务与决策的依据。如 Science Direct 数据库提供了下载前25排名服务，对每季度下载的文章进行排名，把前25名在网上公布并向用户推荐。[10]一些数据库商或网络服务商也运用客服的数据统计出当前的关注热点，并对今后的趋势做出预测，如Google趋势利用用户留下的检索日志记录，以图形和数据方式显示人们对不同主题的关注程度。[11]中国期刊网CNKI以学术关注度统计不同客户搜索CNKI数据库中的文章数量，以图表方式显示关注情况，开发了一个学术趋势搜索。[12]利用它可以了解和分析有关主题的研究历史、当前的研究热点和未来的研究走向，帮助用户找到代表性论文，并可以作为学术评价的依据。

除上述几种推荐方式外，还有基于知识的推荐、基于关联规则的推荐等。将所有这些推荐方法综合起来就成为混合推荐或综合推荐，国外有些数字图书馆已在开发这方面的功能，如斯坦福大学数字图书馆项目中的FAB过滤系统、加州大学伯克利分校的Melvyl书目系统。

5 Web 2.0 环境下的服务

Web 2.0是相对于Web 1.0而言的，Web 2.0具有多种网络形态，如博客、微博、播客、RSS、网摘、社会书签、社会性软件、维基等，用户不仅可以查看内容，还可以提供信息。因此，Web 2.0是去中心化、交互性强的一种网络应用，用户也不再是被动的利用者，他们既是网上信息的使用者，更是内容的提供和建设者。有些人将Web 2.0看成一种理念和服务方式，它给图书馆服务带来的影响既有机遇也有挑战。首先是观念上的变革，其次是服务方式上的改进，另外对工作人员的素质和能力也提出了更高的要求。近年来，图书馆界对Web 2.0的应用关注较多，并提出了图书馆2.0的概念。[13]图书馆2.0给图书馆界带来了变化，也提供了新的研究领域，尤其在服务方面带来的变化较为显著。国家科学图书馆较早使用RSS技术对资源进行整合，建立了国家科学图书馆科技新闻聚合服务系统；中山大学图书馆也利用RSS为用户提供最新动态、新书通报、电子资源等的订阅；台湾大学图书馆的RSS订阅包括图书馆新鲜事、热门推荐、新到资料、最新资讯等内容；上海大学图书馆开发了图书馆新闻聚合系统，不同图书馆的网站或不同的博客上一有新的信息发布，该系统就可以自动采集并通知用户；厦门大学图书馆的图林网志也属于聚合平台，提供RSS订阅服务。美国一些大学图书馆把博客做成一个与专题推荐书目类似的平台，向读者提供有关图书信息，用户在此可以进行讨论。宾州大学图书馆建立了基于标签的资源导航，采用云图方式由用户来推荐相关资源。东北师范大学图书馆利用MSN技术提供参考咨询服务，效果显著。在Web 2.0的技术应用中还有维基方式。如图书馆为了解决某方面的问题，通过维基平台让大家提出有关工作建议；有的图书馆把维基做成一个信息资源评论的工具，如厦门大学图书馆，这样馆员就可以同读者进行双向交流。维基还可以被用来提供定题服务，如上海中医药大学图书馆采用维基提供专题信息服务。维基在图书馆的传统工作如编目等方面也能发挥重要作用，OCLC的联合编目就采用了维基方式，会员单位通过维基平台提供评论、注释和数据。上海图书馆的DC元数据研究项目也采用了维基方式进行讨论。随着网络技术的进一步完善，应用方式不断进行推陈出新，可以预料，Web 2.0在图书馆服务方面还有很大的发展空间。

6 虚拟社区服务

虚拟社区（Virtual Community）又称网络社区（Network Community）、赛博社区（Cyber community）和数字社区（Electronic Community）等，是指在网络空间进行频繁的社会互动形成的具有文化认同的共同体及其活动场所，是一个基于网络信息技术支持的参与者之间的互动，并且在参与者之间形成一种社会关系。虚拟社区为图书馆用户提供信息交流与共享平台，为用户管理与教育培训提供条件。利用虚拟社区可以了解用户的信息需求、进行用户的素质教育和介绍有关服务的信息。虚拟社区有利于促进信息服务的水平和质量的提高，可以利用虚拟社区进行信息推荐服务，进行读者的在线调查，分析大家关注的热点图书和相关问题等。虚拟社区可以把具有相同兴趣爱好或者相同专业背景的学习者组成同一个群组，在群组里交流、互动、协作，组成学习的社会网络，增加社区成员学习的机会，提供学习的资源方法和策略。虚拟社区有利于成员发现和解决问题的能力，促进其素质的提高，进而推动图书馆培训教育的发展。[14]

7 移动服务

近年来，各种移动数字化设备令人目不暇接，如手提电脑、手机（普通手机与智能手机）、MP3、MP4、平板电脑、电子阅读器、掌上游戏机、PDA、MID、上网本、GPS、电子相册、手持电视、录音笔等。移动设备在图书馆有着广阔的应用前景，可以为用户随时随地提供服务，实现无处不在的图书馆（Ubiquitous Library）的理念。图书馆移动服务的形式包括多种，如手机短消息服务、移动业务办理、移动互联网、移动数字阅读等。手机是图书馆移动服务运用最广的终端设备，它可以使图书馆及时向用户提供诸如活动通知、新书通报、信息提醒等服务，也可以协助用户远程办理业务，如书目查询、参考咨询、预约借书、续借、付费等。目前，国内外已有不少图书馆开通了手机业务。如芬兰赫尔辛基工业大学图书馆利用芬兰 Portaliy 软件公司的 Libnet 软件，运用手机为用户提供到期提醒、续借、预约、书目查询、参考咨询等服务[15]；上海图书馆、济南市图书馆、辽宁省图书馆、吉林省图书馆等均利用手机短信为用户提供多样化信息服务。2008 年，中国国家数字图书馆开馆，移动数字图书馆也同时开放。国家图书馆的移动数字图书馆服务以智能手机为媒介，采用先进的动态内容分发技术，为读者提供国图动态、文化快递、书刊推荐、资源检索等频道内容。随着 WAP、3G、Wifi 等通信标准和技术的颁布与实施，利用无线设备浏览互联网已成为现实。为了将图书馆的服务延伸至移动互联网，图书馆有必要开发移动网页。2010 年 1 月，美国国家医学图书馆开通了 MedlinePlus 移动网站，可以自动识别设备种类，并以最佳方式显示，如根据屏幕大小自动调整字体。[16]移动数字阅读也是移动设备的一个重要应用领域，以电子纸为显示技术的电子书阅读器近年来发展相当迅速，如亚马逊的 Kindle、Barnes & Noble 的 Nook、索尼电子阅读器、汉王电纸书、盛大 Bamboo 等。另外，苹果系列产品如 iPad、iPhone、iPod touch 等通过阅读应用程序也可以提供良好的移动数字阅读支持。

在移动数字阅读领域，图书馆承担何种角色，应发挥何种功能，目前许多图书馆都在积极地探索和尝试。国家图书馆、上海图书馆、广州图书馆等分别与超星、金蟾软件、汉王等公司合作，向用户提供阅读器的借阅服务；超星移动图书馆已经开发专门的APP，并且在许多图书馆利用。国外如美国 Sullivan County 公共图书馆为公众提供了类似服务。从技术上讲，实现移动服务仍然有一些问题需要得到解决，如阅读习惯、数字图书的版权问题、信息的完整性、大容量传输、信息组织与管理等。因此，从未来一段时间来讲，图书馆还需要不断摸索，以找到一个对作者、出版社与发行商、图书馆和读者都有利的业务模式。

目前数字化技术发展相当迅速，以智能化、立体化、泛在化为特征的新技术和设备不断涌现。智能化强调服务的主动性，系统在非人工或少人工干预的情况下主动分析用户的需求，并自动为用户提供个性化的推荐与提醒服务；立体化是指功能多元化，强调通过统一的入口使用户尽可能多地获得多种信息和服务；泛在化强调服务的无处不在，无时不在，如“7×24 图书馆、移动数字图书馆”等。[17]一系列新型的数字媒体的出现将为图书馆数字化服务带来广阔的发展空间。数字媒体技术的最终目的是为用户提供良好的服务，因此，“以人为本”、“人性化”成为当代技术和服务研发的主旨，在图书馆数字化服务中，如何面向用户的需求，根据数字化技术特点提高数字媒体和资源的可用性成为一个重要的研究课题。

参考文献

[1] 中国图书馆学会. 图书馆服务宣言［EB/OL］.［2010-08-08］. http://www.lsc.org.cn/CN/index.html.

[2] 黄晓斌，夏明春. 论图书馆数字资源的整合［J］. 图书情报工作，2005（1）：50-54.

[3] 黄文，董秋生. OpenURL 在数字图书馆的应用［J］. 现代图书情报技术，2009（4）：72-74.

[4] 许萍华. Metalib/SFX 的增值服务［J］. 贵图学刊，2010（3）：42-43.

[5] 北京师范大学图书馆［EB/OL］.［2010-08-08］. http://www.lib.bnu.edu.cn/index.jsp.

[6] 马明，武夷山. Don R. Swanson 的情报学学术成就的方法论意义与启示［J］. 情报学报，2003（3）：259-266.

[7] 董慧，等. 基于本体的数字图书馆检索模型研究［J］. 情报学报，2006（4）：451-461.

[8] 黄晓斌. 网络数据库的提醒服务及其应用［J］. 图书馆建设，2008（7）：90-92.

[9] 黄晓斌. 数字图书馆推荐系统研究［J］. 情报资料工作，2005（4）：53-56.

[10] Science Direct. TOP25 Hottest Articles［EB/OL］.［2010-08-08］. http://top25.sciencedirect.com/.

[11] Google Trends［EB/OL］.［2010-08-08］. http://www.google.com/trends.

[12] CNKI 学术趋势［EB/OL］.［2010-08-08］. http://trend.cnki.net/.

[13] 范并思. 图书馆2.0：构建新的图书馆服务［J］. 大学图书馆学报，2006（1）：2-7.

[14] 黄少宽，黄晓斌. 网络虚拟社区及其在图书情报的应用［J］. 情报理论与实践，2008（1）：109-111.

[15] 卢福. 移动设备在图书馆的应用［J］. 图书馆学刊，2010（1）：5-6.

[16] Loren Frant. Mobile MedlinePlus：Health Information On-the-Go［J］. NLM Technical Bulletin，2010（1）：12-14.

[17] 张文秀，朱庆华. 泛在网络下的信息服务［J］. 新世纪图书馆，2008（3）：23-26.

教师简介：

潘燕桃，女，中山大学文学学士、理学硕士、管理学博士。现任中山大学资讯管理学院教授、博士生导师。主讲“信息资源共享”、“信息获取与利用”等本科生课程，以及“图书馆学研究方法论”、“信息资源共享研究”等硕士研究生课程。研究方向包括信息资源管理、图书馆学教育、信息资源共享、信息素质教育、图书馆用户教育与培训、公共图书馆思想、图书馆权利、信息组织与检索等。出版学术著作与专业教材9部，发表中英文学术论文40余篇，主持和参加国家级、省市级科研项目近20余项，获得各级教学和科研奖励10余项。1997年至1998年任美国威斯康星大学麦迪逊校区图书馆学信息学研究院访问学者，2005年至2006年任美国加州大学伯克利校区信息系统与信息管理学院访问学者，2014年7月至2015年1月任英国伦敦大学学院信息研究学系访问学者。兼任教育部高等学校图书馆学学科教学指导委员会委员、中国图书馆学会学术研究委员会资源建设与共享专业委员会成员、广东图书馆学会理事会理事与学术委员会副主任委员、中山大学图书馆与资讯科学研究所副所长。联系方式：puspyt@ mail. sysu. edu. cn。

所选论文“The Propagation of the Library Rights Ideology in Mainland China：A Case Study”原载于《图书资讯学研究》（台北）2013年第8卷第1期

The Propagation of the Library Rights Ideology in Mainland China：A Case Study*

Yantao Pan

Abstract：This paper examines the case of “The Warmest Library in History” and discusses how the library rights ideology has been propagated in Mainland China in recent years, from the perspectives of the planning and promotion activities of professional organizations, advocacy and appeals of professional journals, the scholarship of academics, and the mass media's reporting and influence. This study reveals how the case and the attention it received reflect the progress and positive effect of the propagation of the library rights ideology in China. The people of China have begun to be awakened to those rights, but there is a long way to go until they are fully realized, and theoretical research and practice on library rights in Mainland China are still in their infancy. It is a long-term, arduous and historical mission, and there is an urgent duty for library professionals in China to advocate for making policies on library rights, to protect and preserve those rights, to make people more conscious of those rights, and to conduct more research on library rights theory and practice. Research methods employed in this paper include case study and historical analysis.

Keywords：Propagation of the library rights ideology； “The Event of the Warmest Library in History”；Case

---

* This paper is a keynote speech at “2012 Conference on Information Capital, Property, and Ethics” (ICPE), Shin Hsin University, Taipei, December 10th, 2012.

study on library rights; Hangzhou Public Library

1 Introduction

In January 2011, in Mainland China, while many people were on their way back home for Chinese New Year family reunions, a micro-blog message triggered a hot debate among netizens. In a very short time, it had been forwarded over sixteen thousand times and was reviewed over four thousand times. [1] The message was about how Hangzhou Public Library (HPL) welcomed homeless people to use the library. Because this happened in an unusually frigid winter season when all around the country people were suffering from cold weather and traffic congestion while struggling to make their way back home for the Chinese new year celebrations, what HPL did for homeless people had made them feel much warmer. Netizens thus named HPL "The Warmest Library in History".

This message had not only been forwarded and reviewed many times, but also caused a very heated discussion from different perspectives among the public, netizens and mass media all over the country. Scholars from different disciplines also began to conduct research on this case. Some researchers in library science conducted research on this story as a case study on library rights (See Literature Review).

This case has lead academics and library professionals in China to ask: What are library rights? Actually the phase "library rights" originally comes from *the Library Bill of Rights* which was adopted by the American Library Association (ALA) in 1939 and last amended in 1996. [2] Based on a study of *the Library Bill of Rights*, ALA's existing definition and ALA's Office of Intellectual Freedom mission statement, we defined library rights as the equality and freedom of individuals to use the library[3].

Several library related events① took place in Mainland China between 2004 and 2005, such as "The Event at National Library of China"[4], "The Event at Xinyang Normal University Library"[5], and "The Event at Suzhou Library"[6], those events refer to the unpleasant experiences of the users and the criticism of library services that followed. They were exposed and reported by the mass media and made the public began to turn their eyes to libraries, library service and library rights. The events gave the public a negative impression of library service. On the contrary, "The Event of the Warmest Library in History" (EWLH) made a positive impression on the public and mass media about libraries.

The most interesting part of the story is that the original source of this message came from a report published in November 2008 that originally received very little attention. [7] According to the report, it took place at the beginning of October 2008 when HPL's new building opened to the public and also welcomed homeless people. A librarian at HPL confirmed that they had actually

① More details about these library related events, please See DISCUSSION.

begun welcoming homeless people to use the library since 2003. [8] That is to say, it received much more attention and aroused much more public debate around the country two years after it was first reported, and an astonishing eight years after it happened.

The emergence of this case brought about the issues discussed in this paper. Why did it happen? What made it happen? Why is it considered a case of library rights? What is the connection between the propagation of the library rights ideology and this case? How has the library rights ideology been propagated in Mainland China? It is hypothesized that this caused so much public debate eight years after it occurred because of the propagation of the library rights ideology in Mainland China. It indicates that Chinese people have gradually been awakened to their library rights. It is the fruit of the joint effort from the library professionals, the public and the mass media, and it is also because of the propagation of the library rights ideology in Mainland China.

In the present paper, EWLH is examined. Additionally, the paper explores how the library rights ideology has been propagated in Mainland China, from the perspectives of the planning and promotion activities of professional organizations, advocacy and appeals of professional journals, the scholarship of academics, and the mass media's reporting and influence.

2 Research Methods

Research methods employed in this paper include case study and historical analysis. EWLH is discussed in depth in this paper. The details of the case and its nationwide reverberations will be described and analyzed, its implication and connection to the propagation of the library rights ideology and the case itself will be revealed. This is a typical case of the propagation of the library rights ideology, based on three following facts:

First, this case might be the most famous library related event in Mainland China. Before "The Event at National Library of China" (2004), the public and mass media did not pay much attention to libraries. This was the first time that libraries, library service and library rights received so much attention and were debated so fervently in such a short time. Therefore, it is a very special case that needs to be studied.

Second, this case took place in a public library and it is about homeless people and their rights to use the library. All discussion on this case, both by the new mass media and the traditional mass media, focused on the library rights of homeless people, though they talked about it in different terms, such as cultural rights, equal rights, and the right to access the library.

Third, the timing of this case and the timing of the development of the propagation of the library rights ideology is an exact match. This story actually happened in 2003, it was first reported in 2008, and became a topic of discussion in 2011. Since 2000, researchers have paid increasingly more attention to library rights, and it has become one of the most popular research topics after "The Event at the National Library of China". Professional organizations, journals, scholars in library science and the mass media have been continually promoting and advocating for the library rights ideology between 2000 and 2010.

Historical analysis was also used in this paper. Related materials were collected by: (a) browsing the websites of professional library organizations and associations such as the Library Society of China's (LSC) website and the websites of library societies of different provinces, seminars and activities related to library rights from 2000 to 2011; (b) investigating the conference proceedings at library and library science field; (c) exploring the columns and articles in journals and books related to library rights by searching related databases and the annual indexes of professional periodicals in library science from 2000 to 2011; (d) examining messages, news and articles about EWLH, and collecting, synthesizing and analyzing information on scattered pieces of news both from traditional mass media and new media on the Internet, including micro-blogs, blogs and social networks. In collecting research materials for this paper, an extensive literature review was conducted.

3 Literature Review

As a result of a literature search and review, up to now case studies on library rights from the perspective of propagation of the library rights ideology in Mainland China have not yet been found.

The following literature reviews attempt to demonstrate and support the hypothesis, and will only focus on reviewing three parts: the first part is the overall research on library rights, the second part is the columns and articles in journals and books related to library rights, especially related to the propagation of the library rights ideology published in Mainland China, the third part is literature about EWLH.

In Mainland China, research on library rights started in the 2000s. Since 2004, research in the area of library rights has increased in popularity. Before 2000, the phrase "library rights" had not yet been used, and instead, phrases such as "intellectual freedom", "library freedom", "the right to use the library freely" and "rights of library users" were more common. [9] According to literature reviews in this area, Cheng Huanwen might be the originator of the phrase, "图书馆权利", which can be translated into English as "library rights". In July 2004, Cheng proposed and insisted that library rights should be one of the major topics at the 2005 LSC Annual Conference when he was consulted by the secretary general of LSC. [10] In December 2004, when they issued the Call for Papers, LSC finally decided the theme for the 2005 annual conference would be "People-oriented Innovative Services", and the sub-themes were "Library Science from the Humanities Perspective" and "Library Rights", Upon the announcement, Cheng explained that "library rights" refers to the right to equal access, the right to free access of materials and services, free library services, and library services to people with special needs. [11] In January 2005, for the first time, library rights were officially discussed at the 2005 Library Society of China Summit Meeting, held at Helongjiang University, Haerbin. [12] Since then, more and more researchers have focused on the idea of library rights and began to use the phrase "library rights". As this phrase increased in popularity, library right has become one of the most popular research areas among library professionals in Mainland China. Since 2004, the research in this area has entered a stage of fast development. The number of articles showed a trend of rapid growth. The major topics include the theory of library rights, intellectual freedom, information equity, rights of readers, and case studies on library rights, library systems, professional ethics, the policy of library rights.

According to a literature survey, three journals, *Library*, *Library Development*, and *Document, Information & Knowledge* are especially pertinent. Each column and topic in Table 1 was determined by title of columns, and each topic was determined by title of articles and close examination of the full texts themselves. The numbers, columns and topics listed in Table 1 and Figure 1 showed the subsequent development and change of research in library science in Mainland China between 2000 and 2010: (a) Research on this area began in 2000, and reached a peak in 2005 and 2006, and then dropped. The timing of the activities organized by LSC is consistent with the research trend, and it was also the reaction in the library profession to the library related events in Mainland China which took place in 2004 and 2005. (b) Topics changed from library freedom in 2000 to knowledge freedom in 2003, and to library rights, rights of users and intellectual freedom after 2005. That showed that research on this area became more in-depth (See Table 1 and Figure 1).

Table 1 Columns & topics on library rights in professional journals

Name of Journal	Column/Topic	Year	No. of Articles	No. of Authors
Library	Library Freedom	2000	1	1
	Library Freedom	2002	1	1
	"New Perspectives in New Century: A Dialogue on Knowledge Freedom"	2003	3	3
	"Forum on New Library Movement in the 21st Century"	2005	27	36
		2006	20	23
	Library rights, library freedom, rights of library users, intellectual freedom...	2007	8	12
		2008	11	16
		2009	15	20
		2010	11	13
	Total		97	125
Library Development	"Move to the Age of Rights"	2005	32	41
		2006	29	33
	Library rights, library freedom, rights of library users, intellectual freedom...	2007	2	3
		2008	8	9
		2009	2	4
		2010	7	8
	Total		80	98

Continue Table 1

Name of Journal	Column/Topic	Year	No. of Articles	No. of Authors
Document, Information & Knowledge	"Disadvantaged Groups & Knowledge Equity"	2005	5	7
	Library rights, library freedom, rights of library users, intellectual freedom···	2007	5	5
		2008	2	3
		2009	1	1
	Total		13	16

Source: Collecting data from annual index of the above three journals (If the authors published two or more articles in the same column of the same journal, it was counted as one).

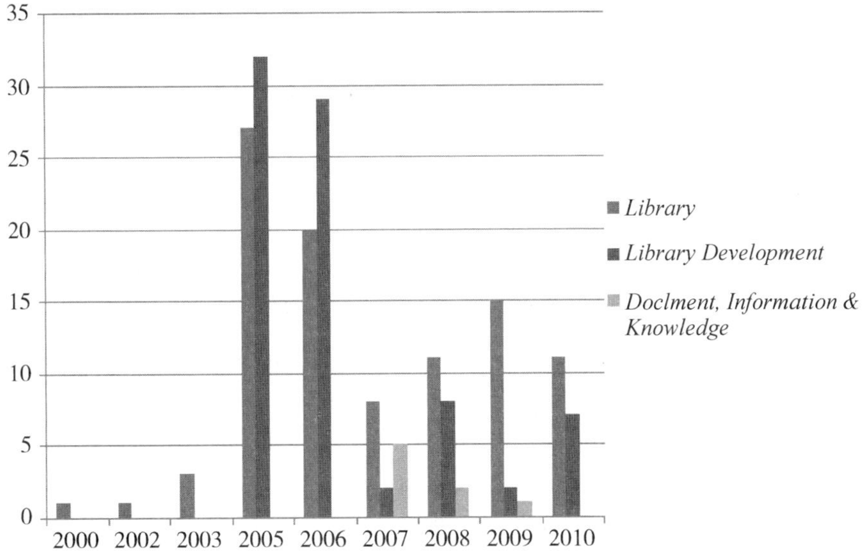

Figure 1 Number of articles on library rights in professional journals

Library is the earliest journal that focused on and advocated for library rights in Mainland China, by publishing two papers about library freedom in 2000[13] and 2002[14]. It also published two columns: "New Perspectives in New Century: A Dialogue on Knowledge Freedom" (2003) and "Forum on New Library Movement in the 21st Century" (2005-2006), in total sixty-two authors published fifty articles on library rights in these two columns. Major topics include intellectual freedom, information freedom, library freedom, library spirit and library rights (See Table 1).

Library Development is another journal which published many columns and articles on library rights. From 2005 to 2006, the journal included the column: "Move to the Age of Rights", and a total of seventy-four authors published sixty-one articles on library rights on this column, articles' topics ranged from library rights, library freedom, rights of library users, intellectual freedom, information rights, laws and policy of library rights.[15] After this column was published, about nineteen articles on library rights were published in this journal from 2007 to 2010. They discussed the status of research, knowledge freedom, the relationship between library rights and other subjects, such as library values, government responsibility, and library cards, library freedom, and information equity (See Table 1).

Document, *Information & Knowledge* is another important journal. In the 1st issue of 2005, a column entitled "Disadvantaged Groups & Knowledge Equity" was published. Seven authors published five articles in this column. Their topics are about knowledge aid to vulnerable groups, information freedom, public library spirit, libraries being open to the public and library equity (See Table 1).

Among the scholars who conducted research on library rights in Mainland China, five scholars, including Cheng Huanwen (程焕文), Cheng Yanan (程亚男), Fan Bingsi (范并思), Jiang Yongfu (蒋永福) and Li Guoxin (李国新)① have published the most on library rights. The following is a list of the publications and an analysis of the contents:

➢ Cheng Huanwen has published three books, one textbook, fifteen journal articles, and 131 blog articles, and completed one research project funded by the National Social Science Foundation ("A Study of Library Rights") in this area. His three books are: (a) *A Study of Library Rights* is the first book titled with the phrase "Library Rights" in Mainland China. Basic theory, the library rights related policies, and case studies were included in this book.[3] (b) *Rights and Professional Ethics of Library* is a collection of nearly 124 policies the rights and professional ethics regarding library from more than thirty countries.[16] (c) *Users Are Always Right* is a collection of sixty articles about the "Users Are Always Right" concept from the heated debates which took place on the web and in academic journals.[17] *Information Resource Sharing* is the first textbook which introduced contents related to library rights in Mainland China.[18] He also delivered and published more than twenty keynote speeches and journal articles on library rights. They focused on the theory of library rights, library rights and library spirit, library rights and professional ethic, library rights for users.

There is one more thing worth mentioning. Before and after EWLH took place, Cheng published three related articles on his weblog: (a) *The Basic Methods for Public Libraries to Solve the Problems about the Homeless People* provided some solutions to help homeless people keep clean when they used libraries.[19] (b) *An Answer to Netizen: Letting the Homeless People in Library to Get Heat Is a Basic Cultural Right* indicated that he strongly supported what the director of HPL did during EWLH.[20] (c) *The Case of the Homeless People Entering Hangzhou Public Library Is the Milestone of the Propagation of the Library Rights Ideology* might be the only one article which discussed the same subject as the current paper and supports its hypothesis. In this article, he pointed out: "The case of the homeless people entering HPL is a milestone for the propagation of the library rights ideology, and it is a symbol of the new starting point of the

① Names are in alphabetic order.

propagation of the library rights ideology in the second decade in the new century. If we ignore this milestone, we will lose this great opportunity to propagate the library rights ideology."[21]

➢ Cheng Yanan has published twelve widely acclaimed journal articles on library rights, which focused on the rights of library users, library rights and library spirit, library rights and library service, and the right for citizens to read. From the statements provided below, we can see that her views are: (a) "The development of the rights of readers requires the elimination of all obstacles which restrict the implementation of and the goal of fairness in library services."[22] (b) "How to be aware of the rights of readers from the perspective of the legal system, how to maximize the cultural rights for citizens, protecting the rights of readers, and promoting intellectual freedom are issues which should never be neglected."[23]

➢ Fan Bingsi has published two books and thirteen articles on library rights and seven of his articles have been influential in academia. His book, *Fair Use of Library Resources* discussed library resources and service, core values and equity of library service, information equity, rights and equity of library service.[24] His second book, *New Library Science in China: Progress and Its Problems* is a collection of his twenty-five articles from 1986 to 2005, these articles discussed the library professions' consciousness of rights, public library spirit, the development of the systems for information equity and information guarantee.[25] His articles focus on intellectual freedom, systems for information equity, public library spirit and library rights case studies in foreign countries. He considered library rights as the rights of citizen and library, and his definition of library rights has two important aspects: "First, library rights in social meaning, they are the rights for citizen to accept library service. Second, professional rights of librarians, they are the rights for librarians to maintain the efficient operation of libraries. Library rights should be the unity of these two rights."[26]

➢ Jiang Yongfu has published the largest number of materials on library rights in Mainland China. In total he has published two books, two textbooks and twenty-nine articles. His first book, *The Research on Information Freedom and Its Limitation*, the first book on information freedom in Mainland China, focused on the freedom to access information, the freedom to cognize information, free information expression and the freedom to access information on the Internet.[27] His second book, *A Study of the Modern Public Library System* discusses the unique value of the public library and issues regarding public library administration in China.[28] He also published two textbooks, *An Introduction to Library Science*[29] and *Foundations of Library Science*[30], which introduce contents related to library rights. His articles concentrate on information freedom, freedom of knowledge, information rights and information equity. He stated: "Libraries are social institutions that ensure intellectual freedom, and the core value of the library profession is to ensure citizens' rights of intellectual freedom."[31]

➢ Li Guoxin is another scholar who started researching library rights early. He has published one book and ten journal articles. In his book, *A Study of the Library Legal System in Japan*, he studied library freedom.[32] His research focused on library freedom, intellectual freedom, laws and policies related to library rights, case studies on library rights in foreign countries. He considered library rights as the rights of professional librarians. After conducting his study on library rights in the U. S. A. and Japan, he concluded that library rights are the rights of library professionals, giving them the freedom to take social responsibility. [33]

Based on the number of their publications and the number of times they have been read and cited, the publications of these five scholars can be considered the most important literature on library rights in Mainland China.

Not long after EWLH took place, in Mainland China, four related research articles were published in journals of Library and Information Science. In an article by Si Jiaojiao, she concluded that EWLH is a successful case of library public relations because of HPL's prompt and positive reactions to the debate in micro-blogs and their efforts of promoting the concepts of library service. [34] According to Yang Lizhi, EWLH was thought of as a good example of advocacy for libraries and the importance of advocacy work for libraries. [35] In another research article by Si Jiaojiao, taking into consideration the impact of micro-blogs on libraries, the necessity for and strategies for libraries to provide a micro-blog service were addressed. [36]

Compared with the above three articles, a research article written by Guo Xiaomin, shares the most similarities with the current paper. There are two similarities between these two articles: (a) both of them are case studies on the same case; (b) both of them focus on library rights. Guo raised two guiding questions in her article. Firstly, why did this issue attract so much attention? Provided that people's rights to free and equal access to library service had not yet been fully realized. Secondly, how could library professionals be inspired to think about this issue and then take action? It was limited in scope for the propagation of library rights and lacks an understanding of civil library rights. [37]

The above articles have not discussed EWLH from the perspective of the propagation of the library rights ideology, as I conducted in the present paper. And I have taken the research further in this area by connecting this case and library rights, especially the propagation of the library rights ideology in Mainland China.

4 Discussion

On January 18, 2011, He Lantai (贺阑泰), a netizen from Taiwan, posted a message on his micro-blog. He talked about how HPL welcomed homeless people to the library to read, which some users felt was unacceptable. While receiving complaints about that, Chu Shuqing, director of HPL said: "I have no right to refuse them to come in to the library to read, but you have the right to choose to leave." He Lantai praised the director as a decent person. This blog was widely read and disseminated in a very short time on many web portals and bulletin board systems. Up to March 3, 2011, his micro-blog had been forwarded 16,797 times and received 4,478 comments and reviews. [1] The issue was reprinted and reported extensively by mass media outlets such as China Central Television, Xinhuanet, People's Daily Online, Guangming Online, YAHOO! NEWS, SINA, and ifeng. com. At the time, reporters rushed to the HPL seeking interviews.

In summary, there were three different opinions on this case. First, most of the mass media and netizens praised HPL and the director, and called it "the Library in Heaven". [38] He was considered a hero. [1] Second, some netizens thought it unfair to other library users and worried they would be disturbed by homeless people. [1] Third, some netizens and mass media outlets stated that this is what a public library is supposed to do and there is nothing to be surprised about. [39]

Regarding these opinions, it must be mentioned that both netizens and the mass media discussed social equity and civil rights in following ways:

➢ "Whether homeless people have time or not, whether they are willing to go to library to read or not, they should be entitled to the same rights as other citizens." [40]

➢ "I support the director, please respect the homeless and respect people who earn a living by working hard with their hands. They have the same civil rights as everyone else including the right to read in a library and so on." [41]

➢ "No matter beggars or scavengers, both of them should have basic rights conferred by the law, there is no doubt that the rights to access to culture and knowledge and to read are included." [42]

➢ "For homeless people being allowed to go in the library and read is common sense. After it has become a popular topic in the news, this is a mockery of fairness; praising common sense diminishes the value of common sense." [39]

➢ "Hangzhou Public Library has been commended for opening to all people, it shows people's aspiration and desire for equal rights, and shows that more and more people understand that all humans are equal and consciousness of citizenship about human beings created equally and has been gradually disseminated. For the sake of equality, libraries should achieve the goal of equal rights for knowledge." [38]

Among library professionals, this case also gave rise to an animated and lively discussion. Up to now, six articles have been published in three academic journals. Dozens of articles have been published in blogs and received hundreds of comments and reviews. In summary, there are three different opinions about this case: (1) Those who supported HPL, argued that reading in the library is a basic right for homeless people[20]; (2) Those who disagreed with the HPL, felt it was unacceptable to let homeless people go in the library and read. One article titled, "*The Library's Open to Beggars Is Just a Bluff*", became a target during discussions[43]; (3) Those who neither agreed nor disagreed thought it difficult in practice. [44]

According to the message on He Lantai's micro-blog, the source of that story was originally from an article "The Civilian Tropism of a Luxurious Library", written by Wan Runlong, a journalist at *Wen Wai Po*, and published on November 19, 2008. The article reports that HPL opened their new building to the public before National Day in 2008. Soon the library became a very popular place for people to go because it was open to all people, and there was no deposit and no handling charges and so on. Some homeless people went into the library to read. HPL only requested that they washed their hands before reading. Some users felt that this was unacceptable, they complained to Director Chu Shuqing that it was disrespectful to the other users. Chu answered, "If you don't like to share the same space with homeless people, you may choose a different reading area of library. And I am sure you can find another comfortable place to read in our library. "[7] For some reason, at that time, the article drew very little attention. Why does the same story resonate so differently at two different times?

Another interesting point to mention, the director and librarians at HPL were very surprised at the heated discussions and debates it had caused and the interviews from the mass media. There are two reasons: First, HPL regarded welcoming homeless people as a responsibility it should undertake as a public library; Second, the library did not think it would become a piece of news, because they had welcomed homeless people since 2003. "Should it be news?" The librarians asked the reporters during interviews. [8]

If it had not been for the propagation of the library rights ideology, and the subsequent rediscovery of the case, then this story and its widespread media coverage would not have happened. This case is a manifestation of the public's attention to library rights, and is also a result of the propagation of the library rights ideology. In order to have a better understanding of how the library rights ideology has been propagated, how it induced public awareness of library rights, and why this case occurred, it is necessary to be discussed from the four following perspectives.

4.1 The planning and promotion of professional organizations

Since 2002, as a professional organization, LSC has organized various kinds of activities to propagate the library rights ideology, such as follows:

(A) Establishing a special committee. After the Sixth Academic Committee of LSC was established in 2001, in consideration of the importance of issues such as library spirit, library law, intellectual property, librarians' professional ethics and library rights for citizen, Cheng Huanwen proposed to establish the Library Laws and Intellectual Property Committee (LLIPC) at the meeting of chairman for the arrangement of professional research committees under the Academic Committee. This proposal was unanimously endorsed by the participating chairmen and vice chairmen, and Cheng was unanimously held up as the founding chairman of the committee by participants. LLIPC was formally established in 2002. The committee is charged with planning and organizing academic research and activities concerning library laws, intellectual property, library rights, professional ethics for librarians and library spirit. [3]155-156

(B) Making and adopting professional policies, including *The Code of Ethics for Chinese Librarians* (trial implementation) (CECL) and *The Library Service Manifesto* (LSM). They are the symbols of great progress of development of ethics for librarians in China.

After the drafting, revision, interpretation, and a nationwide review of comments from May to September, 2002, LSC completed the final version of CECL on December, 2002. A book *entitled The Code of Ethics for Chinese Librarians* (trial implementation) was published by Beijing Library Press on March, 2003, which included the full text and interpretation of CECL, and Chinese translation of the code of ethics which was published by the major library professional organizations in foreign countries. CECL was officially released during the National Library Service Week on May, 2003. There are eight items, 120 words in the main body of CECL. Its main content includes ideology of the profession, professional attitude, professional ability, professional discipline and professional relationships. This is the first Code of Ethics for library professionals in Mainland China, and a sign of the library profession entering the age of self-discipline. [45]

Fan Bingsi proposed to draft LSM at the 2007 LSC Summit Meeting in Suzhou on December, 2006, which should show the core values of the library profession. Fang Bingsi and Ni Xiaojian (倪晓健) were selected to be the leaders of a project to draft "the Core Values of Library Profession in China and *The Library Service Manifesto*". After the first draft of LSM was completed on June, 2007, it took sixteen months to request comments and complete discussions and revisions. The final version was finished on April, 2008. It was released at the 2008 LSC Annual Conference in Chongqing on October, 2008. Once it launched, it caused enormous repercussions both among library professionals and the public. Six famous journals in library science published its full text in a prominent position, and many mass media outlets released it. It includes seven sections, in total about 500 words. It fully reflected the thoughts about public welfare, equality and freedom, humanistic concerns, and sharing and collaboration. This was a major event with landmark significance, which could go down in the history of the development of libraries in China. This is the first professional commitment to library services for the public. [46]

Table 2 Academic activities on library rights held by LSC

Time	Activity Title	Topic
July 2002	Special Topic Forum 2002 LSC Annual Conference	Legislative Process of China's Library Laws: Dialogues with Government Officials
August 2003	Special Topic Forum 2003 LSC Annual Conference	Development of Ethics for Librarians & Library Legislation Environment
November 2004	The Second Youth Academic Forum, LSC	Library and Rights of Librarians
January 2005	2005 LSC Summit Forum	Library Rights
July 2005	The Third Forum on Library Laws & Intellectual Property 2005 LSC Annual Conference	Library Rights
July 2006	The Third Forum on Library Laws & Intellectual Property 2006 LSC Annual Conference 2007 LSC Summit Forum	Development of Library Legislation Environment in China: Protective Laws & Self-Regulation

Continue Table 2

Time	Activity Title	Topic
August 2007	The Third Forum on Library Laws & Intellectual Property 2007 LSC Annual Conference	Development of Library Law & Harmonious Development of Libraries
July 2010	The Ninth Forum 2010 LSC Annual Conference	Safeguard Rights to Read& Enjoy the Happiness of reading

Source: Library Society of China Website (http://www.lsc.org.cn/CN/index.html).

(C) Organizing academic activities (See Table 2). From 2002 to 2010, LSC organized more than ten activities related to library rights. More than half of these activities were held by LLIPC. This is evidence that LLIPC has played a very important role in the propagation of the library rights ideology. After a topical analysis on these activities, three themes emerged: (a) Between 2002 and 2010, the topics of library legislation went through three stages: From 2002 to 2004, it was discussed from the government's perspective. From 2005 to 2007, it was discussed from the library's perspective. And from 2008 to 2010, it was discussed from the user's perspective. (b) From 2002 to 2003, it turned from the legislative process and legislative environment, and to rights of librarians and library rights (2004-2005), and to library law (2006-2007), and to safeguard rights to read (2010) . (c) The gradation of these activities showed a parabolic trend. From just a special topic forum at the LSC Annual Conference in 2002 and 2003, to a specialized conference in 2004, and to a summit meeting in 2005 when it peaked, then went back to a special topic forum at the LSC Annual Conference in 2006, 2007 and 2010. It proves that library right was one of the most popular research areas among library professionals in Mainland China in 2005.

By establishing a special committee, making and adopting professional policies and organizing academic activities, LSC has created a professional environment and a professional platform, and established a professional team to promote and propagate the library rights ideology in Mainland China. That not only forced library professionals, but also the mass media and the public to begin to pay more attention and understand the role of libraries and library rights.

4.2 Advocacy and appeals from professional journals

As was mentioned in the "Literature Review", *Library*, *Library Development*, *Document, Information & Knowledge* are three prominent journals which have published many columns and articles on library rights. There are three things worth mentioning (See Literature Review & Table 1):

(a) *Library* is the journal which published the most articles on library rights in Mainland China between 2000 and 2010, it also published two celebrated columns in 2003 and 2005: "New Perspectives in New Century: A Dialogue on Knowledge Freedom" (2003) and "Forum on New Library Movement in the 21st Century" (2005-2006). The latter column was a very famous academic discussion rather than a movement, not only because of its large number of articles, but also its overwhelming influence on promoting the library spirit, propagating library rights ideology and the review of the practical problems in the library profession, and it had important historical value and practical significance in the history of libraries in Mainland China.

(b) By publishing the column "Move to the Age of Rights", *Library Development* published the largest number and concentration of the articles in this area in the period (2005-2006).[47] For this reason, the journal became the most famous base camp of research on this area and propagation of the library rights ideology.

(c) *Document, Information & Knowledge* is another prominent journal. Although the number of articles on library rights published in this journal was not large, the articles carried much weight, and made a great impact in the area among library professionals.

By publishing columns and articles on library rights which were read, cited and discussed, professional journals in library and information science have become powerhouses in advocating and appealing for the library rights ideology. That has strongly supported and promoted the research on library rights, and made more and more librarians and library staff understand library rights and become aware of their responsibilities to protect and guarantee the library rights of users.

4.3 Research and propagation by scholars

Among the scholars who conducted research on library rights and propagated the library rights ideology in Mainland China, the following five scholars are considered the most outstanding scholars based on the large number of their publications, keynote speeches, and their participation in all kinds of activities across the country and that the great impact they have brought to this field since 2000s. The following are some details showing how they have propagated library rights ideology:

Cheng Huanwen not only coined the phrase "图书馆权利" (library rights), and published numerous publications, but he has also completed the first project with the phrase library rights in the title in Mainland China funded by the National Social Science Foundation ("A Study of Library Rights") . The resulting study is called "*A Study of Library Rights*".[3] The book was placed in the "National Achievements Library of Philosophy and Social Sciences" in 2011 by the National Planning Office of Philosophy and Social Sciences. Furthermore, it received a very high evaluation from library professionals at home and abroad, and it was considered as the most important work on library rights in Mainland China. *Information Resource Sharing* was published on July, 2004[18], and won the second prize for "Outstanding Achievements in Philosophy and Social Science of Guangdong Province". It is not only widely used by many universities and received unanimous positive evaluation from scholars, faculty members and students in and out of the university, but also caused a greater academic and social response. Up to now, it was cited

503 times①, twenty review papers have published in thirteen journals, and 123 related articles have published on forty-one weblogs, and the course of "Information Resource Sharing" was named "the National Fine Course" in 2007.[48] In particular he capitalized on every chance to propagate the library rights ideology through giving lectures and interviews, chairing academic discussions, authoring columns in journals.

Another item worthy of mention is that he started a weblog "Cheng Huanwen Says" (程焕文如是说) in May, 2006, and it had 734, 845 visitors and 656 articles had been published up to September 6, 2009. Among these articles, there were 131 articles related to library rights and library spirit, and three articles were related to EWLH. Based on its influence and popularity on the Internet, ideas regarding library rights, library spirit and professional ethics for librarians had been spread across the country.

Cheng Yanan was the former director of Nanshan Library, Shenzhen. As the only one practitioner (not an academic) among the five outstanding key scholars she has published 12 widely acclaimed journal articles in this area which focused on the rights of library users and the right for citizens to read. She also took advantage of every opportunity to promote library rights. Her work was important in helping propagate the library rights ideology.

Fan Bingsi is another active scholar who contributed to the propagation of the library rights ideology at various academic activities. One item worthy of mention is that between 2004 and 2008, he started the "Weblog of Lao-Huai" (老槐的博客) which had become very popular among library professionals at that time, and it had 491, 410 visitors and 622 articles had been published on it until it was closed on October 24, 2008.[49] On his weblog he published sixty-six articles on library rights which captured much attention.

Jiang Yongfu has the largest number of publications on library rights in Mainland China. His studies concentrate on information freedom, freedom of knowledge, information rights and information equity. According to the number of publications he has published and the number of times they have been cited in the publications of others, his influence has been especially important.

Li Guoxin is another scholar who started researching library rights early. He has published one book and ten journal articles. His research focused on library freedom and the rights of librarians and library users. Not only did he propagate the library rights ideology through scholarly activities and lecturing, but he also offered related courses for graduate students. That was probably the first time library rights issues became the primary content of a graduate level course in Mainland China.

Because of the major impact of their research, professional, and academic activities of, they have not only become the most famous researchers and leading experts on library rights in Mainland China, but also have helped library professionals, the public, and the mass media understand library rights and be more aware of their library rights. Additionally, they continue to

① It is a retrieval result from CNKI (http://www.cnki.net/).

encourage and support library professionals and to protect and guarantee the library rights of users.

4.4 Influence of the mass media

Since 2004, the mass media and netizens have turned their eyes to libraries and library service. This is due in part to library related events in Mainland China such as "The Event at National Library of China" (2004), "The Event at Xinyang Normal University Library" (2004), and "The Event at Suzhou Library" (2005). It shows that Chinese people have gradually come to be awakened to their library rights. While all of these events have evoked heated discussions about library service, library fees and charges, and the use of rare books both in the paper media and on the web, the mass media played an important role in making people more conscious of their rights.

(a) "The Event at National Library of China". On October 14, 2004, Zhou Jiwu, vice editor in chief of Jinan University Press published an article in *Southern Weekend* describing details of two of his most unpleasant experiences of borrowing books at the National Library of China. In his article, he quoted the *IFLA/UNESCO Public Library Manifesto 1949* to point out that the way the National Library of China charged and treated its users is "a brazen infringement on the public library ideology".[4] It was promptly copied and forwarded by Internet users and the mass media all over the country, the article evoked a strong response from the public. People shared their indignation at the author's experiences and supported his opinion. Some scholars in library science joined in discussions. In a weblog article, Fan Bingsi said, "A normal user quoted the *IFLA/UNESCO Public Library Manifesto 1949* to criticize fee-driven services at the National Library of China, it is a signal of progress in concepts of library science and librarianship in our country and it shows the public has begun to understand and accept the spirit of the *IFLA/UNESCO Public Library Manifesto 1949.*"[50]

(b) "The Event at Xinyang Normal University Library". Just two months after "The Event at National Library of China", on December 11, 2004, *Dahe Daily* reported that Xinyang Normal University Library charged students for seats in the reading room. After this news was released, it promptly drew the concern of the mass media and netizens. As a result of the intervention from the local government and professional associations, Xinyang Normal University Library immediately stopped charging and apologized to the public.[5] During this event, students from Xinyang Normal University called *Dahe Daily* to report this issue, and the mass media played a positive role in helping to minimize the detrimental impact. The case shows that the public has begun to be awakened to their rights to library service.

(c) "The Event at Suzhou Library". On March 9, 2005, Qi Yongxiang, a professor from Peking University published an article on the website "Academic Criticism" describing how Suzhou Library refused him when he tried to copy or transcribe a rare book. He also criticized Suzhou Library by quoting *IFLA/UNESCO Public Library Manifesto.*[6] "Academic Criticism" is a website which has quite a powerful hold in academic circles. This article was forwarded and reprinted by major mass media outlets, popular portal sites, and thousands of netizens in a very short time. It is worthwhile to note that, compared to the reaction to "The Event at National Library of China", reaction to "The Event at Suzhou Library" was quite different. Both Qi's article and the mass media's comments and reviews together with the netizens' lively discussion, not only helped express their feelings of dissatisfaction, anger and censure, but also gave suggestions to solve those problems. This fully demonstrates that the public have already been conscious of their library rights and it acted rationally.

Obviously, in all of above mentioned events, especially in EWLH, the mass media, including traditional media and new media, played a very important role in propagating and promoting the library rights ideology. As popular and useful communications tools, new media, such as portal sites, blogs, micro-blogs, instant messaging tools (like QQ, Skype, Weixin), E-journals, and social networking sites, is worth a special mention. It is digital, often having characteristics of being manipulated, networkable, dense, compressible, rapid, and interactive. If there was no new media, EWLH would not take place.

5 Conclusion

In summary, the reason why EWLH has drawn people's attention and caused much public debate eight years after it occurred, it is due to the great progress and positive effect of the propagation of the library rights ideology in Mainland China. Firstly, this case is a manifestation of the public's attention to the library rights. The public in China have not only begun to pay attention to public libraries, but also they begin to care about their rights to access to library, especially begin to care about the rights of people with special needs, like homeless people. Mass media and many people reported or expressed their opinions related to library rights, cultural rights, rights to use library and rights of homeless people. Secondly, it is also because of the tireless hard work and promotion of professional organizations, the advocacy and appeals of professional journals, the propagation and research of scholars, and the reporting of the mass media that have made an increasing number of people aware of their library rights, and have begun to pay attention to protecting and safeguarding their own and others' library rights.

In accordance with *The Constitution of the People's Republic of China*, everyone, regardless of sex and age or wealth, has basic cultural rights to equal and free access to the library. Whether they read in the library or they just enjoy the heat in the winter and air conditioning in the summer, the homeless people are also certainly entitled to those rights. It is quite a normal thing in many countries, though it still has not become an accepted notion in Mainland China. Therefore, there is still a long way to go until the library rights ideology is fully realized in China.

This study did not only enrich the research on library rights, but also propagated the library rights ideology, provided historical experience and a realistic reference for the development of librarianship in China and globally. Meanwhile it also shows that it is a long-term, arduous and historical mission, and there is an urgent duty for library professionals in China to advocate for making policies on library rights, to protect and preserve those rights, to make people more conscious of those rights, and to conduct more research on library rights theory and practice.

References

[1] He L. Micro-blog of He Lantai [EB/OL]. (2011-01-18). http://weibo.com/1281007134/60L0uJTenbB? tt.

[2] American Library Association. Library Bill of Rights [EB/OL]. (1996-01-23). http://www.ala.org/advocacy/intfreedom/librarybill/.

[3] Cheng H, Pan Y, & Zhang J. A Study of Library Rights [M]. Beijing, China: Xuexi Publishing House, 2011.

[4] Zhou J. A Story about Borrowing Books at National Library of China [N]. Southern Weekend, 2004-10-14 (D30).

[5] He Z. Students Complain about Xinyang Normal University Library Selling Seats to Readers, Library Director Replied They Are Charging Administration Costs [N]. Dahe Daily, 2004-11-11 (08).

[6] Qi Y. Library or Book Collecting Hall? A Story Happened at Rare Book Department of Suzhou Library [EB/OL]. (2005-03-10). http://www.acriticism.com/article.asp? Newsid=6157&type=1003.

[7] Wan R. The Civilian Tropism of a Luxurious Library [EB/OL]. (2008-11-19). http://pinglun.eastday.com/p/20081119/ula3992454.html.

[8] Yu C. Hangzhou Public Library: Our Doors Are Always Open to the Homeless. Jinghua Times [EB/OL]. (2011-01-24). http://society.people.com.cn/GB/8217/13800893.html.

[9] Pan Y. A Study of Public Library Ideology in China between 1949 and 2009 [M]. Guangzhou, China: Sun Yat-sen University Press, 2011.

[10] Cheng H. The Realist Library Spirit and the Library Spirit Realism [J]. Journal of Academic Libraries, 2006, 24 (4): 2-14.

[11] Library Society of China. Call for Papers of 2005 LSC Annual Conference [EB/OL]. (2005-03-19). http://www.lsc.org.cn/c/cn/news/2005-03/19/news_730.html.

[12] Bi H. Rights Is Awakening, Passion in the Discharge: A Summary of the 2005 LSC Summit Meeting [J]. Library Development, 2005, 28 (1): 12-14, 29.

[13] Li G. On the Japanese "Library Freedom" [J]. Library, 2000 (4): 12-16, 20.

[14] Li G. A Few Opinions on the Theory of the Freedom of Library [J]. Library, 2002 (1): 16-21.

[15] Jiang Y, & Bi H. Move to Age of Rights: For the New Columns in 2005 [J]. Library Development, 2004, 27 (6): 1.

[16] Cheng H, & Zhang J. Rights and Professional Ethics of Library [M]. Guilin, China: Guangxi Normal University Press, 2007.

[17] Cheng H, & Wang L. Users Are Always Right: The Hottest Topic of Library Science in China in the 21st Century [M]. Guangzhou, China: Guangdong People's Publishing House, 2008.

[18] Cheng H, & Pan Y. Information Resource Sharing [M]. Beijing, China: Higher Education Press, 2004.

[19] Chen H. The Basic Methods for Public Libraries to Solve the Problems about the Homeless People [EB/OL]. (2008-04-14). http://blog.sina.com.cn/s/blog_4978019f01008y3g.html.

[20] Chen H. An Answer to Netizen: Letting the Homeless People in Library to Get Heat Is a Basic Cultural Right [EB/OL]. (2011a-01-20). http://blog.sina.com.cn/s/blog_4978019f01017gkw.html.

[21] Chen H. The Case of the Homeless People Entering Hangzhou Public Library Is the Milestone of the Propagation of the Library Rights Ideology [EB/OL]. (2011b-01-25). http://blog.sina.com.cn/s/blog_4978019f01017gp5.html.

[22] Cheng Y. To Rethink the Reader's Rights [J]. Library Tribune, 2005, 25 (6): 99-101.

[23] Cheng Y. On the Reader's Rights: What Can't Be Ignored in Libraries [J]. Library Tribune, 2004, 24 (6): 226-229.

[24] Fan B. Fair Use of Library Resources [M]. Beijing, China: National Library of China Publishing House, 2010.

[25] Fan B. New Library Science in China: Progress and Its Problems [M]. Beijing, China: Beijing Library Press, 2007.

[26] Fan B. On Librarian's Consciousness of Library Right [J]. Library Development, 2005, 28 (2): 1-5.

[27] Jiang Y. The Research on Information Freedom and Its Limitation [M]. Beijing, China: Social Sciences Academic Press, 2007.

[28] Jiang Y. A Study of the Modern Public Library System [M]. Beijing, China: Intellectual Property Publishing House, 2010.

[29] Jiang Y. An Introduction to Library Science [M]. Haerbin, China: Heilongjiang University Press, 2009.

[30] Jiang Y. Foundation of Library Science [M]. Beijing, China: Intellectual Property Publishing House, 2012.

[31] Jiang Y. Ensuring Intellectual Freedom: The Core Value of Library Profession [J]. Library, 2003, 12 (6): 1-4.

[32] Li G. A Study of the Library Legal System in Japan [M]. Beijing, China: Beijing Library Press, 2000b.

[33] Li G. Definition, Realization and Protection on Library Rights [J]. Library Development, 2005, 28 (1): 1-4.

[34] Si J. Public Relation Events of Libraries Caused by a Micro-blog: Analysis of Public Relations in the "Micro-blog Event" of Hangzhou Public Library [J]. Library Development, 2011, 34 (4): 79-81.

[35] Yang L. The Public Discussion Triggered by a Piece of Micro-blog: The Thoughts about the Publicity Work of Public Libraries [J]. Journal of the Library Science Society of Sichuan, 2011 (6): 53-55.

[36] Si J. Practice of Library Providing Micro-Blog Service [J]. Library Journal, 2011, 30 (5): 31-34.

[37] Guo X. Popularity Situation of Civil Library Rights in China: From the Excessive Attention to the Case of Beggars Entering Hangzhou Public Library [J]. Library Development, 2011, 34 (8): 20-25.

[38] Wang X. A Library Treating People Equally Is a Heaven on Earth [N]. Changsha Wanbao, 2011-01-20 (A11).

[39] Chuan-Hua. The More We Praise a Library Letting Homeless People in the More We More Are Ironical about Ourselves [N]. Guangzhou Daily, 2011-01-25 (A2).

[40] Lu J. Homeless People in Library Is a Scene in Heaven! [EB/OL]. (2011-01-19). http://bbs1.people.com.cn/postDetail.do?view=1&id=106884336&bid=1.

[41] Tian-Ya. Hangzhou Public Library Is Open to All Readers Including Homeless People [EB/OL]. (2011-01-19). http://www.tianya.cn/publicforum/content/free/1/2082894.shtm.

[42] Zhang B. Heaven Should Look like a Library [N]. Beijing Morning Post, 2011-01-20 (22).

[43] Tu-Mao. The Library's Open to Beggars Is just a Bluff [EB/OL]. (2011-01-24). http://libseeker.bokee.com/55601515.html.

[44] Ji-Ren-Luan-Tan. Library and Homeless People Can Not Simply Stop at Chatting about [EB/OL]. (2011-01-10). http://blog.sina.com.cn/s/blog_4d5a923b0100owre.html.

[45] Library Society of China. The Code of Ethics for Chinese Librarians (Trial Implementation) [M]. Beijing, China: Beijing Library Press, 2003.

[46] Library Society of China. The Library Service Manifesto [J]. Journal of Library Science in China, 2008, 34 (6): 5.

[47] Jiang Y. Farewell after Passion Discharging: Concluding Remarks of "Move to Age of Rights" [J]. Library Development, 2006, 29 (6): 1.

[48] Cheng H, & Pan Y. Information Resource Sharing [EB/OL]. (2006-09-15). http://jpkc.sysu.edu.cn/2005/xinxi/index-xg.htm.

[49] Lao-Huai. The 4th Anniversary of My Blog: It Is Time to Say Goodbye [EB/OL]. (2008-10-24). http://oldhuai.bokee.com/6825314.html.

[50] Lao-Huai. About "The Event at National Library of China" [EB/OL]. (2004-11-20). http://oldhuai.bokee.com/258002.html.

教师简介：

陈定权，男，华中师范大学计算机科学理学学士、工学硕士，中国科学院文献情报中心管理学博士。2003 年起任教于中山大学，现任教授、硕士生导师。主讲“数字图书馆研究”、“数字图书馆关键技术”、“信息资源建设”、“信息检索”、“管理信息系统”、“信息管理研究方法与前沿”、“数字图书馆”等课程。主要研究方向为电子资源管理、数字图书馆（侧重服务和资源）、图书馆技术管理。主持科研项目 4 项，发表论文 40 余篇，出版著作 1 部。曾应美国驻华大使馆邀请，赴美国参加“国际访问者计划（IVLP）”活动，考察美国图书馆管理；威斯康辛大学麦迪逊校区图书馆学信息学研究院访问学者。兼任中国图书馆学会会员、广东省图书馆学会会员，广东省高等学校“千百十工程”第四批培养人（校级），第三届广东省宣传思想战线“十百千工程”优秀人才培养对象（社科类，第三层次）。联系方式：chendq@ mail. sysu. edu. cn。

所选论文《图书馆在关联数据运动中的角色解析》原载于《图书馆建设》2014 年第 3 期

图书馆在关联数据运动中的角色解析*

陈定权，卢玉红①

摘　要：关联数据是在现有万维网技术与架构上实现各类数据、信息和知识之间语义关联的一种规范，最终目的是让用户能从更大范围准确地获取信息。图书馆因其自身总结图书馆领域的关联数据项目的基础上，分析图书馆应用关联数据的可行性，其在关联数据运动中可以扮演关联数据的发布者、关联数据德尔信度验证者、关联数据的消费者及关联数据应用中的组织与协调者，秉持大胆研究、谨慎实践的态度，承担起图书馆可以承担的角色和任务。

关键词：关联数据；图书馆；角色分析

On the Libraries' Roles in Linked Data Movement

Dingquan Chen，Yuhong Lu

Abstract： Based on the existing technology and the architecture of World-Wide-Web，linked data is the standard which could realize semantic associations of different kinds of data，information and knowledge，its final aim is to help users access information in the wider range. Because of advantages of resources and technologies，libraries have the feasibility of applying linked data. In the linked data movement，libraries could play four roles as

* 本文得到 2011 年度中山大学青年教师培育项目“关联数据的理论与实践研究”（项目批准号：11wkpy28）的资助。

① 卢玉红，成都中医药大学图书馆助理馆员。

follows: the publisher, the trust verifier, the consumer, the organizer and the coordinator of linked data, and take the attitude of researching boldly, practicing prudently, and undertake their roles and tasked that libraries have the ability to undertake .
Keywords: Linked data; Library; Role analysis

2006年7月，有“互联网之父”之称的蒂姆·伯纳斯·李（Tim Berners-Lee）首次提出了关联数据（Linked Data）的概念。[1]一直以来，人们都希望把网络中原来没有关联的数据互联起来，构建一个结构化、富含语义、便于机器理解的数据网络（Web of data），以便在这个数据网络的基础上构建智能的应用。而关联数据的出现恰恰能促成这一构想的实现。

关联数据提出后，国内外掀起了轰轰烈烈的关联数据运动，参与的机构呈多样化趋势，不仅仅有信息技术界、出版界，政府和图书馆等机构也积极参与其中，跃跃欲试，试图在这场运动中有所作为。目前图书馆领域已经出现了一些相应的关联数据应用，本文将对这些应用进行总结，在把握目前图书馆领域关联数据应用状况的基础上，从图书馆的职能出发，多层次深入解析图书馆在关联数据运动中可以承担的角色，试图为图书馆参与关联数据运动提供参考。

1 关联数据概述

“关联数据”提出者蒂姆·伯纳斯·李认为，关联数据是一种致力于建立数据之间关联的规范，这种规范使得人们可以通过HTTP/URI机制获取数字资源[1]；维基百科定义其为语义网的主题之一，认为它是一种发布结构化数据的方法[2]；夏翠娟等认为关联数据是语义网的一种轻量级实现方式，它能让Web代理通过简单通用的HTTP URI规范直接访问文档中的数据，是实现数据网络的关键方法[3]；金斯利·艾德森（Kingsley Idehen）认为关联数据是网络中的一种富链接机制，它致力于将超文本链接转变为超数据链接[4]；白海燕则侧重从语义方面进行定义，认为关联数据是用来在语义网中使用URI和RDF发布、共享、连接各类资源，强调建立已有信息的语义标注和实现数据之间关联的方式[5]；郭少友则认为关联数据是指根据一定的原则进行组织并发布到Web上的数据，它遵循RDF和SPARQL标准并包含与外部数据之间的链接，可以直接通过HTTP /URI机制进行获取[6]。虽然目前关联数据还没有统一的定义，但大部分对关联数据概念的解读都认为关联数据是一种实现数据关联的规范或者方法，即认为关联数据不是某一种技术，而是利用多种技术来指导数据之间语义关系的创建，起到一种工具性、指导性的作用。

综上所述，笔者认为关联数据是在现有万维网技术与架构上，实现各类数据、信息和知识之间语义关联的一种规范。它利用URI命名数据，采用RDF在网络上发布和链接数据，并通过HTTP揭示和获取这些数据。目的是通过对万事万物及其相互之间关系进行机器可读的描述，使现有的文件网络进化为一个富含语义的、互联互通的数据网络。[7]

2 图书馆与关联数据

关联数据作为一种语义信息的编码、发布和利用方式，它的最终目的是为了让用户能从更大范围内准确地获取信息，而便捷高效的信息获取一直以来都是图书馆努力的目标，无论怎么解读关联数据，它都跟图书馆有着无法割舍的联系。

2.1 图书馆领域的关联数据应用实践分析

关于关联数据应用，爱尔兰国家图书馆的数字企业研究所（Digital Enterprise Research Institute，DERI）在技术报告《关联数据应用——关联数据使用的起源与挑战》（*Linked Data Applications*：*The Genesis and the Challenges of Using Linked Data on the Web*）[8]中给出了两种解释：一是将关联数据应用到不同领域，即将不同领域的数据发布为关联数据仓储；二是指以关联数据仓储为基础而构建的 Web 应用，这类 Web 应用被称为“关联数据驱动的 Web 应用”，主要关注如何在 Web 上消费和操作关联数据，即利用不同关联数据仓储中的数据来支持应用。目前图书馆界的关联数据实践还主要集中在第一类，据不完全统计，有 10 多个国家级图书馆发布了关联数据集，而这些数据集的数据类型主要是各类名称或主题规范数据以及书目数据（表 1）。

表 1　图书馆领域的关联数据应用实践情况统计

发布的数据类型	图书馆
名称或主题规范数据	美国国会图书馆、德国国家图书馆、法国国家图书馆、日本国会图书馆、捷克国家图书馆、芬兰国家图书馆、西班牙国家图书馆、联机计算机图书馆中心（以下简称 OCLC）
书目数据	瑞典国家图书馆、匈牙利国家图书馆、大英国家图书馆、德国国家经济图书馆、西班牙国家图书馆、OCLC

从上面的统计可以看出目前图书馆领域在关联数据应用实践上具有以下几个特点：

（1）基本上都是国家层面上的大型图书馆在进行关联数据的发布。国家图书馆一般技术强大，数据基础和资金都比较雄厚，而小型的图书馆一般都没有太多属于自己的数据，因此国家层面上的大型图书馆最有可能成为关联数据的最先尝试者。

（2）发布的数据主要是主题规范数据、名称规范数据和书目数据，因为这些数据都是图书馆界的原生数据，是属于图书馆界所有的数据。

（3）目前我国还没有图书馆正式发布数据，大部分数据发布应用实践都是由国外图书馆完成的。

目前，基于已经发布的关联数据仓储来构建 Web 应用在图书馆领域没有成型的案例，大多数学者都还是从理论的角度来探讨这类关联数据应用。当图书馆发布的数据仓储渐成规模，且有着稳定的用户需求时，基于关联数据仓储而推出各种服务也就是顺理成章了。

2.2 图书馆应用关联数据的可行性

关联数据运动正在兴起，能否在这场运动中有所作为以及如何作为是现代图书馆积极思考的问题。图书馆自身资源与技术的优势，让正处于转型与变革的图书馆具备应用关联数据的可行性。

传统图书馆作为知识主要保存者与提供者的地位正在被各种商业性信息服务机构所威胁，商业性服务机构在信息技术和因特网的推动下，其服务内容不断渗透到原本属于图书馆的各种信息服务领域，有时候甚至比图书馆做得更好，传统的图书馆信息服务领域正不断被蚕食，优势也在逐渐丧失。图书馆在这样的情况下开始尝试转变，在努力保住自己核心竞争力的同时，也积极学习和借鉴其他类别信息服务机构的有益经验，以期以开放的姿态融入整个信息社会的信息交换与共享交流体系中去。而关联数据的出现，为正处于变革与转型当中的图书馆提供了一个历史机遇，它在帮助图书馆融入数据网络、扩大自身资源范围、强化与外界信息的共享与交换、提升图书馆服务能力等方面都会有所作为。

虽然网络资源内容丰富，但缺乏必要的组织和质量控制，资源发布有很大的随意性，用户往往需要花很大的精力才能找到真正有价值的信息。而长期负担保存人类文明、传播文化重任的图书馆则在长期的实践中积累了丰富而系统的文献资源，其价值毋庸置疑。另外，这些经过精心加工与组织的高质量资源是图书馆参与关联数据运动的“资本”，如果它们能够融入数据网络，那无疑可以对数据网络的发展起到极大的推进作用。

图书馆在长期的数据加工与组织工作实践当中，培养了一大批擅长知识组织和知识管理的专业人才，他们掌握处理信息的方法，能很好地鉴别信息的价值，积累了大量的知识服务经验，他们所拥有的经验和所掌握的方法与技能也是图书馆所拥有的一大笔财富。如果将图书馆工作人员所掌握的工作知识与技能应用到数据网络中去，那必将有助于数据网络变成一个更有序、更有价值的信息空间。

处于变革与转型之中的图书馆，如果能够抓住关联数据运动的发展机遇，以“资源”为阵地，倚重专业技能与专业人才，必将会在关联数据运动中取得令人瞩目的成绩，开辟图书馆信息服务的新阵地。

3　图书馆在关联数据运动中的角色定位

按照创新扩散理论，技术的接收者大抵分为创新者、早期接受者、早期的大多数、后期的大多数和落伍者。在早期接受者与早期的大多数之间，存在着一个死亡陷阱（图1）[9]，新技术的推出或应用存在很大的风险，稍有不慎，前期投资就付诸东流。尽管图书馆开始尝试性地参与到关联数据运动，但关联数据毕竟还是一个新兴事物，未来发展前景尚未可知，或持续发展下去，或可能遭遇某种不可预见的瓶颈而停滞夭折。尽管很多机构对关联数据的前景持积极乐观的态度，但目前各类参与机构总体上是“摸着石头过河”，谨慎前行。在这种形式尚不明朗、机遇与风险并存的情况下，图书馆应该基于自身的基本职能，找准自己的角色，既不能贸然行事，浪费资源，影响图书馆基本职能，但也不能过于谨慎，一无所成，错失发展良机。

3.1　关联数据运动中的角色及其任务

汤姆·希斯和克里斯蒂安·比泽尔在他们的著作《关联数据——推动网络进入全球

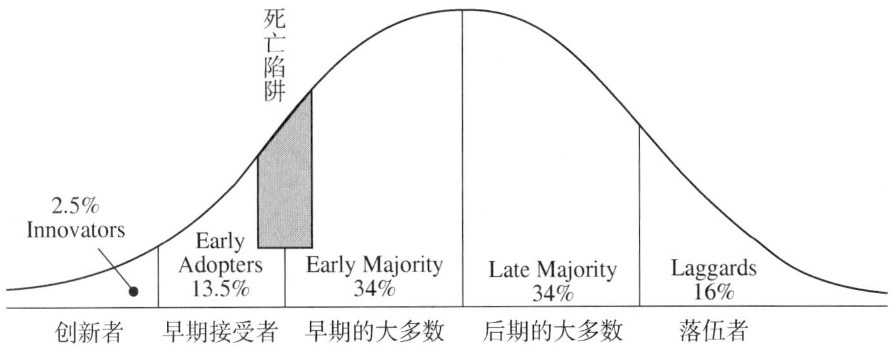

图1　创新扩散过程中的死亡陷阱[9]

空间时代》中提到关联数据的基本架构由下到上由四个部分组成，依次是数据发布层、关联数据网络、数据存取整合和储存层、应用层（图2）[10]。这个关联数据架构中表明了关联数据运动中可能存在着关联数据的发布者、信度验证者和消费者三种角色。

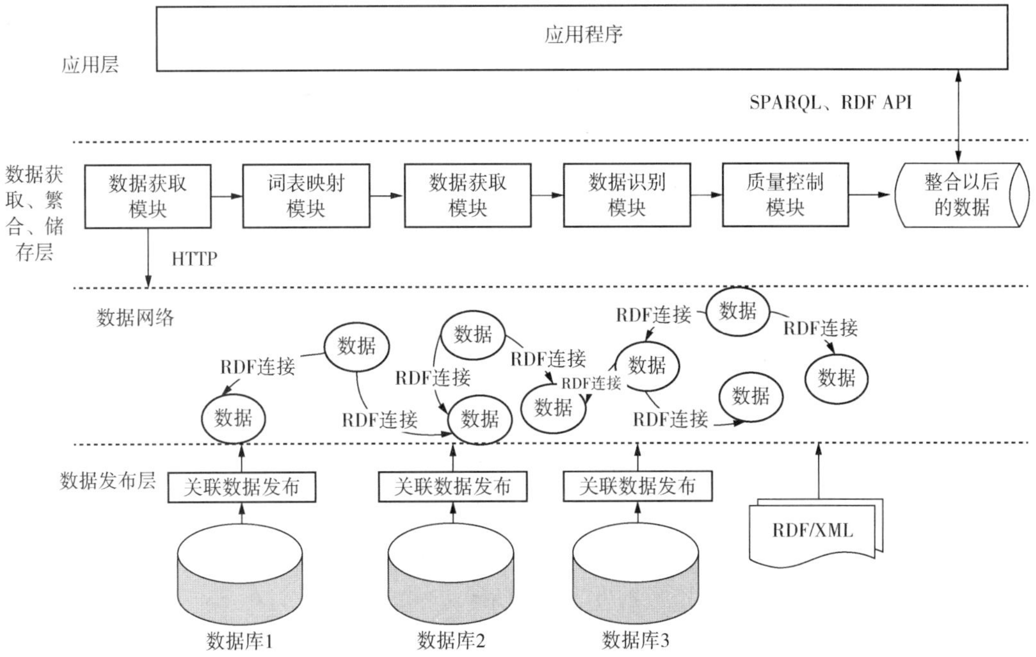

图2　关联数据的基础架构图[10]

（1）关联数据发布者。关联数据发布者存在于数据发布层中，关联数据的发布技术门槛不是很高，组织或者个人只要遵守关联数据四原则[1]，把自己拥有的数据发布出来就可以成为关联数据发布者。

（2）关联数据信度验证者。关联数据信度验证者存在于数据存取整合和储存层中，这一层可以提供一系列基础服务，如本体词汇维护、不同本体词汇之间的相互映射、数据标识的规范控制、数据源辨别等。关联数据网络形成一定规模后，关于关联数据的可信度问题就会随之而来。关联数据网络是一个开放的数据环境，如何建立有效的机制来确保数据的可信度、辨别出可靠的数据将成为数据网络发展的关键。[11]关联数据信度验证者的主要任务就是确定数据的来源，追溯数据由谁提供、这些数据通过哪些程序处理过、谁保存过这些数据等。

（3）关联数据消费者。关联数据应用层则是由关联数据的消费者组成。关联数据的发布最早是由一些大学实验室和一些小公司的研发人员来进行，随着关联数据得到越来越多人的关注，一些政府机构和大企业都纷纷加入到关联数据发布者的行列中。截止到2010年9月，关联数据网络中大约已经包含了317亿条RDF语句，有约3.95亿个RDF链接。[12]随着时间的推移，网络中的关联数据将会越来越多，这就为机构或个人消费关联数据提供了数据基础。

（4）关联数据运动的组织与协调者。除上述三种角色之外，从关联数据基础架构整体环境来看，还应该存在一个组织与协调者的角色。目前发布关联数据的机构和个人都还是自发的，只是因为发布关联数据的机构还不是很多，因此重复发布的现象还不是很严重；但是当关联数据得到普及，大量机构和个人都把自己的数据发布为关联数据时，就会出现各自为政、数据混乱的现状。因此就需要一个权威的组织来对关联数据的发布进行协调和统一，预防混乱现象的出现。

3.2 图书馆可以承担的角色

上述不同角色对于参与的图书馆有不同的要求。图书馆是否能胜任这些角色，还要依据图书馆自身的能力来判断，也就是要根据图书馆的职能和所处的层次来决定。

3.2.1 图书馆的基本职能与角色的判定

图书馆在关联数据运动中的角色定位不能脱离图书馆的基本职能。图书馆的基本职能包括收集、整序文献并提供使用[13]，对基本职能的再次解读有助于图书馆在关联数据运动中寻找合适的角色定位。

（1）收集文献。图书馆的一个最重要的职能就是收集人类文献，致力于收集文献的图书馆可以被看作人类知识的集体宝库，对人类社会具有无可取代的作用。而关联数据希望建立一个覆盖全球的数据网络，图书馆书目信息库可以成为数据网络的重要组成部分，就此来看，图书馆可以承担数据发布者的角色。

（2）整序文献。图书馆的另一个重要职能就是对文献进行筛选和优化，并对文献进行分类、标引、编目等操作，使其得到充分揭示并有序化。另外，图书馆整序内容的粒度不断细化，不再局限在文献单元层面上，而是已经开始深入到对知识单元的层面。图书馆在整序文献单元和知识单元的长期实践过程中积累了丰富的经验，培养了大量的专业人才，这为图书馆成为关联数据信度验证者提供了现实条件。

（3）提供使用。收集和整序文献的目的都是为了提供使用，只是不同时代、不同性质的图书馆服务范围会存在差异。虽说图书馆中包含了人类的大部分文献，但是这些文献并不一定是完整的。在现代图书馆提倡以用户为中心的大环境下，为了能更好地为用户服务，图书馆必须借助于外部力量来完善自身的资源与服务，因此图书馆如果加入关联数据运动，就极有可能成为关联数据消费者。

3.2.2 图书馆层次与角色的判定

从图书馆的职能来分析角色是把图书馆看作一个整体，但是在具体的实践过程中，各个图书馆还是会因为能力与规模的不同而存在角色的差异，因此再从宏观、中观和微观三个层面来细分角色会更准确，更具有指导意义。在这里，宏观意义上的图书馆主要是指国家级图书馆、国际大型的图书馆联盟，如美国国家图书馆、瑞典国家图书馆、OCLC 等；中观层次的图书馆是指图书馆联盟或者图书馆行业协会等，如 CALIS；微观层次上的图书馆则是指具体单个图书馆。具体分析见表 2。

表 2　图书馆在关联数据应用中的角色解析

层　次	发布者	信度验证者	消费者	组织与协调者
宏观：国家图书馆、世界级图书馆联盟	√	√	√	√
中观：地区性图书馆联盟、行业图书馆协会	√	√	√	√
微观：图书馆个体	√	—	√	—

（1）关联数据发布者。从表 2 可以看出，所有图书馆都可以成为关联数据发布者。可能会有人质疑，除了国家图书馆或者大型联合目录外，大部分单个图书馆没有属于自己的数据资源，如何可以发布关联数据？这是因为有些图书馆有自己的特藏，虽然特藏是每个图书馆的重量级资源，但以关联数据形式发布数据资源并不影响资源的访问，只需要对最终链接到的数字资源本身做访问限制即可。[14]

另外，德国国家图书馆的简・汉纳曼与尤尔根・坎特认为，数据网络由里向外分为三层：核心层、中间层（地幔层）、外表层，核心层是其他两层的基础，因此其数据应该是稳定而可靠的[15]，他们认为包括图书馆在内的各类文化机构应该是这个核心层的主要数据提供者。而宏观和中观层次上的图书馆，在长期组织信息、为用户服务的过程中，形成了大量的高质量的规范主题数据、规范名称数据、图书馆数据标准等，这些数据都是由专业人员进行维护的，稳定而可靠，可以发布为核心层数据。

因此，所有类型的图书馆都可以成为关联数据的发布者，宏观和中观层次上的图书馆还是核心数据的发布者，一般的图书馆个体则可以以关联数据形式发布其特色资源或特色馆藏。图书馆领域现有的关联数据应用实践也恰恰说明，图书馆能够成为关联数据的发布者。

（2）关联数据的信度验证者。宏观和中观层次上的图书馆可以成为数据信度验证者。

要成为关联数据信度的验证者，除拥有大量专业人员外，更重要的是要有由专业人员长期修订和维护的高质量的规范数据。这些规范数据记录了人名和机构名的变迁历史，可以成为追踪数据来源的基础数据，这就为数据可信度验证与溯源提供基础。[16] 规范数据的修订和维护是不可能由单个图书馆来完成的，只能由国家级图书馆、世界级图书馆联盟，或者是地区级图书馆联盟、行业性图书馆协会来组织实现，因此它们才有能力来承担数据信度验证者的角色。

（3）关联数据的消费者。图书馆既要让数据“走出去”为他人所用，也要“引进来”一些自己所需要的数据，形成一个无界、自由穿越的数据网络。图书馆可以把自己的特色数据或馆藏数据发布成关联数据，也可以利用外界的关联数据来丰富图书馆资源，以便为用户提供更全面、更准确的信息服务。只要图书馆愿意并且技术允许即可，任何图书馆都可以消费和使用关联数据。

（4）关联数据应用中的组织与协调者。关联数据关系到整个信息社会，不再局限于某个机构或某个行业。为了能更好地建设关联数据网络，需要有个组织或者机构统一组织和协调，高屋建瓴，以全局眼光看待和分析问题，注册和登记关联数据，如同元数据登记机构，有助于发现和使用关联数据集。目前，国家级图书馆或世界性图书馆联盟可以担此重任。行业图书馆联盟或地区级图书馆联盟也可以组织和协调本地区或本行业的关联数据，完成关联数据集的登记和管理工作，类似于元数据二级登记机构。但最终图书馆界能否承担如此重任，除了跟图书馆自身发展有着关系外，还跟外界的发展态势以及图书馆与外界之间的博弈有着密切关系，这实际上决定了是谁来主导关联数据建设的问题。这跟中国早期的数字图书馆研究与建设的历史情形较为类似。当时中国是由图书馆界而非 IT 界来主导数字图书馆建设，导致中国数字图书馆的建设出现了“重资源与服务，轻技术”的乱象，作为国家信息基础设施之一的中国数字图书馆工程却未能培育出来有影响的商业技术方案，我国数字图书馆建设几乎成为国外技术产品的试验田。

4 结　　语

虽然图书馆积极寻求转变，需要新的技术、产品或服务来为自己注入新的活力，但是由于经费不足、专业受限、技术力量薄弱等缘故，图书馆更应该慎重思考，科学定位图书馆的角色和任务。从目前图书馆现有的进展来看，部分图书馆已经成为关联数据的发布者，同时也在积极借鉴其他行业的经验，努力成为关联数据的消费者。关联数据的信度验证者、组织与协调者则还在探索之中。无论图书馆怎样看待关联数据以及采取什么样的应对措施，关联数据依然是循其自身规律逐渐向前推进，但最终结果还不得而知，充满了未知数。在新技术概念眼花缭乱、层出不穷的今天，作为非营利的机构，图书馆最好还是积极关注外界进展，大胆研究，同时立足于图书馆的实际情况，谨慎实践，承担起图书馆能够承担的角色和任务，根据用户的实际需求，推出高效能的服务，切不可为了关联数据而关联数据。大胆研究，谨慎实践，也许这是当今图书馆应对关联数据运动的基本态度吧。

参考文献

[1] Berners-Lee T. Linked Data [EB/OL]. [2012-01-12]. http://www.w3.org/DesignIssues/LinkedData.html.

[2] Linked data [EB/OL]. [2013-02-26]. http://en.wikipedia.org/wiki/Linked_data.

[3] 夏翠娟，刘炜，赵亮，等. 关联数据发布技术及其实现 [J]. 中国图书馆学报，2012 (1)：45-54.

[4] Idehen K. Creating, Deploying and Exploiting Linked Data [EB/OL]. [2013-01-22]. http://virtuoso.openlinksw.com/pre sentations/Creating_Deploying_Exploiting_Linked_Data2/Creating_Deploying_Exploiting_Linked_Data2_TimBL_v3.html# (8).

[5] 白海燕. 基于关联数据的书目组织深度序化初探 [C/OL] [2012-07-20] //2010 图书馆前沿技术论坛：关联数据与书目数据的未来. http://www.kevenlw.name/downloads/Bibliographic data.pdf.

[6] 郭少友. 关联数据的动态链接维护研究 [J]. 图书情报工作，2011，55 (17)：112-116.

[7] 刘炜. 关联数据：概念、技术及应用展望［J］. 大学图书馆学报，2011 (2)：5－12.

[8] Hausenblas M. Linked Data Applications：The Genesis and the Challenges of Using Linked Data on the Web［R/OL］［2012－08－02］. http：//wtlab. um. ac. ir/parameters/wtlab/filemanager/LD_resources/other/lod-app-tr-2009－07－26_0. pdf.

[9] 摩尔. 跨越鸿沟［M］. 赵娅，译. 北京：机械工业出版社，2009：25.

[10] Bizer C. Evolving the Web into a Global Data Space［EB/OL］. ［2013－01－04］. http：//dl. acm. org/citation. cfm? id＝2075915.

[11] Hannemann J. Linked Data for Libraries［EB/OL］. ［2012－01－18］. http：//www. ifla. org/files/hq/papers/ifla76/149-hannemann-en. pdf.

[12] W3C. Linking Open Data［EB/OL］. ［2012－01－18］. http：//www. w3. org/wiki/SweoIG/TaskForces/CommunityProjects/LinkingOpenData.

[13] 吴慰慈. 图书馆学基础［M］. 北京：高等教育出版社，2004：92.

[14] 关联数据的图书馆应用问题［EB/OL］. ［2011－01－20］. http：//catwizard. blogbus. com/logs/3326580. html.

[15] Hannemann J，Kett J. Linked Data for Libraries. World Library and Information Congress：76th IFLA General Conference and Assembly［EB/OL］［2012－07－29］. http：//www. ifla. org/files/hq/papers/ifla76/149-hannemann-en. pdf.

[16] 林海青，楼向英，夏翠娟. 图书馆关联数据：机会与挑战［J］. 中国图书馆学报，2012 (1)：55－65.

教师简介：

肖永英，女，武汉大学管理学学士、硕士，英国女王大学金融与信息学院信息研究博士。1995年任教于中山大学资讯管理学院，副教授，图书馆学硕士生导师。主讲“参考咨询研究”、“参考工作与学科服务”、“信息服务”、“英文经典专业著作选读”等课程。研究范围包括参考咨询服务、信息用户与服务。已出版著作4部，发表论文50余篇。兼任中国图书馆学会会员，广东省图书馆学会阅读指导委员会委员。联系方式：issxyy@mail. sysu. edu. cn。

所选论文“An empirical study of everyday life information seeking behavior of urban low-Income residents in the Haizhu District of Guangzhou”原载于 *Chinese Journal of Library and Information Science* 2011年第4卷第2期

An Empirical Study of Everyday Life Information Seeking Behavior of Urban Low-Income Residents in the Haizhu District of Guangzhou*

Yongying Xiao, Lanman He①

Abstract: This paperre ports an investigation on everyday life information seeking behavior of urban low-income group in the Haizhu District of Guangzhou. Empirical data were collected via in-depth interview with low-income urban residents and were analyzed using qualitative methods. This paper discusses the research findings based on the more noticeable results of information seeking behavior among these people. Our approach touches on a focused study of such issues as what the role of information seeking in their everyday life is, what information they care about, which information channels they prefer to use, which factors influence their information seeking behavior, how difficult it is to seek the information they need, and how they use public libraries. Based on our research findings, we propose that public libraries should provide customized information services for urban low-income residents according to the unique characteristics of their information seeking behavior in everyday life.

Keywords: Everyday life information seeking (ELIS); Information behavior; Urban low-Income residents

---

* This study is supported by the postgraduate summer science and research training scheme of Sun Yat-sen University in 2010.

① 何兰满，中山大学资讯管理学院2010级图书情报学硕士生，目前在中山大学东校区图书馆工作。

1 The Background and Purpose of This Study

1.1 Background

Everyday Life Information Seeking (ELIS) is the acquisition of various types of informational (both cognitive and expressive) elements which people employ to conduct themselves effectively in their daily life or to solve problems not directly connected with their performance of occupational tasks.[1] In 1970s, large-scale surveys were made to investigate citizens' information needs and information seeking behavior such as Dervin's survey on the information needs of Seattle's citizens.[2] However, this type of quantitative surveys became more infrequent by the end of 1970s. Instead, qualitative research methodologies on this topic have made inroads, which have been gradually accepted by the library and information science (LIS) scholarly communities. The empirical research on ELIS has since attracted more attention from LIS scholars. Moreover, more research projects were delved into, though on a smaller research scale, the study of people of different social strata in the practice of ELIS. A good example is Chatman's study of the information behavior of the working poor by the adoption of an ethnographic method.[3] Since Savolainen's first introduction of ELIS in 1995, this conceptual orientation about information needs and information seeking behavior of a particular social stratum toward its "way of life" has become gradually a high profile research issue among LIS scholars in Europe and in the USA. Research in this field has also been fruitful, as indicated by the Biennial International Conference of Information Seeking in Context (ISIC), in which ELIS is featured as one of the most important conference themes.

Overseas scholars have paid a great deal of attention to the information behavior of economically deprived social groups in the ELIS field. Childers & Post first studied the information behavior of low-income people in an information-poverty context.[4] In 1970s, Greenberg & Dervin found that low-income people depended a lot on television for their information intake, which is not only an important source of information and of new knowledge in their ELIS pursuit, but also a device for alleviating the boredom of their monotonous life routine.[5] From the 1980s to the 1990s, Chatman conducted extensive research of everyday life information behavior of various economically deprived social groups such as low-income women, janitors and low-skilled workers. As a result, several theories were formulated such as information poverty, life in the round and normative behavior[6-8], which have had great impact on the field of everyday life information behavior research. In the beginning of the 21st century, Spink & Cole conducted a survey on the information seeking channels of African-Americans low-income households in their daily life.[9] Hersberger, using the theory of social networks, studied the information needs and information sources of homeless populations.[10-11]

In China, several scholars have conducted empirical researches on the information needs and information behaviors of urban disadvantaged groups. The opportunities for knowledge acquisition of peasant workers (sometimes also called *rural migrant workers*) in big cities such as in Beijing, Shenzhen and Wuhan were examined, and raised the public outcry for public libraries to take the responsibility in creating and providing educational and cultural services to rural migrant workers. Such has been advocated repeatedly by Prof. Wang Zizhou and his several other colleagues at Beijing University. [12-14] In Chengdu, a southwest city in Sichuan province, the information needs of such disadvantaged groups as the disabled and peasant workers in their daily life were investigated. [15] The information needs and information seeking behavior of urban disadvantaged groups, both biologically and sociologically speaking, were studied, and the barriers hindering their information seeking activities were also analyzed. [16] In addition, the impact of information technology on the information behavior of the information disadvantaged groups in Liuzhou, a medium-sized city in Guangxi Zhuang Autonomous Region, was also investigated. [17] It should be noted that, as far as the research on the information behavior of the urban disadvantaged groups is concerned, Chinese scholars have paid more attention to such disadvantaged groups as rural migrant workers and the disabled, and their research have put more emphasis on the opportunities of information/knowledge acquisition of these groups. In comparison, the information needs and information seeking behavior of urban low-income residents have been overlooked generally speaking.

1.2 Purpose

According to the recent report on the development of Chinese cities issued by the Chinese Academy of Social Sciences, the urban impoverished population in China can be classified into 3 categories: (1) peasant workers; (2) laid-off workers who used to work in state-owned enterprises; (3) recently-graduated university students who have, most probably, not yet been employed, but taken residence temporarily in urban impoverished areas. [18] In the Chinese LIS field, scholars have paid more attention to the information needs of rural migrant workers, whereas research papers on urban low-income residents such as laid-off workers are scarce and rare in between. Because of the geographic areas (most in urban villages, where these urban low-income people dwelled), their living conditions have substantial impact on the process of urbanization in China. Based on the method of in-depth interview, our study aims to take a closer look at the information needs and information seeking behaviors of urban low-income residents in their daily lives, so as to help public libraries provide better customized information services so as to fulfill their institutional mandate of providing universal and equitable access to public cultural services.

2 Research Design

2.1 Definition of urban low-income residents

Urban low-income residents are people who, because of social, personal and other reasons, can not acquire necessary/sufficient income to sustain a normal living standard and live in an impoverished state. These people are of a specially disadvantaged group during the process of urban economic development and the accumulation of social wealth. [19] According to the statistics from the Chinese Academy of Social Sciences in 2010, most of the urban impoverished population is of age between 40 and 50 years old, who live beyond their means and dwell in poor housing conditions. Urban low-income residents are populated in diverse geographical areas in China. Using the principle of convenient sampling, we chose the urban low-income residents in the Haizhu District of Guangzhou in Guangdong Province as the targeted participants of our study.

2.2 Research methodology

In-depth interviews are an important method to gather research data for a qualitative analysis. It is also a commonly applied method in ELIS research. Bates proposed that narrative and episodic interview techniques are qualitative research methods that sustain a person-centered paradigm of human information seeking behavior and also provide a particularly useful methodological framework for studies of ELIS behavior. [20] We also believe that personal interview techniques are especially useful for collecting research data on such disadvantaged groups as urban low-income residents for the study of their ELIS behavior due to their lack of sufficient electronic communication tools. Therefore, we opted for the in-depth interview method for gathering sufficient qualitative data from the targeted interviewees for our research purposes.

An interview guide was formulated according to our research purpose. ① Considering that urban low-income residents normally would apply for and receive their low-income welfare benefits from their residents' neighborhood committees, we contacted the officials at those neighborhood committees who did the liaison work for us to contact the potential participants for our research. All of these participants dwelled in the jurisdictions of various residents' committees in the Haizhu District. In this way, we were able to select 50 urban low-income residents from 22 residents' committees to be our study participants. We conducted our actual investigation in July 2010.

Prior to the interviews, a pre-training session for interview skills was given to the field interviewers. ② We especially emphasized that field investigators should explain our research purpose clearly to the interviewee and also to assure him/her the confidentiality of the information that they provided was protected. After the interview, the field investigator would give the participant a gift or tutor his/her child homework as a token of appreciation. Each interview lasted for approximately 30 minutes, and the places for conducting these interviews varied anywhere from the participant's home, work place and office of a participant's own resident

① The interview guide can be available from the authors if needed.

② Investigators were selected from library science students at School of Information Management, SYSU, including Ailing Zeng, Minfei Liang, Haiyan Deng, Qiuting Chen, Yanmin Liang, Yi Lin, Suiyan Liu and Fuyong Cao. Most of them have fluent Cantonese language skill, which are a necessity for the success of the interview process. The authors would like to express our sincere appreciation to them.

committee. Because the field investigator conducted the interviews via the liaisonwork of residents' committees, all the interviewees were quite happy to participate in our study.

However, some of them did not answer all the questions asked, especially with regard to the question of how difficult it was for them to acquire information in their daily life. One of the interviewees did not reveal her educational level for unspecified reason. As most of the participants were not willing to be recorded during the interview session, the field investigators could only take notes manually during the interview session. They wrote down the high points within 24 hours after the interview had completed. The submission time of those interview notes varied slightly somewhat within the specified time frame depending on the length of the field investigator's notes and the duration of his/her memory retention. All the transcripts of the interview were coded manually. When the related transcript of an interview was cited in the paper, the code of the transcript was indicated accordingly (e. g. , 01).

3 Basic Information about the Interviewees

3.1 Age and gender

The interviewees are from various neighborhoods of the Haizhu District. Their age ranges from 17 to 78 years old. As indicated in Figure 1, 68% of the intervieweds (34) are of age between 40 and 59 years old, who are usually breadwinners in their families. As far as the gender is concerned, 72% of the intervieweds (36) are women, whereas 28% of them (14) are men. Therefore, there were far more women than men who participated in our study. It is shown that the reasons for family poverty are varied. The breadwinner of the family (most often the husband) usually suffers from a serious disease or a divorce or has passed away resulting in a single parenthood situation. As most of the children from these families are still at school, the interviewees who can participate in our study are therefore mostly women.

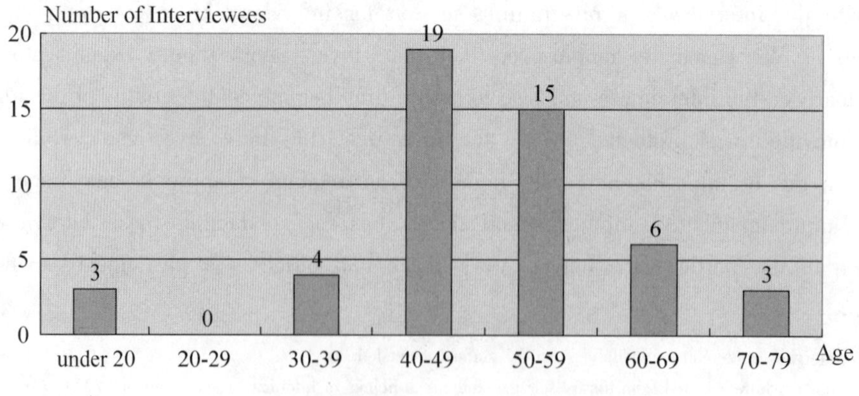

Figure 1 Age distribution of the interviewees

3.2 Educational level

As indicated from Figure 2, the overall educational level of the interviewees is relatively low. 44% of them received a 9-year compulsory education; 26% of them received only a primary education; whereas 18% of them received a senior high school education or vocational education. There is one participant who has received a college education. It is worth noting that, four surveyed participants were almost illiterate. One surveyed participant would not reveal her educational background.

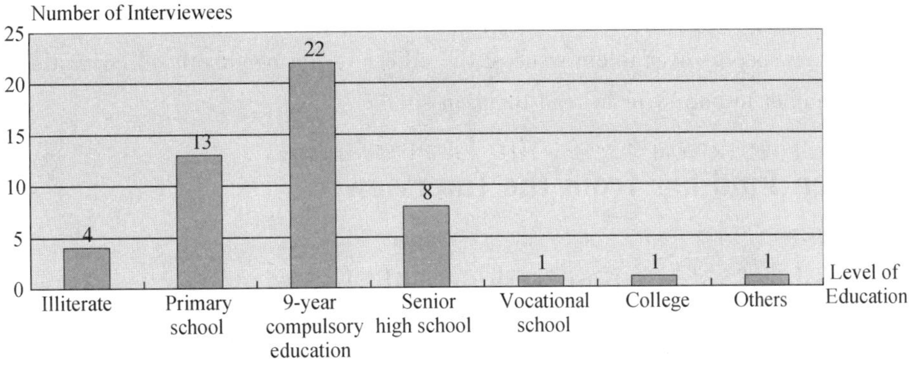

Figure 2 The level of education of the interviewees

3.3 Employment status

Figure 3 shows the employment status of the interviewees. 44% of them (22) were not employed, either because of an illness, old age, low educational level, a lack of skills, or because they were preoccupied with a family member who suffered a chronic illness. Some of them lived strictly on a government welfare program. 38% of them (19) held temporary jobs such as domestic aide or served as a volunteer at the office of their residents' committee. Only 8% of them (4) had stable jobs, 4% of them (2) were self-employed; one was operating as

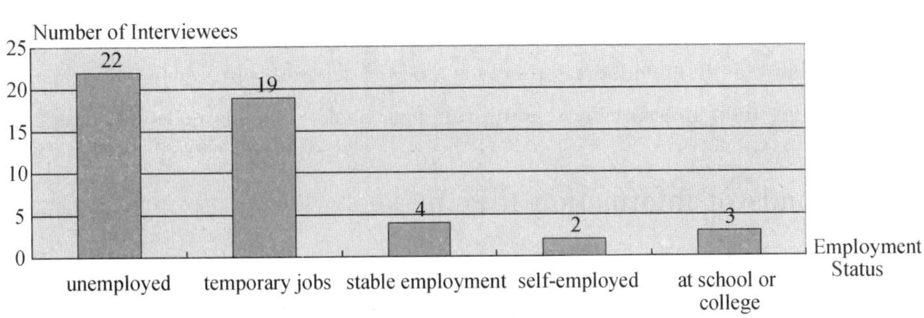

Figure 3 The employment status of the interviewees

a newsstand owner and the other, as a copy shop owner. In addition, 6% of them (3) were high (or vocational) school students from urban low-income families.

3.4 Living condition

All of the interviewees are registered citizens in the city of Guangzhou. Most of them live in a shabby, secluded urban village (e.g., Kangle village) where low-income people live in densely populated blocks. Most of urban low-income residents live in poor housing conditions. However, they do usually have a television set in their homes. 30% of them have their own personal computers at home, most of which have Internet access. There are no public libraries in most of these neighborhoods. Nonetheless, there are possibly small collections of books, magazines and newspapers availablein some of the offices of the neighborhood committees for the local residents either to borrow or to read them on site.

4 Research Findings from the Interviewees

4.1 The role of information in their daily lives

Information plays a very important role in the daily lives of urban low-income residents as they face family, work or emotional problems. Previous research publications on this topic indicated that low-income people acquire their needed information primarily via traditional mass media or from interpersonal communication. Yet at the same time, low-income people are described as if they were living in a seemingly dysfunctional world. The fact is that these urban low-income residents are incapable of taking full advantage of the critically needed information at will for solving the problems that they are facing.[21] For instance, one interviewee has a daughter who suffers from an illness of "attention-deficient hyperactivity disorder" (ADHD). She obtained a certain amount of information about this disease sporadically from her doctors or from some children's health magazines. Other than this, she had no idea of where else she could get this illness related information. In addition, it is shown from our investigation that not all problems of these low-income people can be solved simply by an informational therapy. In several other cases, these interviewees also expressed a need of emotional support and of companionship from their immediate family members, relatives and/or friends. In a few other cases, they resorted to alleviating their pressure by reading religious books, novels or simply watching TV.

4.2 What kinds of information they need

As indicated from Figure 4, urban low-information residents need all kinds of information in conducting their daily lives more effectively. They include but not limited to such essential information as those about medical care, education and healthy living. The information they need are very practical and their information seeking behaviors are very closely related to their daily necessities. In our investigation, more than half of the interviewees claimed that medical care information was what they needed most. 80% of them had at least one family member who suffered from a disease, which was a primary cause of their poverty. Under such circumstances, they needed information not only about medical care, but also about medical welfare programs by which they could better manage their medical expenses. Educational information ranked the second most needed information for them. 84% of them had at least one child who was still at school. As such, educational expenses were an obvious financial burden on the family. To help their children do better at school, most of the parents were very interested in reading about educational information, especially about information regarding to scholarship and stipulations for possible remissions of tuition and miscellaneous fees. Information about healthy cooking and living are also needed as many of them believed that a healthy lifestyle was helpful to reduce their medical expenses.

Moreover, they were more interested in reading about or listening to the societal news, such as local news on robbery, riots, natural disasters and man-made accidents. Some of the interviewees claimed that watching or listening to this kind of news was helpful in keeping them aware of events that happened around them so as to keep them away from troubles and misfortunes. 12% of the interviewees said that they needed not to get any information proactively as they were usually told by their friends and neighbors about those pieces of information that they needed to hear. Our research survey found that the urban low-income residents definitely have a need about many kinds of practical and entertaining information for their well-being and/or survival. However, it is also sadly true that they are often not aware of their true information needs themselves. As suggested by Chatman, life of the poor is full of information problems, but they are not active in seeking information and they also do not know how to express their problems. Previous research publications on ELIS also show that the information need of urban low-income people is very similar to that of such disadvantaged groups as rural migrant workers and the disabled, but there are some differences between them. Therefore, we need to delve more deeply into the information need of the urban low-income people, so as to provide more customized information services for them.

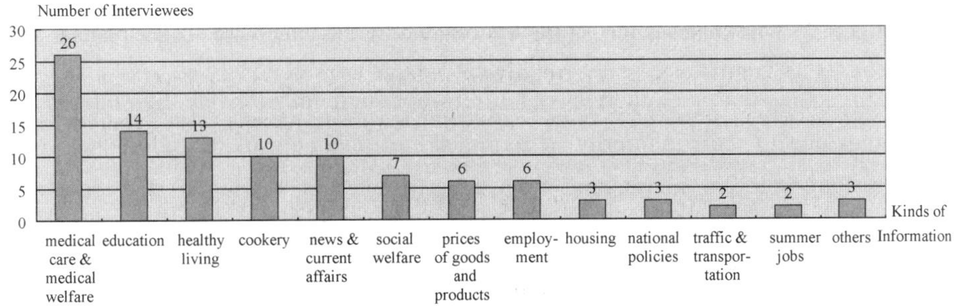

Figure 4　The kinds of information the surveyed participants care about

4.3 Channels for acquiring the information they need

Various channels for the interviewees for acquiring information are indicated in Figure 5. Firstly, they tend to obtain everyday life information from mass media, especially from local television programs and newspapers. This research finding echoes the findings of earlier research works in the USA, such as those authored by Greenberg & Dervin[8] and Chatman[9]. Secondly, the residents' committees are an important source for low-income people to acquire their everyday life information, especially those about medical care and education. It is shown that the officials at the residents' committees often help the low-income residents apply for medical welfare. This is because most of them are not familiar with the relevant policies, not to mention how to apply for them. Thirdly, interpersonal communication is another important channel for the interviewees to acquire everyday life information. They tend to resort to their family, friends and other people who are in the same social stratum as themselves in getting and passing on the needed information. Whenever they are not able to acquire certain information, they would try to get help from such individuals who are in a higher social stratum (as defined by the higher level of income and other tangible assets) or have specialized training in a certain field such as medical doctors or government officials. As suggested by other Chinese scholars, the principle of least effort is especially applicable to the information seeking behavior of the information disadvantaged group, and it is only when they can not solve their problems in a more convenient way that they will resort to other solutions.[17]

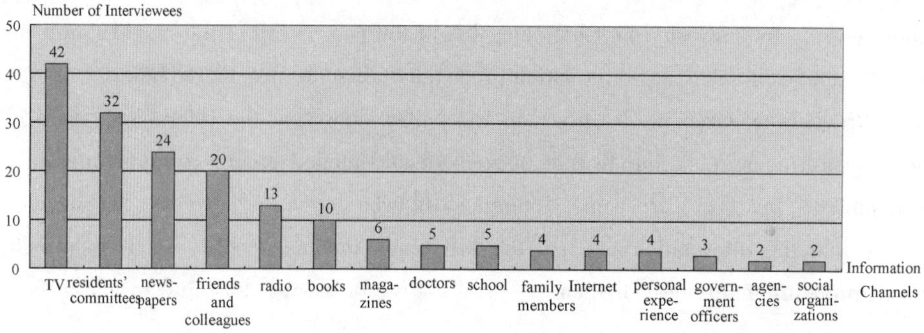

Figure 5 The channels for getting information by the interviewee participants

It is worth noting that the interviewees rarely obtain their everyday life information from printed resources due to their inferiority in terms of the timeliness of the information. Some of them would acquire relevant information from government offices such as the Social Security Bureau and the Civil Affairs Bureau. They claimed that the information from the residents' committees is often either not timely enough or out-of-date. Since the information about medical care or education is very closely related to their everyday lives, they need to pay special attention to the most updated information for such. It should also be noted that these interviewees rarely acquire information via the Internet. One of the reasons is that they do not know how to use computers. Whenever they need some kind of information, they would ask their children or friends for assistance. Moreover, some of them do not have the motive to learn how to use computers as they think that they are too old to learn. This research finding also validates the findings of other Chinese scholars that the information seeking behavior of the disadvantaged groups is confined within the traditional media and these urban low-income residents have not been benefited from the development of information and communication technologies in any significant way in their information seeking activities.

4.4 Factors affecting the information seeking behavior

Pursuant to Savolainen's ELIS model, which is a typical model to elaborate the role of social and cultural factors that affect people's ways of preferring and using information resources in everyday life settings, we attempt to analyze the information seeking behavior of the interviewees in order to have a better understanding of the information behavior of urban low-income people.

4.4.1 Material capital

Poverty is a major characteristic of low-income people. It is shown that money is the most important factor in affecting both their prioritization of certain subject-specific information needs and the selection of their preferred means in accessing such needed information. As mentioned before, most of the study participants are interested in the information related to medical care, education and healthy living (Interviewee No. 10, No. 34). It is also noted that the study participants seldom use printed resources to satisfy their information needs. The reasons for this are not just because of their low educational level, but also because that those printed resources such as books and magazines are involved with a higher cost of money (No. 04, 14 & 37). For example, No. 04 said, "I do not buy books at bookstores because they are too expensive. I would rather buy them on bookstands. Although the books there are pirated ones, they are much cheaper. Sometimes I would spend 1 Yuan to buy *Guangzhou Daily* for reading current events. I would read it from cover to cover. I need to make the most value of my hard-earned money."

4.4.2 Social capital

Social capital consists of someone's social relationships and resources. Because of economical, cultural, biological and other reasons, low-income people usually live in a small world. [22] They often have a strong sense of family-tie and are usually preoccupied with the handling of all kinds of domestic chores in fulfilling their filial responsibilities in their daily lives. In addition, they are seldom in contact with others for their information needs because of their low self-esteem. Therefore, urban low-income people lack the social capital, which may curtail their options for information accessing channels. For example, one interviewee (No. 36) was looking for jobs via job agencies. Although it cost him money, he said, "It is difficult for me to look for jobs by myself. I rarely keep in touch with my relatives and friends. Or I should say that they are probably not willing to contact us, because they worry that we might want to borrow money from them."

4.4.3 Cultural and cognitive capital

Cultural and cognitive capital can be acquired by educational training and it can be converted into economic capital. As mentioned before, the overall educational level of the interviewed participants are relatively low. Most of them have just received a 9-year compulsory education. A few of them are even illiterate. The educational level can have a great impact on people's information seeking behavior. Those who are less-educated can often have a sense of low achievement, which to some extent affects their interest in learning and in seeking needed information. As for the illiterate interviewees, most of them revealed that they had no special preference in getting any kind of information as in most cases they receive information in a passive way. When asked about whether they would occasionally read books, learn how to use computers or go to libraries, their answers were generally negative.

4.4.4 Current situation of life

Current situation of life is the context in which information users live. Information needs arise from information problems, and information seeking behaviors arises from contexts. In other words, the environmental context affects how people define information and how they use information. It is revealed from our investigation that the study participants who have family members suffering from an illness would place a premium value on medical care and welfare information, whereas those who have children at school would assign foremost importance to school-related educational information. For example, An interviewee (No. 37)'s husband has been suffering from a cancer illness for several years, which has prevented their daughter from attending the kindergarten due to their family's financial difficulties. She needs relevant information about the cancer disease her husband has. As the family has already spent a fortune to pay the medical care of her husband, she cannot afford at the same time to bear the cost of the educational expenses for her daughter. She is looking for information about which kindergarten maybe most suitable for her daughter.

In addition, we found that a person's age has a substantial impact on his/her information seeking behavior and attitude toward information. For those adults whose children are still at school, they care a great deal about school-related educational information. They often obtain their needed information via the Internet. For those whose age is between 30 and 59 years old, they are more interested in information about medical care, children's education and housing, in a descending order, which all are closely related to their everyday life. People of this age group tend to acquire information from TV programs and interpersonal communication. For those whose age is 60 and over, they care more about the information on healthy living and medical welfare. Moreover, they depend a lot on the residents' committees to pass on the information that they need in their everyday lives.

4.4.5 Values and attitudes

Values and attitudes can have great influence on people's initiatives to acquire information. It is found that some of the study participants are open-minded, optimistic, and they tend to take their initiatives to acquire information (No. 13). On the other hand, there are also some who are pessimistic towards life and they tend to passively receive information from others such as from the officials at the residents' committees. An interviewee (No. 44) who suffers from a chronic illness of hypertension said, "I do not need too much information. Owing to my old age, I easily forget what I have read. So, if I can get some information, that's fine with me. Otherwise, I do not care too much about it."

4.5 How difficult it is to acquire everyday life information

As far as the easiness in accessing everyday life information is concerned, our research finding indicates that 42% of the interviewed participants said that it is "easy" or "relatively easy". 28% of them said that it is "not very easy" or even "very difficult", whereas the rest of them basically did not give any clear answer. In their everyday lives, urban low-income people would encounter various problems but they manage to solve some of these problems by sharing personal experiences of similar situations. Sometimes, they are aware of their information needs, especially with regard to social welfare and expert opinions. However, they usually acquire this type of information via interpersonal communication or via mass media. Such tactics do not seem to fully satisfy their information needs. As suggested by some Chinese scholars, personal and social factors often contribute an invisible barrier for the urban disadvantaged groups to acquire the information they need. Personal factors consist of material, cultural, social capitals, current situation of life, values and attitudes in the ELIS model, whereas social factors refer primarily to the lack a nationally centralized platform of information resources and a social networking infrastructure at large in China.[16]

5 Use of Libraries

As suggested by *the ILFA/UNESCO Public Library Manifesto*, public library should be the local center of information, making all kinds of knowledge and information readily available to its users. The service of the public library should be provided on the basis of equality of access for all, regardless of age, race, sex, religion, nationality, language or social status.[23] Therefore, to provide information service for urban low-income residents is one of the major responsibilities of public libraries.

5.1 Use of libraries by the interviewees

As indicated in Figure 6, 86% of the study participants said that they have never used libraries, 6% of them said that they used to go to libraries, but they stopped using them anymore for some unspecified reasons. 8% of them said that they do go to libraries. The libraries they use are mostly public libraries such as Guangzhou Children's Library, Guangzhou City Library and Haizhu District Library. A lot of them would read in the library while taking their children there. Apart from public libraries, the children of some interviewees would go to school libraries. It is shown that the current situation of library use by urban low-income residents is left much to be desired. Public libraries are far away from meeting their information needs. Compared with the research findings on the library use by rural migrant workers in China[12-14], we can see that library service rendered to urban low-income residents is even more untenable. This phenomenon should be seriously addressed by researchers and practitioners in the Chinese LIS field.

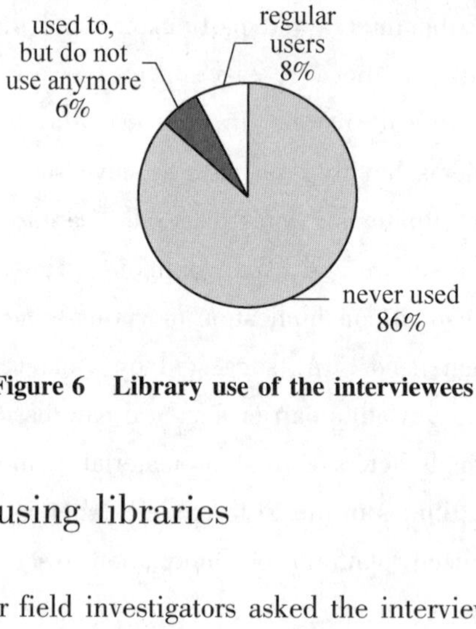

Figure 6 Library use of the interviewees

5.2 Reasons for not using libraries

During the interview, our field investigators asked the interviewed participants why they do not use libraries. They gave us various reasons as follows: (1) they do not have time. They are too busy and preoccupied with either their jobs, or for taking care of their family members. Some of them feel "under too much pressure", and they "have no mood to go to the library". (2) They know very little about library's full-range information service operations. Some of them do not know where their local public libraries are located, whereas some of them mistook bookstores as libraries. (3) Physical reasons, such as old age, bad vision and poor health. Any one of such malaises could pose an overwhelming obstacle inhibiting them from going to a library. In addition, some of them mentioned that there are books and magazines to read or borrow in the office of the residents' committees, and therefore there is no need for them to visit libraries.

5.3 Suggestions of library services for urban low-income residents

Based on the investigations we carried out on the information seeking behavior of urban low-income residents, we put forward suggestions for public libraries to provide customized information services:

· To promote and improve public library service delivery to urban low-income residents, especially to provide fee-free and practical information that is closely related to their everyday lives. Public libraries should also exempt their fees from applying for a library card and should offer them free access to the Internet. For those who are not familiar with the physical layout, resources and services of their local public libraries, public libraries should offer them a series of good library orientation programs.

· Public libraries should develop a collection of specialized digital resources and related information searching tools for urban low-income residents. There should be specialized network resources on library websites for this special group. To help them better benefit from information and communication technology, free training courses should be provided in order to improve their information and computer literacy skills.

· Public libraries should organize various readers' activities for urban low-income residents. We believe that public libraries should be a public space for all residents in the community. The organization of readers' activities is helpful for them not only to cultivate their reading habits, but also to acquire more social capitals and thus to have more channels for them to acquire information.

· Public libraries should provide outreach service to neighborhoods where urban low-income residents live by cooperating with official of the residents' committees. It is revealed from our study that urban low-income residents depend a lot on officials of the residents' committees for acquiring the information they need. In offices of the residents' committees where there are books and magazines available for local residents to read or borrow, public libraries can offer group loan services. Of course, the development of community libraries in these neighborhoods would be a far better solution.

6 Conclusion

As a special social group, urban low-income residents have attracted more attention by LIS scholars and practitioners. Our study has revealed that the information seeking behavior of urban low-income residents has unique characteristics in terms of their capital resources, values, attitudes and current situation of life. The utilitarian value of information is of great importance to them. Their information seeking behavior is very much oriented toward the actual necessities of their everyday lives. They care about the information which can satisfy their basic everyday life needs, rather than on entertainment and recreation. Most of the time, they are not aware of their information needs, even when they do have access to most of the information. They are only rudimentarily knowledgeable about using a very limited number of channels for acquiring information, which is also constantly undermined by their poor information literacy skills. With an aim to develop a universal, equitable public cultural service system in China, public libraries should provide more customized and effective information services for urban low-income residents.

Qualitative and quantitative methods are two complementary research methodologies in social science research. In our study, we primarily adopted qualitative approach. However, in our future research, we need to combine our study with an added quantitative approach in order to achieve more objectivity and validity in our research findings.

Finally, we need to point out that, our research samples were only limited to the Haizhu District of Guangzhou due to the limited funding and manpower made available for us to conduct this research project. It is obvious that we need to expand our research further into other districts of the city in order to enhance the credibility of our analytical interpretations. Also, because Guangzhou is a microcosm of the better-developed cities in China, it is desirable that we should also investigate the situation of urban low-income residents in other cities of China for a comparative analysis. Specifically, we need to examine, at our next opportunity, whether there are any differences of information seeking behaviors among urban low-income residents in different geographical areas of China. If there are some differences indeed, then we also need to delve into more deeply the reasons for such differences.

References

[1] Savolainen R. Everyday Life Information Seeking: Approaching Information Seeking in the Context of "Way of Life" [J]. Library & Information Science Research, 1995, 17 (3): 259 - 294.

[2] Dervin B. The Development of Strategies for Dealing with the Information Needs of Urban Residents [M]. Washington, DC: US Department of Health, Education and Welfare, Office of Education, Office of Libraries and Learning Resources, 1976.

[3] Chatman E A. The Diffusion of Information among the Working Poor [M]. Berkeley: University of California, 1983.

[4] Childers T. The Information-Poor in America [M]. Metuchen: Scarecrow Press, 1975.

[5] Greenberg B, Dervin B. Mass Communications among the Urban Poor [J]. Public Opinion Quarterly, 1972, 34 (2): 224 - 235.

[6] Chatman E A. Information, Mass Media Use, and the Working Poor [J]. Library and Information Science Research, 1985, 7 (2): 97 - 113.

[7] Chatman E A. Opinion Leadership, Poverty, and Information Sharing [J]. RQ, 1987, 26 (3): 341 - 353.

[8] Chatman E A. Life in a Small World: Applicability of Gratification Theory to Information-Seeking Behavior [J]. Journal of the American Society for Information Science, 1991, 42 (6): 438 - 449.

[9] Spink A, Cole C. Information and Poverty: Information-Seeking Channels Used by African American Low-Income Households [J]. Library & Information Science Research, 2001, 23 (1): 45 - 65.

[10] Hersberger J A. Everyday Information Needs and Information Sources of Homeless Parents: A Study of Poverty and Perseverance [M]. Indiana: Indiana University, 1998.

[11] Hersberger J A. Everyday Information Needs and Information Sources of Homeless Parents [J]. New Review of Information Behavior Research, 2001, 2: 119 - 134.

[12] Gao X, Hou W, Wang Z. Report of the Peasant Workers' Capability of Acquiring Knowledge in Beijing and their Requirements for Libraries [J]. Library, 2008 (4): 4-10.

[13] Dong K, Zhang K, Cheng L, et al. Report of the Peasant Workers and Capability of Acquiring Knowledge in Wuhan and their Requirements for Libraries [J]. Library, 2008 (4): 11-17.

[14] Wu L, Wu Z, Zhu H, et al. Report of the Migrant Workers and Capability of Acquiring Knowledge in Shenzhen and their Requirements for Libraries [J]. Library, 2008 (4): 18-24.

[15] Li G. Modern Public Library Users: Needs, Behaviors and Structure [M]. Chengdu: Sichuan University Press, 2010.

[16] Wang S. An Exploratory Study of Information Acquisition of Urban Disadvantaged Groups in China [J]. Document, Information & Knowledge, 2004 (1): 34-36.

[17] Shi D. The Impact of Information Technology Development on the Information Behaviors of the Vulnerable Groups [J]. Library & Information Work, 2008, 52 (11): 75-77.

[18] Pan J, Wei H. Report of the Development of Chinese Cities: No. 4 [M]. Beijing: Social Sciences Academic Press, 2007: 133-150.

[19] Chen Y. Social Welfare [M]. Beijing: China Renmin University Press, 2009: 259-260.

[20] Bates J A. Use of Narrative Interviewing in Everyday Information Behavior Research [J]. Library & Information Science Research, 2004, 26 (1): 15-28.

[21] Chatman E A. Knowledge Gap, Information-Seeking and the Poor [J]. Reference Librarian, 1995, 49/50: 135-145.

[22] Chatman E A. The Impoverished Life-World of Outsiders [J]. Journal of the American Society for Information Science, 1996, 47 (3): 193-206.

[23] Gill P. The Public Library Service: IFLA/UNESCO Guidelines for Development [M]. Shanghai: Shanghai Scientific and Technological Literature Publishing House, 2002: 97-99.

[24] Li Y, Zhang Q. Social Science Research Methods and their Application in Economics [J]. Heilongjiang Social Sciences, 2007 (4): 61-63.

教师简介：

张靖，女，中山大学管理学学士、管理学硕士、历史学博士。2008 年起任教于中山大学资讯管理学院，现为副教授、硕士生导师，2012 年起任副院长。主讲“图书馆学基础”、“图书与图书馆史”、“信息与社会”、“文献保护与修复”等本科生课程，以及“书史”、“信息与社会”、“未成年人信息服务”等研究生课程。研究方向包括信息不平等、未成年人信息服务、公共图书馆事业、书史、图书情报与档案管理教育等。主持科研项目 21 项，出版学术专著 5 部，在国内外学术刊物及学术会议上发表学术论文 50 余篇，获各级教学和科研奖励 10 余项。2010 年加拿大政府研究专项基金访问学者，2014 年美国国际访问者领导项目访问学者，2015 年美国岭南基金访问学者。高等学校“千百十工程”培养对象。兼任美国德雷克塞尔大学图书馆、信息与社会研究中心研究人员，《广州大典》与广州历史文化研究重点基地研究人员，中山大学文献遗产保护与修复研究创新基地研究人员，中山大学图书馆与资讯科学研究所研究人员。联系方式：zhangj87@ mail. sysu. edu. cn。

所选论文《广东省图书馆权利状况调查》原载于《图书情报知识》2015 年第 2 期

广东省图书馆权利状况调查*

张　靖，苏日娜①，何靖怡②，梁丹妮③

摘　要：论文在图书馆权利理论研究持续升温和逐步成熟的背景下，以广东省公共图书馆为对象，作图书馆权利状况调查研究。调查以美国图书馆协会《图书馆权利法案》及其阐释政策群为理论基础，结合课题组关于中国图书馆业界以及民众对图书馆权利问题了解情况的预测，建构了包括权利享有、权利认知、权利观念和权利期望四个方面的图书馆权利状况调查指标体系，并以之作为依据，设计了面向多阶随机抽样确定的到馆用户和馆员两类样本的两份问卷和访谈提纲。论文呈现了通过问卷调查所得的总体数据，以反映广东省图书馆权利基本情况；进而借由地区间、市县间、用户与馆员间、享有与观念间的复合性对比，证明了图书馆权利状况差异的存在及其程度，并对其成因加以分析；与此同时，论文还揭示实践领域在图书馆权利上的隐性需求，以及在图书馆权利上有所反映而实际上可能对更多具体实践产生影响的存在问题。

关键词：图书馆权利；公共图书馆；广东省；美国图书馆协会《图书馆权利法案》

---

* 本文系国家社会科学基金项目“公民权视域的社会弱势群体公共信息服务权益研究”（项目批准号：12CTQ011）成果之一。

① 苏日娜，中山大学资讯管理学院硕士研究生。
② 何靖怡，中山大学资讯管理学院硕士研究生。
③ 梁丹妮，中山大学资讯管理学院硕士研究生。

A Survey of People's Library Rights in Guangdong Province

Jing Zhang, Rina Su, Jingyi He, Danni Liang

Abstract: The theoretical study of library rights has been developed with great attention since 2004 in China. Against this background, this paper tries to carry out an empirical study and applies a questionnaire and interview survey on people's library rights in Guangdong Province. Adopting the library rights policy system of American Library Association's *Library Bill of Rights* and its interpretations as the theoretical foundation, while the authors' hypothesis on the understanding about library rights of practitioners and people is also considered, it constructs an investigation target system including four dimensions, namely, the possession, recognition, sense and expectation of library rights, according to which, different questionnaires and interview outlines are designed for the different samples of users and librarians, both drawn randomly through multistage sampling. This paper pictures the general information about the people's library rights in Guangdong Province by presenting the data collected through questionnaires. Then it proves the differences, as well as their degree and causes of formation, by doing a complex analysis which takes the factors of region, administrative level, user or librarian, possession or sense into account. Meanwhile, it reveals some implicit demands of the practical areas on library rights, as well as some existing problems which affecting not only the library rights buts also many more practical issues. Eight tables. Nine figures. Ten references.

Keywords: Library rights; Public libraries; Guangdong Province; ALA's *Library Bill of Rights*

1 研究背景

自2004年被列入中国图书馆学会次年年会议事日程，2005年成为中国图书馆学会年度峰会讨论最为热烈的议题、相关课题获得国家社科基金立项资助、多种刊物设立相关专栏起，图书馆权利成为中国图书馆学界的热题，热度持续至今。[1]当前的图书馆权利研究主题主要包括：①图书馆权利的界定；②图书馆权利的法律和道德渊源；③图书馆权利体系；④国外图书馆权利政策；⑤国外图书馆权利案例；⑥国内图书馆权利运动（新图书馆运动）；⑦国内图书馆权利案例。研究方法以基于文献的历史研究法、内容分析法和案例研究法为主。研究角度或各有侧重，研究内容则集中为图书馆权利的理论研究。未见除案例之外的对于中国图书馆权利状况的社会调查。

图书馆权利在学界的升温，并不等于业界的关注，更不能代表广大社会民众对于这一问题甚至这一概念的了解乃至认知。在一个对图书馆权利概念的认知几乎刚刚起步的社会环境中，对图书馆权利状况进行调查，其困难可想而知。然而一门社会科学对于一个领域的研究，必然是要在理论探讨的逐渐积累之上，直面社会。论文尝试以广东省公共图书馆为样本，作图书馆权利状况调查研究。

2 调查设计与实施

2.1 调查重点及调查对象说明

图书馆权利是指民众利用图书馆的平等和自由。[1]自由所关怀的是个人权利，平等则更加注重普遍权利；自由所关心的是形式上的法律平等，平等所侧重的则是实质上的经济地位平等。二者是社会制度正义必不可少的两项重要内容。[2]图书馆制度正义同样包括平等权利和自由权利，二者均是图书馆制度正义的核心内容和根基。[1]对于中国民众图书馆权利状况的调查，应同时考察自由权利和平等权利；然而，相对而言，平等权利，即民众利用图书馆的平等，更为笔者所关注，是调查和研究的重点。这一重点的选择，与图书馆权利这一概念的来源——美国图书馆协会（American Library Association，以下简称ALA）《图书馆权利法案》（*Library Bill of Rights*，以下简称《法案》）——中图书馆利用者的平等权利要相对先于其自由权利的观点相一致。“这不仅是因为没有平等就不可能有真正的自由，而且还是在于在权利的救济和保障上，作为社会机构一部分的图书馆自身能够承担的有关图书馆利用者的平等权利的责任和义务要重于或者多于有关图书馆利用者的自由权利的责任和义务，因为在履行权利救济和保障的责任和义务中，对于图书馆利用者的平等权利的救济和保障基本上在图书馆自身的可控职责之内，而对于图书馆利用者的自由权利的救济则不尽然。”[1]

结合图书馆权利的含义、研究视角和重点，以及经费和人力决定的可操作范围，笔者将主要样本地域限定在广东省。虽然图书馆权利的概念界定中并未对图书馆的类型有所特指，但在中国，与高校图书馆、中小学图书馆、专业图书馆等有较明显服务对象范围的几种类型图书馆相比，公共图书馆的服务对象是所服务区域的全体民众，更能体现“民众利用图书馆的平等和自由”权利。因此，调查对象限定为公共图书馆及其用户和馆员。

2.2 抽样与样本

调查采用多阶抽样，各阶段抽样框和样本抽取方法如下。

一阶：地区。结合广东省区域发展不平衡的实际情况，将调查地区划分为珠江三角洲和粤东西北地区。其中珠江三角洲包括广州、深圳、珠海、佛山、江门、东莞、中山、惠州和肇庆9个地级行政区划单位（即地级市）；粤东西北地区包括汕头、潮州、梅州、汕尾、揭阳、河源、湛江、茂名、阳江、云浮、韶关和清远12个地级行政区划单位。[3]地区间民众利用图书馆的平等状况及其差异是调查和研究期望反映的情况，因此，调查在第二阶段抽取地级行政区划单位时将考虑两个地区的样本比例。

二阶：地级行政区划单位。除地区间民众利用图书馆的平等状况及其差异外，课题还期望通过调查了解市县间①民众利用图书馆的平等状况及其差异。地级行政区划单位管

① 虽然城乡间的图书馆权利差异是论文期望通过调查了解的情况，但受限于经费和人力，课题组暂时无法在省域范围内开展面向基层图书馆的随机调查，拟另以个案调查的方式进行；在此次调查中，仅以对应不同级别行政区划的不同图书馆级别，反映地、县两级行政区划单位间之差异。

辖市辖区、县级市、县和自治县等县级行政区划单位。考虑经费和人力所及的最大范围，调查将二阶抽样概率定为45%，即在珠江三角洲地区抽取4个、在粤东西北地区抽取5个地级行政区划单位。由于广州和深圳这两个副省级城市不仅在行政区划上与其他地级城市有所区别，并且在图书馆事业的发展程度上也与其他城市存在距离，因此，在进行区域概率抽样之前，先将这两个城市抽出作为样本。则抽样框调整并编码如图1所示。继而采用随机抽样的方式，抽出珠江三角洲地区的Ⅰ1佛山、Ⅰ2珠海和粤东西北地区的Ⅱ1汕头、Ⅱ3梅州、Ⅱ8茂名、Ⅱ11韶关和Ⅱ12清远作为样本。加上广州和深圳（接序编码为Ⅰ8、Ⅰ9），二阶样本确定为9个地级行政区划单位。

Ⅰ.珠江三角洲：**Ⅰ1佛山**、**Ⅰ2珠海**、Ⅰ3东莞、Ⅰ4中山、Ⅰ5江门、Ⅰ6惠州、Ⅰ7肇庆、**Ⅰ8广州**、**Ⅰ9深圳**

Ⅱ.粤东西北地区：**Ⅱ1汕头**、Ⅱ2潮州、**Ⅱ3梅州**、Ⅱ4汕尾、Ⅱ5揭阳、Ⅱ6河源、Ⅱ7湛江、**Ⅱ8茂名**、Ⅱ9阳江、Ⅱ10云浮、**Ⅱ11韶关**、**Ⅱ12清远**

注：黑体字者为抽中样本。

图1　广东省图书图书馆权利状况调查二阶抽样框

三阶：公共图书馆。三阶抽样的抽样框由二阶样本中的9个地级行政区划单位的省、市、区、县级公共图书馆构成。以地级行政区划单位样本为基础，结合各样本所辖市辖区、县级市、县和自治县等县级行政区划[4]，2010年《广东统计年鉴》对广东各市的公共图书馆的统计情况[5]，以及广东省图书馆学会网站和各图书馆网站等信息，形成三阶抽样框，如表1所示。表1中各级图书馆共计74个，其中省级1个（广东省立中山图书馆），副省级4个（广州图书馆、广州少年儿童图书馆、深圳图书馆、深圳少年儿童图书馆），市级7个，区级33个，县级29个。考虑到市县间民众利用图书馆的平等状况及其差异是课题期望通过调查了解的情况，因此，除广州少年儿童图书馆和深圳少年儿童图书馆①外的10个市级及以上图书馆自动作为样本，再在各地级行政区划单位中，随机抽出与其中市级以上图书馆数量相等的区级或县级图书馆作为样本，样本数为20。

表1　广东省图书馆权利状况调查三阶抽样框

编码	Ⅰ1佛山（6个）		Ⅰ2珠海（4个）		Ⅰ8广州（15个）		Ⅰ9深圳（8个）	
	图[1)]名称	级别	名称	级别	图名称	级别	图名称	级别
1	**佛山市图**	市级	**珠海图**	市级	**广东省立中山图**	省级	**深圳图**	副省级
2	禅城区图	区级	香洲区图	区级	广州少年儿童图	副省级	深圳少年儿童图	副省级
3	南海区图	区级	斗门区图	区级	**广州图**	副省级	宝安区图	区级
4	高明区图	区级	**金湾区图**	区级	白云区图	区级	龙岗图	区级
5	三水区图	区级			番禺图	区级	盐田区图	区级

① 与其他图书馆相比，这两个图书馆以未成年人这一特定的用户群体作为服务对象，课题组拟另作调查研究。

续表 1

编码	Ⅰ1 佛山（6 个）		Ⅰ2 珠海（4 个）		Ⅰ8 广州（15 个）		Ⅰ9 深圳（8 个）	
	图名称	级别	名称	级别	图名称	级别	图名称	级别
6	**顺德区图**	区级			**海珠区图**	区级	南山图	区级
7					花都区图	区级	罗湖区图	区级
8					黄埔区图	区级	**福田区图**	区级
9					萝岗区图	区级		
10					荔湾图	区级		
11					南沙区图	区级		
12					天河区图	区级		
13					越秀区图	区级		
14					**增城市图**	县级		
15					从化图	县级		

编码	Ⅱ1 汕头（8 个）		Ⅱ3 梅州（10 个）		Ⅱ8 茂名（5 个）		Ⅱ11 韶关（9 个）		Ⅱ12 清远（9 个）	
	图名称	级别	图名称	级别	图名称	级别	图名称	级别	图名称	级别
1	**汕头图**	市级	**梅州剑英图**	市级	**茂名图**	市级	**韶关图**	市级	**清远图**	市级
2	金平区图	区级	**梅江区图**	区级	**高州图**	县级	新丰县图	县级	**清城区图**	区级
3	龙湖区图	区级	五华县图	县级	化州图	县级	**乐昌市图**	县级	清新县图	县级
4	澄海区图	区级	梅县图	县级	信宜图	县级	南雄市图	县级	英德市图	县级
5	濠江区图	区级	蕉岭县图	县级	电白县图	县级	翁源县图	县级	佛冈县图	县级
6	**潮阳区图**	区级	大埔县图	县级			曲江区图	区级	阳山县图	县级
7	潮南区图	区级	平远县图	县级			仁化县图	县级	连州图	县级
8	南澳县图	县级	兴宁市图	县级			始兴县图	县级	连南瑶族自治县图	县级
9			丰顺县图	县级			乳源县图	县级	连山壮族瑶族自治县图	县级
10			梅县松口图	县级						

1）表中“图”均为“图书馆”的省略。

说明：黑体字者为抽中样本。

四阶：图书馆到馆用户、图书馆馆员。四阶抽样的第一类抽样框为三阶样本中的 10 ～ 40 个①到馆用户。第二类抽样框为三阶样本中的若干馆员。

① 视问卷发放当天具体图书馆的到馆用户量而定。

2.3 调查指标体系的建构

课题组选定 ALA《法案》及其阐释这一图书馆权利政策群作为建构调查指标体系的理论基础。一则，图书馆权利源自对 ALA《法案》英文“Library Bill of Rights”的翻译，图书馆权利理论的建构理应回归本源。二则，《法案》及其阐释这一系列政策，是国际图书馆界目前所知的最为完备的一个图书馆权利相关政策体系。之所以称其完备，首先，这一政策体系由统一的图书馆机构——ALA——制定、采用和修订，意味着其中所体现的价值观以及行文风格的一致性；其次，这一体系内的政策有主有辅、有简有详——《法案》为主为简，相关阐释为辅为详；再次，该政策体系结构分明——由《法案》、阐释、关于某一阐释的问与答三种类型政策组成逐级详细、逐级补充、逐级完善的三级体系结构；最后，跟进图书馆界不断出现的新问题或老问题的新情况，不断有解决新问题的新阐释补充，同时也不断对原有阐释进行修订，以适应老问题的新情况。[6]

以 ALA《法案》及其阐释这一图书馆权利政策群作为理论基础，结合关于中国图书馆业界以及民众对图书馆权利问题了解情况的预测，研究建构了如表2 所示的图书馆权利状况调查指标体系。

表2 图书馆权利状况调查指标体系

一级指标	二级指标	调查对象	对应问卷题项
图书馆权利享有情况	使用频率	用户	用户问卷：题一
	使用遭拒	用户	用户问卷：题二
	影响因素（用户）	用户、馆员	用户问卷：题三 馆员问卷：题三
	影响因素（图书馆）	用户、馆员	用户问卷：题六 馆员问卷：题六
图书馆权利认知情况	知道权利	用户、馆员	用户问卷：题九 馆员问卷：题一
	认可权利	用户、馆员	用户问卷：题十 馆员问卷：题二
图书馆权利观念情况	影响因素（用户）	用户、馆员	用户问卷：题四、五 馆员问卷：题四、五
	影响因素（图书馆）	用户、馆员	用户问卷：题七、八 馆员问卷：题七、八
图书馆权利期望情况	义务承担	用户、馆员	用户问卷：题十一 馆员问卷：题十一
	权利实现指标	用户、馆员	用户问卷：题十二、十三 馆员问卷：题九、十、十二

2.4 问卷问题与访谈提纲的设计

针对前述四阶抽样所得的图书馆到馆用户和图书馆馆员两种不同类型样本，笔者分别依据所建构的调查指标体系设计了两份问卷。受篇幅所限，完整问卷将不在此处呈现。问卷中与调查指标体系相对应的问题，如表2所示。调查问题以问卷形式呈现，在实际调查过程中，接受过训练的调查人员在受调查者填写问卷的同时进行访谈。在接受调查的到馆用户填写问卷时，调查人员将依次根据问题一、二、三、四、五、六、七、八、十三的问卷填写情况与受调查者进行面对面访谈沟通。例如根据选项，询问具体每周/月/年使用图书馆的次数，了解被拒绝使用图书馆的详细情况，了解各种因素如何影响用户使用图书馆，如何影响图书馆对图书报刊等资料的收藏和提供使用，询问原因，并从中尝试提取典型案例。调查人员还需在一位到馆用户完成问卷后，在相应问卷上补充记录受调查者的性别、年龄段（青少年、中青年、中老年）① 等情况。在接受调查的图书馆馆员填写问卷时，调查人员将依次根据问卷填写情况与受调查者进行面对面访谈沟通（内容与上述针对用户的访谈相似）。调查人员还需在一位到馆用户完成问卷后，在相应问卷上补充记录受调查者的性别、工作时间、职位、是否具有图书馆及相关学位等情况。

2.5 问卷发放与回收

此次调查采取课题组成员实地发放、现场回收问卷，并结合访谈②的数据收集方式。自2012年7月至9月，课题组共发放问卷544份，其中，用户问卷发出443份，馆员问卷发出101份。发出问卷全数回收。回收的用户问卷有效问卷数为428份，有效率达96.61%；回收的馆员问卷有效问卷数为100份，有效率达99.01%。总体问卷有效率为97.06%。以下对有效问卷反馈数据进行呈现和分析。

3 问卷调查总体数据呈现

此处呈现的是分别以图书馆到馆用户和馆员为样本，通过问卷调查所得的总体数据。不同地区、不同群体的情况差异，以及访谈调查所得数据等，将在第4部分结果分析中综合反映。

3.1 以到馆用户为样本的调查结果

（1）权利享有情况。接受调查者使用图书馆的频率情况如图2所示，超过半数的到馆用户表示每周会使用图书馆一次。86.45%的接受调查者表示在使用图书馆时未曾遭遇过拒绝。在13.55%有过被拒遭遇的用户中，曾被拒绝使用图书馆的某些服务的占接受调

① 由此，课题组可以对用户群体（男性群体、女性群体、未成年人群体、成年人群体等）间的权利享有情况对比分析。笔者另有专文探讨。

② 5%的图书馆的馆员调查因工作原因未能进行访谈。

查到馆用户的7.71%，曾被拒绝使用某些馆藏资源的占3.97%，曾被拒绝入馆的占1.87%。根据亲历或知道之事，44.16%的接受调查者认为图3中的因素会影响用户对于图书馆的使用，85.98%的接受调查者认为图4中的因素会影响图书馆对于图书报刊等资料的收藏和提供。

（2）权利认知情况。86.68%的接受调查者表示，在此次调查之前，已知道民众拥有平等和自由地使用图书馆以满足自身教育、文化和信息需求的权利。图5反映了接受调查者所认可的这一权利的重要程度的情况。

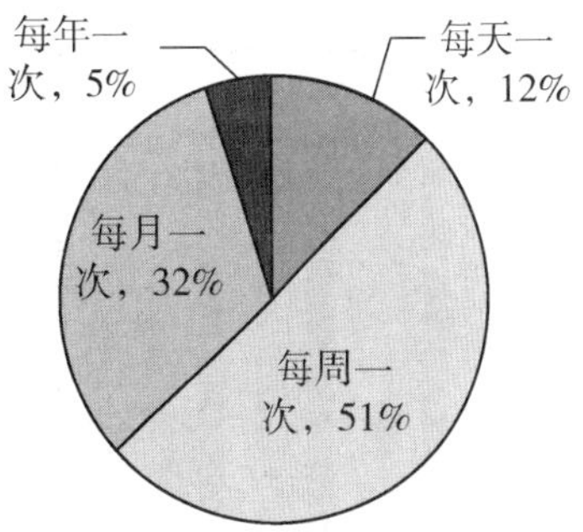

图2 用户使用图书馆的频率

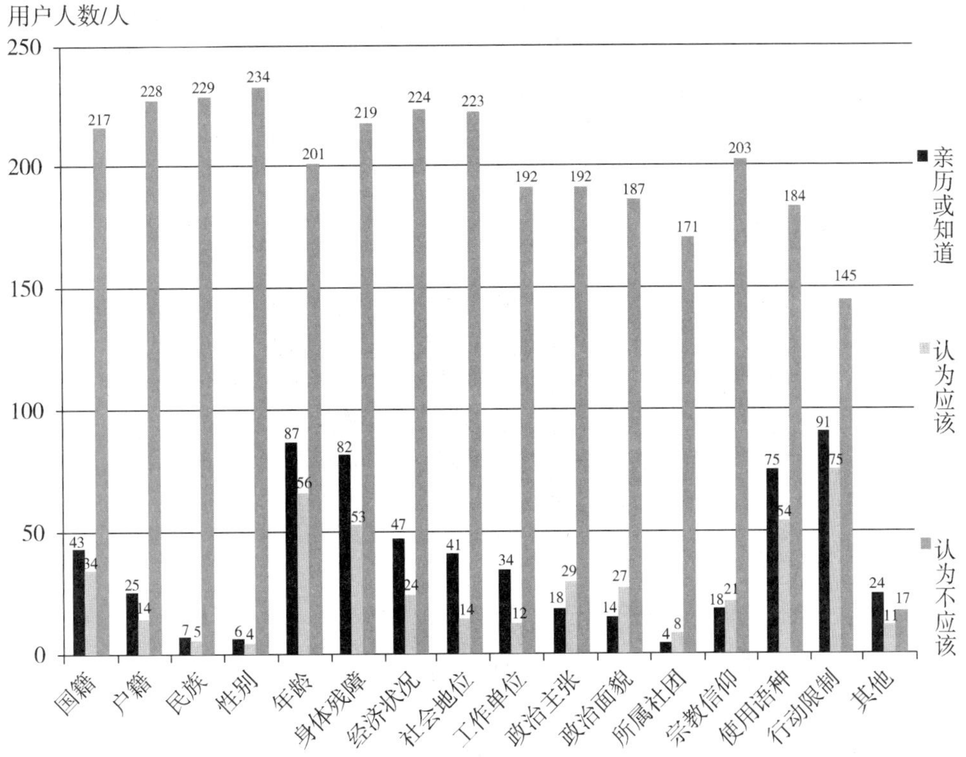

图3 影响用户使用图书馆的因素（用户角度的事实与观点）

（3）权利观念情况。对于可能会影响用户使用图书馆的因素，接受调查者持“应该”或“不应该”观点的情况如图3所示，其中43.46%的用户认为图3中的所有因素都不应该影响用户对于图书馆的使用。对于可能会影响图书馆收藏和提供图书报刊等资料的因素，接受调查者持“应该”或“不应该”观点的情况如图4所示，其中18.22%的用户认为图4中的所有因素都不应该影响图书馆的资料收藏和提供。

（4）权利期望情况。对于民众图书馆权利的维护，接受调查者认为相关政府部门

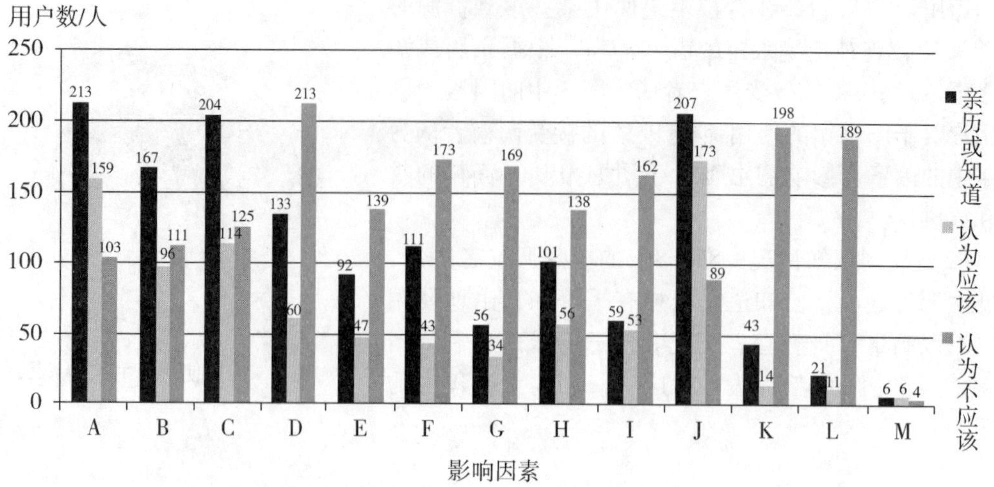

A. 用户需求；B. 收藏政策；C. 获得资料难易程度；D. 资料价格；E. 资料所反映的意识形态；F. 资料所代表的社会政治主张；G. 资料所倡导的宗教信仰；H. 资料所认同的价值观；I. 资料所表达的学术观点；J. 资料是否包含暴力色情等内容；K. 作者的社会身份；L. 出版者的社会身份；M. 其他

图4　影响图书馆收藏和提供资料的因素（用户角度的事实与观点）

（342 人，79.91%）、图书馆和图书馆员（319 人，74.53%）、相关法规（293 人，68.46%）、图书馆协会/学会（265 人，61.92%）均应承担这一义务。在反映民众图书馆权利实现情况的指标方面，调查反馈情况如图 6 所示，所有拟定指标都得到过半数的接受调查者所认可。

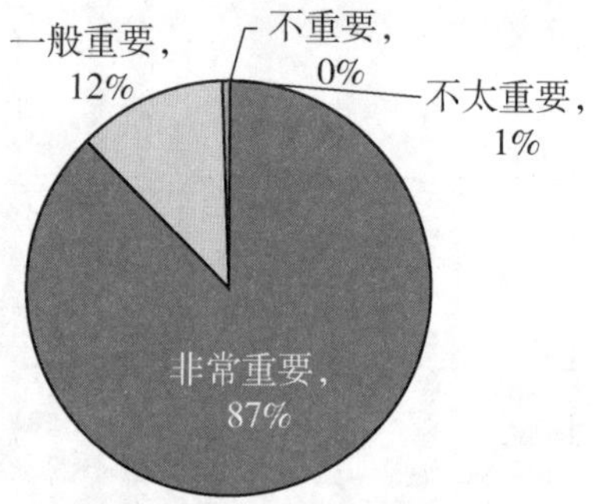

图5　用户所认可的图书馆权利重要程度（用户角度）

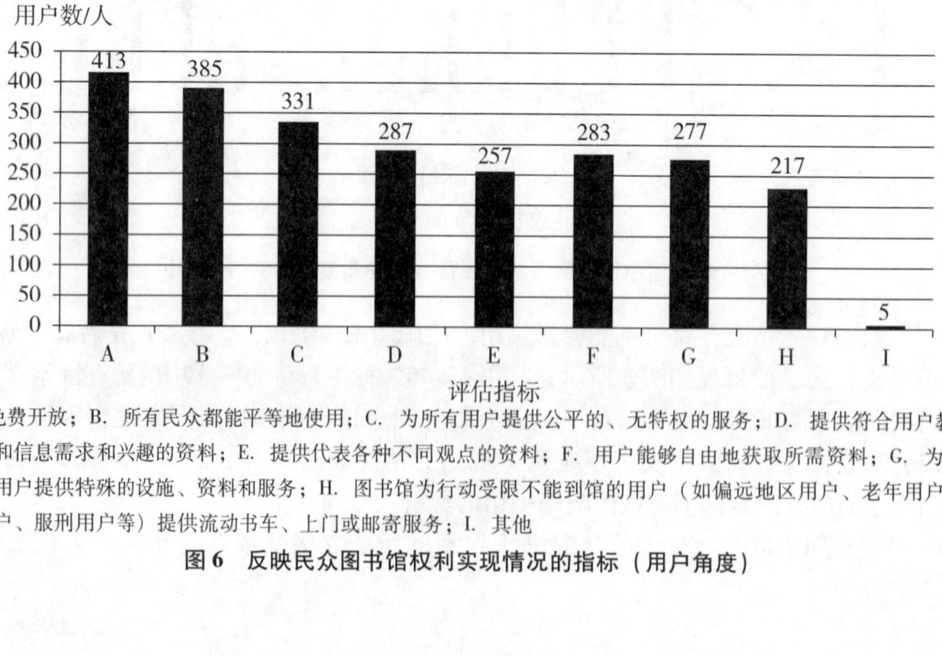

A. 免费开放；B. 所有民众都能平等地使用；C. 为所有用户提供公平的、无特权的服务；D. 提供符合用户教育、文化和信息需求和兴趣的资料；E. 提供代表各种不同观点的资料；F. 用户能够自由地获取所需资料；G. 为身体残障用户提供特殊的设施、资料和服务；H. 图书馆为行动受限不能到馆的用户（如偏远地区用户、老年用户、医院用户、服刑用户等）提供流动书车、上门或邮寄服务；I. 其他

图6　反映民众图书馆权利实现情况的指标（用户角度）

3.2 以馆员为样本的调查结果

（1）权利享有情况。根据亲历或知道之事，67%的馆员认为图7中的因素会影响用户对于图书馆的使用，92%的馆员认为图8中的因素会影响图书馆收藏和提供图书报刊等资料。

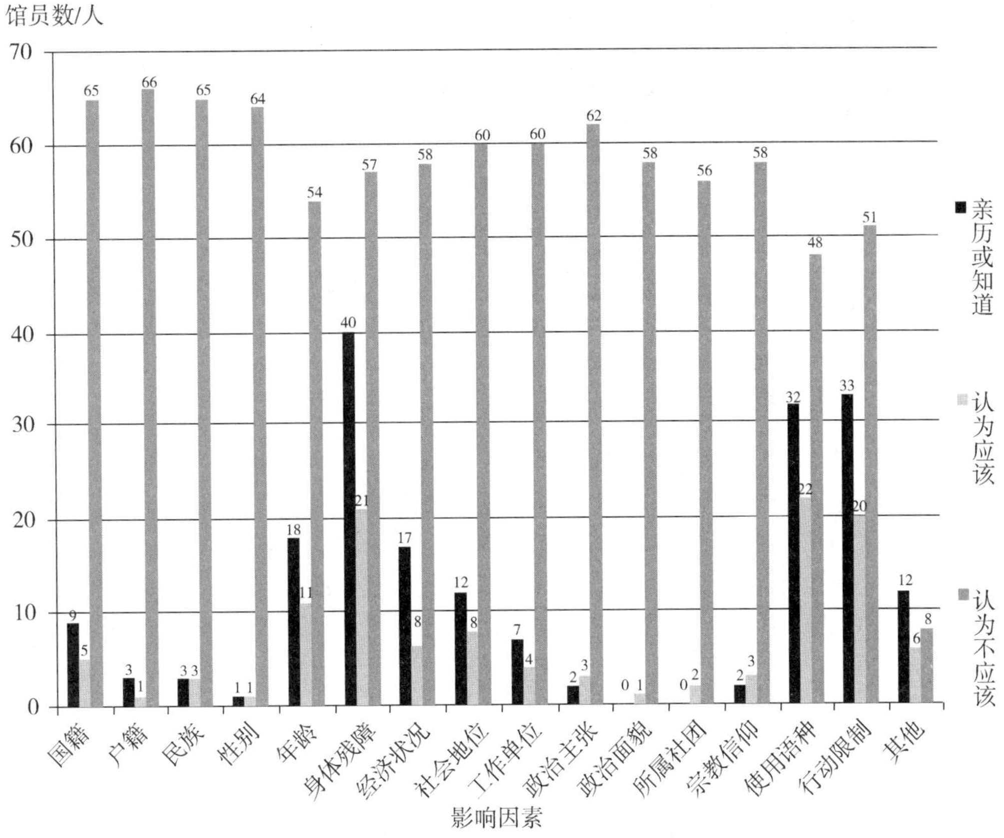

图7 影响用户使用图书馆的因素（馆员角度的事实与观点）

（2）权利认知情况。99%的接受调查的馆员表示知道民众拥有平等和自由地使用图书馆以满足自身教育、文化和信息需求的权利。82%的馆员认为这一权利对于民众非常重要，18%认为一般重要。

（3）权利观念情况。对于可能会影响用户使用图书馆的因素，接受调查者持“应该”或“不应该”观点的情况如图7所示，其中有45%的馆员认为图7中所有因素都不应该影响用户对于图书馆的使用。对于可能会影响图书馆收藏和提供图书报刊等资料的因素，接受调查者持“应该”或“不应该”观点的情况如图8所示，其中8%的用户认为图8中的所有因素都不应该影响图书馆收藏和提供资料。

（4）权利期望情况。对于民众图书馆权利的维护，接受调查者认为相关政府部门（81人，81%）、图书馆和图书馆员（78人，78%）、相关法规（72人，72%）、图书馆

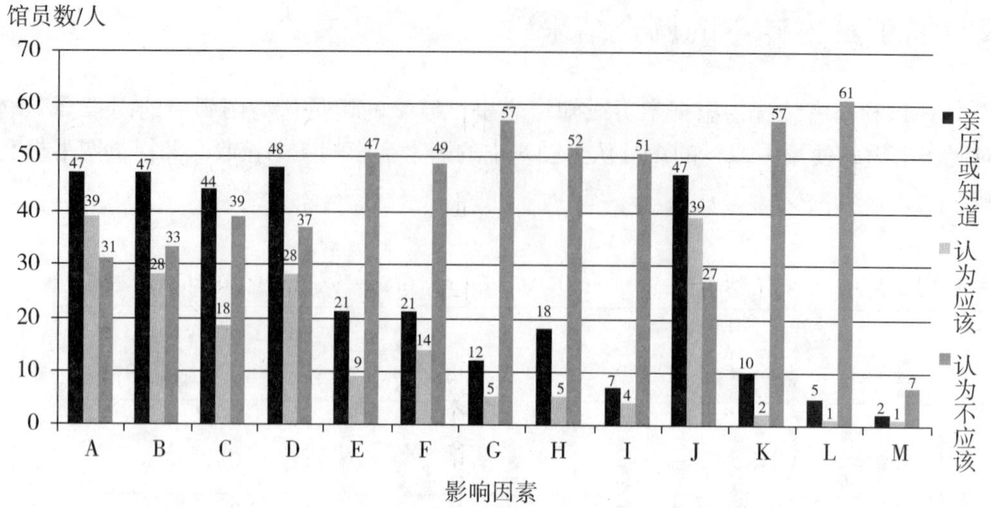

A. 用户需求；B. 收藏政策；C. 获得资料难易程度；D. 资料价格；E. 资料所反映的意识形态；F. 资料所代表的社会政治主张；G. 资料所倡导的宗教信仰；H. 资料所认同的价值观；I. 资料所表达的学术观点；J. 资料是否包含暴力色情等内容；K. 作者的社会身份；L. 出版者的社会身份；M. 其他

图8　影响图书馆收藏和提供资料的因素（馆员角度的事实与观点）

协会/学会（49 人，49%）均应承担这一义务。在反映民众图书馆权利实现情况的指标方面，调查反馈情况如图9 所示，所有拟定指标都得到六成以上的接受调查者所认可。接受调查者表示，对于图书馆和图书馆员而言，完成反映民众图书馆权利实现情况的指标的关键点或难点包括：经费保障（91 人，91%），相关法规、政策保障（69 人，69%），人力资源保障（61 人，61%），图书馆权利观念、理念和文化的培育（56 人，56%）。

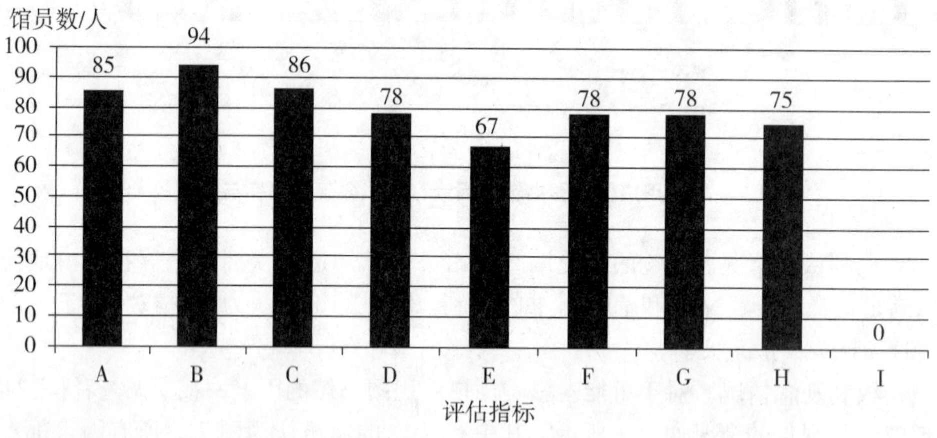

A. 免费开放；B. 所有民众都能平等地使用；C. 为所有用户提供公平的、无特权的服务；D. 提供符合用户教育、文化和信息需求和兴趣的资料；E. 提供代表各种不同观点的资料；F. 用户能够自由地获取所需资料；G. 为身体残障用户提供特殊的设施、资料和服务；H. 图书馆为行动受限不能到馆的用户（如偏远地区用户、老年用户、医院用户、服刑用户等）提供流动书车、上门或邮寄服务；I. 其他

图9　反映民众图书馆权利实现情况的指标（馆员角度）

4 调查结果分析

此次问卷及访谈调查所得数据丰富，从不同的角度作不同的采撷，为不同的目的可以对之进行多样化的分析。以下选择若干点展示调查所得。小标题仅对其中一个或两个变量加以强调，但实际的对比常常结合多个变量进行复合性分析。

4.1 地区间、市县间到馆用户权利享有情况对比分析

调查的第一阶和第二阶抽样策略使得课题可以在了解地区间、市县间民众利用图书馆的平等状况及其差异之外，对地区及市县两个变量作复合性考察。地区的划分主要是考虑经济情况的不同，而对应行政区划的图书馆级别则主要反映图书馆规模和服务范围的不同，因此，为分析之便，笔者将地区化约为经济情况这一较宏观的变量，将图书馆级别化约为图书馆规模及服务范围这一较微观的变量。

数据显示，较发达的珠江三角洲和欠发达的粤东西北地区接受调查的图书馆用户在图书馆权利的享有上，存在差异。

如表3所示，两类地区接受调查的到馆用户中，每月使用图书馆一次或以上者比率颇高，说明本次调查所反映的是图书馆固定用户而非随入（walk-in）用户的图书馆权利状况。

表3 珠江三角洲和粤东西北地区到馆用户图书馆权利享有情况比较

单位：%

图所属地区	每月使用图一次或以上	使用图时遭遇过拒绝	使用图时受到某些因素的影响（亲历或知道）	图收藏和提供使用资料时受到某些因素的影响（亲历或知道）
珠江三角洲	85	10.01	54.90	86.70
粤东西北地区	94	19.46	64.90	84.71

两类地区最明显的差异反映在到馆用户使用图书馆时受到某些因素影响的情况上。与珠江三角洲相比，粤东西北地区的受访用户表示亲历过或知道此种情况的要高出10个百分点。而在具体的影响因素上，珠江三角洲对于用户使用图书馆影响程度最高的四个因素是用户使用的语种、身体残障、所受的行动限制以及性别，粤东西北地区则是用户所受的行动限制、身体残障、性别以及语种，次序略有不同，但项目完全一致。其中，用户身体残障、所受的行动限制以及使用的语种几个因素，反映出残障用户、行动受限用户（如偏远地区用户、老年用户、医院用户、服刑用户等）、小语种用户等社会弱势群体，较明显地受其弱势成因的负面影响，未能与其他群体的民众平等地享有图书馆权利。如果说上述三个因素受到普遍的关注与其所对应的社会弱势群体在图书馆使用上的明显特征——身体残障需要特殊的空间、设施和资料，行动受限用户需要馆外服务，小语种用户需要小语种资料——不无关系，那么，性别因素所呈现的高影响程度则出乎调查者的预期。在ALA《法案》及其阐释这一图书馆权利政策群中，性别因素包括性、性别认同、性别表现或性取向。[7] 国内的图书馆权利研究，对于前述几种社会弱势群体关注较

多，而对于性别因素及其对民众平等使用图书馆的影响等问题，则尚未加以重视，此次调查恰恰反映了这方面的现实需求。

两类地区次明显的差异反映在到馆用户使用图书馆时遭遇拒绝的情况上。珠江三角洲有近10%的受访用户表示曾经有过此类遭遇，粤东西北地区则有近20%。其中，绝大部分案例是被拒绝使用某些馆藏资源或被拒绝使用某些服务，被拒绝进入图书馆的案例在两类地区均很少见（小于2%）。从访谈记录分析，受访用户的图书馆使用遭拒案例中，有相当一部分是由于用户不了解或者不理解具体图书馆的规章制度所致，如有用户表示“不知道不带身份证会被拒绝使用某些服务”、“中文图书外借处没有证无法进入”、“少儿部和成人部分开，在小时候曾经被拒绝进入成人部”、“昨晚过来，儿童馆已经下班了，把孩子放在大厅”等。如果抛却上述个案，则到馆用户使用图书馆时遭遇拒绝的实际情况应优于10.01%和19.46%两个比率。但是，这也反映出图书馆内部规章制度制定和宣传工作中存在着的问题：一则规章制度在制定时可能未对具体资源或服务的特点以及用户对之的需求进行全面的调研，导致规章制度不合理；二则未能以较好的方式向用户告知和解释规章制度，使用户能够了解、理解并接受，从而使得规章制度得以有效实施。

在到馆用户所亲历或知道的图书馆收藏和提供使用资料时受到某些因素影响的情况上，两类地区之间在百分比和高影响因素上基本没有差异。首先，两类地区在这一情况的百分比，均要远远高于上述到馆用户使用图书馆时受到某些因素影响的情况的百分比。如果我们将用户使用图书馆的感受称为直接的图书馆权利体验，而将图书馆为了实现用户的图书馆权利所需的在资料收藏和提供上的空间和自由称为间接的图书馆权利体验，则调查显示，前者要大大优于后者。其次，两类地区用户根据亲历或知道的情况，认为对于图书馆资料收藏和提供使用影响程度最高的四个因素依次为图书馆用户的需求、资料是否包含暴力色情等内容、获得资料难易程度以及资料的价格。其中图书馆用户的需求是从正面影响图书馆的资料收藏和提供使用，后三个因素则是从负面对之造成影响。其他国际图书馆界颇为关注的诸如资料所反映的意识形态、资料所代表的社会政治主张、资料所倡导的宗教信仰、资料所认同的价值观、资料所表达的学术观点、资料作者的社会身份、资料出版者的社会身份等因素对于图书馆资料收藏和提供的影响，却很少为国内的图书馆用户所感受。

通过表4的统计，得出反映市县间图书馆到馆用户图书馆权利享有情况的相关数据。进而如表5所示，市县间接受调查的图书馆用户在图书馆权利的享有上的差异不如地区间的差异明显，地区间在三种情况上的百分比差值接近10（即10个百分点），而市县间仅有一种情况的百分比差值超过5。

表4　市级及以上与区级/县级图书馆到馆用户图书馆权利享有情况比较

图级别	每月使用图一次或以上		使用图时遭遇过拒绝	
	不分地区	不同地区	不分地区	不同地区
市级及以上*	90%	珠江三角洲86%， 粤东西北地区95%	14.2%	珠江三角洲12.67%， 粤东西北地区15.75%
区级/县级**	88.59%	珠江三角洲84.67%， 粤东西北地区92.52%	15%	珠江三角洲7%， 粤东西北地区23%

续表 4

图级别	使用图时受到某些因素的影响（亲历或知道）		图收藏和提供使用资料时受到某些因素的影响（亲历或知道）	
	不分地区	不同地区	不分地区	不同地区
市级及以上*	63.65%	珠江三角洲 56.66%，粤东西北地区 70.64%	87.79%	珠江三角洲 90.16%，粤东西北地区 85.42%
区级/县级**	56.15%	珠江三角洲 53.14%，粤东西北地区 59.16%	83.62%	珠江三角洲 83.24%，粤东西北地区 84%

* 对应市级行政区划单位，** 对应县级行政区划单位。

表 5　地区间、市县间到馆用户图书馆权利享有情况差异度

对比单位	每月使用图一次或以上	使用图时遭遇过拒绝	使用图时受到某些因素的影响（亲历或知道）	图收藏和提供使用资料时受到某些因素的影响（亲历或知道）
地区间*	9	9.45	10	1.99
市县间**	1.41	0.8	7.5	4.17

* 两类地区间该项百分比之差的绝对值，** 市、县间该项百分比之差的绝对值。

免费开放的公共图书馆，对于经济情况较差的民众而言，是更为重要的公共信息/文化服务机构，则粤东西北地区图书馆的“常客”用户应较珠江三角洲为多，调查数据与这一推断相符。一般情况下，区级/县级图书馆较市级及以上图书馆的服务规模及范围为小、服务对象更为集中，则其“常客”用户应较后者为多，然而调查数据与这一推断不符，区级/县级图书馆中每月使用图书馆一次或一次以上的到馆用户比例反而低于市级及以上图书馆。即经济情况与图书馆使用频率反相关，图书馆规模及服务范围与之正相关，二者复合作用的结果，便是粤东西北地区的市级图书馆 95% 的到馆用户每月使用图书馆一次或一次以上，而珠江三角洲的区级/县级图书馆则要少将近一成。结合用户和馆员的访谈，笔者认为，市级及以上图书馆在服务宣传方面的优势，应是其“常客”用户多于区级/县级图书馆的主要原因。

市县间在到馆用户使用图书馆时遭遇拒绝的情况上基本没有差异，但表 4 中所反映出的不同地区的区级/县级图书馆在这一情况上的 7% 与 23% 的差距却颇为显眼，而这一差距也是造成前述地区间次明显的差异的直接原因。多个相关数据表明：对于到馆用户使用图书馆时遭遇拒绝的情况，图书馆的规模及服务范围这一单一变量与之负相关，但影响程度很小，百分比差值为 0.8（表 5）；经济情况这一单一变量与之负相关，反映影响程度的百分比差值为 9.45（表 5）。当两个变量复合作用时，反映影响程度的百分比差值骤升至 16。为何在经济情况较差地区的规模及服务范围较小的图书馆中，较常出现使用图书馆遭拒的情况？从访谈反馈，笔者认为，前述图书馆内部规章制度制定和宣传工作中存在问题依然是主要原因，其中某图书馆“图书价格高于一定标准无法外借”的规定，是特别突出的案例，此处进一步反映出图书馆在内部规章制度制定上的随意性和自由度。

规章制度虽多只是简简单单的文字条款，但却处处体现着主体图书馆的管理和服务理念。如果能对图书馆内部规章制度作一较大范围的调查，不失为一种反映图书馆权利情况、图书馆服务现状、图书馆事业发展的最为简单却颇为有效的途径。

市县间最明显的差异反映在到馆用户使用图书馆时受到某些因素影响的情况上。由表5所得，市级及以上图书馆的受访用户表示亲历过或知道此种情况的要比区级/县级图书馆高出近7.5个百分点。性别、行动限制、残障和语种仍然是影响程度较高的因素。市级及以上图书馆规模较大、服务范围较宽、服务对象较广泛，因此，面向残障用户、行动受限用户、小语种用户等社会弱势群体提供服务的概率较高，如前所述，弱势群体在图书馆权利的享有上较明显地受其弱势成因的负面影响，所以，市县之间出现了这一差距。而在图书馆收藏和提供使用资料时受到某些因素的影响上，市级及以上图书馆的受访用户表示亲历过或知道此种情况的百分比也较区级/县级图书馆高。从具体因素看，一方面，影响程度最高的四种因素依然是图书馆用户的需求、资料是否包含暴力色情等内容、获得资料难易程度以及资料的价格；另一方面，区级/县级图书馆的用户在资料内容（如资料是否包含暴力色情等内容、资料所代表的社会政治主张等）对资料收藏和提供产生影响方面有较多的体验反馈，而市级及以上图书馆的用户则较常提及收藏政策产生的影响。

4.2 用户与馆员间的权利认知和期望情况对比分析

在图书馆权利的认知情况上，馆员方面的数据均优于用户，但双方的差距并不如调查者预期的显著。85.18%的用户和99%的馆员表示在接受这次调查前已经知道民众拥有平等和自由地使用图书馆以满足自身教育、文化和信息需求的权利，对于一个讨论不到10年的话题，这样的认知度不可谓不高。我们可以将之解读为图书馆界近年来宣扬现代图书馆理念、普及图书馆权利意识方面的努力和成效，也可以将之解读为图书馆为民众所平等和自由地使用本就是自然而然、不言自明的权利。在图书馆权利的重要性上，82.65%的用户和85.33%的馆员认为非常重要。在上述反映知道权利和认为权利非常重要两个相关情况的两组数据之间，馆员的反馈展现出更大的差距，虽然绝大部分馆员均知道图书馆权利，但有相当一部分馆员并不认可图书馆权利对于民众而言是非常重要的。以地区、市县等因素作复合分析，更为细划的数据突出了粤东西北地区的馆员，他们之中认为权利非常重要的仅占76%。面向馆员的现代图书馆理念、图书馆权利的进一步宣扬，应多加关注这一地区。

关于反映民众图书馆权利实现情况的指标，问卷中拟定了八项。如前所述，所有拟定指标都得到过半数的到馆用户、六成以上的馆员所认可。关于八项指标的重要程度，有仅填写一项和为多项排序的不同反馈方式。如表6所示，综合两种反馈所得数据，八项指标均有用户认为是反映民众图书馆权利实现情况重要性最强的指标，馆员方面则未见有受访者选择第8项。八项指标中，最多用户和最多馆员认可的最重要指标相同，即图书馆的免费开放最能体现民众图书馆权利的实现情况；认为第1项或第2项指标重要性最强的两类受访者实际上已经占据了各自类别的80%左右。数据显示，用仅填写一项的方式反馈者，到馆用户的选项较馆员丰富，除第5项外，其他各项均有用户认为是最重要的指标，馆员的选择则仅涉及三项。如果将用户的反馈理解为民众对自己图书馆权利实现情况的期望，而将馆员的反馈理解为他们对民众图书馆权利期望的假设，则两者之间是存在差异的。

表 6　到馆用户与馆员对于图书馆权利实现指标认可情况比较

单位：%

反映民众图书馆权利实现情况重要性最强的指标	仅填写一项		两种反馈	
	用户	馆员	用户	馆员
1. 免费开放	32.76	36.36	52.8	58.82
2. 所有民众都能平等地使用	27.59	54.55	25.6	23.53
3. 为所有用户提供公平的、无特权的服务	15.52	0	7.47	1.96
4. 提供符合用户教育、文化和信息需求和兴趣的资料	13.79	9.09	4.53	3.92
5. 提供代表各种不同观点的资料	0	0	2.13	3.92
6. 用户能够通过图书馆自由地获取所需资料	5.17	0	2.13	5.88
7. 为身体残障用户提供特殊的设施、资料和服务	3.45	0	2.67	3.92
8. 为行动受限不能到馆的用户提供流动书车、上门或邮寄服务	1.72	0	2.67	0

关于民众图书馆权利维护之义务的承担者，到馆用户与馆员的反馈情况如表 7 所示。第一，最多用户和最多馆员认为应该承担该义务的均是相关政府部门，而最少用户和最少馆员认为应该承担该义务的均是图书馆协会/学会。第二，选择第 1、2、4 三项的馆员百分比均高于用户百分比，而选择第 2 项的，前者却低于后者；第 2 项将图书馆协会/学会从其他各项中凸显出来。笔者认为，用户最少选择图书馆协会/学会，与图书馆协会/学会在民众中较低的认知度有关，访谈数据显示，不少用户不知道图书馆协会/学会的存在。而馆员最少选择图书馆协会/学会，则只能从图书馆协会/学会的职能定位中寻找解释。回到前文，不论是“图书馆权利”这一中文术语的本源，还是此次调查的理论基础，均与 ALA 这一图书馆协会密切相关，两相比照，反映出国内外图书馆协会/学会（至少在图书馆权利问题上）的职能定位有较大的差异。差异应该引发反思，而一些用户在通过此次调查知道了图书馆协会/学会之后，提出了“由图书馆协会/学承担图书馆权利理念的宣传和普及”之建议，或可作为反思的另一种动力。

表 7　到馆用户与馆员关于民众图书馆权利维护之义务的承担者意见比较

单位：%

受访者	1. 图书馆、图书馆员	2. 图书馆协会/学会	3. 相关政府部门	4. 相关法规
用户	72.04	60.77	74.70	63.62
馆员	80.07	48.53	82.00	73.37

4.3 权利享有与权利观念间的对比分析

为在图书馆权利享有与权利观念之间作对比性观察，笔者首先统计了各个图书馆中最多和次多到馆用户和馆员认为不应该影响用户使用图书馆的因素以及认为不应该影响图书馆资料收藏与提供的因素，以之作为权利观念情况的反映，进而提取到馆用户和馆员所亲历或知道的影响用户使用图书馆以及影响图书馆资料收藏与提供的情况中前述因素的反馈百分比，以之作为权利享有情况的反映。① 为便于讨论，且称这一百分比差值为权利享有与权利观念之相对差距值，该值应在0至1之间取值，值越大，代表用户的图书馆权利享有与权利观念之间的差异越明显。

如表8所示，用户在图书馆权利享有和图书馆权利观念之间存在差距，而二者在图书馆收集和提供资料方面的差距较为明显。具体数据显示，有四个图书馆在用户使用图书馆方面的享有与观念相对差距值为0；在图书馆收集和提供资料方面，有一个图书馆的享有与观念相对差距值高达62.22%，而差距值高于30%的图书馆有四个。前文4.1中指出，调查显示，用户直接的图书馆权利体验要大大优于其间接的图书馆权利体验，而此处的差距值这一数据，再一次说明了用户的间接图书馆权利需求没有得到充分的满足。而用户图书馆权利总体状况的进一步改善，有待相关各方从图书馆的资料收集和提供方面着力加强。

表8 到馆用户权利享有与权利观念之比较

单位：%

图级别		权利享有与权利观念之相对差距值	
用户使用图	市级及以上	5.83	平均：5.42
	区级/县级	5.00	
图收集和提供资料	市级及以上	16.39	平均：20.49
	区级/县级	24.59	

5 结　　语

论文呈现了以广东省公共图书馆的到馆用户和馆员为调查对象所反映的中国图书馆权利现状及其在地区间、市县间、用户与馆员间、享有与观念间的差异情况。一方面，调查呈现了丰富的实证数据，并以之证明了差异的存在及程度，进而对成因加以分析；另一方面，调查还发现了实践领域在图书馆权利上的一些隐性需求，以及在图书馆权利上有所反映而实际上可能对更多具体实践产生影响的一些存在问题。

① 上述基本数据与具体图书馆相联系，不在文中反映。

参考文献

[1] 程焕文，潘燕桃，张靖. 图书馆权利研究 [M]. 北京：学习出版社，2011.
[2] 范进学. 权利政治论：一种宪政民主理论的阐释 [M]. 济南：山东人民出版社，2003：267.
[3] 广东省统计局. 从更深层次探索推进广东区域协调发展探析 [R/OL]. [2014 - 09 - 02]. http://www.gdstats.gov.cn/tjfx/t20080620_59831.htm.
[4] 2011 年广东省行政区划 [EB/OL]. [2014 - 09 - 02]. http://www.xzqh.org/html/show/gd/23996.html.
[5] 广东省统计局. 广东统计年鉴：2010 [J]. 北京：中国统计出版社，2010.
[6] 程焕文，张靖. 图书馆权利与道德 [M]. 桂林：广西师范大学出版社，2007：319.
[7] ALA. Access to Library Resources and Services Regardless of Sex, Gender Identity, Gender Expression, or Sexual Orientation [EB/OL]. [2014 - 09 - 02]. http://www.ala.org/advocacy/intfreedom/librarybill/interpretations/accesslibrary.

教师简介：

唐琼，女，安徽大学管理学学士、中山大学管理学硕士，武汉大学管理学博士。2009年起任教于中山大学资讯管理学院，副教授，硕士生导师。主讲“图书馆管理”、“目录学”、“信息服务营销”、“信息伦理与政策”等本科生课程，以及“信息服务质量管理”等研究生课程。研究方向包括数字信息资源管理、信息服务质量管理、信息政策和信息服务营销。主持及参与十余项国家级、省部级科研项目，出版著作3部，发表论文30余篇，获多项科研奖励。2015年美国伊利诺伊大学香槟分校访问学者。华人图书馆员协会(Chinese American Librarians Association)出版委员会2015—2016年度共同主席(Co-chair)。联系方式：tqiong@ mail. sysu. edu. cn。

所选论文《采用因子分析法构建数字资源选择标准体系的研究》原载于《大学图书馆学报》2011年第2期

采用因子分析法构建数字资源选择标准体系的研究*

唐　琼

摘　要：在汇集整理数字资源选择标准初始集合的基础上，开展专家问卷调查，进行数字资源选择标准重要性及适用性的调查研究，采用因子分析法进行数据统计和分析，提炼精简出关联度最强、最具代表性的选择标准，在此基础上遴选适用性得分高于4分的选择标准，由此构建具有一定合理性和可操作性的数字资源选择标准体系。

关键词：因子分析；数字资源；选择标准

A Study on Establishing a Selection Criteria System of Digital Resources Based on Factor Analysis

Qiong Tang

Abstract: Based on the collection of the initial collection of selection criteria of digital resources, this paper conducts a questionnaire survey of experts to establish a selection criteria system of digital resources, and uses factor analysis to extract the criteria which are of the strongest correlation degree, and are able to explain the measuring purpose of the original selection criteria system. On this basis, the criteria which get scores about applicability higher than 4 are chosen, and finally a representative and applicable selection criteria system is established.

---

* 本文系国家社会科学基金资助项目“信息资源公共获取中的质量保障政策研究”（10CTQ011）及中国博士后科学基金第四十七批面上资助二等资助项目（20100470971）研究成果之一。

Keywords: Factor analysis; Digital resource; Selection criterion

1 引　　言

馆藏资源是图书馆功能发挥与服务效益实现的基础。数字环境下，信息资源的状态、用户需求、图书馆运行模式等正在发生转变，传统环境下发展的资源选择标准应用于数字资源的选择具有很大局限性。开展数字资源选择标准研究，有利于提高图书馆数字资源选择工作的科学性和规范性、实现图书馆资源配置的最优化、提升数字资源建设的效果和效益，最终为图书馆创新服务模式、拓展服务空间、实现持续发展提供支持和保障。数字资源选择标准研究为国内外图书馆理论与实践界所重视。然而，如何建立既能反映用户需求，同时又具有代表性和实际应用价值的数字资源选择标准体系，目前仍处在不断探索中。本文在结合已有学者及机构的相关研究、国内外馆藏发展政策中的现行选择标准基础上，提出数字资源选择标准初始集合，继而采用因子分析法，通过实证研究的方式，验证其在图书馆资源选择业务实践工作中的重要性及适用性，最终构建数字资源选择标准体系。

2 研究方法

2.1 建立数字资源选择标准体系初始集合

数字资源选择标准体系初始集合建立在对已有研究及馆藏政策的考察基础之上。数字资源选择标准研究是国内外相关研究的热点问题之一。霍里曼（Curt Holleman）认为，资源选择的四个基本标准——质量、与图书馆的关联性、功能技术和成本在数字环境下依然有效；但它们的实际含义、判断方法发生了变化，而且数字资源的选择将变得更加复杂和困难。[1]这涉及授权许可协议、多样化的定价模式、设备、空间、资源类型的取舍、技术支持、供应商支持等多种因素。[2]此外，数字资源选择与本地馆藏的实际状况相符合也是选择决策中需考虑的重要因素。[3]李（Leslie A. Lee）和吴（Michelle M. Wu）认为，根据不同图书馆战略发展目标、馆藏发展政策中陈述的不同需求，数字资源的选择决策也应有所不同。但他们同时指出，数字资源的内容、功能、长期使用、用户以及成本标准在众多数字资源选择决策中是通用的。随着新技术的发展，数字资源的表现形式可能日新月异，图书馆必须定期评估审核数字资源的选择标准，并根据环境的变化适时调整。[4]国内学者罗春荣、曹树金认为应从用户需求、资源内容、使用的方便程度、使用与运行环境、成本效益、后续服务等6个方面考察数字资源选择问题。[5]肖珑和张宇红从数字资源内容、检索系统及功能、使用情况、价值与成本核算、出版商/数据商服务、长期保存6个方面提出选择评估数字资源的指标。[6]张晓林等结合中国科学院国家科学数字图书馆数字资源建设的需要，提出了数字资源采购的总体原则、资源内容要求、资源利用要求、支持性服务的要求、支持互操作与集成的要求、长期保存要求等。[7]该研究突破了仅考虑数字资源内在价值的局限，对于实践具有重要的参考价值。

此外，一些研究组织、图书馆联盟等在该领域的研究也很活跃。如图书馆共同体国际联盟（ICOLC）发布并两次修订了《关于当前电子资源选择与购买及首选策略的声明》[8]，数字图书馆联盟（DLF）发布《商业电子资源选择与保存：问题与实践》报告[9]，就数字资源选择的多项重要问题展开讨论，包括许可制度、价格模型和购买模式、长期保存与使用、选择政策与策略计划、机构经费及组织、用户支持、持续评价及使用统计信息、数字资源管理的综合系统等。

从国内外图书馆组织、图书馆制定的馆藏发展政策、资源引进等政策来看，现行数字资源选择标准主要涉及以下方面：资源内容的评鉴、系统功能及技术的要求、资源成本的评估、资源许可协议的规定、资源供应商及其服务的考虑和资源长期保存的考察等。[10-15]如针对资源内容，美国国家农业图书馆《电子资源选择政策》就提出了如下标准："资源需反映准确性、完整性、客观性及权威性或包含提供指向这类信息的链接；资源的责任机构应易于确定；资源应来源于公认的权威人士、出版者、协会或政府机构；资源应及时更新从而足够有用，无论何时，时效性对于资源的主题而言都是十分重要的。"[16]

对上述研究及馆藏政策中提出的数字资源选择标准进行内容分析，可将其归纳为资源质量、资源使用、资源服务、资源契合、资源成本、资源风险六个维度，并提炼出相关的测评标准（表1）。其中，资源质量、资源使用、资源服务是从微观角度提出的选择标准维度，属于对资源本身特质的考察；资源契合、资源成本、资源风险是从较为宏观的角度提出的选择标准维度，即主要兼顾数字资源自身特征以外的外部因素影响。宏观和微观是相对的，完整的数字资源选择标准是两者的有机结合。

表1　图书馆数字资源选择标准的初始集合

维度	测评标准
A 资源契合	A1 与图书馆发展契合 A11 与本馆发展目标一致 A12 能够支持本馆开展的服务
	A2 用户反馈意见 A21 用户对该资源满足需求的总体感知 A22 该资源是用户查找相关信息的主要来源之一 A23 用户对资源的推荐
	A3 能够有效补充已有资源
B 资源质量	B1 内容的完整性 B11 收录数据量 B12 收录内容时间跨度 B13 本校学科覆盖率 B14 全文出版物收录比例

续表 1

维度	测评标准
B 资源质量	B2 内容权威性 B21 核心出版物比例 B22 同行评审刊数量 B23 出版商声誉 B24 作者权威性
	B3 内容时效性 B31 内容更新频率 B32 与对应纸本资源相比出版的及时性
	B4 内容准确性
	B5 内容客观性
C 资源使用	C1 使用范围与方式 C11 授权用户的界定符合图书馆服务开展的需求 C12 授权使用地点的界定符合图书馆服务开展的需求 C13 授权使用方式符合本馆需求 C14 允许文献传递
	C2 检索系统功能 C21 检索系统的有效性 C22 检索系统的易用性 C23 检索系统的易学性 C24 检索系统的可控性 C25 检索系统的帮助功能
	C3 支持资源集成与整合
D 资源服务	D1 提供规范的使用统计数据
	D2 提供免费试用期
	D3 提供培训支持
	D4 售后服务响应时间及效果
	D5 资源长期保存的支持 D51 资源供应者提供数字资源的长期保存 D52 长期保存方式满足本馆要求 D53 长期保存资源访问费用的合理程度 D54 长期保存资源的使用方式符合图书馆开展服务的要求

续表 1

维度	测评标准
E 资源成本	E1 成本构成 E11 资源价格接受程度 E12 年涨价幅度接受程度 E13 软硬件购置成本的合理程度 E14 设备维护成本
	E2 成本效益 E21 数字资源登录次数 E22 数字资源检索或下载次数 E23 人均使用量 E24 人均服务成本 E25 全文下载成本
F 资源风险	F1 版权风险的处理
	F2 合同风险的处理
	F3 尊重用户隐私

2.2 调查设计与实施

本次调查的目的在于：明确调查对象对本研究提出的各个图书馆数字资源选择标准重要程度以及适用性的认知，实现数字资源选择标准的复选和优选过程，并由此确立最终的图书馆数字资源选择标准体系，从而验证研究假设："尽管不同群体对数字资源选择标准的认识存在差异，但寻找和确立一套具有代表性和适用性的图书馆数字资源选择标准体系是可能的。"

2.2.1 调查对象的确立

以中国国家图书馆主页、中国教育和科研计算机网提供的导航为样本获取的途径，两者去重后共计 303 家图书馆。这些图书馆分布于中国大陆各个地区，涵盖了"211 工程"高校图书馆、省级公共图书馆、直辖市或部分副省级城市公共图书馆以及科研图书馆。此外，也包括很多各地区具有代表性的中型图书馆。以订购数字资源在 3 种以上为样本选择的标准，最终确立了 273 家图书馆（表 2）。

表 2 抽样框调查对象所在图书馆类型分布

图书馆类型	高校图书馆	公共图书馆	国家图书馆	科研图书馆
数量（百分比）	205（75.09%）	51（18.68%）	1（0.37%）	16（5.86%）

笔者以邮件及电话访问的方式了解该馆负责数字资源建设的馆长、部主任或馆员联系方式。原则上是每家图书馆确定一位调查对象，另考虑到网络调查问卷回收率普遍较

低的问题，部分图书馆如果能够获得超过一位业务涉及数字资源建设专家的联系方式，均将其列为调查对象。

2.2.2 调查问卷的设计

问卷共分为三个部分：第一部分是调查对象的基本资料，第二部分调查图书馆数字资源选择业务的基本情况，第三部分考察调查对象对本研究提出的图书馆数字资源选择标准重要性以及适用性的认知。根据提出的图书馆数字资源选择标准初始集合设计问题，每一问题均涉及选择标准的重要性及其在图书馆的适用性两个方面。其中，适用性是指该标准在调查对象所在图书馆实践工作应用的可能性，它与图书馆现实条件限制、数据的可得性相关联。采用李克特（Likert）5 分量表，设置 5 个评分等级供调查对象选择。分数越高，表明重要程度越高或适用性越强。通过小规模调查测试，依据部分调查对象提出的意见对问卷进行了多次修改，最后确定正式的调查问卷。

2.2.3 调查的实施

设计网络调查问卷，通过电子邮件将问卷的链接地址发送给调查对象。2008 年 12 月 1 日至 15 日，为第一个调查周期；根据问卷回收的情况，于 2008 年 12 月 15 日至 30 日，向调查对象再次发送问卷。本次调查共发放问卷 300 份，回收 132 份，回收率为 44%。依据答题数超过 40 道（即≥总题数的 2/3）即为有效问卷的判断标准，回收的有效问卷为 125 份，有效率为 41.67%。其中，国家图书馆共征集了 5 位数字资源建设专家的意见，回收问卷涉及的图书馆共计 121 家。

2.3 统计分析方法

因子分析（亦称为因素分析）主要用来研究多个变量之间的相互关系，是多元统计分析的一个重要分支。它运用对诸多变量的相关性研究，剔除多余变量，从而实现用假设的少数几个变量来表示原有变量的主要信息。[17]因子分析所具备的这种特点和优势，使其在社会学、经济学、管理学、医学等领域都得到了广泛应用。如宋健采用层次分析法和因子分析方法构建地区信用环境的评价指标体系和评估模型[18]；刘举等运用因子分析法构建我国综合大学创新能力评价指标体系[19]；徐革运用因子分析中的主成分分析法重新构建电子资源综合评价指标[20]，但其仅从数学角度考察了其可行性，并未开展相关的实证研究。本研究将根据选择标准重要性调查结果，运用因子分析法提取选择标准，再结合选择标准的适用性调查结果实现该标准体系的优化。

3 研究结果分析

3.1 调查问卷的信度和效度分析

应用 SPSS 软件计算 Cronbach 内在信度系数值，得到各维度下选择标准的重要性和适用性的 Cronbach 系数均大于 0.8，说明本次调查的测度问题具有内在一致性。采用独立样

本 T 检验测度本次问卷调查的外在信度（即不同时间进行测量时调查表结果的一致性程度）。将第一次和第二次问卷发放后回收的有效问卷进行独立样本 T 检验发现，除“资源风险”在适用性方面两次调查的 P 值小于0.05外，每一标准维度重要性和适用性的 P 值均大于0.05，可以认为总体上两次调查结果不存在显著差异，调查样本所在总体分布一致，本研究设计的问卷及调查实施具有一致性和稳定性。

一般认为，效度考察的是研究所使用的工具及方法能否有效反映研究的问题，以及在多大程度上有效反映。问卷样本的重要性和适用性效度的 *AVE* 系数分别为0.71和0.73，均大于0.5，符合统计学对于问卷结构效度的要求，表明研究工具真实体现了研究所依据的理论结构。

上述调查结果的信度和效度分析表明，调查问卷设计及调查结果具有较好的一致性、稳定性和有效性，能够反映样本所在总体的分布情况。

3.2 选择标准的重要性因子分析

利用因子分析法实现复杂变量的简化，往往是利用一组观测值实现的。考虑到选择标准适用性是标准体系制定的参考依据，因此，本研究将调查对象对选择标准重要性感知得分作为因子分析的观测值，实现选择标准初始集合的第一次优化。具体过程如下：

首先，评估本次调查应用因子分析的可靠性。因子分析的受试样本数量一般不得少于100人。[21]本研究获得的样本量为125人，符合因子分析对样本量的要求。再对调查数据进行 *KMO* 取样适当性度量和 Bartlett 球形检验。因子分析的 *KMO* 值为0.861，大于0.80；Bartlett 球形检验的近似卡方值为4096.339（自由度为1128），达到0.05的显著，代表各变量（每一选择标准即为一个变量）间有共同因素存在，均说明适合进行因子分析。

其次，运用SPSS软件的因子分析功能，选择主成分分析法抽取因子，并采用最大方差旋转法旋转主轴，以取得选择标准体系主要的因子结构。以特征值为1作为抽取因子的标准。表3说明共抽取出11个共同因子，其中总和栏为特征值，“初始特征值”中“总和”栏的总和刚好等于变量数48。

表3　说明的总方差

成分	初始特征值			旋转前因子方差及其贡献		
	特征值	占方差的比例/%	累积比例/%	合计	占方差的比例/%	累积比例/%
1	16.479	34.331	34.331	16.479	34.331	34.331
2	2.887	6.015	40.347	2.887	6.015	40.347
3	2.335	4.865	45.212	2.335	4.865	45.212
4	2.154	4.488	49.699	2.154	4.488	49.699
5	2.016	4.200	53.899	2.016	4.200	53.899

续表 3

成分	初始特征值			旋转前因子方差及其贡献		
	特征值	占方差的比例/%	累积比例/%	合计	占方差的比例/%	累积比例/%
6	1.846	3.846	57.745	1.846	3.846	57.745
7	1.447	3.014	60.759	1.447	3.014	60.759
8	1.392	2.899	63.658	1.392	2.899	63.658
9	1.220	2.541	66.200	1.220	2.541	66.200
10	1.177	2.453	68.652	1.177	2.453	68.652
11	1.104	2.300	70.952	1.104	2.300	70.952
……						
48	0.053	0.110	100.000			

确定抽取的因子数（即 11 个因子）后，得到旋转后的成分矩阵，整理各个因子及其相关变量、因子负荷量的值，得到表 4。

表 4　整理后的旋转成分矩阵主要数值

共同因子	变量（因子负荷量的值）
1	内容的客观性（0.745）；内容的准确性（0.699）；内容更新的频率（0.648）；检索系统的帮助功能（0.642）；检索系统的可控性（0.528）；检索系统的易学性（0.475）
2	版权风险的处理（0.838）；合同风险的处理（0.785）；尊重用户隐私（0.726）；用户对该资源满足需求的总体感知（0.572）；用户对资源的推荐（0.478）
3	资源长期保存方式满足本馆要求（0.687）；资源供应者提供数字资源的长期保存（0.680）；长期保存资源访问费用的合理程度（0.603）；长期保存资源的使用方式符合图书馆开展服务的要求（0.600）；检索系统的有效性（0.467）
4	提供对用户培训的支持（0.701）；售后服务响应时间及效果（0.663）；提供免费试用期（0.551）；提供规范的使用统计数据（0.477）；检索系统的易用性（0.441）；出版商的声誉（0.439）；作者的权威性（0.422）
5	人均使用量（0.685）；数字资源的登录次数（0.673）；数字资源的检索或下载次数（0.626）；该资源是用户查找相关信息的主要来源之一（0.483）
6	能够支持本馆开展的服务（0.752）；能够有效补充已有资源（0.689）；本校学科的覆盖率（0.657）；与本馆发展目标及使命一致（0.630）；支持资源集成与整合（0.497）
7	软硬件购置成本（0.829）；全文下载成本（0.775）；年涨价幅度接受程度（0.703）；资源价格接受程度（0.538）
8	授权使用地点的界定符合图书馆服务开展的需求（0.786）；授权用户的界定符合图书馆服务开展的需求（0.736）；授权使用方式符合本馆需求（0.660）；允许文献传递（0.490）

续表4

共同因子	变量（因子负荷量的值）
9	核心出版物比例（0.734）；同行评审刊数量（0.721）；全文出版物收录比例（0.632）
10	设备维护成本（0.746）；人均服务成本（0.711）；与对应纸本资源相比出版的及时性（0.402）
11	收录的数据量（0.814）；收录内容的时间跨度（0.712）

旋转后的成分矩阵根据各共同因子中变量（在调查问卷中以题项表示）的因子负荷量的大小排序，各共同因子所包含的变量见表4。同一共同因子下各变量的因子负荷量绝对值均大于0.4，表明共同因子对这一变量的解释度足够，关系紧密度较好，符合因子分析的要求。根据多数研究者编制层面的实际经验，一个层面的题项数最少在3题以上，否则题项太少，无法测出所代表的层面特质，其内容效度会不够严谨。因此在因子分析时，如果共同因子所包含的变量数目只有2个或1个，可以考虑将此共同因子及相关变量删除。[21]此外，考虑到越靠后的因子敏感度越小，即最后一个因子对整体的贡献率最小，因此，将第11个共同因子及其变量“收录的数据量”和“收录内容的时间跨度”删除。重复上述步骤，直至共同因子所包含的变量数大于或等于3。相关结果见表5。

表5　因子分析次数及删除的选择标准

因子分析次数	*KMO* 值	Bartlett 球形检验 *Sig.* 值	不符合要求的选择标准
第一次	0.861	0.000	收录的数据量 收录内容的时间跨度
第二次	0.866	0.000	人均服务成本 设备维护成本
第三次	0.872	0.000	作者权威性
第四次	0.874	0.000	无

第四次因子分析因旋转后的成分矩阵中，各共同因子包括的变量均大于3个，数目适当，符合内容效度的要求；此时共同因子数量由11个简化为9个。通过上述因子分析得到的各因子之间的变量（即选择标准）关联度最强，能够较好解释原有标准体系所要测度的目的。上述分析过程共删除5个选择标准，这也从一定程度上说明提出的图书馆数字资源选择标准初始集合已经具有较好的代表性和关联度。

在未能辨析若干变量之间相互关系的条件下，通过获得这些变量的实际测度值，以因子分析为主要途径，能够实现对各个变量关系的归纳和综合，这也是部分研究将隶属于共同因子的变量归为同一类别的原因。与上述研究不同的是，本文在借鉴已有研究的基础上，已经提出了图书馆数字资源选择标准体系的6个维度，并分析提取若干选择标准分别解释这6个维度，即归类这一过程已经完成。本研究运用因子分析法，主要目的在于分析各选择标准之间的相关关系，以各变量形成的共同因子内容效度较强、对整体选择标准体系解释能力强为标准[5]。根据这一判断依据，每次因子分析后变量数（即选择标准数）少于3个的共同因子不符合要求，将其删除，从而使得保留的各变量之间相关性和代表性最强。

3.3 选择标准的适用性分析

本研究采用的是李克特5分量表测度选择标准的适用性。选择标准适用性得分为1，表明其在调查对象所在图书馆无法应用；若得分为5，表明其在调查对象所在图书馆非常适用。即得分越高，适用性越强。以选择标准的适用性得分大于或等于4作为筛选的阈值(因为大于或等于4分即表明该标准在调查对象所在图书馆数字资源选择实践中能够较好地应用)。统计经过因子分析筛选的选择标准适用性得分，结果如表6所示。

表6 适用性得分低于4的选择标准

选择标准	适用性得分
用户对该资源满足需求的总体感知	3.88
同行评审刊数量	3.94
内容客观性	3.96
检索系统的帮助功能	3.96
支持资源集成与整合	3.94
长期保存资源访问费用的合理程度	3.95
数字资源的登录次数	3.95
人均使用量	3.96
尊重用户隐私	3.88

很多数字资源选择标准虽然非常重要，但由于缺乏支持数据等现实条件的限制，并不能在实践工作中得到很好的应用。表6中共有9个选择标准在图书馆资源选择工作中适用性相对较弱。以“人均使用量”（检索或下载总次数与目标用户比值）为例，该指标是测度资源使用效益的重要支持性数据，但由于一些客观因素的存在，使得现实中获得相关数据存在一定困难，如部分资源供应商未提供使用统计数据，部分图书馆数字资源管理系统不具备资源访问统计的功能；此外，目标用户的范围界定存在模糊性，其具体数量难以确定，对于公共图书馆、国家图书馆而言更是如此。因此，以“人均使用量”作为选择比对的标准不太现实。

本研究以选择标准适用性调查结果平均数大于4作为一个衡量的尺度，但各个图书馆的实际情况存在差别。对不同类型图书馆的统计发现，除了“尊重用户隐私”和“用户对该资源满足需求的总体感知”这两个选择标准的适用性得分均低于4分以外，表6中所列的未能符合适用性的选择标准在一些图书馆是可以应用的。以“支持资源集成与整合”标准为例，调查的科研图书馆专家对于该标准在其图书馆适用性的感知得分就为4.14，这可能与调查对象所在图书馆开发了数字资源统一检索平台，已经对数字资源相关标准及协议是否支持集成整合有了较为深入的认识和详细的规定有关。如中国科学院国家科学图书馆就规定资源提供商必须支持数据内容、数据组织和数据利用的标准化和开放性要求，应该积极协助中国科学院国家科学图书馆建立开放的集成应用环境。[7] 因此，图书馆可将调查结果中未能符合适用性的选择标准作为参考性标准，依据实际情况决定其是否选用。

调查对象结合自身工作实践也提出了一些其他影响数字资源选择的因素。例如资源使用方面，提出要考虑“利用率统计功能”、“利用效果”、“并发用户数限制”，“使用的方便性问题应是资源使用首要标准”；资源成本方面，提出应考虑“外文数据库是否需要支付国际流量费”，“不同学科资源的评价标准难以统一，如新学科的使用成本肯定较高，但没有开始，永远也不可能有高利用率，用户的需求和使用积极性还要靠培养”；资源服务方面，专家指出仅考察资源供应商是否提供使用统计数据是不够的，还应要求其直接提供使用分析报告；合同风险方面，专家指出“因不可抗拒造成的使用中断的补偿：如地震、光缆中断、数据维护等导致的数据库实际使用时间低于合同规定的时间，应有延期或退补偿机制”，“数据库商家对影响用户使用情况的赔偿措施应作为考核标准。数据错误、不全、对方服务器问题造成服务中断等情况经常发生。但由于未能在合同中详细约定，出现这种状况以后图书馆得不到任何赔偿”。

此外，也有部分专家指出，虽然研究提出的选择标准涵盖面较广，但过多的选择标准反而会增加数字资源选择实践工作的复杂性，增加工作成本。为使选择标准体系在实践中具有更好的应用性，结合专家提出的评论性意见，最后修订的图书馆数字资源选择标准体系在层次划分和标准表述方面均进行了修改和简化。考虑到在不同图书馆应用时还需确定各个选择标准的权重，而在层次划分上，多一层级就会带来工作量的增大，故将原有三级选择标准体系简化为两级：第一级为标准体系的维度，第二级为具体的选择标准。此外，对部分内涵相近、能够揭示同一现象的选择标准加以归并处理，以避免标准数量过多带来资源选择过程应用的复杂化，具体包括：

（1）将“资源质量”维度下“与对应纸本资源相比出版的及时性”归入“内容更新频率”。

（2）将“资源使用”维度下“授权用户的界定”和“授权使用地点的界定”合并为“授权适用范围”，将“允许文献传递”归入“授权使用方式”标准的考察。

（3）将“资源服务”维度下“提供规范的使用统计数据”修改为“提供规范的使用统计数据报告”，将“资源供应商提供资源的长期保存”和“长期保存方式满足本馆要求”合并为“数字资源长期保存方式”。

（4）考虑到现有数字资源定价方式的复杂化及其对资源选择工作带来的影响，“资源成本”维度下增加一个标准“资源定价模式”，“软硬件购置成本”归入“资源价格”标准中，“全文下载成本”修改为“全文下载成本/检索成本”，从而全面反映全文数据库、二次文献数据库等的使用效益。“数字资源的检索和下载次数”的适用性得分为 4.27，但考虑到仅考察检索和下载次数在测评资源使用效益方面的实际意义并不大，而检索和下载次数事实上是考察“全文下载/检索成本”的基础数据，故保留“全文下载/检索成本”即可达到测评目的。

（5）将原有的“版权风险”标准细化为“版权争议材料的处理”和“对资源非法使用的界定和控制”，将“合同风险”细化为“合同对双方责任义务约定的合理性”和“合同文本表述清晰”。

最终修正后的图书馆数字资源选择标准体系包括 6 个判断维度、31 个选择标准（图 1）。

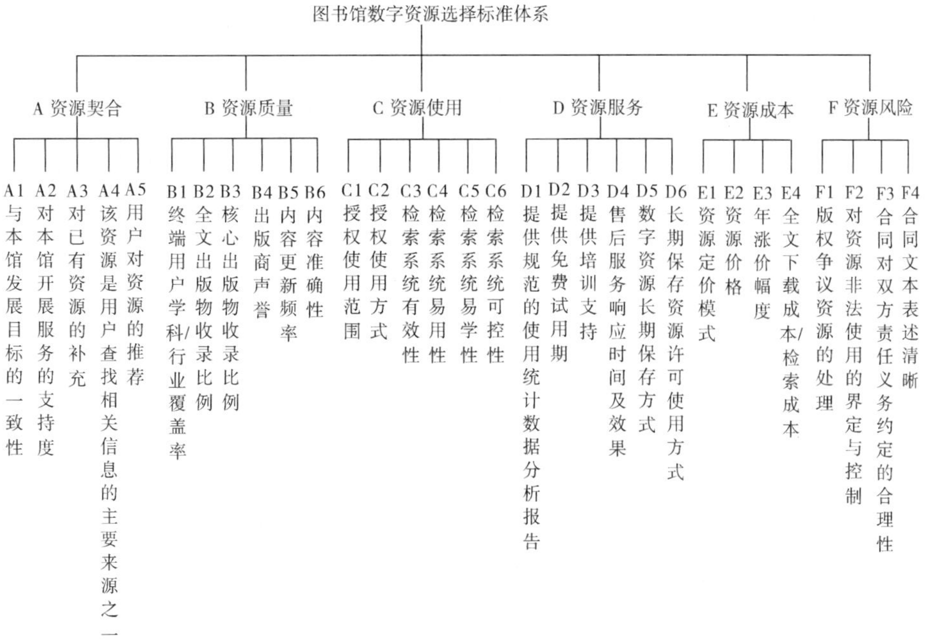

图 1　图书馆数字资源选择标准体系

4　研究结论

从国内外已有研究及图书馆馆藏发展政策中提出的数字资源选择标准来看，虽然不同群体对于数字资源选择标准的认识存在差异，但综合来看，可将其归纳为 6 个方面：资源质量、资源使用、资源服务、资源契合、资源成本、资源风险。本研究以这 6 个方面为图书馆数字资源选择标准体系设计的维度，结合图书馆发展实际，提出相关选择标准，得到图书馆数字资源选择标准体系的初始集合。在此基础上，通过专家问卷调查法验证各选择标准的重要性和适用性，采用因子分析等统计分析方法提炼、确立一套关联度、代表性和适用性均较强的图书馆数字资源选择标准体系。本研究的调查对象来自高校图书馆、公共图书馆、科研图书馆和国家图书馆从事数字资源选择相关工作的实践专家，最终确立的图书馆数字资源选择标准体系是在综合其意见的基础上得出，在不同类型、规模的图书馆均有较为普遍的应用价值。

参考文献

[1] Holleman C. Electronic Resources: Are Basic Criteria for the Selection of Materials Changing [J]. Library Trends, 2000, 48 (4): 694 - 710.

[2] Clayton P, Gorman G E. Managing Information Resources in Libraries: Collection Management in Theory and Practice

[M]. London: Library Association Publishing, 2001: 94.
[3] Johnson P. Selecting Electronic Resources: Developing a Local Decision Making Matrix [J]. Cataloging and Classification Quaterly, 1996, 22 (3/4): 9 - 24.
[4] Lee L A, Wu M M. Do Librarians Dream of Electronic Serials? A Beginner's Guide to Format Selection [J]. The Bottom Line: Managing Library Finances, 2002, 15 (3): 102 - 109.
[5] 罗春荣，曹树金．电子馆藏及其发展政策研究［J］．大学图书馆学报，2001（2）：37－41．
[6] 肖珑，张宇红．电子资源评价指标体系的建立初探［J］．大学图书馆学报，2002（3）：35－42．
[7] 张晓林，宛玲，徐引篪，等．国家科学数字图书馆数字资源采购的技术要求［J］．中国图书馆学报，2004（4）：14－19．
[8] International Coalition of Library Consortia. Statement of Current Perspective and Preferred Practices for Selection and Purchase of Electronic Information (Update No. 2, pricing and economics) (2004) [OL]. [2010 - 01 - 25]. http://www.library.yale.edu/consortia/2004currentpractices.htm.
[9] Jewell T D. Selection and Presentation of Commercially Available Electronic Resources: Issues and Practices (2001) [OL]. [2010 - 01 - 25]. http://www.clir.org/pubs/reports/pub99/contents.html.
[10] CALIS 引进资源工作组．CALIS 引进资源工作规范（2006）［OL］．［2010－02－21］．http://www.calis.edu.cn/calisnew/images1/070913/4.doc.
[11] CONCERT 电子资源选择政策［OL］．（2006－04－17）［2010－02－21］．http://info.zjei.net/content/tsghy_0111/article01.doc.
[12] Library of Congress. Electronic Resources, Selection Guidelines (2004) [OL]. [2010 - 02 - 25]. http://www.loc.gov/acq/devpol/electronicselectionguidelines.html.
[13] 国家图书馆．国家图书馆文献采选条例（2002）［OL］．［2010－02－25］．http://www.nlc.gov.cn/old/res/caixuan.htm.
[14] Hongkong University Library. Electronic Resources Collection Development Policy [OL]. [2010 - 02 - 21]. http://lib.hku.hk/cd/policies/erp.html.
[15] Electronic Access to Information Resources Committee of California State University. Principles for CSU Acquisition of Electronic Information Resources (2005) [OL]. [2010 - 02 - 21]. http://seir.calstate.edu/ear/docs/principles.doc.
[16] National Agricultural Library. Electronic Resources Selection Policy [OL]. (2002 - 04 - 15) [2010 - 02 - 21]. http://www.nal.usda.gov/about/policy/coll_dev_add2.shtml.
[17] 林杰斌，林川熊，刘明德，等．SPSS 12 统计建模与应用实务［M］．2 版．北京：中国铁道出版社，2005：496．
[18] 宋健．基于 AHP 和因子分析的地区信用环境指标体系构建的实证研究［J］．中国软科学，2006（6）：111－119．
[19] 刘举，刘云，曾诚．基于因子分析法的综合大学创新力指标研究［J］．科学学与科学技术管理，2007（10）：111－114．
[20] 徐革．重构电子资源综合评价指标的主成分分析法［J］．图书情报工作，2004（2）：32－34．
[21] 吴明隆．SPSS 统计应用实务——问卷分析与应用统计［M］．北京：科学出版社，2003：67．

教师简介：

周旖，女，中山大学管理学学士、历史学博士。2010年起任教于中山大学资讯管理学院，硕士生导师。主讲“信息资源共享”（国家级精品课程）、“文献保护与修复”（广东省教改课程、校级双语课程）、“外国档案管理”、“社会科学研究方法”、“文献标引”、“图书与图书馆史”（广东省精品资源共享课程）等本科生课程。研究方向包括文献保护项目管理、文献保护教育、馆藏日常维护、图书馆与档案馆的社会角色、公共信息政策、档案职业资格认证与档案学教育、教会大学图书馆史与藏书史、近代图书馆史与藏书史、邹鲁校长与中山大学校史。主持和参加科研项目近30项，出版学术专著2部，在专业核心期刊上发表学术论文近30篇，获各级教学和科研奖励近10项。2014年多伦多大学信息学院访问学者。高等学校985基地项目“文献遗产保护与修复研究创新基地”成员。联系方式：zhouyi37@ mail. sysu. edu. cn. 。

所选论文《岭南大学图书馆中文善本书研究》原载于《图书资讯学刊》（台北），2012年第10卷第1期

岭南大学图书馆中文善本书研究[①]

周　旖

摘　要：论文所研究的“岭南大学”特指以1888年建校的格致书院为前身，一脉发展而来，并于1952年院系合并时停办的广州岭南大学。岭南大学图书馆旧藏中文善本书的主体现保存于广州中山大学图书馆，是其馆藏中文古籍善本之重要来源之一。论文从数量、来源和特色三个层面对岭南大学图书馆旧藏中文善本书进行介绍和分析，并通过岭南大学的办学方针、教育理念和学术研究等角度的研究解释善本馆藏特色的成因。岭南大学图书馆在抗日战争爆发前藏有经、史、子、集各类善本图书共计174种，善本图书是以曾钊的旧藏为主体，其来源还包括徐甘棠、潘宗周、徐绍桢、甘翰臣等人的捐赠，方志类善本的建设则与美国国会图书馆亚洲部中国方志的建设有一定的联系。馆藏中文善本书的特色体现在多明本和抄本，重视对明代史料和明人文集的收集，在广东地方志和广东文献的收藏方面尤其突出。

关键词：中文善本；广东地方志；广东文献；藏书建设；岭南大学图书馆

Study of Chinese Rare Books of Lingnan University Library

Yi Zhou

Abstract: The Lingnan University in this article specifically refers to the Guangzhou Lingnan University, whose

---

① 论文系广州市哲学社会科学规划课题青年项目“岭南大学旧藏中外‘岭南文献’研究”（项目编号：11Q01）系列研究成果之一。

forerunner was a Christian college, which was built in 1888 and ceased operations in 1952 because of the adjustment of disciplines throughout the country. The main part of Chinese rare books of Lingnan University Library are now being stored in Sun Yat-sen University and have become an important source of its Chinese rare books collection. This article intends to analyze the quantity, sources, and characteristics of these Chinese rare books, and explain the cause of characteristics by doing research on the guiding principle, education concept, and academic research of Lingnan University. Before the breaking-out of Anti-Japanese War, Lingnan University had 174 kinds of Chinese rare books. It comprised predominantly Zhao Zeng's collections, and also donations from Gantang Xu, Zongzhou Pan, Shaozhen Xu, Hanchen Gan, etc. The construction of rare local records had been influenced by the Asian Division of the Library of Congress of the United States. The prominent characteristics of the existing collection include: (1) it comprises a large quantity of prints and manuscripts of the Ming Dynasty; (2) it particularly highlights the historical and literary records of the Ming Dynasty; and (3) it has an outstanding collection of Guangdong local records and literature.

Keywords: Chinese rare books; Local records of Guangdong Province; Documents on Guangdong Province; Collection developing; Lingnan university library

1 引　言

“岭南大学”这一机构名称可指代广州岭南大学、香港岭南大学、中山大学岭南（大学）学院以及韩国岭南大学。本论文中之“岭南大学”特指以1888年建校的格致书院为前身，一脉发展而来，并于1952年院系调整时停办的广州岭南大学。论文中所研究之中文善本书在岭南大学停办后，其主体现保存于广州中山大学图书馆，成为其馆藏中文古籍善本之重要来源之一。

广州岭南大学是一所由广州海内外基督教人士发起筹办的教会大学。[1] 其特别之处在于她是20世纪30年代期间中国13所基督教新教大学中唯一一所不属于任何教派和组织所有的学校。岭南大学，初称格致书院（Christian College in China），1884年由美籍传教士香便文牧师（Rev. B. C. Henry D. D.）及哈巴牧师（Rev. A. P. Happer D. D.）等向美国长老会传道万国总会（American Presbyterian Board of Foreign Mission）提议倡办，1886年募得2.5万美元，是年4月脱离总会另立董事局主持一切，1888年开校于广州沙基金利埠（即今广州六二三路）。此后历经停办、几经迁徙，于1904年定永久校址于广州河南康乐，校舍不断增加，学务持续扩充，图书、仪器、标本之设备亦日渐完善。[2]

20世纪20年代，“非基运动”在中国境内蔓延，随着该运动与反帝运动力量的合流，[3] 各行各业纷纷要求收回相关主权，于教育界即要求收回教育主权。在这种历史背景下，岭南大学成为中国首个完全收归国人自办的教会大学。1927年1月11日，私立岭南大学校董会正式成立，宣布学校为私立的、中国人主权的，举钟荣光博士为校长。[1]19 1945年纽约基督教大学联合董事会制定中国战后复兴基督教计划，其内容包括拟将现有大学分两等办理，岭南大学与燕京大学两所学校被列入第一等。[4]

岭南大学图书馆成立于1906年，其始为教员阅书参考室，规模甚小，初设于马丁堂，与博物标本室合建。其时所藏书籍，多属西文，均为美国人士捐赠。随着书籍日增，先与博物标本室分离，继而于1915年迁入新建成之格兰堂。1917年岭南学堂升级为大学，馆务亦随之逐渐扩充。1919 年始设专职馆长之职，聘图书馆专门人才特嘉（Jessie Douglass）女士为馆长。其上任后，积极整顿，对于分类、编目、购订、出纳种种手续，力图改善。

作为一所由美国传教士提议创办的大学，成立之初的岭南大学图书馆藏书以英文书籍为主，但也拥有若干中文藏书，并在历年购买和接受捐赠过程中数量有所增加，但是图书馆始终没有聘请专人整理中文书籍，更无从事中文藏书的部门。1919 年春，彭美赉（Owen E. Pomeroy）委任教授陈德芸襄理图书馆中文藏书事宜，自此中籍部成立，陈德芸为主任。[5]中籍部藏书的基础主要来自 1920 年陈德芸亲赴上海北平各处劝捐所得之 16000 余册书籍。

1928 年，科学院建成后，校址既增，图书馆遂由格兰堂迁往马丁堂二楼全座，稍事扩充后复得取用一楼、二楼全座及三楼之一部分。抗日战争爆发前，岭南大学图书馆的藏书总量居全国大学图书馆之第五名。[6]

1950 年 6 月爆发的抗美援朝战争使中美关系恶化，这一政治上的正面冲突反应在文化、教育界，表现为中国政府决定加快清理教育界所受英美文化的影响，学习苏联教育改革的思路，通过院系调整建立起一套“苏联模式”的社会主义大学制度，把私立大学和教会大学全部改为公立。[7]128岭南大学在这一场高等教育改革中最终停办。

1952 年，根据中央院系调整的方针和原则，岭南大学与原中山大学、华南联合大学和广东法商学院四所院校的理科各系合并组成一所新的综合性大学——中山大学；原中山大学、广东法商学院原有的商科和华南联合大学的财经学院并入新的中山大学；岭南大学文学院除教育系外，文科各系也并入新的中山大学文学院。岭南大学文学院的教育系并入华南师范学院（今华南师范大学）。原中山大学、岭南大学、华南联合大学的工科各系和广东省工业专科学校调整组成新建立的华南工学院（今华南理工大学）。原中山大学农学院和岭南大学农学院共同组成新建立的华南农学院（今华南农业大学）。原中山大学医学院、岭南大学医学院与光华医学院组成华南医学院（后称中山医科大学，现为中山大学医学院）。[7]130

根据以上院系调整的方案，岭南大学图书馆的藏书也进行了相应的移交，故图书馆藏书的流布情况如下：原理科及人文科学相关藏书的主体现保存于中山大学图书馆，原善本古籍、“中国问题研究”西文出版物等专藏的主体亦保存于中山大学图书馆；因原华南医学院现为中山大学医学院，故原分配给华南医学院的岭南大学医学藏书亦尽数藏于中山大学北校区图书馆；原教育类藏书现存于华南师范大学图书馆；原工科类藏书现藏于华南理工大学；原农学类藏书现藏于华南农业大学。

自 1952 年院系合并至今已有近 60 年的时间，期间中国社会又经历了种种变化，岭南大学图书馆被划分至各个学校的旧藏，因各种原因多有流入旧书市场中，或以废纸变卖，于是藏书一再易手，或存或废。而当年岭南大学图书馆堪称特色并著称于世的中文善本古籍、“中国问题研究”西文出版物、西文理科学术期刊和 1911 年至 1937 年的日报全份亦难逃厄运，其收藏、建设及至后来的散佚情况均有待研究和考证。

2 馆藏中文善本书之数量

据岭南大学《馆藏善本图书题识》[8]1凡例所言，岭南大学图书馆将符合如下三条标准的文献作为善本图书：一为图书馆历年所藏之元、明刊本及旧抄、稿本；二为清代刊本中的稀见佳本，如《粤海关志》、《粤闽巡视纪略》等；三为各流传较少的刊本、抄本和稿本。对于流传广泛的书籍，即使价值昂贵，亦不作为善本。

论文所研究的岭南大学图书馆馆藏中文善本书以抗日战争爆发前的收藏为主，原因有二：第一，岭南大学图书馆所藏善本书绝大多数入藏于抗日战争爆发之前，而在1937年到1952年岭南大学停办这15年间，因先后经历抗日战争、解放战争以及受战后经济和局势的影响，入藏的善本图书数量不多；第二，抗日战争期间，馆藏善本图书多有损毁、丢失，实际较战前已不甚完整，1952年院系调整时藏书又被调拨分配，故抗日战争爆发后直至岭南大学停办这一阶段善本图书的增益、散失情况有待继续深入研究。

据对岭南大学1937年版的《馆藏善本图书题识》的统计，在抗日战争爆发前图书馆藏有经、史、子、集各类善本图书共计174种，11302卷，另不分卷者654册，其中以明刻（刊）本为最多，抄本次之，馆藏最早的版本为元刊本。在所有善本书中，史部数量为最多，其次为子部，再次为集部，而经部善本图书数量为最少；若以二级类目观之，则属地理类的方志善本数量为最多，其次多者分别为明别集类和类书类。各类中文善本图书的数量分布情况与岭南大学的办学方针和教学理念，以及图书馆历年来在藏书建设中重点建设的学科相吻合。抗日战争前岭南大学图书馆藏善本图书的具体统计数据如表1所示，对于每种图书的统计，若分卷则统计卷数，不分卷则统计册数，并以数字加“c”表示册数。

表1　抗日战争前岭南大学图书馆馆藏善本图书统计

分类		抄本		稿本		元刊本		明刻（刊）本		明评阅本		清刻（刊）本		民国印本		合计	
		种数	卷册	种数	卷册	种数	卷册	种数	卷册	种数	卷册	种数	卷册	种数	卷册	种数	卷册
经部	易类	2	18					1	4							3	22
	礼类							3	157							3	157
	春秋类							2	42							2	42
	四书类							1	4							1	4
	乐类	1	10													1	10
	小学类	2	36	1	4c			3	78			3	44			9	158+4c
	小计	5	64	1	4c			10	285			3	44			19	393+4c
史部	正史类	2	250+5c					1	85	2	493					5	828+5c
	编年类	4	254					2	63							6	317
	纪事本末类	1	1c									1	5			2	5+1c

续表 1

分类		抄本		稿本		元刊本		明刻（刊）本		明评阅本		清刻（刊）本		民国印本		合计	
		种数	卷册	种数	卷册	种数	卷册	种数	卷册	种数	卷册	种数	卷册	种数	卷册	种数	卷册
史部	杂史类	3	26 +1c				3	281								6	307 +1c
	诏令奏议类	4	12 +27c									2	323			6	335 +27c
	传记类	1	1					2	34 +1c							3	35 +1c
	地理类	8	768					6	71			12	272	1	22	27	1133
	政书类	2	100					4	358							6	458
	目录类	1	4													1	4
	史评类	1	101					3	40							4	141
	小计	27	1516 +34c					21	932 +1c	2	493	15	600	1	22	66	3563 +35c
子部	儒家类					2	30	1	1c			1	66			4	96 +1c
	兵家类	4	59					3	263							7	322
	农家类	2	20													2	20
	天文算法类	3	42					1	72			1	42			5	156
	术数类	2	130													2	130
	艺术类							1	20							1	20
	杂家类	1	30					4	153			1	50			6	233
	类书类							10	2274							10	2274
	丛书类	2	498c					1	71			3	886			6	957 +498c
	小说类							1	64c							1	64c
	道家类	1				1	8									2	8
	小计	15	281 +498c			3	38	22	2853 +65c			6	1044			46	4129 +564c

续表 1

分类		抄本		稿本		元刊本		明刻（刊）本		明评阅本		清刻（刊）本		民国印本		合计	
		种数	卷册	种数	卷册	种数	卷册	种数	卷册	种数	卷册	种数	卷册	种数	卷册	种数	卷册
集部	唐别集	1	20					2	10			1	30			4	60
	宋元别集	1	4					2	64							3	68
	明别集							18	311+4c			2	65			20	376+4c
	清别集	1	23									3	53			4	76
	总集类	1	1					2	17			3	2222+48c			6	2240+48c
	诗文评							2	270							2	270
	词曲类							1	20			3	20			4	40
	小计	4	48					27	592+4c			12	2390+48c			43	3130+52c
合计		51	1909+532c	1	4c	3	38	80	4762+70c	2	493	36	4078+48c	1	22	174	11302+654c

3　馆藏中文善本书之来源

岭南大学图书馆馆藏中文善本书的来源主要为徐甘棠、潘宗周、徐绍桢和甘翰臣四人所赠，另有图书馆从广东藏书家顺德温氏后人和书肆处所购温氏及南海曾钊旧藏。而顺德温氏、徐甘棠、潘宗周、徐绍桢和甘翰臣等人的藏书中亦多曾钊故物，就《馆藏善本图书题识》的著录观之，在 174 种馆藏善本图书中，钤有曾钊藏书印的善本图书达 70 种，而其他未钤有曾钊藏书印的图书中亦有属于曾钊者，故可以说岭南大学的善本图书是以曾钊的旧藏为主体。现将善本图书的各来源分述于下。

3.1　曾钊面城楼旧藏

岭南大学图书馆大批购入曾钊旧藏主要是在 1935—1936 学年度。据这一年度的馆务报告记载，时图书馆以极低廉的价格购入曾钊旧藏佳本颇多，如明刊本之《两朝从新录》、《昭代典则》、《夏桂洲先生文集》、《思玄集》、《想玄集》、《屏山集》、《冯琢庵文集》、《百可亭摘稿》、《韦苏州集》、《祝氏集略》、《弥雅翼》（正德本棉纸）、《邱文庄公集》、《礼记集说》（棉纸）、《礼记注疏》（棉纸）、《頖宫礼乐疏》等 30 多种。[9] 加之在 1935—1936 学年度前后陆续购入的曾氏藏书，到抗日战争爆发前岭南大学图书馆馆藏善本中有其旧藏至少不下70种。何多源在为岭南大学《馆藏善本图书题识》所作的自序中有言：

益年来顺德温氏旧藏曾钊抄本善本逐渐流出，此种抄本善本，多为宋明史书，明人文集，近日绝少流传者。本馆以其罕见传稀，且不少为国内孤本，而亦为研究明史之重要史料，故特为尽量购求，而旧藏主人亦以本馆藏有此种图书较其私人保存为有用，亦愿以较通行本为廉之书价让与本馆。[8]1

曾钊（1793—1854），字勉士，又字敏修，广东南海人士，1825年（道光五年）选乙酉科拔贡，官合浦教谕，调钦州学正，1826年秋举学海堂学长。[10]16曾钊是清代广东地区的著名藏书家。同为粤省著名藏书家的吴兰修曾言：

岭南地湿，易长蠹鱼，藏书无至二百年者，吾家守经堂藏本多于勉士，而旧椠不及焉。勉士尝云：当无聊时，阅古人书目，亦自快意。可想见其癖好矣。[10]17-18

周连宽在《广东藏书家曾钊》一文中则评价道：

清嘉庆、道光两朝，广东出了许多著名的学者，或以诗文雄于时，或以经学道行为世所宗仰，或以史地金石之学见称于当代，而藏书之富，则以曾钊为最。……昔洪北江谓藏书家有数等，即考订家，校雠家，收藏家，赏鉴家，掠贩家。叶焕彬则谓考订校雠可合并之，统名著述家。除掠贩家已入市贾之流，为学者所耻为之外，举上述诸家而褒之者，吾粤曾勉士，可当之而无愧。[11]

曾钊一生喜读书，亦喜藏书，每遇古本辄爱不释手，“即力所不及，亦必多方购求之。既得之后，又必寝食其中，校讹正谬，剖析异同”[11]，故所藏图书“多有题跋，丹黄殆遍，经勉士审订者，钤一‘善本’二字印章”[10]16。其藏书之所初名“古输廖山馆”，后因地方潮湿、狭窄，又筑“面城楼”储之，所藏图书一般钤有“面城楼藏书印”、“曾钊之印”、“曾氏珍本印”、“曾钊印”、“曾钊面城楼藏书印”、“勉士”。

曾氏因博通掌籍，故长于训诂，著有《周礼注疏小笺》和《面城楼集》。陈璞在《面城楼集序》中云：

勉士劬于学，考据精确，最长于核证典礼，辨证经传。生平抱用世志，战守兵法，无不研究。道光辛丑、壬寅间，夷事孔棘，制府祁墳，檄令修碉筑坝，募勇团守。旋因议款，敌兵不至，而所支帑不能报销者至三十二万余金，倾家不偿，坐此免官，藏书数万卷，并质于人。[10]18

此文中所述及之事即指鸦片战争时期，曾钊受命带兵抵御外敌，修筑蚺蛇洞等炮台。钊为恂恂儒者，而胸罗十万甲兵，其为建造炮台，殚精竭虑，创“之”字型台，以勾股之法测定炮台射线，极富现代科学原理。然因事起突然，动工仓促，未及逐一收集工程凭证，故事后清理账目，不能报销者达32万余金，又因祁墳故去，对立者以此事讦之，以致曾钊被免职，倾家荡产亦不足抵偿缺欠，故其藏书全部散出。[11]

曾钊面城楼藏书散出后，大部分为顺德龙山温澍梁所得，其藏书之处名“漱绿楼”；另一部分则入于顺德大良龙凤镳的六篆楼。温澍梁为温汝适、温汝能之族人，清代龙山温氏家族声名显赫，一直晴耕雨读，诗书传礼，温汝适曾官至兵部侍郎。[12]《群书跋·万卷菁华前集》云：“温氏族人有澍梁者，善收藏，颇称富有，而以出自面城楼者为善本”。龙凤镳，字伯鸾，官某部员外，其家族亦“累代显宦，藏书丰富，六篆楼所藏，不少精椠”[10]61-62，其中既收有李文田太华楼藏书，又收有曾钊旧藏部分。

后来温氏藏书、龙氏藏书亦陆续流出，其中部分为岭南大学图书馆收入，故岭南大学图书馆抗日战争前所藏曾钊旧藏中，除钤有曾氏各类藏书印以外，还有20种善本图书上同时钤有温氏各类藏书印，如岭南温氏印、岭南温氏珍藏印、岭南温树材珍藏印、龙山温氏珍藏印、漱绿楼藏书印、漱绿楼书画印、漱绿楼印、顺德温季材之印、顺德温氏藏书印、顺德温氏家藏印、顺德温氏所藏金石书画之印、顺德温氏印和温澍梁藏书印；有5种善本图书上同时钤有龙凤镳各类藏书印，如六篆楼藏书印、六篆楼印和六篆山堂印。

此外，依据岭南大学图书馆1935—1936学年度馆务报告可知，《馆藏善本图书题识》中收录的《夏桂洲先生文集》、《冯琢庵文集》、《韦苏州集》和《邱文庄公集》，虽未著录曾氏藏书印，但是也为曾氏旧藏。另有《两朝从新录》、《弥雅翼》和《礼记注疏》亦为曾氏旧藏明代佳本，但在《馆藏善本图书题识》中未有著录。而岭南大学图书馆所藏温澍梁旧藏中的《历代名臣奏议》、《两浙海防类考续编》、《千一疏》和《五朝小说》，以及六篆楼旧藏中的《经籍志》、《何氏类镕》、《古今逸史》、《唐诗纪》和《观象玩占》等书上未钤有曾钊藏书印，故是否为曾氏旧藏尚不可知。

3.2 徐甘棠赠书

《馆藏善本图书题识》中所载有17种书籍为岭南大学校友徐甘棠捐赠，其中11种为明代刊本，多为曾钊、温澍梁和龙凤镳旧藏。徐甘棠（1875—1935），广东花县人，早年肄业于培英学校，聪颖强记，刻苦卓绝，独好西学，“年最少而成绩为全校冠”。1897年被聘为格致书院教员，并始于教学之余专攻国学，研习诗词。1905年，徐甘棠一方面兼任夏葛医学院化学教授，一方面“以国内西学仅具皮毛，欲求精深，非从外国求之不可”，而在岭南学堂学习英文。1907年徐甘棠赴美留学，为筹集学费而在美担任青年会总干事兼《大同日报》记者，积极宣扬革命，主笔三年，稍有余蓄，即入俄克拉何马州立大学（University of Oklahoma）学习数学，获学士学位后入西北大学研究院，获数学硕士学位。1917年徐甘棠回国，1918年受聘于商务印书馆，编辑数学及大学辞典，旋任江苏省教育会月刊总编辑，月刊停办后就南京高师数学教授职。1921年徐甘棠返粤，担任广东高师数学教授，高师改组为广东大学后，出任数学系主任，后又担任工专、执信、培英等校教授，兼教务主任。广东大学改国立中山大学后，徐甘棠受聘为教务主任兼教授，不久又赴南京，历任教育厅秘书、民政厅秘书、南京立法院秘书。1927年后徐甘棠返回广东，先后担任广州工务局局长秘书、市府秘书长兼教育局长、市立第二中学校长、培英教务长、中山大学教务主任、建设厅秘书长。1932年，邹鲁重掌国立中山大学，徐甘棠再次被聘为教授，兼广东通志馆主任。1935年5月31日，徐甘棠因急性肾炎病逝。[13]

徐甘棠的文章“气格苍古，上追秦汉”，中年以后对国学研究饶有兴趣，并由此产生搜集古籍的爱好，积书数万卷，以经史子集为最多，其中不乏海内孤本，渐成广东知名藏书家。徐甘棠去世后，其夫人罗秀云将其所遗中西文藏书赠予岭南大学图书馆，计西文书80册，以数学书籍为主；中文书1222种，20057册，[14]其中包括丛书54种，类书9种，经籍64种，史乘77种，方志123种，文集250种，杂类645种[15]。其赠书中有明代汲古阁刊本的《中州集》、清内府刻本桃花纸的《（御纂）朱子全书》等善本17种，书上钤有“徐甘棠藏书印”。所赠清道光刻本《粤海关志》流传颇少，是研究清代广东海关制度、设置及贸易情况的重要参考文献；明正德戊寅（1518）刊本《四川志》为海内外孤本，朱士嘉《中国地方志综录》载海内外图书馆所藏《四川志》只有嘉靖本、万历本、康熙本等，刊刻年代均晚于徐甘棠赠给岭南大学图书馆的《四川志》。

3.3 潘宗周赠书

潘宗周（1867—1939），字明训，广东南海人。少时供职上海洋行，后任沪英租界工部局总办，经商成巨富，以巨资藏书，尤重宋刻，编有《宝礼堂宋本书录》四卷，附录一卷，收入20年所积宋版书99种107部，元本6种6部，是书目由张元济作序。[16]潘宗周藏书之处名为宝礼堂，藏书上一般钤有“南海潘明训珍藏印”。徐信符《广东藏书纪事诗》中载：

宗周虽执业商廛，壮岁获交宜都杨守敬，慨然有收书之志。喜储宋椠，初以百种为限，后已逾限矣。其眼识极高，元明以下，视之蔑如也。从袁克文购得宋刊《礼记》，乃南渡后三山黄唐所刻，旧藏曲阜孔氏，海内传为孤本。潘氏适构新居，因颜其堂曰“宝礼”。[10]115-116

明清以来的广东藏书家中，以宋本收藏著称者惟有丰顺丁日昌之持静斋，潘氏宝礼堂则为后起者。宝礼堂藏书中有杨守敬旧藏，亦多黄丕烈“百宋一廛”、汪士钟“艺芸精舍”、郁松年“宜稼堂”、杨氏“海源阁”、韩应陛“读有用书斋”散出之物，袁世凯洪宪失败后，所藏善本旧椠十之六七为潘氏所得。

岭南大学图书馆共藏有元本3种，分别为《（纂图互注）荀子》、《（纂图互注）扬子法言》和《冲虚至德真经》，均为潘明训所赠，而此三种书在《宝礼堂宋本书录》中均无著录。其中《冲虚至德真经》为杨守敬旧藏，有宜都杨氏藏书印、杨印守敬、杨氏小像和弘前医涩汪氏藏书记朱印。杨守敬的藏书曾以国币3.5万元鬻诸国民政府，后政府将大部分藏书交与故宫博物院保存，并由该院何澄一编成《观海堂书目》付梓行世，岭南大学图书馆所藏《冲虚至德真经》为此书目内未载之书，《国立北平图书馆善本书目》中亦未载有此本。[8]55-56此外，收入岭南大学图书馆《馆藏善本图书题识》的潘明训赠书还有明刊本《（东莱先生音注）唐鉴》、明万历郑云斋刊本《（笺注决科）古今源流至论》、吴门缪曰芑仿宋刊本《李太白集》和清乾隆三年五色套印内府刻本《（御选）唐宋文醇》。

3.4 其他捐赠来源

岭南大学图书馆藏中文善本书，除来自前述徐甘棠和潘宗周的大宗捐赠外，得自徐绍桢和甘翰臣的捐赠亦不少，何多源在《馆藏善本图书题识》自序中有言珍藏善本有赖于徐甘棠、潘宗周、徐绍桢和甘翰臣所赠。

在《馆藏善本图书馆题识》中，著录有“徐固卿赠”者计有6种，其中4种为明本，2种为旧抄本，《资治通鉴》、《宋元通鉴》均为明天启年间陈仁锡评阅本，而明万历刊本《南征录》则为清宗室怡府明善堂旧藏。徐绍桢（1868—1934），字固卿，广东番禺人。

其先父徐子远曾参总督节署慕，而娴于经术，家富藏书，藏书处名为通介堂、水南楼、攟云阁。徐绍桢继承家学，收藏甚富，中光绪甲午科（1894）广东乡试举人，嗜书并精版本研究，虽历任军职、戎马一生，却始终书卷相随。徐绍桢于光宣间在南京治兵，于后湖湖神庙之左建藏书楼，藏书不下20余万册，因辛亥起义，藏书尽为张勋所焚。民国成立，徐绍桢历任南京卫戍总督、孙中山广东军政府广州卫戍总司令、总统府参军长、广东省长和内政部长等职，并重新搜求图书。寓居北平时期，与琉璃厂书肆来往最密，所藏复充牣，著有《学寿堂题跋》。其晚年因境遇所迫，藏书散佚，珍本无存。[10]112-114

甘翰臣是在沪经商的广东中山人士，曾担任上海公和祥码头买办、怡和洋行总办，并担任岭南大学上海分校的校董。[17]甘翰臣生前在上海筑有非园、愚园，好藏金石书画，与沪上文化界素有往来，与康有为、叶恭绰、朱祖谋、梅兰芳、程砚秋等人均有交情。抗日战争胜利后，其女甘恕先曾将其生前收藏的30多件广东文物交原广东文献馆馆长简又文携归广州，其中包括现藏于广东省博物馆的“刘猛进碑”。[18]岭南大学图书馆抗日战争前藏有的善本图书中，有3种为甘翰臣所赠，分别为明黄国琦刊本《册府元龟》、清康熙四十九年内府刊本《渊鉴类涵》和殿板初印《（钦定）全唐文》。

作为一所大学图书馆，其收藏的善本图书必然是多年来涓滴搜罗而致。岭南大学图书馆所藏的善本图书除通过各种管道而购得的曾钊、温澍梁、龙凤镳旧藏，以及得自徐甘棠、潘宗周、徐绍桢和甘翰臣赠书外，还有其他相当广泛的来源。如哲学史家、民俗学家容肇祖就曾为岭南大学图书馆搜购文献，馆藏明刻官书精品《春秋经传》、旧抄本《光孝寺志》、清道光南海吴氏筠清馆刊本《石云山人集》等都来自容肇祖的搜购，其中《光孝寺志》书有容肇祖题跋，《石云山人集》书前有容肇祖手录之该书作者吴荷屋传。

由于当时对采访文献的文字记载有限，而保存下来的档案和相关文献亦非齐全，因此很难逐一查析每种书的具体来源。但由馆藏善本图书上钤印的藏书章，或可窥见藏书的渊源，以下所列即为馆藏善本图书上钤有的除曾钊、温澍梁、龙凤镳、徐甘棠和潘宗周藏书印以外的其他家藏书印：陈澧印、兰甫印、登斋藏书印、栋臣印、方氏碧琳琅馆藏书印、冯钤士印、衡阳常氏藏书印、弘前医涩汪氏藏书记朱印、黄芝仙印、璜川吴氏图书印、汲古阁印、静观亭图书印、毛氏子晋印、明善堂所藏书画印记、明善堂珍藏书画之印、南海式之苏氏所藏印、南海苏氏藏书印、南海苏式印、晴臯印、汤子寿读书印、吴琯圆形小印、吴氏家藏印、锡山李氏珍藏之印、阳湖陶氏印、杨守敬小印、杨氏小像、杨印守敬、宜都杨氏藏书印、赵氏鉴藏印、朱彝尊印和竹垞藏本印。

3.5 方志类善本书的来源

据表1《抗日战争前岭南大学图书馆馆藏善本图书统计》数据可知，岭南大学图书馆在抗日战争前藏有中文善本书共计174种，其中地理类的善本书共计27种，超过史部善本书种数的三分之一，为数量最多的二级类目。另据中山大学图书馆藏岭南大学档案缩微胶卷Ree136中的档案 *List of Rare Books in Chinese to be Filmed* 显示，1940年2月岭南大学图书馆将一批馆藏中文善本图书制成缩微胶卷，其中明清两代修纂的广东各地方志数量已达89种，较之1937年出版的《馆藏善本图书题识》中收录的种数多出了62种之多。这从一个侧面反映出岭南大学图书馆在藏书建设过程中，对地方志收集的重视程度。从来源上看，岭南大学图书馆所拥有的方志类善本书多来自搜购，并以曾钊旧藏为主。而以目前笔者所掌握档案资料线索分析之，岭南大学图书馆对方志的采购或与美国国会图书馆亚洲部的方志存在一定的联系。

广东省档案馆收藏的岭南大学档案中，有一通1919年9月2日中籍部主任陈德芸向特嘉馆长汇报中文书籍整理的手续及将来之计划的信函，函中言：

……顾中籍分部，迄无善法，经史子集既不适宜包罗新籍，若仿杜威十目类书法按之，旧籍又多未合，今拟按照施永高先生所列书目，暂用旧法，其新籍可编入旧门类者，仍行附入，……[5]

函中所言之“旧法”是指当时美国国会图书馆对中文书所采用的五部分类法，而函中提及的施永高（Walter T. Swingle），又作施永格，是美国农业部的植物学专家、农林学专家，有志于把中国的优良蔬果种子移植到美国，他发现中国地方志有关于土壤和植物的记载，于是向美国政府建议扩大对中国方志的收集。[19] 1918年4月至1919年7月间，施永高代表美国国会图书馆到中国各省采访地方志，搜购了大量典籍。他通过张元济等版本目录学专家的帮助，收集了413种地方志，其中包括2种省志、87种府志、324种县志，既有官修地方志，亦有非官修地理著作，其中很多即使在中国都已经非常罕见。[20]回国以后，他仍继续为美国国会图书馆间接地采购，直到1928年止。美国国会图书馆现藏的中国旧方志，有一半以上是1928年以前入藏的，该馆大规模的入藏中国方志要归功于施永高。[19]

岭南大学图书馆拥有施永高所列之书目，除参考其分类法以外，也将其作为购书的参考，以施永高当时在中国国内搜集书籍的类别观之，或可推测岭南大学图书馆在当时购入了大量方志类的文献，而其目的也是为支持该校农科教学和研究。另据《岭南大学文献目录：广州岭南大学历史档案数据》[2]的英文档案索引可知，施永高在1919—1921年间以及1928—1929年间，与岭南大学的格兰（W. Henry Grant）先生、晏文士（Dr. Charles K. Edmunds）校长和香雅各（Rev. James M. Henry）校长有多通往来函件，故据此也可推测两所图书馆之间在方志收藏方面应该存在一定的联系，而具体情况仍需要在获取此方面档案内容之后做深入研究。

3.6 1937年后对广东藏书家旧藏的访购

抗日战争爆发后至岭南大学停办的15年间，岭南大学图书馆也陆续购入了若干广东藏书家散佚出的旧藏。李文田泰华楼藏书的精华在抗日战争期间运存香港，广州、香港相继沦陷后，藏书流散，但寄存于北平燕京大学的明代野史得获保全，周连宽和容庚曾赴平拜访李文田之孙李劲庵，为岭南大学图书馆选购明人集部及其他明刻本数十种，取价均廉。又有李劲庵清理出水渍损失的图书一大批，依重量计价出售，周连宽为岭南大学图书馆选得有李文田朱笔批校之图书如下[21]：

（1）《汉书地理志水道图说》七卷，清陈澧撰，咸丰陈氏刻；

（2）《古今尚书经说考》三十三卷，《叙录》一卷，清陈乔樅撰，同治刻；

（3）《脚气集》二卷，宋章茗水撰，宝颜堂秘笈本；

（4）《地球韵言》四卷，清张之洞编，光绪二十八年广州明道堂刻；

（5）《问奇类林》三十五卷，明郭良翰撰，明万历六年刻；

（6）《外国师船表》十六卷，清许景澄撰，光绪十二年石印。

徐信符的南州书楼藏书抗日战争期间亦运往香港，寄存于香港大学，并以港币 9000 余元之价格售出含宋元刻本在内的善本一批。抗日战争后余存图书运返广州。1948 年徐信符病逝，其女又选出善本一批，分装十箱运往澳门，将除广东文献以外的书籍售予澳门富商姚某。此后周连宽访南州书楼，为岭南大学图书馆选购广东文献一批，其中罕见之本包括[21]：

（1）《粤大记》三十二卷（缺卷一、二、卅、卅二），明郭棐编，明万历刻；

（2）《广州府志》六十卷，清张嗣衍等修，乾隆二十四年刻；

（3）《粤秀书院志》十六卷，清梁廷枏撰，道光二十七年刻；

（4）《广州乡贤传》四卷，清潘楳元辑，道光十九年刻；

（5）《温氏家集》十二卷，清温承恭等撰，咸丰元年家刻，卷端有徐信符题记云："此书原版毁于咸丰七年，后欲重刻而未果，故流传极少。"

4 馆藏中文善本书之特色

4.1 版本特色

岭南大学图书馆馆藏中文善本书的特色之一是多明本和抄本。在抗日战争前馆藏的 174 种善本图书中，明代刊刻之本有 80 种，抄本 51 种，其中多为曾钊旧藏，其数量明本和抄本各不下 35 种。在各类明本中，馆藏《宋之问集》的版式、字体与《四部丛刊续编》景印常熟瞿氏铁琴铜剑楼所藏之本均不相同，还有诸如凌蒙初朱墨本《韦苏州集》、绿野堂刊本《许文穆公集》、明万历间新安黄一桂刊本《苍霞草》、明万历南昌胡见原刊本《頖宫礼乐疏》、明嘉靖壬子三衢夏相宠摹宋版校刊《古今合璧事类备要》、明嘉靖元年葑溪堂刊本《韩（雍）襄毅公传》、明万历仁寿堂刊本《（新编簪缨必用）翰苑新书》、明万历郑云斋刊本《（笺注决科）古今源流至论》、明天启陈仁锡评阅本的《资治通鉴》和《宋元通鉴》、明黄国琦刊本《册府元龟》、明内府刊本《重修玉篇》以及明隆庆海盐夏儒刊本《奚襄琐言》等，这些明代文献不但为明史各方面的研究提供了第一手的资料，也在版本学上为有明一代刊刻的文献留存了许多宝贵的实物。

抄本中有残缺已久的《（咸淳）临安志》，抄自毛氏所得宋椠本，原书一百卷，岭南大学图书馆藏本存九十五卷，阙卷六十四、九十、九十八至一百，而该书的振绮堂汪氏刻本、瞿氏铁琴铜剑楼藏本亦阙如上卷，仅有当时的国立北平图书馆存有九十六卷，该书为幸存下来的宋人地志中唯独较详细者。[8]25 馆藏抄本《中兴礼书》存三百二十五卷，阙五十五卷，该书在《四库全书》中没有著录，书世罕传，清代徐松曾从《永乐大典》中辑出一百五十卷，但未刊行；海宁蒋光煦有家传抄本，但未经校勘，讹误颇多；当时国立北平图书馆亦有藏本，但缺卷较岭南大学图书馆藏本的缺卷多。《馆藏善本图书题识》中言：

此书系宋高孝两朝之大典章制度，足以补正《宋史通考》等书者甚多。书中之郊祀御札、明堂御札、郊祀祝册、表文祝文各门，及吉凶礼中所载之表议各篇，均为高宗时之重要文字，尤可贵者，《宋史·乐志》所载乐章，有词无谱，此书乐曲旁注律吕，他书所无，为研究古乐之重要参考资料。[8]35

其他少见的抄本还有《金史补》5册，此书缪荃孙只藏有残稿2册，《艺文志二十种引得》未有著录，可能未有刊本行世。《太平寰宇记》为毛晋汲古阁旧藏，流入曾钊之手，最后为岭南大学图书馆所得，所藏之本较上元焦氏、昆山徐氏、秀水朱氏等藏本所缺均少，且每卷末附校正一页。《太乙统宗宝鉴》馆藏二十卷，续编十二卷，此书《四库全书》列入存目，仅二十卷，《读书敏求记》中记载钱曾家藏有2本，故岭南大学图书馆所藏之抄本可能为当时最全者。另有守经堂影宋抄本《三朝北盟会编》、四库传抄本《齐民要术》、明红格抄本《观象玩占》、满汉对照之稿本《大清全书》等，均为精心缮写之本。

关于广东雕版刻书始于何时，已难考察。1941年，黄慈博在《广东文物》上发表《广东宋元明经籍椠本纪略》一文，记载宋代广东刻本17种，元代广东刻本3种，明代广东刻本不下百种，周连宽则言明初广东刻本以及清代道光前广东刻本流传下来者已不多。[22]而岭南大学图书馆保存了大量广东各地方志和粤人文集。方志包括广州、番禺、南海、顺德、东莞、从化、龙门、增城、香山、新会、三水、新宁、清远、新安、韶州、曲江、乐昌、翁源、英德、博罗、鹤山、惠州、归善、雷州、琼郡等地，这些郡县方志旧刻的留存，保存了广东各地刻书的实物；粤人文集中有不少明清两代广东刻本，尤多明万历年间和清道光年间刻本，明万历刊本《百可亭摘稿》九卷，每半页十行，行二十字，双边白口，上单鱼尾，白棉纸，所刻字体清朗，堪称广东刻本中的精品。[8]60粤人文集中还有不少广东藏书家私家刊刻之本，如清康熙三间书院刊本《广东文选》、道光南海吴氏筠清馆刊本《石云山人集》等。这些文献为研究广东刻本的用纸、版式、字体，以及广东刻书事业情况，提供了实证参考。

4.2 明代史料和明人文集

叶德辉《藏书十约》中关于购置文献之法写道："置书先经部，次史部，次丛书。"[23]而岭南大学图书馆在中文古籍方面的购书政策十分不同于传统的藏书观，与其他图书馆亦相异。岭南大学图书馆对各类文献的采访均受学校办学方针和教育理念的影响，依据学校的课程设置和教学、研究方案进行选购，注意文献的材料价值和研究价值。岭南大学的办学方针一贯坚持发展实用科学，注重与广东社会的融合，即使在20世纪30年代的国学研究热潮中，亦有冷静的态度和相应的办理政策。因此岭南大学图书馆所藏中文善本图书中经部数量最少，史部图书数量最多，尤其重视明代史料和明人文集的搜集，前者的数量占史部善本图书数量超过三分之一，后者的数量占集部善本图书数量的一半。

据对《馆藏善本图书题识》的统计，岭南大学图书馆抗日战争前收有明代史料善本24种，明代兵书善本2种，明人文集善本21种。明代史料善本中有编年类2种，纪事本末类6种，诏令奏议类4种，传记类2种，地理类6种，政书类4种，其中不少为清代的禁毁书籍，在当时已绝少流传。如明万历年间陈于廷刊之《纪录汇编》三种，二百一十六卷，共66册，明代沈节甫辑，采辑嘉靖以前明代君臣杂记，分卷编次。以同一史实集中，因现存元至明初期间史料匮乏，此汇编实有管窥之效，足为研究明史之参考。清代该书被列入禁毁书目，流传甚少。

《今言》四卷，明郑晓著，刊于明嘉靖二十一年，书前有郑晓自序，每半页八行，行十六字。此书记明代洪武至嘉靖一百八十余年间国政朝章、兵戎邦计等方面的史事，凡344则，其中的许多记载可补史之缺佚，正史之谬误，为研究明代前期社会的政治、经济、军事、文化提供了宝贵数据。目前海内外各图书馆所藏的《今言》一书有嘉靖四十五年项笃寿刻本、万历四十二年彭宗孟刻本、清顺治三年李际期宛委山堂刻本等9种版本。根据台湾的"国家图书馆"中文古籍书目数据库检索的结果，现存《今言》较早版本的有美国伯克莱加州大学东亚图书馆明嘉靖四十五年项笃寿刻本，台湾"国家图书馆"和东京大学东洋文化研究所的明嘉靖四十五年刊本，其他各图书馆所藏均为嘉靖四十五年以后的版本，从时间上来看均晚于当时岭南大学图书馆的藏本。

史部诏令奏议类下的《大明宣宗章皇帝宝训》十二卷二册，为旧抄本，现已被中山大学图书馆收藏，据中国国家图书馆中国古籍善本书目显示，大陆其他图书馆再无藏本。据台湾的"国家图书馆"中文古籍书目数据库检索联合导航系统显示结果，仅台北故宫博物院图书馆藏有明刊本的五卷，东京大学东洋文化研究所藏有五卷，即所藏之卷数远少于中山大学图书馆现藏的旧抄本十二卷。《馆藏善本图书题识》中载：

此书北平图书馆善本书目、故宫善本书目均未载，内阁藏书目录则有以下之著录："帝训一册全，宣宗章皇帝御制，首君德，终驭夷，凡二十四条，分四卷，抄本。"查本馆所藏凡十二卷，首敬天，终驭夷狄，凡七十三条，较内阁藏本多八卷，即多49条，据千顷堂书目则载此书凡十五卷，正统三年修，今馆藏卷数虽较千顷堂书目所载者少三卷，然遍查各家书目，均无著录，即内阁书目亦仅存四卷，查内阁书目系明孙能传等编，可知明代此书已残缺不完，今馆藏之本想已成人间孤帙矣。[8]18－19

其他如抄本《皇明诰敕》、抄本《历朝奏疏》、抄本《郭给谏疏稿》、明嘉靖元年葑溪堂刊本《韩（雍）襄毅公传》、明崇祯间刻本《皇明世法录》、明万历廿三年刊本《荒政汇编》等均为版本极罕见的明代史料。明刊本《三镇边务总要》五卷，由明人李如樟编纂，其曾任都指挥签事及广西延绥总兵官，其兄如柏任蓟镇副总兵，并官镇辽东。是书记载了明代沿长城一线的辽镇、蓟镇和昌镇的边防、戍务情况，有关道里险夷、形势冲缓、夷酋多寡、住牧远近等问题俱编其中，[8]29是研究明代边防事务、边关社会及北方游牧民族的珍贵资料。岭南大学所藏之本现存中山大学图书馆，经检索中国国家图书馆中国古籍善本书目联合导航系统，未发现大陆其他图书馆有藏。检索台湾中文古籍书目数据库发现，台湾的各图书馆及美国国会图书馆、哈佛大学图书馆、东京大学东洋文化研究所等机构也无该书。清乾隆重刊本《吴江水利考》，为明代沈氏所作，书前有嘉靖沈启序，王世贞所撰传赞，书中记载苏、松、常、镇、杭、嘉、湖七郡水利，总结明代治水的经验和教训。《明史·艺文志》中，《吴江水利考》作四卷，岭南大学图书馆藏本为五卷，卷首有吴江水利图，该书现存中山大学图书馆，南京图书馆未有藏本。就笔者所查尚未见大陆其他图书馆或台湾的图书馆有藏，国外如美国国会图书馆、哈佛大学图书馆也均无是书。

岭南大学图书馆亦收有不少明代兵书，其中可称为善本者有《纪效新书》十八卷和《水师辑要》一卷，均为旧抄本。《纪效新书》是戚继光在东南沿海平倭战争期间练兵和治军经验的总结，全书分六秩（礼秩、乐秩、射秩、御秩、书秩、数秩）十八篇，由東伍篇始，至水兵篇结束，各系以图而为之说，对于研究明代之兵法、兵士操练及兵营制度有重要的参考价值。尤其是书中记录了戚继光调任浙江抗倭期间东南沿海的地形、我情与倭情，其史料价值自不言而喻。《水师辑要》内容包括船式说、各船说、配船水兵、赶绘船备用器械、配驾官兵等，保留了明代各类船舶之说明和图解，尤其是对澎湖海战前后明郑在役的战船详加剖析，亦足作为明史研究之参考资料。

注重对明人文集的收藏也是岭南大学图书馆馆藏特色之一。在传统藏书观念中，诗文集为等而下一类的文献，尤其是明代的作品，更不足取。在清代叶德辉的《藏书十约》中集部之购置显然为最次一等。明代祁承㸁则认为：

盖文集一事，若如今人所刻，即以大地为书架，亦无可安顿处，惟听宇宙之所自为消磨。则经几百年而不消磨者，自有一段精彩，不可埋没也。[24]

可见传统藏书家对文集一类文献的收藏态度。然岭南大学图书馆却对明人文集着意收集，其中原因之一并非在乎这些文集的文学价值，而是关注其史料价值。自陈寅恪之后，诗文证史的研究方法被广泛应用，所以明人文集的史料价值更加凸显。传统藏书观念下前人对明人文集的轻视，使得大量明人文集到近代已成“孤本”，故有幸保存下来的这类文献亦显得弥足珍贵，此也为岭南大学图书馆注意购求明人文集的原因。

岭南大学图书馆馆藏明人文集中的善本，许多在清代时已被列入禁毁书目，流传稀少，有的藏本至今已寥寥无几。如明万历卅五年刊本《冯琢庵文集》（又名《冯宗伯文集》）四卷、明万历刊本《李沧溟先生集》卅二卷、明天启刊本《邱文庄公集》廿四卷、明绿野堂刊本《许文穆公集》、明隆庆海盐夏儒刊本《奚襄琐言》四卷、明崇祯刻清康熙间印《桂洲文集》十八卷、明万历刊本《南征录》六卷等，在大陆、港、澳、台及其他国家的图书馆都已是绝少见之本。

明嘉靖刊本《王氏家藏集》，又名《浚川集》，馆藏十八卷，内含《浚川公移集》三卷，《浚川驳稿集》二卷，《浚川内台集》三卷，《浚川奏议集》十卷，清代时亦为禁书，流传不多。目前仅知此书在台湾的收藏卷数较为丰富，如台北故宫博物院图书馆藏有嘉靖十五年至四十年刊本四十一卷，“国家图书馆”藏有嘉靖十五年至四十年刊本《王氏家藏集》四十一卷，内台集七卷，慎言十三卷，雅述二卷，丧礼备纂二卷；海外则有美国国会图书馆收藏的明嘉靖间刻本《王氏家藏集》四十一卷，内台集七卷。另据中国国家图书馆中国古籍善本书目联合导航系统、台湾中文古籍书目数据库检索可知，目前大陆有多个图书馆以及美国伯克莱加州大学东亚图书馆、澳门大学国际图书馆均有藏，但是残缺情况不一。比对上述图书馆的收藏可知，虽然岭南大学图书馆所藏之卷数并不多，但是其所藏的《浚川公移集》三卷、《浚川驳稿集》二卷和《浚川奏议集》十卷均为其他图书馆所无者，可谓孤本。《馆藏善本图书题识》有言：

此书为清代禁书，故流传甚少，国立北平图书馆藏有是书，较本馆所藏者多诗二十卷文廿一卷，但无奏议集公移集驳稿集等，浙江省立图书馆藏公移集驳稿集，但无奏议集，范氏天一阁藏有奏议集，但残缺不完（见重编天一阁书目），本馆所存者想为孤本矣。[8]61-62

4.3 广东地方志与广东文献

苏轼暮年流放岭南，曾有“九死南荒吾不恨”的诗句。事实上广东因僻处南疆，自周秦以来就被冠以“荒蛮”之名，“虽羲叔申命于虞书，疆理兴于轴周雅，然征文不足，考献无从”。[25]1秦汉之后，岭南地区相继置郡，至此“华风南寖，岭海文物，遂蒸蒸日上。晋室东迁，中原文物随侨郡而南，南北之风会，乃大殊于昔。隋唐以来，人文蔚起，声教日隆。迄自海通以远，文献之盛，麟麟炳炳，赫赫烜烜，昭人耳目，而征文考献，缵述代有其人。是故卷帙浩繁，包罗万象”[25]1。

然而千年来有关岭南的艺文典籍因被忽视而日沦以泯，明代粤人伦以训曾语“吾邦自秦汉以来几二千载，其文献之录”，“皆缺有间矣”，“荒脱而不核”，“叛涣而无统”。[26]直至明代中叶，“白沙、甘泉之学”的出现以及稍后的黄佐及其弟子对百越先贤事迹的著述、对广东文物的表彰，才使岭南“文化荒漠”的状态有所改变，并对广东学术与人文精神走向产生了深远影响。此后历四百年之人文积累，至清朝嘉庆、道光年间，大儒阮元督粤，为岭南带来了治学新观念，广东学术在沉寂百年后风气为之一变。广东文人间开始了新一轮的“广东文献整理与挖掘”风气，且此风下贯民国。[26]

但是直至民国时期，广州的典型形象仍是东西方贸易的重要港口、“新思潮”与“革命”的策源地，广东本土文化与学术仍然不入主流学术的法眼，故对粤文化的研究依旧有赖于广东学人。岭南大学在当时是广东文化研究之中心，陆键东在《近代广东人文精神与冼玉清学术》一文中曾这样描述岭南大学的学术研究情况：

> 以可称为广东学术重镇的刊物《岭南学报》为例，从民国二十年（1931）起，有关岭南文化研究的论文与文献开始出现，且逐年增多，并最终形成该刊物风格的一个大特色。民国二十三年（1934）至二十四年（1935），《岭南学报》以两期的篇幅先后刊布“广东专号”上、下两辑，集中刊发十三篇关于“广东文献”的研究论文。风气下新一代研究广东文化的年轻学者崛起，其中有终身对“岭南文化研究”情有独钟者多人，如冼玉清、饶宗颐、汪宗衍、罗香林、容肇祖、何格恩等。[26]

与学校这一研究重点相应，岭南大学图书馆在收集广东地方志和广东文献方面亦不遗余力，并日渐形成特色。

方志的价值在于提供纂修当时某一地区有关自然、社会、人文、天文、地理等各方面的资料，可供作各种方面学术研究的参考。岭南大学图书馆对方志的着力收藏可上溯到1919年筹建中籍部之时，尤其重视广东地方志，其原因就在于地方志中记载的自然、天文和地理方面的资料对于学校农学院的教学、研究工作具有十分重要的意义。进入20世纪30年代后，岭南大学图书馆加大对地方文献的搜罗，或重资购买，或向藏家借抄，至抗日战争爆发前共入藏广东方志计105种，涵盖广东70余县，[25]253－254而广东省下辖县的总数为94个（据美国哈佛大学哈佛燕京学社汉和图书馆馆长裘开明在1938年度之后的历年馆长报告中提交的资料均为广东省行政分区总数为108个，或统计的标准不同）。

据当时的统计，在抗日战争前收有广东方志数量最多的是国立北平图书馆，计有166种；其次为上海东方图书馆，计有136种；再次为北平故宫博物院图书馆，计有109种。岭南大学图书馆拥有的广东地方志数量位居全国第四，当时的广州市立中山图书馆拥有广东方志102种，中山大学图书馆拥有广东方志94种，均位于岭南大学之后。而在国外，美国国会图书馆在1937年前藏有广东方志79种，哈佛大学哈佛燕京学社汉和图书馆则为6种，日本内阁文库则为43种，均不及岭南大学图书馆拥有之数量。[25]251－252

在岭南大学图书馆拥有的众多广东方志中，有不少善本、珍本，甚至孤本，在1937

年出版的《馆藏善本图书题识》中，作为善本收入地理类的文献有27种，其中8种为广东各地方志，分别为：

（1）博罗县志，十四卷，清陈裔虞修，清乾隆二十八年刻本；

（2）澄迈县志，十卷，谢济韶修，李广先等纂，嘉庆二十五年刊本，六册；

（3）鹤山县志，十二卷，刘继纂修，乾隆十九年，四册；

（4）鹤山县志，十二卷附卷末一卷，徐香祖修，吴应逵纂，道光六年，五册；

（5）徐闻县志，十五卷，王辅之，清宣统三年闰六月，徐城锦文斋刊本；

（6）崖州志，廿二卷卷首一卷，钟元棣修，张雋、邢定纶等纂，光绪卅四年编修，民国三年重印本；

（7）丰顺县志，八卷，王承鋆修，许普济、吴鹏等纂，光绪十年编纂，仝年刊印，五册；

（8）长宁县志，十卷，高炳文修，冯兰纂，道光十九年刊本。

遗憾的是岭南大学图书馆上述8种方志现已不知去向。通过中国国家图书馆中国古籍善本书目联合导航系统及台湾中文古籍书目数据库检索发现，仅台北故宫博物院图书馆藏有清乾隆二十八年刊本的《博罗县志》十四卷，而乾隆十九年的《鹤山县志》现在台北故宫博物院图书馆、中国科学院南京地理研究所有存，其他6种版本在系统中未见。据《馆藏善本图书题识》的记载，清宣统三年闰六月徐城锦文斋刊本的《徐闻县志》当时只有广东省立中山图书馆及岭南大学图书馆有存各一部，现省馆一部仍存于馆。而经过对美国国会图书馆和哈佛大学图书馆书目的检索发现，仅哈佛大学图书馆藏有嘉庆二十五年刊本的《澄迈县志》。由此，岭南大学图书馆当时苦心搜集的广东各地方志的珍贵程度可见一斑。

据中山大学图书馆藏岭南大学档案缩微胶卷Ree136中的档案显示，至1940年底，因抗日战争局势的恶化，时在香港的岭南大学图书馆开始着手将馆藏文献制成缩微胶片，并由岭南大学美国基金会黄念美（Olin D. Wannamaker）秘书、何士健（Harold B. Hoskins）、加利（Melbert B. Cary, Jr.）负责与美国Committee on Scientific Aids to Learning、香港大学等机构联系相关事宜。1940年2月14日，时任岭南大学教务长的朱有光致函黄念美，请其筹备经费将函后所附的91种书籍制成缩微胶片，其中89种为明清两代修纂的广东各方志。此89种广东各地地方志中不包括前述所提收入《馆藏善本图书题识》的8种方志，可能是抗日战争爆发后，美国基金委员会以及岭南大学利用国学图书专项经费从多方搜购而得的。经检索中国国家图书馆中国古籍善本书目联合导航系统、美国国会图书馆在线书目检索系统和哈佛大学图书馆在线书目检索系统发现，此89种方志中有很多在大陆已属罕见，在美国国会图书馆和哈佛大学图书馆也少有入藏。

除善本方志外，岭南大学图书馆所藏地理类善本中还包括关于广东海关、边防以及专志方面的文献，如清杜臻撰《粤闽巡视纪略》五卷（清康熙经纬堂刻本），明李韡辑、清康熙李文焰重辑《海珠志》十一卷（乾隆李琯增刻编次，抄本），清梁廷枏撰《粤海关志》三十卷（清道光刻本），罗国器辑、马符录编梓《西樵志》四卷（明万历刊本），何厚宣、顾光合修《光孝寺志》（旧抄本）、清梁廷枏撰《粤道贡国说》（清道光刻本）等，现均已被中山大学图书馆收藏，除《粤道贡国说》外，广东省立中山图书馆也藏有上述各书，其他海内外图书馆可能有藏者不多。

历代以来所产生并保存下来的有关广东之文献，除了方志以外，还有大量的关于史地、民族、学术、经政、艺文、社会、教育、实业和物产方面的文献。据笔者仅对李景星收录于《广东研究参考资料叙录·史地篇初编》中方志以外的文献加以统计，就得出文献369种，其中史地文献52种，乡土志139种，关于名胜古迹之文献40种，游记31种，边防志2种，舆图50种，家谱7种，总传20种，个人传记15种，年谱3种。而实际保存下来的有关广东的文献数量必然远远不止于此，因李氏在自序中表示尚有史地篇续编以及民族、学术等各篇因经费问题尚无法出版。而李景星对《广东研究参考资料叙录》的编纂，主要还是以岭南大学图书馆的收藏为基础，辅以其他各图书馆之书目加以补充，可见岭南大学图书馆在广东文献方面收藏之富。

截至抗日战争爆发前，岭南大学图书馆馆藏广东文献中可称得善本者计有15种。有汇集唐、宋、明三代粤人所作事理疏议、礼类杂文、事类杂文、理类语录和事类语录的明刻本《岭南文献轨范补遗》（六卷，明杨瞿崃编），是书现仅中国国家图书馆、山西图书馆、广东省立中山图书馆、中山大学图书馆和“中央图书馆”台湾分馆有存。有明代粤人之文集，如陈献章撰、湛若水注《白沙诗教解》（存八卷，明隆庆元年刊本），庞尚鹏撰《百可亭摘稿》（九卷，明万历刊本），区越撰、余一鹏校、周鲲编《区西屏集》（十卷，明万历刊本），区元晋著、郭梦得校《区奉政遗稿》（十卷，明万历四年刊本），李时行的《李驾部集》（五卷，清乾隆刊本），黄瑜的《双槐岁抄》（十卷，明刊本）。

陈献章，号白沙先生，为有明一代广东大儒，后人还称之为“广东书坛第一家”，其所开创的白沙学派对广东后世的学术与人文产生了深远的影响，《白沙诗教解》是白沙门中的标准教材，其研究价值不容忽视。现是书藏于中山大学图书馆，广东省立中山图书馆、中国国家图书馆和港、澳、台地区及其他国家的图书馆均未见有藏。《白沙诗教解》另有乾隆刻本传世，但颇有异同，其中明刻本中的《夷狄犯中国》一首乾隆本无。李时行为明代“南园后五先生”之一，生平著述甚多，可流传下来者仅有《李驾部集》和《青霞漫稿》，岭南大学图书馆所藏的这部《李驾部集》已被中山大学图书馆收藏，此外中国国家图书馆、广东省立中山图书馆、华盛顿大学东亚图书馆、澳门大学国际图书馆也有收藏。《双槐岁抄》为笔记随录类文献，收文220篇，清代时入全毁书目之内，其中所载之事对研究明代广东地方势力的转变以及乡土文化有重要的参考价值。

至所收藏的清代粤人文集数量则更多，其中重要且传世稀少者有如记清代禁烟御夷情况的《夷氛闻记》（五卷，清梁廷枏撰，清刊本），《馆藏善本图书题识》云：

> 由葡人入澳起，逮英人因禁烟肇事议款开五港后，迄广东阻遏入城止，所有内外臣工之奏议，当事御夷之得失，声叙极为明晰，为研究鸦片战争不可少之参考书。[8]12

清代广东著名学者、藏书家的作品，诸如陈澧的《东塾遗稿》和《东塾类稿》，吴荣光的《石云山人诗集》和《石云山人集》，温汝能的《粤东诗海》，以及梁廷枏的《圆香梦杂剧》等，在当时除广东一些私家藏书外，大抵也只能在岭南大学图书馆等为数不多的几所图书馆得以一见。而在今天，上述各书只有中国国家图书馆、广东省立中山图书馆、中山大学图书馆、台湾“中央研究院”中国文哲研究所图书馆、台湾东海大学图书馆、东京大学东洋文化研究所等为数不多的几所图书馆有收藏，且并非每部都有入藏。

5 结　语

岭南大学图书馆堪称特色的专藏有四类，一为系统、完整的期刊收藏，二为1911年至1937年的日报全份，三为善本古籍，四为“中国问题研究”西文出版物。在此四类中，期刊收藏中的西文学术期刊为全国之首，全份日报收藏在大陆地区图书馆中为少见，仅有善本古籍和“中国问题研究”西文出版物在种类和数量上，难与其他以典藏善本书籍和西文中国学书籍而著称的图书馆比拟。但是在其馆藏中文善本书中，亦有海内孤本，为他馆所无者，而这些善本藏书除其书籍本身的价值以外，更体现了岭南大学所特有的教育理念和办学方针，折射出学校在20世纪30年代教会大学国学研究热潮中的冷静坚持与学术独立的精神，为观察近代中国的学术转型提供了某些侧面的视角。

应该说岭南大学图书馆设立中籍部，并逐渐入藏了为数不少的中文善本书，是其办学目的走向世俗化和中国化的结果，同时与教会学校采用中文教学的趋势密不可分。早在1890年基督教传教士会议上，狄考文（Calvin Wilson Matteer）就列举了用中文施教的种种优势：可以消除英文教育的最根本困难，保证学生学完各项课程；能够弥补学生中文知识的缺陷，使之赢得本国地位和声望；有助于学生更有效地应用知识；有助于学生和其他人进行沟通和扩大影响等。[27]广东教会学校在这方面是全国领先的，不同的是，由于粤语是广东的通用语言，所以学校一般采用粤语教学。岭南大学也不例外，当时大学部还将国文、中国文学等课程设为选修课。

从另外一个方面来说，岭南大学虽为教会大学，但是其具有不属于任何教会的特殊性质；岭南大学又是所有教会大学中，华人参与学校管理最早、掌握实际权力最大的一所教会学校，钟荣光自1899年即协理校务，学校的各管理阶层都有中国人。而岭南大学的农科教育更是在广东省政府、广东基督教教育会和一些著名中国商人的支持下成立起来的。故岭南大学的世俗化和中国化进程明显快于其他教会大学，在商科、农科的教学方面也更注重结合中国尤其是广东的实际情况，使毕业生能够满足中国社会的需要。正是这样的教育方针，决定了图书馆非常重视中文馆藏的充实和建设，尤其是关乎广东方志和广东文献的收藏，进而为后人留下了一批宝贵的文献资源。

总之，岭南大学一直以来在教育理念和办学方针上所坚持的特色，以及后来在国学研究的潮流下所作的相应调整、对岭南文化的研究与关怀，对图书馆的藏书建设产生了既深且远的影响，使包括中文善本书在内的各类馆藏，在内容和结构方面都形成了鲜明的“岭南”特色。反过来透过这些藏书，可以感受到当时的岭南大学矗立于中国的最南端，面朝大海，直面东西方文明冲击与交融的风雨，在教育和学术上最先沾染近现代化的气息，其办学理念、教育思想以及学术研究取向，在当时可能并不合乎潮流、不为重视，但是于今天看来却显得依旧亲切而不过时。如今，岭南大学已经停办半个多世纪，但是其藏书主体仍然保存于广州中山大学图书馆，被一代又一代的研究者、教师和学生使用。浏览当年的目录，翻阅发黄的旧籍，岭南大学作为一所大学所肩负的使命跃然纸上：保守知识和理想、解释知识和理想、探求真理、训练人才，是为“岭南精神”的重要组成部分，是对大学独立精神的弘扬。

参考文献

[1] 经费来源、校董会沿革与现状以及对学校之作用［A］. 广州：广东省档案馆，全宗号：38－1－19.

[2] 李瑞明. 岭南大学文献目录：广州岭南大学历史档案资料［M］. 香港：岭南大学文学与翻译研究中心，2000：19－21.

[3] Latourette K S. A History of the Expansion of Christianity，Vol. Ⅶ：Advance Through Storm［M］. New York：Harper and Brothers，1945：348.

[4] 私立岭南大学卅四年度第二次校务会议记录（1945年12月5日）［A］. 广州：广东省档案馆，全宗号：38－1－14.

[5] 陈德芸致特嘉之中文馆藏建设［A］. 广州：广东省档案馆，全宗号：38－4－182（3－6）.

[6] 调查中国之图书馆事业［J］. 图书馆学季刊，1936，14：680－684.

[7] 陈国钦，袁征. 瞬逝的辉煌：岭南大学六十四年［M］. 广州：广东人民出版社，2008.

[8] 何多源. 馆藏善本图书题识［M］. 广州：岭南大学图书馆，1937.

[9] 廿四年度图书馆馆务报告撮要［N］. 私立岭南大学校报，1937－01－15，9（9）：133－135.

[10] 徐信符. 广东藏书纪事诗［M］. 香港：商务印书馆，1963.

[11] 周连宽. 广东藏书家曾钊［N］. 大公报·艺文周刊，1963－12－22.

[12] 李健明. 走进顺德·龙山温家［N/OL］. 珠江商报，2007－02－02［2009－09－30］. http：//www. sdlib. com. cn/typenews. asp？id＝938.

[13] 黄受照. 徐甘棠同学事略［N］. 私立岭南大学校报，1935－06－30，7（20）：278－279.

[14] 本校一年来之进展［N］. 私立岭南大学校报，1936－11－29，9（6）：82.

[15] 图书馆消息［N］. 私立岭南大学校报，1935－09－30，8（2）：18－19.

[16] 潘祖荫，潘宗周. 滂喜斋藏书记·宝礼堂宋本书录［M］. 上海：上海古籍出版社，2007.

[17] 司徒荣. 广州岭南大学上海分校的旧事［EB/OL］.［2009－09－06］. http：//www. lingnan. net/lnrj/LNSH/LNDD/GUANG. HTM.

[18] 隋广州前陈散骑侍郎刘府君墓铭并序［EB/OL］.（2009－02－23）［2009－09－06］. http：//www. gdwh. com. 71mmcn/whyc/2009/0223/article_1213. html.

[19] Hwa-Wei Lee. The Chinese Collection and Sinological Resource in the Library of Congress［R］.（据美国国会图书馆亚洲部主任李华伟的演讲《美国国会图书馆中文馆藏与汉学研究资源》PPT）

[20] 特木勒，居蜜. 跋美国国会图书馆藏明刻本《两镇三关通志》［J］. 史学史研究，2006（3）.

[21] 周连宽. 羊城访书偶记（三）·广东藏书家近况［J］. 广东图书馆学刊，1986（2）：13－16，40.

[22] 周连宽. 羊城访书偶记（二）·广东刻本［J］. 广东图书馆学刊，1986（1）：5－9.

[23] 叶德辉. 藏书十约［M］. 上海：古典文学出版社. 1957：43.

[24] 黄裳. 天一阁被劫书目前记［J］. 文献，1979（2）：99.

[25] 李景星. 广东研究参考资料叙录·史地篇初编［M］. 广州：岭南大学图书馆，1937（8）.

[26] 陆键东. 近代广东人文精神与冼玉清学术［C/OL］.［2009－10－12］//周义. 冼玉清研究论文集. 香港：中国评论学术出版社，2007. http：//gb. chinareviewnews. com/crn-webapp/cbspub/secDetail. jsp？bookid＝7689&secid＝8606.

[27] 狄考文. 如何使教育工作最有效地在中国推进基督教事业（1890年）［G］//陈学恂. 中国近代教育史教学参考资料：下册. 北京：人民教育出版社，1987.

教师简介：

宋琳琳，女，武汉大学管理学学士、管理学硕士、管理学博士。2011 年起任教于中山大学资讯管理学院，副教授，硕士生导师。主讲“信息描述”、“文献分类”、“文献标引”、“定密理论与实务”等本科生课程。主持及参与科研项目近 10 项，发表论文 40 余篇。联系方式：songlinl@ mail. sysu. edu. cn。

所选论文《大型文献数字化项目元数据互操作的调查与启示》原载于《中国图书馆学报》2012 年第 9 期

大型文献数字化项目元数据互操作的调查与启示*

宋琳琳，李海涛①

摘　要：本文选取了 8 个国内外知名的大型文献数字化项目为调查对象，从模式级、记录级、仓储级 3 个层次，对上述调查对象采用的元数据互操作方式进行了调查研究，结合案例分析了映射、集成、协议和 API 等 4 种主要方式的实现路径，并为我国大型文献数字化项目开展元数据互操作提出建议。

关键词：大型文献数字化项目；元数据标准；互操作

Metadata Interoperability in Mass Digitization Project: The Survey and Suggestion

Linlin Song, Haitao Li

Abstract: This paper reports a study on the metadata interoperability carried in 8 famous mass digitization projects at home and abroad. It summarizes 7 means that used in metadata interoperability from 3 levels, such as schema, record and repository; and analyses 4 main means through case study as mapping, integration, OAI and API. The paper finalizes with recommendations to further improvement on metadata interoperability for Chinese mass digitization projects.

Keywords: Mass digitization projects; Metadata standard; Interoperability

大型文献数字化项目是指大型机构或是多个机构合作开展，以创建数字信息资源、提供数字信息服务为目的，通过扫描、拍照等转换技术，将传统的非数字型资源转换成

---

* 本文系国家社科基金项目“社科化网络环境下信息组织的理论与方法创新研究”（项目编号：10BTQ023）及中山大学青年教师培育计划“大型文献数字化项目的信息组织研究”（项目编号：20000 - 3161107）的研究成果之一。

① 李海涛，中山大学资讯管理学院，副教授，硕士生导师。

计算机可以读取和识别的数字资源的工作。其信息组织的主体主要有政府机构、文化遗产保护机构、非营利机构和IT公司；信息组织对象的来源、类型、格式多样，主要包括图书、期刊、报纸、手稿、地图、书籍、乐谱、录音资料、电影、印刷制品、照片和建筑制图等珍贵文献。主客体的多样性必然导致大型文献数字化项目信息组织过程中多种元数据标准并存。这虽然满足了不同资源、不同领域、不同系统及其应用的需要，但却为分布式信息环境下的大型文献数字化项目的资源集成服务带来诸多问题和挑战：一方面不同类型的信息资源倾向于采用特定的元数据方案，另一方面用户又希望通过统一接口获取满足需求的各类信息资源。元数据的多样性和信息资源需求接口的单一性，使得大型文献数字化项目的元数据互操作势在必行。

在异构、分布式网络环境下，元数据互操作是互操作的基础及保障。本文通过调查国内外知名大型文献数字化项目信息组织中元数据标准及其互操作的开展情况，以期全面掌握数字化项目互操作领域的发展概况，为该领域元数据仓库的建立、元数据检索和服务的集成，以及跨系统的整合检索奠定基础。

1 调查对象与内容

1.1 调查对象

结合大型文献数字化项目参建主体的国别、性质与类型，本文选择了大学数字图书馆国际合作计划（China Academic Digital Associative Library，CADAL）、中国国家图书馆数字图书馆工程（数图工程）、谷歌图书（Google Book）、欧洲数字图书馆（Europeana）、开放图书馆（Open Library）、HaithTrust、加州数字图书馆（California Digital Library，CDL）、美国记忆（American Memory，AM）共8个国内外知名的大型文献数字化项目作为调查对象，通过实地调研、深度访谈、登录各项目网站及查阅与其信息资源建设相关文献等方式，进行分析研究。

1.2 调查内容

元数据互操作是指不同的元数据格式间的信息共享、转换和跨系统检索等相关问题，为用户提供一个统一的检索界面、确保系统对用户的一致性服务。元数据互操作框架和层次是本次调查开展的参考。张晓林将元数据互操作框架划分为数据内容、编码规则、元素语义、元素结构、标记格式、交换格式、通信协议7个层面[1]；DC元数据互操作层次模型包括共享术语定义、形式语义互操作、语法描述级互操作、纲要描述级互操作4个级别[2]；毕强等将元数据互操作划分为语义互操作、语法互操作、协议互操作3个层面[3]。

曾蕾等按照实现互操作性的水平把元数据互操作分别3个级别，即模式级、记录级、仓储级[4]；其中元数据模式级互操作指不同元数据标准之间的互操作，其实现方法包括元数据衍生、元数据应用纲要、元数据映射、通过中心元数据格式进行转换、元数据框架、元数据注册等。元数据记录级互操作主要解决信息系统元数据记录的集成和转换，实现方法主要有数据转换、数据重用及整合。元数据仓储级互操作主要解决从不同的数据源中采集元数据的问题，以便实现跨库检索服务，实现方法包括 OAI 协议、主题规范档文件映射、值域共现映射、丰富记录等方法。参考上述框架，本文将其具化为 7 种主要方式，其具体应用情况如表 1 所示。

表 1　大型文献数字化项目元数据互操作方式调查结果

项目	模式级		记录级		仓储级		
	映射	注册	转换	集成	协议	API	关联数据
CADAL	√				√	√	
数图工程	√			√	√		
American Memory	√	√	√	√	√		
Google Book			√			√	
Europeana	√	√	√	√	√	√	√
Open Library	√				√	√	
HaithTrust	√			√	√	√	
CDL	√				√	√	

2　调查结果分析

2.1　常用的元数据互操作方式

2.1.1 映射

元数据模式级互操作通常发生在数据记录被创造出来之前，是对现有元数据的派生与修改；相较于其他互操作方式，元数据映射在项目创建的初始阶段应用，可从根本上提高互操作的范围，因此被大型文献数字化项目广泛采用。元数据映射又称元数据对照，是指两个元数据标准之间元素的直接转换。它是对存在于不同应用领域的元数据格式进行转换，通过一对一、一对多、多对一及多对多等多种映射方式，解决语义互换及统一检索问题。

通过调查发现，8 个知名大型文献数字化项目在数字对象描述方面均结合实际需求，自建了新的元数据标准；其中 87.5% 的调查对象采用元数据映射，但由于各个项目的需求和发展目标不一致，所映射的对象也存在差异，如表 2 所示，并呈现以下特点：

表 2　大型文献数字化项目自建元数据标准的映射对象

项目名称	描述方式	映射对象
CADAL[5]	自建元数据标准	MARC
数图工程[6]	自建元数据标准	DC CNMARC MARC21

续表 2

项目名称	描述方式	映射对象
Europeana[7]	自建元数据标准	EAD MARC
Open Library[8]	自建元数据标准	DC
HaithTrust[9]	自建元数据标准	PREMIS
CDL[10]	自建元数据标准	DC
American Memory	自建元数据标准	DC ONIX FGDC UNIMARC GILS

（1）MARC、DC 作为通用的元数据标准是最常用的映射目标，与 MARC 映射主要是为方便与原始文献建立关系，如 CADAL、数图工程、Europeana 等；与 DC 映射主要是为了满足数字资源采集、检索和使用的需求，如 CDL、Open Library 等，如表 3 所示。

表 3　Open Library 的元数据标准与 DC 元数据标准之间的映射

OL metadata	DC	OL metadata	DC
author	dcterms：creator	subject_place	dcterms：coverage
contributions	dcterms：contributor	subject_time	dcterms：coverage
title	dcterms：title	genre	dcterms：type
subtitle	dcterms：title	language	dcterms：language
by_statement		description	dcterms：description
physical_format	dcterms：format	table_of_contents	dcterms：tableOfContents
other_titles	dcterms：alternative	notes	dcterms：description
work_title	dcterms：alternative	LC_classification	dcterms：subject
edition		ISBN	dcterms：identifier
publisher	dcterms：publisher	LCCN	dcterms：identifier
publish_place	dcterms：publisher	URL	
pagination	dcterms：extent	source_record_loc	
number_of_pages	dcterms：extent	source_record_id	
DDC	dcterms：subject	publish_date	dcterms：date
subject	dcterms：subject	publish_country	

（2）特定功能需求，大型文献数字化项目肩负着促进资源利用、推动数字资源长期保持等多项使命，因此在元数据互操作中也应兼顾。HaithTrust 为了实现其对数字资源长期保存的功能，将其自建的元数据标准与保存元数据标准（Preservation Metadata

Implementation Strategies，PREMIS）进行映射。

2.1.2 集成

集成是属于元数据记录级互操作，主要发生在元数据记录生成之后。很多大型文献数字化项目在建设前并没有发现相似资源的存在，或是没有考虑互操作问题，因此在项目建设过程中，元数据记录已经产生，映射等模式级互操作方式无法有效满足已赋值的元数据互操作需求。这就需要借助转换、重用、集成等方式，实现各个项目的元数据记录间的整合。

集成方式则将元数据标准作为一个可以分解并整合的框架，将来自不同项目的元数据记录参照其内容属性分别集中到该框架的不同模块中，如描述元数据、结构元数据和管理元数据；再将这些模块在统一的框架下进行整合，从而实现互操作。调查结果显示，87.5%的大型文献数字化项目采用了集成的方式，但是具体的实现途径各有不同，如表4所示。

表4 大型文献数字化项目元数据互操作之集成方式实现途径

项目 方式	数图工程	American Memory	Google Book	Europeana	Open Library	HaithTrust	CDL
METS		√		√		√	√
RDF	√			√			
其他方式			√		√		

（1）METS。大型文献数字化项目在数字化加工的过程中，实现了文献载体和格式的转变，而以数字图像存在的数字资源所需元数据元素和原始文献存在区别，因此很多机构就会重新建立新的标准，从而忽视了原始文献元数据的整合应用，这必然会造成资源的浪费。METS最大的优势在于，构建了由不同模块（描述、管理、结构等）组合而成的统一框架，该框架不受模式、词汇、应用程序等限制，利用XML语言对简单或复杂的数字对象的不同类型的元数据进行编码；可以根据属性将不同来源的多条记录整合到一个模块中，形成一条新的记录。

CDL将METS作为其建立数字资源仓储和提供服务的基础，其数字对象指南（*CDL Guidelines for Digital Objects*）认为METS可以共享数字对象的共同特征，如内容文件格式、元数据编码标准，并且还包括足够的细节，以使METS的创造者和加工人员在创建和处理METS的编码数字对象时符合特定的配置文件。[10]在对数字对象进行描述的过程中，CDL为节约项目建设成本并重用已有资源，会借鉴来自原始文献书目数据以及其合作方的描述元数据，从中选择最贴切的记录并采用XML描述整合到METS框架中，从而作为CDL最终的描述元数据记录。

（2）RDF。大型文献数字化项目的建设目的之一就是促进资源的推广应用，尤其是IT公司，其参建主要目的就是将获取的数字资源整合到其现有的网络资源与服务中。在网络已是用户获取资源的主要途径的大环境下，遵循网络资源描述规则是增强数字化获取的资源在网络中的辨识度的首选方案。

资源描述框架（RDF）是 W3C 为网络资源“提供的一个机制，整合多个元数据方案”。RDF 并没有定义描述资源所用的词汇表，而是定义了一些描述规则，在遵循统一规则的前提下，人们就可以使用自己的词汇表描述任何资源。该规则包括 3 个核心要素，分别是命名空间（nameplace）、XML 语言、RDF 声明。首先，命名空间是元数据标准构成的基础，元数据标准的创建方或维护机构为了定义每一个术语，保障其长期可用性并确定它所归属的元素集，都会通过一定的规则或是惯例约束等方式赋予其命名空间。而用 XML 描述的命名空间可能被定义以允许来自不同框架的元素整合成单一的资源描述。而 RDF 声明则可以基于不同的时间和目的，链接多种资源描述，从而实现了元数据的互操作。

Europeana 的数据模型 Europeana Data Model（EDM）建立在各类成熟标准基础上，为收集、链接和丰富来自不同数据提供方的数据提供了一个框架，利用 RDF 对元数据进行语义描述，可以重用并集中不同词汇，而且还可以保护原始数据并开展互操作。具体如图 1 所示，其中深色的元数据是 EDM 创建的，浅色的元数据则来源于其他成熟的元数据标准。[11]

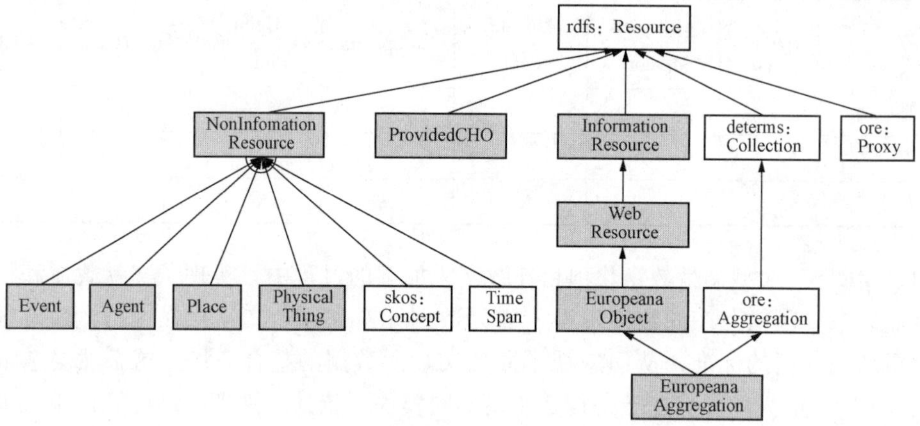

图 1　EDM 的 RDF 构成及来源

此外，为了适应语义网的发展，Europeana 将其数字资源的相关数据都采用 OpenLink Virtuoso 或 4Store 等 RDF 存储方式，其目的是方便在语义环境中，Europeana 的元数据可以通过关联数据有效揭示，提高资源可用性。[12]

（3）其他方式。有的项目并没有利用现有的框架或规则，而是根据项目建设的需要，采用其他方式集成元数据。以 Google Book 为例，其拥有超过 100 个书目数据的来源，包括图书馆、出版商、零售商以及评论和书封的聚集者，收集了 8 亿条数据记录，包含超过 1 万亿个数据字段。Google Book 将这些获得的记录转化为简单的数据结构，但没有添加 URI，并通过几种不同的方式转化为 Google 可以利用的状态。初始的元数据结构储存在一个类似于 SQL 的数据库中，用于简单的检索。其大体流程为：首先利用解析算法进行处理，从中抽取特殊意义的信息如记录号、条形码等，再利用聚类算法、文本相似度匹配等技术进行综合，择优筛选并最终形成一条元数据记录。[13]

2.1.3 协议

大型文献数字化项目通常由多个机构合作完成，数字化成果多为分布式存储，且存在由于规划导致的异构状态。当要实现上述分布式异构资源的集成检索时，项目参加方面临的一个重要问题是检索结果很少以一致、有系统和可信赖的格式出现；究其原因还是因为各个检索结果来自采用不同元数据标准的数据库，或是采用一些特殊的描述规则。解决这种问题还需通过协议、聚合和值共现映射等开展仓储级的元数据互操作。在上述方案中，OAI（Open Archives Initiative）协议是大型文献数字化项目普遍采用的一种互操作解决方案，在本次调查中使用率达75%。

AM利用OAI协议不仅实现了参建机构的元数据互操作及采集整合，并以此为途径将其资源开放给其他相关项目使用。首先，AM将来源于AM、全球门户（Global Gateway）、印刷品及图片部在线目录、历史新闻数据库（Chronicling America）和其他参建机构的元数据进行采集整合；然后，针对不同类型文献的元数据分别进行聚类，大致归为图书、手册、地图、海报、影片、音频、期刊等10类；再根据各个类别的具体情况，分层次地提供基于OAI协议的开放采集，其中照片类的元数据集最多，共有27个数据库可供采集，而大多数类别中仅有1个数据库开放。同时，为了满足用户对于不同格式元数据的需求，AM共提供了DC、MARC XML和MODS等3种格式的元数据以方便采集，并且还提供了一些遵守OAI协议的预先编制的元数据采集请求编码供有需要的机构参考，如图2所示。

利用OAI协议进行元数据互操作，除了遵循协议本身的要求外，数据提供方和数据采集方都应该进行更规范化的操作。首先，数据提供方需要建立一个动态的元素集，提供更详尽的描述。除了遵守OAI标准提供简单的DC外，还应公开便于使用和管理的多种元数据格式，并尝试在一定的框架下使元数据尽量标准化；对元数据进行必要的清洗，使其不包含任何过时的和特殊的编码；与其他服务提供方建立可共享的元数据算法、技术和战略，并为服务提供方提供一个框架图，尽可能朝着兼容多种编码方式的方向努力。[14]而对数据采集方而言，应在元数据采集后建立一个子集，用以判断相关的集合，并进行抽取以方便索引和展示。

2.1.4 API

除了常规的元数据互操作方式外，直接面向资源与服务的“API调用与处理”方式也被大型文献数字化项目广泛应用于信息资源整合，60%的调查对象都提供了可供调用的API。该方式是元数据互操作的高级实现形式，以封装好的包含元数据描述记录的API为基础，通过检索将需求信息与API内包含的元数据进行匹配，并将匹配的API进行调用、加载，从而形成针对特定需求的新资源与服务。当然，该方式实现的前提是其他项目提供了可供调用的API。CDL通过API调用整合了两个项目的资源：PubMed和NSDL资助的地球科学门户。Google为了提高信息资源描述的质量，获取了超过100家书目信息供应方的书目记录，其中很多就是通过调用相关机构的API实现的，如通过调用Worldcat的API，Google可以获取Worldcat中几乎全部的书目信息。

其实现过程主要包括检索匹配、调用、转换格式、加载等环节。以Open Library为

```xml
<?xml version="1.0" encoding="UTF-8" ?>
-<OAI-PMHxmlns="http://www.openarchives.org/OAI/2.0/"        xmlns:xsi="http://www.w3.org/2001/XMLSchema-instance"
 xsi:schemaLocation="http://www.openarchives.org/OAI/2.0/ http://www.openarchives.org/OAI/2.0/OAI-PMH.xsd">
    <responseDate>2012-02-23T13:06:14Z</responseDate>
    <request                    verb="GetRecord"                    identifier="oai:lcoa1.loc.gov:loc.gmd/g3791p.rr002300"
metadataPrefix="oai_dc">http://memory.loc.gov/cgi-bin/oai2_0</request>
- <GetRecord>
- <record>
- <header>
    <identifier>oai:lcoa1.loc.gov:loc.gmd/g3791p.rr002300</identifier>
    <datestamp>2005-11-21T17:08:59Z</datestamp>
    <setSpec>gmd</setSpec>
    </header>
- <metadata>
-<oai_dc:dc     xmlns:oai_dc="http://www.openarchives.org/OAI/2.0/oai_dc/"     xmlns:dc="http://purl.org/dc/elements/1.1/"
xmlns:xsi="http://www.w3.org/2001/XMLSchema-instance"
xsi:schemaLocation="http://www.openarchives.org/OAI/2.0/oai_dc/ http://www.openarchives.org/OAI/2.0/oai_dc.xsd">
    <dc:title>New railroad map of the state of Maryland, Delaware, and the District of Columbia. Compiled and drawn by Frank
Arnold Gray.</dc:title>
    <dc:creator>Gray, Frank Arnold.</dc:creator>
    <dc:subject>Railroads--Middle Atlantic States--Maps.</dc:subject>
    <dc:description>Description derived from published bibliography.</dc:description>
    <dc:publisher>Philadelphia</dc:publisher>
……
    </oai_dc:dc>
    </metadata>
    </record>
```


图2　AM提供的基于简单DC格式的OAI请求内容（节选）

例，首先要解决的是如何准确地获取信息，通过GET方式请求将用户的检索词与API中提供的元数据进行检索标识的匹配，如ISBN、OCLC标识符、LCCNs号和OLIDs（Open Library内部的标识符）。如果API中保存有相关信息，就将其进行调用。如果只是调用一个API，那就可以将符合要求的数据进行分析整合，通过修改Html DOM的方式直接实现客户端浏览器页面的更改；如果同时调用多个数据库，则需要将返回的结果进行综合处理，通常采用将调用返回的多个XML数据混合到一个XML文档中，并且使用XSLT将这个文档转化为一段XHTML代码，然后把这段XHTML代码加载到相关网页中即可，从而实现了架构于元数据互操作基础上的资源与服务集成。

利用API开展元数据互操作的优势在于，资源提供方已经将资源分门别类地封装成不同类型的API，API内的具体元数据的值可能发生变化，但是所生成的API却不会有变动。而且服务提供方所调用的也不是具体的内容而是这些API，就不再因为具体赋值的变化而影响整个元数据互操作的开展。这就意味着服务提供方不必再根据内容的变化而不停地维护资源链接，只要获取了相关资源的API进行解析和链接即可，这就大大减少了工作负担。

2.2 其他元数据互操作方式

除了2.1总结的大型文献数字化项目常用的元数据互操作方式外，还存在其他的互操作方式，如注册、转换、关联数据等。在此次调查中，虽然这些方式的应用率不高，但其在元数据互操作方面的作用却不能忽视。

2.2.1 注册

元数据注册系统（Metadata Schema Registry，MR）是由DCMI提出，对元数据定义及其编码、转换、应用等规范进行发布、注册、管理和检索的系统，以支持开放环境中元数据的发现、识别、调用以及在此基础上的转换、挖掘和复用。它根据统一的标准模型（ISO/IEC 11197）进行语义、编码、标准解析和转换，按照领域或者主题建立元数据规范目录列表，并映射到各自所对应的物理信息资源，并以Web服务的形式在网络进行发布，通过元数据从语义层面的关联和协同可以有效地进行信息资源的整合，支持智能检索、定题服务、主题聚类、内容挖掘等知识服务，从而实现信息资源的开发和增值。

Europeana的元数据注册系统EuMDR（Europeana Metadata Registry）是用来管理和发布该项目参建方所使用的元数据数据模型和具体元素，并实现不同数据模型之间的转换。除了实现上述功能外，EuMDR还将作为系统的组成部分被整合到Europeana环境中，为其他服务提供支持，如REPOX可以利用EuMDR将原始元数据转换成ESE或EDM等不同的元数据框架，方便用户查询。[15]

2.2.2 转换

转换主要是指信息资源的描述方式从一种元数据标准转为另一种元数据标准。在这个转换过程中，最重要的问题就是在转换过程中将面临数据丢失或失真。如果转换过程中包含了数据值，尤其是目标格式比源格式更加细化，包含更多细节元素时，就必须将源元数据记录分解为更细小的单元，如从DC到MARC的转换，从而导致数据失真；反之，则会造成数据的丢失。此外，如果元数据的取值需要参考受控词汇，也会让转换变得更加复杂。正因为上述情况的存在，在开展元数据标准转换时应该制定相应的操作指南予以辅助。这也是阻碍该方式在大型文献数字化项目中有效应用的关键。AM利用LC创建的转换工具MODS，先实现MODS与MARC、MODS与DC的转换，继而实现MARC、MODS、DC三种标准之间的转换，如表5所示。

表5 American Memory中MODS、DC、MARC三种标准之间的转换

MARC	MODS	DC
130，210，241，242，245，246，730	<titleInfo>题名	Title
100，111，700，711，712，720	<name>名称	Creator，Contributor
06	<typeOfResource>数据类型	Type
08	<genre>题材	Type

续表5

MARC	MODS	DC
008/07 - 10，15 - 17，033，044，250，260，07，310，321	<originInfo>来源资源	Publisher，Date
008/35 -37，041	<language>语言	Language
006，007/11，13，008/23，29，256，300，856	<physicalDescription>物理特性描述	Format
520	<Abstract：>摘要	Description
505	<tableOfContents>目录	Description
008/22，521	<targetAudience>适用对象	
245，5XX	<note>附注	Description
034，045，255，600，610，611，630，650，651，653，752	<subject>主题	Subject，Coverage
050，060，080，082，084，086	<classification>分类号	Coverage
534，440，490，700，710，711，730，740，760 -787，800 -830	<relatedItem>相关款目	Source，Relation
010，020，022，024，028，037，856	<identifier>识别号	Identifier
852	<location>位置	
506，504	<accessCondition>取得条件	Rights
	<part>	
	<extension>延伸信息	
001，003，005，008/00 -05，940	<recordInfo>纪录信息	

2.2.3 关联数据

关联数据作为社会网络环境中信息资源整合的新技术，虽然还处于研究阶段，但其超越了格式框架的限制，代表未来网络资源应用发展的方向，值得关注。

关联数据采用RDF数据模型，利用统一资源标识符（URI）命名数据实体，来发布和部署实例数据，从而可以通过HTTP协议揭示并获取这些数据，同时强调数据的相互关联以及有益于人机理解的语境信息。[16]

关联数据之所以可以用于元数据的互操作，是因为关联数据打破了传统元数据的存在形式，不再局限于某一模式或应用框架中，而是将元数据标准中的每一个元素都用RDF三元组的方式进行描述，然后发布在网络中并部署实例数据，利用元素之间的关联，通过HTTP协议进行整合。

在这种情况下，要进行信息资源整合或是集成检索，就不必再考虑不同元数据标准之间的差异，只需要将符合检索要求的RDF三元组进行集成就可获取想要的信息资源。假设图书 *The Organization of Information* 在CDL中有其书目信息，在Google Book Search中有用户对其评论。通过元数据采集或转换，很难采集到Google中的用户评价；但是如果采用关联数据，关于该书的每条信息都可以用 RDF 表示，这样即使是不同的来源，无论其内容是否为元数据标准规定的核心元素，只要它们有一个匹配点（如图 3 所示，ISBN 号匹配），便可以实现两个数据集的关联，从而实现元数据互操作的最终目的。

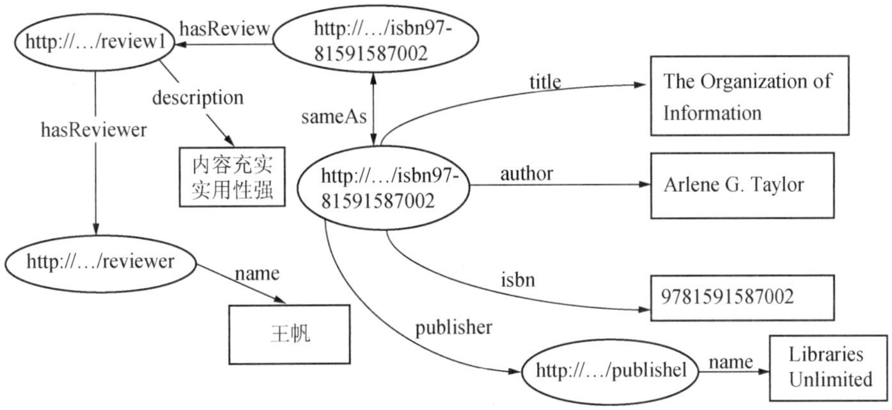

图 3　应用关联数据的元数据互操作

Europeana 在 data. europeana. eu 中已发布了关于文本、图片、视频、音频等类型的 240 万条开放数据，这些数据来自欧洲 15 个国家的 200 多个文化机构，其中很多数据就来自其他机构提供的开放关联数据，如法国国家图书馆、瑞典国家图书馆等。Europeana 收集的数据范围广泛，不仅包括传统的书目记录，还有维基百科描述、用户标签与评论、社会网络活动、用户照片及视频等。经过整理后再以关联数据发布的数据，不仅内容得到丰富，而且可关联的范围也得到拓展。Europeana 开展关联数据项目的主要目的是帮助 Europeana 成为欧洲文化信息的权威来源，及欧洲文化遗产宣传推广的重要渠道。[17]

3　对我国大型文献数字化项目元数据互操作的启示与建议

3.1　启　示

通过上述调查，笔者认为目前大型文献数字化项目元数据互操作正朝着细粒度、去格式化的方向发展。

3.1.1　细粒度

所谓细粒度，是指随着元数据描述和揭示程度的不断加深，强调对数字对象具体特征的全面描述和各元素内在关系的深度揭示，传统的基于框架模式的转换将逐渐减少，而更倾向于面向具体元素的关联。这就意味着在今后元数据互操作实践中，不仅应该关注各项目采用的元数据标准和框架，更重要的是看其对具体元素的描述方式和开放程度，这才是提高其互操作性的基本保障。

3.1.2 去格式化

所谓去格式化，与细粒度相辅相成，在对数字对象描述深入细致的要求下，元数据互操作正在经历由形式到内容的转变，即将对格式一致、兼容、转换的关注逐渐转移到元数据元素描述的可读性与规范化。在统一的描述语言和规则中，即使其描述对象、描述深度、取值的受控词汇、来源框架差异显著，但由于其互操作对象由关于数字对象的一条完整格式记录转换为描述该数字对象某一具体特征的内容元素，互操作中就将格式障碍降到最低。

3.2 建　议

为了迎合这种发展趋势，我国大型文献数字化项目元数据互操作应从以下方面着手改进。

3.2.1 应将元数据互操作纳入项目建设规划

元数据互操作是信息资源整合的基础，大型文献数字化项目通常由多个机构合作建设，而信息资源整合是项目发展中必须面对的问题。通过上述调查笔者发现，越是在项目建设初期，开展元数据互操作的方式越多样，工作量和工作难度相对越小。所以，在我国大型文献数字化项目建设发展的过程中，应在项目规划阶段就考虑元数据互操作问题。首先应调查了解相似项目和相关资源，选择或构建一种适合当前资源环境的元数据标准，既要保证该标准能尽可能详尽描述项目的数字资源，又要与其他通用标准进行映射，还可以构建元数据注册系统，吸纳其他相关标准及元素，成为不同元数据框架转换的中介，从而避免项目建成后的弥补与修正。

3.2.2 推进新技术在元数据互操作中的应用

调查显示，我国的大型文献数字化项目采用的元数据互操作方式较为单一，主要集中在元数据映射和集成采集协议等方面，这种情况会直接影响互操作的广度与深度。所以，丰富元数据互操作方式是目前我国大型文献数字化项目互操作建设中面临的主要问题。因此，新技术的应用势在必行。如调查中显示的关联数据在 Europeana 的应用，可以细化信息资源描述的粒度，元数据标准中的每一个元素都可以以 RDF 的形式表示实例数据。这样就可以打破元数据模式和应用框架的局限，提高资源被发现的概率；同时还可以将存在于网络中的各类相关资源进行链接，从而扩大可用资源的范围。

3.2.3 构建逻辑模型

元数据互操作的逻辑模型是指关注元数据内容而非元数据格式的互操作方式。这就要求打破目前元数据互操作的格式界限。就大型文献数字化项目而言，所调查的 8 个项目均自建了元数据标准，相应的就有 8 种不同格式，所以元数据的格式无法穷尽，实现不同格式之间的互操作工作量过大，而且范围过于宽泛。如果构建元数据互操作的逻辑模型，则互操作的关注点就从形式转移到内容，可以采用通用标识语言 XML 构建一种中介格式，如将 MARC 数据记录转换为 MARC XML 格式，然后以此格式为中介，与其他文档格式、元数据格式和网络文档进行转换，将格式对元素内容的影响降到最低；或以此为基础建立统一描述规则（如 RDF）来描述每一个元素。由于 XML 是网络环境中普遍应用的结构化语言，在同一种语言下进行转换障碍较少，也便于搜索引擎的理解与反馈，从而可以有效实现项目资源与网络资源的整合，以及与外部系统的跨系统、跨平台应用。

3.2.4 构建统一的元数据框架

首先，大型文献数字化项目通常由多个机构合作开展，而且这些机构性质多样，不同性质机构采取的元数据标准存在很大差异。例如，商业公司以检索为目的，其元数据标准相对简洁；文化遗产保护机构基于长期保持的目的，元数据著录详实丰富。即使机构的性质相同，由于自身固有的一些特点，所采用的标准也不尽相同，如图书馆通常采用 MARC，档案馆采用 EDA，有的博物馆则采用 DC。所以在这种情况下，建立一个统一的元数据框架显得尤为重要，这也是大型文献数字化项目的元数据互操作面临的特有问题。

其次，大型文献数字化项目所涉及的文献种类和格式多种多样，要实现项目内部数字资源的有效识别、传递和应用，就必须构建统一的元数据框架。就目前我国大型文献数字化项目发展的现状来看，针对具体类型的文献，如古籍、拓片、甲骨、家谱、舆图等的元数据标准已经建立，但是统一的元数据框架尚未搭建完成，可以借助于元数据注册系统予以全面收集，也可以构建基于 FRBR 模型的 RDA 要素集，不仅可以对所有类型文献的描述元素进行全面呈现，而且可以借助于 FRBR 揭示的关系路线，有效地建立作品、形式、载体、单件等不同实体间的关系。

3.2.5 开展知识组织系统的互操作

本文所调研的元数据互操作是互操作层面的一个基本问题，也是目前大型文献数字化项目在互操作领域采取的主要措施。除此之外，还存在很多高级别的互操作问题，其中知识组织系统的互操作就是目前本领域面临的难题之一。曾蕾等认为：“元数据的互操作看似简单，一旦一些元素已经赋值，而且其取值于受控词汇时，就会使情况变得十分复杂，难免会造成互操作过程中数据的失真或遗失。”[4] 目前基于术语表、叙词表、本体等的互操作研究已经广泛开展，也取得了很多成果，但多是针对某一具体领域，如农业、教育行业等；大型文献数字化项目的文献资源涉及学科广泛，年代跨度大且类型多样，需要用到多种受控词汇，可以借助本体、SKOS、NKOS 等数据模型，发现知识组织系统中的内容概念及其相互关系，利用这些关系可以构建、复用知识组织系统，进而从根本上保障互操作的质量与效果，为信息资源的无缝链接与应用奠定基础。

参考文献

[1] 张晓林. 元数据研究与应用 [M]. 北京：北京图书馆出版社，2002.
[2] 黄田青，刘炜. DC 元数据年度进展（2009）[J]. 数字图书馆论坛，2009（12）：40－44.
[3] 毕强，朱亚玲. 元数据标准及其互操作研究 [J]. 情报理论与实践，2007（5）：155－164.
[4] Zeng M L, Qin J. Metadata [M]. New York：Neal-Schuman Publisher Inc，2008.

[5] CADAL. CADAL元数据规范草案（Version 2.0）[R/OL]. [2015-03-07]. http://www.cadal.cn/cnc/cn/jsgf/CADAL_metadata_2004.pdf.

[6] 北京大学图书馆. 国家图书馆核心元数据标准 [EB/OL]. [2015-03-07]. http://www.nlc.gov.cn/sztsg/2qgc/sjym/files/2.pdf.

[7] Europeana. European Library Metadata [EB/OL]. [2015-03-07]. http://www.theeuropeanlibrary.org/portal/organisation/handbook/display_en.html.

[8] Open Library. Open Library Metadata [EB/OL]. [2015-03-07]. http://openlibrary.org/about/infogami-dc.

[9] HathiTrust. HathiTrust Metadata [EB/OL]. [2015-03-07]. http://www.hathitrust.org/hathifiles_description.

[10] CDL. Guidelines for Digital Objects [EB/OL]. [2015-03-07]. http://www.cdlib.org/services/dsc/contribute/docs/GDO.pdf.

[11] Isaac A. The Europeana Data Model [EB/OL]. [2015-03-07]. http://pro.europeana.eu/documents/866205/13001/EDM_v5.2.2.pdf.

[12] Haslhofer B, etc. Europeana RDF Store Report [EB/OL]. [2015-03-07]. http://www.europeanaconnect.eu/documents/europeana_ts_report.pdf.

[13] Murray P. Mashups of Bibliographic Data: A Report of the ALCTS Midwinter Forum [EB/OL]. [2015-03-07]. http://dltj.org/article/mashups-of-bib-data/.

[14] Tennant R. Bitter Harvest: Problems & Suggested Solutions for OAI-PMH Data & Service Providers [EB/OL]. [2015-03-07]. http://roytennant.com/bitter_harvest.html.

[15] Europeana. D5.1.1 Europeana Metadata Registry [EB/OL]. [2015-03-07]. http://pro.europeana.eu/documents/12117/1000137/The-Europeana-Metadata-Registry.

[16] Linked Data FAQ [EB/OL]. [2015-03-07]. http://structureddynamics.com/.

[17] Europeana Linked Data [EB/OL]. [2015-03-07]. http://pro.europeana.eu/linked-open-data.

教师简介：

曹树金，男，武汉大学管理学学士、硕士，中山大学管理学博士。现任中山大学资讯管理学院院长，教授、博士生导师，中山大学国家保密学院常务副院长。主讲“信息检索与检索语言；信息检索；检索语言”、“电子商务与电子政务研究”、“网络信息组织与利用”、“网络信息组织与利用”、“电子商务与电子政务中的信息管理”、“保密督查”、“保密学概论”等课程。是教育部新世纪优秀人才支持计划入选者。研究方向包括信息组织与信息检索、用户信息行为、网络信息管理、电子商务与电子政务、企业信息化、保密学理论、图书馆战略管理。主持科研项目20余项，出版学术专著10部，在国内外学术刊物及学术会议上发表学术论文80余篇。1994年任美国加州大学洛杉矶分校访问学者。兼任国家社会科学基金学科规划评审专家，全国科技名词审定委员会图书馆、情报与文献学名词审定委员会专家，教育部高等学校保密管理专业教学指导分委会委员，中国索引学会副理事长，中国图书馆学会理事及信息组织专业委员会副主任，中国科技情报学会理事，广东图书馆学会副理事长及学术委员会主任，广东社会科学情报学会副会长，广东科技情报学会常务理事及情报教育专业委员会主任，《中国图书馆分类法》编委等。联系方式：caosj@ mail. sysu. edu. cn。

所选论文《我国图书情报领域研究者对网络信息资源的利用分析》原载于《情报学报》2014年第33卷第9期

我国图书情报领域研究者对网络信息资源的利用分析*

曹树金，李洁娜①

摘　要：本文采用引文分析的方法，基于网络信息资源聚合研究的展开要求，对特定领域研究者网络信息资源的利用情况和需求进行探讨。首先，提出探究研究者网络信息资源利用的网络引文分析框架，从资源整体利用情况和以单篇论文为单位的个体利用情况两个方面分析图书情报领域研究者对网络信息资源的利用情况。接着，参照框架对2010—2012年发表的图书情报领域会议论文、期刊论文、博/硕士学位论文分开进行计量分析，发现其中主题分布、域名分布、类型分布、URL深度分布、研究者利用数量、利用类型、利用目的等的规律，总结图书情报领域网络信息资源利用的特征和需求，得到对图书情报领域网络信息资源聚合研究的相关启示。

关键词：网络引文；引文分析；网络信息资源；网络信息资源聚合

---

* 本文系国家社科基金重大项目“基于特定领域的网络资源知识组织与导航机制研究”（项目批准号：12&ZD223）的研究成果之一。

① 李洁娜，中山大学资讯管理学院情报学硕士研究生。

The Analysis of the Researchers' Utilization of Web Resources in the Field of Library and Information Science

Shujin Cao, Jiena Li

Abstract: Based on the requirement of the research of web resources aggregation, the paper explores the researchers' utilization of web resources through the method of citation analysis. The paper establishes a citation analytical framework to explore the researchers' utilization of web resources. The framework analyses the utilization of web resources from two aspects, the situation of the whole utilization and the particular utilization of web resources. Then, according to the framework, conference papers, journal articles, graduate thesis in the field of Library and Information which were published from 2010-2012 are quantitative analyzed separately. The paper analyzes web citations' topics, domain names, website type, the URL depth, the quantity and purposes of utilization and so on, and concludes the characteristics and needs of utilization of web resources in the field of Library and Information. Some proposals for web resources integration also be put forward.

Keywords: Web citation; Citation analysis; Web resources; Web resources integration

1 引　言

网络信息资源数量庞大，增长迅速，形式多种多样，来源分散，质量参差不齐，研究者对网络信息资源的选择和利用情况必然与对传统信息资源的使用情况不同，他们如何进行选择，主要选择哪些资源，对网络信息资源又有着怎样的需求，这些都是数字时代下需要探讨的问题。另外，如何能通过深度聚合特定学科领域需要的网络信息资源，让研究者更加准确快捷地搜索并获取所需要的学术信息，即如何实现网络上分散资源的整合利用已经成为亟待解决的研究课题。为进行此课题的研究，必须首先对特定领域研究者选择和利用网络信息资源的情况有较深入的了解，并在此基础上总结研究者的聚合需求。国内外对网络信息资源的特征、使用情况及需求等已经作了一定程度的研究，但笔者发现很少研究针对特定学科领域网络信息资源聚合的角度，因此，现有研究结果还不足以为网络信息资源聚合提供足够的理论准备。鉴于此，本文分析图书情报领域研究者对网络信息资源的选择和利用情况，也以从深度聚合的角度探讨相关问题并对已有的研究结果进行补充为目的。

董小英等学者采用问卷调查的方法，对我国学术界互联网用户的背景、用户利用互联网资源的现状、用户的信息查询行为、用户对互联网信息资源的评价和用户对未来互联网服务的期望五个方面进行了分析和讨论。[1]而更多学者通过网络引文计量分析来了解网络信息资源的使用情况。网络引文即参考文献中著录内容含有网址（URL）的引文[2]，一篇论文的网络引文就是该论文引用的网络信息资源。宋歌[3]、谭芳兰[4]、张洋等[5]、薛卫双等[6]分别在2001—2010年不同时期对我国图书情报学期刊所载论文的网络引文的各种特征量进行统计分析，探讨网络学术资源开发与利用的相关问题，分析的特征量包括网络引文的数量、语种、域名、类型、网站被引频次、高频被引网站、篇平均网络引文量、作者情况等。

本文也是采用对网络引文的计量分析来进行研究。因为通过对网络引文进行深入的统计及数据挖掘分析，来研究特定学科网络信息资源使用情况，比访谈和问卷调查等方式更具有客观性、实用性与针对性。[7]同时，笔者发现，尽管已有不少论文运用网络引文的实证分析方法探究研究者利用网络信息资源的情况，但是通过对网络引文的分析还能得到更多的信息，特别是能够为网络信息资源聚合提供理论指导的信息，如研究者使用网络信息资源的目的、网络信息资源来源网站的具体类型等，而已有研究较少深入分析这方面的内容。本文增加了对这些内容的分析，也是对目前研究现状的一种补充。

另外，现有研究的样本基本来源于期刊所载论文，而没有考虑学位论文、会议论文的网络引文。学位论文与会议论文同样是学术研究成果的重要组成部分。学位论文是在导师的严格审核和直接指导下，用 2 ～ 3 年时间才完成的科研成果，还必须通过院校或研究所的专家评审答辩后才能通过，其论文质量有保障。而且，研究生在撰写论文的过程中，往往要查阅大量的国内外文献资料，使参考文献呈现多而全面的特点，这是学位论文与期刊论文、会议论文最大的区别。[8]对于会议论文，鉴于定期举行会议，会议论文讨论的研究课题紧扣当下热点，且审查速度较快，而期刊论文受限于比会议论文更为细致的评估标准，研究人员必须不断地修改自己的文章，直到它与审稿委员会成员提出的建议一致。因此，期刊论文缺乏会议论文所具有的时效性和新颖性。[9]基于学位论文、会议论文同期刊论文存在的差异以及它们在学术研究上的重要性，笔者认为有必要将学位论文、会议论文与期刊论文一起列为研究对象，以得到更加全面、客观、充分的研究结果。这也是本文对网络引文研究发展方向提出的新的思考。

2 分析框架

图书情报领域网络信息资源聚合是指将来自多个分布、异构的，能够在图书情报领域用户专业学习、学术研究与管理决策中发挥作用的，不同粒度的结构与非结构化的网络信息资源整合在一起。因此，网络信息资源聚合需要了解研究者利用的网络信息资源的主题、来源、类型、利用目的等的分布规律。借鉴已有的网络引文研究内容，并增加进行网络信息资源聚合研究需要的并可以从网络引文中获得的信息（如网络信息资源的主题分布、网页类型分布、网站类型分布等），笔者建立如图 1 所示的分析框架，并将分析内容划分为整体利用情况和个体利用情况两方面。整体利用情况主要指研究者利用网络信息资源的广度、深度、集中度和所利用资源的稳定性，个体利用情况分析主要立足于单篇论文分析研究者引用网络信息资源的数量、类型和目的。

3 图书情报领域网络引文定量分析研究

3.1 数据来源

本文探究的是当前图书情报领域网络信息资源的特征和需求，同时考虑到网络引文衰减规律的影响，笔者选取 2010 年到 2012 年发表的图书情报领域的期刊论文、会议论

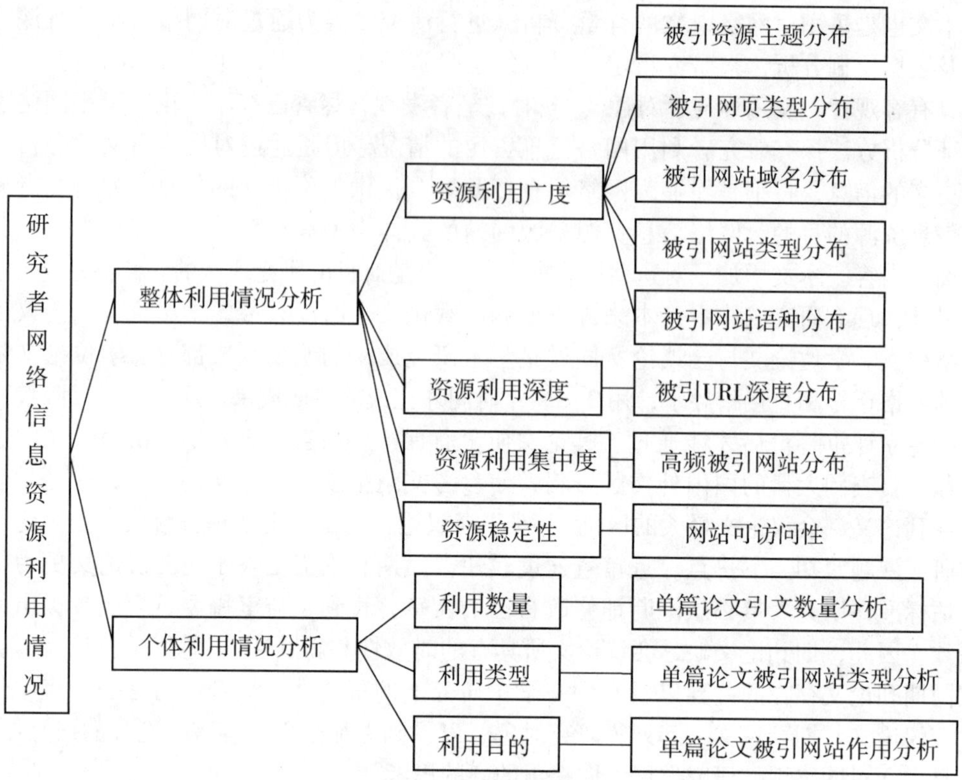

图1　网络引文分析框架

文、学位论文进行分析。对于期刊论文，选择《中国图书馆学报》、《图书与情报》、《情报理论与实践》这三种期刊为分析样本。期刊论文的引文通过 CSSCI 引文数据库下载，再从中抽取网络引文。对于学位论文和会议论文，笔者采用的方法是在 CNKI 博硕士文献/会议文献的检索页面下，将学科领域选定为"信息科技"下的"图书情报与数字图书馆"，再选定发表时间以及增加参考文献包含"http"或"www."这个检索条件进行检索，获取包括网络引文的文献。由于 CNKI 无法直接下载参考文献，所以笔者是先将论文下载下来，再抽取其中的网络引文。考虑到数据处理能力的限制，笔者对包含网络引文的期刊论文、会议论文、学位论文进行随机抽样（利用 SPSS 20 中选择个案的功能，会议论文每年选择 50 个样本，期刊论文每年选择 60 个样本，学位论文每年选择 65 个样本，以时间为随机数种子），记录这些文献的网络引文，再利用 Excel 和 SPSS 进行分析。抽样情况及网络引文的可获得率如表 1 所示。

表 1　数据样本基本情况

文献		文献发表量/篇	含网络引文的文献总量/篇	含网络引文的文章所占比例/%	样本文献数量/篇	样本包括的网络引文量/条	篇均网络引文/条	样本网络引文可获得率/%
2010 年	会议论文	542	113	20. 85	50	127	2. 54	61. 98
	期刊论文	624	321	51. 44	60	287	4. 78	61. 75
	学位论文	390	307	78. 72	65	608	9. 35	61. 38
	总和	1556	741	47. 62	175	1022	5. 84	61. 56
2011 年	会议论文	328	72	21. 95	50	137	2. 74	65. 19
	期刊论文	600	302	50. 33	60	185	3. 08	62. 98
	学位论文	498	344	69. 08	65	483	7. 43	58. 17
	总和	1426	718	50. 35	175	805	4. 60	60. 48
2012 年	会议论文	415	102	24. 58	50	135	2. 70	76. 00
	期刊论文	570	285	50. 00	60	353	5. 88	75. 36
	学位论文	494	301	60. 93	65	682	10. 49	71. 43
	总和	1479	688	46. 52	175	1170	6. 69	73. 13
总和		4461	2147	48. 13	525	2997	5. 71	65. 78

说明：通过软件 Web Link Validator 5. 7 进行链接检测，可获得率为可以访问的网络引文网址数量所占的比例。

由表 1 可知，学位论文引用网络引文的现象最为明显，2010—2012 年都有超过 60% 的文献包含网络引文，且篇均网络引文量超过 7 条；其次是期刊论文，包含网络引文的文献占 50% 以上，篇均网络引文量在 4 条左右；会议论文也有超过 20% 的文献引用了网络引文，篇均网络引文量在 2 ～ 3 条。不过，这三种文献在三年间对网络引文的利用频率并没有明显的增长，甚至有细微的下降，这表明图书情报领域研究者对网络信息资源的利用已经到达一种较为平稳的状态，其他较早时期相关文献提到的飞速增长的势头已经过去，研究者对网络引文的利用渐趋理性。此时利用网络引文对研究者网络信息资源的使用情况进行分析应该能获得更客观、有价值的结果。样本的网络引文可获得率为 65. 78% 。

3. 2　整体利用情况分析

3. 2. 1　资源利用广度分析

（1）被引资源主题分布。笔者浏览采集到的 2012 年所有能够成功链接的网络引文，记录网络引文的主题，并利用 Excel 宏操作将会议论文、期刊论文、学位论文三种文献的全部网络引文主题分布情况绘制成标签云图，如图2所示。图中括号内的数字表示主题出现的频次。为了消除单篇论文网络引文数量的影响，如果在同一篇论文中引用了多篇相同主题的网络引文，这多篇网络引文的主题频次只记为1。

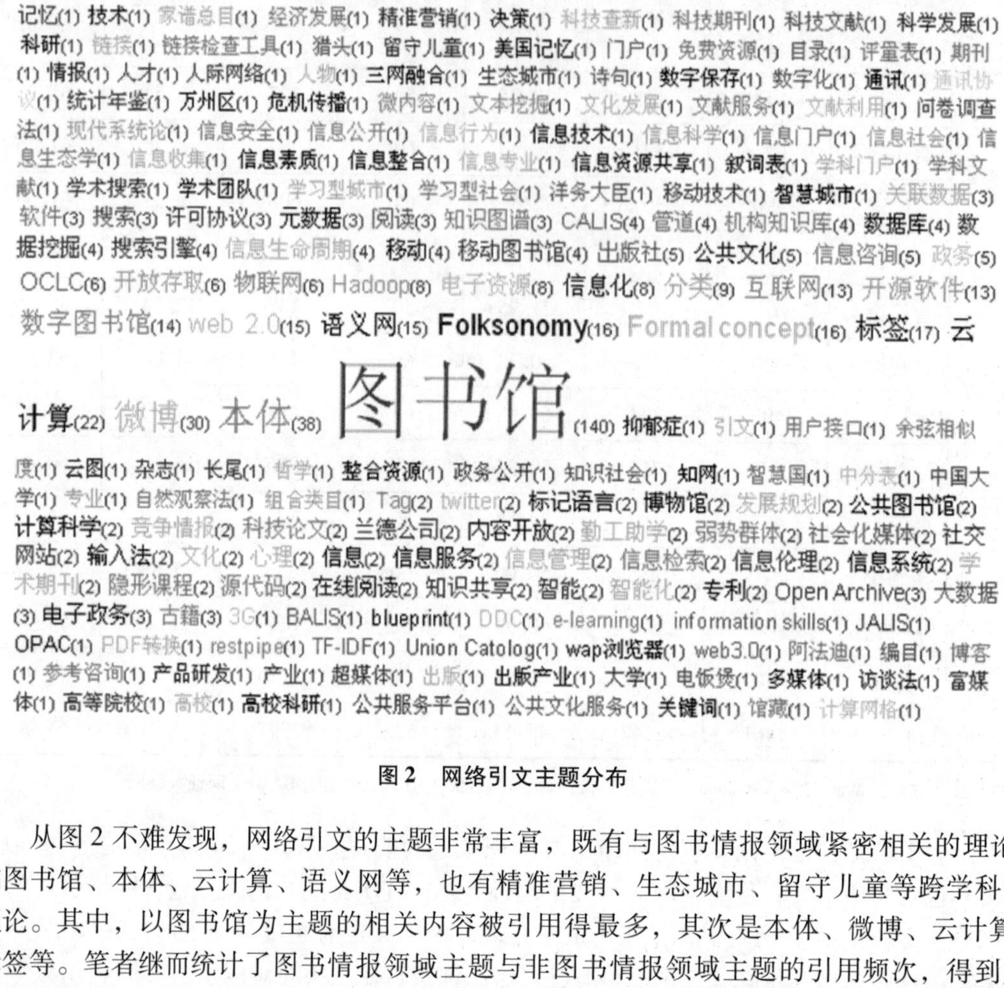

图2　网络引文主题分布

从图2不难发现，网络引文的主题非常丰富，既有与图书情报领域紧密相关的理论，如图书馆、本体、云计算、语义网等，也有精准营销、生态城市、留守儿童等跨学科的理论。其中，以图书馆为主题的相关内容被引用得最多，其次是本体、微博、云计算、标签等。笔者继而统计了图书情报领域主题与非图书情报领域主题的引用频次，得到如表2的数据。有18.38%的网络引文是非本学科领域的理论，比重较大。这一方面是因为图书情报学具有交叉学科性质；另一方面也是因为随着网络的发展，网络的便捷性日益凸显，网络信息资源的质量逐渐提高，通过网络来获取自己不熟悉领域的信息是一种高效率的途径。其中，会议论文的跨学科引用情况最为显著，有35.29%的网络引文是非图书情报领域的内容，笔者认为这与会议论文的特点有关。会议论文时效性最强，论文中会更多引用与政治形势、时代特点、前沿学科相关的内容，而这些内容往往最先在网络上发布，因此，会议论文参考较多非图书情报领域的网络引文。而期刊论文与学位论文的网络引文在主题上分布情况相似。

表 2　网络引文主题分布情况　　单位：%

论文	图书情报领域	非图书情报领域
会议论文	64.71	35.29
期刊论文	83.66	16.34
学位论文	83.44	16.56
总体情况	81.62	18.38

（2）被引网页类型分布。为了了解图书情报领域研究者对网络信息资源文本格式的需求，笔者对 2010—2012 年网络引文的网页类型进行了统计，结果如表 3 所示。

表 3　网络引文网页类型分布　　单位：%

年份	html/htm/shtml	PDF	xls/doc/PPT	动态网页	其他
2010	32.39	10.27	0.59	42.86	13.89
2011	36.89	12.55	1.25	39.25	10.31
2012	35.73	16.58	0.43	35.21	12.05

动态网页是指与静态网页相对的，通过网页脚本和语言自动处理、自动更新的页面，多以 .asp、.aspx、.php、.jsp 结尾[10]。其他主要是一些只以网站、主机形式或 IP 地址著录的引文。由表 3 可以看出，2010 年到 2012 年网页类型引用变化最明显的是对 PDF 的引用，且呈现增长的趋势。PDF 能够跨平台显示任何源文档的原貌（包括字体、格式、颜色和图形等），且压缩的 Adobe PDF 文件比源文件小，易于传输与存储；同时，它还是页独立的，可以单独处理各页，每次下载一页在网页上快速显示，而且不会降低网络速度。[11] 因此，PDF 越来越成为网络学术资源的标准格式。[12]

会议论文、期刊论文、学位论文网络引文的网页类型如图 3 所示。可见，在会议论文中，研究者们引用 PDF 格式资源的情况并不显著。笔者认为这和会议论文的特点有关，会议论文更多参考时下最新的前沿信息，这类信息较少以 PDF 格式存在，所以，会议论文更多地参考动态网页或者以 html/htm/shtml 等静态网页格式呈现的资源。三种文献都较少引用网络 Excel 表格、Word 文档、PPT 文档等资源。

（3）被引网站域名分布。通过对网络引文的高层域名进行分析，可以了解网络信息资源的来源和分布集中情况。笔者统计发现网络引文较常见的类别域名有 .com（工商金融等企业）、.edu（教育机构）、.org（非营利性组织）、.ac（科研机构）、.gov（政府部门）、.net（互联网络的信息中心和运行中心）。类别域名可能在网站中充当顶级域名，也可能充当二级域名，如 .com，本文提取该网址的二级域名进行统计。不同域名在三种文献的网络引文中的分布情况如图 4 所示，其他指著录为 IP 地址、网址中无类别域名只有国别域名以及属于其他类别域名如 .mil、.info、.name 等的网站。

由图 4 可知，会议论文引用域名的频率为 .com > .edu > .org > .gov > .net > .ac，期刊论文为 .org > .com > .edu > .gov > .net > .ac，学位论文为 .com > .org > .edu > .gov > .net > .ac。三种文献的引用情况接近。从全球范围来看，.com 网站在所有网站中比例最高，其次是 .net，但是网络引文中引用 .net 的比例较少，可见，研究者们对网络信息资源是有

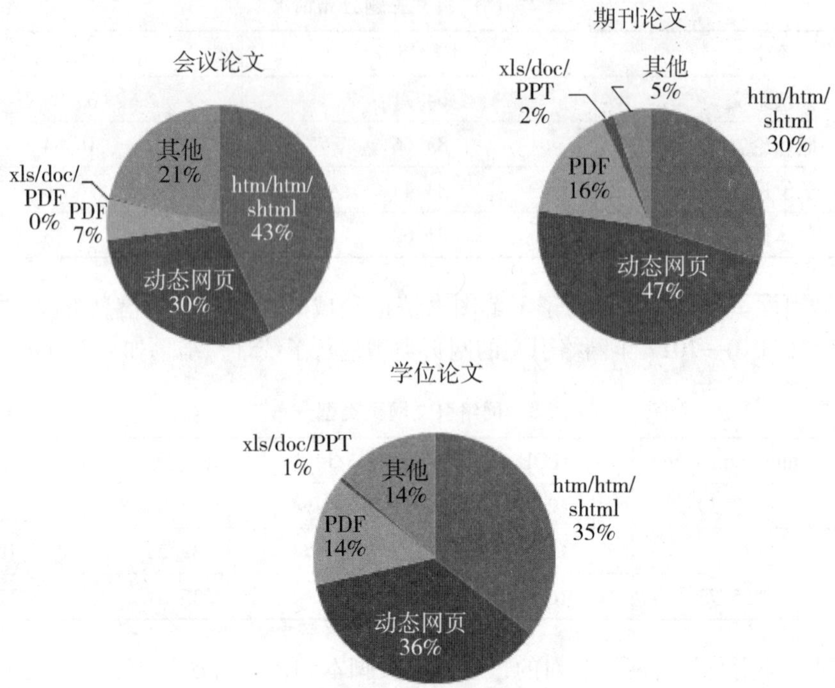

图3　被引网页类型分布情况

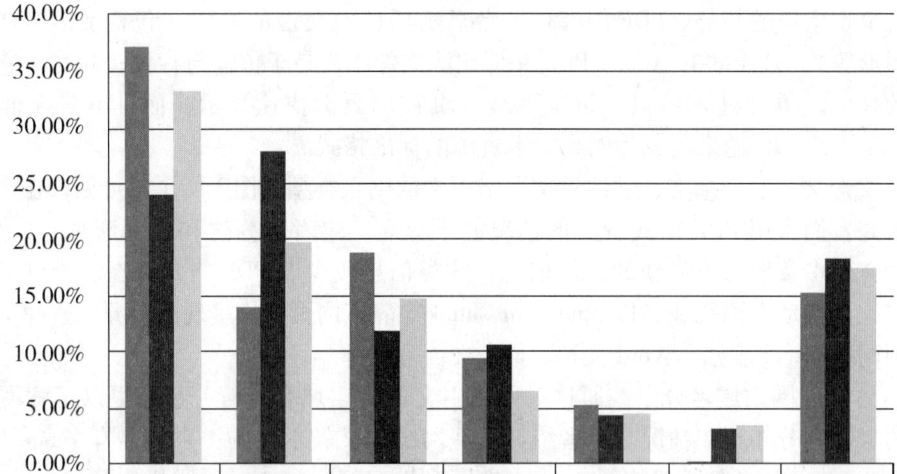

	com	org	edu	gov	net	ac	其他
■会议论文	37.09%	13.78%	18.80%	9.52%	5.26%	0.25%	15.29%
■期刊论文	23.88%	27.76%	11.88%	10.67%	4.36%	3.15%	18.30%
■学位论文	33.22%	19.80%	14.83%	6.54%	4.62%	3.50%	17.48%

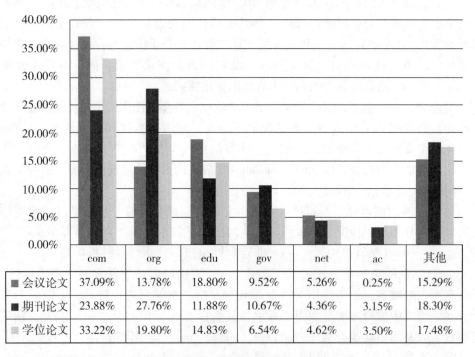

图4　被引网站类别域名分布情况

选择性地使用的。. com、. org、. edu 的网站中包含了较多可信度较高、质量较好、满足图书情报领域研究者学术需求的网络信息资源。本文同时对 2010—2012 年类别域名使用频率进行统计，发现差别不大，在此不赘述。

值得注意的是，笔者对国家或地区级域名也进行了统计，发现图书情报领域研究者除了引用中国域名和国际域名的资源外，还有引用其他国家或地区域名的资源，如表4 所示。我们可以发现图书情报领域网络信息资源的来源非常广泛，研究者们具有较强的外文资源使用意识和能力。并且，对其他国家或地区资源的引用频次逐年有所增加，来源也有愈加广泛的趋势。英国、德国、中国台湾地区、加拿大的资源参考较多。

表4　引用其他国家或地区域名分布情况

国家级域名	国家或地区	频次			总频次
		2010 年	2011 年	2012 年	
uk	英国	41	24	35	100
de	德国	6	7	40	53
tw	中国台湾	20	14	9	43
ca	加拿大	7	9	9	25
au	澳大利亚	11	6	2	19
it	意大利	3	1	13	17
hk	中国香港	6	5	4	15
us	美国	2	3	9	14
jp	日本	7	4	2	13
fr	法国	1	1	9	11
at	奥地利	2	0	8	10
es	西班牙	2	5	3	10
nl	荷兰	2	3	2	7
nz	新西兰	2	0	3	5
dk	丹麦	1	2	2	5
br	巴西	1	0	3	4
pt	葡萄牙	0	0	3	3

说明：除了中国域名（. cn）、国际域名（. com、. net、. org 等）的国家或地区域名分布情况。

（4）被引网站类型分布。尽管通过网站的域名可以了解网络信息资源的来源，但是域名的分类比较宽泛，不足以帮助我们建立对网络引文来源网站的清晰认识。本文对网站进行更具体的分类，以更深入地探究图书情报领域网络信息资源利用的特征和需求。本文的分析基于网址的服务器级别，即根据 URL 中 hostname（主机名）来分析，它是指存放资源的服务器域名（显著特点是在 URL 中有“/”符号与其他部分分隔开）。[13]

中国互联网络信息中心按照主题性质的不同，将网站分为政府网站、企业网站、商业网站、教育科研网站、个人网站、其他公益性网站以及其他网站七类。笔者通过观察采集到的网络引文并参考互联网信息中心的分类，将网站类型分为政府网站、机构网站（包括企业与非营利组织）、商务网站、教育科研网站、个人网站、新闻网站、在线百科全书、信息门户网站和其他网站九类，并按获取途径对一些类目再进行细分，得到如表5所示的网站类型体系。

表5 网站类型体系

分类		网站举例	参考内容
政府网站		中国广州政府（http://www.gz.gov.cn）	引用资源主要为政务信息、年鉴、统计报告等
机构网站		IBM公司主页（http://www.ibm.com/cn/zh/），香港大学图书馆长联席会（http://www.julac.org/）	引用资源主要为机构介绍及机构提供的相关信息资源
商务网站		亚马逊（http://www.amazon.com）	主要作为数据采集源或实证分析对象
教育科研网站	开放存取期刊	First Monday（http://firstmonday.org/），e-print archive（http://arxiv.org/）	引用资源为相关文献，多为外文文献
	文献导航网站	CALIS（http://www.calis.edu.cn/）	多是文献来源或网站整体引用作为实证分析对象
	学术协会/机构网站	OCLC（http://www.oclc.org/），Council on Library and Information Resources（http://www.clir.org/）	多引用该协会提供的相关信息或该协会的简介
	专业论坛	Naples Forum（http://naple.mcu.es/），人大经济论坛（http://www.pinggu.org）	引用资源为特定专业的信息
	开源软件/协议标准提供网站	hadoop（http://hadoop.apache.org/），The DARPA Agent Markup Language（http://www.daml.org/）	使用该开源软件资源或引用相关技术文档说明
	大学网站	Computer Science-Duke University（http://www.cs.duke.edu/）	引用大学或学院相关信息
	图书馆网站	上海图书馆（http://www.library.sh.cn/）	引用资源为该图书馆的规章制度、年鉴报告等
	学术会议网站	Joint Conference on Digital Libraries（http://www.jcdl.org/），3rd Central European Conference in Regional Science（http://www.cers.tuke.sk/）	引用资源多为与该会议相关的理论成果
个人网站	个人主页	danah boyd（http://www.danah.org/）	多引用作者提供的信息资源或其研究成果
	博客	郭崇慧的博客（http://blog.sciencenet.cn/home.php?mod=space&uid=34250）	多引用作者提供的信息资源或其研究成果
	微博	暨南大学图书馆微博（http://e.weibo.com/1998400881/ycoYJyBZu）	多为实证分析对象

续表 5

分类		网站举例	参考内容
新闻网站		新华网（http://www.xinhuanet.com/）	引用相关的新闻信息
在线百科全书		百度百科（http://baike.baidu.com/）	多参考相关名词定义
信息门户网站	综合信息门户	搜狐网（http://www.sohu.com/）	多引用门户提供的信息资源
	地方信息门户	中国西藏网（http://www.tibet.cn/）	引用门户提供的信息资源
	专业信息门户	比特网（http://www.chinabyte.com/），OntologyPortal（http://www.ontologyportal.org）	引用资源为特定专业的相关理论知识
其他	社区网站	豆瓣（http://www.douban.com/），Flickr（http://www.flickr.com/）	多为数据采集源或对整个站点引用，作为实证分析对象
	文档共享平台	道客巴巴（http://www.doc88.com/）	多参考平台上文献资源
	搜索引擎	Quintura（http://quintura.com/）	对整个站点引用，多作为示例或实证分析对象

资料来源：表格中列举的网站例子均来源于采集的网络引文。

笔者按照表 5 的分类体系，统计采集到 2012 年所有可打开网络信息资源的网站类型，得到被引网站类型分布如图 5、图 6 所示。由图 5 可知，教育科研网站在三种文献中都占据最大的比重，会议论文占 48.24%，期刊论文占 47.71%，学位论文占 38.80%。这里的教育科研类网站不只包括域名为 .edu 的网站，还包括域名为 .org 的学术机构主页、学术会议主页、开源软件下载网站、协议标准说明网站等学术类网站。可见图书情报领域引用的网络信息资源仍较多来自学术网站。在细分类目中，会议论文和期刊论文引用最多

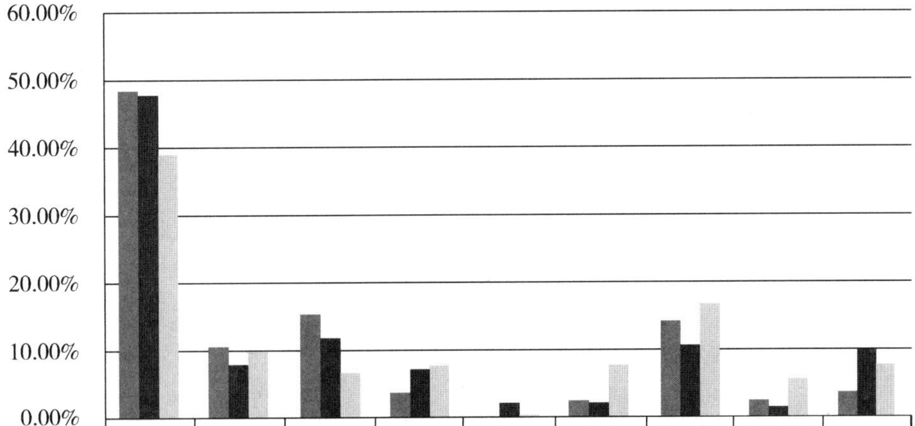

	教育科研网站	在线百科全书	政府网站	机构网站	商务网站	个人网站	信息门户网站	新闻网站	其他
会议论文	48.24%	10.59%	15.29%	3.53%	0.00%	2.35%	14.12%	2.35%	3.53%
期刊论文	47.71%	7.84%	11.76%	7.19%	1.96%	1.96%	10.46%	1.31%	9.80%
学位论文	38.80%	9.58%	6.66%	7.47%	0.32%	7.63%	16.56%	5.36%	7.63%

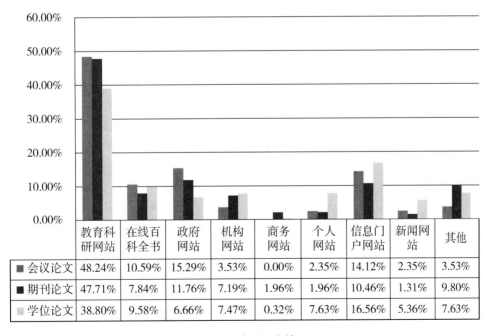

图 5　被引网站类型分布情况（1）

的是图书馆网站，而学位论文引用最多的是专业信息门户。专业信息门户指经过组织、有序化和人工处理、专家排选、定期检查处理的某一学科或某一领域的信息导航系统。如 SocialBeta（http://www.socialbeta.com/）专注于社会化媒体这一领域的研究和资源共享，便是一个社会化媒体的专业信息门户网站。可见，专业信息门户网站也是图书情报领域网络信息资源的重要来源，应予以重视。

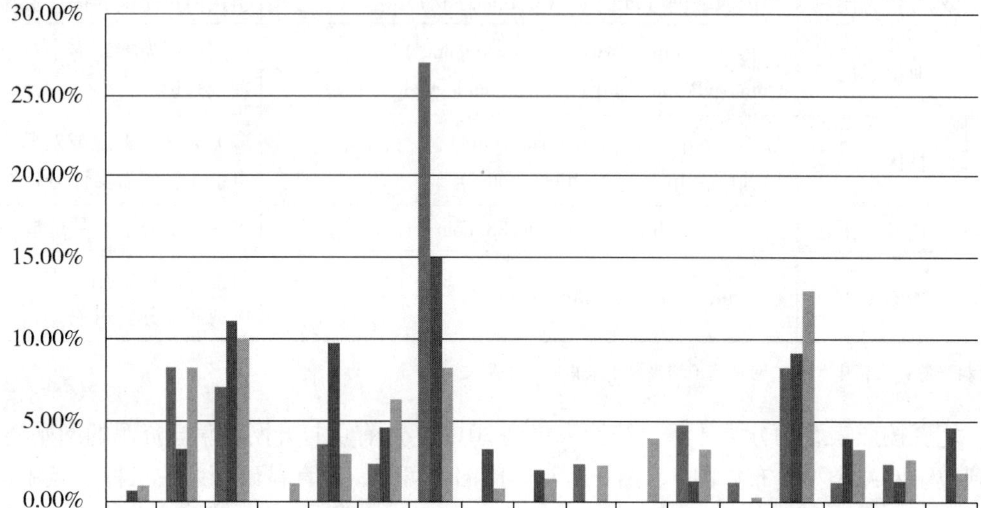

	开放存取期刊	文献导航网站	学术协会/机构网站	专业论坛	开源软件/协议标准提供网站	大学网站	图书馆网站	学术会议网站	个人主页	博客	微博	综合信息门户	地方信息门户	专业信息门户	社区网站	文档共享平台	搜索引擎
	教育科研网站								个人网站			信息门户网站			其他		
会议论文	0.00%	8.24%	7.06%	0.00%	3.53%	2.35%	27.06%	0.00%	0.00%	2.35%	0.00%	4.71%	1.18%	8.24%	1.18%	2.35%	0.00%
期刊论文	0.65%	3.27%	11.11%	0.00%	9.80%	4.58%	15.03%	3.27%	1.96%	0.00%	0.00%	1.31%	0.00%	9.15%	3.92%	1.31%	4.58%
学位论文	0.97%	8.28%	10.06%	1.14%	2.92%	6.33%	8.28%	0.81%	1.46%	2.27%	3.90%	3.25%	0.32%	12.99%	3.25%	2.60%	1.79%

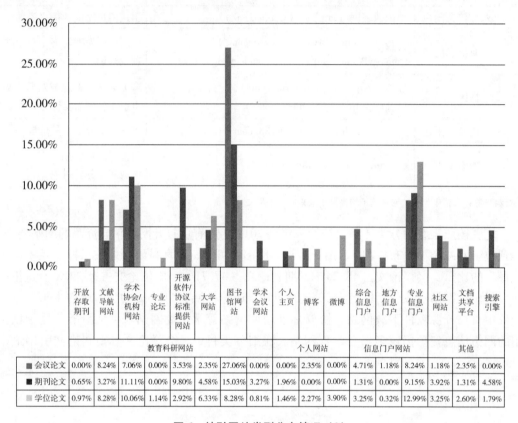

图6　被引网站类型分布情况（2）

学术协会/机构网站被引用的频率也很高。由图6可知，会议论文的网络引文来自学术协会/机构网站的占所有网络引文的7.06%，期刊论文的占11.11%，学位论文的占10.06%。学术协会/机构网站指学术型组织的主页，如OCLC（联机计算机图书馆中心）主页（http://www.oclc.org/）提供中心成员、产品及服务、新闻及活动等的信息，便归入学术协会/机构网站。文献导航网站也被引用较多，文献导航网站指如CSSCI、Calis、CiteSeer等提供文献索引的网站。笔者观察发现作者对这类网站大多是整体引用，即将这类网站作为论点的例证或实证分析的对象，而比较少引用网站中全文型的信息。对商务网站、搜索引擎、社交网站的引用也存在这样的情况。

网站引用类型的整体分布情况如图7所示，可见教育科研机构网站在图书情报领域网络信息资源中的重要地位。

（5）被引网络信息资源语种分布。本文通过统计网络引文来源网站的语种来获得被引网络信息资源的语种分布情况，得到如图8的结果，对于少数日语、德语、法语等的网

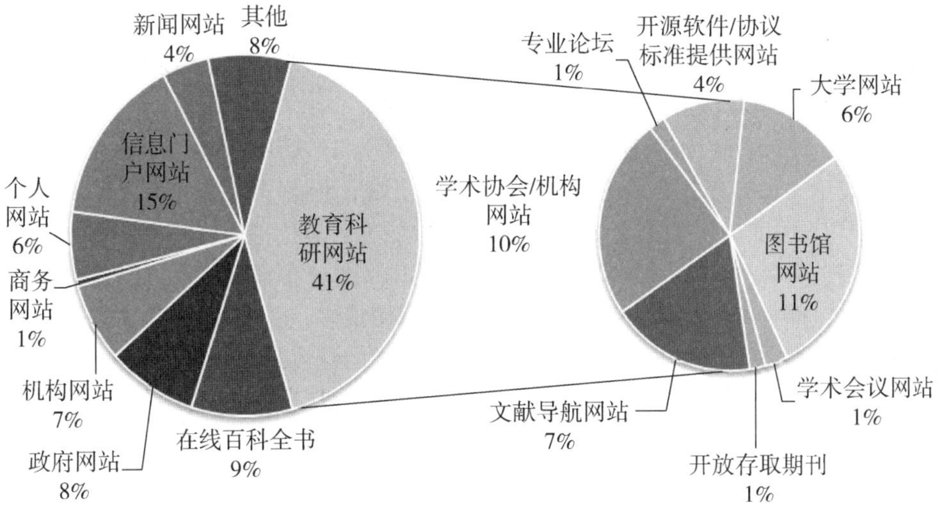

图7　被引网站类型总体分布情况

络资源以及没有标出题目的网络引文归入其他类。除了会议论文，其他两类论文都较多地参考了外文的网络信息资源，外文大部分是英文。结果反映了图书情报领域研究者掌握和使用外国文献的能力较高，对外文文献有较高的需求。笔者认为会议论文引用外文网络信息资源较少的原因在于会议的主题（较多涉及图书馆和信息服务）需要更多地参考我国的信息资源；期刊论文和学位论文主题范围较广，参考的网络信息资源相较之下会分布较广。2010—2012 年，三种文献总体来说对中文和英文网络信息资源的使用频次较为接近，英文资源的利用略高于中文资源。

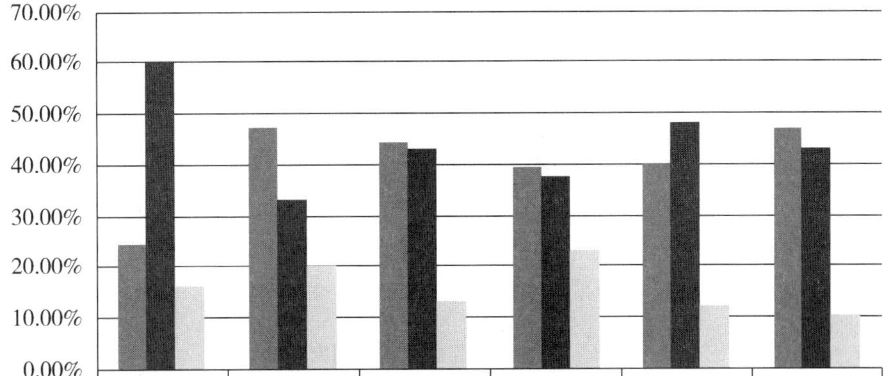

	会议论文	期刊论文	学位论文	2010	2011	2012
英文	24.31%	47.15%	44.22%	39.43%	39.75%	46.75%
中文	59.65%	35.09%	42.98%	37.57%	48.07%	42.91%
其他	16.04%	19.76%	12.80%	22.99%	12.17%	10.34%

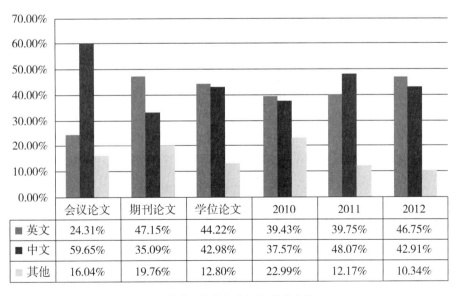

图8　被引网络信息资源语种分布情况

3.2.2 利用资源深度分析

资源利用深度，需分析被引 URL 的深度分布。本文这样描述 URL 深度：网址中每增加一个“/”，就认定其深度加 1；若没有“/”或“/”在 URL 末尾，则深度为 0。[13] 例如 http://informationr.net/ir/6-1/paper90.html 的深度为 3。URL 深度为 0 表示论文对该网站整体引用或论文虽参考了较深层次的网络信息资源，但著录不完整。笔者统计了所有网络引文的 URL 深度。不管是会议论文、期刊论文还是学位论文，引用最多的都是深度为 2 的网络信息资源。2010—2012 年网络引文 URL 深度分布情况基本一致，图 9 是 2012 年的分布情况，都是深度为 2 的网络信息资源被引用最多。三种文献 URL 深度小于或等于 5 的网络引文都占了 95% 以上。会议论文网络引文的深度最大为 9，期刊论文和学位论文网络引文的深度最大为 11；中文网络引文的深度最大为 11，英文网络引文的深度最大为 10。

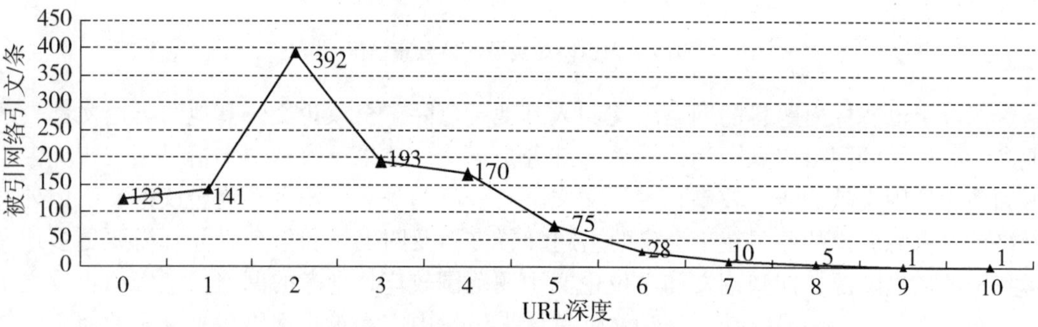

图 9 2012 年被引网络信息资源 URL 深度分布情况

3.2.3 利用资源集中度分析

本文主要对服务器级别的网站进行频次分析，即把主机名相同的网址聚集分析，得到较高频被引网站列表（表 6）。在这些高频被引网站中，除了百度百科、百度文库和新华网，其他网站都是学术性较强的网络资源，包括图书情报领域的相关协会组织、信息技术领域具有权威性的网站和具有相当影响力的文献导航库。由表 6 可以发现研究者在网络信息资源的利用上有一定的集中度，倾向于引用本领域相关协会组织提供的信息，但是集中度并不强，网络信息资源的来源非常广泛。

表 6 高频被引网站及其访问率情况

网站主机名	网站名称	频次			总频次	可访问率/%
		2010 年	2011 年	2012 年		
baidu	百度百科	27	24	43	94	99.38
sina	新浪网	13	12	13	38	84.62
wikipedia	英语维基百科	10	9	9	28	84.21

续表6

网站主机名	网站名称	频次			总频次	可访问率/%
		2010年	2011年	2012年		
ifla	国际图书馆协会联合会	8	6	12	26	50.00
w3	World Wide Web Consortium (W3C)	8	3	13	24	84.75
xinhuanet	新华网	6	10	6	22	72.73
cnnic	中国互联网信息中心	6	6	9	21	28.00
oclc	联机计算机图书馆中心	7	4	9	20	83.33
people	人民网	6	7	7	20	95.83
tsinghua	清华大学	14	0	5	19	81.25
arl	Association of Research Libraries	9	6	4	19	79.17
gov	中华人民共和国中央人民政府门户网站	5	6	7	18	68.42
calis	Calis联合书目数据库	4	5	7	16	94.12
ala	美国图书馆协会	8	3	5	16	35.29
nlc	中国国家数字图书馆	5	3	7	15	47.37
stanford	斯坦福大学	8	3	4	15	82.35
google	Google	3	3	8	14	93.33
dlib	D-Lib电子杂志	6	4	3	13	68.75
sciencenet	科学网	3	7	3	13	68.75
loc	国会图书馆	3	1	8	12	78.57
citeseerx	CiteSeer引文索引系统	3	1	7	11	95.45
china	中国网	3	6	1	10	90.00

3.2.4 资源稳定性分析

如果访问不到网络引文指向的网络信息资源，即使资源的质量再高也无济于事，网络引文的可访问性一直是研究的热点，国外更针对这个问题积极构建互联网档案馆。可见，网络信息资源的可访问性意义重大。因此，本文认为有必要通过网络引文的可获得性探究利用对象网站的稳定性。本文统计了高频网站的可访问率，使用公式Ⅰ，得到表6的“可访问率”一列。其他被引网站也可以基于此公式计算可访问率。

$$\text{可访问率} = \frac{\text{可访问的与高频网站同主机名的引文网址}}{\text{所有与高频网站同主机名的引文网址}}。 \qquad (\text{Ⅰ})$$

由表6可知，高频被引的国际图书馆协会联合会主页、中国互联网信息中心、美国图书馆协会、中国国家数字图书馆的网站稳定性都不高，可访问率小于50%，这意味着很多重要的信息会随着时间的流逝而消失。针对这种情况，笔者认为图书情报领域网络信息资源聚合过程中应该采取能够更久地保存资源的策略，满足图书情报领域研究者的研究需求。

3.3 个体利用情况分析

3.3.1 利用数量分析

本文统计不同类型文献2010—2012年每篇论文引用的网络引文数量，发现会议论文的网络引文数量较少，集中在每篇引用1～3条网络引文；期刊论文也基本上集中在每篇论文引用1～3条网络引文，但引用4条以上网络引文的比例较会议论文大；学位论文篇均网络引文的数量较多，且集中在5～20条，这与学位论文篇幅较长，本身参考文献总数就较期刊论文、会议论文多有关（表7）。

表7 单篇论文网络信息资源利用数量分布 单位：条

网络引文篇数	学位论文			期刊论文			会议论文			总计
	2010年	2011年	2012年	2010年	2011年	2012年	2010年	2011年	2012年	
[50，76]	0	0	3	0	0	1	0	0	0	4
[30，50)	4	0	3	0	0	0	0	0	0	7
[20，30)	3	5	4	2	0	1	0	0	0	15
[10，20)	16	14	8	9	2	11	1	3	1	65
[5，10)	15	20	12	7	11	8	5	4	7	89
4	3	4	7	6	6	4	2	3	6	41
3	6	4	12	11	10	8	7	10	4	72
2	7	6	6	8	9	9	14	9	10	78
1	11	12	10	17	22	18	21	21	22	154

3.3.2 利用类型分析

笔者统计每篇论文的网络引文量以及引用的网络信息资源来源网站的类型（分类体系见表5），用SPSS分析发现网络引文量与网站类型数量之间并没有相关性，也就是说，并不是作者引用的网络引文越多，其引用网站的类型越丰富。对2012年的样本进行统计发现，在141篇论文中（共175篇论文，34篇论文的网络引文超过一半无法获得，则不予以统计）只参考了一种网站类型的论文有52篇，占所有论文的37%；参考两种网站类型的论文有34篇，占24%；参考三种网站类型的论文有23篇，占16%；参考四种以上类型网站的论文有32篇，占23%（表8）。参考网站类型最多的一篇论文共参考了14种类型的网站。研究者们对于网络信息资源的使用是基于论文主题的，根据主题研究的需要寻找网络上相应的信息资源，而往往相关的信息资源会被存储在相似类型的网站中，因此，一篇论文参考的网站类型会集中在3种之内。

由表8也可发现，52%的会议论文参考了一种类型网站，26%的会议论文参考了两种类型的网站，13%的会议论文参考了三种类型网站，参考三种以内类型网站的会议论文比例占91%；47%的期刊论文参考了一种类型的网站，23%的期刊论文参考了两种类型的网站，13%的期刊论文参考了三种类型的网站，参考三种以内类型网站的期刊论文比例占83%；22%的学位论文参考了一种类型的网站，24%的学位论文参考了两种类型的网站，21%的学位论文参考了三种类型的网站，合67%的学位论文参考了三种以内类型的网站。由此，不管是会议论文、期刊论文还是学位论文，论文参考的网站类型都较多在1～3种，且只参考一种网站类型的论文占据较高比例。

表8　单篇论文网络信息资源利用类型数量分布　　单位：篇

网站类型数量	会议论文	期刊论文	学位论文	总计
1	16	22	14	52
2	8	11	15	34
3	4	6	13	23
4	1	3	3	7
5	1	4	6	11
6	0	0	2	2
7	1	0	4	5
≥8	0	1	6	7
总计	31	47	63	141

3.3.3　利用目的分析

在前面被引网站类型分布分析中也有提到，作者标注网络引文，大部分是因为参考了该网址对应网页的内容；但是，当作者将网站作为证明论点的例子或者是实证分析的对象时，也会将对象网站的URL标注为网络引文。如在论文《学术型开放存取期刊的质量评估》中，作者的网络引文［24］DOAJ. http://www. doaj. org. 2012便不是参考了该网址的内容，而是将开放存取期刊DOAJ作为质量评估实验的对象。笔者发现按表5的网站类型体系分类，商务网站、文献导航网站、微博、社区网站、搜索引擎这几种类型的网站经常被作者整体引用。如论文《社会标签的应用功能分析》里引用商务网站亚马逊，是将其作为电子商务网站嵌入标签的成功案例；又如论文《心理学在图书馆用户服务工作中的运用研究》引用搜索引擎Google Scholar，是将其与图书馆的功能搜索进行对比；再如论文《基于社会标签的推荐系统研究》引用社区网站Delicious、Flickr、CiteULike，说明什么是社会标签。

本文认为，图书情报领域研究者对网络信息资源的引用基于两种目的，一种是对内容的参考，一种是对网站整体的引用。在进行网络信息资源聚合时，我们只需考虑研究者出于第一种引用目的所需要的网络信息资源。

对2012年的网络引文样本进行统计，80.33%的网络引文是研究者对网络信息资源内容的参考，19.67%的网络引文是研究者出于对网站的整体引用为目的而使用网络信息资源。笔者统计发现，175篇论文中，有109篇论文的网络引文都是基于第一种目的——内容参考，其比例为62%；有60篇论文，即34%的论文引用网络信息资源既有第一种目的也有第二种目的；另外，有6篇论文，即4%的论文对网络信息资源的引用仅出于对网站整体引用的目的。

4 总结与讨论

本文通过定量方法，对图书情报领域的三种文献（期刊论文、学位论文、会议论文）2010—2012年网络引文引用情况进行分析，在整体利用方面，发现：①利用的非图书情报领域主题内容大概占20%；②对PDF网页类型的引用呈现增长的趋势；③.com、.org、.edu是被引用最多的网站域名；④英国、德国、中国台湾地区、加拿大域名的资源被引用较多，且对其他国家或地区资源的引用频次逐年有所增加；⑤本文将网站类型分为九类，发现教育科研网站、信息门户网站、政府网站被引用频次较高，教育科研网站中图书馆主页、学术协会/机构主页是研究者参考的主要来源；⑥中文和英文网络信息资源的使用频次较为接近，英文资源的利用略高于中文资源；⑦URL深度为2的网络信息资源被引用最多，URL深度小于或等于5的网络引文占了95%；⑧研究者在网络信息资源的利用上倾向于引用本领域相关协会组织提供的信息，但是集中度并不强，网络信息资源的来源非常广泛；⑨被引信息资源的可获取率在65%左右，一些高频被引的网络信息资源可获取率小于50%。在个体利用方面，发现：①会议论文和期刊论文篇均引用1～3条网络引文，学位论文篇均网络引文集中在5～20条；②论文参考的网站类型都较多在1～3种，且只参考一种网站类型的论文占据较高比例；③80%的网络引文基于参考引用网页内容的目的，20%的网络引文是对网站整体的引用。以上是图书情报领域研究者利用网络信息资源的总体情况，会议论文、学位论文、期刊论文的情况略有不同，在上文中笔者都进行了统计和分析。本文的数据来源较为全面，力图补充此前仅仅通过期刊论文数据得到的研究结果。

基于上文的分析结果，笔者认为，图书情报领域具有交叉学科的性质，需要参考的不只有本学科领域的网络信息资源，还需要本学科领域外的信息资源。对于学科外信息资源需求的满足，由于学术性要求较低，主题广泛，可以通过提供在线百科全书、机构网站、相关信息门户网站等的入口链接即可。对于图书情报领域网络信息资源的需求，教育科研类网站，特别是这类别中的图书馆网站、学术协会/机构网站，被利用频率最高，在进行网络信息资源聚合时应该给予更高的权重。另外，专业信息门户网站提供较深入、全面、可信的专业信息，学者对这类网站的引用也较为普遍；随着开源思想的传播以及图书情报领域研究技术需求的提高，开源软件/协议标准提供网站的网络信息资源越来越受到重视。这两类网站也可作为聚合本学科领域网络信息资源的首选。网络信息资源的来源不能只局限于中文网站和美国、英国等国家的网站，还应该包括德国、意大利、日本、加拿大等国网站。

在聚合细节上，域名为.com、.org、.edu的应赋予较高权重；在进行网络信息资源聚合时可以考虑挖掘深度取URL深度5；对于核心信息资源，尤其是来源于稳定性不高的网站的重要资源，应该建立数据库对这些重要的信息资源进行备份。

网络引文实际上就是研究者使用的网络信息资源，通过对网络引文的分析可以了解学科领域网络信息资源的利用情况和需求。笔者认为，各引文数据库有必要增强网络引文的检索功能，这样才能对更多来源的数据进行分析，获得更全面更客观的研究结果。

参考文献

[1] 董小英，张本波，陶锦，等. 中国学术界用户对互联网信息的利用及其评价［J］. 图书情报工作，2002，(10)：29 -40.

[2] 邱均平. 网络计量学［M］. 北京：科学出版社，2010.

[3] 宋歌. 图书情报学期刊网络资源利用状况探析［J］. 图书情报知识，2007 (2)：79 -82，92.

[4] 谭芳兰. 从 web 引文看网络学术资源开发与利用［J］. 图书馆学刊，2007 (5)：110 -112.

[5] 张洋，张洁. 近年来图书情报期刊引用网络文献的计量分析［J］. 图书情报工作，2010 (2)：40 -44，10.

[6] 薛卫双，郑春厚，王娟. 《图书情报工作》2000—2009 年网络引文衰减规律实证研究［J］. 图书馆界，2012 (1)：56 -60.

[7] 邱均平，宋艳辉. 域名分析法的研究Ⅱ——应用研究［J］. 情报科学，2011 (2)：161 -165.

[8] 葛郁葱. 学位论文的特点及其检索方法［J］. 现代情报，2003 (9)：161 -162.

[9] 李静. 基于信息检索的会议论文与期刊论文相关性分析研究［J］. 情报科学，2010 (7)：1037 -1041.

[10] 网页类型［EB/OL］.［2013 -4 -10］. http://wenku. baidu. com/view/a00bb249fe4733687e21aa1f. html.

[11] 高淑琴. 网络学术资源全文文件格式比较分析［J］. 图书馆界，2004 (2)：28 -33.

[12] 杨思洛，邱均平. 基于中英维基百科的网络引文分布分析［J］. 国家图书馆学刊，2012 (6)：7 -19，38.

[13] Yang S，Han R，Ding J，et al. The Distribution of Web Citations［J］. Information Processing & Management，2012，48 (4)：779 -790.

教师简介：

邹永利，男，武汉大学图书馆学系学士，法国里昂第一大学情报学研究所情报学硕士，法国国家图书情报学院图书馆学硕士，日本庆应大学文学部后期博士课程毕业，北京大学信息管理系博士。2004 年起任教于中山大学资讯管理学院，现任教授，硕士生导师。主讲“跨文化交流与管理”等本科生课程，以及“信息组织与传播”等研究生课程。研究方向包括信息检索、网络信息组织与传播、跨文化交流与管理。联系方式：isszyl@mail. sysu. edu. cn。

所选论文“Non-Topical Attributes of Academic Papers and Implications to Information Retrieval”原载于 *Journal of Library Science in China* 2012 年第 4 期

Non-Topical Attributes of Academic Papers and Implications to Information Retrieval*

Yongli Zou

Abstract: Indexing and searching mechanism based mainly upon topical attributes of documents has been showing certain limitations. The function of the non-topical attributes and their implications to information retrieval and system design are not yet fully explored. By summarizing the non-topical attributes of documents and by analyzing them in light of information needs, information seeking, the author attempts to explore their potentialities to information retrieval and information system design. Based on some non-topical attributes, a system, NSIRS, was developed and evaluated in order to test the ideas brought forward in this article. Finally, the non-topical attributes embedded in some well-known information retrieval systems are discussed as well.

Keywords: Information retrieval; Non-topical attributes; Information need; System design

1 Introduction

The abstraction and representation of the document subjects have been one of the key research issues in library and information science, while non-subject or non-topical attributes of documents are somewhat neglected for their comparative simplicity and unambiguity both in meaning and form. Consequently, few systematic studies about non-topical attributes have been carried out, and as a reflection in practice, the non-topical accesses provided by information

* Project of National Social Science Fund (2010-2012). Project name: Automatic identification and retrieval of Chinese academic documents over the internet-Research and system development based on document style, links and image-text relatedness. Project Number: 10BTQ049.

retrieval systems in general are few and lack of originality. The insufficiency of non-topical accesses might not become a serious obstacle to users of traditional information retrieval systems in which data is highly controlled and the data amount is comparatively limited, but when it comes to information retrieval in the internet where information is huge in number and with a much lower level in control, the same problem may hinder users' retrieval efficiency and users need more effective ways to filter out the large amount of irrelevant documents; if properly used, the non-topical attributes of documents should be able to alleviate this problem for they are particularly effective in excluding or filtering out the non relevant documents. In recent years, search engines as well as structured database retrieval systems have been improving their non-topical access functionality, and the option and originality of non-topical accesses are becoming important indicators of system assessment. [1] This paper attempts to systematically examine the non-topical attributes of academic documents and the significance of those attributes for the theory and practice of information retrieval.

2 Limitations of Subject-based Information Retrieval

Most of the scientific information seeking tasks can be called subject searches. In fact, the majority of the literature on information seeking and information retrieval are concerned with subject searching, and the key issue for researchers becomes how to represent subjects—the subject of documents and the subject of information needs because subject access is actually a matching manipulation of those two kinds of representations. This is not an easy task for the two kinds of representations are different in nature. Whether human or machine, to accurately index the subject of a document is a challenge, even an impossible task, so is for a user to express his information needs accurately and clearly. Thus the matching that a subject-based information retrieval system manipulates is in fact a comparison between two representations that are originally inaccurate. Lack or inadequacy of necessary correspondence in analyzing and representing the concerned subject matters would lead to failure of the search. Studies show that the fact that concepts or query terms used by users for access to information are not used by information system to represent the information objects is the most common cause for failures of information retrievals. [2] In other words, a certain gap or distance exists between the relevant concepts perceived by the two parties involved in regard to the concerned topic or in representing a certain problem situation. Although the full-text search technology to a large extent solved the problem of keywords selection in indexing, subject-based retrieval still can not get rid of its inherent limitations, which is related to the very problem of human understanding and representation of knowledge. [3]

Firstly, it is highly improbable that the words contained in a document may express fully and accurately the concepts of the related subject, however those words are taken as the scale for measuring the information contained by the document in the full-text search mechanism. Of all things, a document is a product in which the author exhibits his thought, purposes, knowledge state, methodologies, expressive ability and preference. The main concepts or terms that make up the text reflect the author's understanding and interpretation of a topic, which are often called "author aboutness". The author aboutness of a subject and its representation through a document are affected by two kinds of limitations, namely the personal one and the social one. The former is understood as the limitations of a person's knowledge structures around the subject, which are always incomplete and inaccurate in relation to the concerned knowledge about the subject. And furthermore the author's representation of his understanding is also affected by personal limitations—the ability to express a subject or problem. The social limitation—the rhetorical requirements for a socially accepted document—is somehow an objective one by nature. Although an author is faced with a huge world of expressions to represent his aboutness of a subject, what he could do is to select from them some finite expressions to accomplish his goal. Eventually, when the document is written, varieties of terms or expressions are left unused that could also have been used to convey the same or similar ideas. Any expression is but one possible form for the concept, ideas, and feelings. Unless supplemental indexing is provided, expressions not used in the work may nonetheless be useful access points for information seekers. Secondly, a subject concept is often time-specific, region-specific and domain-specific, and the same concept may have different forms of expression, and some may have been outdated and unfamiliar for nowadays users, making thus the subject retrieval for the concerned documents difficult. Third, it is difficult for a user to express his information needs, especially the task-oriented information needs accurately and completely with a search term or a coordinate set of search terms, or an elaborated query.[4] Sometimes users are not only unable to use the system prescribed language and format to express his information needs clearly, but even unable to do it in natural language. Subject access, however, assumes that users be able to select appropriately the search terms that represent his information needs and takes the assumption as a prerequisite.

Plato argues in *Meno* that man cannot enquire either about that which he knows, or about that which he does not know; for if he knows, he has no need to enquire; and if not, he cannot; for he does not know the very subject about which he is to enquire.[5] Plato's argument points out roughly the dilemma of the information users seeking information from the subject or topical perspective: lack of specialized vocabulary vis-à-vis the subject of the information needs, coupled with lack of grammatical knowledge vis-à-vis the information retrieval system, reducing the representation of information needs at most to something similar to the real information needs that reflect a user's knowledge structures.[6]

3 Non-topical Attributes

The non-topical attributes of a document refer to attributes that the document possesses but are not directly or necessarily related to its thematic content, or its subject. Table 1-Table 3 list the general non-topical attributes of an academic document, which mainly come from four sources: first, the creative process, during which attributes are generated by the author;

second, the editing and publishing process, during which attributes are added by editors and publishers; third, the information services where attributes are given by information professionals when processing the document for utilization; and last, the utilization process during which such attributes as records of use, users' remarks and evaluation and etc. In this way, a set of non-topical attributes are being formed gradually around a document.

The non-topical attributes fall into two broad categories: internal attributes and external attributes, and the latter can be further divided into two types: explicit attributes and implicit attributes.

3.1 Internal non-topical attributes

The internal non-topical attributes of a document refer to attributes or features that can be found within the document. Some of those attributes are explicit and can be observed directly, while others are implicit or hidden and need to be found out through reading and analysis, such as the stylistic attributes of the document and the author's standpoint and etc. Table 1 and Table 2 list respectively the main types of the explicit and the implicit attributes of documents.

Table 1 Explicit attributes

Type	Content
Document form	Text, graphic, sound, audio-visual, language, etc.
Physical feature	Carrier, size, format, length, play time
Document type	Review, experiment report, textbook, conference paper, etc.
Publishing issue	Date, version, publisher, distributor, etc.
Document component	Title, Abstract:, keyword, directory, text, chart, citation, index, appendices, footnote, references, etc.
Logical structure	Introduction, literature review, methodology, implementation, conclusion, acknowledgement, etc.
Design	Word size, font, layout, color, etc.
Symbol	Punctuation, operator, equation, etc.
Contributor	Author, translator, editor, designer, conductor, director, performer, etc.
Identifier	ISBN, ISSN, etc.

Table 2 Implicit attributes

Type	Content
Research genre	Basic research, applied research, comprehensive study, etc.
Research method	Naturalistic observation, case studies, surveys and interviews, quasi-experiment, controlled experiments, historical method, etc.

Continue Table 2

Type	Content
Research stance	Refutation, falsification, verification, etc.
Readability	Targeted audience, required level of knowledge, etc.
Stylistic features	Special expressions, typical sentences, number or proportion of different language characters, average sentence length, types and ratio of punctuation, etc.
Citation	Number of citations of a particular author or document, in what places an author or a document is cited, etc.

3.2 External non-topical attributes

The external non-topical attributes refer to the attributes that cannot be found or do not necessarily exist in the document. As shown in Table 3, background information of the author, use record, user evaluation and availability belong to this kind of attributes.

Table 3 External non-topical attributes of documents

Type	Content
Author background	Affiliation, occupation, title, position, academic school, social, historical or political circumstances
Utilization	Times of citation, times of being borrowed, times of being clicked or downloaded, etc.
Evaluation	Users' ratings, ranking and remarks concerning the quality or value of the document, etc.
Availability	Costs, delivery time, etc.

4 Implications of Non-topical Attributes

The theoretical and practical implications of non-topical attributes to information retrieval are analyzed here from three perspectives: the nature of the information needs, information filtering, and specific information locating.

4.1 Shedding light on the contradictory nature of information needs

Information needs seem to have two faces or two dimensions: on the one hand, they tend to be vague, general and difficult for users to define with appropriate, clear words; on the other hand, they appear to be very specific, individual, and can not be met only with very specific information. The non-topical attributes of documents may serve to clarify this seemingly contradictory phenomenon about information needs.

The vague dimension of information needs has been clearly discussed in several influential theories. Taylor clearly stated the difficulty of specifying an information need by calling it "a certain incompleteness" in the user's picture of the world-an inadequacy in what we might call his "state of readiness" to interact purposefully with the world around him in terms of a particular area of interest.[7] In Dervin's Sense-making model, information needs are defined as a "gap" in a person's knowledge structures, which prevents the person from moving as he desires and causes in him the need to make sense of the new contextual situation in order to "move" again.[8] Belkin, an enthusiastic advocate of the cognitive approach to information retrieval, considers information needs to be the reflection of an insufficient or anomalous state of knowledge structure, and that a person having information needs means his having an anomalous state of knowledge.[9] In conclusion, information needs are a kind of defect in a person's knowledge structures, which is vague and difficult to define.

Paradoxically enough, when a document or certain information is provided, the information seeker tends to say for certain whether it meets his needs or not, proving thus that information needs are something concrete and clearly-cut, not vague at all. Research on relevance judgment shows that, among the various factors that influence users' judgment, many are confirmed to be of non-topical nature (Table 4).[10-15] It is these clearly defined non-topical aspects or conditions that give information needs their other face—something clear and specific. In addition to be topic related, documents that meet the information needs, or relevant documents must have the required specific non-topical attributes; this is determined by the individuality or particularity of a person's anomalous state of knowledge, or cognitive gap. This individuality or particularity is also known as the "personal construct", which dominates users' relevance judgment of documents.[16] Other investigations[12] also show that scholars frequently examine additional attributes of the text, such as the footnotes, or the acknowledgments, to identify the author's specific point of view, or reference group. From this aspect of the text, the scholar can tell something about the way in which the topic is treated in the text, and about who the author is. This involves more than an assessment of topical relevance, but establishing the author's 'point of view', determining the credibility or authority of the author; and, determining the scholarly community the text is intended to address.

Table 4 User relevance criteria of non-topical nature

1	Research method, purpose, viewpoint, standpoint, values
2	Depth, scope, oriented audience
3	Type and nature of information sources, source reputation
4	geographical location
5	Whether a specific and effective theory or method is proposed
6	Document type
7	Relationship with the theoretical paradigms of the field.

Continue Table 4

8	Relationship with the author
9	Recency
10	Research background
11	Publisher, distributor
12	Document length
13	Author's expertise, status, occupation, degree, affiliation, etc.
14	Accuracy, validity, external verification
16	Availability
17	…

Understanding the non-topical dimension of information needs and improving accordingly the design of information retrieval systems should be helpful to users in expressing their needs more accurately and clearly. Of the two dimensions of information needs (Figure 1), topical dimension is, as mentioned above, difficult to be stated accurately by users, whereas the topic dimension, which does affect their relevance judgment, generally can be stated quite clearly. Therefore, providing users with a richer means of non-topical access during information retrieval will no doubt facilitate their task in describing more easily and accurately their information needs and eventually lead them to the relevant information or required documents.

Information needs
- Topical dimension: the topic or field of required in formation→defect of knowledge structure (ASK, cognitive gap) →difficult to express accurately→uncertain and ambiguous
- Non-topical dimension: type/nature/depth/carrier and etc. →known and may be clearly stated by the user→specific, concrete

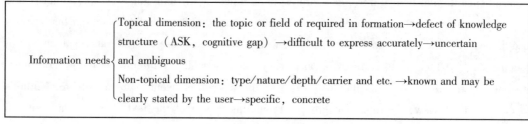

Figure 1　Two dimensions of information needs

4.2　Creating conditions for the filtering functions of information retrieval

Information seeking, to some extent, is not so much a problem of finding information as it is a problem of excluding irrelevant information. Filtering and restricting functions allow users to limit levels and types of documents and thus to manipulate information searching more efficiently.[17] Belkin stated this problem more flatly by saying: "the relationship between information filtering and information retrieval… It seems fair to say, after having examined the foundations of each of these enterprises, that there is relatively little difference between the two, at an abstract level".[18] Computer-based information retrieval systems are more often used as a means of filtering out quickly the large amount of irrelevant information rather than a reliable way of finding accurately the required information.[14] Some well-known information seeking models also reveal that information seekers often start their searching process with non-topical attributes of documents and then frequently use these attributes to control searching process. [14,19] Since people rely on multiple aspects or attributes of texts in their evaluation of the usefulness of a text, they rely accordingly on the same aspects or attributes to approach their target. Therefore, sufficient and suitable filters in an information retrieval system will be a great help for users to eliminate the irrelevant information and shorten the distance between users and required information. The fact that both information needs and documents possess non-topical attributes provides a basis for information system design to integrate more filtering functions of non-topical nature.

Certain structured database retrieval systems allow users to filter retrieval items by document types, research types and research depth, and improve thus the precision rate of retrieval, however by and large, the exploration of non-topical attributes is far from sufficient. As described earlier, the non-topical attributes of documents have at least 20 types, more than 80 sub-types, and many of them can be used as filters to exclude irrelevant documents and to enhance the non-topical retrieval functions of information systems. For example, in addition to some general criteria of classifying documents, documents can also be differentiated by their research nature (evaluation of an existing theory, model or approach, or proposition of a specific theory, model, and etc.), research type (basic research or applied research), research methods (qualitative or quantitative), research purpose (verification or falsification) and etc.

Those attributes of documents can be either indexed or labeled by hand or automatically according to the non-topical attributes of the document. For example, the reference number and citation times of a document can be used as indicators of its certain properties (basic research, applied research, research depth, etc.), chart, graph and formula numbers as indicators of the research methods adopted by the document, utilization as indicators of document quality. Likewise, authors' background, such as their affiliations, academic groups, status, occupation, titles and degrees can also be served as indicators or filters for both information systems and users to locate possible documents of a certain quality or research nature, to track the research results and research trend of peer research institutions, and to access to documents that have a certain research tendency, or take a certain position or point of view, or belong to some academic schools and etc. Other investigations illustrate the same point that, to judge relevance of a specific text, many of the scholars look first at such characteristics of the text as title or author. These document characteristics are most useful in identifying texts which are not interesting to the scholar. [12] Ingwersen calls this kind of information seeking the "access to the vertical knowledge structure" of a field. [20]

4.3 Improving the capability of information retrieval system in more accurately locating specific information

Kircz identified in his investigation four broadly defined groups of readers of scientific papers: non-readers, informed readers, partially informed readers and uninformed readers.[21] Every scientist on different occasions will play all these four roles of readership depending on the stage of the research, and usually uses a very limited part of a long article. The structure of imprinted documents along with the standardized scientific training leads readers of academic articles to possess some form of mental representation for the text's typical structure that allows them to accurately predict a paragraph's location and quickly find the wanted information.

Investigations on document structures also show that although document creators display varying degrees of difference in words and sentences or in styles when introducing or describing an experiment, building or evaluating a model or theory, they demonstrate a very similar, even high standardized style in terms of structure, logic and narrative style due to the common education and scientific training that a scientist receives. Kircz, when discussing in depth the argumentational aspects of a scientific discourse[21], clearly states that the line of argumentation in a scientific article is nowadays standardized to a high degree-hence the availability of different types of style manuals and writer aids. An article has to (dis)prove or comment on an idea or experiment following a well defined path. It therefore becomes perfectly acceptable that, for example, Day can state in his book *How to Write and Publish a Scientific Article*: "Yes, this isa cookbook."[22] The research article in physics conforms to a strict pattern giving uniformity to every work published and therefore the opportunity to judge the work on the basis of more or less standardized criteria.

The reason why readers with a certain educational background can quickly get information they are interested in from a long-winded article or very rapidly browse a document without the need to pass reading it, is because they are familiar with and adept at using those fixed structures and rhetorical features of academic documents. Allen's information need study based on problem-solving model reveals that information needs of different types or different research phases often need information contained in different structural parts to satisfy.[23] This means that the search query entered by a user is a request for information from a particular structure part of the document, rather than for the overall semantic attributes of the document as a whole, therefore a system should provide appropriate functions to meet this kind of information needs in order to improve retrieval precision and relevance. For example, users should be allowed to limit their retrieval within some particular locations of a document, such as footnotes, caption, graphic, formula, diagram, flow chart and so on; likewise, users should also be able to run their search within some specific structural parts of the document, such as background, hypothesis, experiment environment, methodology, findings, conclusions, and etc.

It should be noted that although the structure of a typical scientific document (e. g., introduction, literature review, methodology, implementation, findings and analysis, conclusions, acknowledgement) in general is quite fixed or stereotyped, this structure is not necessarily dominant in all sorts of academic documents, sometimes it may exist in a rather hidden way. This hidden structure, also known as rhetorical or argumentational syntax, can also serve to support the retrieval, such as allowing the user to find only documents in which search terms occur within some defined rhetorical syntax.

Kircz tries to provide a tentative template for an argumentational syntax in the case of an experimental physics article.[21] If a sentence reads "following Einstein we can conclude that", it means that reference is made to other people's work and the conclusions of that work are adopted without discussion. The retrieval system will store it under "references to other people's work". If searchers want to know under what assumptions the concluding inferences of that paper are made, they will retrieve those sentences which belong to the notion "theoretical assumptions", with the expected result that the above mentioned sample sentence will be retrieved. Sillince[24] proposes the categorization of rhetorical syntax and expects that retrieval systems, based on a thesaurus, can automatically identify sentences which fit into the corresponding categories. For example, "in this paper" and "different approach" identify "new approach", and "problem" and "need" identify "problem", and "criticized" and "stagnation" identify "criticism", "enable" identifies "solution", and so on. In such a way, the information locating power of the system may go deep into the hidden structure part of a document.

5 Non-topical Searching Features of Some Current Information Retrieval Systems

Although the non-topical attributes of documents have not yet been given adequate attention, some of the information retrieval systems do provide creative non-topical searching functions. In recent years, many search engines have been strengthening their non-topical search function and as a result, the non-topical ways of accessing to information for users have been gradually enriched. Currently, all the major search engines basically support the use of date, file type, language, domain, country or region, appearing position of search term and other non-topic criteria as filters for users to manipulate their searches. Some search engines support even more sophisticated non-topical search functions, such as directory depth, page depth, file size, case sensitivity, proximity, reading level and so on. AltaVista, supporting almost all the functions listed here, was once the leader in this regard and considered the best search engine for finding online scientific articles. Unfortunately, taken over by Yahoo at the end of May 2004, AltaVista changed-its databases were substituted by Yahoo's and many of its non-topical search functions, including proximity searching, case sensitivity and other features, have disappeared. Based on Notess's comparison of some search engines[25], Table 5 lists the non-topical search features and the search engines that support them.

Table 5　Non-topical search features of some search engines

Feature		Search engine
Proximity	Phrase Search	Ask, Exalead, Gigablast, Google, Live Search, Yahoo! Search
	NEAR	Exalead
	NEAR/#:	Exalead (replace # with a number to specific distance of proximity)
Field searching	Title	Ask, Exalead, Gigablast Google, Live Search, Yahoo!
	Url	Ask, Exalead, Gigablast, Google, Yahoo!
	Link	Exalead, Gigablast, Google, Yahoo!
	Domain	Live Search
	Site	Ask, Exalead, Gigablast, Google, Live Search, Yahoo!
	Filetype	Ask, Exalead, Google, Live Search
	Originurlextension	Yahoo!
	Type	Gigablast
	Ip	Gigablast
	Related	Gigablast
Limits	Date	Ask, Google, Live Search
	Domain	Ask, Gigablast, Google, Live Search
	Containing a media type	Live Search
	Document Directory Depth	Live Search
	Language	Gigablast, Google, Live Search, Yahoo!
	Page Depth	Gone. Formerly at HotBot
File types	PDFs	Gigablast, Google, Live Search, Yahoo!
	MS Word (.doc)	Gigablast, Google, Live Search, Yahoo!
	PowerPoint (.ppt)	Gigablast, Google, Live Search, Yahoo!
	Excel (.xls)	Gigablast, Google, Live Search, Yahoo!
	PostScript (.ps):	Gigablast, Google, Yahoo! (using originurlextension:)
Family filters		Gigablast, Google, Live Search, Yahoo! Search

On the other hand, it is relatively easy for structured database retrieval systems to exploit the potential of non-topical attributes of documents. In fact, the non-topical attributes related functions provided by this kind of systems are comparatively richer, for example, most of them allow users to narrow their searches by document structure (title, keywords, abstract, references, full text, etc.), creator property (author, first author, author affiliation), publishing issue (publication title, year, volume, issue), identifier (classification number, ISBN, ISSN, accession number) and so on. Some systems even support searches by cited references (cited author, cited resource, cited year), by recommending core authors and core journals for a given research areas, making thus information filters more diverse and sophisticated. The document type, one of the typical non-topical attributes, is carefully subdivided as search options in systems like EBSCOhost, ProQuest, Emerald, EI. ProQuest, and the earlier version of Emerald was especially interesting in its exploitation of non-topical attributes of documents.

ProQuest's "document feature" and "document type" options are quite comprehensive and interesting. The document feature option includes nine kinds of graphs: charts, diagrams, engravings, equations, illustrations, maps, photographs, plates, tables (Figure 2), and users can narrow their searches by retrieving only the documents with or without a particular type of graphs; the document type option has a total of 23 categories, 10 sub-categories for users to refine their searches, such as annual reports, monographs, case studies, reviews, cover story, editorials, speeches, statistics and etc.

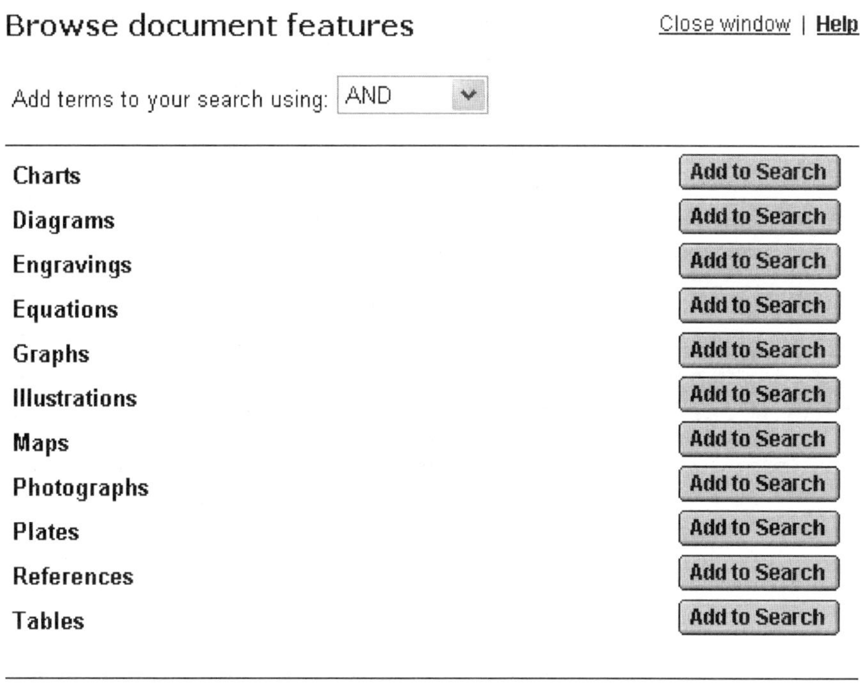

Figure 2 ProQuest's document feature check box

Emerald provided a wealth of non-topical filters through its "content indicator" and "article type" options. The former allows the user to retrieve documents according to the level of their originality, practical implications, readability and research implications, and three levels were given for each of those indicators to meet the diversified needs of users with different retrieval purposes (Figure 3). Emerald's document type option divided documents into case studies, comparative/evaluation, general review, conceptual paper, journalistic, literature review, research paper, review, survey, technical, technical papers, theoretical with application in practice, theoretical with worked example, view point, wholly theoretic (Figure 4). Unfortunately, Emerald has transformed then its interface and the current version has only a simplified article type option, whereas the content indicator option is gone.

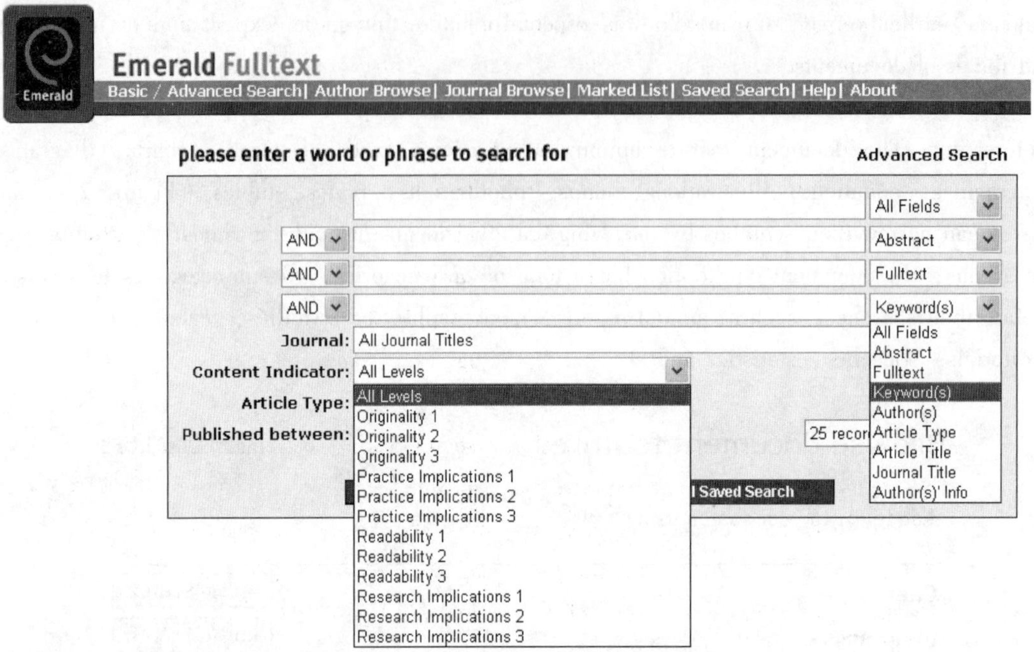

Figure 3　Emerald's content indicator check box

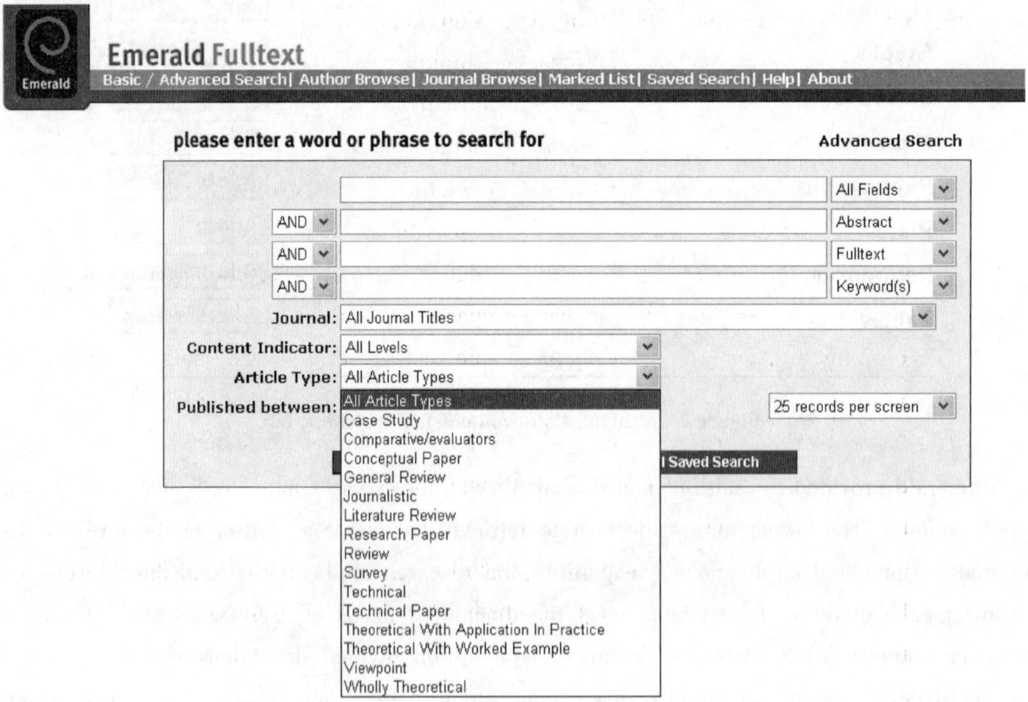

Figure 4　Emerald's article type check box

6 Experimental Study: Non-Topical Attributes and Automatic Identification of Chinese Academic Papers

To test the practical implication of non-topical attributes of documents in information retrieval, an identification program of Chinese academic papers over the internet (NSIRS) has been developed with VC++ 6.0 as platform and ACCESS 2000 as backend database. NSIRS is designed to improve the low precision problem of general search engines in searching Chinese academic papers over the internet. Although Scirus from Elsevier Science Corporation and Google Scholar are devices specially developed to search academic papers over the internet, both of them have some limitations in searching Chinese academic articles: Scirus's coverage of Chinese papers is quite limited, while Google is confined to search mainly the published papers stored in some commercial databases such as Weipu, and Wanfang, and papers that have not been formally published are not sufficiently covered.

NSIRS is actually a re-ranking system of the search results returned by search engines①, composed by three functional modules: pretreatment of initial retrieval, analysis and processing of non-topical attributes, and result processing. Figure 5 shows the work principle of NSIF: first, users conduct searches on Google, and the result pages are downloaded to a temporary database; then the Analysis and Processing Module of non-topical attributes analyzes the search results and assigns each page a corresponding weight according to its unique expression frequency, average sentence length, image-text relatedness, proportion of foreign characters and file size. The unique expressions, divided into structural expressions and rhetorical expressions, refer to the high frequency non-topical expressions somewhat unique to academic documents. Structural expressions include for example the preface, introduction, research background, literature review, research purpose, implications, methodology, findings, conclusions, and acknowledgement and so on; rhetorical expressions include in turn expressions like "based on", "investigation of", "aims at", "analysis of", "research", "model" and so on. Each unique expression corresponds to a default weight and the higher the frequency, the higher weight a page gets. Image-text relatedness refers to whether an image on the page is related or not to the text, in other word, whether it makes part of the academic paper or it is just an interfering image such as ads, or buttons and has nothing to do with the document. Using images or figures, tables and equations to illustrate the research process and results is a major feature of the academic document, and understanding the use of those components may inform users about the papers, the field, and even the way the writer reasons. [26] Consequently, the higher the relatedness of an image to the containing text is, the higher the possibility is for that text being an academic paper. Similarly, the longer the average sentence length and the higher the proportion of foreign characters and the bigger the file size, the more likely the concerned page is an academic

① Currently, NSIRS conducts its search tests on Google.

document, and consequently the higher weight the document will be assigned. Finally, NSIRS re-ranks result pages according to each page's total weight, and export then the re-ranked search results in Google's webpage format.

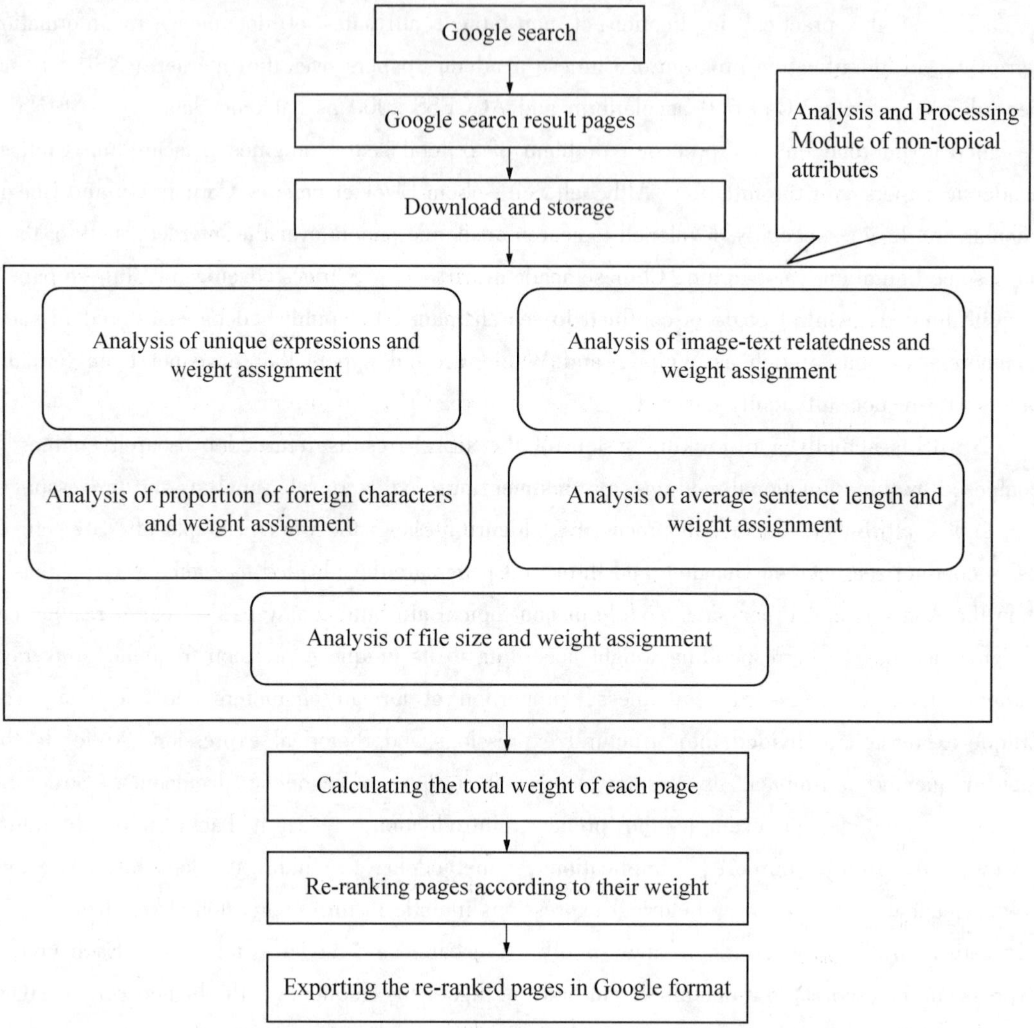

Figure 5 NSIRS's work principle

Evaluation based on first 30 precision measurement[27] shows that NSIRS's effect in improving Google's initial ranking for Chinese academic papers over the internet is evident. Google and NSIRS are compared for precision on the first 30 results for 10 queries. Results show that the first 30 precision of NSIRS's re-ranked results for Chinese academic papers over the internet is basically higher than that of Google's original ones by applying any of the following five non-topical attributes alone: unique expressions, average sentence length, image-text relatedness, proportion of foreign characters and file size. When all those 5 attributes or filters are applied, NSIRS scored a precision rate of 48.2%, increased by 12.5% compared to Google's original precision rate of 35.7%. This result clearly indicates that the non-topical attributes can be effectively applied to the identification and retrieval of Chinese academic document over the internet. It should be noted however, that NSIRS is not yet an independent retrieval tool for Chinese academic documents over the internet, and its collection of non-topical attributes of documents and its parameter system for identifying those attributes are still far from complete.

7 Conclusion

We have examined in this paper the non-topical attributes of academic documents and their implications for information retrieval, which need obviously further study both theoretically and practically, and the development and application of NSIRS also are just a preliminary exploration in this direction. Furthermore, the non-topical attributes of Chinese academic documents are comparatively rich, and consequently the discovery and representation of the logical relationship among them are more complex, and constant efforts are necessary for researchers to find out and test new representation rules. Since NSIRS's rules expansion and clustering function are relatively weak, we plan to establish more standardized rules library and clustering function on the basis of the actual version by using the regular expression as the rule representation tool to build a "Regular Expression Library of non-topical attributes of Chinese academic documents". Hopefully, through this kind of exploration, the implications of non-topical attributes to the knowledge system of Library and Information Science could be made more explicit.

References

[1] Notess G R. Search Engines by Search Features [OL]. [2012-5-12]. http://www.searchengineshowdown.com/.

[2] Kang Y H. Modern Theories of Information Retrieval [M]. Beijing: Scientific and Technological Document Publishing House, 1990.

[3] Hjorland B. Information Seeking and Subject Representation: An Activity-theoretical Approach to Information Science [M]. London: Greenwood Press, 1997.

[4] Vakkari P. Task Complexity, Problem Structure and Information Actions: Integrating Studies on Information Seeking and Retrieval [J]. Information Processing and Management, 1999 (35): 819-837.

[5] Plato. Meno [OL]. [2012-5-1]. http://classics.mit.edu/Plato/meno.html.

[6] Hosono K, Zou Y L. Knowledge Structure for Information Needs and Their Representation: Implication for Information System Design [J]. Library and Information Service, 1999 (1): 1-7.

[7] Taylor R S. Question Negotiation and Information Seeking in Libraries [J]. College and Research Libraries, 1968 (29): 178-194.

[8] Dervin B. From the Mind's Eye of the User: The Sense-making Qualitative-quantitative Methodology [G] // Glazier D, Powell R. Qualitative Research in Information Management. Englewood Colo: Libraries Unlimited, 1992: 61-84.

[9] Belkin N J, Oddy R, Brooks H. ASK for Information Retrieval [J]. Journal of Documentation, 1982 (38): 61-71.

[10] Barry C L. User-defined Relevance Criteria: An Exploratory Study [J]. Journal of the American Society for Information Science, 1994, 45 (3): 149-59.

[11] Park T K. The Nature of Relevance in Information Retrieval: An Empirical Study [D]. Bloomington: Indiana University, 1992.

[12] Cool C, Belkin N J, Kantor P. Characteristics of Texts Affecting Relevance Judgments [C] //14th National Online

Meeting. Medford: Learned Information, 1993: 77 – 84.
[13] Howard D L. Pertinence as Reflected in Personal Constructs [J]. Journal of the American Society for Information Science, 1994, 45 (3): 172 – 85.
[14] Ellis D. A Behavioral Approach to Information Retrieval System Design [J]. Journal of Documentation, 1989, 45 (3): 171 – 212.
[15] Wang P L, Soergel D. A Cognitive Model of Document Use During a Research Project: Study 1. Document Selection [J]. Journal of the American Society for Information Science, 1998, 49 (2): 115 – 33.
[16] Kelly G. A Theory of Personality: The Psychology of Personal Constructs [M]. New York: Norton, 1963.
[17] Marchionini G. Information Seeking in Electronic Environments [M]. London: Cambridge University Press, 1995.
[18] Belkin N J, Croft W B. Information Filtering and Information Retrieval: Two Sides of the Same Coin? [J]. Communications of the ACM, 1992, 35 (12): 29 – 37.
[19] Bates M. The Design of Browsing and Berry-picking Techniques for the Online Search Interface [J]. Online Review, 1989, 13 (5): 407 – 24.
[20] Ingwersen P. Information Retrieval Interaction [M]. London: Taylor Graham, 1992.
[21] Kircz J G. Rhetorical Structure of Scientific Articles: The Case for Argumentational Analysis in Information Retrieval [J]. Journal of Documentation, 1991, 47 (4): 354 – 72.
[22] Day R A. How to Write and Publish a Scientific Article [M]. Philadelphia, PA: ISI Press, 1979.
[23] Allen B L. Information Task: Toward a User-centered Approach to Information Systems [M]. San Diego: Academic Press, 1996.
[24] Sillince J A A. Argumentation-based Indexing for Information Retrieval from Learned Articles [J]. Journal of Documentation, 1992, 48 (4), 387 – 405.
[25] Notess G R. Search Engines by Search Features [OL]. [2012 – 5 – 12]. http://www.searchengineshowdown.com/features/byfeature.shtml.
[26] Nickerson J V. The Meaning of Arrows: Diagrams and other Facets in System Sciences Literature [C]. The Proceedings of the Hawaii International Conference on System Sciences, Big Island, Hawaii, January 3 – 6, 2005: 321 – 331.
[27] Leighton H V, Srivastava J. First 20 Precision among World Wide Web Search Services (Search Engines) [J]. Journal of the American Society for Information Science, 1999, 50 (10): 870 – 881.

教师简介：

张洋，男，华中科技大学工学学士、工学硕士，武汉大学管理学博士。教授，硕士生导师。2006 年起任教于中山大学资讯管理（系）学院。2009 年起担任（系副主任）副院长。主讲“信息管理概论”、“信息计量学”等本科生课程，以及“网络信息计量学”、“网络信息资源的计量与评价”等研究生课程。研究方向包括科学计量学、网络信息计量学、信息资源聚合、馆藏资源语义化、科学评价、网络信息资源评价、大学评价、期刊评价、网络信息交流、社会化媒体计量分析。主持多项国家级、省部级科研项目。已发表论文 60 余篇，出版著作 2 部。2010 年美国锡拉丘兹大学访问学者。中国图书馆学会学术研究委员会图书馆学教育专业委员会委员，广东省科学技术情报学会理事及情报教育专业委员会委员。联系方式：zhyang2@ mail. sysu. edu. cn。

所选论文《基于复杂网络演化模型的三元闭环合著网络研究》原载于《情报学报》2015 年第 34 卷第 1 期

基于复杂网络演化模型的三元闭环合著网络研究*

张　洋，麦江萌①

摘　要：本文通过构建和分析国外图书情报领域的三元闭环合著网络，改进已有的复杂网络演化模型，提出严格三元闭环概念和扩张系数用以研究影响合著网络扩张速度的关键因素。研究表明，学者合著集群的扩张速度，与他跟集群成员合著的均匀程度成正相关关系。扩张系数是对目前合著网络测度指标的一个有效补充。

关键词：合著网络；三元闭环；复杂网络；学术引荐人；信息计量学

A Research of Triadic Closure in Coauthorship Network Based on Evolution Model of Complex Network

Yang Zhang, Jiangmeng Mai

Abstract: The concepts of Strictly Triadic Closure and Expanding Coefficient were proposed in the research of Coauthership network expansion, based on the analysis of current Library & Information Science Coauthership network and an optimized evolution model of Complex Network. It is proven that the expansion of a scholar's coauthorship clique is positively correlated with the homogeneous degree of his/her coauthoring with other

* 本文系国家社会科学基金项目“新型网络环境下学术期刊影响力的计量分析与评价研究”（项目批准号：14BTQ067）和国家社会科学基金重大项目“基于语义的馆藏资源深度聚合与可视化展示研究”（项目批准号：11&ZD152）的研究成果之一。

① 麦江萌，中山大学资讯管理学院硕士研究生。

scholars. Expanding coefficient is considered as a useful supplementary index to the evaluation of Coauthorship network.

Keywords: Coauthorship network; Triadic closure; Complex network; Research facilitator; Informetrics

在信息计量和科学评价领域内，合著和合著网络一直是众多学者关注的重点。通过引入社会网络的分析方法，合著和合著网络研究在近年来取得了显著进展，各种关于合著网络的理论研究和实证研究不断出现，推动合著研究的深入发展。然而，基于社会网络分析方法的合著网络研究大多以静态网络为对象，学者与学者间的合著关系客观存在，分析结果则侧重于描述某特定时间点上学者在整个网络中所处的位置。对于合著网络的动态描述、学者在合著网络中扮演角色的发展演化等问题，在目前的合著网络研究中较少有成果报道。三元闭环合著现象和学术引荐人，是国外学界近年对合著网络研究的新发现，是一种在合著关系下的隐性现象的描述。本研究尝试将动态的复杂网络演化模型用于三元闭环合著现象的研究中，探讨影响合著网络发展速度的因素及其度量指标。

1 文献回顾

1999年，Barabasi和Albert提出了“BA网络模型”，在网络的构造中引入了增长性和择优连接性：增长性指网络中不断有新的节点加入进来，择优连接性则指新的节点进来后优先选择网络中度数大的节点进行连接。[1]基于BA模型的增长性原则，开始出现对于复杂网络演化的研究。此后，不同学者提出了各种各样的演化模型，取得了丰富的研究成果。按照不同的分类方法，可将这些模型分为以下主要类型。

（1）按网络演化的部件划分：①基于点、边的网络演化模型。在网络演化过程中，网络中的节点和边都可以增加或者删除的演化模型。从定义上不难发现，节点的数目存在着增减，而边的数目也存在着增减的模型的典型代表就是BA模型。在BA模型提出后，Klemm和Egufluz在其基础上进行了改进，从而使生成网络不仅具有幂律度分布特性，而且还具有高集聚系数等其他网络特性。[2,3]②基于边的网络演化模型。在网络演化过程中，网络中的节点数目保持不变，但是边可增加或者删除的演化模型。例如，ER模型在给定的节点之间采用随机连边策略产生随机图模型[4]；WS模型在给定的节点之间采用边重连的策略产生小世界网络模型[5]；Newman和Watts提出的NW模型通过在给定的节点之间采用随机加边的策略产生小世界模型[6]。

（2）按是否考虑权重划分：①无权网络演化模型，网络的边没有赋予相应的权值，则该网络就称为无权网络。目前绝大多数的网络模型都是无权的网络演化模型。例如，BA网络模型是目前学者对于网络模型改进中最常见的基础网络模型。根据BA模型的网络增长和择优连接两条规则，这些模型又可以分为两类：修改增长规则的无权网络演化模型，主要由Dorogovtesv和Mendes[7]、Sen[8]提出；修改连接规则的无权网络演化模型，主要由Bianconi等[9]和Li等[10]提出。无权网络演化模型主要针对网络的拓扑演化机制进行研究而不考虑网络的功能、承载业务等，演化结论主要也是通过对网络拓扑结构的评判（是否具有幂律度分布特性、小世界效应等）来验证。而在实际中，我们很难将所有的节点或边都平等地看待，因而，无权网络对于真实网络的贴合情况还有待提高。②加权网络演化模型。对网络中的点或边附加权值，那么该网络模型就成为加权网络演化模型。目前，加权网络演化模型是网络演化模型中的热点，但其复杂性使得研究的发展困难重重。具有代表性的加权网络模型有 DM 模型[11]、YJBT 模型[12]和简单加权演化网络模型 BBV 模型[13]等。加权网络相较无权网络而言，对真实的网络的描述能力得到了明显的提高，它既继承了无权网络的思想和研究方法，又强调了点和边的重要性，因而与目前的真实网络相对接近。

（3）按是否动态变化划分：①静态网络演化模型。在相邻两个时间步内，网络节点及节点之间的关系（边）一直保持不变，则称这类网络为静态网络。目前研究的网络演化模型基本上都属于此类型。②动态网络演化模型。在相邻两个时间步内，网络节点及节点之间的关系（边）具有可变性，则称这类网络为动态网络。Leydesdorff 通过双连接（bi-connected）图形分析算法[14]以及他自己开发的一些小工具[15]，用动态图谱形象地描述知识结构网络，为描述动态网络提供一种直观的描述手段。Ren 和 Beard[16]，以及 Moreau[17]都有对网络的稳定性及相关集体行为进行深入的探讨。目前由于对于网络中集体的动力行为的研究仍然处于一个探索的阶段，而网络的动态演化的复杂性由于因素间的相互影响趋向于不可知的方向，因而相对而言，目前的动态网络演化模型的研究仍处于一个停滞的阶段。

2　概念界定

2.1　三元闭环与学术引荐人

三元闭环合著网络研究近年才刚起步，相关概念最近才出现在国外的文献中，有必要厘清其含义。人与人之间通过某个共同的媒介产生联系，这一概念最先由德国著名社会学家 Georg Simmel 提出。[18]20 世纪 70 年代，美国社会学家 M. Granovetter 依据这一思路提出了两个陌生人通过共同认识的一个人所形成的强联系（strong ties）与弱联系（weak ties）理论，并使用了 Closed Triad 一词用以描述这种三人群体。[19]2006 年，Kossinets 和 Watts 首次使用了“Triadic Closure”一词用于描述两个陌生人通过第三人相互认识的过程[20]（笔者依据其含义，考虑复杂网络的特征，译为“三元闭环”）。他们在对一所大学 43533 名学生、职工的社交网络演化进行实证分析发现，有大量的循环闭环（cyclic closure）存在，其中三元闭环的数目占绝大多数。在三元闭环关系中，存在一个中间人（mutual acquaintance），这个中间人与其他两个人都认识，而这两人可能是陌生人或不相熟的两人。他们的研究发现，这个中间人的角色、地位对于另外两人间关系的强度（tie strength）有着很大的影响。例如，两个学生通过一个教授而认识的关系强度要弱于两个学生通过另一个学生而认识的关系强度。

2013 年，P. S. Cho 等人首次将三元闭环现象与合著现象一起进行研究，并给出合著关系中三元闭环现象的严格数学定义。[21]定义如下：

定义 1：单位时间内的合著图 G_t =（V，E）是由点的集合 V 和带有权重的边的集合

$E=(v_1, v_2)$ 组成。点集 V 中每一个点代表一个独立的研究人员，而边集 E 中的每一条边代表在一个单位时间内研究人员间发生的一次合著关系。

定义2：一个时间段内的合著图 G_T 是由一个按顺序排列的 G_t 的集合组成，且 $i<t\leqslant j$。对于这个集合中的任意一幅图 G_i，其点的性质和意义均不变，只有边发生改变（指特定单位时间 i 内发生的合著关系）。

通过图形化的方式，研究人员被形式化成一个点，一份有 k 个研究人员的出版物则会被形式化成一个具有 k 个点的图，只有单个作者的出版物则不会在图像上显示。依据两个研究人员在单位时间 t 内合著的出版物的篇数多少给图的边赋权重，一般以年作为 t 的衡量单位。

定义3：将两个研究人员 v_1、v_2 间的第一次合作 $\overleftarrow{(v_1, v_2)}t$ 定义边 $e\in G_t$，用以显示 v_1、v_2 间的一次合著关系。

为了方便表达，这一定义使用大写字母代表一个独立的研究者，等价表示为 $\overleftarrow{(v_1, v_2)}$ t，其中 $v_1=A$，$v_2=B$。而由于合著关系是对称的，所以 $\overleftarrow{AB}(t)=\overleftarrow{BA}(t)$。详见图1。

定义4：一条暂时的路径 $ABC(t_1, t_2)$ 等价于 $e_1=(A, B)\in G_{t1}$ 和 $e_{12}=(B, C)\in G_{t2}$。

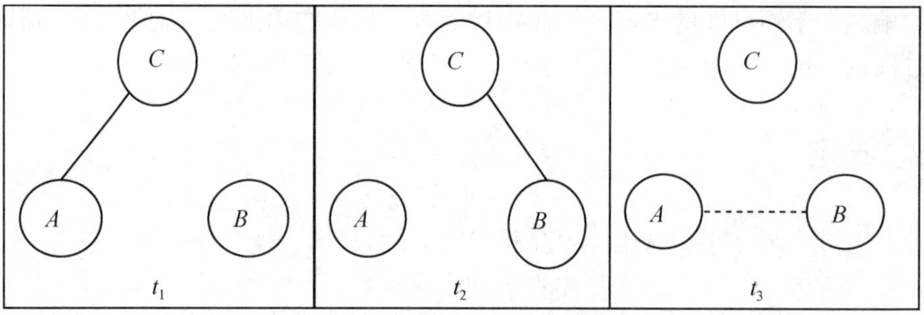

图1

定义5：C 是 $\overleftarrow{(AB)}(t)$ 的 Facilitator（笔者依据其含义，译为"学术引荐人"），当且仅当存在 $\overleftarrow{(CA)}(t_1)$ 和 $\overleftarrow{(CB)}(t_2)$，且 $\max(t_1, t_2)\leqslant t$。我们以 *facil*（$C$，$AB$）表示 C 在促成 A、B 间学术合作的行为，依上述定义可得 *facil*（C，AB）等价于 *facil*（C，BA）。

2.2 熵的原理与应用

"熵"的概念是由 Shannon 在对信息进行度量的时候提出来的。[22] 假设一个通信系统中存在 N 个符号，其中第 i 个符号被传输的概率是 p_i，那么该系统的信息量就定义为：

$$H=-\sum_{i=1}^{N}p_i\log p_i\text{。} \tag{1}$$

此外，Shannon 的信息理论还有两个重要的结论：第一，在不考虑对数的底的情况下，随着概率 p_i 越来越接近均等，信息量 H 会变得越来越大，当所有的概率 p_i 变得完全均等的时候，信息量 H 也达到了最大值。第二，当所有的概率 p_i 完全均等的时候，信息量 H 随着 N 的变大而变大。[23]

2007 年，F. Tutzauer 在一篇研究社会网络的论文中，首次将 Shannon 的熵作为衡量网络中一个节点中心度的指标。[24]他通过实证证明，在信息传递的过程中，假如信息传递者的目标接收者越明确，那么该信息传递的范围就越小；信息传递者的目标接受者越模糊，传递范围越广。

3 三元闭环合著网络直观分析

三元闭环合著现象是合著网络中经常出现的一种现象。本研究采集图书情报领域的实际数据，构建三元闭环合著网络，据此分析学术引荐人在合著网络中所处的位置和所扮演的角色。

3.1 数据获取与处理

本研究选取 2012 版 JCR 中收录的非医学相关的图书情报领域期刊为样本。由于排名靠前的期刊影响因子没有显著差异（相差小于 0.5），所以采用“总被引数”作为排序依据。兼顾考虑样本规模和数据处理能力，最终确定 *MIS Quarterly*、*Jasist* 和 *Scientometrics* 三种期刊作为数据来源。这三种期刊的总被引数均大于 4000 次，与其他期刊相比具有明显优势。在 WOS（Web of Science）平台上下载了这三种期刊所刊载的所有文献为基本的分析对象，检索时间为 2014 年 3 月 1 日。[25]期刊改名的情况在数据采集过程中也有考虑，例如 *Jasis* 改名为 *Jasist*。为了直观地展现合著网络的演化过程，将所有的文献分成 1999—2004 年、1999—2009 年、1999—2014 三个阶段分别进行数据统计与可视化处理。由于三种文献最早可检索到的文献出版日期为 1999 年，所以将开始计数的年份记为 1999 年。通过对各阶段的数据进行清洗，其中 1999—2004 年阶段共获取文献 1381 篇，作者总数 1385 人；1999—2009 年阶段共获取文献 3365 篇，作者总数 4023 人；1999—2014 年阶段共获取文献 5564 篇，作者总数 6924 人。

合著关系数据获取存在数据噪声的干扰问题。Web of Science 已经意识到相应的问题，因此近年来通过在作者姓名的简称后补充全称、增加作者的联系信息（如 E-mail 和机构信息）等相关手段进行改进，以保证作者身份确定的唯一性。但是由于不同阶段期刊对于作者的标注仍然存在差别，例如作者 Wolfgang Glanzel 在 2012 年后的文献被标注为 Glanzel，Wolfgang，在 1999—2012 年间的文献则被标注为 Glanzel，W.。表 1 以作者 Cassidy R. Sugimoto 为例展示了三种主要的不规范问题，这些问题主要在作者位于第二或第三作者角色中时发生。

表 1　作者姓名标注不规范示例

作者字段常用形式	存在问题	不规范形式
Cassidy R. Sugimoto	空格的误用	Sugimoto CR
	全称、简称混用	Sugimoto Cassidy R
	缩写符号“.”的误用	Sugimoto C. R

针对上述问题，本研究已对所收集到的数据利用正则表达式进行清洗，对不同标注方式的同一个作者的文献进行统一计算，避免了同人异名造成的统计误差。另外，本研究着眼于三元合著现象和学术引荐人对于合著网络演化所起的作用，因而在处理作者数据时将一篇文献中所标注出的所有作者皆纳入统计范围内，而没有采用其他研究惯常使用的只统计第一、第二作者的做法，以确保尽可能大地扩大所包含的作者的范围。但是，对于“et al”中无法考究的作者，本文忽略不计。

本文对数据的处理主要通过自编的 Python 脚本进行。该脚本的处理逻辑基本按照本文 2.2 节中引用的三元闭环的定义进行拓展。如学者 A 与学者 C 在时刻 t_1 合著了一篇文献 P_1，学者 B 和学者 C 在时刻 t_2 合著了一篇文献 P_2，而学者 A 与学者 B 在时刻 t_3 合著了一篇文献 P_3。当且仅当 $\max(t_1, t_2) \leq t_3$ 时，把学者 A、B、C 三者的三元合著次数增加 1，并将作者 C 记为学术引荐人。

本文对数据的可视化处理主要使用荷兰莱顿大学科学技术研究中心开发的 VOSViewer 可视化软件。该软件主要运用了基于相似性的可视化思想，是目前在计量分析中应用较为广泛的可视化软件，其可视化结果有利于研究结果的分析和解读。

3.2 初步实验结果分析

通过上面程序的处理后，得到各阶段中作者间存在的三元闭环。通过对上面三组数据构建共现矩阵，并且导入 VOSViewer，得到了以实验数据为基础的合著网络。

图 2 是依据原始数据构建合著矩阵，建立起基本的合著网络；然后将实验后的结果作为节点的标识符标注于原来的网络上。其中，网络中深色的节点为上文中担当学术引荐人的学者，浅色的节点则为从未担当过学术引荐人的学者。每幅图都只列出该时间段内发生过合著关系的学者，而没有列出一篇文献仅有一位学者的情况。节点的面积说明该节点在网络中的重要性，面积越大，则重要性越高。节点与节点间的距离反映节点间联系的紧密程度。从节点间距离的定义可知，两个节点间发生合著关系的次数越多，每次合著中总学者数越少，则权重越大，两个节点间的距离越小。

图 2 清楚地表明了合著网络的演变过程。从图 2 可见，在 1999—2004 年的出版物中，合著情况出现的频率不是十分高。具体体现为整个网络中节点的数目比较少，密度比较低。从图中能大概分出三个合著集群，分别以 W. Glanzel、H. F. Moed、R. Rousseau 和 C. S. Wilson 以及 H. Kretschmer 为核心。在 2004—2009 年，整体的合著网络与前五年没有太多变化，学者的数目也没有呈现大量的增长。但是各个合著集群都围绕其核心有了一定程度的扩展，同时也出现了新的学术引荐人（如 M. Thelwall）。整个合著网络在 2009—2014 年间发生了巨大的变化。具体体现为合著作者数目的大幅度增加，学术研究呈多极化发展。例如，原来的 R. Rousseau 集群中的学者逐渐朝着不同的方向深入发展，进而形成自己的小集群，与原来集群里的成员的研究方向逐渐发生偏离。而类似 W. Glanzel 集群，则维持着其高度的向心力，出现了高密度的点的集群，并逐步将 H. F. Moed 集群吞并进自己的集群中。再如 L. Leydesdorff 则慢慢从网络的边缘位置移动至中心区域，虽然并没有形成明显的集群，但在各分支的发展中起着枢纽作用，沟通着研究中的各个新兴领域。

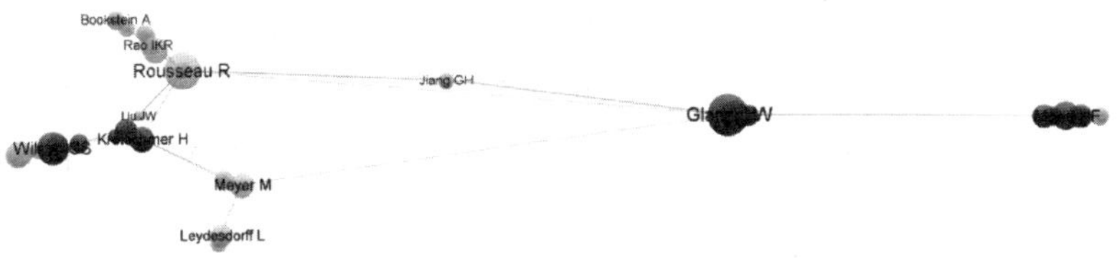

1999—2004年三元闭环合著网络的可视化结果

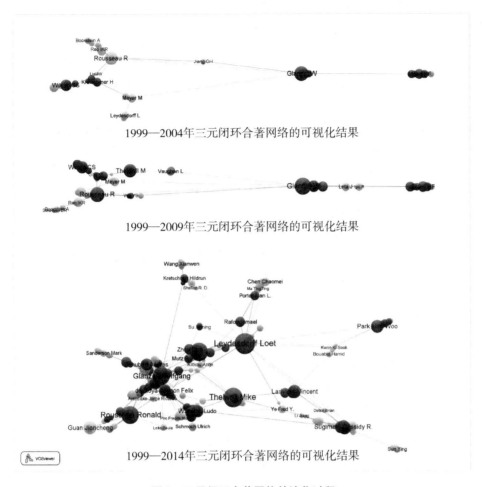

1999—2009年三元闭环合著网络的可视化结果

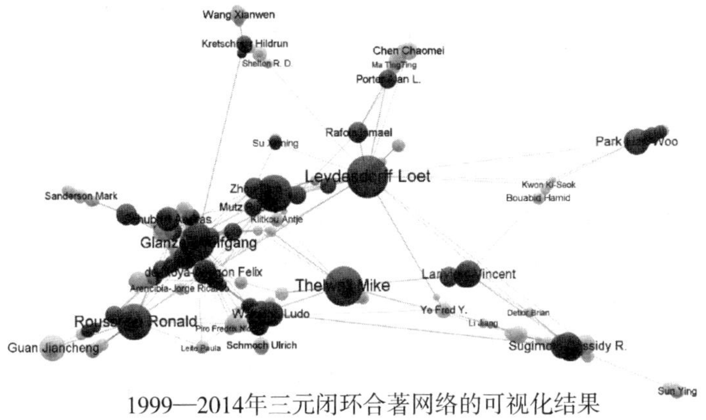

1999—2014年三元闭环合著网络的可视化结果

图2　三元闭环合著网络的演化过程

考察网络中各个学术引荐人及其集群的演变，可以总结出学术引荐人起到的作用：①学术引荐人往往会在合著网络上形成一个稳定的集群，这一个集群会随着时间的推移、新成员的加入，以及与其他集群的交流的加深而逐渐扩大。②无论在网络演化的哪一阶段，学术引荐人都处于网络发展的关键节点上。无论是位于网络中心的枢纽位置，还是各个新兴领域中发展的源头，都会有学术引荐人出现。学术引荐人就相当于整个网络的“关节”一样，决定着整个网络往哪个方向发展，体现了三元闭环现象和学术引荐人在网络演化的关键作用。

3.3　实验结果的修正与分析

虽然以上分析可以从一定程度上反映三元闭环现象在整个网络演化过程中所处的地位和发挥的作用，但是从数据的特征可以发现，三元闭环定义方法存在着某些漏洞，使得统计出来的三元闭环的数据存在很大的系统误差。

考虑下面一种情况：学者 A、学者 B 和学者 C 在时刻 t_1 发表了一篇论文 P_1，学者 A、

学者 B 和学者 C 在时刻 t_2 发表了一篇论文 P_2，学者 A、学者 B 和学者 C 在时刻 t_3 发表了一篇论文 P_3，且 $\max(t_1, t_2) \leq t_3$。那么，依据三元闭环现象的定义和4.1节中的统计口径，学者 A、学者 B 和学者 C 均会作为学术引荐人出现，且会存在分别以他们为学术引荐人的组成三元闭环的学者为 A、B、C 的一条数据，且次数均为1。但是，这样的统计数据是没有实际意义的。因为从这三篇文章的合著情况中可以看出，学者 A、B、C 三人其实并不相互作为学术引荐人存在，他们三个在这段关系中是相互平等独立的三个人存在。而且，对于次数的统计也是不合理的，因为这样的统计方法将原本实际上为一次的三元闭环现象统计成了三次。因此，对于关系密切而一起合作次数比较多的学者，数据重复计算所造成的系统误差会更大。

为消除这一误差，笔者在原定义的基础上，提出“严格三元闭环”的概念，定义如下：如果学者 A 与学者 C 在时刻 t_1 合著了一篇文献 P_1，文献的作者不包含学者 B；学者 B 和学者 C 在时刻 t_2 合著了一篇文献 P_2，文献的作者不包含学者 A；而学者 A 与学者 B 在时刻 t_3 合著了一篇文献 P_3，文献的作者不包含学者 C。当且仅当 $\max(t_1, t_2) \leq t_3$ 时，把学者 A、B、C 三者的三元合著次数增加1，并将作者 C 记为学术引荐人。采用“严格三元闭环”的定义，不仅可以消除上述统计上的误差，也更符合现实情况。只有当学者 A 和学者 B 之前不认识或没有发生过合著关系，而经过 C 的引荐后两人能产生单独合作的成果，才能称得上这种引荐行为的成功之处。所以，严格三元闭环更能反映出引荐行为的本质，更能衡量引荐行为是否成功。

根据上文对于实验存在的系统误差的讨论和修正后，将原来三元闭环的统计标准更改为严格三元闭环后，得出修正后的合著网络，如图3所示。

对比图3和图2可以发现，网络的整体布局没有发生变化，但是网络中深色标注的学术引荐人的数目大大地减少了。究其原因，网络的整体布局没有改变是因为构造网络时边的值的定义方法没有发生改变，所以严格三元闭环的统计方法不会对点与点间相对位置和空间布局造成任何影响。

深色标注的学术引荐人数目的大量减少则与实验数据的结果相吻合。由于删除了大量重复计算的数据，使得对学术引荐人的认定更为严格。例如，C. S. Wilson 和 M. Thelwall 消失了。这一现象表明，这些学者的合著关系只是与几个固定的学者间频繁发生，而且这几个学者间又是相互独立和没有产生后续的合作关系。从而从侧面说明，这一类型的学者在网络上扩展自己学术交流圈子的能力相对比较低。而从学术引荐人所处的位置来看，学术引荐人的位置更加集中在各自集群的核心位置，而且点的面积都比较大。这说明严格三元闭环的统计方法实际上消除了在三元闭环合著关系中跟随核心作者发生合著行为的附庸的影响，而更集中于凸显集群核心作者的扩张作用，这对于呈现网络演化的本质有更好的优化作用。

在原统计方法下，基本网络上的每个分支与网络中心部分的连接处都有学术引荐人的存在。而在新的统计方法下，部分网络分支与网络中心部分的学术引荐人却消失了，如M. Thelwall。对于这一现象一个可能的解释为，该学者在自己所属的新兴领域内，与该分支内的成员的合著水平比较低；或者是由于该领域为新兴领域，学者们为了保持自己在该领域的领先地位，而对于新的发现和新的研究成果选择单独发表论文或只和少部分人合著论文，造成该分支缺乏形成三元闭环的条件。

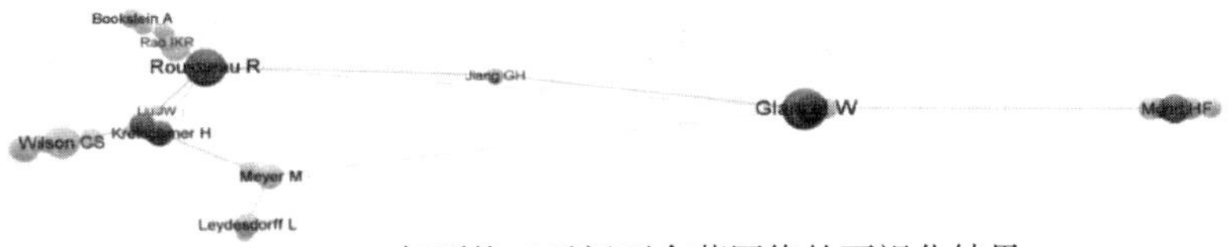

1999—2004年严格三元闭环合著网络的可视化结果

1999—2009年严格三元闭环合著网络的可视化结果

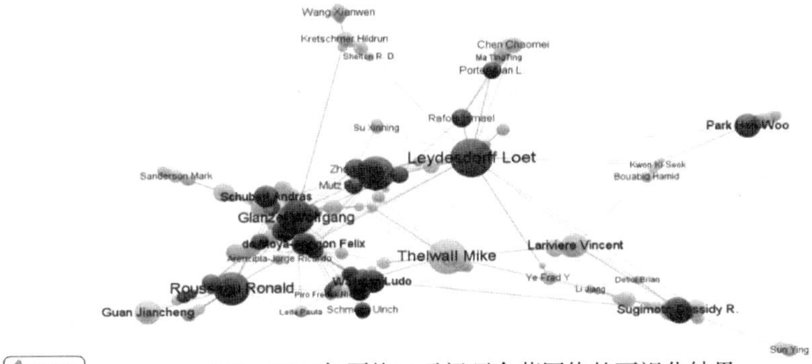

1999—2014年严格三元闭环合著网络的可视化结果

图3　严格三元闭环合著网络的演化过程

3.4　小　结

综合以上分析，主要有以下发现：①不同的学术引荐人在网络的演化过程中呈现不同的发展速度，有的学术引荐人所在的集群发展速度快，集群的扩张规模程度小；有的学术引荐人所在的集群发展速度慢，集群的扩张规模程度小。②学术引荐人在网络中多处于集群核心和分支与核心交接的部位，对网络的发展和扩张起着关键的枢纽和支点的作用。③严格三元闭环合著关系比普通的三元闭环合著关系更能反映数据中真实的三元闭环现象发生的情况和凸显学术引荐人的作用。

此外，通过对网络的直观分析还发现：随着时间的推移，这些学术引荐人新促成的合著关系的数目也有多有少，不同的学术引荐人所在的集群的扩张速度有快有慢。那么，影响学术引荐人促成新的合著关系的因素有哪些呢？影响学术交际圈扩张的因素有哪些呢？这些因素又是如何对学术引荐人促成新的合著关系产生影响，其内在机理又是如何呢？下面，运用复杂网络演化模型，对上述三元闭环复杂网络做进一步的分析。

4　针对学术引荐人的演化模型改进

A. Rapoport在研究信息流通问题的过程中，曾提出一个影响很大的信息流通模型。[26]该模型基于概率论，描述了信息从一个人的交际圈内传递到他的交际圈外的过程。

在此，借鉴这一模型，得到学者 A 在时刻（$t+1$）与小圈子里的其他学者发生合著关系的概率为：

$$1-\left[1-P(t)+P(t)\left(1-\frac{1}{q}\right)^{\alpha}\right]^{q}; \tag{2}$$

学者 A 在时刻（t+1）与小圈子外的学者发生合著关系的概率为：

$$-\frac{1}{m}\log\left[1-P(t)\left(1-e^{-\alpha}\right)\right]。 \tag{3}$$

在考虑双交际圈的情况下，假设学者 A 的交际圈中有 q_1 个学者，学者 C 的交际圈中有 q_2 个学者。学者 C 为学者 A 的交际圈内的学者，而相对应的，学者 A 也是学者 C 的交际圈内学者的一员。假设现存在一个学者 B 在学者 C 的交际圈内，而不位于学者 A 的交际圈内。三者的关系如图 4 所示。

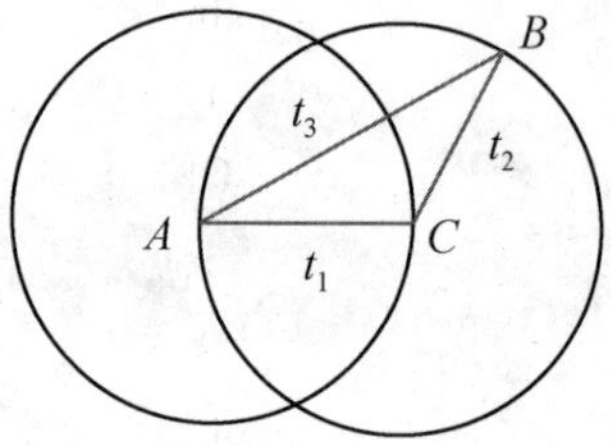

图 4　A、B、C 三个学者的关系

图中位于圆心位置的为该学术交际圈的中心人物，例如学者 A 的学术交际圈即为一个以点 A 为圆心的圆，每个位于学者 A 的交际圈内的学者皆位于圆上。图中所示的为学者 A 与学者 C 的学术交际圈，B 为位于学者 C 的交际圈内，而位于学者 A 的交际圈外的学者。

先考虑学者 C 的交际圈。根据公式（2）可得，学者 C 在时刻 t_1 与学者 A 发生合著关系的概率为：

$$P_{CA}=1-\left[1-P(t_1-1)+P(t_1-1)\left(1-\frac{1}{q_2}\right)^{\alpha_C}\right]^{q_2}。 \tag{4}$$

式中：α_C 为学者 C 的学术交际圈内的度的密度。同理，学者 C 在时刻 t_2 与学者 B 发生合著关系的概率为：

$$P_{CB}=1-\left[1-P(t_2-1)+P(t_2-1)\left(1-\frac{1}{q_2}\right)^{\alpha_C}\right]^{q_2}。 \tag{5}$$

考虑到学者 B 在学者 A 的学术交际圈外，可以认为学者 B 与学者 A 之前并不认识。又因为学者 A 与学者 B 之前并不认识，可以认为学者 C 与学者 A 发生合著关系的概率与学者 C 与学者 B 发生合著关系的概率相互独立，因而，在 $\max(t_1,t_2)$ 时，学者 C 与学者 A 和学者 B 均已发生合著关系的概率为：

$$\{1-[1-P(t_1-1)m_C]^{q_2}\}\cdot\{1-[1-P(t_2-1)m_C]\}^{q_2}。 \tag{6}$$

其中：

$$m_C=1-\left(1-\frac{1}{q_2}\right)^{\alpha_C}。 \tag{7}$$

此时，考虑在学者 A 的学术交际圈内，学者 A 在时刻 t_1 与学者 C 间发生合著关系的概率为：

$$1-\left[1-P(t_1-1)+P(t_1-1)\left(1-\frac{1}{q_1}\right)^{\alpha_A}\right]^{q_1}。\tag{8}$$

式中：α_A 为学者 A 的学术交际圈内的度的密度。而由于合著关系是双向的，在学者 A 的学术交际圈内学者 A 与学者 C 发生合著关系，实际上与在学者 C 的学术交际圈内学者 A 与学者 C 间发生合著关系所描述的同一件事件。因此，公式（4）与公式（8）所描述的是同一事件，所以两条公式的值是相等的，因而有：

$$1-[1-P(t_1-1)m_A]^{q_1}=1-[1-P(t_1-1)m_C]^{q_2}。\tag{9}$$

其中：

$$m_A=1-\left(1-\frac{1}{q_1}\right)^{\alpha_A}。\tag{10}$$

那么，当学者 A 与学者 C 已经发生合著关系且学者 B 与学者 C 已经发生合著关系的情况下，学者 A 与学者 B 间发生合著的概率是多少？此处同样应用贝叶斯公式对这一条件概率进行计算。

S_k 是一个假设，这个假设是下面两种情况的任意一种：

S_1：学者 A 与学者 B 在时刻 t_3 发生了合著关系；

S_2：学者 A 与学者 B 在时刻 t_3 没有发生合著关系。

设事件 D 为“学者 A 与学者 C 在时刻 t_1 发生了合著关系且学者 B 与学者 C 在时刻 t_2 发生了合著关系”，依照式（3）可得：

$$p(S_1)=-\frac{1}{m_A}\log[1-P(t_3)(1-\mathrm{e}^{-\alpha_A})],\tag{11}$$

$$p(S_2)=1-p(S_1),\tag{12}$$

$$p(D\mid S_1)=1,\tag{13}$$

$$p(D\mid S_2)=\{1-[1-P(t_1-1)m_C]^{q_2}\}\cdot\{1-[1-P(t_2-1)m_C]^{q_2}\}。\tag{14}$$

依照题意，本文要求的是 $p(S_1\mid D)$，即“在学者 A 和学者 C 发生合著关系且学者 B 与学者 C 发生了合著关系的条件下，学者 A 和学者 B 发生合著关系的概率”，代入贝叶斯公式得：

$$p(S_1\mid D)=\frac{p(D\mid S_1)p(s_1)}{\sum\limits_{j=1}^{2}p(D\mid S_j)p(s_j)}。\tag{15}$$

并将公式（9）代入结果并整理可得：

$$p(S_1\mid D)=\frac{1}{1+\dfrac{P_{CA}\cdot P_{CB}}{-\dfrac{1}{m_C}\log[1-P(t_3)(1-\mathrm{e}^{-\alpha_C})]}+P_{CA}\cdot P_{CB}}。\tag{16}$$

由公式（16）可以看出，$p(S_1\mid D)$ 只与学者 C 的学术交际圈中的点的数目与度密度相关，而与学者 A 的学术交际圈的点的数目与度密度无关。换句话说，在三元闭环现象中，两个之前不认识的学者最后能否发生合著关系，很大程度上依赖的是学术引荐人交际圈是否足够的广泛，以及学术引荐人的交际圈内部学者间合作的程度的高低。由此可见，学者 C，即三元闭环现象中的学术引荐人，在促成两位陌生的学者间的合作的过程中发挥着重要的作用。在接下来的研究中，本文将基于这一模型改进结果，结合扩张系数的计算，探讨三元闭环现象在合著网络扩张中所起到的作用。需要说明的是，上文所述的基于三元闭环现象对已有模型的改进，仅仅是作为对合著网络扩张过程中三元闭环现象和学术引荐行为发挥的机理作用进行描述，而并非提出一个衡量学术引荐行为的指标。这是因为，本模型是基于概率论对学术引荐行为、三元闭环现象的发生进行模拟，对合著网络演化过程中可能出现的路径进行推导，这是一种预测性的模型。而在现实的合著网络中，两个学者之间有否发生合著关系是一个布尔关系（有就是有，没有就是没有），是一个基于已经发生的合著关系构建起来的网络，具有后验性质。

通过对模型的改进可以发现，在三元闭环合著现象中，两个陌生的学者间能否通过学术引荐发生合著关系，很大程度上取决于学术引荐人交际圈的大小以及交际圈内学者间相互合作的频率。这在某一程度上表明，学术引荐人在促成新的合著关系的形成和促进合著网络扩张的过程中发挥着关键的作用。下面结合扩张系数对学术引荐人的作用进行定量的分析，讨论三元闭环现象在合著网络扩张过程中起到的作用。

5　扩张系数的原理与计算方法

综合上述对演化模型的改进发现，影响学术引荐人促成新的三元闭环合著关系的因素主要是其“学术交际圈内的学者数目”和“学术交际圈内合著发生的频率”。针对这两个影响因素，笔者提出“扩张系数”这一评价指标，用以沟通微观的三元闭环合著现象与宏观的学者学术交际圈的扩张两者间的关系，进而用以衡量学者学术交际圈的扩张速度。下面，对扩张系数的理论原理进行说明，然后给出具体的计算方法。

5.1　扩张系数的原理

对于整个合著网络而言，三位学者之间发生三元闭环合著关系是一个微观层面所发生的现象。从宏观上来看，三元闭环合著现象的累积，能转化成一个学者的学术交际圈的扩张，进而推动整个合著网络规模的扩张。考虑上文4章中，基于复杂网络演化模型所提出的学术引荐人促成新的三元闭环合著关系的影响因素，学术引荐人的圈子内学者的数目和圈子内合著关系发生的频率是两大影响因素。根据 Shannon 的熵的原理以及 Tutzauer 对其的应用可以发现，假如一个学术引荐人只引荐特定的某几位学者发生三元闭环合著关系，那么他所促成的三元闭环合著关系的覆盖范围只会占他整个交际圈范围的很少一部分，数目也会较少；相反，假如他对他交际圈内的学者一视同仁，会均匀地分配学术引荐的机会，那么他所能促成的新的三元闭环合著关系覆盖的范围就会越广，数目也会越多。

从另外一个角度看，学术引荐人的学术交际圈内的每一位学者都有其对应的自己的学术交际圈，学术引荐人与自己交际圈内的学者的合著关系分布越均匀，则他与各个学者对应的交际圈的接触也同样越均匀，他所直接或间接认识到的其他学者的数目也越多，因此也越有可能促成新的不同学者间的合著关系的发生。

扩张系数与改进后模型的联系在于，当学术引荐人交际圈内的学者的数目越多，那么可供学术引荐人选择的合适的学者数目就越多，新的合著关系发生的范围就越广。圈子内发生合著的频率越高，那么学术引荐人就会有越多的机会选择他想要引荐的作者。

总的来说，依据 Shannon 的熵的原理以及 Tutzauer 的应用，学术引荐人在自己的学术交际圈中的合著情况的分布越均匀，那么他越能促成更多的三元闭环现象的产生，进而推动整个合著网络的扩张。

5.2 扩张系数的计算方法

本文在可视化的过程中，每一个作者分别用一个单独的点表示，点与点之间的连边的大小主要根据 Newman 在 2004 年提出的根据合著次数及合著强度共同来计算合著关系网络边权的方法来确定。[27] 这种方法对简单加权的方法进行了一定程度的改进，认为两个作者之间的合著强度不是恒定的，而是根据文献合著作者人数的不同而有所不同，一篇文献著者的数量和合著强度成反比。具体定义如下：

$$W_{i,j}^{d} = \frac{1}{n_d - 1}, \tag{17}$$

$$W_{i,j} = \sum_{d} W_{i,j}^{d} = \sum_{d} \frac{1}{n_d - 1}。 \tag{18}$$

式中：$W_{i,j}^{d}$为论文 d 中，作者 i 与作者 j 之间的合著强度；

n_d 为论文 d 中，合著作者的总人数；

$W_{i,j}$为作者 i 与作者 j 两个节点之间的边权。

这种对于合著网络中边的定义方法根据合著人数的不同，对单篇文献中的合著强度予以区分，对于本文的研究比较合适。两个作者间合著强度越大，则其在图像上的相对距离越近，两者之间的连线越粗。

为了验证本文 4 章的模型改进是否符合实际情况，现基于上文三元闭环原理与 Shannon 的熵的原理提出学者的扩张系数，其具体计算方法如下。

假设一个合著网络中共有 N 个学者，c 个小圈子，在时刻 t 时，一个学者 i 与第 m 个小圈子内所有学者的合著强度为：

$$\text{sum}_m(i) = \sum_{q} W_{i,j}。 \tag{19}$$

式中：q 为小圈子内包含的学者的人数。那么，学者 i 与第 m 个小圈子内所有学者的合作关系强度之和占学者 i 总的合著强度的比例是：

$$R_m(i) = \frac{\text{sum}_m(i)}{\sum_{j=1}^{N} W_{i,j}}。 \tag{20}$$

基于 Shannon 的熵的计算原理（见本文 2.4 节），学者 i 的扩张系数为：

$$EC(i) = -\sum_{m=1}^{c} R_m(i) \log R_m(i)。 \tag{21}$$

在本研究中，将对数的底设为 2。值得一提的是，如果一个学者的合著者都不属于任何一个小圈子，那么该作者的扩张范围为 0，即扩张系数的值为 0。

6 扩张系数与合著网络扩张速度的相关性分析

如上文所述，依据 Shannon 的熵的原理以及 Tutzauer 的应用，提出了扩张系数这一概念和具体的计算方法。笔者通过自编的 Python 脚本计算得出整个合著网络中各个学者的扩张系数，整理后得到最终结果。下面对扩张系数进行直观分析，然后对扩张系数与模型的贴合程度、扩张系数对学者学术交际圈扩张速度进行相关性检验，验证扩张系数度量学者在网络中的扩张能力的信度和效度。

6.1 扩张系数的直观分析

根据扩张系数的定义，扩张系数的取值范围均大于等于零。本研究通过自编的程序计算出各学者在各数据集中的扩张系数，鉴于数据量大，仅列出排名前十位的学者的扩张系数（表2）。

表2 各年度区间扩张系数前十名的学者

排名	1999—2004 年		1999—2009 年		1999—2014 年	
	学者	扩张系数（EC）	学者	扩张系数（EC）	学者	扩张系数（EC）
1	van Leeuwen，TN	1.33	Glanzel，W	2.795	Leydesdorff，L	5.228
2	Chen，H	1.238	Daniell，HD	2.716	Glanzel，W	4.898
3	Glanzel，W	1.041	van Leeuwen，TN	2.433	Thelwall，M	4.882
4	Thelwall，M	0.984	van Raan，A	2.269	Chen，H	4.305
5	Rousseau，R	0.872	Chen，H	2.076	Daniell，HD	4.17
6	Myers，M	0.713	Rousseau，R	1.897	Sugimoto，CR	3.997
7	van Raan，A	0.661	Thelwall，M	1.883	Huang，M	3.604
8	Schubert，A	0.596	Leydesdorff，L	1.74	van Raan，A	3.601
9	Bornmann，L	0.544	Bornmann，L	1.505	Rousseau，R	3.453
10	Leydesdorff，L	0.529	Sugimoto，CR	1.462	Debackere，K	3.376

将表2与图3结合起来分析，可以发现，同一时期的扩张系数并不能很好地描述图像的特征。例如，1999—2004 年间的 M. Thelwall 和 1999—2009 年间的 H. D. Daniell，都没有在当期的图像中出现，但是却在扩张系数的排名上占据非常靠前的位置。但是，扩张系数的统计还是能反映当期图像的大致情况的。各个集群的核心作者，如 1999—2014 年间的 W. Glanzel、R. Rousseau 和 M. Thelwall，都在 1999—2009 年的网络中充当其对应集群的核心学者。

但是，针对有些学者在当期的扩张系数排名非常高，却在下一期的图像出现的现象，将 1999—2004 年的扩张系数与 1999—2004 年的网络、1999—2009 年的网络作对比分析，将1999—2009年的扩张系数与1999—2009年的网络、1999—2014年的网络作对比分析，则扩张系数所描述的结果变得一目了然。例如H. D. Daniell，他的扩张系数在1999—2009年间的得分非常高，但是在1999—2009年间的合著网络间没有凸显他的地位，他却在1999—2014年的合著网络中出现了，而且在该合著网络中占据着网络的核心位置，他所代表的点的面积非常大。同样的情况也发生于1999—2004年的M. Thelwall和1999—2009年的C. R. Sugimoto，他们两个在本期的网络中没有占据很关键的位置，但是在下一阶段的网络中却逐渐成长为自己学术集群的核心学者。同样的道理，W. Glanzel在1999—2009年的扩张系数排名第一，但他在1999—2009年的合著网络中并没有体现出非常重要的地位，却在1999—2014年的合著网络中迅速扩大他的合著圈子和学术集群，成为整个网络的核心之一。

因此，综合上述对于扩张系数结果在合著网络图像上的出现规律，可以总结出，某一阶段的扩张系数的结果主要在下一阶段的合著网络中得以体现。对于这一现象，一个合理的解释是，扩张系数描述的是一个学者在当前网络扩张自己合著圈子的能力，因而它所代表的是一种发展的潜力，代表的是在当前时期自身网络扩大的一个速度。因此，在某一时刻高的扩张系数，其结果要到下一阶段的合著网络中才能体现出来。这与扩张系数的定义和扩张系数所描述的变量是内涵一致的。所以从直观的角度上来说，扩张系数能很好地描述一个学者扩大他的合著圈子的能力。

而横向对比各阶段的扩张系数可知，随着时间的发展，同一个学者的扩张系数在逐渐增加。对这一现象的一个解释是，随着时间推移，一个学者会不断地扩大他自己的合著圈子；随着合著圈子规模的增大，在这个圈子的基础上往外扩张的能力也会增强。例如，一名学者一开始只和两个学者发生合著关系，过了一段时间，经过这两位学者的引荐和介绍，该学者又与其他三位学者发生了合著关系。而此时五个人的合著圈子，对比原来两个人的合著圈子，发生下一段圈子外的合著关系的概率要更高，因为规模越大意味着与外面更多的其他学者有接触的可能。但是依据这一原理可以推断，扩张系数不会无休止地增加，而是增加到一定的程度后就会维持在相对比较稳定的水平上。其原因在于，一位学者的社会交际能力是有限的，他不可能与整个网络中的所有人发生合著关系。因此，扩张系数会由于学者有限的交际能力而趋向于稳定，达到一个动态的平衡状态。

依据上文对于扩张系数的直观分析，结合1999—2014年扩张系数的结果，笔者可以大胆预测：在下一阶段，即接下来的5年时间内，L. Leydesdorff会成为网络中一个重要的增长点，W. Glanzel的集群会进一步地扩大，M. Thelwall的合著圈子也会继续扩大，成为网络中一个举足轻重的学者集群。

6.2 扩张系数与三元闭环数据的相关性分析

在对扩张系数和学者学术交际圈扩张速度进行相关性检验之前，必须对扩张系数与三元闭环的数据进行相关性分析。这是因为，三元闭环合著关系统计数据与扩张系数是依据不同的原理和不同的数学统计方法统计得出的。扩张系数则是基于复杂网络演化模型的结论，从宏观的角度考量学术引荐人促成新的三元闭环合著关系而得出的，有必要对两者之间的相关性进行检验。

在本文对模型的改进及讨论中提到，三元闭环现象实际上是一个学者通过学术引荐人的推荐，与自己学术交际圈外的另外一位学者发生合著关系的一个过程。这一过程涉及学者 A 和学术引荐人 C 两个学术交际圈。对于学者 A 而言，新的合著关系是发生在交际圈外的；而对于学术引荐人 C，新的合著关系是发生在自己的交际圈以内的。因此，对于学术引荐人 C 而言，他越广泛地与他的学术交际圈内的学者发生合著关系，理论上其学术交际圈中任意两个学者发生合著关系的概率也就越高。

而为了描述学术引荐人 C 与其学术交际圈内的学者合著情况的广泛性，本文引入了扩张系数及其计算方法。那么，对于学术引荐人 C，是否他与自己学术交际圈内的学者的合著情况越广泛，他所促成的三元闭环关系就越多呢？针对这一问题，本文将一位学者的扩张系数和引荐人指数，即他充当的三元闭环关系中学术引荐人的次数，用 SPSS 进行 Spearman 相关性计算，计算结果如表 3 所示。

表 3　各年度区间学者的扩张系数与三元闭环数据的相关性分析

	1999—2004 年			1999—2009 年			1999—2014 年		
	扩张系数	三元闭环数目	严格三元数目	扩张系数	三元闭环数目	严格三元数目	扩张系数	三元闭环数目	严格三元数目
扩张系数	1.000	0.688	0.953**	1.000	0.571	0.927**	1.000	0.429	0.810*
三元闭环数目		1.000	0.708*		1.000	0.764*		1.000	0.786*
严格三元数目			1.000			1.000			1.000

说明：*显著性水平为 0.05，**显著性水平为 0.01。表 4 同此。

相关性分析结果显示，一个学者的扩张系数与其充当学术引荐人所促成的严格三元闭环条目数存在着显著的相关关系。其中，1999—2004 年、1999—2009 年两者在显著性水平为 0.01 时显著相关，而 1999—2014 年两者在显著性水平为 0.05 时显著相关。这表明，一个学者的扩张系数与其促成的严格三元闭环关系的条目数间存在着强烈的相关关系。换句话说，一个学者与其学术交际圈中的学者发生合著关系的情况越均匀，那么他所能促成的严格三元闭环关系的数目就越多。同时，由于扩张系数是与学者学术交际圈内的学者的数目是正相关的，所以基本可以排除学者学术交际圈内人数很少但是合著情况分布均匀对于实验结果的影响。

从另一方面可以发现，在三个数据集中，扩张系数与修正前的三元闭环条目数间的相关性不显著。这说明修正前的三元闭环统计方式由于统计上存在系统误差，导致其对于现实情况的描述不够准确，因此与扩张系数缺乏明确的相关关系。这也从定量的角度证明了本文对于三元闭环数目与严格三元数目间差别的结论。

对比修正前的三元闭环条目数和严格三元闭环条目数可以发现，在三个数据集中严格三元闭环条目数与修正前三元闭环条目数都保持着显著性水平为 0.05 的显著相关性，这是由两者间的内在联系所决定的。严格三元闭环的条目数是在原来的三元闭环条目数中通过删除重复计算的三元闭环关系的条目数所得出的，所以两者之间存在相关性是很容易理解的。而从纵向进行比较可以发现，两者之间的 Spearman 相关指数随着时间跨度的拉长而增加，这表明随着整个网络节点数目的增加，三元闭环与严格三元闭环之间的差距越来越小。这一现象的一个合理的解释是，随着节点数目的增加，一个学者会不停地与其他新出现的学者发生合著关系，产生新的三元合著关系。而这些新的三元合著关系会稀释原来三元闭环与严格三元闭环之间的差别，使得两者之间的差别越来越小，因而相关系数越来越大。

观察扩张系数与严格三元闭环条目数的相关性指数可以发现，随着时间跨度的拉长，两者的相关性指数逐步降低，显著性水平也由原来的 0.01 变为 0.05，说明两者间的相关程度随着节点数目的增加变得越来越低。这一现象发生的一个原因是，一个学者的学术交际能力是有限的，他不可能认识整个合著网络里的所有人。换句话说，他的学术的交际圈的扩张范围是有限的。当他的扩张范围达到极限的时候，即使他与自己圈子里的学者的合著情况再均匀，他对于网络扩张的影响力最大也只能作用在他所在的集群之中，而无法影响整个网络的每一个角落，因而其严格三元闭环的条目数也会达到一定的极限，从而使得扩张系数与严格三元闭环条目数的相关程度随着整个网络节点数目的增加而缓慢下降。

总之，通过上述对扩张系数与三元闭环数据的相关性分析，可以发现：①扩张系数与严格三元闭环条目数间存在着强烈的相关关系，但这一相关关系会随着整个网络的节点数目的增长而缓慢下降；扩张系数与修正前的三元闭环条目数间的相关性不显著。②修正前的三元闭环条目数与严格三元闭环条目数间存在着显著的相关关系，这是由于三元闭环与严格三元闭环之间存在着内在的联系。而三元闭环与严格三元闭环之间的差距会随着网络中节点数目的增加而逐渐缩小，这是由于新学者的加入稀释了两者之间重复的条目数。

6.3 扩张系数与学术引荐人的交际圈扩张速度的相关性分析

为了验证 6.1 节中对扩张系数代表学者扩张其学术圈子的能力的讨论，本文将通过计算扩张系数与学者下一阶段增加的度的数目的 Spearman 相关系数，检验学者本阶段的扩张系数与下一阶段度的增加数的相关性。具体过程如下：对于学者 i，他在 1999—2004 年文献集构建的合著网络中的度为 $D_{1999—2004}(i)$，他在 1999—2009 年文献集构建的合著网络中的度为 $D_{1999—2009}(i)$，那么有 $D_{2004—2009}(i) = D_{1999—2009}(i) - D_{1999—2004}(i)$，其中 $D_{2004—2009}(i)$ 为学者 i 在 2004—2009 年间新增加的度的数目。设 $EC_{1999—2004}(i)$ 为学者 i 在 1999—2004 年合著网络中计算出的扩张系数。将在 1999—2004 年合著网络中存在的所有学者的 $EC_{1999—2004}(i)$ 与 $D_{2004—2009}(i)$ 导入 SPSS，并计算其相关系数。依照同样的方法，可以得出 $D_{2009—2014}(i)$，代表学者 i 在 2009—2014 年间新增加的度的数目。同样地，将在 2004—2009 年合著网络中存在的所有学者的 $EC_{2004—2009}(i)$ 与 $D_{2009—2014}(i)$ 导入 SPSS，并计算其相关系数。这里之所以使用度的变化值作为衡量学者合著范围扩大的一个标志，是因为从度的定义出发可知：度的增加代表该点与之前没有建立连接的点间建立起了连接。其现实意义为，一个学者与之前没有发生过合著关系的学者间建立起了联系，这一点与学者合著范围扩大的含义是一样的，所以采用这一指标是合理的。

在这里没有将 $[D_{2004-2009}(i) - D_{1999-2004}(i)] / D_{1999-2004}(i)$ 与 $EC_{1999-2004}(i)$ 导入 SPSS 并计算其相关系数，是基于这样的考虑：学者 i 在前一阶段所积累下来的人脉，会对他下一阶段拓展其合著圈子有正面的影响。假如消除了规模影响，将显得实验的结果不符合实际情况。

从表 4 的相关性检验结果中可以看出，$EC_{1999-2004}(i)$ 与 $D_{2004-2009}(i)$ 的相关性和 $EC_{2004-2009}(i)$ 与 $D_{2009-2014}(i)$ 的相关性都是显著的，而且显著性水平相对较高。这证明了上一节中从直观感受对于扩张系数描述效果的推断是正确的，即：一个学术引荐人在某一阶段的扩张系数与下一阶段该学者学术交际圈增长的速度有着强烈的正相关关系。扩张系数的值越大，则下一阶段学者合著圈子增长的速度就越快；扩张系数的值越小，则下一阶段学者合著圈子增长的速度就越慢。

表 4　扩张系数与学术圈扩张速度的相关性分析

$EC_{1999-2004}$ 与 $D_{2004-2009}$ 相关性分析		
	$EC_{1999-2004}$	$D_{2004-2009}$
$EC_{1999-2004}$	1.000	0.681**
$D_{2004-2009}$		1.000
$EC_{2004-2009}$ 与 $D_{2009-2014}$ 相关性分析		
	$EC_{2004-2009}$	$D_{2009-2014}$
$EC_{2004-2009}$	1.000	0.737**
$D_{2009-2014}$		1.000

6.4 小　结

通过本章对于扩张系数与两个关键指标的相关性分析，可以得出以下结论：①扩张系数与严格三元闭环条目数间存在着强烈的相关关系，证明了扩张系数能正确反映一个学者在微观层面三元闭环合著的情况，两者之间存在着强烈的正相关的关系；②扩张系数与学术引荐人的学术交际圈的扩张速度呈现显著的正相关关系，证明扩张系数能正确描述一个学者在未来一段时间内学术交际圈扩张的快慢，是衡量学术引荐人在网络中位置和角色的一个合理的新的指标。

7　结论与讨论

本研究通过构建和分析国外图书情报领域的三元闭环合著网络，改进已有的复杂网络演化模型，提出了严格三元闭环和扩张系数等重要概念及计算方法，用以研究影响学者合著网络扩张速度的主要因素。主要结论如下：

（1）学术引荐人所在集群的扩张速度，与学术引荐人跟集群内成员合著的均匀程度正相关。他们往往处于学者集群的核心，是自己所在的学者集群与整个网络连接的枢纽。

学术引荐人合著的均匀程度直接决定了他所在学者集群的扩张速度，并对整个网络的扩张速度有影响。

（2）针对三元闭环统计过程中可能出现的系统误差，本研究提出严格三元闭环统计方法。实证研究表明，严格三元闭环统计方法能更准确地描述学者间的学术引荐活动。

（3）为了衡量学术引荐人扩张其学术交际圈的能力，本研究提出扩张系数这一指标，给出了具体的计算方法，并对其信度和效度进行实证验证。结果证明，扩张系数是描述学者扩张其学术交际圈能力的有效指标，对合著网络动态演变研究具有重要价值。[27]

目前的研究仅是初步的探讨，还有许多问题有待进一步的深化研究。在样本期刊的选择上，可以将作者群体的交叉程度考虑进去，以增强代表性。三元闭环的定义也还存在完善的空间。扩张系数可尝试更复杂的关系强度计算方法，以更好地描述学者的扩张能力。此外，目前的研究中对学者角色的描述仍然偏少，可以从更多的角度进行分析。例如，本研究将一篇文章中的所有作者的角色都平等看待。但在现实情况中，作者出现的次序往往反映了作者对文献的贡献程度和作者的重要程度。在未来研究中，将对学者的角色与出现顺序等因素做进一步的探讨。

参考文献

[1] Barabasi A L, Albert R. Emergence of Scaling in Random Networks [J]. Science, 1999, 286 (5439): 509 -512.

[2] Klemm K, Egufluz V M. Highly Cluster Scale-free Networks [J]. Physical Review, 2002, 65 (3): 36 -123.

[3] Klemm K, Egufluz V M. Growing Scale-free with Small World Behavior [J]. Physical Review E, 2002, 65 (5): 57 -102.

[4] Erdos P, Renyi A. On Random Graphs [J]. Publications Mathematics, 1959, 6: 290 -297.

[5] Watts D J, Strogatz S H. Collective Dynamics of "Small World Network" [J]. Nature, 1998, 393: 440 -442.

[6] Newman M E J, Watts D J. Renormalization Group Analysis of the Small World Networks Model [J]. Physical A, 1999, 263: 341 -346.

[7] Dorogovtesv S N, Mendes J F F. Effect of the Accelerating Growth of Communication Network on Their Structure [J]. Physical Review E, 2001, 63 (2): 25 -101.

[8] Sen P. Accelerated Growth in Outgoing Links in Evolving Networks: Deterministic vs. Stochastic Picture [J]. Physical Review E, 2004, 69 (4): 46 -107.

[9] Bianconi G, Barabasi A L. Bose-Einstein Condensation in Complex Networks [J]. Physical Review Letters, 2001, 86 (25): 5632 -5635.

[10] Li Xiang, Chen Guanrong. A Local-World Evolving Network Model [J]. Physical A, 2003, 328 (1/2): 274 -286.

[11] Dorogovtesv S N, Mendes J. F F. Minimal Models of Weighted Scale-free Networks [EB/OL]. [2014 -01 -24]. http://arxiv.org/cond-mat/0408343.

[12] Yook S H, Jeong H, Barabasi A L, et al. Weighted Evolving Networks [J]. Physical Review Letters, 2001, 86 (25): 5835 -5838.

[13] Barrat A, Barthelemy M, Vespignani A A. Weighted Evolving Networks: Coupling Topology and Weight Dynamics [J]. Physical Review Letters, 2004, 92 (22): 228 -701.

[14] Leydesdorff L. Clusters and Maps of Science Journals Based on Bi-connected Graphs in the Journal Citation Reports [J]. Journal of Documentation, 2004, 60 (4): 317 -427.

[15] Leydesdorff L, Persson O. Mapping the Geography of Science: Distribution Patterns and Networks of Relations among Cities and Institutes [J]. Journal of the American Society for Information Science and Technology, 2010, 61 (8): 1622 -1634.

[16] Ren W, Beard R W. Consensus Seeking in Multi-agent Systems under Dynamically Changing Interaction Topologies [J]. IEEE Transactions on Automatic Control, 2005, 50 (5): 655 -661.

[17] Moreau L. Stability of Multi-Agent System with Time-Dependent Communication Links [J]. IEEE Transaction on Automatic Control, 2005, 50 (2): 169 -181.

[18] Ritzer G. Modern Sociological Theory [M]. 7th edition. New York: McGraw-Hill, 2007.

[19] Granovetter M. The Strength of Weak Ties [J]. American Journal of Sociology, 1973, 78 (6): 1360 -1380.

[20] Kossinets G, Watts D. J. Empirical Analysis of an Evolving Social Network [J]. Science, 2006, 311 (5757): 88 -90.

[21] Cho P S, Do H H N, Chandrasekaran M K, Kan M Y. Identifying Research Facilitator in an Emerging Asian Research Area [J]. Scientometrics, 2013, 97 (1): 75 -97.

[22] Shannon C E. A Mathematical Theory of Communication [J]. The Bell System Technical Journal, 1948, 27 (3): 379 -423, 623 -656.

[23] Shannon C E, Weaver W. The Mathematical Theory of Communication [M]. Chicago: University of Illinois Press, 1964.

[24] Tutzauer F. Entropy as a Measure of Centrality in Networks Characterized by Path-transfer Flow [J]. Social Network, 2007, 29 (2): 249 -265.

[25] Thomas Reuters. JCR-SSCI edition [EB/OL]. [2014 -03 -01]. http://webofknowledge.com/JCR.

[26] Rapoport A. Spread of Information Through a Population with Socio-Structure Bias: Ⅰ. Assumption of Transitivity [J]. Bulletin of Mathematical Biophysics, 1953, 15 (4): 523 -533.

[27] Newman M E J. Scientific Collaboration Networks Ⅱ: Shortest Paths, Weighted Networks, and Certainty [J]. Physics Review E, 2001, 64 (1): 16 -132.

教师简介：

路永和，男，东北师范大学理学学士、大连海事大学工学硕士、中山大学岭南学院访问学者。2002 年起任教于中山大学资讯管理学院，副教授。主讲“电子商务”、“电子商务安全与保密”、“企业资源计划”等本科生课程，以及“数据挖掘与决策支持”、“信息系统”、“数据挖掘及其应用”等研究生课程。主要从事电子商务、ERP、数据挖掘、智能信息处理领域的教学、研发及实践等方向的研究。主持国家及省市科研项目 10 项，发表学术论文 20 余篇，其中 SCI 收录的 Q1 区论文 1 篇，EI 收录的论文 4 篇。2015 年香港中文大学访问学者。广东省科技厅、广州市科信局、东莞市科信局、佛山市科信局等各级科技行政部门的科技咨询专家，为广东省内 50 多家企业信息化项目的规划与实施提供咨询与指导。联系方式：luyonghe@ mail. sysu. edu. cn。

所选论文《多因素影响的特征选择方法》原载于《现代图书情报技术》2013 年第 5 期

多因素影响的特征选择方法*

路永和，李焰锋①

摘　要：在特征选择过程中，通过特征选择评估函数得到的词的权值大小决定该词是否作为特征词，然而词的权值受多因素影响，其主要因素有词的重要性、特征性和代表性。从以上几个因素出发，构建新的特征选择函数 TW；通过对词的卡方分布 CHI、信息增益 IG 和新的特征选择函数 TW 作对比实验，验证 TW 能够提高类别中专有词汇的权值，降低常见但对分类不重要的特征的权值；将 TW 作为新的特征选择算法，通过在中文分类语料库上分别采用 KNN、类中心和支持向量机（SVM）3 种分类方法进行实际分类实验，并与其他特征选择算法比较，验证此种特征选择算法的有效性。

关键词：文本分类；特征选择；类别区分；TFIDF

A Feature Selection Based on Consideration of Multiple Factors

Yonghe Lu，Yanfeng Li

Abstract：In the process of feature selection，term's weight determines the term whether it can be a feature. But the weight was affected by many factors，the main factors are term's importance，term's characteristics and term's representative. With the consideration of those factors，a new function *TW*（term weight），based on the importance of the feature and the ability of category distinguishing，is brought to be an improved method to select features. After that，experiments on the comparison between term's *CHI*，term's *IG* and term's *TW* validate that

* 本文系国家高技术研究发展计划（“863”计划）资助项目“农产品全供应链多源信息感知技术与产品开发”（项目编号：2012AA101701）的研究成果之一。

① 李焰锋，中山大学资讯管理学院硕士研究生。

TW can increase the weight of special features in a class and can decrease the weight of unimportant features. Finally, the validity of the new algorithm in feature selection is validated by the classification experiments on Chinese classification corpus by three classifiers.

Keywords: Text categorization; Feature selection; Class discrimination; Term frequency and inverse documentation frequency (TFIDF)

1 引　　言

Web 信息的快速增长使得寻找所需要信息的难度加大，文本分类作为处理大量文本数据的关键技术，可以在一定程度上解决信息快速增长带来的一些问题。向量空间模型 VSM（vector space model）是目前文本分类中最常用的文本表示方法之一。VSM 的基本思想是用词袋法表示文本，将每个特征词作为向量空间坐标系的一维，文本被形式化为多维向量空间中的一个向量，文本之间的相似度用两个向量间的夹角衡量。[1] 也就是说，这个模型把对文本内容的处理简化为向量空间中的向量运算，并且它以空间上的相似度来表达语义的相似度。当文档被表示为文档空间的向量时，就可以通过计算向量之间的相似性来度量文档间的相似性。

采用 VSM 模型进行分类的最关键环节之一是特征选择。好的特征选择算法不但能降低向量空间维数、简化计算，还能去除噪声，从而提高文本分类的准确率和分类速度。

2 相关研究

通常原始特征空间维数非常高，且存在大量冗余的特征，为避免特征维数过高导致影响系统速度和分类效果，通常会对其进行降维处理。降维处理的根本任务是在尽可能保持其信息的完整性的同时对无用的信息进行删减过滤，目前的降维技术主要有特征选择和特征重构。特征选择常用的算法有文档频率（document frequency，DF）、卡方统计（CHI）、信息增益[2]（information gain，IG）和互信息（mutual information，MI）等。

对文本原始特征进行特征选择的通用方法是卡方统计（CHI）和信息增益（IG）。在一定程度上，这两个方法能比较有效地筛选出对分类比较有效的特征词[2]，但方法本身存在不足[3-5]，而且在中文文本分类实验中的表现仍不突出，需要对其进行修正才能适合中文文本分类[6]。因此，有部分学者对传统的特征选择方法进行改进，在其实验中也得到较好的效果。如熊忠阳[7]等分析了卡方统计的不足并提出将频度、集中度、分散度应用到卡方统计方法上，以此来改进卡方统计；在互信息基础上，王卫玲等[8]提出一种既考虑特征与类别之间的关联性，也考虑特征与特征之间的关联性的特征选择算法，以此来选出区分能力强、弱相关的特征。除此之外，学者还提出了基于其他领域知识的一些改进算法，如 Shankar 等[9]引入经济学中的基尼指数，并研究了基尼指数进行加权特征选择问题；Zhenyu Lu 等[10]通过对词的语义进行统计来筛选特征；Khan 等[11]则引入本体论来提取概念术语，从而实现特征选择，通过实验验证了效果比 TFIDF 更好。

国内也有学者将向量权重算法 TFIDF（term frequency-inverse document frequency）应用到特征选择中，但直接应用的效果不是很明显，所以多半会进行改进以使 TFIDF 适应特征选择。直接将 TFIDF 应用到特征选择效果不好的原因是：如果一个词在某个类频繁出现，而在其他类中却极少出现，这样的词应该是具有更高权重的，然而根据 IDF 定义的描述，这样的词却极有可能被赋予较低的权重。此后，不断有学者对如何将 TFIDF 运用到特征选择过程中进行了研究。不少学者将 TFIDF 与传统的特征选择算法结合起来作为新的特征选择算法，并且也取得了不错的效果，如刘海峰等[12]将互信息与改进的 TFIDF 结合起来作为一种新的特征选择算法，提高特征项利用效率等。

以上各种方法普遍存在以下一个或几个问题：①构造或改进的函数中需要更多的统计量；②计算方式复杂，如方差计算等；③仅考虑词的类内类间分布，未考虑词在文本集和文本中的重要性；④未考虑词与类别间的关联性。

因此，本文打算从词在文本集和文本中的重要性、类内的代表性和类间的特征性出发，在不增加更多统计量的基础上，使用较精简的函数来描述词的特征重要性，从而使其更容易在实际中得到应用。

3 特征选择算法的改进

改进的核心思想是：每个词对每个类的区分能力是不同的，其重要性用传统的特征选择评估函数与向量权重计算方法 TFIDF 共同反映，同时该词集中分布的类就是其所属的类，即这个特征词要具有这个类的特征性。事实上，对于某词所属的类存在两种情况：一是该词集中出现在所属类的少数几篇文档中，二是该词均匀出现在所属类的所有文档中。在特征选择的实际过程中，本文的处理方法是：同等条件下，第二种情况下词的权重比第一种情况下词的权重更大一些。

3.1 特征权重定义

对于特定词 t，它具有的区分类别的能力是不同的，并且这种能力最终会影响分类效果，这种能力的大小定义为特征权重 TW（term weight）。特征权重 TW 大小受多因素影响，主要包括以下几个方面[1]：

（1）词的重要性[13]。尽管传统的特征选择评估函数不能完全描述词的重要性，但总体上还是可以体现词的重要性，同时将向量权重计算方法也作为衡量词的重要性的一个因素。若存在一个词，该词的特征选择评估函数值和通过向量权重算法计算得出的权值越大，说明在一定程度上该词越具有重要性，对分类的影响越大。

（2）词的特征性。若存在一个词，该词越集中出现在某个类别文档集中，在其他类别的文档集中越少出现，那么该词越能区分其所在类别集与文本集合中的其他类别集，即该词具有其集中出现的类别集的特征越明显，对分类贡献越大。

（3）词的代表性。若存在一个词，该词越均匀地出现在某个特定类别文档集中，就是说该词能覆盖该类别集中的文档数越多，那么该词越能代表其所在类别集。即该词越能代表其均匀出现的类别集，对分类贡献也越大。

3.2 构造函数

TFIDF 方法因为考虑到了特征词词频等因素，在一定程度上能比较有效地表示出一个词在文档中和语料库文档集合中的重要程度。另外卡方值 *CHI* 和信息增益 *IG* 是常用的特征选择评估函数，故词的重要性采用其中的卡方值 *CHI* 和 *TFIDF* 来共同衡量。由于 *CHI* 不能完全反映词的重要性，为避免使权重失衡，故需对其值进行对数化处理。

从理论上来说，不包含词 t 但属于某个类别的文档越少，即包含词 t 同时属于该类别的文档越多，并且词 t 能在该类别中均匀分布，说明词 t 在该类的代表性越强。本文用 C 来反映词的代表性，其含义为不包含该词但属于该类的文档数。同样，包含词 t 但不属于该类的文档越少，即词跟该类的关系较大，说明词 t 在类别间的分布基本集中在该类中或该类文档都不包含该词。本文用 B 来反映词的特征性，其含义为包含该词但不属于该类的文档数。

词的卡方值 *CHI* 和 *TFIDF* 越大，同时 C 和 B 越小，说明类内分布越均匀，类间分布越集中，那么该词的特征权重越大，越有机会被选为分类特征。因此，本文考虑定义特征权重公式为：

$$TW(t) = \frac{TFIDF \times \log CHI_t}{\log(B_t \times C_t)}。 \tag{1}$$

式中：t 为词；CHI_t 为该词的 *CHI* 值；B_t 为包含 t 但不属于该类的文本数；C_t 为不包含 t 但属于该类的文本数；*TFIDF* 为词 t 的经过对数 TF 处理后的 *TFIDF* 值。

对于某些词，其 $B_t \times C_t$ 值可能为 0 或 1。该值为 0 或 1 的意义是该词只出现在某个类中，很少出现在其他类中，它可能是这个类的专有词汇。理论上，这种词的类区分能力是相对较强的。但在实际分类中，$B_t \times C_t$ 为 0，也有可能是由于分词效果差和语料库不规范导致的。考虑到分词效果和语料库规范问题较难预测和避免，同时也为了解决特殊点的问题，考虑加入 λ 使函数在整数的定义域内取值都有意义。而且通过训练 λ 的取值，还可以减少语料库、分词效果带来的影响。因此，将公式调整为：

$$TW(t) = \frac{TFIDF \times \log CHI_t}{\log(B_t \times C_t + \lambda)}。 \tag{2}$$

式中：λ 为一相对于 $B_t \times C_t$ 很小的常数（在实验中发现取 $\lambda = e^{-7}$ 时分类效果比较好）。

综上所述，改进的特征选择算法为：

$$TW(t) = \frac{TFIDF \times \log CHI_t}{\log(B_t \times C_t + \lambda)} = \log tf_{ik} \times \log\left(1 + \frac{N}{n_k}\right) \times \frac{\log CHI_t}{\log(B_t \times C_t + \lambda)}。 \tag{3}$$

式中：tf_{ik} 表示文档 i 中第 k 个词的词频；N 表示文本集的文档数；n_k 表示文本集中出现该词的文本数。

4 实验过程与结果分析

为验证 *TW* 对表达词权重大小的有效性，实验将 *TW* 与 *CHI*、*IG* 进行对比分析；同时为证明采用 TW 算法进行特征选择的优越性，实验将其分类效果与现有比较典型的三种算法进行比较，包括 DF、CHI 和 IG。

4.1 验证步骤

实验数据集采用复旦大学李荣陆博士提供的中文文本分类语料库中的一部分[14]，选取其中的 9 个类别，分别是体育、艺术、历史、航空、计算机、环境、农业、经济、政治，每个类别 200 篇，按 1∶1 比例选择训练文本集和测试文本集，即训练文本集和测试文本集各 900 篇。实验采用的编程语言是 Java，IDE 环境是 Eclipse，采用中国科学院的中文分词进行预处理，实验流程如图 1 所示。

选取的特征数量有 300、600、900、…、3000。在进行特征选择时分别采用 DF、IG、CHI 和 TW 方法来对比。向量权重计算方法分别采用 TFIDF 和对数处理 TF 的 TFIDF 算法。分类算法分别采用 KNN 分类法、类中心分类法[15]和支持向量机（SVM），其中 KNN 中 k 统一取 10。

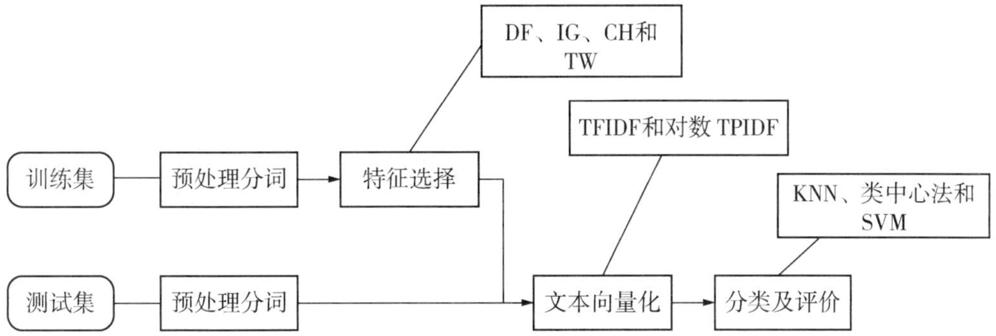

图 1　文本分类实验流程

4.2 评价标准

分类结果评价标准[16]采用宏平均查全率 *MR*（macro-averaging recall）、宏平均查准率 *MP*（macro-averaging precision）和宏平均 *F* 测度值 *MF*（macro-averaging f-measure）等常用标准。

4.3 实验结果

4.3.1 特征权重修正的有效性分析

通过实验发现，*TW* 能提高专有词的权重，同时也能降低常见词的权重。例如，“裁判”集中出现在体育类中，其分布并不会很分散，就是说“裁判”这个词可以区分体育这个类别；“学生”并不会集中出现在某个类，其分布要比“裁判”的分布分散得多。因此，“裁判”的类区分能力比“学生”高，即“裁判”的权重会比“学生”高。实际 *TW* 也反映了这一情况，如表 1 所示（*TF*：词的词频；*A*：包含词同时属于该类的文档数；*B*：

包含词但不属于该类的文档数；*C*：不包含词但属于该类的文档数；*D*：既不包含词也不属于该类的文档数）。

表1 “裁判”与“学生”的对比

词	*TF*	*A*	*B*	*C*	*D*	*CHI*	*TW*
裁判	4	8	1	92	799	55.6818	12.479
学生	10	27	34	73	766	72.8121	6.154

当选取特征词数量为30时，*TW*、*IG*和*CHI*对应的选择结果如表2所示。表中只有27个特征词是因为选取时为避免特征词在每个类的分布不均衡，采取每个类都选取相同数量的词作为特征的做法。也就是说此处的做法是：从9个类中各选取特征评价函数值最高的3个词作为特征词，因此最后只有27个特征而非30个（由于数量差别不大，本文中仍称其有30个特征）。

表2 特征数量为30时各选择函数的特征词对比

序号	*TW*	*IG*	*CHI*
1	运动员	5月	JOURNALOFSOFTWARE1999
2	体重	新华社	体育
3	计算机科学	摘要	联系人
4	拓扑	关键词	博士生
5	收支	参考	航空
6	身高	JOURNALOFSOFTWARE1999	CHINASPORTSCIENCEANDTECHNOLOGY1999
7	IP	体育	农业
8	雕塑	方法	运动员
9	美术	联系人	第18
10	含水量	软件	艺术
11	截面	标题	ACTA
12	外贸	Vol	SCIENTIAE
13	污染物	分类	AERONAUTICALMANUFACTURINGTECHNOLOGY1999
14	写意	正文	作品
15	陈寅恪	研究	创作
16	投资者	航空	品种
17	公顷	本文	标题
18	载荷	应用	栽培

续表 2

序号	*TW*	*IG*	*CHI*
19	地中海	数据	工艺技术
20	对流	农业	正文
21	根系	No	5 月
22	白话文	导师	总统
23	大豆	Keywords	新华社
24	淀粉	文献	原文
25	南非	单位	会见
26	外长	结果	主席
27	杨尚昆	Abstract	百分之三

由表 2 中，可以看到 *TW* 选择的词都是较为专业且具有代表性的，而 *CHI*、*IG* 对专业词的选择较差，如 *IG* 中的“5 月”、“新华社”等词、*CHI* 中的“第 18”、“5 月”等词，这些词对分类的贡献都较小，不仅如此，可能还会成为分类的噪声，对分类结果造成影响。*TW* 中的词则与类别具有较强的联系，许多词都能直接判断出其所属类别，如“运动员”、“计算机科学”等词。

4.3.2 分类效果的有效性分析

采用各种向量权重计算方法和三种不同分类方法最后得到的分类结果的宏平均 *F*1 值的结果如图 2 至图 7 所示。

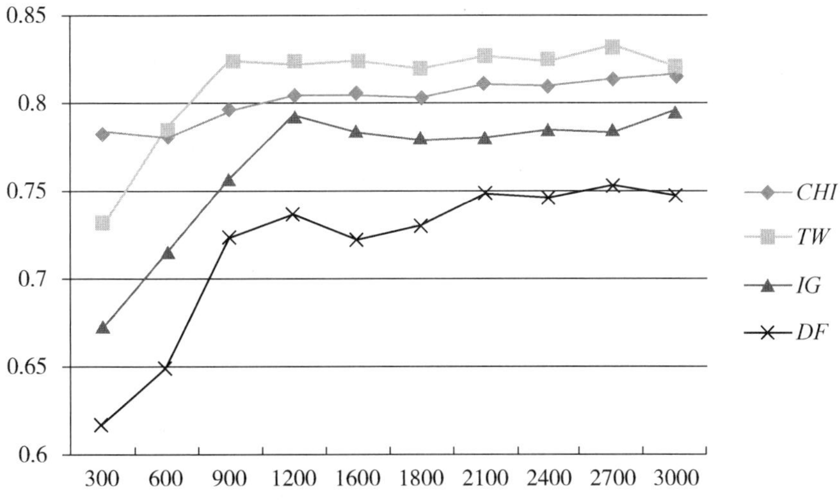

图 2　宏平均 *F*1 值对比——*TFIDF* + KNN 分类法

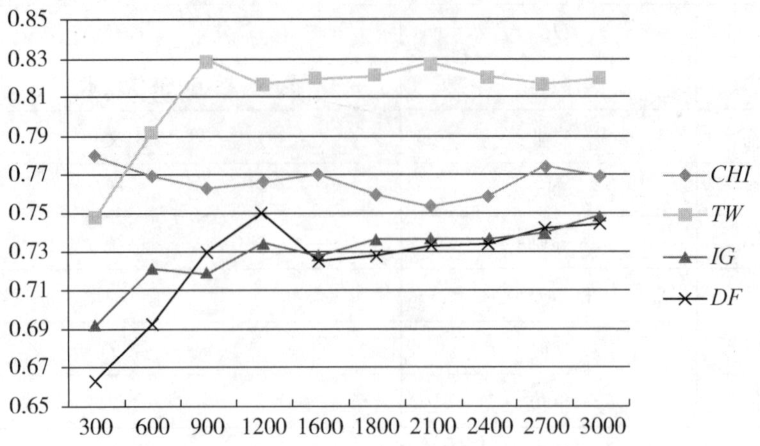

图 3　宏平均 *F*1 值对比——log*TFIDF* + KNN 分类法

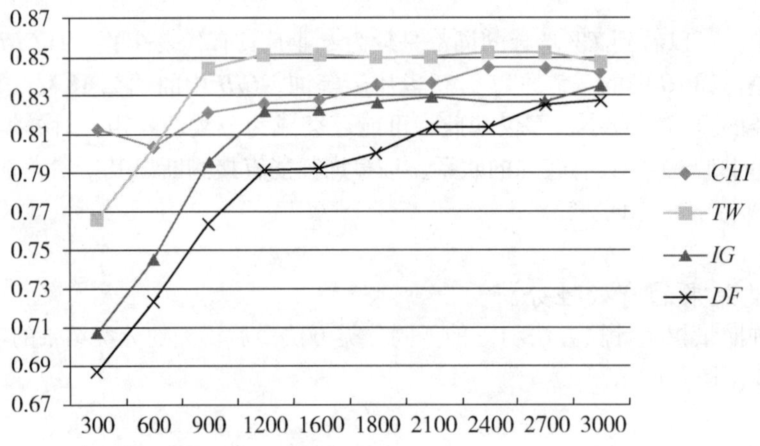

图 4　宏平均 *F*1 值对比——*TFIDF* + 类中心分类法

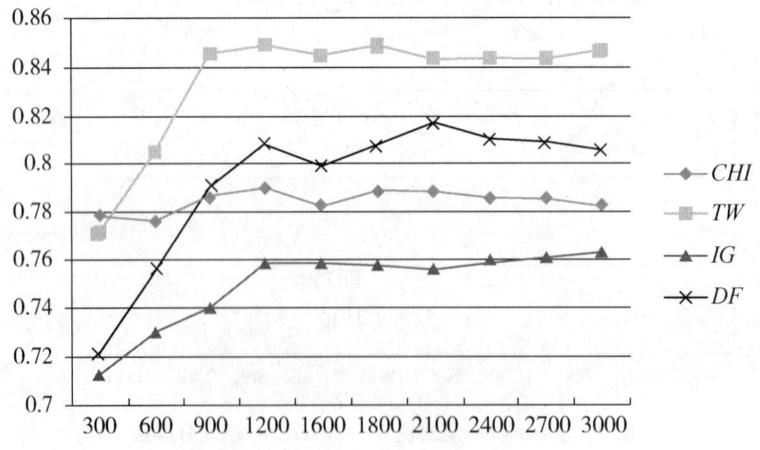

图 5　宏平均 *F*1 值对比——log*TFIDF* + 类中心分类

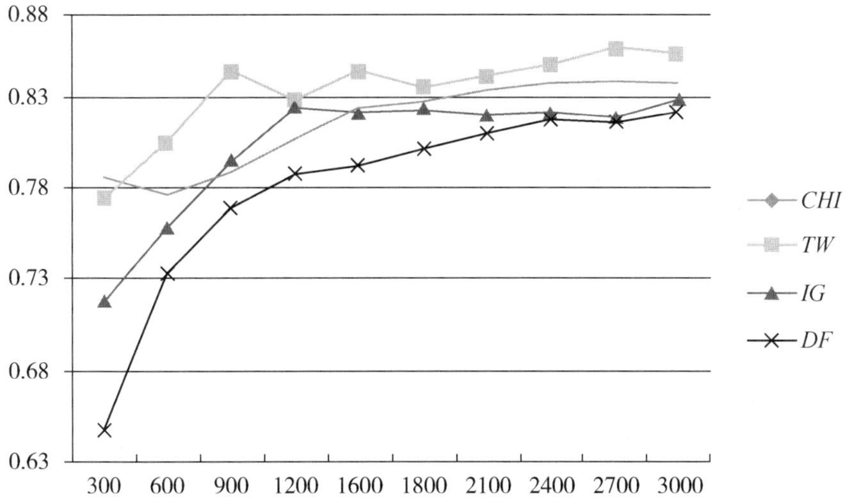

图 6　宏平均 *F*1 值对比——*TFIDF* + SVM 分类法

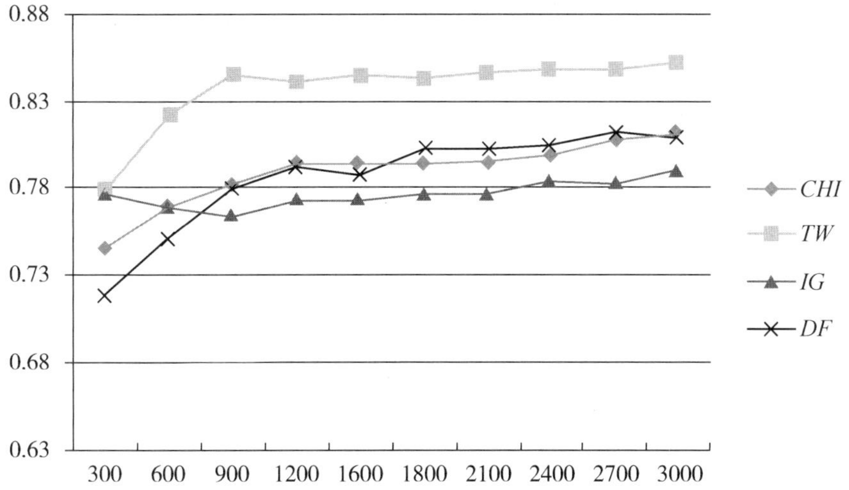

图 7　宏平均 *F*1 值对比——log*TFIDF* + SVM 分类法

从以上几幅图中可以看出：

（1）本文提出的 *TW* 特征选择方法是所有特征选择方法中在实际分类中效果比较好的，相对比传统的 *CHI*、*IG* 和 *DF* 特征选择方法，其宏平均 *F*1 值确实得到了普遍提高，特别是采用 log*TFIDF* 作为向量权重计算方法时。

（2）本文提出的 *TW* 特征选择方法虽然相较于其他三种方法取得了较好的分类效果，但从图中可以发现，在选取特征数量较少时（如特征数量为 300），其表现不如 *CHI* 特征选择方法；但当特征数量较多时，其明显优于其他三种方法。这是因为 *TW* 在选取过少特征时，如果给专有名词过高的权重，那么特征集合中存在过多的专有词，特征就有可能在测试集中基本不出现，这会导致向量模型中存在过多权重为零的特征，出现特征不明显从而影响分类效果的情况。

5 结　　语

本文重点研究了影响特征选择的几个影响因素——词的重要性、特征性和代表性，并在这三个影响因素的基础上提出了 *TW* 特征选择方法，而且用实验验证了该方法的有效性。该方法的前提是认为每个不同的词对分类有不同的贡献权重，这种权重可以反映词的重要性和类别区分能力，通过赋予词这种权重来进行特征选择，从而使分类效果得到提升，但也存在着以下不足：

首先，*TW* 特征选择方法的提出是建立在词的重要性、特征性、代表性三个因素的基础之上。从这三个因素的量化角度来说，虽然本文的量化过程能取得较好的分类效果，但未必是一种最佳的量化方式，还可对其进行更深入的研究并应用于文本分类。另外，在量化过程中还遇到专有词权重的计算问题，对于基本只在某一个类中才出现的词的权重计算问题也需要进一步研究。

其次，*TW* 特征选择方法整合了 *CHI* 和 *TFIDF* 对词的重要性描述，但还存在其他方法可代替 *CHI* 来描述词的重要性，如信息增益 *IG* 等。因此，在对词重要性的描述上还可用其他方法进行优化。

最后，本文用于实验的语料库仅局限于中文，难以验证特征选择算法改进的普遍适用性。因此，在接下来的研究中可以选取更广泛的语料库进行实验，以完善模型从而增强其适用性。

参考文献

[1] 台德艺，王俊．文本分类特征权重改进算法［J］．计算机工程，2010，36（9）：197－199，202．

[2] Shannon C E．A Matheatical Theory of Communication［J］．Bell System Technical Journal，1948，27（3）：379－423，623－656．

[3] Yang Y，Pederson J O．A Comparative Study on Feature Selection in Text Categorization［C］//Proceedings of the 14th International Conference on Machine Learning（ICML '97）．Nashville：Morgan Kaufmann Publishers，1997：412－420．

[4] 张帆，张俊丽．统计频率算法在文本信息过滤系统中的应用［J］．图书情报工作，2009，53（13）：116－119．

[5] 刘庆和，梁正友．一种基于信息增益的特征优化选择方法［J］．计算机工程与应用，2011，47（12）：130－132，136．

[6] 代六玲，黄河燕，陈肇雄．中文文本分类中特征抽取方法的比较研究［J］．中文信息学报，2004，18（1）：26－32．

[7] 熊忠阳，张鹏招，张玉芳．基于 χ^2 统计的基于条件互信息的特征选择算法［J］．计算机应用，2008：28（2）：4513－514，518．

[8] 王卫玲，刘培玉，初建崇．一种改进的基于条件互信息的特征选择算法［J］．计算机应用，2007，27（2）：433－435．

[9] Shankar S，Karypis G．A Feature Weight Adjustment Algorithm for Document Categorization［C］．The 6th ACM SIGKDD Int'l Conf on Knowledge Discovery and Data Mining．Boston，MA，USA，2000．

[10] Lu Z，Liu Y，Zhao S，et al．Study on Feature Selection and Weighting Based on Synonym Merge in Text Categorization［C］//Future Networks，2010．ICFN '10．Second International Conference on．IEEE，2010：105－109．

[11] Khan A，Baharudin B，Khan K．Efficient Feature Selection and Domain Relevance Term Weighting Method for Document Classification［C］//Computer Engineering and Applications（ICCEA），2010 Second International Conference on．

IEEE, 2010: 398 - 403.
[12] 刘海峰, 王元元, 张学仁. 文本分类中一种改进的特征选择方法 [J]. 情报科学, 2007, 25 (10): 1534 - 1537.
[13] 赵小华, 马建芬. 文本分类算法中词语权重计算方法的改进 [J]. 电脑知识与技术, 2009, 5 (36): 10626 - 10628.
[14] 中文文本分类语料库 [EB/OL]. [2011 - 10 - 30]. http://www.datatang.com/datares/detail.aspx? id = 11963.
[15] 柳培林. 基于向量空间模型的中文文本分类技术研究 [D]. 大庆: 大庆石油学院, 2006.
[16] Soucy P, Mineau G W. Beyond TFIDF Weighting for Text Categorization in the Vector Space Model [C]. Proc Int'l Joint Conf Artificial Intelligence, 2005: 1130 - 1135.

教师简介：

马芝蓓，女，山西大学图书情报学系学士，武汉大学图书情报学院硕士、博士。1989—1992 年任教于山西大学信息管理系，助教、讲师。1995—2001 年任教于广东商学院经济信息管理系，讲师、副教授，2001 年起任教于中山大学资讯管理学院，副教授、硕士生导师。主讲“商业秘密保护”、“经济信息伦理与规范研究”、“信息系统设计与组织创新研究”、“信息职业伦理”。研究领域包括经济信息管理与信息保护、经济信息保密与管理、商业秘密及个人信息保护与管理、信息系统设计与组织创新等。发表学术论文 30 余篇，参编著作 3 部。曾兼任广东省图书馆学会宣传教育委员会委员。联系方式：issmzb@mail. sysu. edu. cn。

所选论文《客户信息保护认知模型构建及保护措施探讨》原载于《情报探索》2011 年第 1 期

客户信息保护认知模型构建及保护措施探讨

马芝蓓

摘　要：客户信息管理是现代企业信息管理的重要内容之一，而作为企业商业秘密进行保护的客户信息，又成为企业客户信息管理的重中之重。本文通过建立企业客户信息保护认知模型，分析当前企业在客户信息保护认知方面存在的主要问题，提出从商业秘密信息的基本特征出发来制定企业客户信息保护策略，是有效保护企业客户信息的重要措施之一。

关键词：客户信息；信息保护；认知模型；商业秘密；保护措施

A New Discussion on the Cognitive Models of the Protection of Customer Information and Customer Information Protection Measures

Zhibei Ma

Abstract: Customer information management is one of the important contents of a modern enterprise information management. As a corporate trade secrets to protect customer information, the most important tasks must be the customer information management. In this paper, through the establishment of cognitive models of the protection of customer information and an analysis of the main problems of the protection of customer information in cognitive aspects, to develop the protection strategy of trade secret information from the basic characteristics of corporate customer information is one of the important measures of the effectiveness of the protection of customer information.

Keywords: Customer information; Information protection; Cognitive model; Trade secrets; Protection measures

1 引　　言

客户信息管理是现代企业信息管理的重要内容之一，随着企业客户信息系统的建立，客户信息的真实性、时效性、系统性和集成性为企业赢得了更多的竞争优势；以客户为中心的管理理念的确立，正是这种观念渗透到企业文化核心价值体系中的具体体现。在客户信息成为企业重要的资源的今天，没有客户也就没有企业；反之，拥有更多更好的客户资源，企业才能获得更快、更健康的成长。当今，随着商业竞争日益加剧，客户资源保护问题越来越多地得到了企业的高度关注，在我国市场经济法律保护体制尚未健全的条件下，竞争对手间激烈的客户争夺战愈演愈烈，如银行业、餐饮业、医疗行业等已是狼烟四起。为了适应这一新形势的发展，客户信息管理的范围应从单纯的数据加工、传递、处理、集成、利用向客户信息保护延伸，并逐渐形成新的学科体系。具体表现在：为了获得更持久的竞争优势，企业在为客户提供优质产品和优质服务的同时，客户信息保护意识与保护能力的强弱直接关系着企业的存亡，这几乎是所有企业当前所面临的共同问题。

近10年来，我国商业秘密管理探讨者反复引用一句话："21世纪企业家所犯的最多最致命的错误是泄密。"这从另一个角度说明信息泄密不仅是员工的事，管理者也有着更重要的信息保护的责任。在新形势下，如何更好地保护客户信息这一企业的关键资源，已成为现代企业管理者的必修课。在我国，由于《反不正当竞争法》制定于并实行于20世纪90年代初期，而在90年代后期，特别是加入WTO以后，企业竞争又出现了很多新情况和新形势，尤其使我国中小企业对商业秘密信息的识别与保护力不从心，泄密与窃密案例时有发生，不正当竞争行为严重扰乱了企业的正常生产秩序，使众多企业陷入困境。与此同时，法律跟不上经济形势的迅速发展，企业商业秘密泄密或失窃后难于获得法律援助而使企业遭受巨大损失，企业在发展过程中遇到了前所未有的挑战。2006年出台的《最高人民法院关于审理不正当竞争民事案件应用法律若干问题的解释》，基于对构成商业秘密的客户信息，进行了较有针对性的阐释。本文在总结以往研究成果的基础上，围绕着客户信息资源非法使用（窃密）、非合理使用（泄密）与合理使用（保护）情形，拟从商业秘密信息的基本特征出发，通过建立客户信息保护认知模型并进行相应分析，提高企业客户信息保护意识，探索企业客户信息保护的新思路。

2 信息、企业信息、商业秘密信息、客户信息特征及相关分析

2.1 信息的基本特征

信息的基本特征主要包括信息的真实性、时效性、传递性、共享性、加工性、替代性、可扩散性、可压缩性等方面。本文拟重点强调的是其传播特性，如传递性和可扩散性。

2.2 企业信息的特征

在信息基本特征的基础上，企业信息的特征可归结为真实性、准确性、时效性、价值性、系统性、集成性等方面。本文拟重点强调的是其系统性与集成性，它与我们将要讨论的保密性密切相关。

2.3 商业秘密信息的特征

《中华人民共和国反不正当竞争法》（以下简称《反不正当竞争法》）于1993年9月2日第八届全国人民代表大会常务委员会第三次会议通过，于2007年2月1日起施行。《反不正当竞争法》第十条第三款对商业秘密的界定是指：①不为公众所知悉；②能为权利人带来经济利益；③具有实用性并经权利人采取保密措施的技术信息和经营信息。2006年12月30日，最高人民法院审判委员会第1412次会议通过了《最高人民法院关于审理不正当竞争民事案件应用法律若干问题的解释》（以下简称《解释》），对上述条款中的“不为公众所知悉”，《解释》第九条解释为：“信息不为其所属领域的相关人员普遍知悉和容易获得，且具有所列情形之一的，可以认定有关信息不构成不为公众所知悉：（1）该信息为其所属技术或者经济领域的人的一般常识或者行业惯例；（2）该信息仅涉及产品的尺寸、结构、材料、部件的简单组合等内容，进入市场后相关公众通过观察产品即可直接获得；（3）该信息已经在公开出版物或者其他媒体上公开披露；（4）该信息已通过公开的报告会、展览等方式公开；（5）该信息从其他公开渠道可以获得；（6）该信息无需付出一定的代价而容易获得。”因此，根据《反不正当竞争法》及《解释》中的相关条款，商业秘密信息特征可归纳为秘密性、经济价值性、实用性、保密性等方面。这其中，秘密性与信息扩散性是相互矛盾的，商业秘密信息的保密性是防止其在未授权条件下进行扩散的；与此同时，企业信息的系统性与集成性构成企业信息的秘密性及采取保密措施的必要性，是企业客户信息保护的关键环节。

2.4 客户信息与可构成商业秘密信息的客户信息特征

2.4.1 客户信息

客户信息，习惯上称为客户名单，是指经营者将其作为交易对象的客户名录、地址以及其他资料。[2] 由此可见，客户信息内容十分丰富，客户名单不能顾名思义地理解为客户的名单，而是指企业所记录的与客户交易的全部信息的集合。

2.4.2 可构成商业秘密信息的客户信息特征

客户信息是否构成商业秘密信息，一直是司法鉴定中的难点。《解释》第十三条（1）：商业秘密中的客户名单，一般是指客户的名称、地址、联系方式以及交易的习惯、意向、内容等构成的区别于相关公知信息的特殊客户信息，包括汇集众多客户的客户名册，以及保持长期稳定交易关系的特定客户。

3　企业客户信息保护认知模型建构及其应用

3.1　企业客户信息保护认知模型Ⅰ——客户信息中的公知信息（一般信息）与特殊客户信息（可构成信息保护的客户信息）及相关分析

笔者认为，客户信息中的公知信息可视为企业中的一般客户信息，对于一般客户信息的使用，并不构成商业秘密泄密和窃密；特殊信息即构成商业秘密的客户信息则是企业保护的重点。笔者通过建立企业客户信息保护认知模型Ⅰ（图1），更直观地定位这两部分信息及相互转换的关系，使企业更合理地确定客户信息的保护范围、确定不同性质客户信息保护的原则与方法，企业还可根据自身的实际情况进行调节客户信息保护范围，使客户信息保护具有动态平衡能力，更好地实现客户信息保护的有效性。具体地讲，模型Ⅰ中的 C_1 代表一般客户信息；C_2 代表可构成信息保护的客户信息；V 代表在 C_1、C_2 间可进行调节而发生变化，如在一定的条件下可向 C_1 或 C_2 转化的客户信息。下面分为四种情形进行讨论。第一种情形，当 V 的面积增大，表明 C_1、C_2 重叠程度加大，企业客户信息保护范围随之加大；第二种情形，当 V 面积减小，企业客户信息保护范围随之减小，客户信息保护范围相应缩小；第三种情形，$V = C_1 = C_2$，将在模型Ⅱ中进行讨论；第四种情形，$V = 0$，将一般客户信息完全作为非保护信息，现代企业这种情形已不多见，故此情形暂不讨论。在模型中 V 变量的调节，目的是增强企业信息保护的动态性和灵活性，改变以往企业信息保护僵化的做法，使企业根据风险因素的影响程度及时调节信息保护的力度和范围。换言之，公知信息与特殊客户信息在企业经营管理过程中并不是一成不变的，两者也不是泾渭分明，而是可以相互转化的。转化的条件可从信息特征分析得出。例如，随着技术的进步，原来作为商业秘密加以保护的客户信息已成为可共享的公知信息；随着经营管理水平的提高，原来的公知信息经过深加工又转换成为商业秘密信息……这个过程随着企业的发展而不断发展，这一相互转换过程也将持续进行。因此，企业客户信息保护不可能是一劳永逸的，信息保护政策也不应该是一成不变的，企业需要在具体的信息保护实践中不断调整和完善信息保护策略。而客户信息保护手段的不断完善，始终是需要企业面对的第一道竞争门槛。这又回到本文开头提到的，没有客户就没有企业这一论题上来。

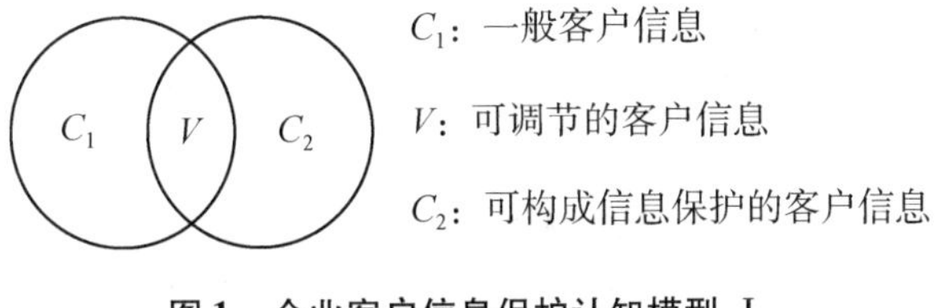

图1　企业客户信息保护认知模型Ⅰ

3.2 企业客户信息保护认知模型Ⅱ

随着竞争的加剧，企业对客户信息采取了不同程度的保护措施。尽管如此，客户信息的泄密与窃密仍时有发生，由此而使企业蒙受巨大经济损失的案例层出不穷。究其原因，笔者认为，这些案例的发生，与当前企业对客户信息保护及可构成企业商业秘密信息保护的区别在认识上的差异有密切的关系。因此，本文在模型Ⅰ（图1）的基础上进一步延伸，通过建立客户信息保护认知模型Ⅱ（图2）来进一步说明提高企业客户信息保护措施的有效性才是更重要的。

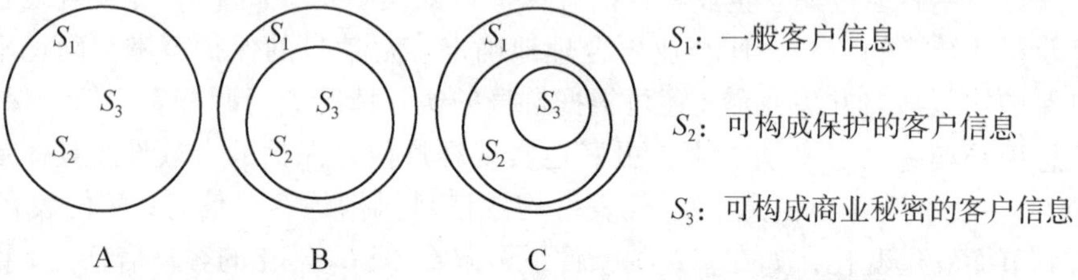

图2　企业客户信息保护认知模型 Ⅱ

模型Ⅱ中反映了当前企业对客户信息保护的三种较有代表性认识及采取的相应的客户信息保护的方法，具体来说，A 情形反映出企业对三类客户信息 S_1、S_2、S_3 实行无差别化保护，即 $S_1 = S_2 = S_3$，即凡是客户信息就是商业秘密信息并可以获得法律保护。在此认识指导下，信息保护范围十分宽泛，这不仅会增加企业信息管理的成本，而且也过度限制了客户信息的有效使用，信息资源在企业不能被充分利用，束缚了企业的手脚，对企业竞争优势的发挥产生不利影响。这是对法律所提供保护的商业秘密认识上存在误区。B 情形反映了企业将可构成保护的客户信息与可构成商业秘密加以保护的客户信息混为一谈，并且认为凡是可以构成企业保护的信息就同样可以获得法律的保护，即 $S_1 > S_2$，$S_2 = S_3$。这反映出对相关法律条款的认识还存在盲区。C 情形可明确区分出三类不同客户信息保护程度的差异，将客户信息保护范围确定在基本合理的范围之内，对企业自身的职责与将来有可能行使的法律所赋予的权利清晰到位。在客户信息中，只有特殊客户信息才可构成商业秘密信息，客户信息只有在符合法律规定的条件，才可能得到法律相应的保护，即 $S_1 > S_2 > S_3$。

3.3 相关分析

通过以上讨论，笔者认为，用客户信息代替客户名单，可以更好地反映客户信息的内涵。早期的客户信息因内容相对简单而称之为客户名单，在企业纷纷实施数据库营销的今天，“客户名单”这一概念继续沿用已不能涵盖客户信息中所包含的丰富内容，也容易造成人们的误解和信息保护不到位的情况。通过模型Ⅰ，可将企业客户信息原本具有的动态集合特征体现出来。这其中包括两个方面的含义：其一是企业要对客户信息进行周期性更新，以确认信息的真实性和准确性，及时了解客户信息的变化，同时对客户信息异动进行监测；其二是不同的企业对客户信息加工的深度是千差万别的，如零售巨头沃尔玛的客户信息系统为业界所称道，也是该企业保持竞争优势的有效手段。因此，用客户信息代替客户名单的提法，可赋予其更多的内涵，对重新认识客户信息资源并予以合理保护，具有更积极的意义。通过模型Ⅱ，可较好地识别当前企业信息保护的程度，特别是可构成保护的客户信息与可构成商业秘密的客户信息之间的区别。对前者可进行预防性保护，有效的预防性保护措施在最大限度地为企业降低信息泄密与窃密风险的同时，还可以降低企业打官司的成本和信息二次泄露的新风险，可谓一举两得。

因此，我们强调加强企业可构成保护的客户信息的管理，是一种主动防范风险的积极措施。结合模型Ⅰ和模型Ⅱ来看，企业客户信息的保护应是有计划、有侧重、分层次、重实效来进行的，同时，也是从管理者到员工每个人的责任，而非仅是一个部门（如档案部门）和几个部门（如销售部门和公关部门等）自己部门内的事，客户信息保护应是企业全员共同参与、共同监督的集体行动与组织行为。认识到这一点，对于更有效地进行企业客户信息保护也是十分重要的。

3.4　当前企业客户信息使用情形与保护状态分析

3.4.1　企业客户信息使用中的几种情形

（1）非法使用。《解释》第十四条认为当事人指称他人侵犯其商业秘密的，应当对其拥有的商业秘密符合法定条件、对方当事人的信息与其商业秘密相同或者实质相同以及对方当事人采取不正当手段的事实负举证责任。其中，商业秘密符合法定条件的证据，包括商业秘密的载体、具体内容、商业价值和对该项商业秘密所采取的具体保密措施等。由此可见，非法使用可根据《反不正当竞争法》的相关条款及《解释》来进一步认定。与此同时，选择法律途径带来的另外一面是企业内部更多信息的披露，而过多的信息披露对企业是双刃剑。因此，企业对客户信息采取预防性保护对于防止信息未授权使用，会对企业自身有更多积极的作用。

（2）非合理使用。企业在客户信息使用过程中可能出现泄密的情形，如需要保护的客户信息没有达到法律认定的被保护的要求，致使信息保护在实际操作过程中出现的辨析难点主要涉及客户信息的秘密性如何进行判断以及权利人所采取的保密措施合理性如何认定的问题。《解释》第十条有关信息具有现实的或者潜在的商业价值，是能为权利人带来竞争优势的，应当认定为《反不正当竞争法》第十条第三款规定的“能为权利人带来经济利益、具有实用性”。以上问题不能妥善解决，客户信息非合理使用的情形就不会自行减少。

（3）合理使用。在合乎法律和企业规定的前提下，授权企业正确使用客户信息的情形，如图2中C所示的情形。

3.4.2　当前企业客户信息保护状态分析

当前企业客户信息保护存在困惑较大的方面主要表现在对客户信息保护范围的认定上。对客户信息保护，企业存在三种情形：过度保护，如对公知信息的保护；失度保护，如信息保护不足；适度保护。其中最需要关注的是被泄露和窃取的信息因没有采取法律认可的保护措施，给企业带来了严重的后果却不能得到相应的法律援助的情形在企业中较为普遍。在相关案例分析中，笔者讨论如下三种主要情形：

（1）缺乏保护状态（信息共享性的过度使用）。如果权利人没有采取必要的信息保密措施，若被他人使用则不属于侵犯商业秘密行为。这包括两种情形：①信息保护意识薄弱，没有对关键客户信息加以必要的保护；②虽然采取了保护措施，但不能构成法律所认可的保护形态，也视为缺乏保护状态。

（2）过度保护状态（信息保密性的过度使用）。信息保护意识强烈，但观念上还存在一定的误区，将客户信息保护范围无限扩大，将一些公知信息作为保密信息，除增加企业的管理成本外，还会对企业产生禁锢，增加了企业自我利用客户信息的难度，同样不利于企业的发展。

（3）适度保护（有效保护）状态。理论上对客户信息进行适度保护是十分明确的，但在实际执行过程中却较难把握。特别是由于不同的企业构成商业秘密的客户信息千差万别，没有统一的可执行标准，操作难度大。企业只有根据自身情况加以把握。也就是说，每个企业必须结合自身的特点，如根据核心竞争优势等企业生存与发展的关键要素，制定本企业的客户信息保护执行标准。这样，一旦企业客户信息泄露，当需要法律救助时，能够使企业经济受损程度减少。

4 客户信息保护措施讨论

4.1 预防性保护措施

对企业客户信息进行积极的预防性保护措施，借助于预防医学术语可称之为一级保护措施。除相关责任人之外，本文观点认为应从企业全员负责的角度出发，即信息保护，人人有责，但因责任有大小之分，因此可根据组织结构形态对权责的分配，确定承担责任大小，在签订保密协议责任条款中加以区别，预防的重点是各级管理者和相关责任人。

4.2 补救性保护措施（法律措施）

在一级保护措施防范不利的情形下，启动二级保护措施，即补救性措施。通过事先采取符合法律要求的信息保护措施，实施法律援助，使权利人通过法律程序来挽回企业全部或部分损失，以减少企业更多的损失。从法律角度看，认定权利人所采取了的保密措施，须满足《解释》第十一条所列如下七种情形之一：①限定涉密信息的知悉范围，只对必须知悉的相关人员告知其内容；②对于涉密信息载体采取加锁等防范措施；③在涉密信息的载体上标有保密标志；④对于涉密信息采用密码或者代码等；⑤签订保密协议；⑥对于涉密的机器、厂房、车间等场所限制来访者或者提出保密要求；⑦确保信息秘密的其他项合理措施。

4.3 综合性保护措施

在以上保护措施基础上，综合性保护措施是应对日益复杂的竞争形势的新思考，其效果有待企业在实践中不断摸索与积累。主要思路有：①预防性保护措施与补救性保护措施并重。企业在实施信息保护的过程中，双管齐下，事前与事后措施配套，可提高可构成商业秘密的客户信息保护的效果。②结构化保护措施，预防性保护措施与补救性保护措施是以时间为序列展开的线性保护手段。之所以提出结构化保护措施是基于多重保护的思考，扩充预防性保护措施手段，如技术保护手段与行政保护手段并重、重点保护措施与一般保护措施并重、管理者及相关责任人与其他员工全员参与并重等。此外，企业还可根据具体的实际情况，制定出适合本企业的客户信息保护的有效措施。

5 结　　论

综上所述，笔者提出的观点有三：一是用“客户信息”替代“客户名单”，从商业秘密信息特征出发，对企业客户信息进行更有效的保护；二是将企业客户信息特征分为三大类，即一般客户信息、可构成保护的客户信息及可构成商业秘密的客户信息，并将企业客户信息保护视为动态、持续、可调节的保护过程；三是对当前企业客户信息保护的几种状态及利弊进行了分析与评价，为今后企业客户信息保护提供了较为有效的认识手段与保护措施。因此，我们强调加强企业可构成保护的客户信息的管理，是一种主动防范风险的积极措施。结合模型Ⅰ和模型Ⅱ来看，企业客户信息的保护需要从有计划、有侧重、分层次、重实效等几个方面来进行，同时，注重加强从管理者到员工的全员责任感，而非仅仅作为一个部门（如档案部门），或几个部门（如销售部门或公关部门）内部的事，客户信息保护应是企业全员共同参与、共同监督的集体行动与组织行为。认识到这一点，对于更有效地进行企业客户信息保护也是十分重要的。

参考文献

[1] 熊青．论商业秘密犯罪中非法获取行为的设置问题及解决之道 [J]．法制与社会，2009 (1)：111－116.
[2] 檀民．商业秘密的保护与管理 [J]．企业管理，2008 (1)：82－83.
[3] 李明，等．试论商业秘密的保护 [J]．理论月刊，2008 (10)：121－123.

教师简介：

聂卉，女，中山大学工科硕士、博士。2002 年起任教于中山大学资讯管理学院，副教授，研究生导师。主讲“英文经典专业著作选读”、“中文信息处理”、“离散数学”、“信息分析与决策”等课程。研究方向包括网络信息抽取与挖掘、智能信息检、知识管理、商务智能、电子商务在线评论观点挖掘等。已在本领域的一类及重要期刊发表论文 30 余篇，在国际会议发表论文若干篇。主持和参与国家、省部级课题多项。2011 年赴美访学，在亚利桑那大学 Eller 管理学院信息管理系的人工智能实验室参与科研工作，参与指导教授的“商务智能”课题的研究。联系方式：issnh@ mail. sysu. edu. cn。

Textual Characteristics Based High Quality Online Reviews Evaluation and Detection*

Hui Nie

Abstract: With the rapid growth of internet, a wealth of product reviews has been spread to the web. The user-generated on-line information varies greatly in quality, which making harder for review readers to identify the most useful reviews and understand the true underlying quality of a product. In this paper, we studied the problem of evaluating and detecting high-quality product reviews. We particularly examined how the textual aspect of a review affects the perceived usefulness of it. Based on a real-world data set, our results indicate that the text-specific characteristics are significantly associated with the perceived helpfulness of reviews. A review is perceived to be useful if the content of the review focusing on the given subject, with rich information and being moderately expressed in subjective ways.

Keywords: User-generated content; Text mining; Product reviews; Sentiment analysis

1 Introduction

With the rapid growth of internet, the way that people express themselves and interact with others has changed. They post reviews of products at commercial sites and express their viewpoints in various social media websites. [1] The *user-generated* content contains valuable information that can be exploited for many applications. In e-commerce, particularly, there has been an increasing interest in mining opinions from reviews in recent years. A growing number of consumers wade through online product reviews to gauge their purchase decisions and many merchants are expected to focus on the on-line *word of mouth* by which they can understand the consumers' need and make further predictions for the market trends. Regardless of customers or

* This work is support by the National Science Foundation of China (Grant No. 61100080).

merchants, all review readers need to seek unbiased evaluation of their target products or brands, by leveraging information from multiple reviews. [2] However, the *user-generated* reviews are so over whelming that make individuals harder to identify the valuable information and understand the true underlying quality of the product. Even worse, the *user-generated* reviews often vary greatly in quality due to the lack of editorial and quality control. Low-quality or even spam reviews are mixed with the valuable ones, causing trouble to users who expect to obtain useful information. Obviously, if the *user-generated* contents are need to be exploited effectively, it is crucial to have a mechanism capable of assessing the quality of reviews and extracting the high-quality reviews from the high volume of original information.

In the social psychology literature, message source characteristics have been found to influence judgment and behavior[3], and it has been often suggested that source characteristics might shape product attitudes and purchase propensity. Review readers, as a rule of thumb, pay more attention on review content than other information aspects when seeking the peer-reviewers' opinions, which implies, to the large extent, the vote for the *usefulness* of a review depends on the textual content. Based on the idea, we believe that deeply analyzing the textual aspects of reviews should be the most direct and effective way to detecting the quality of reviews. Therefore, we place special emphasis on how the textual aspect of a review affects the perceived usefulness of it. To address the problem, a simple but well-established framework for assessing review quality has been designed to examine the nature of *helpfulness*. A stream of NLP① technologies, e. g. Chinese words segmentation, POS② tagger and sentiment analysis, has been fully employed to extract the corresponding text-specific characteristics. Then, we conducted the study by integrating an explanatory econometric analysis with a supervised machine learning technology, decision tree classification. The purpose of the study is maximizing the utility of online information by investigating the most influential factors for evaluating the quality of user-generated content and intending to seek an effective approach for predicting the perceived helpfulness of reviews.

2 Related Work

Our research program is inspired by the works of Ghose. [3-5] Ghose's work[3] is the first study that integrates econometric, text mining, and predictive modeling techniques to a complete analysis of the information captured by *user-generated* online reviews in order to estimate their *helpfulness* and economic impact. In addition, Jindal's research[1] and Zhang's work[2] are also relevant to our study. In these studies, review evaluation is typically viewed as a ranking or identification problem resolved with regression models or classification techniques. In the process of model training and testing, most of them used the ground-truth derived from users' votes of *helpfulness* provided by websites. And multiple information aspects, such as the numerical review

① NLP: Natural Language Processing.

② POS: Part-of-Speech.

data (e. g. Star-level) were investigated for building a prediction model. However, from the perspective of users' perception for reading, multiple information aspects might not specifically uncover the nature quality of a review. Hence, our study places the special emphasis on the influences exerted by the content-specific characteristics.

Actually, feature representation and selection plays a crucial role in the quality evaluation for information sources. In the related studies, Liu[6] presented a classification-based approach for low-quality reviews detection and three aspects of reviews, namely *informativeness*, *readability* and *subjectiveness*, have been selected as metrics to evaluate the quality of reviews. Otterbacher[7] designed as much as seventeen quality metrics on five factors, such as the relevancy, reputation and representation, to evaluate reviews. And Zhang[2] investigated the predicting task from text sentiment analysis point of view. A diverse set of language-specific features has been incorporated to build the prediction model and the results indicated the perceived utility of a review highly depends on its linguistic style. Therefore, the NLP-related text analysis is emphasized in the relevant researches. In [3 – 5], Ghose employed the NLP toolkit *Lingpipe*① to get the subjective-specific features of reviews. In [2], Zhang collected the shallow syntactic features by using existing lexical resources. And [6] adopt a sentiment analysis tool to solve the problem of subjective features extraction. Since our study focus on Chinese e-commerce website, text mining techniques for Chinese language were employed to fulfill the tasks of textual analysis and opinion mining. To the best our knowledge no prior work has combined text mining with economic methods to evaluate the utility of online Chinese reviews.

3 Research Design

This research is focused on investigating the influence of textual features for high-quality review identification and intents to define a valid specification to evaluate the quality of user-generated contents. In view of the research objective, the content-oriented evaluation mechanism study has been conducted and three main research questions are posed as follows:

Question 1: What are the influential textual features for evaluating the quality of reviews and how could we obtain the textual features by utilizing NLP-based technologies.

Question 2: How do the textual features and ways of combination exert impacts on the *helpfulness* of reviews?

Question 3: How do we utilize the Machine Learning (ML) approach to discriminate between high-quality reviews and low-quality reviews in the light of text-specific features?

3. 1 Metrics system for reviews quality evaluation

Based on Wang's study[8], data quality is divided into four major categories: intrinsic

① LingPipe is a tool kit for processing text using computational linguistics. http://alias-i. com/lingpipe/.

quality, contextual quality, representational quality and accessibility. Intrinsic quality emphasizes information have quality in their own right, such as subjectivity and objectivity. And contextual quality focuses on the natures relevant to completeness and quantity, commonly relevant to the writhing style, such as the length of information. Generally, longer texts contain more information; however, some studies suggest tediously long texts might exert negative impact on people's reading experience. As representational quality, is commonly referred to nature of readability which can be measured by characters-to-sentences ratio or words-to-sentence ratio. Learning from Wang's analysis, a metrics system has been designed for our task of content-oriented quality evaluation, shown as Table 1. As can be seen, we have incorporated 6 textual features of reviews across on three types.

Table 1 The metric framework for reviews quantity evaluation

Type	Feature Variables	Explanation
Subjectivity	*Avg_Sub*	The average probability of a review being subjective
	Avg_SD	The average standard deviation of the subjectivity probability
Readability	*Num_wd*	The length of the review in words
	Num_sen	The length of the review in sentences
	Num_wd_sen	The words-to-sentence ratio
Informativeness	*Topic_relevancy*	The similarity between review with product specification

Generally speaking, a high-quality product review is a reasonable mixture of subjective valuation and objective information. *Subjectivity* reflects the reviewers' viewpoints, while *objectivity* is more relevant to factual descriptions. *Topic-relevancy* tells readers what the content is about, reflecting the relevance between a product and a review description in our study case. Regarding *readability*, item bodies the level of understanding. According to our definition, the reviews with high scores on *readability* are more complex and harder to be understood. [9] Empirically, all the features should to some extend have effect on the perceptions of the on-line review readers; therefore, the features space in the statistical learning framework ought to capture thesecharacteristics.

3.2 Text-specific features extraction

The objective of textual analysis is to collect text-specific features; the input of analysis model is the original textual aspects of a review; and the output is a group of textual features defined in Table 1. As shown in Figure 1, the features extraction task is carried out in three phases, pre-processing, sentimental analysis and similarity calculation. Due to our study is for Chinese language, FundanNLP① is employed.

① FundanNLP is a tool kit for Chinese natural language processing. http://code.google.com/p/fudannlp/.

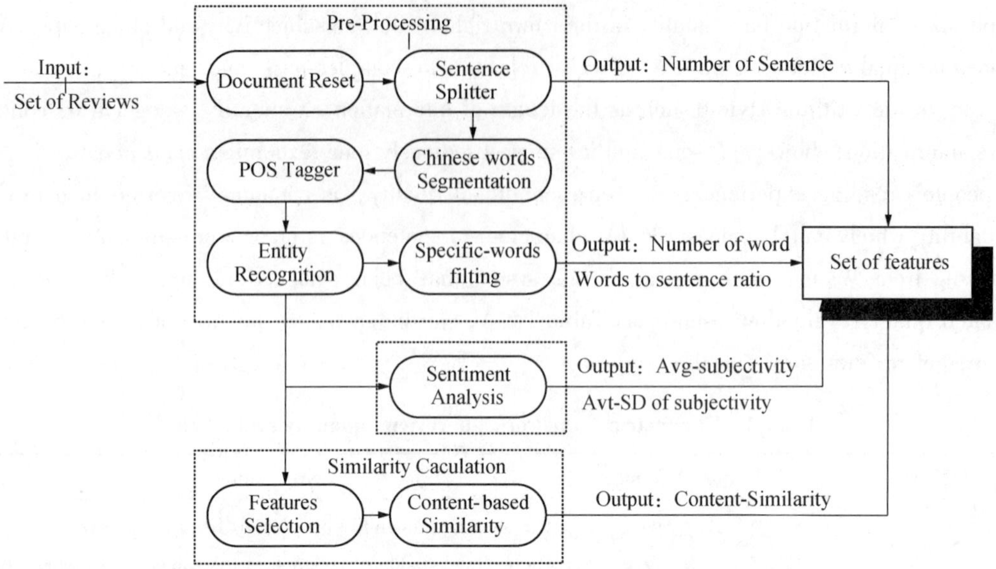

Figure 1　The framework of textual analysis processing

In the stage pre-processing, the fundamental text processing and textual features extraction are performed. *Sentence Splitter* is used to segment the text into sentences according to the segmentation mark; then, by using *Chinese word segmentation*, the sentences are further spitted into the Chinese words. Afterwards, each word is annotated with a part-of-speech tag and an entity type respectively by *POS Tagger* and *Entity Recognition*. Finally, *Words filter* extracts the feature words for the further analysis. Adjectives and Adverbs in the text, for instance, are chosen for sentiment analysis, meanwhile, text-specific features relevant to *readability* (e. g. *Num_sen* and *Num_wd*) are also obtained in the stage.

Regarding *Subjectivity* features, the average probability of a review being subjective and the average standard deviation of the subjectivity probability designed in[3] are adopted to describe sentiment factors implied in a review's textual content. The formula of the average probability of a review is showed as follow:

$$Avg\_Sub(R) = \frac{1}{n}\sum_{i=1}^{n} Pro_{subjectivity}(Sentence_i).$$

Where n is the number of sentences in review R and $Sentence_i$ ($i = 1, 2, \cdots, n$) is the sentences that appear in review R and represents the probability of $Sentence_i$ being subjective. In [3], two types of information, the objective information, listing the characteristics of the product and the subjective information, in which the reviewers give a very personal description of a product, were presented. Empirically, a helpful review should present several aspects of a product and provides convincing opinions with enough evidence as well, which means both types of information should be included in a review. Since a review may be a mixture of objective and subjective sentences, the standard deviation of the subjectivity probability for the review has been defined to describe the statue of mixture:

$$Avg\_SD(R) = \sqrt{\frac{1}{n}\sum_{i=1}^{n}[Pro_{subjectivity}(Sentence_i) - Avg\_Sub(R)]^2}.$$

We employed a machine learning based approach to predicting the probability of a sentence being subjective. By manually annotating the training set, a subjectivity classifier based on linear regression has been constructed. Performance of the classifier was evaluated by 10-fold cross-validation on the test set, which is promising as the accuracy of the classifier is above 0.85.

Topical relevancy embodies the semantic content of a review. A helpful review can be commonly taken as the main reference that users need to read before making their purchase decision on a product, which indicates that the content of a review should be written closely around a given product. The similar situation is conceivable between a customer review and an editorial review; the latter approximates a relatively objective and authoritative view of the product. Based on the understanding, similarity between customer reviews and the official evaluation for products has been adopted to quantify the feature of *topical relevancy*. The standard cosine similarity in Vector Space Model (VSM) with TF * IDF term weighting are used. The processing framework is showed as Figure 2.

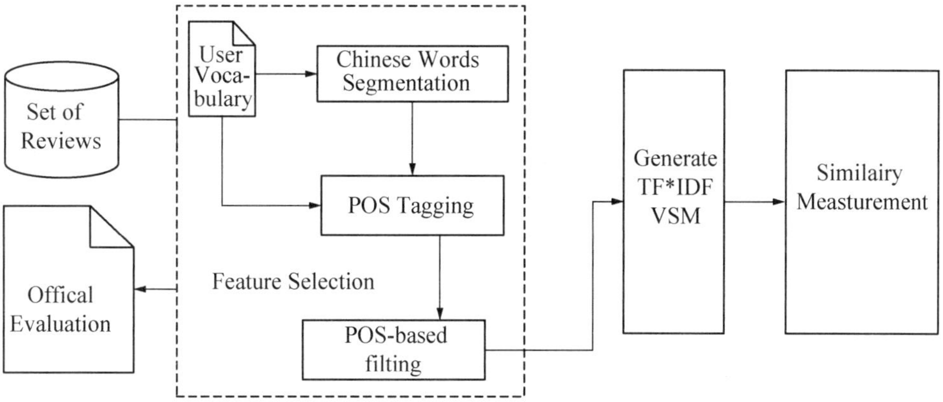

Figure 2 The processing framework for topical relevancy measurement

3.3 Explanatory econometric analysis model

Once we have derived the textual features of each review, we aim to look into how the textual features and ways of combination exert impacts on the quality of reviews. Here, the quality of a review refers to the perceived *helpfulness* of the review since the high-quality reviews are commonly with high score of *helpfulness*. So, in our explanatory econometric model, *helpfulness* is the dependent variable and the textual features variables are the predictors. Before presenting the model, we need test the following hypothesis:

Hypothesis 1: All else equal, a change in the *subjectivity* levels in a review will be associated with a change in the *helpfulness* of that reviews.

Hypothesis 2: All else equal, a change in the *readability* of a review will be associated with a change in the *helpfulness* of that review.

Hypothesis 3: All else equal, a change in the *topical relevancy* of a review will be associated with a change in the *helpfulness* of that review.

According to the hypothesis above, a linear specification for our *helpfulness* estimation has been defined as:

$$R_{helpfulness} = \alpha + \beta_1 \ln(R_{Num\_wd}) + \beta_2 R_{Num\_sen} + \beta_3 R_{Num\_wd\_sen} + \beta_4 R_{Avg\_sub} + \beta_5 R_{Avg\_SD} + \beta_6 R_{Topic\_relevancy} + \varepsilon.$$

The unit of observation in our analysis is a review R. The dependant variable $R_{helpfulness}$ is the radio of helpful votes to total votes received for a review. Independent variables, R_{Avg_sub} and R_{Avg_SD} are used to capture the level of subjectivity in a review; R_{Num_wd}, R_{Num_sen} and $R_{Num\_wd\_sen}$ quantify the degree of informativeness; and $R_{Topic\_relevancy}$ embodies the semantic content feature of a review. In our model, the influence of features derived from the textual aspect of a review is emphasized; we do not consider all possible information aspects (e. g. features about reviewers). Actually, from the view of review readers, the content, containing the most specific information, might be their major concern when they determining whether a review is useful or not.

3.4 The rule-based prediction model

Although the explanatory study can uncover what kinds of factor influence the perceived *helpfulness* of a review, another objective is to examine, given an existing review, how well we can predict it's *helpfulness* on the basis of the content. The *helpfulness* of each review in our data set is defined by the votes of the peer customers. In our predictive framework, we attempt to build a binary prediction model that can classify a review as being helpful or not. Therefore, the first step, the continuous variable *helpfulness* (*helpfulness* $\in$ (0, 1)) is converted into a binary one. The threshold is set to mark all reviews that have *helpfulness* as helpful and others are not helpful. Then, as a rule-based approach, the decision tree model has been selected to perform the task of prediction; since classification rules can make people better understand the result. In the process of constructing the tree, the splitting feature is specifically selected based on the *information gain* which being interpreted as the informational value of creating a branch on the feature. Basically, higher the information gain of an attribute is, more influential the attribute is for classification; so, the predictive ability of attribute can be examined according to the structure of tree.

For better understanding how decisions being made, given the decision tree, we also need to convert the numeric attributes into nominal variables. A clustering algorithm is specifically used. For instance, according to R_{Avg_sub} and R_{Avg_SD} the *subjectivity* is converted into a nominal variable with three-styles: *highly subjective*, *moderately subjective* and *weakly subjective*. *Topical relevancy* is ranked into *strong*, *less strong* and *weak*, and the *informativeness* is also categorized into three types according to the length of the review in words: *large*, *medium and small.*

4 Experiments & Analyses

4.1 Data collection

As the most commercially marketable IT-specific website in China, www.zol.com.cn has been chosen to be our source of data. By using a web spider toolkit—Locoy①, we collected totally 1,569 original reviews about an *Moto mobile phone* (*ME* 525) from the website. A parsing program has been developed to automate the data extraction. Textual aspects of reviews are the major target data. Certainly, the total number of voters and the number of useful voters has been extracted, used as the ground-truth to approximate the target value of the regression model and the decision tree model as well.

4.2 Experiments and analyses

Based on the data set described above, we firstly approximate the predictive variable, as follow:

$$R_{helpfulness} = \frac{R_{Num\_helpful\_voters}}{R_{Num\_total\_voters}}.$$

Then, we obtained the relevant predictors by running a stream of textual analysis (Section 3.2). Two major studies have been conducted to investigate the quality of reviews. The first one (Section 3.3) investigates the influence exerted by textual features, attending to determine the most predictors for assessing the *helpfulness* of a review by using regression analysis. The second one (Section 3.4) is designed for validating the reliability of regression model and attempt to obtain an effective rules for detecting high quality reviews.

4.2.1 Estimating the quality of reviews

The experiment is conducted on the platform of *R* Language②. The correlations between the predictive variables and a group of independent variables have been examined, as shown in Figure 3. More distinct results are obtained by use of the regression analysis, as shown in Figure 4.

① http://www.locoy.com/.

② *R* is a language and environment for statistical computing and graphics. http://www.r-project.org/.

```
> newdata2 <- subset( mydatafram,!(Num_sen<3 || Avg_SD == 0),select = c
+ (Ln_Num_wd,Num_sen,Num_wd_sen,Avg_sub,Avg_SD,Topic_relevancy,Helpfulness))
> x<-newdata2[,c("Ln_Num_wd","Num_sen","Num_wd_sen","Avg_sub","Avg_SD","Topic_relevancy","Helpfulness")]
> y<-newdata2[,c("Ln_Num_wd","Num_sen","Num_wd_sen","Avg_sub","Avg_SD","Topic_relevancy","Helpfulness")]
> cor(x,y)
                  Ln_Num_wd     Num_sen  Num_wd_sen     Avg_sub     Avg_SD Topic_relevancy Helpfulness
Ln_Num_wd        1.00000000  0.80628739  0.06272398 -0.08629804  0.3247757      0.30319656  0.38123191
Num_sen          0.80628739  1.00000000 -0.17032697 -0.05548273  0.2666340      0.25963865  0.30820670
Num_wd_sen       0.06272398 -0.17032697  1.00000000  0.08950960 -0.2309435     -0.02099942  0.03706644
Avg_sub         -0.08629804 -0.05548273  0.08950960  1.00000000 -0.7572519     -0.02040985  0.04362200
Avg_SD           0.32477574  0.26663400 -0.23094348 -0.75725185  1.0000000      0.12013733  0.06699940
Topic_relevancy  0.30319656  0.25963865 -0.02099942 -0.02040985  0.1201373      1.00000000  0.21435293
Helpfulness      0.38123191  0.30820670  0.03706644  0.04362200  0.0669994      0.21435293  1.00000000
```

Figure 3 Correlation analysis for $R_{helpfulness}$ with the relevant independent variables (Screenshot)

```
> summary(fit)

Call:
lm(formula = Helpfulness ~ Ln_Num_wd + Num_sen + Num_wd_sen +
    Avg_sub + Avg_SD + Topic_relevancy + Avg_sub:Topic_relevancy,
    data = newdata4)

Residuals:
     Min       1Q   Median       3Q      Max
-0.61536 -0.23655  0.04496  0.21533  0.46321

Coefficients:
                         Estimate Std. Error t value Pr(>|t|)
(Intercept)            -8.287e-01  2.381e-01  -3.481 0.000549 ***
Ln_Num_wd               1.873e-01  4.201e-02   4.458 1.05e-05 ***
Num_sen                -8.974e-04  1.846e-03  -0.486 0.627118
Num_wd_sen             -9.927e-04  3.162e-03  -0.314 0.753709
Avg_sub                 5.754e-01  2.208e-01   2.606 0.009483 **
Avg_SD                  1.194e-01  1.899e-01   0.629 0.529583
Topic_relevancy         1.167e+01  3.813e+00   3.060 0.002350 **
Avg_sub:Topic_relevancy -1.339e+01  4.967e+00  -2.697 0.007277 **
---
Signif. codes:  0 '***' 0.001 '**' 0.01 '*' 0.05 '.' 0.1 ' ' 1

Residual standard error: 0.2634 on 439 degrees of freedom
Multiple R-squared:  0.2046,    Adjusted R-squared:  0.1919
F-statistic: 16.13 on 7 and 439 DF,  p-value: < 2.2e-16
```

Figure 4 The result of regression analysis (Screenshot)

From the Figure 3, we can see that $\ln R_{Num\_wd}$ and R_{Num_sen} have the relatively strong correlation with $R_{helpfulness}$ compared to other variables; the corresponding correlation coefficients come to 0.3812 and 0.3082 respectively. And correlation between $R_{Topic\_relevancy}$ and $R_{helpfulness}$ is 0.2143, being on the second place. Moreover, we notice that there is no significantly relevant between the subjective features of a review with its *helpfulness* as we intuitively expected, e.g., correlation between R_{Avg_sub} and $R_{helpfulness}$ is only about 0.0436.

From the Figure 4, it is clearly shown that the change in $\ln R_{Num\_wd}$ or $R_{Topic\_relevancy}$ of a review leads to the change of $R_{helpfulness}$ and significantly. Regarding sentimental factors, R_{Avg_sub} has positive influence on the helpfulness of the review in statistical significance; but, R_{Avg_SD} does not exert significantly impact on the usefulness. No significant influence also comes to the other two independent variables $R_{Num\_wd\_sen}$ and R_{Num_sen}. Beyond that, in the process of optimizing the regression specification, we further detected the impacts led by the interaction of two variables. The product term of R_{Avg_sub} and $R_{Topic\_relevancy}$ is significantly put negative influence on usefulness of a review, suggesting the change rate of the usefulness might decrease with the increase of topical relevancy and subjective level. Namely, the relationship between sentimental factors and usefulness of a review is also associated with its content. A review with rich content and high topic correlation can be perceived to be useful respectively; but a review might not be recognized as being much useful if it's over emotional even if the content is closely related with product-specific subject.

Since not all features are statistically significant with the *helpfulness* of a review, we obtain the best two models according to the value of *adjusted* R^2 by exploring models on all possible feature subsets. As shown in Figure 5, the best two models are on the top row, being described by the variables $\ln R_{Num\_wd}$, R_{Avg_sub}, R_{Avg_SD}, $R_{Topic\_relevancy}$, and $R_{Avg\_sub} \cdot R_{Topic\_relevancy}$ and with the highest value of *adjusted* R^2 (about 0.2), which indicates the two models can account for up to 20 percent of *adjusted* R^2 and the major influential factors for evaluating *usefulness* of reviews are *Num_wd*, *Avg_sub*, *Avg_SD* , and *Topic_relevancy* respectively.

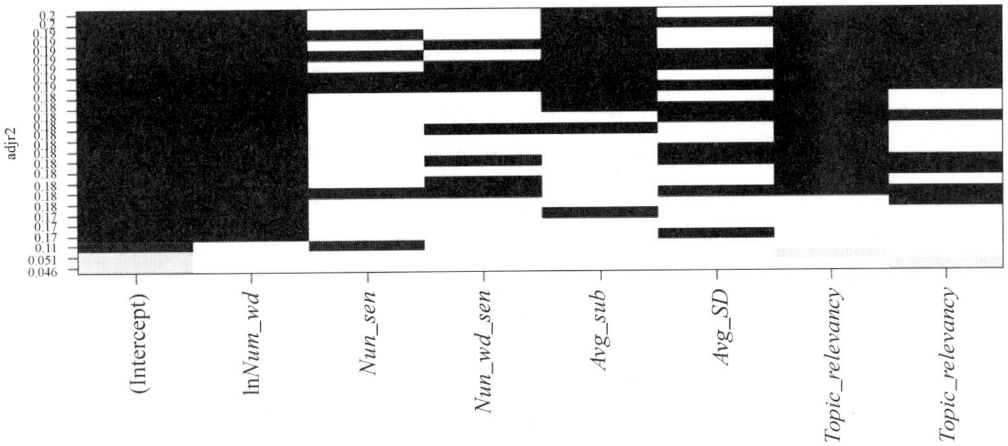

Figure 5 Rank the explanatory models based on the *adjusted* R^2

Furthermore, relative importance for the predictor variables has also been measured. Relative importance can be thought of as the contribution each predictor makes to R^2, both alone and in combination with other predictors. An approach for measuring the metric, which closely approximates the average increase in R^2 obtained by adding a predictor variable across all possible sub_models, has been employed in our experiment. As shown in Figure 6, it is clear ln*Num_wd* has the greatest relative importance, followed by *Topic_relevancy* and subjective factors, in that order.

4.2.2 Detect the quality of reviews by decision tree

According to the analysis in Section 3.4, we use the decision tree to examine whether, given an existing review, how well can we predict the *helpfulness*, i.e., of a review that was not included in the data used to train the predictive model. The influential factors obtained from the

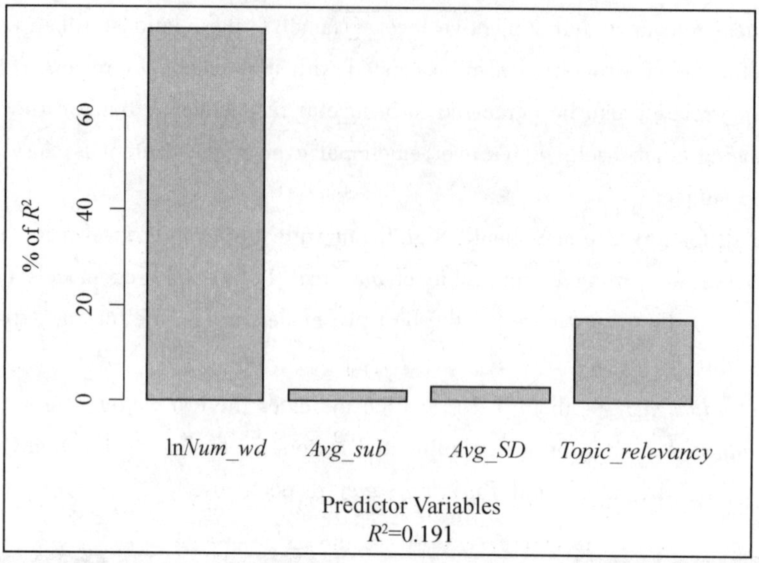

Figure 6　Relative importance for the predictor variables

optimal model in section 4. 2. 1 have been used as the features to build the classifier and Rapid Miner① was employed to conduct the classification experiment. The evaluation results are based on stratified 10-fold cross validation on our experimental data set. The resulting performance of the classifier is satisfactory. The classification accuracy comes to 82. 6%.

Another interesting result is the tree model obtained. As shown in Figure 7, we can see that *Num_wd* is the first attribute being tested, followed by the *topic relevancy* and the *sentimental types* in that order. Based on the decision tree approach, the result indicates *Num_wd* is the biggest attributor to the classification, namely, it exert the most significant influence on detecting useful reviews. The second most powerful classification features is *topic relevancy*, then followed by *subjectivity* associated with predictors R_{Avg_sub} and R_{Avg_SD}. The result is consistent with the results of regression analysis in section 4. 2. 3. Beyond that, routing down the tree according to the values of the attributes tested in successive nodes, we can find a set of easy-understanding rules for determining whether a review is helpful or not. For example:

Rule* 1**: if (*Num_wd* = *large* **and** *Topic_relevancy* = *Strong* **and** *Sentimental style* = (*moderate* **or** *weak*) *then* (**The review is *helpful)

Rule* 2**: if (*Num_wd* = *large* **and** *Topic_relevancy* = *Strong* **and** *Sentimental style* = *high*) then (**The review is *not helpful)

***Rule* 1** implies when the content of a review is informative and detailed on a specific subject interested by review readers and being moderately expressed in subjective ways, it is commonly perceived to be helpful; whereas, ***Rule* 2** reveals reviews with high topical relevancy but over-subjective content regardless of being positive or negative, tend to be perceived as excessive

① Rapid Miner: The world-leading open-source system for data mining. http://rapid-i.com/content/view/181/190/.

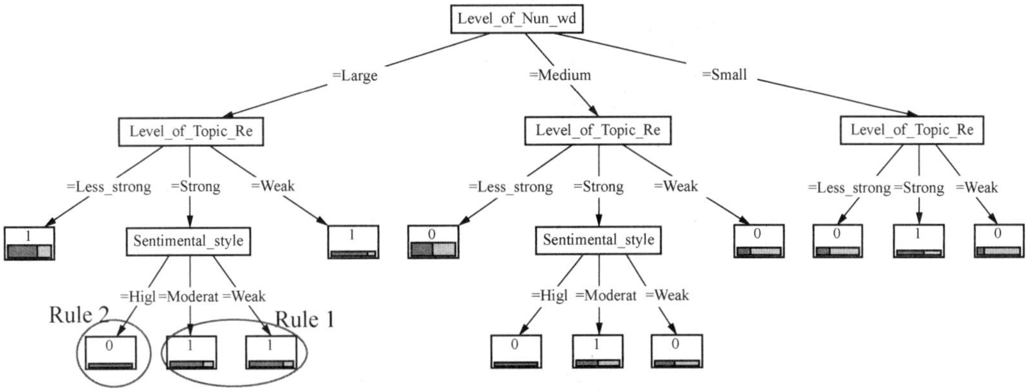

Figure 7 The Decision Tree Model for detecting the helpfulness of reviews (screen shot)

assessments and have a significant possibility of being identified as uselessness, which can be explained by the negative influence exerted by the interaction of R_{Avg_SD} and R_{Topic_sim} in the regression model in 4. 2. 1. Clearly, classification rules derived from the tree model make review readers get more intuition about the detection procedures.

5 Conclusion

In this paper, we studied the problem of evaluating and detecting high-quality product reviews. We particularly examined how the textual aspect of a review affects the perceived usefulness of it. To address the problem, a simple but well-established framework for assessing review quality has been designed to examine the nature of *helpfulness*. A stream of NLP technologies, e. g. Chinese words segmentation, POS tagger and sentiment analysis, has been fully employed to extract the corresponding text-specific features. We conduct the study by combining an explanatory econometric analysis and a supervised machine learning technology, decision tree classification.

Based on a real-world data set, our econometric analysis reveals that the text-specific characteristics, including quantity of content, topical relevancy and extent of subjectivity, are significantly associated with the perceived helpfulness of the review. The optimal model demonstrates a review is perceived being useful if the content of the review focusing on the given subject, with sufficient information and being expressed in moderately subjective ways. Additionally, by using the decision tree classifier, we also examine the relative importance of the three broad feature categories: *subjectivity*, *informativeness* and *topic relevance*, and find *informativeness* plays the most important role in detecting the *helpfulness* of reviews. Beyond that, the good performance of the tree-based classifier further indicates the high-quality reviews can be discriminated from the low-quality ones only by examining their textual features.

In summary, our study suggests we can quickly estimate the quality of a review by performing an automatic stylistic analysis according to its textual content and sentimental characteristics and we can straight forwardly indentify the product reviews expected to be helpful to the online customers and show them at first time on the commercial websites without any biases resulted from the lacking of voters.

References

[1] Jindal N, Liu B. Analyzing and Detecting Review Spam [C]. Seventh IEEE International Conference on Data Mining (ICDM '07), 2007: 547-552.

[2] Zhang Z, Varadarajan B. Utility Scoring of Product Reviews [C]. Information and Knowledge Management (CIKM '06), 2006: 51-57.

[3] Ghose A, Ipeirotis P G. Estimating the Helpfulness and Economic Impact of Product Reviews: Mining Text and Reviewer Characteristics [J]. IEEE Transactions on Knowledge and Data Engineering, 2011, 23 (10): 1498-1512.

[4] Ghose A, Ipeirotis P G. Designing Ranking Systems for Consumer Reviews: the Impact of Review Subjectivity on Product Sales and Review Quality [J]. Workshop Information Technology and System, 2006.

[5] Ghose A, Ipeirotis P G. Designing Novel Review Ranking Systems: Predicting the Usefulness and Impact of Reviews [C]. Electronic Commerce (ICEC '07), 2007: 303-310.

[6] Liu J, Cao Y. Low-quality Product Review Detection in Opinion Summarization [C]. Of 2007 Joint Conference on Empirical Methods in NLP and CNLL, 2007: 334-342.

[7] Otterbacher J. "Helpfulness" in Online Communities: A Measure of Message Quality [C]. Proc of the 27th International Conference on Human Factors in Computing Systems (CHI '09), 2009: 955-964.

[8] Wang R Y, Strong D M. Beyond Accuracy: What Data Quality Means to Data Consumers [J]. Journal of Management Information System, 1996, 12 (4): 5-34.

[9] Foltz P W, Laham D, Landauer T K. Automated Essay Scoring: Applications to Educational Technology [J]. Ed Media, 1999.

教师简介：

杨利军，男，云南大学理学硕士，中山大学理学博士。2002 年毕业于中山大学并留校工作，2006 年 6 月起任教于中山大学资讯管理学院，副教授，硕士生导师，中国档案学会影像技术委员会委员。主讲“专门档案管理”、“管理统计学”、“线性代数”、“电子文件管理”等本科生课程，以及“信息计量学”、“信息系统设计与组织创新研究”、“档案学专题研究”、“档案学研究方法论”等研究生课程。主持及参与 7 项国家级、省部级科研项目，发表论文 30 余篇，其中同时被 SCI、EI 收录 1 篇，被 EI 收录 2 篇。联系方式：ylj@mail. sysu. edu. cn。

所选论文《低被引期刊论文学术价值的评价方法研究》原载于《情报理论与实践》2014 年第 7 期

低被引期刊论文学术价值的评价方法研究*

杨利军，万小渝①

摘　要：以论文被引频次为基础的评价方法逐步得到学术界的认同，但当前多数方法对低被引论文的评价存在不足。本文在分析期刊论文被引频次特征的基础上，构建了对低被引论文最终被引频次的估计模型；经实证检验，本文提出模型的计算结果与实际有较好的吻合。据此，得出结论：①部分低被引的期刊论文确实存在高学术价值；②对低被引期刊论文的学术价值可采用分段评价方法，对于发表时间小于 3 年的低被引论文采用综合指标体系进行评价，达到或者超过 3 年的低被引期刊论文的学术价值采用数学模型进行评价。

关键词：低被引论文；被引频次；学术价值；评价方法

Study on Evaluation Methods for Academic Value of Low-Cited Journal Articles

Lijun Yang，Xiaoyu Wan

Abstract： Evaluation methods based on citation frequency of article have been gradually recognized in academic circles, but most methods currently have deficiency in evaluating low-cited articles. Based on analysis of the characteristics of journal article citation frequency, an estimation model for final citation frequency of low-cited articles was constructed in this paper; it was verified through experiment that the calculation results from the model proposed in this paper fit well with the actual situations. Thus, it was concluded that: (1) some low-

* 本文是国家社会科学基金“低被引论文对情报学研究热点、方法及经典理论的影响及实证研究”（项目批准号：11CTQ027）的部分研究成果。

① 万小渝，中山大学资讯管理学院情报学研究生。

cited journal articles indeed have high academic value; and (2) low-cited journal articles can be evaluated for academic value by stage, in other words, the comprehensive index system method can be used to evaluate the academic value of low-cited journal articles having been published for less than 3 years and the mathematical model method can be used to evaluate the academic value of low-cited journal articles having been published for 3 years or more.

Keywords: Low-citedarticle; Citation frequency; Academic value; Evaluation method

1 引　言

学术界当前对期刊论文学术价值的评价方法多数都是基于被引频次展开的，被引频次被看作衡量学术价值的重要标准。但是，相关研究表明这些方法（如 H 指数及 H 型指数）仍存在不足——只关注高被引的期刊论文，忽略了低被引期刊论文的学术价值贡献[1,2]，使得评价结果缺乏真实性。事实上，一篇期刊论文是否为高被引往往需要较长时间来验证，由于发表时间较短而导致的低被引论文并不意味着其永远为低被引。特别地，当前的部分评价仅看被评者近期的成果，使得这些评价方法在应用上也存在不足。基于以上背景，本文将在前期研究的基础上，对低被引（当前“图书馆、情报与文献学”为小于等于 9 次）期刊论文[3]学术价值的评价方法展开研究，以期提高科研评价方法的科学性。

2 期刊论文学术价值评价方法的文献分析

根据文献调查，学术界对期刊论文学术价值评价方法主要包括定性评价、定量评价、综合评价（定性与定量相结合）。定性评价是评价主体通过阅读和讨论等形式对评价对象的相关方面用文字语言进行描述的方法[4]，其主要形式是同行评议。虽然同行评议是当前我国评价社会科学成果的主要方法，但存在主观性太强、同行专家难以选择、评价成本高等不足之处。[5-7]

为了避免定性评价的主观性，学术界不断探索定量评价方法，主要分为“以刊代文”和基于被引频次的学术价值评价两类。“以刊代文”的评价方法简单易行，相对于同行评议客观性更强，因此该方法一直是成果评奖、职称评定、学位授予以及科研考核等的主要方法，亦是评价科研人员或机构科研能力和学术水平的主要方式。[8]然而“以刊代文”将论文的学术价值完全等同于期刊等级，这种评价方式过于绝对化，且部分评价结果与事实不符合，因此该方法也遭到学术界众多学者的质疑和反对。[9-11]基于被引频次的学术价值评价方法主要是指依据论文获得的被引频次来评价该论文的学术价值，如 H 指数以及 H 型指数。虽然这种方法计算简便，但忽略了论文被引频次与发表时间的关系。对此 Anderson 提出了锥形 H 指数[2]，根据其推导出的矩阵可以计算出每篇论文的学术价值。我国学者也引入时间因素结合被引频次提出了一种综合计算论文学术价值的方法[12]；但有学者对此提出异议，认为该方法未能完全反映时间因素[13]。事实上，文献［12］及［13］都存在“获得相同被引频次的论文，经计算所得的学术价值有可能会不同”的问题——这不符合科研评价的公平原则。

定性评价方法容易受到主观因素的影响，并且评价过程复杂，所需时间长；定量评价有时又过于简单，无法评价比较复杂的对象。因此，学术界开始对定性与定量相结合的综合指标体系评价方法进行研究，将评价指标分为定性和定量两大类：定性指标包括科学性、创新性、规范性、可读性等，定量指标包括期刊等级、期刊影响因子、被引频次、参考文献数等。[14-19]

综上分析，当前对期刊论文学术价值的评价还不够科学合理，主要不足包括三点：①对低被引期刊论文学术价值揭示不足；②虽然已有学者意识到被引频次和发表时间在评价过程中的重要性，但由于现有的评价方法都未能真正理清二者的关系，基于此所建立的评价方法就不能真实反映出期刊论文的学术价值；③部分评价体系过于复杂，导致可行性差，很难在实践中得到推广。因此本文将从期刊论文被引频次的特征分析入手，在此基础上建立基于被引频次的低被引期刊论文学术价值评价方法。

3　期刊论文被引频次特征分析

3.1　数据的选取

参照中国学术文献网络出版总库（CNKI）、中文社会科学引文索引（CSSCI）、中国科教评价网以及中文核心期刊要目总揽，我国“图书馆、情报与文献学”领域主要的期刊总共有 18 种。参照中国知网引文数据库的期刊被引统计数据，总体上，18 种样本期刊刊载论文被引高峰期为发表之后的 2～4 年，随后几年被引频次逐年减少，当论文的发表时间超过 10 年后，则很少再被引用，其总被引频次将趋于稳定，可认为发表 10 年后获得的总被引频次就是该论文的最终被引频次（也可称为总被引频次）。因此本文选取 2001 年刊载论文的被引频次为分析对象，按照 CNKI 数据库图书情报类期刊刊载高被引论文百分比进行等距抽样，抽取《中国图书馆学报》、《图书馆》、《图书与情报》作为样本进行期刊论文被引频次的年代分布特征分析。

3.2　逐年累计被引频次与总被引频次的关系分析

大部分期刊论文发表之后，在一段时期内其累计被引频次将随着论文发表时间的增长而不断提高，当增长时间足够长时（当前“图书馆、情报与文献学”这一时间大约为 10 年），其累计被引频次不再随着被引时间的增长而显著提高，只是无限趋于总被引频次。

为了发掘逐年累计被引频次与总被频次的关系，本文利用 SPSS 18.0 对每篇论文逐年累计被引次数与总被引频次作 Person 相关性分析，结果如表 1 所示。

由于论文的被引具有滞后性，当论文发表时间为 1 年时，大部分论文都处于未被引状态，从而导致在刚刚发表的时候累计被引次数与总被引次数的相关性很低，且论文发表的前 3 年其逐年累计被引频次与总被引频次的相关性水平均较低；当论文发表时间达到 3 年之后，各年累计被引频次与总被引频次的相关性已达到较高水平。如《中国图书馆学报》在第 3 年时其载文的累计被引频次与总被引频次的相关性已经达到 0.924。

表1 样本逐年累计被引次数与总被引次数的相关性分析

发表时间	《中国图书馆学报》		《图书馆》		《图书与情报》	
	Pearson 相关性	显著性（双侧）	Pearson 相关性	显著性（双侧）	Pearson 相关性	显著性（双侧）
1 年	0.562**	0.000	0.495**	0.000	0.468**	0.000
2 年	0.837**	0.000	0.806**	0.000	0.583**	0.000
3 年	0.924**	0.000	0.854**	0.000	0.833**	0.000
4 年	0.963**	0.000	0.905**	0.000	0.876**	0.000
5 年	0.979**	0.000	0.932**	0.000	0.886**	0.000
6 年	0.985**	0.000	0.955**	0.000	0.925**	0.000
7 年	0.990**	0.000	0.969**	0.000	0.962**	0.000
8 年	0.995**	0.000	0.985**	0.000	0.978**	0.000

说明：**表示在0.01水平（双侧）上显著相关（下同）。

因此，当论文发表时间小于3年时，本文采用综合指标体系方法来预测期刊论文的总被引频次；当论文的发表时间达到或者超过3年时，本文用对应的累计被引频次按照某种计算方式（数学模型）来预测某一篇论文的总被引频次。

4 总被引频次的综合指标体系预测方法

4.1 评价指标的选取

客观公正是评价期刊论文学术价值的基本要求，这要求选取的评价指标应尽量全面、客观，能最大限度地反映期刊论文的学术价值；并且选取的指标应当相对精炼，以确保评价方法的效率和可行性；选取的评价指标要有区分度，即根据所选指标能够将评价对象按照某一属性区分开来，为择优去劣提供依据。由于定性评价指标相对复杂、主观性强且评价成本较高，因此，本文去除定性评价指标，选取纯定量的指标，主要包括以下三个：

（1）被引频次。一方面，被引频次不仅显示了期刊论文被引使用和受研究者重视的程度，而且直接反映了该期刊论文在学科发展过程中所起的作用，在一定程度上反映出期刊论文的学术价值。[20] 同时由于被引频次是一个纯客观性指标，避免了同行评价的主观性等缺点，因此被引频次得到了广大学者的认可，被广泛应用于科研评价中。另一方面，随着国内外引文数据库的不断成熟和当前学术研究（引用）的不断规范，使得用被引频次来评价期刊论文的学术价值成为可能。因此，本文将被引频次作为评价期刊论文学术价值的主要指标之一。

（2）所在期刊论文被引频次的数学期望。“以刊代文”的方法操作简便，因而被广泛应用于科研评价中。然而，以期刊总体的学术水平来评价某篇论文的质量，认为优秀期刊上刊登的一定是优秀论文，这一推论在逻辑上并不合理，因此这种方法的合理性也遭到很多学者的质疑。[21] 事实上，2005 年图书馆、情报与文献学领域的“权威期刊”[22] 刊载的论文也只有 55.72% 的文章是高被引。并且刊物等级排序和期刊影响因子与 2001—2005 年高被引论文百分比的平均值只存在弱相关性（Person 相关性系数），其中与中国科教评价网排序的相关性系数为 -0.665，与中文核心期刊要目总揽排序的相关性系数为 -0.616，与中文社会科学引文索引排序的相关性系数为 -0.722，与期刊影响因子的相关性系数为 0.701。上述数据表明，将期刊等级直接用于评价期刊论文学术价值存在一定的不合理性。

一定时期内，事物某一属性的数学期望代表该事物在这一属性上的总体水平，因此数学期望经常被用于判断不同对象之间在某一属性方面的优劣程度。例如预测一个射击队员完成一次射击后的可能得分，就是根据该射击队员的射击数学期望值来判断的。因此，本文认为在一定时期内，发表在某期刊上的论文最终可能获得的总被引频次也可以用该期刊载文被引频次的数学期望值来预测。事实上，2001—2005 年图书馆、情报与文献学领域期刊的被引期望的平均值与平均高被引比例的相关性为 0.97（Person 相关性系数）。因此，在某篇论文发表之后的一定时期内，可以用其所在期刊的论文被引期望来预测该论文在未来最有可能获得的总被引频次。

（3）论文的发表时间。期刊论文最终获得的被引频次，除了论文自身的质量因素外，论文发表的时间长短是众多外在影响因素中最主要的方面。2000 年《中国图书馆学报》刊载的 136 篇学术性论文，经过近 11 年的被引积累，最终有 80 篇论文成为高被引，占总刊文量的 58.82%。在 80 篇高被引论文中，有 66.25% 是经过 2～4 年的被引才成为高被引，有 32.5% 则需要 5 年以上的被引积累才能成为高被引。《情报学报》大部分的高被引论文形成时间则更长。《情报学报》在 2000 年刊载的 69 篇高被引论文中，有 57.97% 需要经过 4～7 年的被引积累才能成为高被引，有 26.09% 则需要 7 年以上的时间才成为高被引。

数据表明，无论是《中国图书馆学报》还是《情报学报》，2000 年刊登的论文中 99% 在当年都是低被引（《情报学报》的这一比例在 2002 年还有 89.62%），而这些在 2000 年处于低被引的文章，最终分别有 58.82% 和 65.09% 的论文成为高被引。如果在 2000 年只用被引频次来衡量这些论文的学术价值的话，无疑这些论文都只是具有较低的学术价值。因此，基于被引频次的学术论文评价必须考虑论文的发表时间。

4.2 综合指标体系的分数合成方法研究

经过文献分析，评价期刊论文质量常用的分数合成方法有指标加权求和、层次分析法、模糊综合评价法、基本分乘系数等。指标加权求和是将各个指标得分乘以其对应的权重再分别累加而得到最终分值，指标加权求和的方法常用于具有相互补偿性的指标体系中，在某一个指标上得了低分，可以通过在其他指标上得到高分来补偿。层次分析法可以认为是模糊综合评价法的一种特例，二者均是对评价对象从多个因素进行综合评价的方法，是当前常用的综合评价分数计算方法，但二者的指标权重大多是由人为确定，主观性较强。基本分乘系数是指在计算某一对象的总体得分时，以某一个指标的得分为核心，其他指标得分对该指标得分进行调整。由于本研究选取的各指标不涉及指标得分之间的相互补偿，以及为了避免个人主观判断随意性的影响，本研究在计算综合指标得分时选用基本分乘系数的方法，基本表达式为：X = 实际被引频次 + int① （期刊被引频次的数学期望 × 论文发表时间得分系数）。

4.3 评价指标的分数计算方法

（1）所在期刊论文被引频次的数学期望值。参照 CNKI、CSSCI、中国科教评价网以及中文核心期刊要目总揽，选取图书馆、情报与文献学领域的 18 种代表性期刊为例，利用 CNKI 获得这些期刊 2001—2005 年载文的被引数据，运用上述计算方式，得到 2001—2005 年各个期刊的论文被引期望的平均值，结果如表 2 所示。

表 2　期刊被引频次的 5 年平均被引期望值　　单位：次

刊名	期望值	刊名	期望值	刊名	期望值
A1	23	A7	11	A13	8
A2	19	A8	11	A14	7
A3	19	A9	10	A15	7
A4	13	A10	9	A16	6
A5	10	A11	8	A17	6
A6	11	A12	8	A18	5

说明：A1 ～ A18 代表的期刊依次是：《中国图书馆学报》、《情报学报》、《大学图书馆学报》、《图书馆论坛》、《图书馆工作与研究》、《情报理论与实践》、《图书馆》、《图书情报知识》、《图书情报工作》、《情报科学》、《图书馆建设》、《现代图书情报技术》、《图书与情报》、《国家图书馆学刊》、《情报杂志》、《情报资料工作》、《图书馆学研究》、《图书馆杂志》。下同。

（2）论文发表时间得分系数计算方法。当一篇论文刚发表时，可以通过所在刊物的论文被引期望值进行预测其最终最有可能获得的总被引频次，据此估算该论文的学术价值。但随着被引时间的不断增长，被引期望值逐渐转为真实被引频次，论文的学术价值也逐渐由实际的被引频次来表现，对论文学术价值的评估就不能再依靠所在刊物的论文被引期望值来预测评估，而是应该根据实际的被引频次进行精确评估为了分析实际被引频次的形成过程，进而确定论文发表时间的得分系数，本研究选取图书馆、情报与文献学领域额的 18 种期刊为例，分析 2001 年 18 种期刊载文在 2001—2011 年的逐年的被引情况。

数据显示，图书馆、情报与文献学领域的期刊论文刚刚发表时一般很少被引用，被引高峰期是在论文发表后 2 ～ 4 年（以发表的当年为第 1 年算起，下同），此后随着发表时间的增长被引次数逐渐减少，大部分论文超过 7 年以后就很少获得被引。总体上，在论文发表的第 1 年，很少获得被引，此时的学术价值还没有转化为实际被引频次，因此在计

---

① int 表示向下取整，例如 int（2.7） =2，下同。

算时会因为论文发表时间较短而在发表时间得分系数上获得较高的分数。当论文发表4年后，平均累计被引频次占总被引频次的48%；当论文的发表时间为8年时，累计被引频次与总被引频次的比例达到90%。可见随着发表时间的增长，期刊论文的学术价值逐渐表现为实际被引频次，在计算总被引频次时，论文在发表时间方面的得分系数也逐渐减小。为使得计算结果更接近期刊论文被引分布规律以及确保研究结果更准确，本文依据实际的平均累计被引百分比进行论文发表时间方面得分系数的计算，具体计算方式为：

$$K_t = 1 - A_t。$$

式中：K_t 表示第 t 年时论文在时间方面的得分系数；A_t 表示第 t 年时平均累计被引百分比。因此，论文发表时间的得分系数如表3所示。

表3　论文发表时间得分系数

年份	系数	年份	系数	年份	系数
1	0.9720	5	0.4225	9	0.1025
2	0.8094	6	0.3327	10	0.0444
3	0.6519	7	0.2526	11	0
4	0.5194	8	0.1722		

4.3　综合评价指标体系的分数合成及实证研究

假设某期刊论文的实际被引频次为 N，发表时间的得分系数为 K_t，所在期刊的论文被引期望值为 E，则一定时期内该期刊论文的总被引频次 X 可以表示为：

$$X = N + \text{int}(E \times K_t)。$$

例如，当某篇论文发表2年后，实际获得6次被引，所在期刊的论文被引期望值为10次，则该论文的总被引频次的计算为：

$$X = 6 + \text{int}(10 \times 0.8094) = 14。$$

依据上述方法，以2001年《中国图书馆学报》、《图书馆》、《图书与情报》三种期刊的载文为数据进行实证分析。通过对低累计被引频次的预测结果进行统计，检验综合指标体系预测方法的有效性，结果如表4所示。

表4　高低被引预测准确度

发表时间	《中国图书馆学报》	《图书馆》	《图书与情报》
1年	59.86%	34.33%	59.55%
2年	50.00%	31.25%	76.14%

表4是指当前为低被引的论文，通过综合指标体系的计算后准确判断是否为高被引的百分比。从表4得知，《中国图书馆学报》的准确度在50%左右，《图书与情报》在60%左右，而《图书馆》相对较低，为30%左右。虽然整体上看准确度都不高，但相比于传统的“以刊代文”方法已有很大提高。

5 总被引频次的数学模型预测方法

5.1 总被引频次的条件均值

由前文的分析可知，当期刊论文发表了3年之后，其累计被引频次与总被引频次之间存在较高的线性相关，因此，分别选取三种期刊2001年载文的前3～6年累计被引频次（*R*）与总被引频次（*N*）进行分析。由于本文探索的数学模型是为了解释给定*R*值下*N*的期望值或条件均值的轨迹，因此先计算给定*R*值时*N*的条件均值。限于篇幅，此处只列出给定*R*值为0～9次时*N*的条件期望值，结果如表5所示。

表5 给定*R*值下*N*的期望值 单位：次

R	《中国图书馆学报》				《图书馆》				《图书与情报》			
	3年	4年	5年	6年	3年	4年	5年	6年	3年	4年	5年	6年
9	28.7	14.3	17.0	10.8	17.4	15.8	11.0	11.6	18.8	16.7	12.0	13.8
8	26.0	14.6	12.3	8.7	24.0	12.0	13.0	10.6	19.5	26.0	15.0	12.0
7	19.3	13.3	8.1	8.9	17.3	14.0	9.7	9.0	12.5	12.0	10.5	14.7
6	13.8	14.8	9.7	7.7	14.5	12.4	8.6	6.8	23.0	11.2	11.4	8.7
5	17.0	9.0	7.9	6.8	8.8	10.5	7.0	7.4	15.2	11.0	10.8	8.6
4	11.1	7.5	7.3	7.0	12.6	5.2	5.9	4.9	14.0	12.0	10.8	9.2
3	9.0	6.2	5.4	5.0	6.8	5.0	5.0	5.6	9.5	8.8	6.6	4.1
2	6.3	5.1	3.1	2.9	6.4	4.9	3.9	3.3	7.4	5.1	4.5	3.4
1	4.4	2.2	2.0	1.9	4.7	3.1	2.8	2.3	5.2	5.2	2.3	2.3
0	1.8	0.8	0.5	0.1	2.1	1.4	1.2	1.0	3.0	1.4	1.3	1.1

表5是指给定某年累计被引频次下的条件均值。例如，表中的28.7（次）的意思是指，经过3年的累计被引之后，当某篇发表在《中国图书馆学报》上论文频次达到9次时，则该论文的总被引频次最有可能是28.7次。

5.2 条件均值的总体线性回归分析

为考察预测效果，本文利用SPSS 18.0统计分析工具对各年累计被引频次下总被引频次均值的变化特征进行线性回归分析，回归分析结果如表6所示。

表 6　样本期刊总被引频次条件均值的线性回归分析结果

发表时间	《中国图书馆学报》				《图书馆》				《图书与情报》			
	R	R^2	调整 R^2	标准估计误差	R	R^2	调整 R^2	标准估计误差	R	R^2	调整 R^2	标准估计误差
3 年	0. 910[a]	0. 828	0. 823	24. 7	0. 844[a]	0. 712	0. 695	23. 6	0. 864[a]	0. 747	0. 727	9. 8
4 年	0. 955[a]	0. 912	0. 910	16. 4	0. 897[a]	0. 804	0. 795	17. 2	0. 911[a]	0. 830	0. 821	7. 6
5 年	0. 976[a]	0. 953	0. 952	11. 7	0. 929[a]	0. 863	0. 858	11. 2	0. 859[a]	0. 738	0. 725	10. 1
6 年	0. 983[a]	0. 967	0. 966	9. 6	0. 949[a]	0. 901	0. 897	12. 5	0. 910[a]	0. 829	0. 821	8. 0

a. 预测变量：（常量）。下同。

如表 6 所示，分析结果的判定系数 R^2 都较高（最大值为 1），表明线性回归的结果对数据拟合得较好，大部分总被引频次条件均值的变异，都能由累计被引频次来说明。总体上，随着发表时间的增长，拟合优度越来越好（判定系数 R^2 接近 1），且复相关系数 R 越趋近于 1。这是由于发表时间越长，累计被引频次就越接近总被引频次。相比之下，当论文发表时间相同时，《中国图书馆学报》的拟合优度最好，且《中国图书馆学报》刊载论文的总被引频次只需经过较短时间（3 ～ 4 年）就能被累计被引频次很好地解释（预测）；《图书馆》,《图书与情报》的拟合优度相对较低。

5. 3　条件均值的分段线性回归分析

当论文的发表时间较短时，大部分的期刊论文都集中于低累计被引区域，而高累计被引次数下的总被引频次分布又相对分散，因此可以对总被引频次相对集中或分散的区域单独进行线性回归分析，即根据累计被引频次下总被引频次的分布特征，将累计被引频次分为高低被引两个区域（以低被引标准为界限），分别对两个区域内不同累计被引次数下总被引频次均值的演变轨迹进行线性回归分析。

（1）低累计被引次数下总被引频次均值演变轨迹的线性回归分析。利用 SPSS 18. 0 统计分析工具，对不同低累计被引次数（表 5 中累计被引次数小于 10 次的部分）下总被引频次的均值分布规律进行线性回归分析，结果如表 7 所示。

表 7　样本期刊低累计被引次数的线性回归分析结果

发表时间	《中国图书馆学报》				《图书馆》				《图书与情报》			
	R	R^2	调整 R^2	标准估计误差	R	R^2	调整 R^2	标准估计误差	R	R^2	调整 R^2	标准估计误差
3 年	0. 975[a]	0. 951	0. 945	2. 1	0. 926[a]	0. 857	0. 839	2. 8	0. 866[a]	0. 751	0. 720	3. 5
4 年	0. 964[a]	0. 930	0. 921	1. 5	0. 960[a]	0. 922	0. 912	1. 5	0. 865[a]	0. 748	0. 717	3. 7
5 年	0. 959[a]	0. 920	0. 910	1. 5	0. 977[a]	0. 954	0. 949	0. 9	0. 924[a]	0. 854	0. 836	1. 8
6 年	0. 974[a]	0. 948	0. 942	0. 8	0. 984[a]	0. 968	0. 964	0. 7	0. 951[a]	0. 904	0. 892	1. 6

从表7可看出，所测算的判定系数 R^2 值都较高，表明线性回归分析的结果对数据拟合得较好。相比于总体线性回归分析结果，低累计被引次数区域的判定系数 R^2 在整体上均较高，表明低累计被引次数的线性回归拟合优度更好。低累计被引区域线性回归标准估计的误差值要远远小于总体线性回归分析的误差，表明低累计被引次数的线性回归结果与实际值的误差相对较小，拟合精度更高。同时，相比于总体线性回归分析结果，低累计被引区域的线性回归模型达到较高的拟合优度所需要的时间更短，并且标准估计的误差值更小。

（2）高累计被引次数下总被引频次均值演变轨迹的线性回归分析。采用同样的方法对不同高累计被引频次下（累计被引次数大于9次）总被引频次均值分布特征进行线性回归分析，结果如表8所示。

表8 样本期刊高累计被引次数的线性回归分析

发表时间	《中国图书馆学报》				《图书馆》				《图书与情报》			
	R	R^2	调整 R^2	标准估计误差	R	R^2	调整 R^2	标准估计误差	R	R^2	调整 R^2	标准估计误差
3年	0.876[a]	0.767	0.757	29.6	0.742[a]	0.551	0.487	36.6	0.260[a]	0.068	-0.243	17.5
4年	0.941[a]	0.886	0.882	18.7	0.860[a]	0.739	0.719	22.7	0.816[a]	0.666	0.624	10.7
5年	0.970[a]	0.941	0.940	13.1	0.901[a]	0.811	0.800	14.0	0.682[a]	0.465	0.412	13.3
6年	0.980[a]	0.960	0.959	10.7	0.933[a]	0.870	0.862	16.0	0.826[a]	0.681	0.655	10.4

分析可知，在三种期刊中，只有《中国图书馆学报》在发表时间达到4年及以后的判定系数 R^2 大于0.85，表现出较好的拟合优度；《图书馆》与《图书与情报》的判定系数 R^2 值都较低，拟合效果不好。相比于被引频次条件均值的总体线性回归结果，发表时间相同时，此次回归分析的判定系数偏小，拟合优度不如总体线性回归结果。例如，表8中《中国图书馆学报》发表时间为3年时判定系数 R^2 的值为0.767，而表6中对应的值为0.828。

5.4 总被引频次数学模型预测方法的设定

由前文的分析可知，低累计被引频次下总被引频次条件次均值分布规律的回归结果一直保持很好的拟合优度，而对于高累计被引次数区域，总体线性回归分析结果具有更高的拟合优度。因此当论文的发表时间大于2年时，本研究将预测某篇期刊论文最终获得总被引频次（X）的方法设定为：当累计被引频次 N 小于10次时，采用低累计被引频次下总被引频次条件均值分布规律的回归模型进行预测；当累计被引频次 N 大于9次时，采用总体线性回归模型进行预测。各自回归分析所得的系数和常量如表9和表10所示。

表9 总体线性回归分析的结果

发表时间	《中国图书馆学报》				《图书馆》				《图书与情报》			
	3年	4年	5年	6年	3年	4年	5年	6年	3年	4年	5年	6年
常量 w	1.35	-0.28	-0.44	-0.06	0.27	-1.99	-2.12	-2.49	0.84	3.17	4.60	3.32
系数 r	2.48	1.91	1.60	1.40	2.60	2.05	1.76	1.60	2.98	1.75	1.39	1.32

表 10　低累计被引区域的回归分析结果

发表时间	《中国图书馆学报》				《图书馆》				《图书与情报》			
	3 年	4 年	5 年	6 年	3 年	4 年	5 年	6 年	3 年	4 年	5 年	6 年
常量 w	0.69	1.23	0.26	1.02	2.00	1.20	1.35	1.13	4.38	2.08	2.25	0.93
系数 r	2.90	1.68	1.57	1.10	2.10	1.61	1.21	1.14	1.87	1.96	1.39	1.52

当论文的发表时间大于 2 年时，预测该论文的总被引频次 X 的方法为用实时累计被引频次 N 乘以对应的系数 r 再加上对应的常数 w，为便于计算，同样对最终的计算结果取整，其表达式如下：

$$X = \mathrm{int}(r \times N + w)。$$

5.5　总被引频次数学模型预测方法的实证分析

根据前文分析的总被引频次数学模型预测方法，对 2001 年三种期刊刊载的论文进行实证分析。计算方法是，依据某篇论文的各年累计被引次数按照数学模型的计算方法，预测该论文最终可能获得总被引频次，并将预测结果与实际值进行对比分析，分析结果如表 11 所示。

表 11　样本期刊总被引频次预测实证分析结果

发表时间	《中国图书馆学报》			《图书馆》			《图书与情报》		
	低被引个数	高低准确个数	准确率	低被引个数	高低准确个数	准确率	低被引个数	高低准确数	准确率
3 年	95	80	84.2%	132	112	84.8%	81	66	81.5%
4 年	84	73	86.9%	124	115	92.7%	74	59	79.7%
5 年	77	64	83.1%	112	104	92.9%	71	59	83.1%
6 年	67	61	91.0%	111	107	96.4%	68	58	85.3%

表 11 中各列值分别表示：论文发表的时间、累计被引次数为低被引的论文个数、准确预测出累计被引次数为低被引的论文在最终是否为高被引的个数、本文模型的预测准确率。

由实证分析可知，随着发表时间的增长，数学模型对总被引频次的预测结果标准差更小，预测结果更准确；在较短的发表时间内，对累计被引次数为低被引的论文其总被引频次是否为高被引的预测准确度均已达到 80% 以上。如表 11 所示，当发表时间为 3 年时，累计被引频次为低被引的论文总共有 95 篇，以前 3 年的累计被引频次为基础，通过数学模型对这 95 篇论文进行总被引频次预测分析，其中准确预测到 29 篇高被引论文和 51 篇低被引论文，总计准确预测到 80 篇，准确度为 84.2%。实证结果表明回归分析所得数学模型对总被引频次的预测较好；相对于高累计被引区域，低累计被引区域回归分析结果的误差更小，其数学模型对总被引频次的预测更准确。总之，经过实证分析表明，通过回归分析得到的数学模型比较理想，能较准确地预测某篇论文的总被引频次。

6 总　结

低被引期刊论文学术价值的评价是一个复杂的过程，本文从纯定量角度对低被引期刊论文学术价值的评价方法进行了探讨。将论文发表时间纳入评价体系中，对发表在不同时间段的论文采用不同的评价方法，从而提高了期刊论文学术价值的评价结果的准确性。

参考文献

[1] 聂超，朱国祥. H指数在科研评价中的缺陷及其对策 [J]. 情报理论与实践，2009 (11)：1-2.
[2] Anderson T R, Hankin R K S, Killworth P D. Beyond the Durfee Square: Enhancing the H-Index to Score Total Publication Output [J]. Scientometrics, 2008, 76 (3): 577-588.
[3] 杨利军，万小渝. 期刊论文低被引标准的界定方法 [J]. 情报理论与实践，2013，36 (7)：51-53.
[4] 叶继元. 人文社会科学评价体系探讨 [J]. 南京大学学报，2010 (1)：97-110.
[5] 陈进寿. 从人际关系谈同行评议制的改进 [J]. 中国科学基金，2002 (3)：182-184.
[6] 马晓光，连燕华，沈全锋，等. 同行评议中专家识别研究 [J]. 研究与发展管理，2003 (3)：68-72.
[7] 赵黎明，徐孝涵，张卫东. 对同行评议专家的反评估分析 [J]. 中国科学基金，1995 (1)：62-66.
[8] 欧翠珍. 核心期刊在广东高校科研奖励机制中的应用及其评价 [C] //第四届中国科技期刊发展论坛论文集. 北京：中国科学技术出版社，2008：213-220.
[9] 金铁成. 科技论文评价中存在的三大误区 [J]. 中国科技期刊研究，2004 (3)：284-286.
[10] 刘艳阳，吴丹青，吴光豪，等. SCI用作科研评价指标的思考 [J]. 科研管理，2003 (5)：59-64.
[11] 卢秉福，霍丽华. 刍议SCI在科研评价体系中的作用 [J]. 科研管理，2007 (增刊)：180-183.
[12] 徐建国. 定量分析评价科技论文质量 [J]. 情报学刊，1985 (6)：22-23
[13] 杨建明. "定量分析评价科技论文质量" 得与失 [J]. 情报学刊，1987 (5)：51-52.
[14] 任全娥. 人文社会科学成果评价研究 [M]. 北京：中国社会科学出版社，2010：241-257.
[15] 卜卫，周海宏，刘晓红. 社会科学成果价值评估 [M]. 北京：社会科学文献出版社，1995：158-170.
[16] 何川. 科技期刊论文质量的评价指标与方法 [C]//科技编辑出版研究文集：第八集. 成都：四川科学技术出版社，2005：80-83.
[17] 李学孟，李倩. 科技论文质量量化指标初探 [J]. 郑州工学院学报，1996 (2)：114-118.
[18] 杨亚晶，左惠凯. 高校学术论文质量评估及其数学模型 [J]. 现代情报，2005 (11)：191-192.
[19] 潘峰. 科技论文质量定量评估数学模型研究 [J]. 昆明理工大学学报，1996 (2)：6-10.
[20] 张静. 引文、引文分析与学术论文评价 [J]. 管理论坛，2008 (1)：33-38.
[21] 汪再非，杨国祥. 学术期刊对科研的评价作用 [J]. 科技管理研究，2006 (11)：170-172.
[22] 刘宇，叶继元，袁曦临. 图书情报学期刊的分层结构：基于同行评议的实证研究 [J]. 中国图书馆学报，2011 (192)：105-114.

教师简介：

徐健，男，2000年在西安交通大学获学士学位，2003年在中山大学获硕士学位，2010年在中国科学院获情报学博士学位。2003起任教于中山大学资讯管理学院，副教授，硕士生导师。主讲“信息技术与档案馆”、“网络开发工具与技术”、“数据结构”等课程。主要研究方向为智能信息处理、术语相似度计算及应用技术、网络用户情感分析。目前主持一项教育部社会科学项目“从科技文献中挖掘术语相似性及其在知识发现中的应用”，一项国家社会科学基金项目“用户评论情感分析及其在竞争情报服务中的应用研究”，并参与多项国家、省部级科研项目工作。已发表研究论文40余篇，学术专著1部。2014年1月至2015年1月美国印第安纳大学计算与信息学院访问学者。联系方式：issxj@mail. sysu. edu. cn。

所选论文《基于多种测度的术语相似度集成计算研究》原载于《情报学报》2013年第6期

基于多种测度的术语相似度集成计算研究*

徐　健

摘　要：在对当前术语语义相似度集成相关研究进行分析的基础上，针对典型集成方法存在的不足，构建了基于多种测度的术语相似度集成计算模型。首先对集成计算模型的设计思路进行论述；其次提出了在模型中应用的相似度网络初始化算法、术语语词相似度改进算法、术语语境模板相似度改进算法以及基于搜索引擎的术语相似度改进算法，并实现了该集成计算模型；最后对该模型中所使用的各种相似度测度计算性能指标以及完全计算SVM集成和条件计算SVM集成性能指标进行对比评测。实验证明，该计算模型的F_1综合性能达到0.8797，并能缩短32%的计算时间，有效提升了术语相似度综合计算性能。

关键词：术语相似度；相似度集成；相似度计算

Term Similarity Integration Computation Model Based on Multiple Measure

Jian Xu

Abstract: Based on analysis of current study on term semantic similarity integration, the paper construct a multiple measure based term semantic similarity integration computation model. Firstly, the paper discusses the designing of integration computation model. Secondly, similarity network initialization algorithm, improved lexical similarity algorithm, improved context similarity algorithm and improved similarity algorithm based on

* 该文系国家社会科学基金项目“用户评论情感分析及其在竞争情报服务中的应用研究”（项目编号：11CTQ022）成果之一。

search engine are presented, and the model are realized. Finally, comparative experiments are conducted under condition of all kinds of improved similarity algorithms, fully computing SVM integration model and conditional computing SVM integration model. Experiments show that the model reaches 0.8797 on F_1 measure, and can shorten computing time up to 32%, therefore, effectively improve the comprehensive performance of term similarity calculation.

Keywords: Term similarity; Similarity integration; Similarity computation

1 引　　言

术语代表了特定的领域概念，如实体、过程以及功能等。通过对术语之间相似度的计算，能够为术语规范化、识别同义/近义词、术语聚类、基于实例的机器翻译等自然语言处理和知识挖掘任务的开展提供重要支持。[1-2] 在本体构建和知识库构建任务中，通过计算术语语义相似度，能够发现术语之间存在的新关系，并在此基础上实现本体自动构建。[3-4]

目前已经有学者从不同角度提出了多种术语相似度计算方法，但从整体来看，各种相似度算法计算性能还存在提升空间，在计算适用范围方面也面临种种限制。本文在对当前术语相似度集成相关研究进行分析的基础上，针对典型方法存在的不足，构建了基于多种测度的术语语义相似度集成计算模型。首先对基于多种测度的术语语义相似度计算模型的设计思路进行论述，在此基础上描述了集成计算模型实现过程，最后对该模型中所使用的各种相似度测度计算性能指标以及该模型在完全计算和条件计算情况下的集成性能指标进行对比评测，以验证该模型的实际效果。

2 相关研究

由于术语间的相似性度量是多种自然语言处理任务和知识发现任务开展的重要基础，因此对术语之间的语义相似度的研究具有较长的历史，到目前为止大致经历了三个阶段的发展。

（1）从 20 世纪 70 年代到 90 年代初的相似度概念相关研究阶段。这个阶段重点解决术语语义相似度的概念如何界定，以及基于概念界定，如何进行术语语义相似度的有效计算问题。具有代表性的理论有：Hindle[5] 从互信息（mutual information）的角度提出了他对相似性测度的理解，并将基于互信息的语词相似度计算方法应用于英语语词的分类任务中；Resnik[6] 从信息内容（information content）的角度对分类体系中的类目相似度进行了描述，他认为分类体系中类目的相似性可以通过它们之间共有的信息量来衡量。

（2）从 20 世纪 90 年代初到 2000 年前后的简单相似度计算方法研究阶段。该阶段研究重点放在如何找到简单、有效的单一相似度指标，进行术语相似度计算。最具代表性的算法有：Bourigault[7] 等人提出，术语的语词构成，也就是中心词（head）和修饰部分（modifiers）可以作为测度语词相似性的重要标志，并在一个半自动术语抽取的系统中，借助术语中心词和修饰部分特征来构造候选术语网络，进而便利了人工对候选术语的验证；Hearst[8] 认为特定句法形式可能传达了术语之间的某种关联性，可以通过找到更多的句法模板，并识别这些句法模板所暗示的语义关联，来发现实体之间的特定语义关系。

（3）从2000年前后到目前的多相似度指标集成方法研究阶段。该阶段相关研究主要集中在如何将多种术语相似度指标有效集成来提高相似度计算精度，以及基于搜索引擎等网络资源的术语相似度计算问题。具有代表性的理论有：Goran 等人[9]使用线性加权方法，将基于语词相似度的指标、基于句法相似度的指标和基于语境相似度的指标进行了综合，得到更加全面和精确的语词相似度测度。基于搜索引擎等网络资源的术语相似度计算方法将相似度计算所依赖的文集范围扩大到了整个 Web，因此能够较好地解决基于有限文集的相似度计算方法中因实例数过少而无法计算的问题。具有代表性的算法有：Bollegala 等人[10]认为可以将搜索引擎命中数指标和语词在结果页面的摘要中出现的模式指标进行综合，训练二类的支持向量机来计算语词之间的相似度。

国内关于语词相似性的研究主要集中在以下四个方面。

（1）利用语义知识库计算词语语义相似度的算法研究。具有代表性的算法有：荀恩东等人[11]借助 WordNet 的同义词词集、类属信息、意义解释构造向量空间，计算英语词语的相似度。刘群等人[12]提出了一种利用知网中词义所用义原之间关系来计算词语相似度的方法。李素建等人[13]提出了加权合并同义词词林的词义相似度和知网语义表达式的义原相似度的词语相似度计算方法。徐硕等人[14]针对传统算法未考虑原子术语顺序差异对构建原子术语对应关系的影响，提出了一种基于同义词词林的双序列对比中文术语语义相似度计算方法。还有较多相关研究在此基础上提出了基于知网或同义词词林的词语相似度计算改进算法。[15-19]这类算法的相关研究最多，针对一般词语相似度计算也能取得较好的效果。但是对于特定领域术语相似度计算而言，术语间存在的相似性与其在一般意义上的相似性可能有所不同。例如，一般意义上来讲“医生”与“护士”应该是相似的，都属于医务工作者；但是在卫生医疗领域中，更强调“医生”与“护士”之间的差异而非相似性。因此，基于 WordNet、知网或同义词词林等通用语义知识库的相似度算法对于识别特定领域术语相似度而言并不完全适用。

（2）基于领域本体的概念相似度计算研究。代表性算法有：滕广青等人[20]通过提炼概念的对象（外延）与属性（内涵）构建概念格，进而通过比较概念格相似度来获得概念之间的相似度值。徐德智等人[21]基于领域本体中节点之间最短路径及各边的权值，并据此计算概念间的语义相似度。张忠平等人[22]提出一种综合考虑语义距离和本体库统计特征的概念间相似度计算方法，将概念的深度、语义重合度以及概念间强度的影响因素也引入计算过程。周剑烽[23]在基于本体的一般相似度计算模型基础上加入了实例、概念和实例的关系以及实例间的关系等因素，取得了较好的相似度计算效果。这类算法主要借助领域本体中概念的位置信息以及语义信息计算相似度，在进行特定领域概念相似度计算时能取得不错的效果，但是受制于领域本体存在及质量的先决条件，使得该方法存在一定的适用局限性。

（3）基于网络资源的语词相似度计算研究。典型算法有：盛志超等人[24]基于维基百科的页面链接信息，通过模仿人类联想的方式计算不同词之间的相似度。徐健等人[25]将语义上下文和领域上下文引入检索式构造过程，借助搜索引擎检索命中数来计算特定领域术语相似度。这类算法依托丰富的网络知识资源进行相似度计算。由于计算过程中需要大量的网络访问，使得这类算法在时间性能上并不存在优势。

(4) 基于语词的各种语义相似度计算方法的应用研究。例如，占飞等人[26]利用WordNet和上下文信息进行词语相似度计算，并用于生成英文辅助写作时的相关提示词。吴健等人[27]基于本体进行词汇语义相似度计算，用于进行Web服务的相似度计算。胡俊峰等人[28]基于上下文词汇向量空间模型近似描述词汇的语义，在此基础上开发了具有词义联想功能的唐宋诗搜索引擎。

在众多术语相似度测度相关研究中，有三种类型相似度测度受到广泛关注：①利用术语在单词级别和/或单词集合级别的语词构件相似特征，来计算术语之间相似程度的语词相似度测度[9,30-31]；②通过测量术语在语句中出现语境的相似性来间接衡量术语相似度的语境模板相似度测度[5,9,32-33]；③利用网络知识资源来计算术语相似度的相似度测度[34-37]。在对这些相似度测度进行分析后，不难发现它们存在着鲜明的计算特性。本文从优点、缺点两个方面对这些相似度测度的特点进行了总结（表1）。

表1　三种类型的相似度测度特点分析

项　目	优　点	缺　点
语词相似度测度	不需要训练语料，可以直接计算相似度，准确率较高	只能从“形”上计算相似度，计算召回率不高
语境模板相似度测度	召回率相对较高	需要对语料进行解析来获取术语语境模板，计算效果受语料库质量和大小影响
基于网络知识资源的相似度测度	Web语料库容量大，能够有效解决基于特定语料库计算时的实例稀缺性问题	需要访问网络，计算效果受到搜索引擎或特定知识资源性能的制约，计算速度较慢

从表1可以看到，上述相似度测度在适用性和计算效果方面各有优劣，具有很强的互补性。如果能将各种术语相似度测度进行有机集成，应该能够突破各种相似度测度单独计算时存在的局限性，获得更好的综合计算效果。

目前术语相似度测度集成的相关研究可以归纳为三种思路，分别是以章成志[38]和Goran等人[9]的相关研究为代表的基于线性加权的集成方法，以Neshati等人[32]的相关研究为代表的基于神经网络的集成方法，以及以Bollegala等人[10]的相关研究为代表的基于SVM（Support Vector Machine，支持向量机）的搜索引擎相似度测度集成方法。基于线性加权的集成方法具有原理简单、易于实现的优点，但是各项相似度测度权值设定难于确定，而不合理的权值设定会影响到集成的整体效果。基于神经网络的集成方法具有对非线性数据快速建模的能力，能够通过对训练集的反复学习来调节自身的网络结构和连接权值，但是神经网络从某种意义上可以看作一种启发式的学习机制，本身有较强的经验成分。SVM是Cortes和Vapnik于1995年首先提出[39]，它在解决小样本、非线性及高维模式识别中表现出许多特有的优势，目前已在关系类型探测[40]、文本分类[41-42]等任务中得到成功应用。基于SVM的集成方法克服了传统神经网络存在的问题，在特定训练样本的学习精度和无错误地识别任意样本的能力之间寻求最佳折衷，以获得最好的推广能力。目前基于SVM的相似度测度集成研究较少，Bollegala等人的研究也只是将SVM应用于搜索引擎相似度测度的集成研究。

3 术语相似度集成计算模型设计

本文针对当前术语相似度集成相关典型方法存在的不足，构建了基于 SVM 机器学习实现各种类型术语相似度测度集成的计算模型。利用 SVM 快速学习和自动分类的特点，对多种改进的术语相似度测度计算方法进行集成，并将条件计算流程引入集成计算过程中，以期提升计算效果，减少集成计算时间。

术语相似度测度集成计算可分为两个阶段，分别是学习阶段和计算阶段。在学习阶段，使用语词相似度测度、语境模板相似度测度、基于搜索引擎的相似度测度以及人工判断结果构成的向量集合，自动训练得到 SVM 分类模型。在计算阶段，可以采用具有条件判断机制的相似度计算流程简化部分相似度计算。对于达不到条件判断阈值的术语对可使用在学习阶段训练获得的分类模型对其进行自动分类，以判断其相似性。

基于多种测度的术语相似度集成计算模型的学习阶段模型设计如图 1 所示。

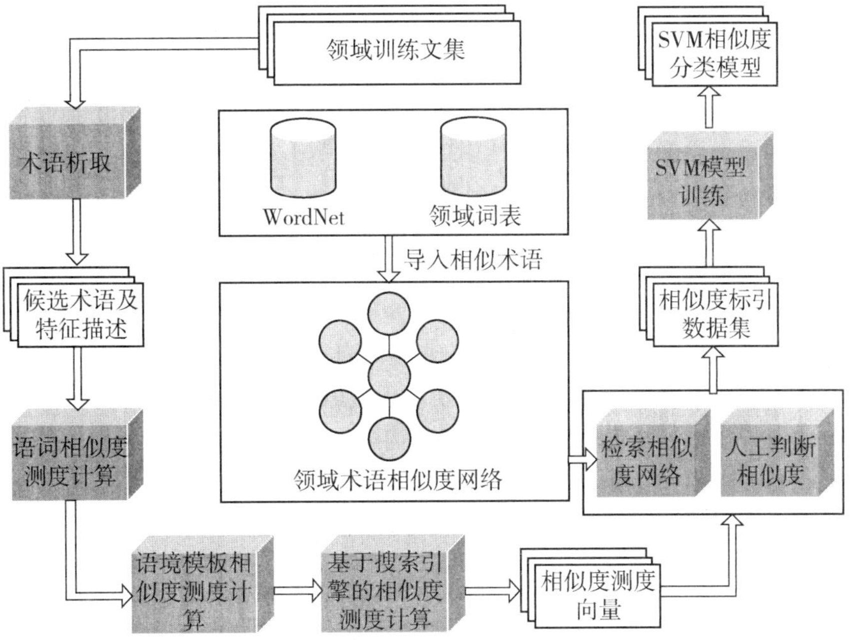

图 1　基于多种测度的术语相似度集成计算——学习阶段模型

基于多种测度的术语相似度集成计算模型的计算阶段模型设计如图 2 所示。

在上述两个模型中，虽然基本模块功能类似，但是由于学习阶段和计算阶段的目标设定有所不同，因此各模块所起到的效用以及计算流程设计等方面也存在较大差别。

（1）领域术语相似度网络的初始化和应用。领域术语相似度网络在模型中提供了相似术语对保存、检索等功能。在学习阶段，可以从 WordNet[43] 或领域词表导入相关领域中自动判断为相似的术语，并记录术语间相似程度，形成基本的领域术语相似度网络。以 WordNet 为例，该词表以同义词、异形词、反义词等方式揭示了语词之间的相似关系。

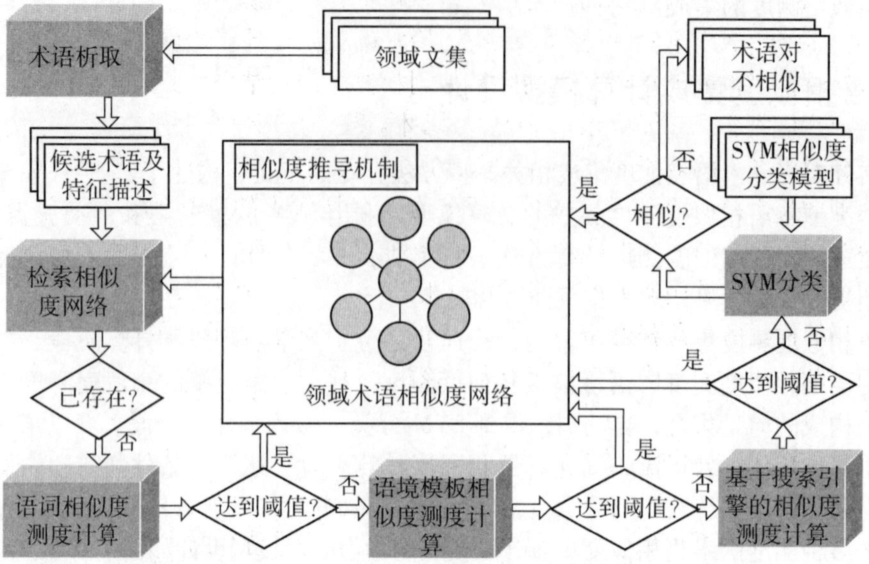

图2　基于多种测度的术语相似度集成计算——计算阶段模型

通过检索WordNet的方式，快速获得部分候选术语的相似语词集合。在构造学习阶段所使用到的训练集时，通过检索相似度网络可以自动判断部分术语对的相似度结果，从而减轻人工判断负担。在计算阶段，可以首先用待计算术语对在相似度网络中检索，如果已经通过检索就可以判断出术语对之间存在相似关系时，后续流程操作将提前终止，以有效减少总体计算时间消耗。此外，计算过程中被判断为相似的术语对会被保存到相似度网络中。在经过大量的相似度计算后，可以形成基本覆盖特定领域的术语相似度网络。该网络可以直接作为相似度判断的快捷工具，也可为领域内的其他处理任务（如基于术语相似度关系的术语聚类任务）提供高效、可复用的优质数据源。

（2）语词相似度、语境模板相似度以及基于搜索引擎的相似度测度计算。在学习阶段，训练集的各种相似度测度被分别计算，以构造出相似度测度向量，用于进行SVM分类模型训练。在计算阶段，各种相似度测度计算模块间加入了阈值条件判断。一旦某个计算步骤的术语相似度测度计算结果大于设定阈值，则该术语对被判断为相似并保存到领域术语相似度网络中，而后续流程中的操作将会提前终止，从而节省了整体计算时间。

（3）SVM相似度分类模型训练与应用。在学习阶段，当所有训练集中的术语对完成各项相似度测度计算和相似度标引后，使用SVM模型训练工具对其进行训练，获得相似度分类模型。在训练阶段，利用学习阶段获得的SVM分类模型，对各种相似度计算获得的相似度测度进行集成，为术语间的相似关系作出最终判断。

4　术语相似度集成计算模型实现

4.1　相似度网络初始化

相似度网络是将特定领域内通过计算判断为相似的术语表示为节点，将术语之间的相似关系表示为节点之间连线而构造的网络。在集成计算模型内，相似度网络的构建可以有效避免术语相似度重复计算。在每次开始术语相似度计算之前，先通过术语相似度网络进行检索，如果能够检索到，则直接得到相似度判断结果。此外，相似度网络还可以提供相似度检索、推导等功能，并可为领域术语聚类等知识发现任务的开展提供支持。

术语相似度网络的效用随着网络规模增长而增长。因此，如何让术语相似度网络以更快的速度增长也是一个值得考虑的问题。本文以抽取出的所有领域术语作为检索词，通过调用开源软件 JAWS[44] 提供的 WordNet 检索接口，在 WordNet 3.0 中检索获取相似术语，并将这些术语及其相似关系存储到术语相似度网络中。在对 537 个基因工程领域术语进行 WordNet 检索后，共获得 94 个术语对应的 1540 个相似关系。在后续的相似度计算过程中，被判断为相似的术语对会不断增加到该相似度网络中。

4.2 术语语词相似度测度计算

在现有的主要术语相似度计算思路中，基于语词构成特征的术语相似度计算思路基本不需要除术语本身以外的其他语料资源支持，其计算具有直接性和快捷性等特点，因此得到了广泛的应用。本文中所使用的语词相似度算法在 Nenadic 算法[9] 基础上进行了两方面改进，使其综合计算性能得到有效提升。

（1）在 Nenadic 算法中，术语中心词和术语修饰词的匹配计算都是基于单词直接匹配来实现的。通过实验观察发现，一些相似术语对的中心词互为字面形式不同的同义词、近义词，这就导致了 Nenadic 算法在计算这类术语时容易失效。例如，在相似术语对“Genetic Mutation”（基因变异）和“Genetic Variation”（基因变异）中，术语中心词“Mutation”和“Variation”互为同义词，但在术语字面形式上相差较大，因此无法通过 Nenadic 算法获得有效计算结果。本文在中心词匹配过程中引入 WordNet 同义词、近义词检索功能，以中心词部分的语义匹配来替代字面匹配，从而达到提升相似度计算效果的目的。此外，对于那些修饰词以及在 WordNet 中查询不到的中心词而言，采用 Nenadic 算法中的简单字面匹配方法很难对相似术语对“visualisation”（可视化）和“visualization”（可视化）作出正确判断。本文采用编辑距离法与词干法相结合的方法，通过术语词语的模糊匹配来解决上述问题。这里词干算法使用了当前应用较为广泛的 Porter Stemmer 算法[45]，编辑距离算法使用了公认效果较好的 Jaro-Winkler distance 算法[46]。两术语组成单词之间的相似度计算采用如下公式：

$$sim(w_{t1i},w_{t2j}) = \begin{cases} d_w(w_{t1i},w_{t2j}), & \text{if } d_w(w_{t1i},w_{t2j}) \geq 0.8 \\ 0, & \text{if } d_w(w_{t1i},w_{t2j}) < 0.8 \\ 1, & \text{if}(w_{t1i} \,\&\, w_{t2j}) \in head\ words \,\&\, w_{t1j} \in Synonyms(w_{t2i}) \end{cases} \quad。\qquad (1)$$

式中：w_{t1i}和 w_{t2j}分别表示术语 t_1 和 t_2 中的任意子序列。$sim(w_{t1i}, w_{t2j})$ 表示两术语中任意子序列之间的相似度。$Synonyms(w_{t2j})$ 表示通过查询 WordNet 获得的中心词 w_{t2j}的同义词、近义词集合。如果两词为各自所属术语的中心词，则先检索 WordNet 判断两者是否互为同义词、近义词，如果是则返回值 1，否则按两个一般单词来计算相似度。$d_w(w_{t1i}, w_{t2j})$ 表示通过编辑距离公式计算获得的单词 w_{t1i}和 w_{t2j}之间的编辑距离。通过实验观察确定这里的相似度阈值取 0.8 较为合适。$d_w(w_{t1i}, w_{t2j})$ 计算首先采用 Porter Stemmer 算法获取待计算单词的词干表达，然后采用 Jaro-Winkler distance 算法计算单词之间的编辑距离。

（2）根据英语语言学研究成果，与术语中心词距离越近的修饰词在相似度计算时所贡献的权重应该越大。[47] 以术语对“induced pluripotent stem cell”（诱导多能干细胞）和“embryonic stem cell”（胚胎干细胞）为例，两者的修饰词分别为“induced”、“pluripotent”、“stem”以及“embryonic”、“stem”。与其他修饰词相比，距离术语中心词最近的术语修饰词“stem”的语义修饰限定作用最为明显，而随着与术语中心词的距离增加，术语修饰词的语义表达能力逐次下降。本文认为，可以根据与术语中心词之间距离的远近特征为术语修饰词分配不同的相似度权重，从而更加客观地体现术语之间的相似程度。公式（2）作为相似度权重的分配函数，对中心词和修饰词进行统一权重分配。

$$Weight(w_{t1i}, w_{t2j}) = \frac{\frac{1}{d(w_{t1i})+1} + \frac{1}{d(w_{t2j})+1}}{2} \text{。} \tag{2}$$

式中：$d(w_{t1i})$ 表示词语 w_{t1i} 与 t_1 术语中心词之间的距离；$d(w_{t2j})$ 表示词语 w_{t2j} 与 t_2 术语中心词之间的距离。随着修饰词与中心词之间的距离增大，$Weight(w_{t1i}, w_{t2j})$ 会越来越小。

对上述公式进行综合后得到术语语词相似度计算公式（3）：

$$LS(t_1, t_2) = \frac{\sum_{i=0}^{|t_1|-1} \max_{j=0}^{|t_2|-1} sim(w_{t1i}, w_{t2j}) \cdot Weight(w_{t1i}, w_{t2j})}{\sum_{l=0}^{\max(|t_1|,|t_2|)-1} \frac{1}{l+1}} \text{。} \tag{3}$$

式中：t_1 和 t_2 为需要计算语词相似度的术语对；$sim(w_{t1i}, w_{t2j})$ 表示术语 t_1 中第 i 个单词与术语 t_2 中第 j 个单词之间的相似度值；$Weight(w_{t1i}, w_{t2j})$ 表示根据与各自术语中心词之间的距离，为 w_{t1i} 和 w_{t2j} 分配的相似度权重；分母中 l 的取值范围为［0，max（|t1|，|t2|）］，即下限为0，上限为 t_1 和 t_2 两个术语单词个数的最大值。分母确保了整个计算结果始终处于［0，1］范围内。

在集成计算模型中，术语语词相似度测度计算排列在计算流程的第二步，是由其准确率高、计算速度快的特点所决定的。将语词相似度计算安排在靠前的位置，当计算结果达到设定阈值时，就可以认为该术语对相似，从而提早结束计算流程，为大规模术语相似度计算节约时间。

4.3 术语语境模板相似度测度计算

在集成计算模型中的第三步是术语的语境模板相似度计算，本文在 Goran 等人[9] 提出的基于 N-Gram 语境模板截取和匹配的相似度计算方法基础上，对语境模板的获取机制进行了改进。

Goran 等人所采用的基于 N-Gram 语境模板截取和匹配的方法，与基于窗口的方法相比提升了语境特征质量，但是语境特征仍然局限在术语邻近位置（与 N-Gram 语境模板截取时的 N 值相关），因此对于语句中相距术语位置较远、却具有强句法关联的语境模板特征难于获取，也就不能更加全面、客观地反映术语语境。本文借助句法依赖关系构造语境模板，试图突破基于窗口的计算方法以及基于 N-Gram 语境模板截取方法的局限性，在全句范围内解析获得术语的高质量语境模板特征，以期有效提升计算效果。在这一过程中，句法依赖关系的获取精度直接影响着语境模板相似度计算结果。本文使用 Stanford Dependencies[48] 来实现句法依赖关系解析。Stanford Dependencies 能够将语句中的语词依赖关系以二元组的形式表示出来，并对关系类型进行了标注。这些关系并不局限于与术语直接邻接的语词，那些相隔距离较远的语词间关系也可以被较好地解析出来。根据 Daniel 等人[49] 的评测结果，Stanford Dependencies 的解析 F_1 综合测度达到 87.2%。此外，Stanford Dependencies 解析获得的模板在长度上适中，均为两部分语词构成的模板，这为模板匹配操作提供了便利条件。

以下面的句子为例：

"Several nutrient-controlled pathways, which regulate cell growth and proliferation, metabolism and stress resistance, have been defined in yeast."

在对目标术语"nutrient-controlled pathways"（营养控制路径）使用"TermX"进行替换后，经过句法解析获得的与目标术语直接相关的依赖关系如图 3 所示。

```
nsubjpass ( define-18, TermX-2 )
nsubj ( regulate-5, TermX-2 )
amod ( TermX-2, several-1 )
rcmod ( TermX-2, regulate-5 )
```

图 3　与目标术语直接相关的依赖关系示例

从解析结果可以看到，在整个语句范围内与目标术语有依赖关系的语词都被标示出来。这些二元关系并不局限于术语出现的位置附近。例如，"nsubjpass（define-18, TermX-2）"表示名词"nutrient-controlled pathways"和动词"define"之间的被动关系。在使用基于窗口的相似度算法和基于 N-Gram 的语境模板截取算法时，由于受到窗口大小限制或 N 值限制，很难捕获该语境特征。本文在获取语句中所有依赖关系之后，对其中与目标术语直接相关的、能够反映术语语境特征的依赖关系进行过滤，可得到高质量的术语语境模板。与 N-Gram 语境模板截取方法相比，该方法所获得的语境模板在语义表达质量上有较大提升，所获得的无效语境模板数量也有明显减少。

基于上述模板获取方法的术语语境相似度计算公式为：

$$CS(t_1,t_2)=\frac{2\times\sum_{i=1}^{m}|CP_{it1}\cap CP_{it2}|\times CPValue(CP_i)}{a+\sum_{j=1}^{n}|CP_j|\times CPValue(CP_j)+\sum_{k=1}^{l}|CP_k|\times CPValue(CP_k)}。\tag{4}$$

式中：$CS(t_1, t_2)$ 表示术语 t_1 和术语 t_2 的语境模板相似度计算结果；m 为与 t_1 和 t_2 相关联的总模板数；n 为 t_1 相关联的语境模板数；l 为 t_2 相关联的语境模板数；$|CP|$ 为某种语境模板出现的次数；$CPValue(CP)$ 为模板类型的重要度分值。分子表示 t_1 和 t_2 关联模板的匹配数与模板类型重要度分值乘积的总和，分母表示 t_1 和 t_2 各自相关模板的出现次数乘以模板类型重要度的总和。当术语 t_1 和 t_2 对应的模板完全匹配时，CS 值应为 1，否则为一个小于 1 但大于等于 0 的相似度值。为确保分母始终不为 0，应该为分母加上一个很

小的值 a，如0.001。

4.4 基于搜索引擎的术语相似度测度计算

在集成计算模型中的第四步是基于搜索引擎的相似度计算。与特定语料库中术语共现能够反映术语间相似度的原理类似，在Web网络庞大的语料文档库中的术语共现特征也能被用来作为衡量术语间相似程度的测度。目前已经有学者在利用搜索引擎计算术语相似度方面进行了探索，提出了基于检索命中数的术语相似度算法，典型的有Web-PMI算法[34]、LC-IR算法[50]和Google Distance算法[51]。由于术语本身具有较强的领域特征，直接将这类算法应用于特定科研领域术语相似度计算的效果并不十分理想。

本文结合以下三种方法以引入领域限定因素，提高检索结果质量，并进而提升相似度测度计算效果：

（1）在检索式中添加领域核心词作为领域限定，从而有效减少检索结果的歧义发生，提高检索结果的领域相关度，并间接提升算法效果。

（2）借鉴Sean等人[35]提出的方法，在构造检索式时加入提示词"synonyms"、"antonyms"来实现语义限定，以获取质量更高的检索结果。

（3）以"NEAR"运算符构造检索式能够进一步提高检索返回命中结果的质量。Kenneth等人[11]认为，在较小的语境窗口中的共现可以看作语词之间具有相似性的一个指标，并且如果两个语词在越多的窗口中共现，则它们越相似。可以通过"NEAR"运算符限定两个术语的共现语境窗口大小，则检索结果应能更为准确地反映目标术语对的相似程度。

本文综合运用了以上三种方法来构造具有领域特征的检索式。由于典型算法Web-PMI在适用性和计算效果方面表现都相对较好[35-37,50]，因此本文将上述限定因素引入Web-PMI计算过程，以期获得更好的计算效果。改进后的Web-PMI计算公式为：

$$\text{改进的}\ Web\text{-}PMI(P,Q)=\begin{cases}0 & \text{if } hits(P_{domain}\ NEAR\ Q_{domain})\leqslant c\\ \log_2\left(\dfrac{\dfrac{hits(P_{domain}\ NEAR\ Q_{domain})}{N}}{\dfrac{hits(P_{domain})}{N}\times\dfrac{hits(Q_{domain})}{N}}\right) & \text{otherwise}\end{cases}\text{。} \tag{5}$$

式中：P 和 Q 分别为需要计算相似度的两个术语；P_{domain} 表示术语 P 对应的具有领域限定特征的检索式；$hits$（P_{domain}）表示该检索式检索返回的命中数；$hits$（$P_{domain}\ NEAR\ Q_{domain}$）表示采用"*NEAR*"联合符连接两个具有领域限定特征的术语进行检索返回的命中数；N 为搜索引擎索引的文档规模，这里设置为100亿。当术语 P 和 Q 联合检索的命中数小于等于 c 时，相似度计算结果直接赋值为0。根据实验观察，这里设置 $c=5$ 较为合适。考虑到本文在改进算法上的设计特点，实验中确定采用AltaVista作为搜索引擎进行相似度计算。该搜索引擎可以支持"AND"、"NEAR"等运算符，对检索式的长度也有较宽松的限制，为算法实验提供了较为理想的平台。[52]

由于计算所使用的语料库为Web网络资源，所以该方法受到语料库大小和质量的影响较少，计算准确率和召回率也相对较高；但是该方法在计算过程中需要多次获取搜索引擎检索结果，计算时间较长。因此，该方法作为最后一步相似度测度计算引入集成计算模型。

4.5 相似度测度的 SVM 集成

SVM 模型训练和相似度测度集成功能通过在 LIBSVM 2.9[53] 开源软件的基础上进行开发实现。基于 SVM 的相似度测度集成流程涉及以下 5 个主要步骤：

（1）将训练集转换为 LIBSVM 要求的特定数据格式。为便于一致处理，需要首先将训练集中的相似度测度向量表达为 LIBSVM 要求的规范数据格式。

（2）进行数据缩放规范化处理。为了尽可能减少部分向量分量变化范围大造成对分类结果的干扰，这里使用数值范围 [-1， +1] 对训练集中所有向量分量进行规范化。

（3）核函数最优参数获取。实验中采用的 SVM 核函数为 RBF 核函数，该核函数比较适合维数不高、训练数据量不算特别大的情况，对于相似度测度集成实验是适用的。本实验中采用 LIBSVM 提供的 Grid. py 工具为核函数测试获得最优参数设置。

（4）使用最优参数进行模型训练。输入上一步获得的最优参数，运行 LIBSVM 提供的 Train 工具自动训练获得用于术语相似度判断的 SVM 模型。

（5）测试集计算。在对测试集进行转换数据格式以及数据规范化操作后，使用上一步获得的 SVM 模型对其进行自动分类，获得相似度判断结果。

5 术语相似度集成计算模型评测

5.1 实验数据

本文采用从电子期刊 Springer 网站[54] 下载的基因工程领域专业期刊摘要共 502 篇作为实验测试文集。将其中核心期刊 *Journal of Genetics* 的 82 篇摘要进行术语抽取和人工判断，获得 272 对相似术语和 272 对不相似术语。本文还针对不同规模训练集对 SVM 相似度指标集成效果的影响进行了实验，证明只要测试集规模控制在至少 100 对术语以上，就能够获得比较理想的训练效果。因此随机选取经过人工标注的 300 对术语作为学习阶段的训练集，剩余 244 对术语构成测试集，用于计算阶段测试。[55-56]

5.2 实验过程

实验按照如下步骤依次进行，对各种相似度测度改进算法的计算效果和术语相似度集成效果进行评测。

（1）在相同的实验数据集基础上，分别应用上文中所提出的术语语词相似度测度改进算法、术语语境模板相似度测度改进算法、基于搜索引擎的术语相似度测度改进算法进行计算，并将其计算效果与基准算法进行比较分析，以验证各种改进措施的有效性。

（2）依照第 3 节所提出的学习阶段模型，进行人工标引训练集、相似度网络初始化，并使用改进的语词相似度测度、语境模板相似度测度、基于搜索引擎的术语相似度测度对训练集进行计算，将计算结果存储到相应术语对的相似度测度向量中。基准测度（即Nenadic 语词测度、Nenadic 语境模板测度以及 Web-PMI 测度）也对相同训练集进行了计算，并将计算结果保存下来，以便于后续集成计算效果的对比评测。

（3）在对所有训练集中的术语对进行各项相似度测度计算和相似度标引后，使用SVM 训练工具分别对各种改进测度组合条件下的实验集进行模型训练和自动分类，以验证各种改进相似度测度对集成模型的真实贡献以及相互之间的互补效果。

（4）在训练集上进行训练，获得改进相似度测度的集成 SVM 分类模型和基准测度集成 SVM 分类模型。分类模型将用于计算阶段对术语相似度测度向量的自动分类处理。

（5）采用基准测度的完全计算 SVM 集成对测试集中的术语对进行相似度计算，为评估基于改进相似度测度的 SVM 集成效果做好准备。

（6）采用改进测度的完全计算 SVM 集成对测试集中的术语对进行相似度计算。这里的完全计算是指先将术语对各种相似度测度都计算出来，再基于这些测度构成的向量和SVM 相似度分类模型进行相似度测度集成以获得最终计算结果。

（7）依照第 3 节所提出的计算阶段模型，采用改进测度的条件计算 SVM 集成对测试集中的术语对进行相似度计算。在计算时，若某一术语相似度测度计算结果超过判断阈值，则认为已经能够判断出该术语对相似，从而提早结束该术语对的后续计算步骤，节约计算时间。通过条件计算和完全计算的计算效果、时间花销比较，以验证条件计算术语相似度集成模型的真实性能。

5.3 实验结果

对术语相似度计算的效果评测一般采用准确率、召回率、F_1 测度这三个指标。[34,57] 本实验中沿用了文本分类任务中对于准确率、召回率和 F_1 测度的定义。[58]

准确率计算公式为：

$$precision = \frac{\text{正确判断为相似的术语对数量}}{\text{所有被算法判断为相似的术语对数量}}。\tag{6}$$

召回率计算公式为：

$$recall = \frac{\text{正确判断为相似的术语对数量}}{\text{所有人工判断为相似的术语对数量}}。\tag{7}$$

综合准确率和召回率的 F_1 测度计算公式为：

$$F_1 = 2 \times \frac{precision \times recall}{precision + recall}。\tag{8}$$

各种相似度测度计算性能指标如图 4 所示。

从图 4 可以看到，各种改进相似度测度在综合计算性能上相比对照测度有明显提升。其中，改进的术语语词相似度测度在 F_1 测度指标上达到 0. 7992，比 Nenadic 语词相似度测度高出 13% 以上，改进的术语语境模板相似度测度和改进的 Web-PMI 测度也比相应的对照测度分别高出 5% 和 4% 。实验表明，上文中所提出的各种相似度测度改进方法是可行且有效的。另外，从各种相似度测度的准确率表现也可以看到，基于语词的相似度测度准确率表现最好，其次是基于语境模板的相似度测度和基于搜索引擎的相似度测度。而在以部分召回率的损失换取较高准确率的情况下，基于语词相似度测度能够获得更高

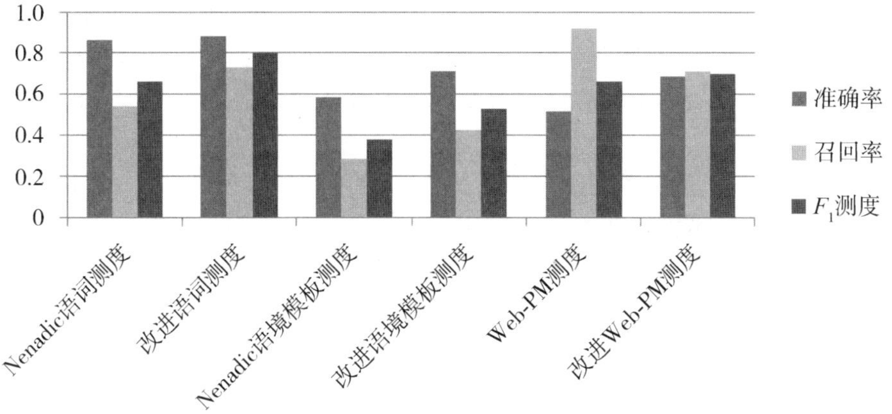

图 4　各种相似度测度计算性能指标

的准确率，这正是相似度测度集成阶段条件计算流程中将其安排在靠前位置的原因。

在对改进语词测度、改进语境模板测度以及改进 Web-PMI 测度进行组合后，得到 4 种测度组合形式，然后分别以所得到的各种测度组合形式为输入，进行 SVM 自动分类。各种测度组合形式的分类准确率、召回率、F_1 测度如表 2 所示。

表 2　各种改进测度组合的 SVM 自动分类结果

改进测度组合	准确率	召回率	F_1 测度
[改进语词测度，改进语境模板测度]	0. 8443	0. 8879	0. 8655
[改进语词测度，改进 Web-PMI 测度]	0. 8846	0. 7863	0. 8326
[改进语境模板测度，改进 Web-PMI 测度]	0. 8529	0. 7436	0. 7945
[改进语词测度，改进语境模板测度，改进 Web-PMI 测度]	0. 8790	0. 9008	0. 8898

从图 4 与表 2 中数据的对比可以看到，相对于各种改进测度单独作为分类标准时的性能表现而言，改进测度组合的分类效果存在不同程度的提高。即使是 F_1 测度最低的改进语境模板测度与改进 Web-PMI 测度组合，其 F_1 测度也比单独采用改进语境模板测度获得的 F_1 测度值 0. 5312 和单独采用改进 Web-PMI 测度获得的 F_1 测度 0. 698 有明显提升。当同时采用三种改进测度的组合进行 SVM 分类时，分类的 F_1 测度是所有 4 种组合中最高的，这说明各种单一改进测度之间存在优势互补的特性。

在进行基准测度的完全计算 SVM 集成、改进测度的完全计算 SVM 集成和改进测度的条件计算 SVM 集成后，对性能指标进行统计，如表 3 所示。

表 3　三种 SVM 集成性能指标对比

项目	准确率	召回率	F_1 测度
基准测度完全计算 SVM 集成	0. 7436	0. 7130	0. 7278
改进测度完全计算 SVM 集成	0. 879	0. 9008	0. 8898
改进测度条件计算 SVM 集成	0. 8069	0. 9669	0. 8797

从表 3 可以发现，改进测度的 SVM 集成计算综合性能比基准测度 SVM 集成计算有较为明显的提升。条件计算 SVM 集成的 F_1 测度达到了 0.8797，相比基准测度 SVM 集成计算 F_1 测度提高了 15%。这表明各项相似度测度的算法改进的确对于 SVM 集成的计算效果提升有正面影响。

从表 3 中还可以发现，改进测度的完全计算 SVM 集成和条件计算 SVM 集成的 F_1 测度分别为 0.8898 和 0.8797，相差仅为 1%，但是两者的平均计算时间却存在较大差别。采用条件计算 SVM 集成模型能够有效减少大量相似度计算时所花费的总时长。在 2.1 GHz 双核 CPU、2.5 G 内存、Windows XP 操作系统、MyEclipse 6.5 + JDK 1.6 开发环境下，采用 SVM 完全计算和 SVM 条件计算的平均耗费时间如表 4 所示。

表 4　SVM 集成计算的平均时间耗费表

算法	术语对相似度计算平均耗费时间/ms
改进测度完全计算 SVM 集成	41762.5
改进测度条件计算 SVM 集成	28355.5

从表 3 可以看到，在采用条件计算 SVM 集成的情况下，计算所需的平均耗费时间有大幅度减少，条件计算 SVM 集成平均耗费时间仅为完全计算 SVM 集成平均耗费时间的 67.9%。在确保准确率和召回率的情况下，SVM 条件计算为大规模术语相似度计算节约了时间。

6　结　　论

从以上实验分析可知，基于多种测度的术语相似度集成计算模型主要有以下三个特点：

（1）无论是术语的语词相似度测度、语境模板相似度测度还是基于搜索引擎的相似度测度，在单独作为术语语义相似度判断依据时都具有一定的局限性。本文认为，可以将术语相似度判断看作一个分类问题，而 SVM 快速学习和自动分类的特点，使其成为集成各种相似度测度、获得术语相似度判断结果的良好工具。利用 SVM 进行相似度测度集成的主要优势在于：通过训练获得分类器既有效综合了各种术语相似度测度，又省去了加权综合集成方法中加权值难于确定的麻烦。基于 SVM 的集成计算模型能够在仅需提供少量相似度人工标引训练集的情况下，通过自动学习形成 SVM 分类模型，并以领域术语相似度网络为基础，实现领域术语语义相似度的快速计算。此外，该模型在克服各种术语相似度测度片面性的同时，降低了相似度测度之间的相互干扰作用。实验证明，采用 SVM 集成多种相似度测度的方法是可行的，计算结果与各种单项相似度测度相比表现得更好。

（2）各种相似度测度计算所需时间相差较大，速度最快的是基于语词特征的相似度测度计算，较慢的有基于语境模板特征的相似度测度计算和基于搜索引擎的相似度测度计算。此外，不同相似度测度在准确率、召回率方面也表现出较大差异性。Goran 等人[9]的实验表明，尽管基于语词特征的相似度测度具有相对较低的召回率，但其判断准确率可以高达 90% 以上，而基于语境模板特征的相似度测度则具有更加突出的召回率表现。

针对这些计算特点，本文在集成模型中设计了条件计算流程，在部分相似度测度计算后就可能已经可以判断术语对的相似程度，从而终止后续计算。实验结果证明，条件计算机制的引入能够大幅节省计算时间。

（3）基于 SVM 的集成模型中应用了多种改进的术语相似度测度计算方法。在基于语词的术语相似度测度方面，提出了将 WordNet[43] 和编辑距离计算应用于术语语词匹配，并根据术语修饰词的位置赋予特征权重的改进算法；在基于语境模板特征的术语相似度测度方面，提出了基于句法依赖关系自动构造术语语境模板，进而通过语境模板匹配计算术语相似度的算法；在基于搜索引擎的术语相似度测度方面，提出了基于领域限定网络检索的相似度算法。此外，在模型中构建相似度网络，可以减少术语相似度重复计算，提供相似度检索、推导功能。以上各种措施的综合应用有效提升了术语语义相似度计算的整体效果和适用性。

实验结果证明，基于多种测度的术语相似度集成模型在计算性能方面有较大提升，F_1 测度达到了 0.8797。与完全计算 SVM 集成相比，条件计算 SVM 集成模型能够节省 32% 的计算时间。

参考文献

[1] Chen P, Lin S. Automatic Keyword Prediction Using Google Similarity Distance [J]. Expert Systems with Applications, 2010, 37 (3): 1928 - 1938.

[2] Sánchez D, Batet M. Semantic Similarity Estimation in the Biomedical Domain: An Ontology-Based Information-Theoretic Perspective [J]. Journal of Biomedical Informatics, 2011, 44 (5): 749 - 759.

[3] Novalija I, Mladenić D, Bradeško L. OntoPlus: Text-Driven Ontology Extension Using Ontology Content, Structure and Co-Occurrence Information [J]. Knowledge-Based Systems, 2011, 24 (8): 1261 - 1276.

[4] Shih C, Chen M, Chu H, et al. Enhancement of Domain Ontology Construction Using a Crystallizing Approach [J]. Expert Systems with Applications, 2011, 38 (6): 7544 - 7557.

[5] Hindle D. Noun Classification from Predicate-Argument Structures [C]. Proceedings of the 28th Annual Meeting of the Association for Computational Linguistics, 1990 (1): 268 - 275.

[6] Resnik P. Using Information Content to Evaluate Semantic Similarity in a Taxonomy [C]. Montreal: Proceedings of IJCAI-95, 1995 (1): 448 - 453.

[7] Bourigault D, Jacquemin C. Term Extraction-Term Clustering: An Integrated Platform for Computer-Aided Terminology [C]. Athens: European Chapter of the Association of Computational Linguistics, 1999, 15: 19 - 22.

[8] Hearst M. Automatic Acquisition of Hyponyms from Large Text Corpora [C]. Nantes: Proceedings of the 14th International Conference on Computational Linguistics, 1992 (1): 539 - 545.

[9] Goran N, Irena S, Sophia A. Automatic Discovery of Term Similarities Using Pattern Mining [C]. Taipei: International Conference on Computational Linguistics, 2002 (1): 1 - 7.

[10] Bollegala D, Matsuo Y, Ishizuka M. Measuring Semantic Similarity between Words Using Web Search Engines [C]. Banff, Alberta, Canada: International World Wide Web Conference Committee, 2007 (1): 757 - 766.

[11] 荀恩东，颜伟. 基于语义网计算英语词语相似度 [J]. 情报学报，2006，25 (1): 43 - 48.

[12] 刘群，李素建. 基于《知网》的词汇语义相似度计算 [J]. Computational Linguistics and Chinese Language Processing, 2002, 7 (2): 59 - 76.

[13] Sujian L, Jian Z, et al. Semantic Computation in Chinese Question-Answering System [J]. Journal of Computer Science and Technology, 17 (6): 933 - 939.

[14] 徐硕，朱礼军，乔晓东，等. 基于双序列比对的中文术语语义相似度计算的新方法 [J]. 情报学报，2010，29

(4): 701 - 708.

[15] 张亮，尹存燕，陈家骏. 基于语义树的中文词语相似度计算与分析 [J]. 中文信息学报，2010，24 (6)：23 - 30.

[16] 林丽，薛方，任仲晟. 一种改进的基于《知网》的词语相似度计算方法 [J]. 计算机应用，2009，29 (1)：217 - 220.

[17] 田久乐，赵蔚. 基于同义词词林的词语相似度计算方法 [J]. 吉林大学学报：信息科学版，2010，28 (6)：602 - 608.

[18] 王小林，王义. 改进的基于知网的词语相似度算法 [J]. 计算机应用，2011，31 (11)：3075 - 3077.

[19] 刘青磊，顾小丰. 基于知网的词语相似度算法研究 [J]. 中文信息学报，2010，24 (6)：31 - 36.

[20] 滕广青，毕强. 基于概念格的跨本体映射中概念相似度计算方法 [J]. 情报学报，2012，31 (4)：390 - 397.

[21] 徐德智，王怀民. 基于本体的概念间语义相似度计算方法研究 [J]. 计算机工程与应用，2007，43 (8)：154 - 156.

[22] 张忠平，赵海亮，张志惠. 基于本体的概念相似度计算 [J]. 计算机工程，2009，35 (7)：17 - 19.

[23] 周剑烽. 基于本体的语义相似度计算模型改进 [J]. 情报杂志，2010，29 (12)：144 - 151.

[24] 盛志超，陶晓鹏. 基于维基百科的语义相似度计算方法 [J]. 计算机工程，2011，37 (7)：193 - 195.

[25] 徐健，肖卓. 基于领域限定网络检索的术语相似度计算 [J]. 情报理论与实践，2012，35 (6)：109 - 113.

[26] 占飞，刘挺. 面向英文辅助写作的词语相似度应用研究 [J]. 智能计算机与应用，2011，1 (1)：51 - 58.

[27] 吴健，吴朝晖，李莹，等. 基于本体论和词汇语义相似度的 Web 服务发现 [J]. 计算机学报，2005，28 (4)：595 - 602.

[28] 胡俊峰，俞士汶. 唐宋诗中词汇语义相似度的统计分析及应用 [J]. 中文信息学报，2002，16 (4)：39 - 44.

[29] Sheila T, Craiga K, Steven M. Learning Object Identification Rules for Information Integration [J]. Information Systems, 2001, 26 (8): 607 - 633.

[30] Smith T F, Waterman M S. Identification of Common Molecular Subsequences [J]. J Mol Biol, 1981, 147 (1): 195 - 197.

[31] Yeganova L, Smith L, Wilbur W J. Identification of Related Gene/protein Names Based on an HMM of Name Variations [J]. Computational Biology and Chemistry, 2004, 28 (2): 97 - 107.

[32] Neshati M, Hassanabadi L. Taxonomy Construction Using Compound Similarity Measure [J]. Lecture Notes in Computer Science, 2007, 4803: 915 - 932.

[33] Church K W, Hanks P. Word Association Norms, Mutual Information, and Lexicography [C]. New Brunswick: Proceedings of the 27th Annual Conference of the ACL, 1989: 76 - 83.

[34] Danushka B, Yutaka M, Mitsuru I. Measuring Semantic Similarity between Words Using Web Search Engines [C]. Proceedings of WWW2007. Banff, Alberta, Canada: International World Wide Web Conference Committee, 2007: 757 - 766.

[35] Sean M F, Dmitri M, Margaret A S. Combining Web-Based Searching with Latent Semantic Analysis to Discover Similarity between Phrases [C]. On the Move to Meaningful Internet Systems 2006: CoopIS, DOA, GADA, and ODBASE, Montpellier, 2006: 1075 - 1091.

[36] Yih W, Christopher M. Improving Similarity Measures for Short Segments of Text [C]. Proceedings of the Natural Conference on Artificial Intelligence, London, 2007: 1489 - 1495.

[37] Roberto J B, Ma Y, Ramakrishnan S. Scaling up All Pairs Similarity Search [C]. Proceedings of the Seventeenth World Wide Web Conference, Korea, 2007: 131 - 140.

[38] 章成志. 基于多层特征的字符串相似度计算模型 [J]. 情报学报，2005，24 (6)：696 - 701.

[39] Support Vector Machine [EB/OL]. [2012 - 12 - 06]. http://en.wikipedia.org/wiki/Support_vector_machine.

[40] Gumwon H. Relation Extraction Using Support Vector Machine [J]. Natural Language Processing-IJCNLP, 2005 (1): 366 - 377.

[41] Yang B, Zhang Y, Li X. Classifying Text Streams by Keywords: Using Classifier Ensemble [J]. Data Knowledge Engineering, 2011, 70 (9): 775 - 793.

[42] Fu J, Lee S. A Multi-Class SVM Classification System Based on Learning Methods from Indistinguishable Chinese Official

Documents [J]. Expert Systems with Applications, 2012 (2): 3127 -3134.
[43] Christiane F. WordNet: An Electronic Lexical Database [M]. Cambridge, MA: MIT Press, 1998: 292 -296.
[44] Java API for WordNet Searching (JAWS) [EB/OL]. [2012 -12 -06]. http://lyle.smu.edu/~tspell/jaws/index.html.
[45] The Porter Stemming Algorithm [EB/OL]. [2012 -12 -06]. http://tartarus.org/~martin/PorterStemmer/.
[46] Jaro-Winkler Distance [EB/OL]. [2012 -12 -06]. http://en.wikipedia.org/wiki/Jaro-Winkler_distance.
[47] 刘莎. 名词短语中修饰语排序的认知原因 [J]. 科教文汇, 2007 (10): 198 -199.
[48] Marneffe M C, Manning C D. Stanford Typed Dependencies Manual [EB/OL]. [2012 -12 -06]. http://nlp.stanford.edu/software/dependencies_manual.pdf.
[49] Daniel C, Marneffe M C, Daniel J, et al. Parsing to Stanford Dependencies: Trade-offs between Speed and Accuracy [C]. In 7th International Conference on Language Resources and Evaluation, 2010: 1628 -1632.
[50] Derrik H. Which Statistics Reflect Semantics? Rethinking Synonymy and Word Similarity [C]. In International Conference on Linguistic Evidence, Tubingen, 2004: 265 -284.
[51] Rudi C, Paul V. The Google Similarity Distance [J]. IEEE Transactions on Knowledge and Data Engineering, 2007, 10 (3): 370 -383.
[52] How to Use AltaVista [EB/OL]. [2012 -12 -06]. http://www.cs.tut.fi/~jkorpela/altavista/.
[53] LIBSVM 简介 [EB/OL]. [2012 -12 -06]. http://www.blog.sh/user3/warisa/archives/2006/75791.html.
[54] Springer Link [EB/OL]. [2012 -12 -06]. http://www.springerlink.com/.
[55] 徐健. 人工智能领域人工判断为相似的测试术语集合. [EB/OL]. [2012 -12 -06]. http://wenku.baidu.com/view/66fab87b5acfa1c7aa00ccbc.html? st =1.
[56] 徐健. 人工智能领域人工判断为不相似的测试术语集合. [EB/OL]. [2012 -12 -06]. http://wenku.baidu.com/view/46b61084d4d8d15abe234ebc.html? st =1.
[57] Peter T. Mining the Web for Synonyms: PMI-IR Versus LSA on TOEFL [C]. Berlin: Proceedings of the Twelfth European Conference on Machine Learning, 2001: 491 -502.
[58] 宗成庆. 统计自然语言处理 [M]. 北京: 清华大学出版社, 2008: 352 -353.

教师简介：

武琳，女，郑州大学管理学硕士、武汉大学管理学博士。2006 年起任教于中山大学资讯管理学院，副教授，硕士生导师。主讲“情报学基础”、“企业管理咨询基础”、“信息组织：导论”、“信息管理概论”、“信息管理研究方法与前沿”等本科生课程，以及“信息组织与检索”等研究生课程。研究方向包括网络信息资源管理、数字信息服务、数据科学管理、研究数据服务。主持国家社会科学和教育部人文社会科学项目多项，发表专业论文 30 余篇，参编著作 3 部。2010 年美国雪城大学信息学院访问学者。兼任美国信息科学与技术学会会员（ASIS & T）、中国科技情报学会竞争情报分会会员、广东图书馆学会会员。联系方式：wulin2@ mail. sysu. edu. cn。

开放数据驱动城市创新

——以 Smart Disclosure 为例*

武　琳，伍诗瑜[①]

摘　要：近几年开放数据运动在全球范围内掀起了一股浪潮，欧美出现了一种新型开放数据服务方式——Smart Disclosure，本文主要介绍了英美 3 个典型项目：英国的 Money Advice Service、“midata”，美国的“蓝绿按钮”，分析了该类项目主要开放的数据类型，并讨论了项目的经济价值，提出推进我国 Smart Disclosure 的四种途径——全面开放政府数据、鼓励企业开放数据、规范数据开放标准、积极寻求多方合作，为我国开放数据运动提供实践发展策略，从而更充分利用开放数据驱动城市创新。

关键词：开放数据；Smart disclosure；开放数据运动

Open Data-Driven City Innovation：Take Smart Disclosure for Example

Lin Wu，Shiyu Wu

Abstract：Worldwide tide of Open Data Movement was swept from Europe to USA in recent years；the emergence of a new open data service pattern—Smart Disclosure is looming. This paper described three typical projects：the Money Advice Service，“ midata” and “blue-green button”，and analyzed major open data types of this model. The economic value of the project was also discussed. There are four ways to promote our nation Smart Disclosure：comprehensive open government data，to encourage enterprise open data，open data standards，and multilateral cooperation. Practical development strategies for China’s Open Data Movement were provided to make full use of open data in driving city innovation construction.

Keywords：Open data；Smart disclosure；Open data movement

① 伍诗瑜，中山大学资讯管理学院本科生。

1 引　言

2009 年美国颁布《开放政府指令》[1] 以及开放政府数据平台 Data. gov 的上线，开放数据运动逐渐席卷全球。从开放政府联盟[2] 到 G8 开放数据宪章[3]，再到全球开放数据指数[4]，各国政府相继制定开放数据政策法令、行动计划推动数据的开放。

目前国内外关于开放数据如何实现创新的研究才刚开始[5]，但是开放数据已然成为大数据时代下重要的数据资产。2013 年 11 月全球知名咨询公司麦肯锡发布的报告《开放数据：释放流动信息的创新能力》[6] 显示，每年大约有 3 万亿美元的经济价值是由开放数据产生的。

2 Smart Disclosure 典型案例剖析

新型的开放数据服务“Smart Disclosure”是基于《助推》（*Nudge*）[7] 一书中的 RECAP 模型——记录（record）、分析（evaluate）、比较可选择价格（compare alternative prices）提出的，其定义为“以标准的、机器可读的形式及时发布复杂信息和数据，以便消费者做出明智的决定”[8]，这是开放数据的又一创新应用形式。我国的开放数据运动正处于起步阶段，了解这种新型的开放数据服务不仅可以提高政府和企业的透明度，还有助于企业创新和消费者决策，助推经济发展。

2.1 英国——MAS 和“midata”

财务咨询服务（Money Advice Service，MAS）[9] 是 RECAP 模型在英国金融领域的实际应用。2011 年 4 月，MAS 正式上线，提供在线、电话以及英国范围内面对面的咨询服务。MAS 是由英国金融服务管理局建立的一个独立机构，它与其他组织合作通过提供免费以及公正的咨询服务来帮助人们管理财务。MAS 收集整理了英国市场内提供的所有关于财产贷款的数据，如果消费者想获得最适合自己的产品，就可以通过 MAS 的在线网页回答一些问题来获得建议。2012 年 4 月，MAS 又增加了债务咨询服务，主要是帮助消费者管理债务以及与提供债务服务的机构一起合作等。

“midata”[10] 项目是英国 Smart Disclosure 的典型例子，主要在银行、手机公司和能源公司三个领域发起。2011 年 11 月，英国政府宣布成立“midata”团队，总共有 26 家企业、消费者团体和监管机构加入了这个团队（表 1），并承诺和政府合作推动 Smart Disclosure，以便让消费者更好地掌握自己的数据。“midata”希望通过鼓励创新来推动企业、消费者和经济的发展，它主要有三个目的：①使更多的企业以电子格式向消费者发布他们的个人数据；②确保消费者可以安全地获取他们的数据；③鼓励企业开发应用程序来帮助消费者有效地使用他们的数据。“midata”项目成立之初是一个志愿项目，但是在 2012 年 11 月，政府宣布如果企业不愿意主动发布数据，他们将会使用法律强制企业发布[11]，即《企业和监管改革法案（2013）》[12]，法案中明确指出哪些机构需要开放数据，向谁开放数据以及开放哪些数据。

表1　英国"midata"项目部分参与成员

领域	企业/组织机构	数据应用方式
能源消费	British Gas EDF Energy E. ON Npower Scottish Power	同意消费者使用有关个人记录的电子数据，并为消费者提供更好的缴费信息
金融	Billmonitor Lloyds Banking Group MasterCard The UK Cards Association Visa	进行手机价格比较；以相同格式为消费者提供 midata 下载服务
信用	Callcredit	为消费者提供过去几个月至3年的存档数据下载服务
隐私身份	Garlik	提供产品和服务使消费者在线掌握他们的个人信息

2.2　美国——蓝绿按钮

美国将 Smart Disclosure 列入开放政府联盟国家行动计划中，承诺推进 Smart Disclosure 进展。[13] 2011 年 7 月，美国科学技术委员会 Smart Disclosure 工作小组成立。2012 年，白宫和美国国家档案馆成功举办了 Smart Disclosure 峰会，会议邀请了很多决策引擎公司参加并发言，涉及医疗、能源、金融、教育等领域。同时，美国还推出了 Smart Disclosure 的官方网站 Consumer. data. gov，截至 2015 年 5 月 15 日，该网站共发布了 235 个数据集和 24 个应用程序。在美国，Smart Disclosure 最早被运用于医疗健康——蓝色按钮（Blue Button）和能源消费——绿色按钮（Green Button）两个领域。[14]

2010 年 8 月美国退伍军人管理局（VA）在它的个人健康在线平台 My Heathe Vet[15] 上推出了一个叫作"蓝色按钮"的互联网应用。通过这个应用，退役军人可以点击电脑屏幕上的虚拟按钮下载医疗记录，包括合同、检测结果、家庭历史以及其他的一些数据，这些数据可以使他们更好地管理个人医疗健康。在蓝色按钮推出后的头两个月时间里，大约有 10 万退役军人请求查看他们的个人健康数据，超过 15 万条个人健康记录被下载。[16] 之后，美国能源部和环境保护署也在 2012 年 1 月正式启动了"绿色按钮计划"，可以为消费者及时提供他们的能源数据。超过 50 家公用事业和电力供应商参与了该计划，保证了超过 6000 万个家庭和企业可以以标准形式安全地获取自己的能源数据。与由政府主导的蓝色按钮不同的是，绿色按钮计划是由产业界主导开展的。[17]

Smart Disclosure 在医疗健康和能源消费领域取得了初步成效后，逐渐被推广到了金融、房地产、教育等领域，催生了各种新兴数据企业和网站（表2）。

表2　美国 Smart Disclosure 在各领域的应用

领域	企业/网站	数据应用方式
医疗健康	FAIRHealth（www. fairhealthus. org/） CakeHealth（cakehealth. com/） HealthGrades（www. healthgrades. com/） ZocDoc（www. zocdoc. com/） UnitedHealth Group（企业）	收集用户的医疗记录信息、支付信息、医院信息帮助用户预测成本、选择医疗方案、预约医生等
能源消费	WattzOn（企业） PlotWatt（企业） FirstFuel（企业） Opower（企业）	利用 Green Button 提供的能源数据为用户提供具体的工具，帮助他们节约能源
金融	Mint. com GetRaised（getraised. com/） HelloWallet（www. hellowallet. com/） BillGuard（企业）	利用劳工部等机构发布的数据提供个人金融管理、判断报酬高低、与他人比较财务状况、纠正不当的信用卡和借记卡收费等服务
房地产	Realtor. com Estately（www. estately. com/） Trulia（www. trulia. com/） Zillow（www. zillow. com/）	利用劳工统计局等部门提供的数据帮助用户做出最佳的买房决策
教育	GreatSchools. org College Scorecard（collegecost. ed. gov/）	通过评分的方式帮助家长和学生选择合适的教育机构

2.3　Smart Disclosure 的数据类型

在信息呈指数增长的大数据环境下，Smart Disclosure 既可以帮助消费者应对令人困惑的市场，同时也能为企业创造新的商机，目前已经在英美两国取得了良好的效果。[18]

桑斯坦提出的 RECAP 模型指出披露的信息可分为两种：一是关于产品价格构成的信息（企业应该向消费者解释产品的用途是怎样影响到总价的），二是关于消费者过去使用记录的数据（假设消费者和这家企业有着长期的交易关系）。[19]霍华德也认为使消费者能够在购买产品以及签订合同时做出明智决定的最有效的方法就是将产品和服务的数据（如定价算法、质量、特点等）与个人数据（如消费记录、信用得分、健康、能源以及教育数据等）结合起来使用（如用于搜索引擎、交互式地图或者移动应用程序中）。[20]据此，可以将 Smart Disclosure 分为四种数据类型，如表3 所示。

表 3　Smart Disclosure 主要数据类型

发布者	产品和服务数据	个人数据
政府	政府发布关于产品和服务的数据	政府发布关于公民的个人数据
企业	企业发布关于产品和服务的数据	企业发布关于公民的个人数据

2.4　Smart Disclosure 的经济价值分析

Smart Disclosure 不仅向个人提供公司的产品和服务数据以及个人数据，帮助消费者决策，同时也促进了企业创新，催生了大量数据产品和新服务，产生了巨大的经济价值。参考美国白宫 Smart Disclosure 工作小组 2013 年发布的报告 *Smart Disclosure and Consumer Decision Making*[21]，其经济价值体现在以下几个方面：

（1）促进明智决策。Smart Disclosure 通过网页和手机 APP 帮助消费者在市场环境中做出明智的决策。其中最典型的例子就是“决策引擎”的产生。“决策引擎”是帮助消费者在医疗健康、能源、教育、金融等领域做出重要决策的工具，消费者可以利用决策引擎比较同一商品在不同网站上的价格，选择最合适的航线、旅行时间等其他因素来满足自己的需求。

（2）节约决策成本。使消费者掌握自己的个人数据，从而使决策变得更简单，节约决策成本。越来越多的决策引擎可以帮助消费者分析自己的个人数据，并为其定制关于产品和服务的个性化服务。例如病人们用他们的医疗数据去选择新的医疗保险项目，房主们使用能源数据找到节约能源的方法，消费者通过他们的个人金融管理工具获取如何管理个人金融的建议等。

（3）助力新兴公司的创立。Smart Disclosure 有助于创立新兴数据公司，创造新的产品和服务，催生了各种类型各个领域的比价网站/决策引擎。例如英国的一个新创网站 CompareTheMarket. com，它是一个关于保险产品的比较网站，消费者只需几次简单的点击鼠标就可以比较来自英国顶级供应商的大量保险服务。

（4）其他经济价值。Smart Disclosure 通过使消费者更简单地做出明智的决策来帮助促进市场更加透明和高效，同时也为市场环境下基于消费数据的创新提供了支持，有利于促进经济发展和增加就业机会。

3　我国 Smart Disclosure 的对策分析

近年来，民生科技已成为各国解决民生问题的重要手段，众多民间创客脱颖而出，政府也在为创业创新搭建新平台。我们应把握好当前社会经济发展的有利环境，抓住机遇，借鉴英美的实践经验和教训，研究 Smart Disclosure 创新的数据消费方式，以推进我国民生科技的快速发展。

3.1 全面开放政府数据

统计显示，在社会的主要领域，政府掌握了超过90%的信息资源[22]，如何利用和开放这些数据成为大数据环境下政府需要解决的重大课题。2015 年 4 月国务院办公厅印发《2015 年政府信息公开工作要点》[23]，要求 2015 年政府数据要全面公开。因此，各级政府都应该主动全面开放数据，并以标准、机器可读的形式将产品和服务数据以及消费者的个人数据提供给消费者无限制地重复使用，提供渠道允许用户申请开放自己需要的数据类型，同时开放应用程序接口（API）鼓励企业和个人利用开放数据开发 APP，实现开放数据的增值利用。

3.2 鼓励企业开放数据

基于学者伊曼（Iemma）针对绿色按钮提出的“绿色按钮运作图”[24]，我们可以得到企业 Smart Disclosure 双向循环图（图 1）。消费者在与企业的交往过程中产生了大量有经济价值的数据，而如今这种数据的控制权是掌握在企业手中的，要实现 Smart Disclosure，第一步就是要将这种数据控制权从企业手中转移到消费者手中[25]，所以政府应当鼓励企业开放数据给消费者。当消费者拥有了自己的个人数据以及公司的产品和服务数据后，就可以将这些数据上传到第三方机构的比较网站（决策引擎）上进行分析，第三方机构则可以将分析结果反馈给政府。这就构成了从政府到企业，到消费者，到第三方机构，再到政府的第一个循环。当各方都获得了相应的经济价值时又促成了第二个循环，即反向循环。这时企业会主动开放数据以及 APIs（应用程序接口）给政府或第三方机构，第三方机构则会开发更多的应用工具来分析数据，帮助消费者决策，而消费者也将主动向企业请求拿回自己的个人数据。

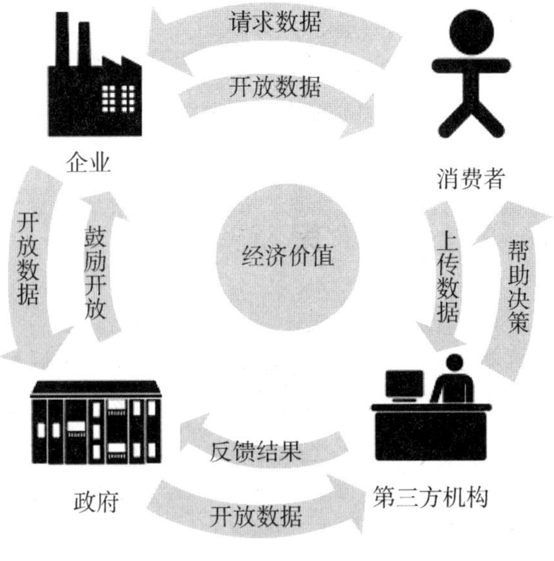

图 1　企业 Smart Disclosure 双向循环图

3.3 规范数据开放标准

我国目前还没有全国性的统一的开放数据平台，虽然部分地区如北京、上海、无锡已经建立了地区性的开放数据平台，但是开放的数据却没有统一的标准格式，有的数据可用，有的不可用，十分不便于用户使用这些数据。虽然建立全国统一的开放数据平台会更有利于数据的使用，但是我国国情复杂，各地区间差异较大，暂时难以建立起统一的数据平台。因此，就目前而言，我国可先制定出数据开放的标准格式，要求各个地方政府和企业使用标准格式、机器可读形式（如 xls、csv）进行 Smart Disclosure，不仅可以提高数据质量，有利于当下用户对数据的使用，还有利于将来建立全国性的数据平台时数据的整合与统一。

目前国际上建立的标准有：关于道路事件的 Open511 标准[26]，用户通过将自己的道路事件放到软件中进行分析便可以充分利用自己的数据；关于合同的开放合同数据标准[27]，它可以帮助利益相关者将数据整合起来，使他们能够更高效地使用合同数据；关于发展合作活动的 IATI 标准[28]，这是一个以及时、全面和前瞻性的方式发布关于发展合作活动信息的框架。

3.4 积极寻求多方合作

我国正处于开放数据的起步阶段，我们需要将眼光投向国际舞台，与英美等国发展良好的合作关系以借鉴其经验，或者借助第三方机构和 NGO 的力量来评价数据的可靠性，等等[29]，积极寻求多方合作，以推进我国开放数据进程。

“中西开放创新对话”（East West Chats）[30]是由中国和美国的团队（休斯敦负责在美国的领导）建立的在线虚拟创新对话，组织开放数据创新的展示，分享最好的实践经验以及发展良好关系。2014 年 9 月 19 日成功举办了中西开放创新首次在线对话，聚集了中美双方在开放数据与城市创新领域的专家、实践者、创新者，共同探讨各自国家在开放创新方面的发展并探索未来合作的可能。紧接着在 11 月 5 日又举办了第二轮对话，主题为“政府提供服务的未来”，讲述了开放数据在全球不同国家是如何被政府运用的，以及它如何改变政府所提供的公共服务。目前类似的国际交流活动还很少，但是随着我国开放数据运动的不断发展，这种交流将显得越来越重要。

4 结　　语

从 Smart Disclosure 在英美两国的发展现状来看，这种新型的开放数据服务确实给政府、企业以及消费者带来了很多益处。但是我国在探讨该服务方式时，要注意消费者的隐私安全必须得到充分的保障。只有在开放和保密之间找到一个最佳平衡点，我国的开放数据运动才能顺利开展。对于国外的经验也不能完全照搬，需结合我国的具体国情将其本土化，探索出城市开放数据创新发展新路径。

参考文献

[1] Open Government Directive [EB/OL]. [2015-5-15]. https://www.whitehouse.gov/open/documents/open-government-directive/.

[2] Open Government Partnership [EB/OL]. [2015-5-15]. http://www.opengovpartnership.org/.

[3] 洪京一. 从 G8 开放数据宪章看国外开放政府数据的新进展 [J]. 世界电信, 2014 (Z1): 55-60.

[4] Global Open Data Index [EB/OL]. [2015-5-15]. http://index.okfn.org/.

[5] Zuiderwijk A, Helbig N, Gil-García J R, et al. Special Issue on Innovation through Open Data: Guest Editors' Introduction [J]. Journal of Theoretical and Applied Electronic Commerce Research, 2014, 9 (2): i-xiii.

[6] Manyika J, Chui M, Farrell D, et al. Open data: Unlocking Innovation and Performance with Liquid Information (2013) [EB/OL]. [2015-5-15]. http://www.mckinsey.com/insights/business_technology/open_data_unlocking_innovation_and_performance_with_liquid_information.

[7] Thaler R H, Sunstein C R. Nudge: Improving Decisions about Health, Wealth, and Happiness [M]. New Haven: Yale University Press, 2008.

[8] Sunstein C. Informing Consumers through Smart Disclosure. [EB/OL]. [2015-5-15]. https://www.whitehouse.gov/blog/2012/03/30/informing-consumers-through-smart-disclosure.

[9] Money Advice Service [EB/OL]. [2015-5-15]. http://moneyadviceservice.org.uk/.

[10] The Midata Vision of Consumer Empowerment [EB/OL]. [2015-5-15]. https://www.gov.uk/government/news/the-midata-vision-of-consumer-empowerment.

[11] Consumer Protection [EB/OL]. [2015-5-15]. https://www.gov.uk/government/policies/providing-better-information-and-protection-for-consumers/supporting-pages/personal-data.

[12] Enterprise and Regulatory Reform Act 2013 [EB/OL]. [2015-5-15]. http://www.legislation.gov.uk/ukpga/2013/24/contents/enacted.

[13] Sayogo D S, Zhang J, Pardo T A, et al. Going beyond Open Data: Challenges and Motivations for Smart Disclosure in Ethical Consumption [J]. Journal of Theoretical and Applied Electronic Commerce Research, 2014, 9 (2): 1-16.

[14] Sayogo D S, Pardo T A, Bloniarz P. Information Flows and Smart Disclosure of Financial Data: A Framework for Identifying Challenges of Cross Information Sharing [J]. Government Information Quarterly, 2014, 31 (S1): S72-S83.

[15] Myhealth [EB/OL]. [2015-5-15]. https://www.myhealth.va.gov/index.html.

[16] Department of Veterans Affairs. Blue Button [EB/OL]. [2015-5-15]. https://www.whitehouse.gov/open/innovations/BlueButton.

[17] Green Button [EB/OL]. [2015-5-15]. http://energy.gov/data/green-button.

[18] Gurin J. Open Data Now: The Secret to Hot Startups, Smart Investing, Savvy Marketing, and Fast Innovation [M]. Columbus: McGraw Hill Education, 2014.

[19] Brodi E. "Product-Attribute Information 'and' Product-Use Information": Smart Disclosure and New Policy Implications for Consumers' Protection [J/OL]. http://ssrn.com/abstract=2142734, 2012.

[20] Howard A. What Is Smart Disclosure? O'Reilly Radar, 2012 [EB/OL]. [2015-5-15]. http://radar.oreilly.com/2012/04/what-is-smart-disclosure.html.

[21] Smart Disclosure and Consumer Decision Making: Report of the Task Force on Smart Disclosure [EB/OL]. [2015-5-15]. https://www.whitehouse.gov/sites/default/files/microsites/ostp/report_of_the_task_force_on_smart_disclosure.pdf.

[22] 首届中国政务大数据开放论坛在京举办 [J]. 电子政务, 2015 (1): 42.

[23] 国务院办公厅印发 2015 年政府信息公开工作要点 [EB/OL]. [2015-5-15]. http://politics.people.com.cn/n/2015/0421/c1001-26879337.html.

[24] Iemma R. Data Ingredients: Smart Disclosure and Open Government Data as Complementary Tools to Meet Policy Objectives [J]. The Case of Energy Efficiency, 2014 (4): 43.

[25] Jennifer Cobb. Smart Disclosure: Innovation in Personal Data. Spruce Advisers, 2012 [EB/OL]. [2015-5-15]. http://www.spruceadvisers.com/smart-disclosure-innovation-in-personal-data/.

[26] Open511: About the Standard. [EB/OL]. [2015-5-15]. http://open511.org/.

[27] The Open Contracting Data Standard [EB/OL]. [2015-5-15]. http://standard.open-contracting.org/.

[28] IATI Standard Is a Technical Publishing Framework Allowing Data to be Compared. This Site Gives Detail on the Standard, How to Implement It and Provides Guidance [EB/OL]. [2015-5-15]. http://iatistandard.org/.

[29] Sayogo D S, Zhang J, Liu H, et al. Examining Trust as Key Drivers in Smart Disclosure for Sustainable Consumption: The Case of I-Choose [C]. Proceedings of the 15th Annual International Conference on Digital Government Research. ACM, 2014: 137-146.

[30] 9月19日中西开放创新首次在线对话 [EB/OL]. [2015-5-15]. http://www.udparty.com/news.php?act=view&id=653.

教师简介：

曹效阳，男，中山大学学士，南京大学商学硕士，中山大学管理学博士。2000 年起任教于中山大学资讯管理学院，讲师。主讲“数据库系统”、“网络信息组织”等本科生课程。近期发表《网络舆情的结构与网络特征分析》等学术论文。联系方式：caoxy@mail.sysu.edu.cn。

基于 AHP 的社区空间犯罪热点预测研究

曹效阳

摘　要：本文总结国内外关于空间犯罪预防的研究成果和预测模型的优劣，并通过对社区犯罪热度影响因素的分析，在相关数据的支持下，提出社区犯罪热点的 AHP 预测模型。最后对中山大学东校区空间犯罪热度进行了评价预测。
关键词：AHP 模型；犯罪热点；犯罪预测

The Study of Spatial Crime Hotspots Prediction Model Bases on AHP

Xiaoyang Cao

Abstract: The paper summarizes the research findings on space crime prevention and the pros and cons of crime prediction model at home and board. With the support of relative data, the author put forward the crime hot spots of community prediction model which bases on AHP. And finally, the author put forward initial idea for building the forecasting system about space crime hot spots with the evaluated prediction of the crime hot spot of East Campus of Sun Yat-Sen University.
Keywords: AHP model; Crime hotspots; Crime prediction

1　国内外有关空间犯罪预测模型的研究

1.1　犯罪预测模型

犯罪预测模型建立方面，国外很早就开始了相关研究，主要方法是通过大量搜集以往的犯罪记录或者罪犯的生存状态，在此基础上利用统计学等相关方法进行建模，然后用犯罪制图等方法进行预测。例如 Matthews、Yang、Hayslett、Ruback 在 *Built Environment and Property Crime in Seattle*, 1998 – 2000: *A Bayesian Analysis* 里面对西雅图、华盛顿等地的犯罪案件进行了大量的统计，建立了空间泊松模型和分析出犯罪环境因子。[2]

目前国外对犯罪预测模型主要有三种：灰色预测模型，数据挖掘预测模型和时间序列分析模型。三者都是基于大量的数据收集，然后用数学方法进行预测的。但其关联因素较少，预测的指标维度也较低，实用性不高。因此，通过建立犯罪预测模型，完善犯罪关联因素以及预测指标维度成为犯罪预测研究的一种有效途径。

1.2 空间犯罪预测模型

早在20世纪后半叶，国外一些学者和规划设计师就公共空间犯罪防控开展了不同程度的研究，并取得了一定的成果，如简·雅各布（1961）对“街道眼”和自然监视的研究、杰弗瑞（1971）提出的通过环境设计预防犯罪（crime prevention through environmental design，CPTED）理念、奥斯卡·纽曼（1972）的可防卫空间理论、R. 克拉克（1992）的“情境犯罪预防”（situational crime prevention）理论等。这些理论和见解试图通过空间环境设计来达到预防和抑制犯罪的目标。经过数十年的发展与融合，通过城市规划设计改善城市物质空间环境，从而阻止和预防犯罪，逐渐成为营造城市公共安全环境的重要手段之一。[9]

其中影响最为广泛的是美国犯罪学家和行为建筑学家奥斯卡·纽曼在《可防御的空间：通过城市设计预防犯罪》一书中提出的“防卫空间理论”。“可防卫的空间”这一思想的理论根据是：利用环境设计改变物理环境的空间样式的功能，以此改变居民的行动方式和增加相互间的社会联系，达到预防犯罪的目的。“防卫空间”主要具有以下四个要素：区域性、监视、外形和环境。

另外，根据环境犯罪学的常规活动理论，其中的中心假设是如果缺少有力的防护能力，作为可能的犯罪者和合适的目标的集中的作用，犯罪在任何时间任何地点都可能发生。常规活动的方法并不否认对于犯罪的发生来说犯罪人犯罪倾向性上的变化，而是考虑到这些倾向性。费尔森（Felson，1998，2002）认为合适目标的选择需考虑四个维度：①目标的价值或需求度；②目标的可见性；③可接近性和逃跑性；④选择的惯性。这四维描述了与犯罪相联的突出的危险因素，包括所有能够便利或妨碍运送目标的条件，如重量、移动性、抵抗度以及是否被锁住等。

2 AHP的社区空间犯罪热点预测模型的基础理论研究

2.1 AHP模型的选取

在选取预测模型方面，考虑到空间因素的多样性和复杂性，笔者采用了层次分析法，简称AHP（analytical hierarchy process），对空间犯罪热点进行建模。AHP是一种定性分析与定量分析相结合的系统分析方法。它把一个复杂问题表示为有序的递阶层次结构，从而使复杂问题能够使用简单的两两比较的形式解决，并且带有很高的准确率。

2.2 影响犯罪热度的空间因素选取

结合费尔森的四个犯罪维度和纽曼的防卫空间四因素，笔者对可视空间下的影响犯罪热度的空间因素进行了分类（表1）。

表1　犯罪热度影响的因素分类

主类别	子类别
监视性	景观障碍物
	空间实物间距离
区域性	建筑密度
	建筑群布局
接近、逃逸可能性	道路网密度
	道路弯曲率
	道路网复杂度

2.3　影响犯罪热度的空间因素研究

2.3.1　监视性研究

（1）景观障碍物。监视作用要发挥至最大，当然需要空间视野的开阔性。所以在城市建筑周围如果有山坡或树林等景观挡住视线，将会不利于防控犯罪。因为犯罪都时常发生在犯罪分子容易藏身，而过往路人无法看到以及被侵害者难以逃脱的场所。

人是公共区域中一个重要的自然监视设施。在公共空间中，群众的存在一方面可以及时制止犯罪的发生，另一方面对犯罪嫌疑人的犯罪心理起到一定的约束。为此，在空间的防控设计中，要注意利用人的监视功能。人的视觉在各距离段的判断效果如表2所示。从表中可以看到，25～28米是可以看清人的面部表情的最大距离。笔者将这一距离称为“最远监视距离”。

表2　人的视觉在各距离段的判断效果

距离/米	效果	实例
35～100	能够根据人的行走姿态判断一个人	球场距离，人们可以根据球员带球姿态、处理球方式分辨是哪个队员
25～35	能够根据印象就能认出人，不需要看面部	按《剧场建筑设计规范》，观众到舞台视距，歌舞剧33 m，话剧28米
0～25	这个距离也能够看清人的面部表情	课室的大小设计一般不超过25米

在以建筑为中心、25米为半径的圆形区域内，如果有山坡、树林等景观，且高度不低于建筑的高度，则在建筑内其视线必将大大受阻。在建筑内对建筑外难于形成有效的自然监视，在建筑外也无法形成对建筑的有效监控。

（2）空间实物间距离。空间实物间距离因素中影响空间监视性的一般有建筑物间距离和光源距离。两者都是通过实物间的协同作用营造空间的良好监视性。

根据纽曼的“防卫空间理论”，在环境设计时应考虑到该区域的合法使用者能够观察到这一区域内的日常活动，以便于发现可疑活动以采取对策。如果两幢或多幢建筑之间距离合适，它们的合法使用者能互相起到监督作用，这样将有助于防控犯罪的发生。相反，如果建筑物之间的距离不合适，不但不利于防控犯罪，还可能诱发犯罪。

2.3.2 区域性研究

（1）建筑密度。建筑密度是建筑基地面积与建筑用地面积的比值。建筑密度低，则留给业主公共活动区域越多，居住舒适度越高，有利于人与人之间的亲密关系的发展；建筑密度高则意味着规划户数多，居住环境拥塞，人员往来频繁，人与人之间关系不紧密，居民的领域感弱，难于形成较好的区域性。

（2）建筑群布局。将建筑单体组合成群体，常见的设计形式有行列式、周边式和散立式（图1）。

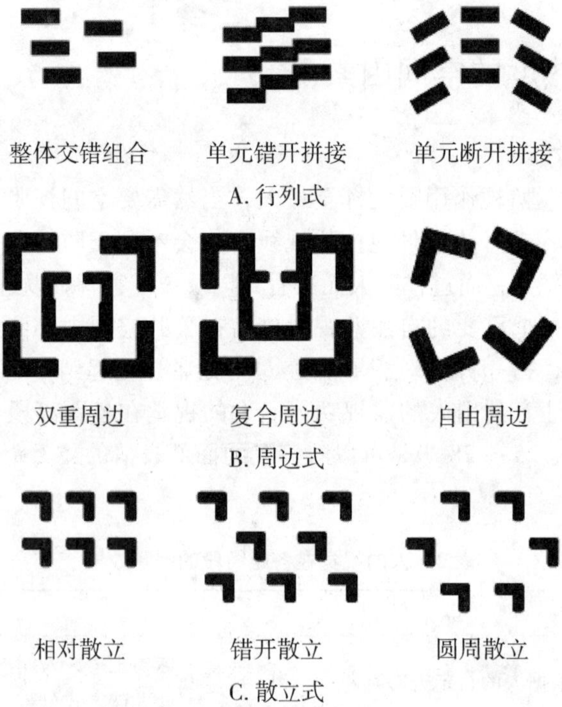

图1　建筑单体组合形式的变化[11]285－297，381－458

周边式，在其中间可以形成一块公共的活动空间，区域内人与人的交流较多，关系就较密切，建筑单体之间形成有效的自然联系。居民之间形成一种良好的互动、亲密关系，能够形成很好的区域性。

散立式的建筑布局，规律性不强。建筑与建筑之间相对独立，不易于形成一块公共的活动区域。人与人之间的关系没那么紧密，区域性不强。

行列式的排布介于上述两者之间。

2.3.3 接近、逃逸可能性研究

（1）道路网密度。就道路网密度这个因素来说，道路网密度越大，连接空间场所之间的道路就越多，道路环境的意向性和可识别性不高，这些都增加了实施犯罪的概率。同时，道路网密度越高，罪犯躲藏和接近目标的机会就越多，管理和监视的难度也加大了。

（2）道路弯曲率。道路弯曲率通过一定路程下位移长短来表示。如图 2，在相同路程下，位移越长，则道路弯曲率越低；位移越短，则道路弯曲率越高。道路 1 和道路 2 路程长度一样，但位移 $S_1 < S_2$。

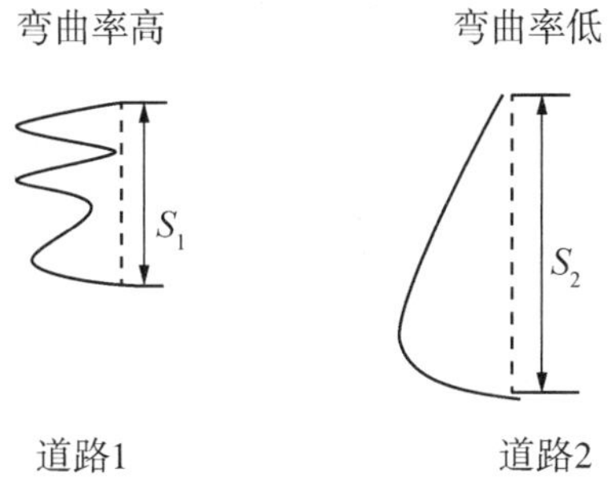

图 2　道路弯曲率表示

与道路网密度对犯罪前接近目标、犯罪后逃逸的难易性的影响原因一样，道路的弯曲率越高，令罪犯有更多的隐蔽物来一步步接近或监视目标，同时也给罪犯逃逸带来了便利。伊藤滋在《城市与犯罪》中列举了城市空间中存在可能发生犯罪的十个空间死角，其中“空间死角”之二：视线受阻，小巷、幽径以及木结构的公寓过多，高层密集住宅相继，住宅过于稠密，使人们的视线受阻，发现有犯罪嫌疑的人不利于追踪，形成难以监视的死角。[17]这与道路的弯曲率息息相关。

（3）道路网复杂度。社区道路系统对犯罪有一定影响。如果某区域对犯罪人很有吸引力的话，道路系统越复杂，则犯罪率越低；道路系统越简单，则犯罪率越高。[18]道路系统简单、明了、四通八达，犯罪分子潜入和逃逸便利，犯罪率比其他形式的道路系统高。

城市道路网复杂度越高，犯罪分子潜入和逃逸所要花费的时间成本和代价越大，其接近、逃逸可能性也比较低，因而对犯罪能起到一定的遏制作用。道路网复杂度可以通过道路与道路之间的交汇点个数来衡量。如果在某一地区道路与道路之间错综复杂，交汇点非常多，那说明道路网复杂度高；如果类似方格网道路，四通八达，交汇点比较少，则道路网复杂度低（图 3）。

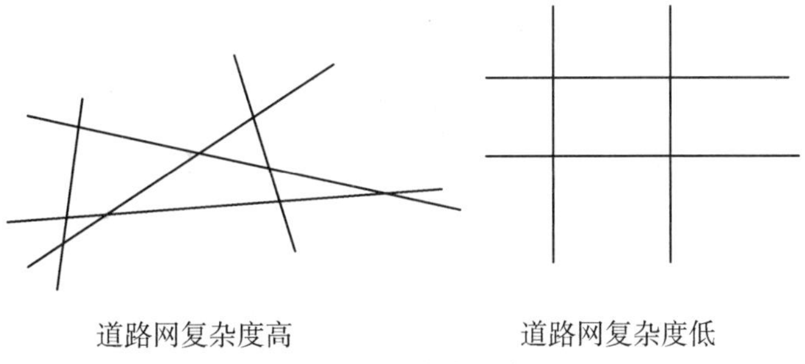

图 3　道路网复杂度表示

3 基于 AHP 的数据收集

用层次分析法建模需要确定递阶结构中相邻层次元素间的相关程度。通过构造两两比较判断矩阵及矩阵运算的数学方法，确定对于上一层次的某个元素而言，本层次中与其相关元素的重要性排序——相对权值。

在如何确定因素两两之间相对权值方面，笔者通过网络、报纸等收集了有预谋的1392 个刑事犯罪案件，收集情况如表 3 所示。

表 3　案件收集情况

单位：个、%

来源	收集案件	相关案件	有效率
报纸	162	79	48.77
网络	1230	704	57.24
总数	1392	783	56.25

通过 Google 地图找到案发地点的所在地，并以之为中心、周围半径约 200 米圆形区域内，对其中牵涉到的因素进行了分析，统计得到各因素出现的次数。为了避免每个人的主观判断对因素分析造成的不统一性，笔者对每个因素在案件中是否出现设置阈值，当达到这个阈值的时候，我们就认为这个因素在案件中起了作用。得到的结果如表 4 所示。

表 4　案件影响因素相关性统计

因素	次数	百分比（次数/案件总数）/%	阈值
景观障碍物	425	54	28 米内没有可以阻碍视线的景观障碍物
空间实物间距离	357	46	存在宽少于 2 米的小巷或者建筑物的距离超过 100 米
建筑密度	374	48	建筑物占划定的区域的面积 60% 以上
建筑布局	323	41	周围建筑物分布无规则
道路网密度	289	37	附近有 3 条以上的道路
道路弯曲率	153	20	有弯曲超过 30 度的道路
道路网复杂度	289	37	道路的交叉点在 3 个以上

4 运用 AHP 对犯罪热度进行建模

按照表 5 的层次结构，经过笔者研讨和发掘，应用萨蒂教授的表度法，即人类判别事物好坏、优劣、轻重、缓急的经验方法，对不同的比较结果给以数量表度，如表 6 所示。

表 5　层次结构

标层 A	准则层 B	因素层 C
犯罪热度	监视性大小 B_1	景观障碍物 C_1
		建筑物间的距离 C_2
	区域性的大小 B_2	建筑群布局 C_3
		建筑密度 C_4
	接近、逃逸可能性 B_3	道路网密度 C_5
		道路弯曲率 C_6
		道路网复杂度 C_7

表 6　数量表度

表度 a_{ij}	定义	解释
1	同样重要	i 元素与 j 元素同样重要
3	稍微重要	i 元素比 j 元素稍微重要
5	明显重要	i 元素比 j 元素明显重要
7	很重要	i 元素比 j 元素很重要
9	极端重要	i 元素比 j 元素极端重要
2、4、6、8	介于上述相邻判断之间	为以上两判断的折衷表度
上述数字倒数	反比较	j 元素比 i 元素重要程度

根据所收集的数据，笔者按照两两判断矩阵的生成方法和结构形式，得了该评价体系的各个层次的两两比较判断矩阵，如表 7～表 10 所示。

表 7

A	B_1	B_2	B_3	W_i	一致性检验指标
B_1	1	2	1	0. 400	$\lambda_{max}=3.000$，$CR=0.000<0.1$
B_2	1/2	1	1/2	0. 200	
B_3	1	2	1	0. 400	

表 8

B_1	C_1	C_2	W_i	一致性检验指标
C_1	1	3	0. 750	$\lambda_{max}=2.000$，CR $=0<0.1$
$C2$	1/3	1	0. 250	

表 9

B_2	C_3	C_4	W_i	一致性检验指标
C_3	1	2	0. 667	$\lambda_{max}=2.000$，$CR=0<0.1$
C_4	1/2	1	0. 333	

表 10

B_3	C_5	C_6	C_7	W_i	一致性检验指标
C_5	1	5	1	0.455	$\lambda_{max}=3.000$，$CR=0.000<0.1$
C_6	1/5	1	1/5	0.091	
C_7	1	5	1	0.455	

根据判断矩阵给出的各个指标之间的相对重要值，可以计算出每个指标在其所在判断矩阵中的权重，以判断矩阵 A（表 7）为例，计算 B_1、B_2、B_3 的权重，即可判断出准则层对于目标层的权重。具体计算步骤为：

（1）将判断矩阵 A、B 中的元素按行相乘：

$$M_i = \prod_{j=1}^{n} a_{ij}, \qquad i = 1,2\cdots,n。$$

（2）计算权重：

$$W_i = \sqrt[n]{M_i} / \sum_{i=1}^{n} \sqrt[n]{M_i}, \qquad i = 1,2,\cdots,n。$$

将判断矩阵 A 中的权重向量填入表 7 中，得到三个准则指标对于目标层的重要排序。同理，分别计算判断矩阵 B_1、B_2、B_3 的权重向量，并填入表 8 ～表 10 中．得到判断矩阵的权重向量后，需要对其有效性进行一致性检验，确保该判断矩阵的有效性，进而科学地反映各个指标的相对重要性。

以 A 矩阵为例，具体检验步骤为：

（1）将判断矩阵与其对应权重向量相乘，如计算 AW_i。

（2）计算判断矩阵的最大特征根：

$$\lambda_{max} = \frac{1}{n}\sum_{i=1}^{n}\frac{AW_i}{W_i}, \qquad i = 1,2\cdots,n。$$

（3）计算一致性指标和选定平均随机一致性指标。其中：

$$CI = \frac{\lambda_{max} - n}{n - 1}。$$

（4）计算一致性指标比率：

$$CR = \frac{CI}{RI}。$$

（5）断定判断矩阵 A 是否通过一致性检验。通常当 $CR=0$ 时判断矩阵具有完全满意的一致性，当 $CR<0.1$ 时判断矩阵具有满意的一致性，则该判断矩阵可以用来做层次分析；否则就要请判断人重新做出相对重要度评价，直到判断矩阵满意为止。

计算得判断矩阵 A 中的 $CR=0$，具有完全满意的一致性，即矩阵 A 为有效矩阵，并把 λ_{max}、CI 和 CR 的值填入表中。

最后，我们得出犯罪热度值的公式为：

$$A=0.300C_1+0.100C_2+0.133C_3+0.067C_4+0.182C_5+0.036C_6+0.182C_7。$$

式中：C_1 ～ C_7 分别为景观障碍物、建筑物间的距离、建筑群布局、建筑密度、道路网密度、道路弯曲率、道路网复杂度。

5 社区空间犯罪热点预测的 AHP 模型实例

5.1 犯罪制图

犯罪热点的分析一般要借助犯罪制图来实现。犯罪制图是以空间地理信息为参照，操作与处理犯罪数据，以可视化形式显示、输出对特定用户有用的信息的过程，是一种有效的情报分析和侦查工具。它是与情报学、侦查学、犯罪学、制图学与地理信息系统等理论技术相结合的综合应用系统，既可以用于警务管理，也可以用于战略情报和战术情报的分析。犯罪制图即可以帮助警务人员确定犯罪热点地区、分析犯罪状况，以采取相应的对策进行警务干预，有效地打击、预防和控制犯罪活动，以及评价警务工作对犯罪干预的有效性。要实现犯罪制图，进而进行犯罪热点分析，首先要利用空间地理信息，提取出犯罪热点地区所普遍具有的空间地理特征，并以这些特征建立犯罪热点地区空间地理预测模型，基于该模型和 GIS 就能在某城市地图信息中预测出犯罪热点地区。在城市各区域的内部存在着犯罪高发区、高发点等，这种不平衡具有一定的必然性，因此，全面掌握犯罪活动的状况，根据空间地理信息寻找和标定犯罪的高发区和高发点，并制定控制和治理措施，是区域（特别是大中城市）犯罪防治的重要环节。

5.2 以中山大学东校区为例进行空间犯罪制图

笔者在 Googlemap 上截取了广州市番禺区大学城中山大学东校区的鸟瞰图（2010 年 11 月 30 日星期二），并依照上述的研究方法对该地区进行了犯罪热度的计算。*C* 值的计算如表 11 所示。

表 11　因素赋值标准

因素	分值计算方法
景观障碍物	景观障碍物和建筑物间距离 2 ～ 25 米赋值 3 分，26 ～ 100 米赋值 5 分，100 米开外或者 2 米之内赋值 7 分
建筑物间距离	建筑物间实际距离占网格大小的百分数乘以 10
建筑群布局	自由式赋值为 2，行列式赋值为 5，周边式赋值为 8
建筑密度	建筑物占地面积占网格面积的百分数乘以 10
道路网密度	道路总长度占网格面积大小的百分数乘以 10
道路弯曲率	网格内道路的平均弯曲率
道路网复杂度	网格内道路交叉的点数

经计算，得出该地区的犯罪热度值如图 4 所示。从图中可以明显地看出，楼房呈行列式布局，并且附近有小山或者树林阻挡视线的地区，犯罪热度值明显比其他地方要高；视野开阔的地方热度值偏低。值得注意的是，图 4 中的 G8—H9 区域属于城中村，建筑分

布散乱，建筑物间距离小，道路弯曲率大，临近主要交通干线，导致该区域的犯罪热度值为整个测量区域之最。结合实际的一些数据来看，该分布具有一定的准确性。

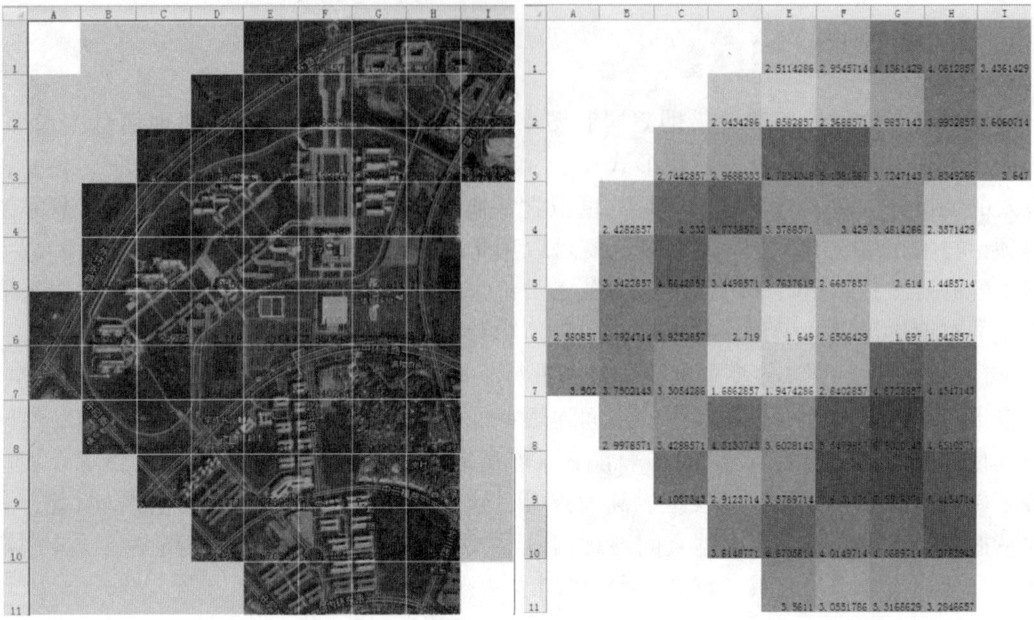

图4 中山大学东校区犯罪热度值分布

6 结 语

空间犯罪热度研究作为国外犯罪预防研究新兴的领域，为预防犯罪、维护社会稳定提供了较为廉价、高效的指导性意见。目前，我国的空间犯罪热度研究还不太成熟，需要更多的研究人员合理利用国外一些较成熟的研究成果，结合我国实际情况，在大量的统计数据前提下，深入挖掘提出更为准确的预测模型，使之为我国预防犯罪、维护社会稳定提供更为精准的参考意见。

参考文献

[1] 犯罪预测 [OL].（2010－12－2）. http://baike.baidu.com/view/151222.htm.

[2] Matthews S A, Yang T C, Hayslett K L, Ruback R B. Built Environment and Property Crime in Seattle, 1998－2000: A Bayesian Analysis [J]. Environmentanning, 2010, 42（6）: 1403－1420.

[3] 史常凯．灰色系统理论在旅游客源地市场预测中的应用 [J]. 高等理科学刊, 2005, 25（3）: 75－78.

[4] 李刚. 数据挖掘技术在侦破网络犯罪中的应用 [J]. 西北民族大学学报：自然科学版, 2006（64）: 58－60.

[5] 吕研昱. 基于时间序列分析的金融事件预测 [J]. 北京印刷学院学报, 2007, 15（6）: 48－51.

[6] 孔一. 犯罪预测：原理与方法 [J]. 青少年犯罪研究, 2004（3）: 48－56, 34.

[7] 陈亮. 犯罪制图的理论与实践进展研究 [J]. 中国人民公安大学学报：自然科学版, 2008, 56（2）: 65.

[8] Eck J E, Chainey S, Cameron J G, et al. Mapping Crie: Understanding Hot Spots [D]. National Institute of Justice, US, 2005.

[9] 蔡凯臻. 通过城市设计干预城市公共空间犯罪防控——英国经验及其启示［J］. 城乡规划·园林建筑及绿化，2008，26（11）：92－95.

[10] ODPM and Home Office. Safer Places：The Planning System and Crime Prevention［M］. London：Thomas Telford Ltd，2004.

[11] 李德华. 城市规划原理［M］. 3 版. 北京：中国建筑工业出版社，2001，285－297，381－458.

[12] 邹晖，胡玲. 恐惧的选择——奥斯卡·纽曼（Oscar Newman）的防卫空间评述［J］. 国外建筑科学，1989（1）：4－10.

[13] 恩里科·菲利. 犯罪社会学［M］. 北京：中国人民公安大学出版社，1990：75－90.

[14] 李玫瑾. 犯罪心理研究在犯罪防控体系中的价值［J］. 中国人民公安大学学报，2005（5）：100－110.

[15] 王发曾. 城市犯罪的移动空间盲区及其综合治理［J］. 河北法学，2007（11）：18－21.

[16] 毛媛媛，戴慎志. 犯罪空间分布与环境特征——以上海市为例［J］. 城市规划学刊，2006（3）：85－93.

[17] 伊藤滋. 城市与犯罪［M］. 夏金池，郑光林，译. 北京：群众出版社，1988.

[18] 徐磊青. 社区安全与环境设计——在“可防卫空间”之后［J］. 同济大学学报：社会科学版，2002，13（1）.

教师简介：

郑重，女，华中师范大学管理学学士，武汉大学管理学硕士、博士。2009 年起任教于中山大学资讯管理学院，讲师。主讲“信息检索”、“文献计量学”、“情报学基础”等本科生课程。主要从事竞争情报、知识管理、用户信息行为、网络信息管理等方向的研究。主持科研项目 5 项，发表论文 10 余篇。2013—2014 年美国威斯康辛密尔沃基分校访问学者。联系方式：zhengzhg@ mail. sysu. edu. cn。

网络舆情视角下中国政府形象评价指标体系之构建*

郑　重，张　星①，聂　冰②

摘　要： 阐述了构建政府形象评价指标体系的意义和作用；在综述国内对政府形象评价指标研究现状的基础上，提出了政府形象评价指标体系的基本框架及其主要内容；以中国汶川地震期间的政府网络舆情治理为案例论述了中国政府处理网络舆情的关键影响因素；最后尝试提出了网络舆情视角下的中国政府形象评价指标体系。

关键词： 电子政务；信息社会；网络舆情；政府形象评价；应急管理

Constructing an Evaluation System of the Image of Chinese Government with Network Public Opinion

Zhong Zheng, Xing Zhang, Bing Nie

Abstract: This paper describes the importance and function of constructing an evaluation system of government image. The domestic studies about the evaluation system of government image were reviewed. The framework and content of an evaluation system of government image were proposed. By taking the case of the management of network public opinion during the Wenchuan Earthquake, the key influential factors of network public opinion were discussed. Finally, we attempted to propose an evaluation system of the image of Chinese government with network public opinion.

Keywords: E-government; Information society; Network public opinion; Evaluation of government image; Emergency management

---

* 本文系广东省 2010 年度哲学社会科学“十一五”规划项目“网络舆情对广东省政府行为的影响力研究”(GD10YTS01)、湖北省教育厅科学技术研究计划优秀中青年人才项目“互联网舆情传播网络的结构测度与演变机制研究”(Q20111602) 研究成果。

① 张星，武汉纺织大学管理学院讲师、博士。

② 聂冰，中山大学资讯管理学院硕士研究生。

1 引 言

网络舆情在中国的发展与互联网在中国的发展息息相关。网络舆情在10余年间的发展令所有传统媒体相形失色，无数网民在其发展过程中贡献了自己的力量，同时完成了当代中国公民个体意识觉醒的过程，网络为这种转变提供了一个自由宽泛的平台。政府形象建设优良与否，取决于政府的实际作为；判定政府形象的优良与否，则来自人们的评价。指标是评价的依据，政府形象评价指标如同“指挥棒”[1]，引领政府形象建设的方向。面对政府形象建设的严峻挑战，贯彻落实科学发展观，建构一套科学、合理、可行的政府形象评价指标体系，衡量出政府形象的优劣，促使政府树立正确的价值理念，增强政府治理能力，提高政府绩效，以满足公民利益需求，符合时代发展的要求。

一个良好的政府形象评价指标体系为政府形象建设提供了一个可量化的标准，为政府形象建设树立参照系，有利于树立正确的政府价值理念。首先，评价指标体系的建构有利于规范政府治理行为。政府的实际作为过程或政府在履行职能、行使公共权力的行为直接影响政府的形象。[2]政府形象评价指标体系将政府行为作为评价政府形象的重要指标，以期通过行为指标的评价，规范政府行为，实现政府自身及其与社会、市场、自然的和谐，树立政府美的形象。其次，评价指标体系的建构有利于提高政府绩效。政府形象不仅取决于政府所倡导和持有的价值理念以及价值理念指导下的政府行为，更取决于政府价值追求指导下的政府行为所产生的绩效。

2 政府形象评价指标研究

在中国，有关政府形象评价指标体系的阐述和分析很少，国内有关政府形象评价指标体系的论述尚未形成一套完整、缜密的逻辑体系。曹随、陆奇主编的《政府机关形象设计与形象管理》借鉴企业形象设计理论和方法研究政府形象设计，系统提出了政府理念的建立，对政府形象提出了全面准确的定位，开创性地建立了政府机关形象的评价指标体系，涉及“环境指标、人员指标、理念指标、目标指标、政策指标、效率指标和效果指标等指标体系”。[3]苏柏佳、赵彦发表的学术论文认为国内专家学者从不同的角度对政府形象评估维度提出了各自的见解，主要分为引用企业形象评估维度来测评政府形象与在政府形象测评时偏重美誉度两类。[4]肖军勇认为，政府形象评价指标体系是由政府价值指标体系、政府行为指标体系以及政府绩效指标体系组成的层级要素体系；他还以郴州为个案研究对象进行实证调研，了解不同群体对政府形象评价指标的选择及对所在政府形象的评价，分析政府形象评价指标体系的理论与实践的相关程度并提出前景展望。[5]这是国内首次对政府形象评价体系做出的完整性论述，笔者认为这种指标体系是比较符合当前政府形象评价实质的，故下文会着重介绍此指标体系，并在此模型基础上提出网络舆情视角下的政府形象评价模型。

结合现代政府形象的内在结构，政府形象评价指标体系的基本框架包括政府价值、政府价值指导下的政府行为、政府价值指导下的政府行为所产生的政府绩效，由此共同组成政府形象评价的金字塔式结构指标体系。

2.1 政府形象评价的价值指标体系

政府价值是政府理念以及信念的集中体现，是政府形象生成与确立的核心因素，也是实现和维护公众利益诉求的前提条件。它整合了政府价值手段和工具手段，层层递进，具有开放性和层级性，是一个完整的体系而非孤立的要素。在这个层级体系中，目的性价值居于金字塔顶端，因为它反映了政府的希望和理想，是人们对于政府行政能力的绝对超越指向；工具性价值则在其统治之下，是政府实现其目的性价值的必备属性（图1）。

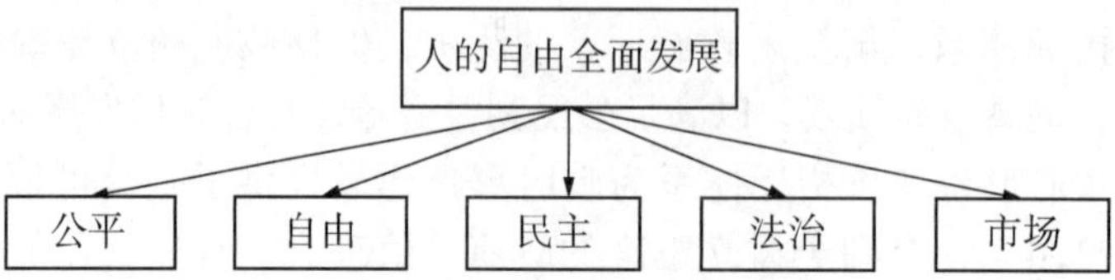

图1　政府形象评价价值指标体系

2.2 政府形象评价的行为指标体系

政府行为是指政府行政机关及其行政人员为谋求公共利益，实施行政管理活动的总称。[6]胡伟在其主编的《政府过程》明确指出，政府过程的行为主要是政府决策和政府执行两个环节。[7]首先，整个政府管理过程围绕着决策的制定和组织实施而展开；其次，政府执行是行政权的集中体现，是贯穿整个政府管理活动的重要环节；再次，政府监督行为是政府决策、执行围绕社会“公共利益”方向发展的重要保证；最后，政府创新已经成为一个全球的趋势。

综上所述，政府决策、执行、监督以及创新共同构成政府过程行为的基本环节，也是政府形象评价的行为指标（图2）。

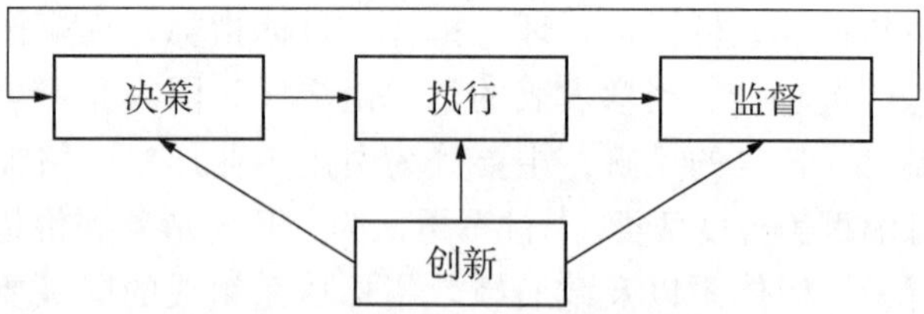

图2　政府形象评价行为指标体系

2.3 政府形象评价的绩效指标体系

综合已有的学术界各种观点，笔者认为，政府绩效是政府在积极履行公共责任的过程中，在讲求内部管理与外部效应、数量与质量、经济因素与伦理政治因素、刚性规范与柔性机制相统一的基础上，所获得的公共产出最大化。评价政府绩效的每一个要素，只能选择关键性要素作为评价政府形象的绩效指标。将政府绩效体系内容作为一个有关政府提供公共物品和公共服务效果（具体体现为政府在促进经济发展、维护社会秩序、优化公共服务以及保护生态环境等方面做出的成效）和程度的横向（与邻区政府绩效）和纵向（与往届政府绩效）优劣比较来进行评估（图3）。

- 政府绩效
  - 提供公共物品和服务的效果
    - 经济发展
    - 社会秩序
    - 公共服务
    - 生态环境
  - 提供公共物品和服务的程度
    - 横向比较
    - 纵向比较

图3　政府形象评价绩效指标体系

2.4　政府形象评价的指标体系

借鉴层次分析法的技术思想，政府形象评价指标体系的各种因素构成的集合被称为因素集。根据前文分析，政府形象评价指标体系的各个层次的因素集（参见表1）分别如下：

H 表示总因素；

A_n 表示第一层因素（$n=1, 2, \cdots, n$）；

B_m 表示第二层因素（$m=1, 2, \cdots, m$）；

则 $H=\{A_1, A_2, A_3\}$（A_1、A_2、A_3 分别表示政府价值、政府行为、政府绩效三个因素）。A_1、A_2、A_3 三个因素又分别由若干子因素构成，诸如政府价值 A_1 就是由其目的性价值 B_1——人的自由全面发展，工具性价值 B_2——民主、法治、公正、效率以及市场两方面因素的反映。表1只反映到评价体系的二级指标。根据实际需要和不同角度，可将评价指标体系按照层次分析法继续划分，并赋予相应权重，即可对政府形象评价进行定量分析。

表1　政府形象评价指标体系

总指标	一级指标		二级指标	
政府绩效评价指标体系 H	A_1	政府价值体系	B_1	目的性价值
			B_2	工具性价值
	A_2	政府行为体系	B_3	政府决策
			B_4	政府执行
			B_5	政府监督
			B_6	政府创新
	A_3	政府绩效体系	B_7	经济发展
			B_8	社会秩序
			B_9	公共服务
			B_{10}	生态环境

3 中国政府处理网络舆情的关键影响因素

毫无疑问，政府在处理网络舆情过程中的某些关键影响因素对政府形象评价有着重要的影响作用，因此对这些关键影响因素的研究也是进行网络舆情视角下政府形象评价的理论依据和参考要素。由于当前政府处理网络舆情的成效良莠不齐，笔者选择了汶川地震时期的网络舆情治理作为一个典型性的分析对象，希望从中窥视政府处理网络舆情的关键影响因素。汶川地震时期的网络舆情实质是一种在突发公共危机状态下的舆情表达与影响，中国政府对这一事件的处理非常成功，并在国际上大大提升了中国政府形象。深刻分析汶川地震时期的网络舆情危机及其治理，对政府如何处理网络舆情，以及哪些因素将影响政府形象提供了可资借鉴的思路与方法。

3.1 中国政府主动的应对态度

网络舆情是一个包含了态度、情感、心理和行为等多层面内涵的综合概念，是一个丰富的“民意表达场域”[8]。汶川地震时期的网络舆情在总体特征上表现为高度的正向一致性，即对政府救援的高度支持、对灾区民众的高度同情、对杜绝谣言的高度自觉。[9]

在汶川地震中，互联网成为反映震情最迅速的信息平台，超过报纸和电视台等传统媒体，同时担负起公众情感宣泄和意见交流的渠道。2008 年 5 月 12 日 14 时 28 分，地震发生；14 点 46 分，新华网就发布了四川汶川发生 8 级强烈地震的权威消息，此时，大多数人们刚从避震的户外陆续回到室内，一上网就能了解到地震的真相。傍晚，温家宝总理飞往灾区指挥救灾的消息在网上发布。截至当晚 10 点，四川地震局已经召开了 6 次新闻发布会。各网站均开设汶川地震专页，比中央电视台更早启动滚动发布震情新闻。汶川地震是新中国第一次对灾情提供即时大规模的发布。地震遇难人数也在网上持续更新，即使统计口径存在出入，有的被埋或失踪人口被误统计为死亡，也通过新闻的动态更新来校正。例如 5 月 15 日某地更正说，先前计入死亡的 500 人已被成功营救，死亡人数相应减少。这种做法在此前的灾难报道中是十分罕见的。这些都表明了我国政府以及最高领导人对此次事件的重视和主动响应。

3.2 政府处理速度和效度

在汶川地震中，中国第一次展示了在大规模突发公共危机事件中的政府网络舆情治理效度。其经验模式体现了网络舆情危机治理的普适性，具有借鉴意义。

一是信息发布的及时权威性。强震发生后不到 20 分钟，中国国家地震台网即向世人发布了地震的震中和震级。震后两小时内重庆市率先发布了此次灾难的首批伤亡数字。此后，官方公布的伤亡情况一路更新。中央电视台中断正常节目的播出，直播四川地震的最新情况。互联网上，官方新闻机构不断发布最新报道，提供最新的死亡人数，以及救援行动、失踪儿童和倒塌医院的细节。及时准确的信息披露有助于政府赢得公众信任，安抚震惊中的人们。地震发生后，北京、广西、上海、重庆等地的地震局分别通过媒体澄清本地将发生强震的不实传言，解除了民众的恐慌情绪。[10]

二是救援行动的公开透明性。中国政府抗震救灾行动之所以能够得到国内国外的普遍支持与赞誉，很重要的原因就在于抗震救灾是在一种开放的环境之中进行的，是一次“直播式”行动。无论是救灾一线还是身处后方，在信息共享方面公众基本达到了无差别性。正是通过这种信息的及时共享，广大网民了解到了政府救灾行动的每个步骤，而政府也通过提高自身行为的透明度，获取了民众的坚定支持。

当前，随着我国社会转型的剧烈变动，社会突发事件频繁发生，对各级党委和政府处置突发事件的能力提出了现实要求。汶川地震作为一起由自然灾害引起的突发公共危机事件，各级政府的总体作为表现得到社会认可。从网络舆情治理的角度而言，在抗震救灾期间，政府对待网络舆情危机的态度表现出了高度的理性平和，在处置的方法上采取了沟通对话的“治理”方式而不是关堵封闭的“控制”方式。这应该是这次公共危机管理中舆情治理的最大经验。

4 网络舆情视角下中国政府形象评价体系

根据前文对政府处理网络舆情过程中关键因素进行分析，笔者认为，在政府处理网络舆情的过程中要得到良好的政府形象评价，关键是在政府处理态度、政府处理速度以及政府处理效度三个方面进行考量。一旦网络舆情事件发生之后，政府要能够迅速作出反应，查找问题根源，及时回应公众疑问，有效解决网络舆情事件，维护政府形象。

4.1 评价角度

（1）政府处理态度。长期以来，我国政府对网络资源的管理都以一种自上而下的强硬方式来推行。政府对网络舆情的消极处理态度实质上是公权力对私人领域的入侵，也就是公权力对私权利的克减。网络的参与性和网民平等的话语权以及发言的匿名性，有利于调动网民参与公共事务管理的积极性。网民积极关注社会问题、发表意见甚至是批评意见，是社会民主、进步的表现，对网上积极、正当的舆论应予以提倡。在深化改革的过程中，一些深层次的矛盾、对现实生活的不满情绪会在网上表露，一些负面的东西会在网上出现，对这些消极的方面应当积极予以引导。

（2）政府处理速度。网民所关注的热点问题是经常变化的，常常是一个热点问题还没有“冷”下来，新的热点问题又出现了；与之相对应，网络舆情的影响也是相互交织的。经常出现的情况是政府在网络宣传上的迟缓，没有找准时间点和合适的切入点，网民迫切需要了解的信息得不到及时的披露，网民的意愿要求也得不到及时的回应。另外，政府在网络语言的使用上也比较呆板，导致网络宣传难以与网民产生共鸣。在“重庆钉子户”、“厦门 PX 项目”等事件中，当地政府的决策遭致网民的批评，面对海量的质疑、批评的帖子，当地政府不得不改变决策。如果政府能及时地披露相关的信息，加强与民众的信息沟通，充分地了解民众意愿，适时采取有效的网络宣传和舆论引导，这样的事件并非不能避免。

（3）政府处理效度。从某种意义上说，政府应对网络舆情需要学习一些操作层面上的处置方式与应对经验，但是更重要的还是要不断强化自身尊重公民权利的意识。当尊重公民的知情权、参与权与监督权已经内化为地方政府的自觉意识，出现网络热点事件时，自会积极对事件展开调查，快速及时地对事件作出处理，并通过吸纳网民与人大代表参与等方式确保调查与处理的公正性，政府形象与公信力自然也就能得到维护；反之，如果地方政府缺乏尊重公民包括知情权、参与权与监督权在内权利的意识，也就必定会在应对网络热点事件上出现处置失当现象，并因此而使政府形象与公信力受到损害。

4.2 评价指标

笔者尝试将前文阐述的政府形象评价指标和政府处理网络舆情的关键因素结合，从网络舆情的视角来进行政府形象评价体系研究。政府处理网络舆情的态度和政府价值指标对应，政府处理网络舆情的速度代表政府行为指标对应，政府处理网络舆情的效度对应政府绩效指标。根据网络舆情特点及政府应对的策略，选择3个一级指标、6个二级指标、12个三级指标来构建政府在处理网络舆情过程中政府形象评价的指标体系。

（1）政府处理态度指标。在政府处理态度方面，选择官方响应度和信息透明度作为二级指标，选择积极响应、官方回应、信息公开和信息完整作为三级指标。官方响应度，即地方党政机构对于突发公共事件和热点话题的响应和表达情况，包含响应速度、应对态度、响应层级（是否有党政主要领导人、部门领导人和警方发声）。信息透明度，即地方党政机构新闻发布的透明度，官方媒体报道情况，互联网和移动通信管理、对外媒体的态度等。

（2）政府处理速度指标。在政府处理速度方面，选择动态反应度和信息及时度作为二级指标，选择政府引导、舆情预警、信息实时和信息更新作为三级指标。动态反应度，即地方党政机构随着舆情的发酵，矛盾的激化或转移，迅速调整立场、更换手法；信息及时度即地方党政机构是否能在事件进程中及时跟进，并迅速作出相关报道。

（3）政府处理效度指标。在政府处理效度方面，选择事件处理度和网络技巧度作为二级指标，选择事件解决、官员问责、信息工具和处理时机作为三级指标。事件处理度，即对网络舆情涉案官员的处理以及网络舆情事件的解决；网络技巧度，即很好地运用网络等新媒体进行信息发布和意见沟通，熟悉网络宣传和引导技巧。

4.3 评价指标体系

根据以上分析，政府形象评价指标体系的各个层次的因素集（图4）分别为：

H 表示总因素；

A_n 表示第一层因素（$n=1, 2, \cdots, n$）；

B_m 表示第二层因素（$m=1, 2, \cdots, m$）；

C_l 表示第三层因素（$l=1, 2, \cdots, l$）.

则 $H=\{A_1, A_2, A_3\}$（A_1、A_2、A_3 分别表示政府处理态度、政府处理速度、政府处理效度三个因素）。A_1、A_2、A_3 三个因素又分别由若干子因素构成，根据实际需要和不同角度，可将评价指标体系按照层次分析法继续划分，并赋予相应权重，即可对基于网络舆情的政府形象评价进行定量分析。

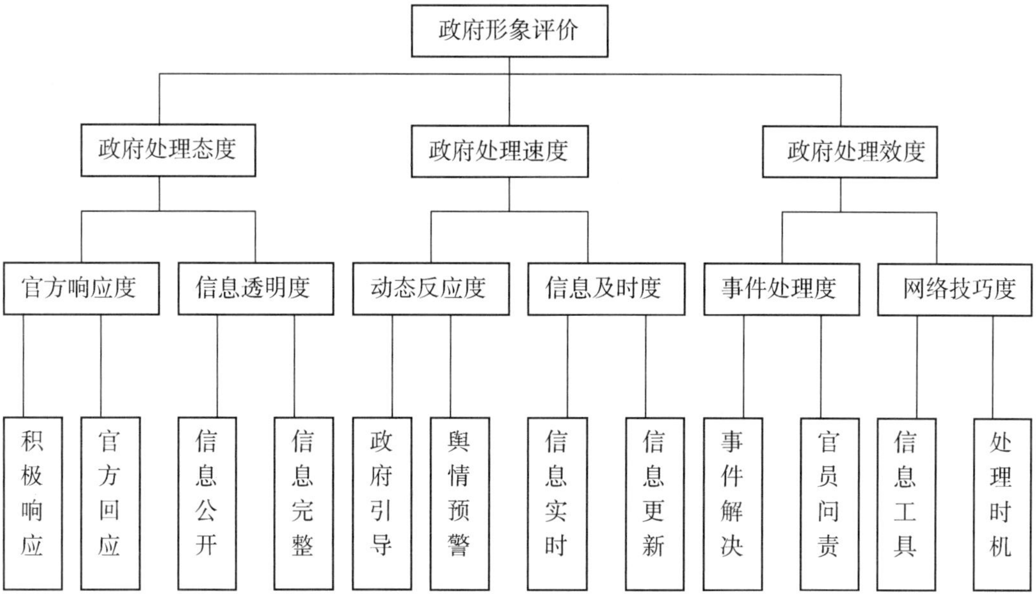

图4　网络舆情视角下政府形象评价指标体系

5　总结和展望

中国的网络舆情在经历了萌芽、初步发展、迅猛发展时期后，逐步进入当前的成熟稳定时期。现阶段的网络舆情以网络舆情热点事件系列化和网络载体变化为最显著表征，前者表现为同类型事件反复出现并无一例外地在网络上积聚大量民意言论，后者则主要体现在微博影响力的扩大、即时通讯工具的广泛应用以及传统网络载体作用减弱三个方面。毫无疑问，一个良好的政府形象评价指标体系可以为政府形象建设提供可量化的标准，为政府形象建设树立参照系，有利于树立正确的政府价值理念。目前学术界对于网络舆情和政府形象的探究多是从理论角度开展，实证研究较少，这必将是以后研究的重点与热点所在。

参考文献

[1] 王东京．中国的难题［M］．北京：中国青年出版社，2006.
[2] 胡宁生．中国政府形象战略［M］．北京：中共中央党校出版社，1998.
[3] 曹随，陆奇．政府机关形象设计与形象管理［M］．北京：经济管理出版社，2002：58.
[4] 苏柏佳，赵彦．政府形象评价维度的解构和重建［J］．台声·新视角，2005（7）：26.
[5] 肖军勇．政府形象评价指标体系的理论与实践［D］．长沙：中南大学，2007.
[6] 俞可平．治理与善治［M］．北京：社会科学文献出版社，2000.
[7] 胡伟．政府过程［M］．杭州：浙江人民出版社，1998.
[8] 曾润喜．我国网络舆情研究与发展现状分析［J］．图书馆学研究，2009（8）：2.
[9] 张静．汶川大地震标志着网络媒体真正步入了主流媒体［N］．新民周刊，2008（6）.
[10] 刘宁．从5·12地震事件中看政府应急管理能力［J］．民办高等教育研究，2008（2）：67－69.

教师简介：

丁玲华，女，武汉理工大学经济学博士，中山大学工商管理博士后。2008 年起任教于中山大学资讯管理学院，讲师。主讲“市场营销学”、“信息经济学”、“国外保密制度”、“经济学原理”等本科生课程。主要从事信息资源产业、数字内容产业等方向的研究。主持科研项目 3 项，发表论文 10 余篇。2013 年美国威斯康辛大学麦迪逊分校访问学者。联系方式：dinglh@ mail. sysu. edu. cn。

所选论文《现代信息服务业区域发展模式的识别与优化》原载于《情报探索》2015 年第 3 期

现代信息服务业区域发展模式的识别与优化*

丁玲华，张倩男①

摘　要： 根据要素导向型、投资导向型和创新导向型三种现代信息服务业的发展模式，建立现代信息服务产业发展模式评价指标体系，运用排序离散多元选择方法建立现代信息服务业区域发展模式的识别模型，对广东省现代信息服务业发展模式进行识别，判断出广东省现代信息服务业处于投资和创新混合导向型阶段，提出广东省现代信息服务业向创新性方向优化发展的对策。

关键词： 信息服务业；产业发展模式；产业优化

An Analysison Identification and Optimization of Regional Developmental Model of Information Service Industry: A Case of Guangdong Province

Linhua Ding, Qiannan Zhang

Abstract: This paper established an index system to evaluate the developmental model of information service industry based on three developmental models: elements-oriented, investment-oriented and innovation-oriented, and then ordered multivariable discrete choice model was used to identify the current developmental model of Guangdong's information service industry. It was shown that Guangdong's information service industry is in the mixed model of investment-oriented and innovation-oriented, and it should be optimized to make it more innovative and creative.

Keywords: Information service industry; Industrial development mode; Industry optimization

---

* 本文系广东省哲学社会科学“十一五”规划项目“广东省现代信息服务业发展模式研究”（项目批准号：09M－01）、中央高校基本科研业务费专项资金资助项目“中国信息服务业演化规律与发展模式研究”（项目批准号：20000－3161109）研究成果之一。

① 张倩男，广东财经大学经济贸易学院副教授，博士。

1 引　　言

产业发展是对产业自身的各种结构及各种影响产业发展的外部因素的内部结构所进行的系统性描述。产业发展模式则是在既定的外部发展条件和市场定位的基础上，通过产业内部和外部的一系列结构所反映出来的一种资源利用方式。[1]迈克尔·波特的产业发展理论认为一个国家产业的发展水平主要取决于其对资源的有效利用水平，产业的发展大致按照要素驱动阶段、投资驱动阶段、创新驱动阶段和财富驱动阶段依次递进。[2]现代信息服务业是横跨信息技术与服务内容所衍生出的新兴服务业[3]，其发展水平同样也取决于各种要素资源的利用水平，如信息技术的研发、信息化基础设施建设、企业战略、资本的可获得性等极大地促进了现代信息服务业的发展[4]。对于发展中国家而言，外商直接投资、信息人才的流动性对现代信息服务业的发展起着极其重要的作用[5]，其中外商直接投资对信息服务业的发展起着至关重要的作用[6]。

产业发展模式有很多种类型，如从产业核心竞争力的角度，可划分为生产要素推动型、城市需求拉动型和相关产业支持型[7]；从推动产业发展的主要因素划分，有要素推动型、投资推动型、创新推动型[8]；从产业融合的角度，可划分为融合发展模式和链式发展模式[9]。适宜的产业发展模式不仅有助于制定符合本地区特点的产业扶持政策，而且有利于优化资源的配置。如何选择适宜本国或本地区的产业发展模式，国内外学者进行了不少相关研究，但大多数的研究以定性研究为主，也有一些学者尝试采用一些定量的分析方法对不同产业的发展模式进行评价和分析。本文综合学者们对发展模式的定量分析方法[10-12]，试图运用排序离散多元选择方法，以广东省为例对区域现代信息服务业发展模式进行识别和判断。

2 现代信息服务业区域发展模式识别模型的构建

2.1 模型概述

在排序多元离散选择模型中，y_i 为观测值，是被解释变量，表示排序结果或分类结果，以0，1，2，3，…，M 表示，x_i 为解释变量，是可能影响被解释变量排序的各种因素。排序多元离散选择模型的一般形式可表示为：

$$y_i^* = x_i \beta_i + u_i。 \tag{1}$$

式中：y_i^* 为潜变量；x_i 为解释变量；u_i 为随机误差项；β_i 为参数向量。观测值 y_i 由指标变量 y_i^* 根据以下规则定义：

$$y_i = \begin{cases} 0 & \text{若 } y_i^* \leqslant \gamma_1 \\ 1 & \text{若 } \gamma_1 < y_i^* \leqslant \gamma_2 \\ 2 & \text{若 } \gamma_2 < y_i^* \leqslant \gamma_3 \\ \vdots & \quad \vdots \\ M & \text{若 } \gamma_M < y_i^* \end{cases}$$

式中：γ_i 是决定观测值 y_i 的门限值，决定 y_i 取值于0，1，2，3，…，M 或其他任意值。此模型要求较高的被解释变量 y_i 和较高的潜变量 y_i^* 相对应，即当 $y_i < y_j$ 时，$y_i^* < y_j^*$。由此，y_i 取每一个指标的概率可由下列式子表示：

$$P(y_i = 0 | x_i, \beta, \gamma) = F(\gamma_1 - x_i \beta),$$
$$P(y_i = 1 | x_i, \beta, \gamma) = F(\gamma_2 - x_i \beta) - F(\gamma_1 - x_i \beta),$$
$$P(y_i = 2 | x_i, \beta, \gamma) = F(\gamma_3 - x_i \beta) - F(\gamma_2 - x_i \beta),$$
$$\vdots$$
$$P(y_i = M | x_i, \beta, \gamma) = 1 - F(\gamma_m - x_i \beta)。$$

式中：F 是随机误差项 u_i 的累积分布函数。若假定误差项服从标准正态分布，则所得的即为有序 Probit 模型；若假定误差项服从 Logistic 分布，则所对的模型则为有序 Logit 模型。

2.2 现代信息服务产业发展模式评价指标体系的建立

本文借鉴相关研究成果[13-17]，将现代信息服务业区域发展模式划分为要素导向型、投资导向型和创新导向型以及介于几种模式之间的混合型发展模式，结合研究目的，在现有经济理论和研究成果的基础之上，遵循系统性、科学性、客观性、可行性等原则，建立了现代信息服务业区域发展模式评价指标体系（表1）。

表1　现代信息服务业区域发展模式评价指标体系

产业发展模式	衡量指标	指标解释
要素导向型	消费群体规模	区域常住人口数量/万人（x_1）
	产业从业人员	产业城镇单位从业人员数/城镇单位从业人员总数×100%（x_2）
	信息网络设施条件	光缆线路长度/公里（x_3）
投资导向型	产业固定资产投资	产业年末固定资产投资额/万元（x_4）
	产业规模	产业增加值/GDP×100%（x_5）
	产业投资环境	实际利用外资额/亿美元（x_6）
创新导向型	产业研究与开发投入	研发经费/GDP×100%（x_7）
	科技创新度	版权合同登记数/份（x_8）
	从业人员素质	研发人数/从业人数×100%（x_9）

2.3 现代信息服务产业区域发展模式评价模型的建立

2.3.1 模型设定

假定 y_i^* 为现代信息服务业发展模式，是一个不可观测的潜变量，可观测的为 y_i，则可建立潜变量 y_i^* 与解释变量 x_i 的线性模型：

$$y_i^* = x_i \beta + u_i。 \tag{2}$$

式中：x_1，x_2，…，x_9 分别表示影响现代信息服务业发展模式的9种因素；β_1，β_2，…，β_9 分别表示各影响因素对现代信息服务业发展模式作用的权重；u_i 为随机误差项，表示影响现代信息服务业发展模式的其他因素。

根据迈克尔·波特的产业发展理论，一个国家或地区的产业发展一般按照要素导向型、投资导向型和创新导向型依次递进。在产业的发展过程中，产业模式可能会出现两种模式甚至是三种模式同时并存的情况。因此，在对现代信息服务业发展模式进行赋值时，y_i^* 和 y_i 的取值分布如表2所示。

表2　y_i^* 和 y_i 的取值分布

y_i	y_i 对应的产业发展模式	y_i^*	y_i 的取值概率
0	要素导向型	$y_i^* \leq \gamma_1$	$F(\gamma_1 - x_i\beta)$
1	要素、投资混合型	$\gamma_1 < y_i^* \leq \gamma_2$	$F(\gamma_2 - x_i\beta) - F(\gamma_1 - x_i\beta)$
2	投资导向型	$\gamma_2 < y_i^* \leq \gamma_3$	$F(\gamma_3 - x_i\beta) - F(\gamma_2 - x_i\beta)$
3	投资、创新混合型	$\gamma_3 < y_i^* \leq \gamma_4$	$F(\gamma_4 - x_i\beta) - F(\gamma_3 - x_i\beta)$
4	创新导向型	$\gamma_4 < y_i^*$	$1 - F(\gamma_4 - x_i\beta)$

2.3.2　数据收集

研究现代信息服务业的发展模式，首先需要明确其定义和界定其范围。由于现代信息服务业产业跨度较大且产业变化较快，目前世界上还没有一个统一的划分标准对现代信息服务业进行分类。综合众多学者及机构组织对现代信息服务业的定义，现代信息服务业是利用计算机和通信网络等现代科学技术对信息进行生产、收集、处理、加工、存储、检索、利用，并以信息产品为社会提供服务的专门行业，主要包括三大类：信息传输服务业、信息技术服务业和信息内容产业。基于数据的可得性和实证研究的需要，本文以现代信息服务业中信息传输、计算机服务和软件业为主要考察对象，对其发展模式进行识别。

用定量的方法来确定现代信息服务业的发展模式是现代信息服务业研究领域的一种新探索。目前国内学者虽从不同角度对现代信息服务业的发展模式进行相关研究，但以理论研究居多，尚未发现有学者对现代信息服务业区域发展模式进行边界赋值和模式认定。本文以现代信息服务业发展模式的评价指标体系为导向，参考近几年学者对我国现代信息服务业发展水平的研究成果[18-21]，对我国31个地区现代信息服务业的各项指标进行综合比较，剔除掉数据缺失的几个地区后，最终选取了12个代表性地区并对其现代信息服务业发展模式进行赋值。本文所使用的12个代表性地区现代信息服务业发展的各项指标基本数据主要来源于《中国统计年鉴》（2013年）、各地区2013年统计年鉴、中经网统计数据库、国家统计局、中国工业和信息化部网站等。

北京、上海、江苏三个地区在创新类指标上具有明显优势，设定这三个地区为创新导向型发展模式，赋值4；天津、辽宁、浙江在创新类指标和投资类指标上均具有明显优势，设定这三个地区为投资与创新导向型发展模式，赋值3；福建、重庆在投资类指标上体现出竞争优势，设定这两个地区为投资导向型发展模式，赋值2；山东、河南在投资和要素类指标上竞争力较强，设定这两个地区为要素与投资导向型发展模式，赋值1；安徽、湖南在要素类指标上竞争力明显，设定这两个地区为要素导向型发展模式，赋值0。

2.3.3 参数估计

由于不同评价指标往往具有不同的量纲和量纲单位，为了使不同单位或量级的指标能够进行比较和加权，首先对12个代表性地区2012年现代信息服务业相关数据进行无量纲处理。经过无量纲处理的原始数据，均转换为无量纲化指标测评值，即各指标值都处于同一个数量级别上，可以进行综合测评分析。无量纲处理的方法有很多，如极值化、标准化、均值化以及标准差化等。本文采取标准化方法，其公式如下：

$$Z_{ij} = (X_{ij} - \overline{X})/\sigma。\tag{3}$$

式中：Z_{ij} 为标准化后的变量值；X_{ij} 为实际变量值；$\overline{X}$ 为变量的算术平均值；σ 为相应的标准差。

利用Eviews 6.0软件对数据进行主成分分析，计算出现代信息服务业发展模式多元离散选择模型中，要素类影响因素区域常住人口数量（x_1）、现代信息服务业从业人员比重（x_2）、光缆线路长度（x_3）的系数值分别为 -0.01279、0.256817、0.072955，投资类影响因素产业年末固定资产投资额（x_4）、产业增加值占GDP的比重（x_5）、实际利用外资额（x_6）的系数值分别为0.180444、0.2354、0.062413，创新类影响因素研发经费占GDP比重（x_7）、版权合同登记数（x_8）、研发人数占从业人数比重（x_9）的系数值分别为0.261864、0.309551、0.22847，将这9个系数值纳入排序多元离散选择模型中确定临界值。

2.3.4 临界值估计

根据计算出的9个影响因素的系数值对已建立的现代信息服务业发展模式的排序多元离散选择模型进行修正，可得出以下三个表达式：

$$X_{要素} = -0.01279x_1 + 0.256817x_2 + 0.072955x_3,\tag{4}$$

$$X_{投资} = 0.180444x_4 + 0.2354x_5 + 0.062413x_6,\tag{5}$$

$$X_{创新} = 0.261864x_7 + 0.309551x_8 + 0.22847x_9。\tag{6}$$

由以上三个表达式，可以得出修正后的现代信息服务业发展模式的排序多元离散选择模型，其表达式为：

$$y_i^* = \alpha_1 x_{要素,i} + \alpha_2 x_{投资,i} + \alpha_3 x_{创新,i} + \varepsilon_i^* \quad (i=0,\ 1,\ 2,\ \cdots,\ N)。\tag{7}$$

采用排序多元离散选择模型对修正后的现代信息服务业发展模式进行计算，结果如表3所示。

根据排序多元离散模型的运算结果，可以得出最终的现代信息服务业发展模式的识别模型，其表达式为：

$$y_i^* = 1.615321x_{要素,i} + 2.312362x_{投资,i} + 1.916652x_{创新,i}。\tag{8}$$

由此，可以得出 y_i 对应的产业发展模式相应的取值范围，如表4所示。

表 3　排序多元离散选择模型计算结果

变量	相关系数	标准差	z 统计量	概率值
要素导向型	1. 615321	5. 175155	0. 31213	0. 7549
投资导向型	2. 312362	1. 72037	1. 344108	0. 1789
创新导向型	1. 916652	1. 426092	1. 343989	0. 179
取值范围				
LIMIT_1：*C*（4）	-2. 01198	0. 735425	-2. 73581	0. 0062
LIMIT_2：*C*（5）	-1. 26664	0. 696111	-1. 8196	0. 0688
LIMIT_3：*C*（6）	-0. 58613	0. 65548	-0. 89421	0. 3712
LIMIT_4：*C*（7）	1. 167594	0. 770781	1. 51482	0. 1298

表 4　现代信息服务业区域发展模式取值范围

y_i 对应的产业发展模式	y^* 的取值范围
要素导向型	$y_i^* \leqslant -2.01198$
要素、投资混合型	$-2.01198 < y_i^* \leqslant -1.26664$
投资导向型	$-1.26664 < y_i^* \leqslant -0.58613$
投资、创新混合型	$-0.58613 < y_i^* \leqslant 1.167594$
创新导向型	$1.167594 < y_i^*$

3　广东省现代信息服务业发展模式的识别与优化

3.1　广东省现代信息服务业发展模式的识别

根据建立的排序多元离散选择模型可对广东省现代信息服务业发展模式所处的阶段进行识别。将表5中的数据标准化后代入现代信息服务业区域发展模式的识别模型，可得出 y_i^* ，其计算结果如下：

$$
\begin{aligned}
y_i^* &= 1.615321x_{要求,i} + 2.312362x_{投资,i} + 1.916652x_{创新,i} \\
&= 1.615321 \times 0.026074 + 2.312362 \times 0.139168 + 1.916652 \times 0.053844 \\
&= 0.467124。
\end{aligned}
$$

根据以上计算结果，结合表4中现代信息服务业区域发展模式的取值范围，可以看出 $0.467124 \in (-0.58613, 1.167594]$ ，由此可以断定广东省现代信息服务业为投资、创新混合导向型发展模式。

表5　广东省2012年现代信息服务业发展的相关数据

指标	数值	指标	数值
区域常住人口数量/万人	10594	实际利用外资额/亿美元	241.0578
现代信息服务业就业人员比重/%	1.4256	研发经费占GDP比重/%	2.1661
光缆线路长度/公里	1054583.50	版权合同登记数/份	102
产业年末固定资产投资额/亿元	381.9407	研发人数占从业人数比重/%	4.8241
产业增加值占GDP比重/%	2.8354		

资料来源：《广东统计年鉴（2013）》。

综合以上分析，广东省现代信息服务业的发展处于投资驱动和创新驱动为主的发展阶段，究其原因主要有以下三方面：

第一，要素驱动因素有较强竞争力。广东省现代信息服务业城镇单位就业人员为18.59万人，仅次于北京，居全国第二位，占城镇单位就业人员比重为1.4%，居全国第八位，说明广东省现代信息服务业发展程度较高，在服务生产、增加就业方面有较大贡献。广东省常住人口为10594万人，居全国第一，较大的人口规模使得现代信息服务业有较大的消费群体，这将有助于扩大对现代信息服务产品的需求。广东省光缆线路长度1054583.5公里，仅次于江苏省，居全国第二，说明广东省具备良好的通信网络设施条件，这为广东省现代信息服务业的发展提供了良好的基础，并极大地促进了现代信息服务业从要素导向型发展模式向投资、创新导向型发展模式进行转变。

第二，投资驱动因素有一定优势。广东省现代信息服务业固定资产投资381.94亿元，居全国第一位，说明广东省现代信息服务业在基础设施方面有较大投入，这将对改善基础设施建设、完善发展环境起到重要作用。广东省现代信息服务业增加值占GDP比重为2.84%，居全国第三位，说明广东省现代信息服务业呈现快速增长态势，产业地位也日渐提高。广东省毗邻港澳，具有优越的地理位置，对吸引外资以及对区域资源进行整合和协调有强大的促进作用。2012年广东省实际利用外资额241.06亿美元，居全国第三位，说明广东省对吸引外资具有较强的竞争力。

第三，创新驱动因素有较大发展潜力。广东省研发经费的投入占GDP的比重为2.17%，居全国第五位，说明广东省对于创新有较强的支持力度。广东省研发人数占从业人数的比重为4.8%，居全国第二位，这将为促进广东省现代信息服务业创新提供强大的人才支持。广东省的版权合同登记数为102份，远远低于北京、上海、江苏这三个创新导向型发展模式的代表地区，说明广东省在知识产权的保护方面有所欠缺。知识产权是现代信息服务业核心竞争力的主要来源，保护知识产权就是鼓励自主创新，就是增强产业的核心竞争力。因此，广东省现代信息服务业在保护知识产权、提高自主创新力方面尚有较大提高空间。

3.2　广东省现代信息服务业发展模式的优化

综合前面的分析，虽然广东省现代信息服务业实现了从要素驱动向投资、创新驱动的转变，目前处于投资、创新驱动为主的发展阶段，但在创新力上与北京、上海等创新地区相比仍有很大差距。因此，广东省现代信息服务业的发展应重点增强创新能力，加快其进一步向创新导向型发展模式优化。结合影响现代信息服务业区域发展模式的九大因素，广东省现代信息服务业发展模式的优化应从以下几方面进行。

3.2.1　加大现代信息服务业基础设施建设力度

信息服务产品的创新及消费都需要有强大的信息网络基础设施作为支撑。因此广东省应继续加大现代信息服务业基础的建设力度，完善信息网络基础设施，优化网络布局，通过新的网络、移动通信等技术，不断提升网络传输服务能力，为信息服务创新提供基础支持条件。

3.2.2　培育新兴的现代信息服务业态

新兴的信息服务业态往往具有高端、高效、高辐射力的特性以及广泛关联性和较高成长性的优势，这对于整个行业效率的提升、发展质量的提高以及内部结构的优化都具有重要作用。广东省应着力培育和发展数字新媒体、空间信息服务、移动即时通讯、移动搜索、在线数据处理和存储等现代信息服务的新业态，培育一批具有自主知识产权、在国内外技术领先、市场占有率较高的产品和企业，从而带动整个区域自主创新能力的提高。

3.2.3　创新现代信息服务业商业经营模式

移动互联网、云计算、物联网、大数据等信息通信技术日新月异，推动产业生态和市场环境发生了深刻变革。在大数据时代，企业拥有数据的规模、价值，以及收集、运用数据的能力，决定其核心竞争力。广东省现代信息服务业应加快实现商业经营模式的创新，不断更高效地整合数据资源，推出符合消费者需求、便捷的信息服务，满足大数据时代消费者对信息获取更加高效、便捷、安全的需要。

3.2.4　加强知识产权的保护

对于现代信息服务业而言，在某个领域拥有知识产权并形成专利，就意味着拥有该领域的最高话语权和市场主导权。从某种程度上来说，知识产权是现代信息服务业核心竞争力的主要来源，而保护知识产权，就是鼓励自主创新，就是增强产业的核心竞争力。广东省应加强对知识产权保护的重视，加大知识产权投入，在国内外申请专利、注册商标、登记著作权、创建品牌，特别是加强数字内容创意企业著作权的登记。

参考文献

[1] 娄勤俭. 中国电子信息产业发展模式研究 [M]. 北京：中国经济出版社，2003：37－72.

[2] 迈克尔·波特. 国家竞争优势 [M]. 李明轩，等译. 北京：华夏出版社，2003：119.

[3] 熊励. 中国三大区域现代信息服务业差异比较与融合发展 [J]. 上海大学学报：社会科学版，2009 (5)：21－28.

[4] Ein-Dor P, Myers M, Raman K S. IT Industry Development and the Knowledge Economy: A Four Country Study [J].

Journal of Global Information Management, 2004, 12 (4): 23 - 49.
[5] Hsiu Hua Chiang. The "Flying Geese Development" Model of the IT Industry in East Asia [J]. Journal of the Asia Pacific Economy, 2008, 13 (2): 227 - 242.
[6] Tan F B, Leewongcharoen K. Factors Contributing to IT Industry Success in Developing Countries: The Case of Thailand [J]. Information Technology for Development, 2005, 11 (2): 161 - 194.
[7] 李艺，秦玉婷. 基于钻石模型的现代服务业发展模式研究 [J]. 沈阳工业大学学报：社会科学版，2003 (1): 77 - 83.
[8] 安筱鹏. 电子信息产业发展模式的探讨 [J]. 现代经济探讨，2005 (7): 38 - 41.
[9] 杨全成. 融合与链式：信息内容产业发展模式探讨 [J]. 中国科技论坛，2011 (3): 49 - 53.
[10] 许娟，孙林岩，何哲. 基于DEA的我国省际高技术产业发展模式及相对优势产业选择 [J]. 科技进步与对策，2009 (1): 30 - 33.
[11] 许明星，王健，胡永仕. 区域流通产业发展模式的识别与优化——以福建省为例 [J]. 北京工商大学学报：社会科学版，2012 (9): 37 - 45.
[12] 陈伟达，景生军. 基于偏离—份额分析的南京市软件服务业发展模式与对策研究 [J]. 东南大学学报：哲学社会科学版，2010 (3): 58 - 63.
[13] 哈进兵，陈双康. 构建现代信息服务业发展水平指标体系的探讨 [J]. 情报理论与实践，2006 (4): 442 - 444.
[14] 李超. 我国各地区现代信息服务业综合评价研究 [J]. 图书情报工作，2011 (14): 49 - 53.
[15] 王炳清，胡平，陆燕萍. 中国分地区信息服务业竞争优势的综合评价分析 [J]. 科技管理研究，2011 (21): 182 - 185.
[16] 程少锋，郑初悦. 信息服务业发展水平评估研究——以宁波市为例 [J]. 科技进步与对策，2007 (6): 155 - 159.
[17] 宋静，曹顺良，雷向欣，王建会. 上海市信息服务业区域竞争力定量分析 [J]. 情报杂志，2011 (9): 117 - 121.
[18] 徐盈之，赵玥. 中国信息服务业全要素生产率变动的区域差异与趋同分析 [J]. 数量经济技术经济研究，2009 (10): 49 - 60.
[19] 温春龙，胡平. 我国各地区信息服务产业的地理聚集分析 [J]. 科技管理研究，2011 (4): 180 - 184.
[20] 陈建龙，王建冬. 我国地方政府信息服务业发展模式和热点领域分析 [J]. 图书情报工作，2009 (24): 55 - 59.
[21] 陈建龙，王建冬. 我国地方信息服务业发展的经济环境和发展阶段分析 [J]. 图书情报工作，2010 (4): 38 - 40.

教师简介：

陈明红，女，西南大学管理学学士，武汉大学管理学硕士、博士。2013 年起任中山大学资讯管理学院讲师。主讲“电子政务导论”、“信息分析与决策”、“网络信息获取”、“信息检索”、“演讲口才与公共礼仪”等课程。研究方向包括移动信息行为、社会化媒体与知识共享、信息分析与多元统计、信息生态与信息资源配置、复杂系统分析与仿真。已在国际期刊、国际会议和国内核心刊物发表相关领域研究论文 20 余篇；参与编写专著及教材 8 部；主持教育部人文社会科学青年项目和中国博士后科学基金面上项目研究，参与多项国家级项目研究工作。广东社会科学情报学会会员和广东省城镇化发展研究会会员。联系方式：chenmhstar@ 163. com。

所选论文《学术虚拟社区用户持续知识共享的意愿研究》原载于《情报资料工作》2015 年第 1 期

学术虚拟社区用户持续知识共享的意愿研究*

陈明红

摘　要：采用社会资本理论和技术接受模型，构建学术虚拟社区持续知识共享的结构方程模型，深入探究学术虚拟社区用户持续知识共享的关键影响因素。以科学网社区用户为调查对象，通过网络调查获得 370 份有效问卷，采用偏最小二乘法（PLS）对模型进行验证。研究结果表明，社会资本、感知有用性和感知易用性均对学术虚拟社区知识共享满意度具有显著的正向影响，并且知识共享的满意度显著地影响持续知识共享的意愿。

关键词：学术社区；虚拟社区；知识共享；持续意愿；社会资本

Research on Knowledge Sharing Continuance Intention in Academic Virtual Communities

Minghong Chen

Abstract: In order to explore key influencing factors of knowledge sharing continuance intention in academic virtual communities, this study builds a continuance intention model of knowledge sharing based on social capital theory and Technology Acceptance Model (TAM). And the model is validated by Partial Least Squares (PLS) method through online questionnaire of 370 valid responses from ScienceNet. cn. The results indicate that social

* 该文系教育部人文社会科学青年项目“信息生态视角下的网络信息资源优化配置研究”（项目批准号：12YJC870004）、国家自然科学基金项目“基于云计算的公共信息服务机制研究”（项目批准号：71263006）、中山大学青年教师培育项目“社会网络视角下的虚拟社区知识共享研究”（项目批准号：1309076）的研究成果之一。

capital, perceived usefulness and perceived ease of use are significantly related to continuance intentions to share knowledge, and users' satisfaction is significantly related to knowledge sharing continuance intention in academic virtual communities.

Keywords: Academic communities; Virtual communities; Knowledge sharing; Continuance intention; Social capital theory

1 引　　言

随着互联网的全面普及与快速发展，虚拟社区成为信息交流和知识共享的重要平台。[1]数字媒体研究集团（Digital Media Research Group）的调查显示，50%以上的网民受到了虚拟社区中相关信息和知识的影响。[2]许多学者参与各种专业社区，通过搜寻、获取和贡献专业知识以传播其研究兴趣、提高学术洞察力和提升学术创新能力。[3]与传统的正式的知识交流相比，学术虚拟社区知识共享具有开放性和便利性，不受时间和空间限制，知识共享效率更高。然而，学术虚拟社区的社会关系松散、管理不规范及知识质量标准缺失等因素可能对知识共享效果和用户持续共享意愿带来负面影响。据统计，虚拟社区用户流失非常严重[4]，33%的用户偶尔在虚拟社区中提问或搜寻知识，经常参与知识共享的用户只有4.4%[5]，不少用户参与一次后就不再问津。这使得许多虚拟社区在创建后不久便走向衰落，不利于虚拟社区的可持续发展。[1]

作为典型的信息系统，虚拟社区的最终成功主要取决于用户的持续参与而不是初始采纳。[6-8]在学术虚拟社区中，知识共享是重要的社区活动，用户持续的知识共享是学术虚拟社区长期发展的关键。然而，学术虚拟社区是依托信息技术而存在的在线社交网络系统[9]，其知识共享过程和结果受到社会资本资源和信息技术的双重影响。本文利用社会资本理论和技术接受模型（TAM）构建学术虚拟社区持续知识共享的社会—技术理论框架，深入探讨用户对学术虚拟社区知识共享的满意度评价及持续知识共享的影响机制，针对性地提出学术虚拟社区持续发展与知识管理策略。

2 文献回顾

2.1 学术虚拟社区中的知识共享

学术虚拟社区是用户以互联网为平台，针对特定主题内容进行学术知识交流与共享并建立网络社会关系的专业在线社区。[10]作为社会价值和社会期望产生的重要场所，学术虚拟社区通过知识交流与共享促进学术知识的开发与利用。[1]根据Usoro等提出的定义，知识共享是知识提供和知识获取的双方或多方的交流互动过程。[11]在学术虚拟社区中，具有共同兴趣、背景或目标的成员利用在线论坛、电子邮件、BBS、Blog和Wiki等社会化媒体，通过对同一学术领域或主题进行提问、回答和讨论进行知识共享。[12]这种依靠互联网建立相互理解和信任而进行的信息交流与知识共享显然比面对面方式受到的影响因素更多[13]，已有学者从技术特性、成本与收益、激励机制、内在与外在动机、社会资本、社会与个人认知、社区氛围等诸多方面广泛研究知识共享意愿[14]，且尤其关注学术虚拟社区的社会性与可用性对知识共享的影响。社会性是指学术虚拟社区促使用户互动以实现共同目标的特性，包括互惠、规范、信任、社会关系、社会影响等内容；可用性是指学术虚拟社区技术系统对于用户完成特定任务的易用程度和有用程度[15]，包括感知有用性、感知易用性、感知相对优势等内容。

2.2 社会资本视角下的知识共享

社会资本是指嵌入在社会关系网络中的各种资源的总和，由结构资本、关系资本和认知资本三个维度构成。[16]其中，结构资本是指社会系统中个人之间的交流结构和联系强度，是社会资本的基础，没有结构资本就没有社会关系，个人便无法获得所需的社会资源；关系资本是指人们通过多次互动所形成的个人关系，主要源于关系网络中人们之间的相互信任和对集体的强烈认同；认知资本是指个人共享代码和含义系统的程度，认知资本能够促进社会系统对集体目标和行为的共同理解和沟通。

知识资源价值的实现不仅依赖于个人知识的存储与创造，更得益于人们之间的社会化互动与交换，诸多研究均已证实社会资本对虚拟社区知识交流、传播和共享具有促进作用，如 Chiu 等的研究指出在线交互联结显著地影响虚拟社区成员之间知识分享的数量[17]；Chang 等的实证研究表明，关系资本会显著地影响个人的知识共享动机[18]；Lin 等提出社会认知资本中的信任因素对学术虚拟社区知识共享行为具有正向影响[3]。可见，社会资本是虚拟社区知识共享的前置动因，利用社会资本理论可从网络结构和组织关系的宏观层面探究知识共享的动力机制。

2.3 技术接受视角下的知识共享

技术接受模型（technology acceptance model，TAM）常用于解释人们对信息技术和信息系统的态度及意愿，该模型利用感知有用性和感知易用性两个主要的行为信念预测用户态度及接受意愿。[19]知识共享总是依托于一定的社会技术系统而存在，系统的可用性对知识共享过程具有重要影响，而可用性主要通过人们对社会技术系统的感知有用性和感知易用性进行测量。如 Hung 等采用 TAM 研究虚拟社区知识共享意愿，指出感知有用性和感知易用性对知识共享意愿具有正向影响。[20]TAM 能够从用户对技术感知的视角很好地解释知识共享意愿和行为，却忽视了社会关系、社会影响等外部因素的影响。为了全面揭示知识共享影响机制，有学者综合社会资本理论和 TAM 构建了知识共享理论模型。如 Phang 提出虚拟社区成员的社交能力和感知易用性是知识搜寻和交换行为的前因变量[21]，Liao 等研究发现社会资本、社会影响、可用性（包括感知有用性和易用性）对虚拟社区知识采纳具有重要影响[21]。

综上所述，学者从社会资本和技术接受两种视角研究虚拟社区知识共享意愿及行为，揭示出社会性和可用性对虚拟社区知识共享具有重要影响，并且以社会资本理论和 TAM 为基础构建的综合模型比单一理论或模型更符合客观实际，具有更好的解释力。然而，已有研究对学术虚拟社区的关注不够，从两种视角综合研究学术虚拟社区知识共享满意度及持续意愿的成果不多，社会性与可用性对知识共享满意度及持续意愿的内在影响机制不得而知。鉴于此，本研究整合社会资本理论和 TAM 模型，构建知识共享的社会—技术综合模型，深入探究学术虚拟社区持续知识共享的动力机制与影响机理。

3　研究模型及假设

将学术虚拟社区知识共享的满意度及持续知识共享意愿的影响因素划分为社会资本与技术接受两个方面，构建理论研究模型（如图 1 所示）。该模型表明，社会资本与技术接受因素通过知识共享满意度对持续知识共享意愿产生影响。其中，社会资本由结构资本、关系资本和认知资本三个变量构成，而结构资本通过社会交互联结进行测量，关系资本和认知资本是二阶变量，分别由两个一阶变量进行测量；技术接受因素包括感知有用性和感知易用性两方面内容。

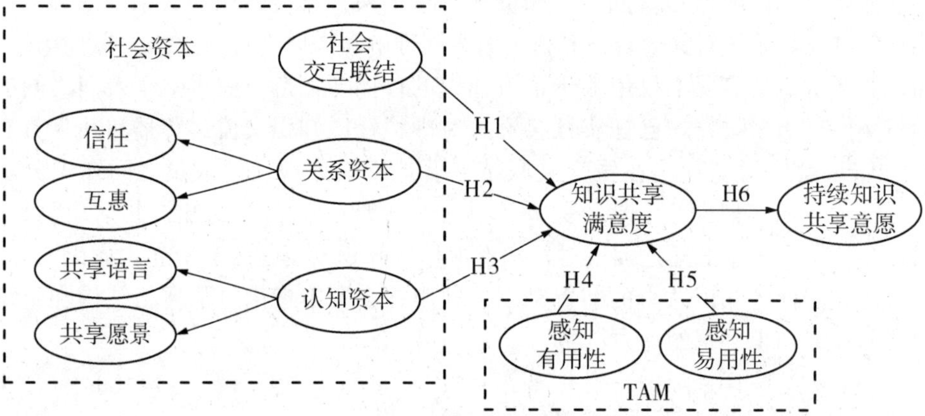

图 1　理论研究模型

3.1　社会资本

知识共享总是嵌入在特定的社会情境中，人们之间的网络结构、关系质量以及共同的社会认知对知识共享效果起着不容忽视的作用。本研究从社会资本的三个维度展开研究，探究结构资本、关系资本和认知资本对虚拟社区知识共享满意度及持续意愿的影响机制。

（1）结构资本与知识共享满意度。结构资本表征的是社会系统中人们相互联结的整体模式。人们通过社会交互联结可以获得他人的知识和其他资源，因而可将社会交互联结视为社会资源流通的渠道。[16] 在学术虚拟社区中，知识共享的各方以提问、回答和讨论等方式进行的对话和联系是一种社会交互联结，社会联结越强，社区用户交换知识资源的频率越高，数量越多。这在已有研究中得到证实，如 Chiu 等指出虚拟社区的社会互动关系能够增加知识交互的强度、频率和广度[17]，Liao 等提出社会交互联结对虚拟社区知识共享采纳态度具有重要影响[21]。本研究将社会交互联结作为结构资本，从交互强度、耗费时间及交流频率等方面测量，并认为社会交互联结关系能够促进知识共享，提升知识共享满意度，社会交互联结与知识共享满意度之间具有如下假设关系：

H1：学术虚拟社区知识共享满意度受到社会交互联结的正向影响。

（2）关系资本与知识共享满意度。关系资本是指社会联系的人格化内容，聚焦于影响个人行为的互动关系，主要包括信任和互惠。其中，信任被视为营造合作环境和促进知识共享的关键因素，从两个方面加以影响：一是信任促使组织成员更愿意参与成员间的对话，使得双方交换的知识更多；二是信任使得成员之间交换知识更加自由。因此，信任程度会影响知识交换的效果，如 Ridings 等对 36 个虚拟社区的调查研究表明用户对他人的信任程度直接影响其知识给予和知识获取的意愿。[22]此外，关系资本的另一变量互惠是指在社会交互过程中，个人对未来的收益预期。根据社会交换理论，知识共享活动的参与者总是对互惠有所期望，这种期望也决定了他们为知识共享付出的时间和努力程度。[17] Davenport 等指出互惠使得用户在分享知识时感到更方便，对知识共享有促进作用[23]；Bock 等提出互惠对知识分享态度有积极影响[24]。可见，以信任和互惠表征的关系资本能够促进知识交流和知识共享，提高对知识和自我需求的理解程度，能够提高用户对知识共享的满意程度。[25]本研究将关系资本视为二阶变量，通过两个一阶变量信任和互惠进行测度，研究二者对知识共享满意度的影响，并提出以下假设关系：

H2：学术虚拟社区知识共享满意度受到关系资本的正向影响。

（3）认知资本与知识共享满意度。认知资本是指社会系统提供的用于共享的含义和推断的资本，主要包括共享语言和共享愿景。[26]从共享语言看，虚拟社区成员若采用共同语言或代码，表明他们有着相似的观点和看法。[26]共享语言对虚拟社区活动的重要作用体现在共享语言能够改善社区用户的相互认知，减少用户间的误解，有助于用户认同社区整体目标并付诸实际。[27]因而，具有共享语言的社区用户具有较强的信息获取和知识交换能力，知识共享的效率和效果更佳。

此外，共享愿景表示用户对社区共同目标的理解和就目标实现达成共识的程度。[27]对于知识共享而言，共享愿景使人们产生共同的行动目标，加强用户对彼此的认同度和社区凝聚力，增强知识共享的驱动力和参与度。已有研究表明，共享语言和共享愿景对知识采纳态度具有积极作用[21]，认知资本对知识共享满意度具有重要影响[25]。据此，本研究将共享语言和共享愿景作为认知资本的一阶变量，研究二者对知识共享满意度的影响，提出以下假设关系：

H3：学术虚拟社区知识共享满意度受到认知资本的正向影响。

3.2 技术接受因素

对于学术虚拟社区，感知有用性（perceived usefulness，PU）是指用户认为利用学术虚拟社区对其工作和学习绩效的提高程度，感知易用性（perceived ease of use，PEU）是指用户认为利用学术虚拟社区的容易程度。TAM 及其应用研究表明，感知有用性和感知易用性对知识共享行为意愿具有显著影响。[21]根据 Oliver 提出的期望确认理论（expectation confirmation theory，ECT），用户的忠实来自他们对产品或服务的高度认同和承诺，进而影响用户再次使用的意愿。[28]如果用户认为学术虚拟社区有用且方便使用，那么他们会增加对学术虚拟社区的使用频率和满意度。因此，本研究认为感知易用性和感知有用性是知识共享满意度的两个前因变量，并提出以下两个假设关系：

H4：知识共享满意度受到感知有用性的正向影响。

H5：知识共享满意度受到感知易用性的正向影响。

3.3 知识共享满意度

在本研究中，满意度是指用户对知识共享是否满足自身需求的主观评价，是用户对知识共享的感知绩效与其期望进行比较的结果。研究表明用户对信息技术或信息系统的满意度直接影响持续使用意愿，例如，Bhattacherjee 以期望确认理论与 TAM 为基础研究信息系统持续使用意愿，发现用户满意度是影响持续使用意愿最重要的因素[6]；Jin 等对网上问答知识社区的研究表明，用户对问题回答的满意度与该用户继续回答问题的意愿正相关[8]；Zhou 等以社会型虚拟社区"第二人生"为研究对象，研究指出用户满意度与持续使用意愿之间具有正相关关系[29]。因此，本研究认为用户对学术虚拟社区知识共享的满意程度与持续知识共享意愿具有如下假设关系：

H6：持续知识共享意愿受到知识共享满意度的正向影响。

4 量表设计与数据收集

4.1 量表设计

研究模型包括 9 个一阶变量和 2 个二阶变量，二阶变量通过对应的一阶变量进行测度。为了提高量表的内容效度，各变量的测度指标均来源于已有研究，每个变量至少包括 3 个测度项，采用李克特 7 级量表进行测度。在正式派发问卷前，邀请科学网用户进行了小样本的预调查，回收有效问卷 43 份，根据问卷分析结果对部分问项进行修改和调整，最终量表及来源参考如表 1 所示。

表 1　变量的测度及来源

变量	测度项	指标内容	来源文献
社会联结（social interaction ties）	SIT_1	我与科学网社区成员保持紧密的在线联系。	Liao & Chou，2012[21]
	SIT_2	我花大量时间与科学网社区成员进行交流。	
	SIT_3	我与科学网社区的一些成员有频繁的交流。	
信任（trust）	TRU_1	即使有机会，科学网社区成员也不会利用他人。	Chiu，et al.，2006[17]
	TRU_2	科学网社区成员能遵守自己对别人许下的承诺。	
	TRU_3	科学网社区成员会真诚对待彼此。	
	TRU_4	我完全信任科学网社区成员。	

续表1

变量	测度项	指标内容	来源文献
互惠 (reciprocity)	REC_1	我知道科学网社区的其他成员会帮助我，所以我帮助他们是理所当然的。	Hau, et al., 2013[30]
	REC_2	我相信当我需要时，科学网社区的成员会帮助我。	
	REC_3	当我在科学网社区中共享知识时，我相信我对知识的疑惑定将得到解答。	
	REC_4	在科学网社区中共享知识可以让我获得更多知识。	
共同语言 (shared language)	SL_1	科学网社区成员使用常用的词汇或术语。	Chang & Chuang, 2011[18]
	SL_2	在讨论过程中，科学网社区成员使用易于理解的方式进行交流。	
	SL_3	科学网社区成员使用易于理解的表达方式发布消息或文章。	
共同愿景 (shared vision)	SV_1	科学网社区成员具有帮助他人解决专业问题的共同愿景。	Liao & Chou, 2012[21]
	SV_2	科学网社区成员具有互相学习的共同目标。	
	SV_3	科学网社区成员具有助人为乐的价值观。	
感知有用性 (perceived usefulness)	PU_1	使用科学网社区能够帮助更快地完成工作任务。	Liao & Chou, 2012[21]
	PU_2	使用科学网社区能够帮助我提高工作绩效。	
	PU_3	我认为科学网社区对我的工作有帮助。	
	PU_4	我认为科学网社区是有用的。	
感知易用性 (perceived ease of use)	PEU_1	我觉得利用科学网社区做我想做的事情很容易。	Kuo & Lee, 2009[31]
	PEU_2	利用科学网社区对我来说很容易。	
	PEU_3	科学网社区的在线互动明了易懂。	
	PEU_4	对我而言，熟练地利用科学网社区是很容易的。	
知识共享满意度 (satisfaction)	SAT_1	我对科学网社区知识共享的经历非常满意。	Jin, et al., 2012[8]
	SAT_2	科学网社区知识共享的经历对我来说是非常愉快的。	
	SAT_3	科学网社区知识共享的经历对我来说是非常满足的。	

续表1

变量	测度项	指标内容	来源文献
持续知识共享意愿（continuance intention）	CI_1	我打算未来继续在科学网社区中共享知识。	Jin, et al., 2012[8]
	CI_2	我期待未来在科学网社区的知识共享能够持续。	
	CI_3	我计划未来在科学网社区中共享知识。	

4.2 数据收集与描述性统计

以全球最大的中文科学社区——科学网为研究环境，选取在科学网上注册并参加过知识共享的用户作为调查对象，广泛搜集各用户邮箱并向其逐一发放网络问卷。经过半年时间，共回收有效问卷370份。表2是对调查样本进行描述性统计分析的结果。由表2可知，在370份有效问卷中，84.86%是男性，70%以上具有副高及以上职称，45岁以下用户大约占80%，自然科学领域用户占大多数（76.49%）。

表2　描述性统计结果

统计量		频次	百分比/%	统计量		频次	百分比/%
性别	男	314	84.86	年龄	<29岁	22	5.95
	女	56	15.14		29～35岁	126	34.05
职称	教授/研究员	117	31.62		36～45岁	152	41.08
	副教授/研究员	167	45.14		>45岁	70	18.92
	讲师/助理研究员	60	16.22	学科	自然科学	283	76.49
	博士研究生	13	3.51		社会科学	36	9.73
	硕士研究生	5	1.35		人文科学	11	2.97
	其他	8	2.16		交叉科学	40	10.81

5 数据分析与假设检验

基于方差的偏最小二乘法（partial least squares，PLS）不要求样本具有正态分布特征，并且能够同时分析测量模型和结构模型。由于本调查的样本数据采用方便抽样方式获得，并不完全服从正态分布，故采用PLS分析数据，检验相关假设。

5.1 测量模型分析

（1）信度评估。采用组合信度 *CR*（composite reliability）、*Cronbach* 和平均萃取方差 *AVE*（average variance extracted）三个指标测量信度。根据Burkink和Chin提出的标准，

当 *CR* 和 *Cronbach* 分别大于 0.7[32]、*AVE* 大于 0.5[33]时，表明调查数据具有较好的一致性，测量模型信度可以接受。以上三个值可直接由 PLS 计算得到，如表 3 所示，所有变量的 *CR* 值均大于 0.8，*Cronbach* 均大于 0.7，除“信任”的 *AVE* 值为 0.55 外，其余变量的 *AVE* 值均大于 0.7，因此，所有变量都具有较好的测量信度。

表 3　信度分析结果

变量	测度项	因子载荷值	平均值	标准差	*CR*	*Cronbach*	*AVE*
社会交互联结	SIT_1	0.89	2.88	1.64	0.94	0.90	0.84
	SIT_2	0.93	2.24	1.32			
	SIT_3	0.93	2.34	1.40			
信任	TRU_1	0.78	5.14	1.37	0.83	0.74	0.55
	TRU_2	0.68	3.59	1.87			
	TRU_3	0.71	3.76	16.8			
	TRU_4	0.79	5.14	1.53			
互惠	REC_1	0.87	5.32	1.47	0.93	0.89	0.75
	REC_2	0.89	5.09	1.44			
	REC_3	0.85	5.52	1.43			
	REC_4	0.87	5.37	1.45			
共同语言	SL_1	0.87	5.03	1.29	0.93	0.93	0.88
	SL_2	0.92	5.13	1.24			
	SL_3	0.90	5.18	1.20			
共同愿景	SV_1	0.91	5.15	1.43	0.93	0.89	0.83
	SV_2	0.90	5.27	1.38			
	SV_3	0.91	5.15	1.44			
感知有用性	PU_1	0.85	5.69	1.21	0.91	0.86	0.71
	PU_2	0.87	4.81	1.39			
	PU_3	0.85	4.72	1.49			
	PU_4	0.81	5.60	1.25			
感知易用性	PEU_1	0.84	5.46	1.28	0.94	0.91	0.79
	PEU_2	0.92	5.30	1.26			
	PEU_3	0.87	4.91	1.33			
	PEU_4	0.92	5.05	1.34			
知识共享满意度	SAT_1	0.93	4.82	1.32	0.96	0.94	0.89
	SAT_2	0.95	5.02	1.29			
	SAT_3	0.94	4.90	1.31			

续表 3

变量	测度项	因子载荷值	平均值	标准差	*CR*	*Cronbach*	*AVE*
持续知识共享意愿	CI_1	0.93	5.38	1.31	0.96	0.93	0.88
	CI_2	0.94	5.64	1.26			
	CI_3	0.94	5.59	1.28			

（2）效度评估。对于聚合效度，可从两个方面进行评估：一是所有变量的因子负载值（loading）都要显著且大于 0.6，二是每个变量的平均萃取方差至少大于 0.5。[34] 表 3 表明，所有变量的因子负载值都大于 0.6，所有变量的平均萃取方差在 0.55 至 0.89 之间，满足聚合效度的最低标准。

对于区分效度，主要通过比较平均萃取方差（*AVE*）的平方根与变量间相关系数进行评估，若某变量 *AVE* 的平方根大于所有与该变量相关的相关系数，则表明该变量的区分效度好。变量间的相关系数（表 4）显示，所有变量 *AVE* 的平方根均大于相应变量之间的相关系数，可见测量模型的区分效度较好。

表 4　变量间的相关系数

	SIT	*TRU*	*REC*	*SL*	*SV*	*PU*	*PEU*	*SAT*	*CI*
SIT	**0.917**								
TRU	0.289	**0.740**							
REC	0.227	0.542	**0.868**						
SL	0.209	0.498	0.702	**0.938**					
SV	0.206	0.471	0.726	0.681	**0.908**				
PU	0.244	0.437	0.667	0.596	0.651	**0.842**			
PEU	0.218	0.376	0.508	0.425	0.449	0.501	**0.888**		
SAT	0.300	0.447	0.592	0.502	0.571	0.573	0.523	**0.942**	
CI	0.248	0.441	0.603	0.570	0.555	0.651	0.469	0.706	**0.937**

说明：斜对角线上的粗体数值表示对应变量 *AVE* 值的平方根。

（3）多重共线性诊断。由于个别变量之间的相关系数较高（如与互惠和满意度相关的少数几个相关系数），容易引起多重线性问题，因而有必要进行多重共线性诊断，以评判研究模型中各自变量之间是否存在严重的相互依赖关系。利用 SPSS 的回归分析模块进行计算，结果表明，方差膨胀因子 *VIF*（variance inflation factor）处于 1.67 至 6.01 之间（符合小于 10 的要求），相容度（Tolerance Values）处于 0.16 至 0.59 之间（符合大于 0.1 的要求）[35]，表明本研究不存在多重共线性问题。

5.2　结构模型分析

结构模型的评估及假设检验需要查看 PLS 运算结果，包括路径系数、显著性水平和因变量被解释的比例（R^2 值），3 个指标如图 2 所示。

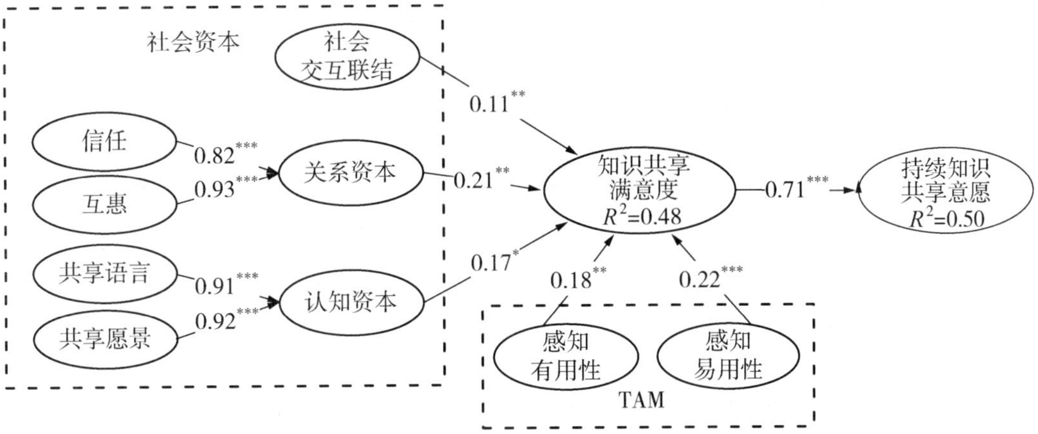

显著性水平 ＊代表 $p<0.05$，＊＊代表 $p<0.01$，＊＊＊代表 $p<0.001$。

图 2　结构方程模型检验结果

由图 2 可知，满意度和意愿的 R^2 值分别为 0.48 和 0.50，说明该结构模型具有较好的预测效果。此外，所有假设关系均得到验证。其中，知识共享满意度对持续共享意愿具有非常显著的影响，影响系数为 0.71，显著性水平为 0.001，假设 H6 成立；知识共享满意度被社会资本和技术接受因素解释了 48% 的方差，其中，结构资本（社会交互联结）对知识共享满意度的影响比较显著，影响系数为 0.11，显著性水平为 0.01，假设 H1 成立；关系资本对知识共享满意度的影响显著，影响系数为 0.21，显著性水平为 0.01，并且关系资本中的信任对知识共享满意度的影响系数为 0.17（0.82 ×0.21），互惠对知识共享满意度的影响系数为 0.20（0.93 ×0.21），假设 H2 成立；认知资本对知识共享满意度的影响是显著的，影响系数为 0.17，显著性水平为 0.05，并且认知资本中的共享语言对知识共享满意度的影响系数为 0.15（0.91 ×0.17），共享愿景对知识共享满意度的影响系数为 0.16（0.92 ×0.17），假设 H3 成立；感知有用性对知识共享满意度的影响显著，影响系数为 0.18，显著性水平为 0.01，假设 H4 成立；感知易用性对知识共享满意度的影响非常显著，影响系数为 0.22，显著性水平为 0.001，假设 H5 成立。

6 讨　论

由测量模型和结构模型的分析结果可知，所有假设均得到验证，所有路径系数均显著。分析各因素对学术虚拟社区知识共享满意度及持续知识共享意愿的影响关系，得到如下启示：

（1）学术虚拟社区知识共享满意度对持续知识共享意愿具有重要影响。学术虚拟社区知识共享满意度到持续知识共享意愿的标准化路径系数为 0.71，并且在 0.001 的水平下显著，表明用户知识共享满意度对持续知识共享的意愿具有非常显著的正向影响作用。这与 Jin 等[8]、Cheung 等[12]的研究结论一致，说明满意度对持续知识共享的意愿具有直接决定性影响。虚拟社区实践发展表明，用户持续参与虚拟社区的信息交流、知识共享等活动是虚拟社区可持续发展的关键，因而需要重视学术虚拟社区用户持续知识共享意愿的影响因素，提升用户对知识共享的满意度。而满意度是用户对学术虚拟社区知识共享的期望与实际感知之间的差异程度，学术虚拟社区管理者需经常调查用户对知识共享的满意度评价，关注用户的实际体验，通过高效的管理与服务，改善知识共享效果，缩小用户期望与实际感知之差异，提高用户满意度，增强用户持续知识共享意愿。

（2）社会资本对学术虚拟社区知识共享满意度具有重要影响。学术虚拟社区知识共享是基于特定情境的社会化活动，受到社会资本的显著影响。[14]其中，关系资本对学术虚拟社区知识共享满意度的影响最大，影响系数为0.21（$p<0.01$）；认知资本的影响次之，影响系数为0.17（$p<0.05$）；结构资本（社会交互联结）的影响作用相对较小，影响系数为0.11（$p<0.001$）。这说明社会资本的三个维度对知识共享满意度均有显著的正向影响，体现于社会资本在一定程度上能够防止或减少“公共地悲剧”现象。如果不考虑学术虚拟社区的社会交互联结、信任、互惠等社会资本的影响和约束，用于共享的知识常常被视为“公共物品”[36]，用户总是希望获取知识而不愿意为此支付任何成本，不愿意贡献自身知识以回馈他人，导致社区中的知识数量日益减少，造成知识共享困境。然而社会资本嵌入于学术虚拟社区，对知识共享过程和结果产生持续性影响。在一个具有共同语言和共同愿景的学术虚拟社区中，若用户之间相互联系紧密且彼此信任，那么用户将会更愿意共享更多高质量知识，知识共享效果更好，用户满意度也越高。因此，学术虚拟社区管理者不仅要关注用户个人的知识量，更要注重社会资本的影响，通过增强用户之间的社会联结、信任、互惠，形成共同的价值观和意义体系，构建学术虚拟社区知识共同体，促进知识的共享与利用。

（3）技术接受因素对学术虚拟社区知识共享满意度具有重要影响。技术接受因素的感知有用性和感知易用性对知识共享满意度的影响非常显著，影响系数分别为0.18（$p<0.01$）和0.22（$p<0.001$），感知易用性的影响稍大于感知有用性，这与预期有一定出入。对于一般社区的知识共享，社区有用性的影响大于易用性；但在学术虚拟社区中，参与知识共享的专家和学者更加关注专业知识的价值和共享条件的便利性，因而社区的易用性对知识共享满意度的影响更大。学术虚拟社区管理者在保证社区有用性的前提下，强化社区的易用性，以用户为中心，利用各种技术手段和管理手段，提高学术虚拟社区的实用价值和操作简便性，提升用户体验，让用户感受到学术虚拟社区的有用性和易用性，以提高用户满意度，增强社区吸引力，形成稳定的用户群，并促进用户持续地参与知识共享。

7 结　论

从社会资本和技术接受两个视角研究学术虚拟社区持续知识共享的意愿，综合考察学术虚拟社区的社会性和可用性对知识共享满意度及持续知识共享意愿的影响，构建了社会—技术理论模型，并以科学网用户为调查对象进行实证研究。结果表明知识共享满意度对持续知识共享的意愿具有非常显著的正向影响，并且社会资本的三个维度（结构资本、关系资本和认知资本）和学术虚拟社区的技术因素（感知有用性和感知易用性）均显著地影响知识共享满意度。理论上，本研究利用社会资本理论和技术接受模型

(TAM)对信息系统持续使用模型进行扩展，从社会性和可用性的视角探究学术虚拟社区持续知识共享的动力机制和内在机理。实践上，本研究对于学术虚拟社区知识管理具有一定的借鉴意义，学术虚拟社区管理者以及相关网站可以从社会性和技术因素两个方面采取针对性措施，促进知识共享。然而，本研究还存在着些许不足：一是结构资本由一个一阶变量社会交互联结进行测量，而另外两个维度关系资本和认知资本是二阶变量，分别由两个一阶变量进行测量，变量分布不均匀，可能会对因果关系造成影响，未来可扩充结构资本，增加其一阶变量；二是只针对科学网社区用户进行调查，样本缺乏多样性，将来可全面调查多个中外学术虚拟社区用户，增加模型的普适性。

参考文献

[1] Chen Y L. The Factors Influencing Members' Continuance Intentions in Professional Virtual Communities—A Longitudinal Study [J]. Journal of Information Science, 2007, 33 (4): 451 -467.

[2] Digital Media Research Group. An Analysis of Consumer Media Contact for Online Shopping, Marketing Intelligence & Consulting Institute (MIC) Research Report [R/OL]. [2013 -12 -26]. http://mic. iii. org. tw/aisp/reports/reportdetail. asp? docid = CDOC20120330003&doctype = RC&smode = 1.

[3] Lin M J, Hung S W, Chen C J. Fostering the Determinants of Knowledge Sharing in Professional Virtual Communities [J]. Computers in Human Behavior, 2009, 25 (4): 929 -939.

[4] Jones Q, Ravid G, Rafaeli S. Information Overload and the Message Dynamics of Online Interaction Spaces [J]. Information Systems Research, 2004, 15 (2): 194 -210.

[5] Development and Evaluation Commission: The Survey Report of Person and Family Households Digital Divide [R/OL]. [2011 -01 -17]. http://www. rdec. gov. tw/public/ Attachment/0121411543371. pdf.

[6] Bhattacherjee A. Understanding Information Systems Continuance: An Expectation-Confirmation Model [J]. MIS Quarterly, 2001, 25 (3): 351 -370.

[7] Butler B S. Membership Size, Communication Activity, and Sustainability: A Resource-Based Model of Online Social Structures [J]. Information Systems Research, 2001, 12 (4): 346 -362.

[8] Jin X L, Zhou Z Y, Lee M K O, et al. Why Users Keep Answering Questions in Online Question Answering Communities: A Theoretical and Empirical Investigation [J]. International Journal of Information Management, 2013, 3 (33): 93 -104.

[9] Lu Y, Yang D. Information Exchange in Virtual Communities under Extreme Disaster Conditions [J]. Decision Support Systems, 2011, 50 (2): 529 -538.

[10] Lee F S, Vogel D, Limayem M. Virtual Community Informatics: A Review and Research Agenda [J]. Journal of Information Technology Theory and Application, 2003, 5 (1): 47 -61.

[11] Usoro A, Sharratt M W, Tsui E, et al. Trust as an Antecedent to Knowledge Sharing in Virtual Communities of Practice [J]. Knowledge Management Research & Practice, 2007, 5 (3): 199 -212.

[12] Cheung C M K, Lee M K O, Lee Z W Y. Understanding the Continuance Intention of Knowledge Sharing in Online Communities of Practice through the Post-Knowledge-Sharing Evaluation Processes [J]. Journal of the Association for Information Science and Technology, 2013, 64 (7): 1357 -1374.

[13] Lin F R, Huang H Y. Why People Share Knowledge in Virtual Communities? [J]. Internet Research, 2013, 23 (2): 133 -159.

[14] Chen C J, Hung S W. To Give or to Receive? Factors Influencing Members' Knowledge Sharing and Community Promotion in Professional Virtual Communities [J]. Information & Management, 2010, 47 (4): 226 -236.

[15] Phang C W, Kankanhalli A, Sabherwal R. Usability and Sociability in Online Communities: A Comparative Study of Knowledge Seeking and Contribution [J]. Journal of the Association for Information Systems, 2009, 10 (10): 721 -747.

[16] Nahapiet J, Ghoshal S. Social Capital, Intellectual Capital, and the Organizational Advantage [J]. Academy of Management Journal, 1998, 23 (2): 242-266.

[17] Chiu C M, Hsu M H, Wang T. Understanding Knowledge Sharing in Virtual Communities: An Integration of Social Capital and Social Cognitive Theories [J]. Online Information Review, 2011, 35 (1): 134-153.

[18] Chang H H, Chuang S S. Social Capital and Individual Motivations on Knowledge Sharing: Participant Involvement as a Moderator [J]. Information & Management, 2011, 48 (1): 9-18.

[19] Davis F D. Perceived Usefulness, Perceived Ease, and User Acceptance of Information Technology [J]. MIS Quarterly, 1989, 13 (3): 319-340.

[20] Hung S W, Cheng M J. Are You Ready for Knowledge Sharing? An Empirical Study of Virtual Communities [J]. Computers & Education, 2013, 62 (2): 8-17.

[21] Liao S L, Chou E Y. Intention to Adopt Knowledge through Virtual Communities: Posters vs Lurkers [J]. Online Information Review, 2012, 36 (3): 442-461.

[22] Ridings C M, Gefen D. Virtual Community Attraction: Why People Hang out Online [J]. Journal of Computer-Mediated Communication, 2004, 10 (1).

[23] Davenport T H, Prusak L. Working Knowledge: How Organizations Manage What They Know [M]. Boston: Harvard Business School Press, 1998.

[24] Bock G W, Zmud R W, Kim Y G, et al. Behavioral Intention Formation in Knowledge Sharing: Examining the Roles of Extrinsic Motivators, Social Psychological Forces, and Organizational Climate [J]. MIS Quarterly, 2005, 29 (1): 87-111.

[25] Sun Y Q, Fang Y L, Lim K, et al. User Satisfaction with Information Technology Service Delivery: A Social Capital Perspective [J]. Information Systems Research, 2012, 23 (4): 1195-1211.

[26] Wasko M M, Faraj S. Why Should I Share? Examining Social Capital and Knowledge Contribution in Electronic Networks of Practice [J]. MIS Quarterly, 2005, 29 (1): 35-57.

[27] Tsai W, Ghoshal S. Social Capital and Value Creation: An Empirical Study of Intrafirm Networks [J]. Academy of Management Journal, 1998, 41 (4): 464-76.

[28] Oliver R L. Whence Consumer Loyalty? [J]. Journal of Marketing, 1999, 63 (1): 33-44.

[29] Zhou Z Y, Fang Y L, Vogel D, et al. Attracted to or Locked In? Predicting Continuance Intention in Social Virtual World Services [J]. Journal of Management Information Systems, 2012, 29 (1): 273-305.

[30] Hau Y S, Kim B, Lee H, et al. The Effects of Individual Motivations and Social Capital on Employees' Tacit and Explicit Knowledge Sharing Intentions [J]. International Journal of Information Management, 2013, 33 (2): 356-366.

[31] Kuo R Z, Lee G G. KMS Adoption: The Effects of Information Quality [J]. Management Decision, 2009, 47 (10): 1633-1651.

[32] Burkink T. Cooperative and Voluntary Wholesale Groups: Channel Coordination and Interfirm Knowledge Transfer [J]. Supply Chain Management, 2002, 7 (2): 60-70.

[33] Chin W W. The Partial Least Squares Approach to Structural Equation Modeling [C] // Marcoulides G A. Modern Methods for Business Research. London: Psychology Press, 1998: 295-336.

[34] Fornell C, Lareker D F. Evaluating Structural Equation Models with Unobservable Variables and Measurement Error [J]. Joumal of Marketing Research, 1981, 18 (1): 39-50.

[35] Mason C H, Perreault W D. Collinearity, Power and Interpretation of Multiple Regression Analysis [J]. Journal of Marketing Research, 1991, 28 (3): 268-280.

[36] Wasko M M, Teigland R. Public Goods or Virtual Commons? Applying Theories of Public Goods, Social Dilemmas, and Collective Action to Electronic Networks of Practice [J]. Journal of Information Technology Theory and Application, 2004, 6 (1): 25-42.

教师简介：

杨锐，男，中山大学理学学士、工学博士。2013 年起任教于中山大学资讯管理学院，讲师。主讲“计算机病毒原理与防护技术”、“微机原理”、“计算机网络”等本科生课程。主要从事多媒体信息安全、保密通信、电子文件鉴定等方向的研究。曾先后作为核心成员参与多项国家自然科学基金和国家“973”科技计划等课题，在国内外重要刊物上发表相关的学术论文 10 余篇，获授权专利 2 项。2008 年 9 月至 2009 年 9 月，曾获国家公派留学基金赴新泽西理工学院访问学习。兼任 Session Chair of APSIPA ASC 2014，Reviewer of IEEE T-IFS。联系方式：Email：yangr23@ mail. sysu. edu. cn。

Additive Noise Detection and Its Application to Audio Forensics*

Rui Yang

Abstract: Digital audio recordings can be manipulated by pervasive audio editing software easily. Often forgery would not be naive splicing. Post-processing would be a part of tampering. Post-processing can eliminate the obvious traces of forgery. Noise can cover audible evidence of forgery and destroy traces of other tampering operations. The detection of additive noise in audio signal is a useful tool for audio forensics. In this paper, we investigate the effect of additive noise on audio signal, and propose a feature named "sign change rate" for detecting additive noise. Via theoretical analyze and extensive experiments, it shows the proposed feature is effective in additive noise detection. Also the method can be a potential tool for forgery localization of digital audio.

Keywords: Audio forensics; Additive noise; Audio forgery; Sign change rate

1 Introduction

Digital audio forensics has recently become a widely studied stream of research in multimedia security. Often audio forgery would not be naive splicing, post-processing would be performed after tampering, and otherwise there will be audible trace of forgery. Adding noise is a common post-processing after audio forgery. Frequently-used audio editing software, such as CoolEdit, GoldWave, Audacity, always has a function of adding noise. Shown as Figure 1, the widely used software Audacity contains an adding white noise function. Nowadays even the user without any knowledge of audio processing can perform adding weak noise to audio recording. The

* This work was supported by NSFC (61202497) and the Open Project Program of the National Laboratory of Pattern Recognition (NLPR).

perceptual quality of the audio is almost not degraded after adding the weak noise. Additive noise may be applied to audio not only to cover audible evidence of forgery, but also in an attempt to destroy traces of other tampering operations. Thus the detection of additive noise in audio signal is certainly significant for the authenticity of the audio and its content.

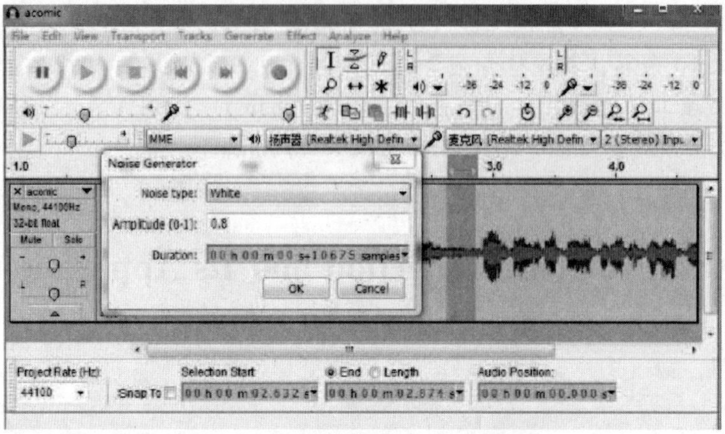

Figure 1 Adding white noise is a function of Audacity

Nowadays the reported work about digital audio forensics focus on forgery detection[1-3], recorder identification[4-5], reverberation[6] and compression history analysis[7-8], but there are no work about post-processing detection on digital audio. Work about detection of additive noise on audio is also not reported. However, in the research area of image forensics, lots of work about post-processing detection have been reported, such as detection of filtering[9], detection of sharpen[10]. Since adding noise is not a good way to hide the forgery trace of image, detection of additive noise on image is of small value in digital image forensics. The case is different for audio, since weak noise is inherent in audio recording, and it doesn't influence the perceptual quality of audio much.

In this paper we focus on additive noise. We propose an additive noise detection method for audio signal. The key idea of the proposed method is that: if the audio signal is processed twice, the modification introduced by the second process is less than the first process. Adding noise is one kind of this process. We introduce a feature named "sign change rate" to measure the modification.

The rest of this paper is organized as follows. In Section 2, we investigate the effect of additive noise on audio signal, and show how it eliminates the traces of forgery. Then we propose the sign-change-rate feature and additive noise detection method in Section 3. The experimental results are shown in Section 4. Finally, we conclude our paper with a discussion and future work in Section 5.

2 Effect of Additive Noise

The forgery trace of audio signal is easily covered by weak noise. Figure 2 shows an example of adding noise to cover evidence of forgery. Several samples of the original audio are removed, and then an obvious change appears at the splicing point. After adding weak noise on the samples around the splicing point, the splicing point is not perceptual again, no matter listing or viewing the waveform.

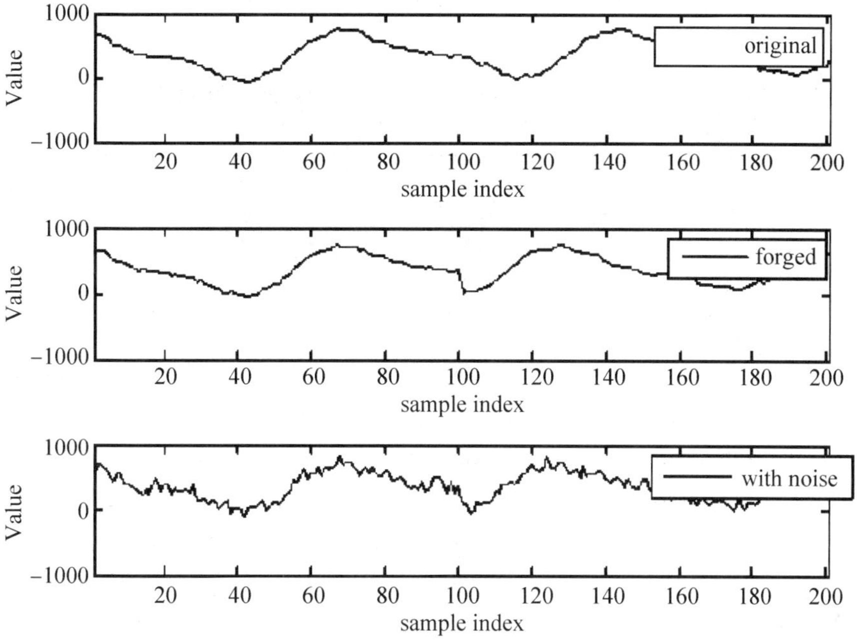

Figure 2 Example of adding noise to cover evidence of forgery

Without a reference signal, it is very difficult to determine speech signal with additive noise or not from the waveform. Since the speech signal is short-time stationary, the values of neighbor samples have a small fluctuation. After adding weak noise, the neighbor samples of speech will overlay with different values, and this will enlarge the difference between neighbor samples. It means that the variance of the differential signal will become larger after adding noise. As shown in Figure 3, the first column shows the differential signal of original speech and speech with additive noise. In order to detect additive noise in speech without reference signal, we actively add white noise to two kinds of speech, and investigate the effect of white noise on the differential signal, as shown in the second column of Figure 3. Since the additive white noise would flip the sign of some value of differential signal, we perform dot product between differential signal and the noise version. Then we find that there are much more negative samples in the dot product for the original speech, as shown in the fourth column of Figure 3. Obviously, few samples changing sign after actively additive noise would be avery strong indication of previously adding noise. In the next section, we will introduce sign change rate to measure the influence by adding noise.

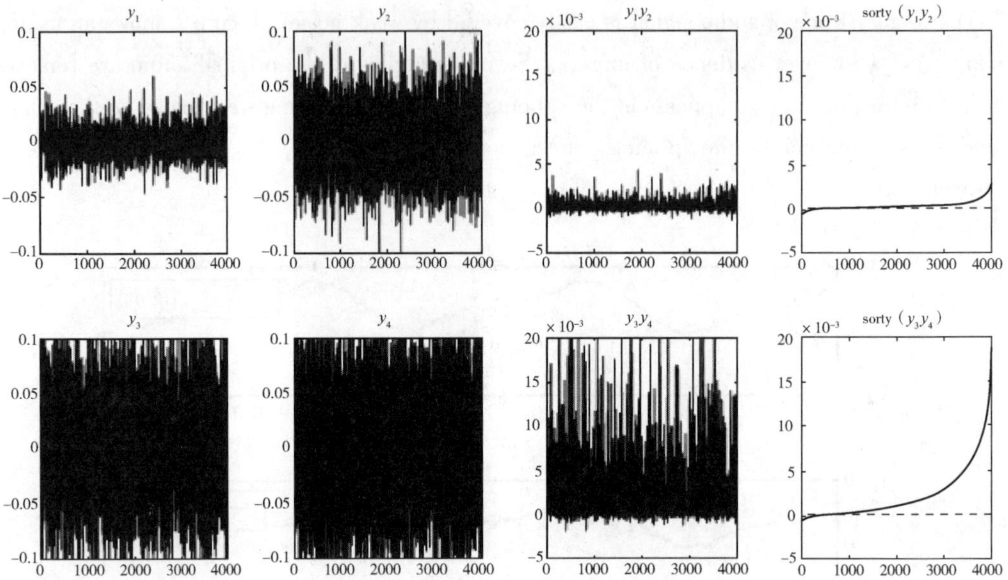

Figure 3 Effect of additive noise on differential signal, the case of original speech is at the top, and the case of noise version is at the bottom

3 Sign Change Rate and Proposed Method

3.1 Sign change rate

Given a sequence X of length L and its processed version $Y = f(X)$, the number of sign change K is the number of element in $\{i \mid x_i * y_i < 0, i = 1, \cdots, L\}$. The sign change rate θ is defined as follow: $\theta = K/L$. We use sign change rate θ to measure the effect of additive noise on the audio signal. To illustrate the sign change rate, we randomly select 100 samples of differential signal of original speech and the noise version, respectively, then observe the sign of dot product between differential signal and differential signal with active noise. As shown in Figure 3, the sign change rate of original speech is obviously larger than that of noise version.

3.2 Theoretical proof

Due to the variation of speech signal, however, theoretical analysis of the general relation between the speech and its noise version is highly non-trivial. For this reason, it is often assumed that the input speech samples are i. i. d. We denote the differential signal of x and $x + n_2$ as y_1 and y_2, respectively. That is $y_1 = \Delta(x)$ and $y_2 = \Delta(x + n_2)$. The case of signal

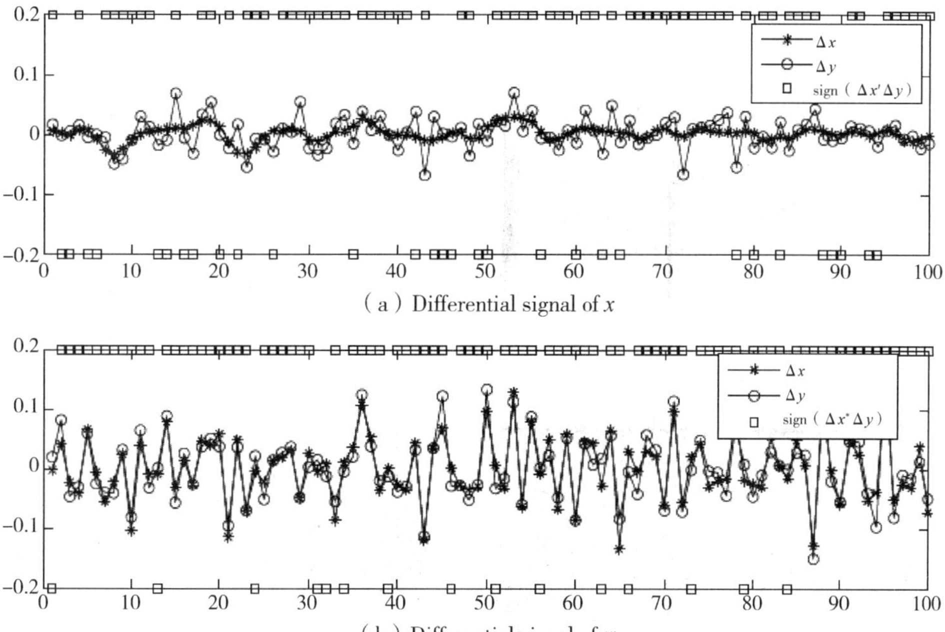

(a) Differential signal of x

(b) Differential signal of x'

Figure 4 Sign change of audio signal after adding noise, the case of original speech is at the top, and the case of noise version is at the bottom

without additive noise:

$$x \sim N(0,\sigma_0^2) \Rightarrow y_1 \sim N(0,2\sigma_0^2), \tag{1}$$

$$x + n_2 \sim N(0,\sigma_0^2 + \sigma_2^2) \Rightarrow y_2 \sim N(0,2\sigma_0^2 + 2\sigma_2^2). \tag{2}$$

We denote the differential signal of $x + n_1$ and $x + n_1 + n_2$ as y_3 and y_4, respectively. That is $y_3 = \Delta(x + n_1)$ and $y_4 = \Delta(x + n_1 + n_2)$. The case of signal with additive noise:

$$x + n_1 \sim N(0,\sigma_0^2 + \sigma_1^2) \Rightarrow y_3 \sim N(0,2\sigma_0^2 + 2\sigma_1^2), \tag{3}$$

$$x + n_1 + n_2 \sim N(0,\sigma_0^2 + \sigma_1^2 + \sigma_2^2) \Rightarrow y_4 \sim N(0,2\sigma_0^2 + 2\sigma_1^2 + 2\sigma_2^2), \tag{4}$$

$$E(\theta_1) = \int_0^{+\infty}\int_{-\infty}^{0} p(y_1,y_2)\,\mathrm{d}y_2\mathrm{d}y_1 + \int_{-\infty}^{0}\int_0^{+\infty} p(y_1,y_2)\,\mathrm{d}y_2\mathrm{d}y_1, \tag{5}$$

$$p(y_1,y_2) = \frac{1}{2\pi\sqrt{(2\sigma_0^2)(2\sigma_2^2)}}\exp\left(\frac{-y_1^2}{2\sigma_0^2} + \frac{-(y_2 - y_1)^2}{2\sigma_2^2}\right), \tag{6}$$

$$E(\theta_1) = \frac{1}{2} - \frac{\arctan\sqrt{\sigma_0^2/2\sigma_2^2}}{\pi}, \tag{7}$$

$$E(\theta_2) = \int_0^{+\infty}\int_{-\infty}^{0} p(y_3,y_4)\,\mathrm{d}y_4\mathrm{d}y_3 + \int_{-\infty}^{0}\int_0^{+\infty} p(y_3,y_4)\,\mathrm{d}y_4\mathrm{d}y_3, \tag{8}$$

$$p(y_3,y_4) = \frac{1}{2\pi\sqrt{(2\sigma_0^2 + 2\sigma_1^2)(2\sigma_2^2)}}\exp\left(\frac{-y_3^2}{2\sigma_0^2} + \frac{-(y_4 - y_3)^2}{2\sigma_2^2}\right), \tag{9}$$

$$E(\theta_2) = \frac{1}{2} - \frac{\arctan\sqrt{(\sigma_0^2 + \sigma_1^2)/2\sigma_2^2}}{\pi}. \tag{10}$$

Since $\sigma_0^2 < \sigma_0^2 + \sigma_1^2$ and arctan(.) is monotone increasing, we can show that $E(\theta_1) >$

$E(\theta_2)$. The difference between $E(\theta_2)$ and $E(\theta_1)$ depends on $\arctan\sqrt{(\sigma_0^2+\sigma_1^2)/2\sigma_2^2} - \arctan\sqrt{\sigma_0^2/2\sigma_2^2}$. Thus the larger σ_1^2, the larger difference between $E(\theta_2)$ and $E(\theta_1)$. The smaller σ_2^2, the larger difference between $E(\theta_2)$ and $E(\theta_1)$.

3.3 Proposed method

Based on the above investigation and theoretical analysis, we find that the speech with additive noise can be recognized by the sign change rate. Given the audio signal x, the process of detecting additive noise in audio is as follow.

1) we add additive noise $n_2 \sim N(0, \sigma_2^2)$ to x;

2) $\Delta(x)$ and $\Delta(x+n_2)$ are calculated respectively;

3) The zero crossing rate zc between $\Delta(x)$ and $\Delta(x+n_2)$ is computed.

4) If $zc < Th$, x is regarded as the one additive noise has been added, otherwise it is without additive noise. The selection of threshold Th is based on the observation of extensive experiment.

4 Experimental Results

To evaluate the performance of the proposed method, we test with lots of speech clips. The data set consists of 384 speech clips. These WAV clips of 5 sec each are downloaded from two publicly available uncompressed audio databases.[11-12] All these WAV clips are of 22.05 kHz, 16 bit, mono. We experimentallyexamine and report if our proposed method can correctly detect the noise version from the original audio in Section 4.1. In addition, the experiment to check if the proposed method can work reliably when the length of audio is short in Section 4.2. Similarly, if the proposed method works as different strength of active noise σ_2^2 are used is reported in Section 5.3. In Section 5.4, we apply the proposed method to locate audio forgery.

The false positive error means that the original speech are determined as noise version, while the false negative error represents the noise version are recognized as original ones. We denote false positive error and false negative error as f_p and f_n, respectively. The accurate rate AR is calculated as $AR = \frac{2-(f_p+f_n)}{2} \times 100\%$.

4.1 Detection of additive noise

We add white gaussian noise of $SNR = 30$ dB to the 384 speech clips, and then save them in the same format as the original ones. Here we get two classes of speech signal: original ones and the noise version. Here we utilize the proposed method to classify the two kinds of speech signal. First, we actively add white gaussian noise of $SNR = 35$ dB to all speech clips. Then we compute the sign change rate of these speech, as shown in Figure 5. Obviously, the sign change rates of the noise version are all around 0.15. However, the sign change rates of the original speech are most above 0.3. The sign change rate between these two classes of speech data has a significant difference. Based on the observation, the threshold is selected as $Th = 0.2$, and the accurate rate AR is 100%.

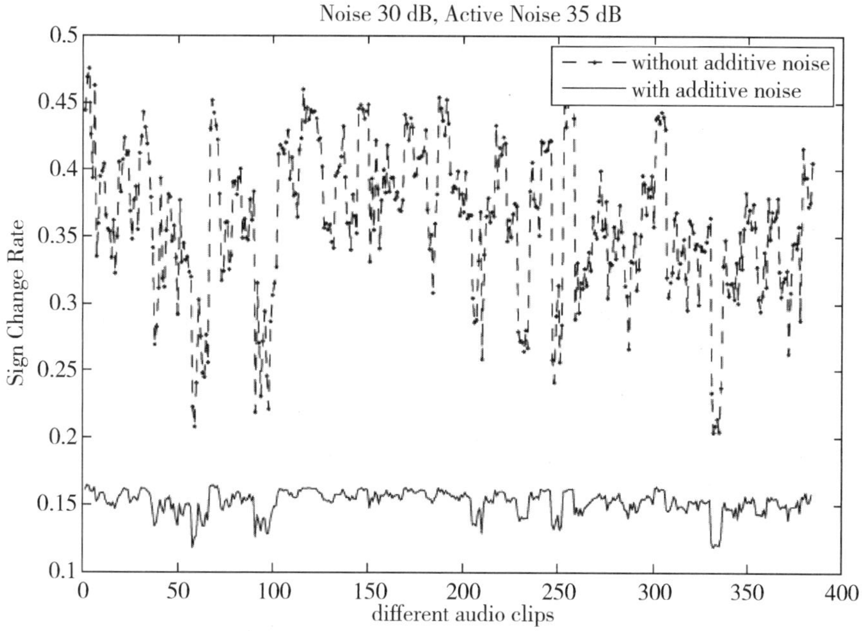

Figure 5 Detection result of 5 s clips using 35 dB active noise

The above experiment investigates the case of noise strength $SNR = 30$ dB. However, is the proposed method valid for additive noise with different strength? We add noise of 20 dB, 25 dB, 35 dB to those 384 speech clips respectively, and save them as the noise ones for classification. Same with the previous detection procedure, we actively add white gaussian noise of $SNR = 35$ dB to all speech clips, and then compute the sign change rate. The results are shown in Figure 6. When the additive noise is of 20 dB, 25 dB and 30 dB, sign change rate between original speech and noise version is distinct. Even the additive noise is as weak as $SNR = 35$ dB, only 5 of 384 original speech clips are misclassified as noise version.

4.2 Different length of audio

From the above experimental results, it is shown that the proposed method performed well on detecting additive noise of 5-sec audio clips. However, in practice, post-processing is only performed on the portion around the forgery position, which may last only 1 second. Hence, it is necessary to test if our proposed method can work for very short clips. For this purpose, we randomly select 1 second and 0.5 second portion of each above clips for testing.

As shown in Figure 7, the same threshold $Th = 0.2$ is applied, only 5 of 384 original

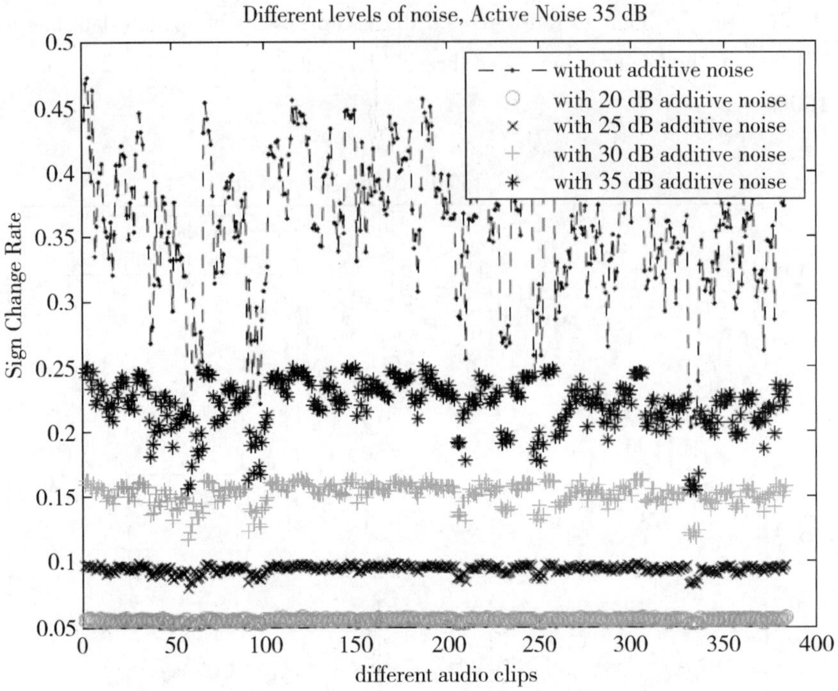

Figure 6 Detection result of different noise levels

speech clips are misclassified ($AR=99.3\%$) for speech of 1 second, but 7 clips are wrong for speech of 0.5 second ($AR=99.0\%$). Can we draw a conclusion that the longer clips the more reliable detection? Yes, we can see that sign change rate is more stable when speech is of 1 second. Since sign change rate is based on statistics, more samples will generate more reliable result.

4.3 The impact of σ_2^2

From Equation (7) and (10), we can find that sign change rate highly rely on the value of σ_2^2, the strength of active noise. Hence, the impact of σ_2^2 on our method should be investigated. The experiment setup is the same as the first one in Section 4.1, except the strength of active noise σ_2^2. This time the active noise is of $SNR = 30$ dB and $SNR = 25$ dB, respectively. As shown in Figure 8, sign change rate between original speech and noise version is always distinct. Comparing with Figure 5, we can see that sign change rate of noise version is upraised, which is in accord with Equation (7). At the same time, the threshold for classification should rise. This shows that the threshold only depends on the strength of active noise, which is under control of the detector.

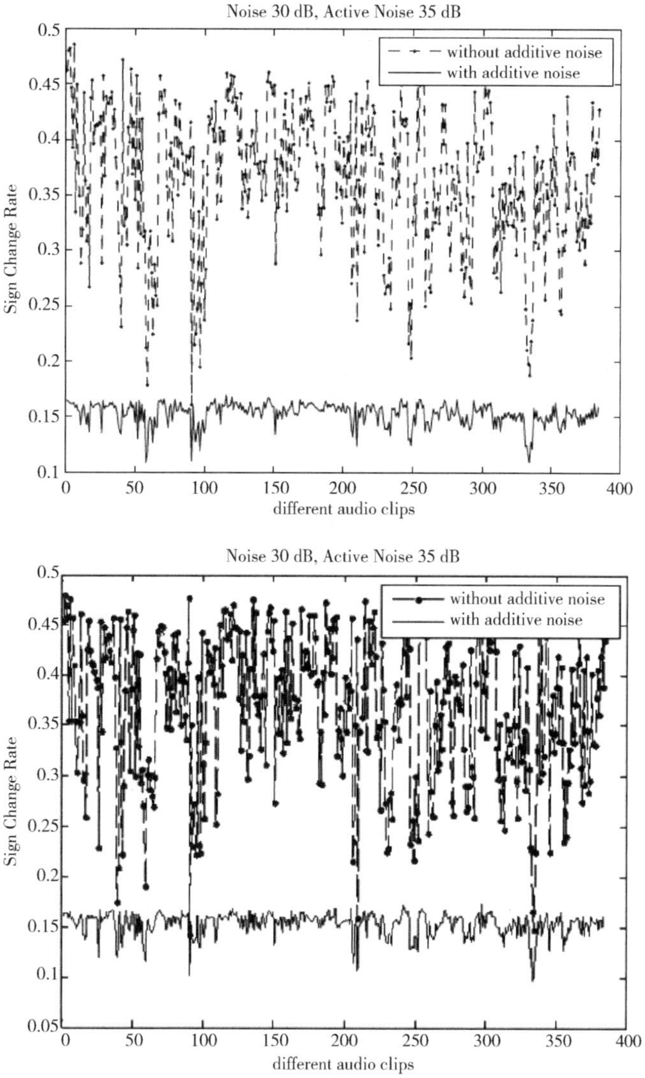

Figure 7 Detection result of speech clips with the length of 1s (top) and 0.5s (bottom)

4.4 Locating forgeries via detecting additive noise

A potential application of detecting additive noise is forgery localization. For example, after insertion or splicing operation, a forger would add some weak noise around splicing positions to eliminate traces. Such kind of forged audio can be identified by our proposed method. For a suspected audio, we can separate it into several audio clips of 1 or 0.5 second (s) length. Using our method to identify each portion, and the forgery will be clearly caught. Also audio recording by combining two recordings can be identified. As shown in Figure 9, an audio recording contains two parts, which are recorded under different environments. We divide the

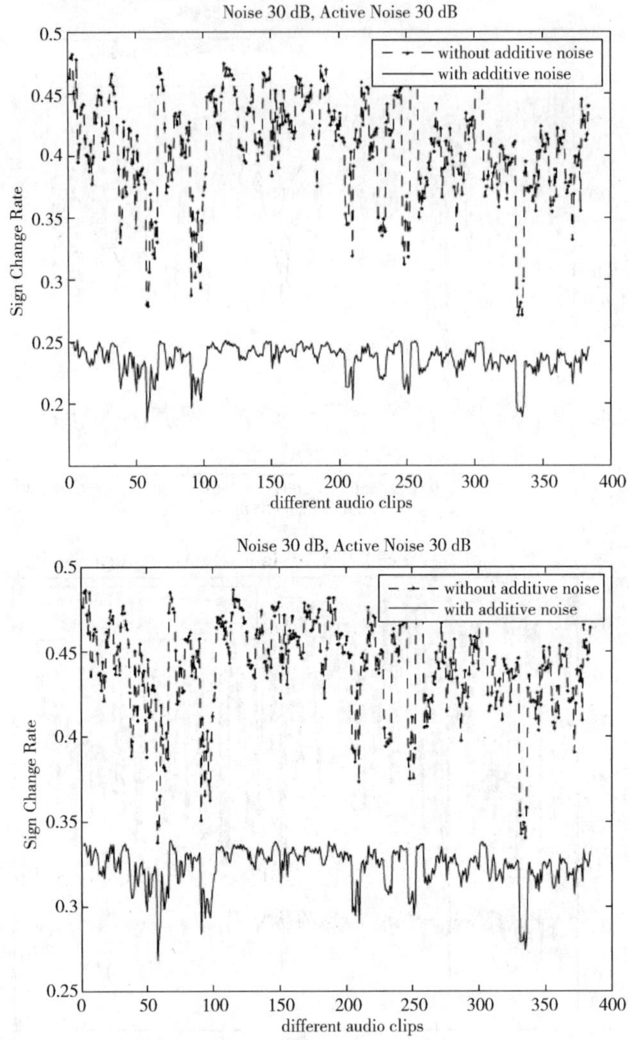

Figure 8　Detection result of speech using 30 dB (top) and 25 dB (bottom) active noise

audio recording into several audio clips of 1 second, add active noise to each clip, and compute the sign change rate.

5　Conclusion

In this paper, we have investigated the detection of additive noise in digital audio. In the broader framework of digital audio forensics, we see this work as a contribution to the problem of examining post-processing of audio. Via theoretical analyze and extensive experiments, it show that sign change rate is effective in additive noise detection. Further, the proposed method can be extended as a forgery localization tool in some audio forensics cases. However, there are still many limitations of the method, such as sign change rate of original speech fluctuates a lot due to

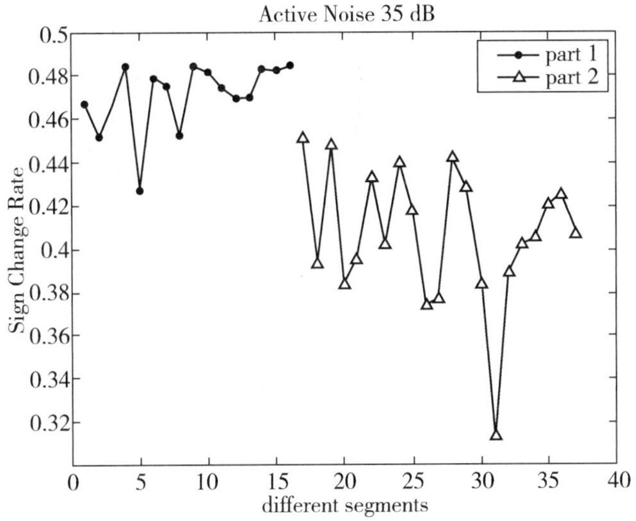

Figure 9 Splicing localization via detecting additive noise

its content, only additive noise is analyzed. In our future work, we will consider apply the method to detect other kinds of noise. Also the quantitative criteria of the classification threshold will be studied.

6 Acknowledgment

This work was supported by NSFC (61202497) and the Open Project Program of the National Laboratory of Pattern Recognition (NLPR).

References

[1] Grigoras C. Digital Audio Recording Analysis: The Electric Network Frequency (enf) Criterion [J]. The International Journal of Speech Languageand the Law, 2005, 2 (1): 63-76.

[2] Farid H. Detecting Digital Forgeries Using Bispectral Analysis [R]. MIT AIMemo AIM-1657, MIT, 1999.

[3] Yang R, Qu Z, Huang J. Exposing Mp3 Audio Forgeries Using Frame Offsets [J]. ACM Transactions on Multimedia Computing, Communications and Application, 2012, 8 (S2): 1-20.

[4] Kraetzer C, Oermann A, Dittmann J, Lang A. Digital Audio Forensics: A First Practical Evaluation on Microphone and Environment Classification [C]. Proc of the Workshop on Multimedia and Security, Dallas, Texas, USA, 2007: 63-74.

[5] Buchholz R, Kraetzer C, Dittmann J. Microphone Classification Using Fourier Coefficients [C]. Proc of the International Workshop on Information Hiding, Darmstadt, Germany, 2009.

[6] Malik H, Farid H. Audio Forensics from Acoustic Reverberation [C]. Proc of the International Conference on Acoustics Speech and Signal Processing, 2010: 1710-1713.

[7] Hicsonmez S, Uzun E, Sencar H T. Methods for Identifying Traces of Compression in Audio [C]. Proc of the 1st International Conference on Communications, Signal Processing, and their Applications, Sharjah, 2013: 1-6.

[8] Yang R, Shi Y Q, Huang J. Detecting Double Compression of Audio Signal [C]. Proc of SPIE 7541, Media Forensics

and Security Ⅱ, 2010.

[9] Yuan H. Blind Forensics of Median Filtering in Digital Images [J]. IEEE Transactions on Information Forensics and Security, 2011, 6 (4): 1335-1345.

[10] Cao G, Zhao Y, Ni R. Detection of Image Sharpening Based on Histogram Aberration and Ringing Artifacts [C]. Proceedings of IEEE International Conference on Multimedia and Expo, 2009: 1026-1029.

[11] sound lab @ Princeton [OL]. [2014-05-10]. http://soundlab.cs.princeton.edu.

[12] The Music-Speech Corpus [OL]. [2014-05-10]. http://www.ee.columbia.edu/dpwe/sounds/.

教师简介：

甘春梅，女，华中师范大学管理学学士、硕士、博士。2013 年起任教于中山大学资讯管理学院。主讲“信息检索”、“市场营销学”等本科生课程。研究方向包括网络信息资源管理、社会化媒体用户行为和人机交互。目前正主持国家自然科学基金青年项目一项，并作为主要参与人参加多项国家级项目。已在国内外学术期刊和会议上发表论文40余篇，出版专著一部、教材一本。多次在西班牙、台北、新加坡等地举办的国际会议如PACIS、ECKM、ISPIM 上受邀进行论文宣讲。2011—2012 年芬兰 Lappeenranta University of Technology 国家公派访问学者。兼任中国保密协会会员。联系方式：ganchm3@ mail. sysu. edu. cn。

所选论文《学术博客的概念、类型与功能》原载于《信息资源管理学报》2015 年第 1 期（《新华文摘》“论点摘编”收录）

学术博客的概念、类型与功能*

甘春梅，王伟军①

摘　要：学术博客发展迅速，日益引起学界的重视。为了挖掘学术博客对科研活动的潜在作用，通过对国外学术博客相关文献的调研分析，揭示学术博客的概念、类型及功能，期望为更好地挖掘学术博客的价值进而改善国内学术博客服务提供理论指导。

关键词：学术博客；博客；概念；类型；功能；Web 2. 0

Definition, Types and Functions of Academic Blog

Chunmei Gan, Weijun Wang

Abstract: Academic blog develops quickly and attracts attentions from academia. To identify potential functions of academic blog plays in scientific research areas, this paper analyzes definition, types and functions of academic blog based on research on related English articles of academic blog. It aims to better recognize values of academic blog and thus provide theoretical guidelines for better blog services in China.

Keywords: Academic blog; Blog; Definition; Type; Function; Web 2. 0

---

* 本文系国家自然科学基金项目“Web 2. 0 环境下科学研究中知识交流与共享机制研究”（71073066）、“基于使用与满足理论的社交媒体使用机理研究：从采纳到持续使用的行为转变”（71403301）和华中师范大学优秀博士学位论文培育计划资助项目“Web 2. 0 科研社区中知识交流与共享的信任机制”的研究成果之一。

① 王伟军，华中师范大学信息管理学院教授、博士。

1 引　言

随着 Web 2.0 在学术领域的应用以及科学 2.0 的发展，学术博客呈指数级增长并日益引起学界的重视。[1] Kirkup 认为，学术博客正成为一种学术实践与新型的学术写作方式，它将成为学界的一项重要活动并成为学者的一种技能；且这种方式正改变着 21 世纪实践者的属性。[2] 国外实践也表明，越来越多的科研实验室、团队和个体使用学术博客来报道成果，讨论问题或共享观点，进行在线合作、在线出版或创建学术身份等。相比之下，虽然国内有不少学者在使用学术博客（如科学网博客、图情博客圈），但其在科研领域发挥的真正作用仍然有所限制。这也是为何近年来不少学者呼吁要改善学术博客服务以更好地发挥其对科研的促进作用。那么，学术博客能够发挥哪些功能，如何应用于科研领域？为了回答这一问题，本文尝试对国外学术博客相关的文献进行综述，从中提炼出学术博客的概念、类型与功能，期望能够为国内学术博客服务的改善提供理论指导。

2 学术博客的概念与类型

2.1 学术博客的概念

尽管现有的诸多文献都使用“学术博客”这一术语，但对学术博客的使用仍处于混淆状态，它的概念并没有得到统一的界定。

Saper 首次提出将学术博客看作一种特定类型的博客，即“Blogademia”；并提出，学术博客没有经过任何同行评审或编辑过程，因而不能将其看作知识产生的一部分。[3] Gregg 认为，学术博客是一种对话式的学术形式，使得学术界之外的读者也能够接触学术工作并参与其中。[4] 通过观察博士生和年轻学术人员的公开博客，Gregg 也将学术博客看作一种亚文化的表达，是一群在其所选择的学术和研究领域中努力生活的人的表达；同时探讨了这一亚文化如何观察并批评学术的角色和功能以及学术内的雇佣实践。[5] Ward 则将学术博客看作一种民族志形式。[6]

与此同时，也出现了一些平行概念，如科学博客（science blog）和知识博客（k-log）。知名博客搜索引擎 Technorati 将科学博客界定为“由在职科学家写的博客，而且必须是关于科学的内容”。Kelleher 和 Miller 将知识博客定义为“专业期刊的在线等同物，传播专业领域内的新知识，包括研究进展、参考文献和观察等”。[7]

综上所述，目前学者认为学术博客是：①主要内容是学术知识的博客；②由科研人员撰写的、以讨论学术相关问题为主的博客。一般来说，学术博客是以博主为中心，及时记录自身的学术观点，同时通过 RSS、回溯、评论和链接来实现自己同相关学术群体的知识交流。[8]

2.2 学术博客的类型

科研人员因不同目的而使用学术博客，因此存在不同类型的学术博客。根据不同的需要，可将其分为不同的类型（图1）。

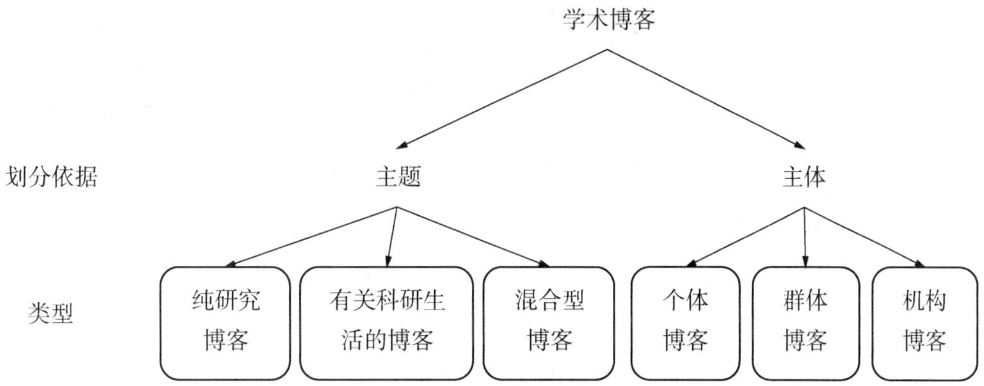

图1　学术博客的类型

2.2.1　纯研究博客、有关科研生活的博客和混合型博客

（1）纯研究博客。纯研究博客涉及的主题与研究相关，类似于学术会议上的演讲与对话。传统上，科研人员使用笔记来记录实验过程和观点等。目前，越来越多的科研人员尝试利用学术博客来记录正在开展的研究的过程、观点以及结果。它为学术交流和研究的传播提供了崭新途径[9]，可使研究过程公开化，研究成果在正式出版前后更容易被他人，尤其是公众获取[10]。具体来讲，科研人员可公开其研究设计、数据搜集过程、早期研究结果和其他研究细节，而这些信息通过传统的渠道（如期刊等）无法获取；也可吸引他人参与到观点讨论中，或寻求对实验的帮助。[11]国外已有不少组织、研究团队利用学术博客来促进持续的交流以及信息的相互补充与完善。例如，"Research Blogging"（http://researchblogging.org/post-list/list/date/all）、"Mathemagenic"（http://blog.mathemagenic.com/phd）。

（2）有关科研生活的博客。这一类型的博客涉及的主题包括广泛的科研生活，如做研究的经历与体会，带领团队或指导学生的经验等，是一种有价值的"理解情绪、氛围、个人感性和自我意识之外知识的方式"[3]。科研人员在博客中随时记录个人感想与体验，与他人分享并讨论相关经历。通过阅读这一类型的博客，用户可从侧面了解科研人员或科研生活。目前，国内的大多数博客属于这一类型，如科学网博客（http://blog.sciencenet.cn/blog.php）。

（3）混合型博客。混合型博客是上述两种类型博客的综合。其既探讨有关研究的内容，也分享有关科研生活的感想。

2.2.2　个体博客、群体博客和机构博客

（1）个体博客。个体博客由单个科研人员撰写与维持，其主体通常是高校教师、科研机构工作人员以及研究生等。各类博客平台为个体博客的存在和发展提供了重要支撑，使得自我出版过程变得更为简单、快捷。为了运营一个高质量的、受欢迎的博客，个体博客需要科研人员投入较多的时间和精力去撰写博文，并通过评论与反馈等方式与读者

进行交互。例如，科学网博客"黄安年的博客"（http://blog.sciencenet.cn/?415）、新浪图情博客圈知名博客"程焕文如是说"（http://blog.sina.com.cn/huanwen）。如果没有高质量的博文、持续的写作和稳定的读者群，个体博客通常很难维持下去。在实际中，很多个体博客已经很少或不再更新，并最终被放弃。通常来讲，这一类型的博客占绝大多数。

（2）群体博客。群体博客通常由两个或以上的、研究领域相同或相近的科研人员撰写并维持，其主体通常是在现实中已互相认识的科研人员（如大学教授）/研究群体或同一领域中任何对该博客感兴趣且愿意贡献的个体。这一类型的博客大多数为研究型博客，即日志多与学术相关。相比个体博客，群体博客关注的主题较为专一和集中，发表的博文质量更高，且能吸引更多的读者。群体博客更容易促进参与主体之间的线上线下合作，激发新想法的产生；也能得到持续的维持。实证研究发现，研究型小组博客主要有两个目标：自我呈现和构建研究群体的身份，促进知识构建中的协作。[12]在国外，这一类型的博客较为常见。例如，"Organizations and Markets"（http://organizationsandmarkets.com/）、"iMechanica"（http://imechanica.org/）。

（3）机构博客。机构博客通常与某一组织（如出版商、期刊等）相关联，由该组织予以维持，其作者可以是一个人或多个人。在社会化媒体时代，诸多组织也纷纷利用不同类型的社会媒体，如博客、维基和社交网络等，来吸引和留住用户，建立自己的用户基础。机构博客通常有着更强的构建基础的优势，因为随着用户转向社会化媒体，他们倾向于信任已经建立的站点或已经存在的实体组织。[13]用户可通过留言和评论等方式与机构博客进行互动交流，以及利用 RSS 订阅等方式随时关注机构博客的动态。例如，"WileyChinaBlog"（http://blog.sciencenet.cn/home.php? mod=space&uid=822310）。

3 学术博客功能的研究现状

根据对国外文献的分析，可将学术博客发挥的功能归纳为：对传统学术活动的冲击，对知识交流与共享的影响，链接的作用，以及学术博客的其他功能。

3.1 学术博客对传统学术活动的冲击

相比传统的学术活动（如交流、出版与评审等），学术博客的兴起与发展对其产生一定的冲击与影响，如渠道、模式、理念等的改变。

传统上，撰写文章将研究成果发表在同行评审的期刊上是交流知识并使科研人员获得认可和声誉的一种重要方式。但学术博客的发展促使通过学术博客形成并传播基于证据的信息也成为学术身份创建的一种有效方式。[14]通过发表活跃日志、发布个人信息、提供出版物或项目列表、参与主题讨论等方式，科研人员能够有效地进行自我呈现与身份创建。[12]此外，博客平台中的出版内容不受限于传统科学出版的流程与规则，提供更加丰富的表现形式，如文本、图片、音频和视频等，并促进更多听众的参与交流与意见反馈。Bukvova 提出，与传统的出版方式不同，学术博客不受限于严格的准则和程序，也能避免同行评审，且不受传统出版严格定义的出版类型的限制；学者可以自由发表任何内容，并接受来自其他读者的评价与意见；更重要的是，学者能够与任何对内容感兴趣的广泛读者群进行开放式交流。[15] Lindgren 认为，学术博客发挥了与传统法律期刊一样的功能，能够产生并传播有关法律相关的知识；此外，学术博客成为个人研究工作早期阶段中提炼想法与获得反馈的一种好方式。[14]

此外，学术博客也催生了“基于博客的评审”。与传统的同行评审不同，这一新型的评审方式以一种开放的、动态的形式吸引那些对博主书稿感兴趣的、具有不同学科背景和经验的读者参与进来，鼓励参与者与博主之间的协作式与讨论式交流。[16] 例如，2008 年，加州大学计算机科学教授 Noah Wardrip-Fruin 尝试开展了一个实验，即在将书稿 *Expressive Processing* 发送给传统出版社送去同行评审的同时，也将书稿分为章节作为每日博文发表在群体博客 Grand Text Auto 中，期望能够接受读者的评论；实验结果显示：评审被视作对话以及时间上的不灵活性。[16] 最终，Noah 获得了高质量的评论，且能直接用于修改书稿。如 Noah 所说，那些可能很少参与书稿评审的读者的加入丰富了基于博客的评审过程。

3.2 学术博客对知识交流与共享的影响

学术博客以一种开放的、透明的方式支持一种新型的对话实践，来自世界各地的不同学科的研究人员参与到讨论中，共享早期结果，或寻求对实验的帮助。[11] 这些特性使得越来越多的科研人员尝试使用学术博客作为信息交流与知识共享的非正式平台。[17] 不少学者提出学术博客能够促进科研人员之间、科研人员与大众之间的跨学科、跨边界的知识交流与共享。

Benton 探讨了自身写作博客的经验以及博客如何从最初与学生的小范围交流扩大到更多感兴趣的读者的公共博客。[18] Park 认为博客能够促进研究、合作与知识的共享。[19] 通过对 12 个研究群体博客进行分析，Luzón 发现，学术博客有助于公开研究小组及其研究成果，向大众开放研究小组的工作并寻求反馈，与小组其他成员保持交流并记录小组活动，与不同研究者讨论感兴趣的话题并就这些话题共享信息或想法，强化社交链接并与社区成员保持联系。[12] Wakeford 和 Cohen 阐述了学术博客如何成功地应用于在线社会研究中，不仅涉及研究者与参与者的信息共享，也涉及跨学科小组间的信息共享。[20] 通过分析学术博客典型案例，Powell 等提出，博客有助于研究方法和结果以一种开放、透明的方式得到快速共享；在适当的引用下，博客和其他新媒体能够在公共环境下对学术研究进行定位，并对新出现的话题提供快速、可靠的信息。[10] Sauer 等指出其所在的研究团队使用学术博客和维基来促进持续的交流以及作为实验室日常工作的补充方式。[21] 通过分析学术博客语言与传统学术文献中的正式语言特征，Stuart 提出，学术博客提供了更快捷的学术讨论方式，为不同科研人员之间的交流提供了平台和机会；学术博客的个性化及其能为科研人员提供补充性观点的特性能够不断促进学术的发展。[22]

3.3 学术博客链接的作用

学术博客包含丰富的链接，且发挥着重要的作用。[23] Ciszek 和 Fu 认为博客中的链接成为一种社会网络机制。[24]通过分析不同学科中的15个学术博客，Luzón 指出，链接是学术博客的基本要素，成为对话、信息传播和知识构建的工具，并有助于促进学者融入在线社区中。[1]此外，Luzón 也归纳总结了已有研究中对博客链接动机的分类，包括向同行表示敬意、交换预先相关的工作、确定方法、提供背景阅读、修改或批评、责备别人的工作、证实主张、鉴别数据、提醒读者即将展开的工作、确认某术语或概念原始出版物以及提高引用工作的权威性等。[1]

Ali-Hasan 和 Adamic 提出博客中用于表达不同关系的三种联结：好友链接、引用链接和评论链接；通过比较分析好友链接和评论链接所形成的社会网络结构，发现不同链接呈现出不同的特征；并指出许多在线关系通过博客形成，并非源于离线关系。[25]通过对日本博客站点 Doblog 中50000位博主的分析，Furukawa 等发现社交关系与读者关系的交互作用，即博主定期阅读他人的博客（定期阅读关系）；进一步利用四种类型的社会网络（即引用、评论、好友和引用通告）的特征对这一关系进行预测。[26]而 Priem 和 Hemminger 发现，博主之间的链接文化与学界的引用文化很相似，科研学者倾向于证实其来源。[27]

3.4 学术博客的其他功能

学术博客的特性为教育等领域提供了信息传播和知识交流的新途径。Putnam 探讨了科学博客有助于在线学习。[13] Churchill 认为，通过博客，教师能够创建一种良好的氛围，使学生感觉到作为课堂的重要组成部分及其需求和意见能够得到认可与解决。[28] Joshi 和 Chugh 认为，博客能够用作教学工具，通过补充其他教学方法和技术来鼓励学生的参与、个人的反映、交流以及批判性思维和写作技能的发展。[29]通过对比实验，George 和 Dellasega 则发现，微博和博客能够保持和扩展学习对话，促使指导者和学生之间的实时对话，并使得家庭作业的完成变成一种动态体验。[30]

此外，学者探讨了使用学术博客的利弊。Lawley 列举了学术博客的好处，包括加速发表、自发性、发表正在进展中的工作且获得反馈的能力、增加个人声音、避开编辑过程、增加分布式同行评审以及支持科研人员与他人建立联系等。[31]与此同时，学术博客也使得科研人员承担一定的风险，如在成果正式发表之前共享的信息和想法被盗取或受到攻击、对可信度的影响以及对传统研究活动时间的占用等。Putnam 则认为，撰写学术博客的好处在于：提高写作技能，通过链接创建兴趣社区，支持科研人员对不同新闻做出快速的反应，并通过更强的资源来支撑其观点；但其弊端体现在：需要大量的时间去管理，如学习新技术的时间、与读者交互的时间和撰写博文的时间，且博客通常被认为不专业。[13]

4 结　　论

学术博客对科研活动具有潜在的促进作用。通过对国外学术博客相关文献的调研与分析，本文归纳总结了学术博客的概念、类型及功能。结果显示：就概念来看，学术博客的主要内容是学术知识，由科研人员撰写的、以讨论学术相关问题为主的博客。就类型而言，根据主题来划分，学术博客包括纯研究博客、有关科研生活的博客和混合型博客；根据主体来划分，学术博客包括个体博客、群体博客和机构博客。就功能来说，学术博客对传统学术活动产生冲击，促进知识交流与共享，链接发挥着重要的作用，以及为教育等领域提供信息传播和交流的新途径。期望本文的分析能够有助于更好地认识与理解学术博客的价值，从而更有效地挖掘其价值。

参考文献

[1] Luzón M J. Scholarly Hyperwriting: The Function of Links in Academic Weblogs [J]. JASIST, 2009, 60 (1): 75 –89.

[2] Kirkup G. Academic Blogging, Academic Practice and Academic Identity [J]. London Review of Education, 2010, 8 (1): 75 –84.

[3] Saper C. Blogademia [J]. Reconstruction, 2006, 6 (4): 1 –15.

[4] Gregg M. Feeling Ordinary: Blogging as Conversational Scholarship [J]. Continuum: Journal of Media and Cultural Studies, 2006, 20 (2): 147 –160.

[5] Gregg M. Banal Bohemia: Blogging from the Ivory Tower Hotdesk [J]. Convergence: The International Journal of Research into New Media Technologies. 2009, 15 (4): 470 –483.

[6] Ward M. Thoughts on Blogging as an Ethnographic Tool [C]. Proceedings of the 23rd Annual Ascilite Conference: Who's Learning? Whose Technology? Sydney, Australia, 2006: 843 –851.

[7] Kelleher T, Miller B M. Organizational Blogs and the Human Voice: Relational Strategies and Relational Outcomes [J/OL]. Journal of Computer-Mediated Communication, 2006, 11 (2): 395 – 414 [2010 – 12 – 02]. http://jcmc. indiana. edu/vol11/issue2/kelleher. html.

[8] Furukawa T, Tomofumi M S, Yutaka M S, et al. Analysis of User Relations and Reading Activity in Weblogs [J]. Electronics and Communications in Japan (Part Ⅰ: Communications), 2006, 89 (12): 88 –96.

[9] Walker J. Blogging from Inside the Ivory Tower [C] //Bruns A, Jacobs J. Uses of Blogs. NewYork: Peter Lang, 2006: 127 –138.

[10] Powell D A, Jacob C J, Chapman B J. Using Blogs and New Media in Academic Practice: Potential Roles in Research, Teaching, Learning, and Extension [J]. Innovative Higher Education, 2012, 37 (4): 271 –282.

[11] Skipper M. Would Mendel Have Been a Blogger? [J]. Nature Reviews Genetics, 2006, 7 (9): 664.

[12] Luzón M J. Research Group Blogs: Sites for Self-presentation and Collaboration [EB/OL]. [2010 –09 –13]. http://unizar. es/aelfe2006/ALEFE06/5. newtechnologies/87. pdf.

[13] Putnam L. The Changing Role of Blogs in Science Information Dissemination [J/OL]. Issues in Science and Technology Librarianship. 2011 (65) [2012 –03 –20]. http://www. istl. org/11-spring/article4. html.

[14] Lindgren L. Is Blogging Scholarship? Why Do You Want to Know? [J]. Washington University Law Review, 2006, 84 (5): 1105 –1108.

[15] Bukvova H. Taking New Routes: Blogs, Web Sites, and Scientific Publishing [J/OL]. Scie Com Info, 2011, 7 (2) [2012 –05 –10]. http://www. sciecom. org/ois/index. php/sciecominfo/index.

[16] Noah W F. Blog-Based Peer Review: Four Surprises [EB/OL]. [2011 – 12 – 19]. http://grandtextauto. org/category/expressive-processing.

[17] 王伟军，甘春梅，刘蕤. 学术博客知识交流与共享心理诱因的实证研究 [J]. 情报学报. 2012, 31 (12): 1026 –1033.

[18] Benton M. Thoughts on Blogging by a Poorly Masked Academic [J/OL]. Reconstruction, 2006, 6 (4) [2010 –01 –12]. http://reconstruction. eserver. org/064/benton. shtml.

[19] Park Y, Heo G M, Lee R. Blogging for Informal Learning: Analyzing Bloggers' Learning Perspective [J]. Educational Technology & Society, 2011, 14 (2): 149 –160.

[20] Wakeford N, Cohen K. Field Notes in Public: Using Blog for Research [C] // Fielding N, Lee R M, Blank G. Handbook of Online Research Methods. London: SAGE, 2008: 307-326.

[21] Sauer I M, Bialek D, Efimova E, et al. "Blogs" and "Wikis" are Valuable Software Tools for Communication within Research Groups [J]. Artificial Organs, 2004, 29 (1): 82-89.

[22] Stuart K. Towards an Analysis of Academic Weblog [J]. Revista Alicantina de Estudios Ingleses, 2006 (19): 387-404.

[23] 王伟军，甘春梅. 学术博客中链接类型与功能研究 [J]. 情报学报，2013，32 (6)：640-652.

[24] Ciszek T, Fu X. Hyperlinking: From the Internet to the Blogosphere [C]. Proceedings of the Sixth International and Interdisciplinary Conference of the Association of Internet Researchers (AoIR), Chicago, USA, 2005. （转引自：Luzón M J. Scholarly Hyperwriting: The Function of Links in Academic Weblogs [J]. JASIST, 2009, 60 (1): 75-89.）

[25] Ali-Hasan N, Adamic L A. Expressing Social Relationships on the Blog through Links and Comments [C]. Proceedings of International Conference on Weblogs and Social Media (ICWSM), Boulder, Colorado, USA, 2007: 1-11.

[26] Furukawa T, et al. Social Networks and Reading Behavior in the Blogosphere [C]. Proceedings of International Conference on Weblogs and Social Media (ICWSM), Boulder, Colorado, USA, 2007: 1-8.

[27] Priem J, Hemminger B M. Scientometrics 2.0: Toward New Metrics of Scholarly Impact on the Social Web [J/OL]. First Monday, 2010, 15 (7) [2011-10-15]. http://firstmonday.org/htbin/cgiwrap/bin/ojs/index.php/fm/article/viewArticle/2874/2570.

[28] Churchill D. Educational Applications of Web 2.0: Using Blogs to Support Teaching and Learning [J]. British Journal of Educational Technology, 2009, 40 (1): 179-183.

[29] Joshi M, Chugh R. New Paragigms in the Teaching and Learning of Accounting: Use of Educational Blogs for Reflective Thinking [J/OL]. International Journal of Education and Development Using ICT, 2008, 5 (3) [2010-10-29]. http://ijedict.dec.uwi.edu/viewarticle.php? id=664.

[30] George D R, Dellasega C. Use of Social Media in Graduate-level Medical Humanities Education: Two Pilot Studies from Penn State College of Medicine [J]. Medical Teacher, 2011, 33 (8): 429-434.

[31] Lawley L. Thoughts on Academic Blogging [EB/OL]. [2012-10-28]. http://many.corante.com/archives/2004/04/01/thoughts_on_academic_blogging_msr_breakout_session_notes.php.

教师简介：

朱侯，男，华中师范大学信息管理与信息系统专业学士、硕士，华中科技大学管理科学与工程专业博士。2014 年起任教于中山大学资讯管理学院讲师。主讲“运筹学”、“管理信息系统”等课程。研究方向包括社会计算与行为模拟、信息预测等。擅长对人类的心理和行为建立可计算模型，并结合数据挖掘、系统仿真等技术模拟网民群体、社会组织等对象的复杂行为，及预测复杂现象的未来趋势等。迄今为止，以第一作者或通讯作者身份在 *Simulation*：*Transactions of the Society for Modeling and Simulation International*、*AISS*：*Advances in Information Sciences and Service Sciences*、《系统工程理论与实践》、《现代图书情报技术》等 SCI、EI 及 CSSCI 期刊发表十余篇学术论文。参与项目包括国家自然科学基金项目“基于系统模拟、心理学和突变论的企业管理组织性能测试研究”（71071065）、国家自然科学基金项目“基于贝叶斯网络和演化博弈的社会化媒体信息传播建模和模拟”（71101059）等。担任期刊 *International Journal of Simulation and Process Modelling* 的匿名审稿人。联系方式；*zhuhou3@mail. sysu. edu. cn*。

所选论文“Adaptation of Cultural Norms after Merger and Acquisition Based on Heterogeneous Agent-Based Relative-Agreement Model”原载于 *Simulation*：*Transactions of the Society for Modeling and Simulation International* 2013 年第 12 期

Adaptation of Cultural Norms after Merger and Acquisition Based on Heterogeneous Agent-Based Relative-Agreement Model*

Hou Zhu，Bin Hu①，Jiang Wu②，Xiaolin Hu③

Abstract：The subject of norm formation and diffusion has gained lots of attention in social science and organizational science in the last decade. This paper explores how public dissenters in acquired firms can affect success or failure of merger and acquisition（M&A）. In the classical relative agreement model[1]，all individuals observe their neighbors' behavior and update their own opinion and behavior following the same rule. This paper proposes a new heterogeneous relative agreement model where individuals update their behavior following different rules after M&A. Simulation experiments show that the time shortly after acquisition is a key period to guide the acculturation in a way consistent with the intent of the acquiring firm，and that the risk of cultural norm reversing

---

* This work was supported by the National Natural Science Foundation of China（grant number 71071065 and number 71101059）.

① Bin Hu，a professor in the School of Management and Director of the Institute of Modern Management in Huazhong University of Science and Technology，China.

② Jiang Wu，an associate professor in School of Information Management in Wuhan University，China.

③ Xiaolin Hu，an associate professor in the Computer Science Department and director of the Systems Integrated Modeling and Simulation（SIMS）Lab at Georgia State University.

after acquisition is influenced by several important factors. Some suggestions for guiding the acculturation process after M&A are also provided.

Keywords: Norms; Merger and acquisition; Relative agreement model; Social network; Agent based model

1 Introduction

Since the 20th century, with waves of enterprise acquisition in the whole world and the painful lessons of its failures, people gradually realize the risk of acquisition. Successful acculturation is a very important factor for the success of cross-cultural acquisition. For example, GE has benefited from cultural integration in cross cultural M&A. On the other hand, cultural difference may lead to failure of business fusion, and prevent capability transfer, resource sharing, organization study, and so on. [2] The greater the cultural difference is, the higher the agency costs is and the greater uncertainty is. [3] Increase of the cultural difference between employees may lead to high personnel mobility, high potential cost, conflict between employees, rupture of internal communication network and high M&A risk. [4] This paper focuses on the mechanism of cultural norm formation and the risk of the acquiring firms' culture being reversed after acquisition.

There are several definitions of cultural norm in the existing literature. Norms can be defined as a set of conventions or behavioral expectations that people in a population abide by. Norms represent a balance between individual freedom on the one hand and the goals of the society on the other. [5] Essentially norms inform an agent, or an individual, on how to behave. Cultural norms, or normative behaviors, are mechanisms that allow large groups of self-interested humans to cooperate together and to coordinate actions[6], thereby providing a solution to the problem of social order . [7] In a special organization, norms are behavior patterns that are typical of specific groups, such as "exchange ideas openly and freely". Such behaviors are learned from workmates, leaders, and many others whose values, attitudes, beliefs, and behaviors take place in the context of their own organizational culture. Ignoring social norms can lead to negative effect for individuals, including being excluded from a group. To establish an organizational norm, one of the populations has to give up its preferred behavior. [8]

To understand the complex psycho-sociological mechanisms involved in the process of cultural norm formation, there have been many researches concentrating on opinion dynamics, culture dynamics and sociophysics. Most of the related models assume that agents are aware of opinions of their neighbors. According to the well-known theory of opinion dynamics-bounded confidence assumption, agents exchange opinions only with the agents holding similar opinions. Opinion exchange occurs when the difference of opinion value is smaller than the confidence bound (also referred to as uncertainty). As a result, original mainstream opinion is more likely to prevail despite disagreement from a small number of individuals. However, in some cases the opinions of an entire group may change significantly. For example, if a single non-conformist expresses his clear attitude and strong certainty of an opinion, some other individuals may become confident in rejecting the previous dominant opinion. In this case, the minority individuals will not have to worry their opinion clashing with others. This scenario differs from the common case where the mainstream opinion prevails in several different ways. First, the public non-conformists attract the minority and repulse the majority. Second, the minority are more confident when they encounter with the public non-conformists, and the attractive influence will be larger as a result. Then such a scenario would decrease the explanatory power of the bounded confidence assumption to explain why a group doubts or overturns its previous opinions in response to a minority view. [9] For example, BYD, a private enterprise in China, acquired several state-owned enterprise and foreign-funded enterprise in recent years, such as Qinchuan Automobile and Sanxiang Bus. However, because the fighting spirit of the private enterprise is incompatible with the easy and stable characteristic of the state-owned enterprise, the rapid growth trend of BYD no longer exists. As another example, GOME acquired Yolo and DAZHONG Electronics several years ago, and became the largest household appliances enterprise. The culture of the original GOME was "the interest of the enterprise is above all". However, the culture of the DAZHONG Electronics was "service happily, live happily". The cultural conflict between GOME and DAZHONG led the employees who were arranged to work in DAZHONG from GOME difficult to execute their tasks and being assimilated by DAZHONG finally. This phenomenon became more remarkable after Mr. Dazhong Zhang who was the founder of DAZHONG Electronics became the Chairman of the Board of GOME.

In research of cultural norm, Nahavandi and Malekzadeh proposed four modes of organizational culture integration[10]; Cartwright and Cooper put forward four types of organizational culture[11]. Their findings are significant as most of the later works are based on their research frameworks. However, the majority of these works only analyzed the feasible match between the culture types and acculturation modes from the perspective of qualitative analysis. They did not cover the risk for the major norms to be reversed by public non-conformists after M&A from the microscopic point of view. Modes of acculturation after M&A include not only integration, assimilation, separation and deculturation but also reversion. Although integration, assimilation and separation are more popular in reality, reversion must also be paid attention to. If the norms of the acquired firm reverse the norms of the acquiring firm, the original external balance of the acquiring firm will be broken and the M&A will be in risk of failure.

Motivated by the above observations, this paper focuses on reversion after M&A. The aim of the paper is to study whether the target firms can reverse the cultural norm of the acquiring firms when there are employees in the target firms expressing non-conformist attitude and behavior publicly after cross-culture merger and acquisition. In this case, traditional homogenous models cannot depict the main characteristics of the public non-conformists. This is because these models do not consider the coexistence of attractive influence and repulsive influence if there are some public non-conformists; and these models do not consider the scenario that the minority will become more confident when they interact with the public non-conformists. We define different behavior updating rules for the majority employees from the acquiring firm, the common minority employees from the target firm, and the pubic non-conformist employees from the target firm, respectively. Our heterogeneous model overcomes the deficiency of classical relative agreement (RA) model that is based on a single updating rule for all individuals. Because of this, our model can describe the reality more accurately.

This paper focuses on the process of norm formation and risk of norm formation after cross-cultural acquisition. This is an important topic in cross-culture acquisition because there is significant risk for the acquiring enterprise if the target enterprise reverses the main cultural norm of the acquiring enterprise. We further extend the relative agreement model to examine the effect of public non-conformists on the probability for the minority to reverse the whole population, and we examine what are the key factors that influence the reversal probability. We also examine what will happen when public non-conformists are located in cohesive community.

The reminder of this paper is organized as follows. Section 2 reviews the literatures about opinion dynamics based on the bounded confidence assumption and the minority reversing theory; section 3 presents the heterogeneous relative agreement model that defines different opinion updating rules for different individuals respectively; section 4 analyzes the relationship between various factors and the probability of minority to reverse the initial mainstream opinion; section 5 concludes the simulation results and discusses the containment; the last section summarizes this study and describes future research.

2 Literature Review

In recent years, there has been a growing interest in the related field of cultural dynamics. The typical questions asked with respect to cultural influence are similar to those related to the dynamics of opinions: What are the microscopic mechanisms that drive the formation of cultural domains? What is the ultimate fate of diversity? Is it bound to persist or all differences eventually disappear in the long run? Whatis the role of the social network structure?[12]

Since last decade, physicists have been working actively in social dynamics, and many models have been designed. Many agent-based cultural dynamics models are proposed to determine how groups reach consensus or how certain individuals or small groups can influence public opinion or behavior. Most of these models, which attempt to model the process of opinion evolving, consider binary opinions.[13,14] Because the opinions in these models are binary or discrete representations, they do not distinguish between hard-core extremists and varying levels of tacit supporters and non-supporters. As such, they can only be used to examine the spread of an opinion to become the minority or majority opinion.

The bounded confidence model[15,16] relaxes the assumption of binary opinions. In the bounded confidence model, opinions are represented as points on an opinion continuum (e. g., anywhere between −1 and 1). Interactions become nonlinear in that agents influence each other only if the distance between their opinions is below a threshold. Some researchers have used the bounded confidence assumption to extend the well-known continuous opinion dynamics models and applied it to various applications involving opinion dynamics research and norm emergence. For example, Groeber et al. (2009) built a simulation model about formation of the local culture among firms in a cluster based on bounded confidence theory.[17] Huang et al. (2011) used opinion to represent the external behavior, such as utterance, emotions, and body language.[9] The relative agreement model is an extension of the bounded confidence model. In the relative agreement model, the level of influence between agents is governed by the distance between opinions and the certainty of the influencing agent, rather than some predefined level of influence.[18] Nevertheless, neither the minority agents nor the majority agents are aware of the type of other agents; they are a swarm of dispersed individuals interacting with others in the society; all agents are homogeneous, but hold different opinions.

The minority issue that the initial minority may win the competition spreading over the entire population has gained much attention in the past. In [19 – 21], Galam et al. focused on the problem of minority opinion under a physical principle called the "inertia principle". The inertia effect means that in an update with equal-size groups, the opinion that preserves the Status Quo is selected locally by all the group members.[19,20] To understand the reason of such a social inertia, previous works have concentrated on analyzing the complex psycho-sociological mechanisms involved in the process of opinion formation. In particular, these works focus on the aspects that a majority of people give up to an initial minority view.[22,23] And a special group of works focus on the influence of extremists. Extremists are people with marginal opinions that are far away from ambivalence. The multidisciplinary innovation diffusion literatures have produced many case studies where an initially small minority of extremists spread their opinion to a majority of the population. Examples include drug use, new cropping techniques, and the introduction of family planning practices.[24] However, there are also extremists whose opinions never become generally accepted, such as those of the Ku Klux Klan.

A lot of works about minority reversing and extremism are based on bounded confidence theory and relative agreement model. The assumptions of the relative agreement model have been shown to be supported well by simulation experiments.[1] Most of these models are based on homogeneous agent society, and the influence between two agents has nothing to do with the type of the individuals. While these models allow for influence based on persuasion (attractive forces), they do not allow for conflicts of opinion to drive opinions further apart (repulsive forces).

Moreover, cultural inheritance is not absorbed from all possible sources randomly: opinion formation is embedded in social interaction.[25] In other words, many behaviors spread through social contact.[24,26,27] As a result, the network structure of who is connected to whom can critically affect the extent to which a behavior diffuses across a population.[24,27 – 32] In an economic context, for instance, it is well known that small cliques of core users can form a niche[33,34] and have a different behavior from the majority. This phenomenon high lights one of the fundamental questions in network dynamics, namely, how could the opinion of a small but cohesive community persist or even be accepted by the majority of the society.[35] If a single non-conformist expresses his or her attitude and antagonism behavior in public place, the opinion evolving process of the whole population will change considerably. Wander and Amblard[36] introduce a repulsive effect between two disagreeing agents. The meta-contrast model[37] allows for both attractive and repulsive influence. However, the homogeneous agent society in these models can not depict the scenario completely.

3 The Heterogeneous Relative Agreement Model

Let us consider a population of N agents, where the agents coming from the target firm is referred to as *minority*, and the rest of the agents coming from the acquiring firm is referred to as *majority*. The population size of minority is *N_minority*, and the population size of majority is *N_majority* where $N\_minority < N/2$ and $N\_minority + N\_majority = N$. We assume that the two enterprises have formed their own cultural norm respectively before acquisition. Further more, the behavioral values of the employees from the target firm are mostly negative and the behavioral values of the employees from the acquiring firm are mostly positive. Generally speaking, the norm of the target firm (minority) is more likely to be assimilated by the acquiring firm (majority). However, there may be several extremely loyal employees in the target firm who will never conform to the norm of the acquiring firm and will express their dissentient attitude publicly. Assume that the population size of these employees is *N _ antagonism*, where *N_antagonism* is smaller than *N_minority*.

Each agent a_i is characterized by two variables, its opinion x_i and its uncertainty u_i, both being real numbers. The opinion x_i and its uncertainty u_i, define the mean and variance of the *opinion segment* of a_i. We define the value range of the opinion of each agent as $x \in [-1,1]$, and the value range of uncertainty as $u \in (0,1]$. More specifically, the opinion segments of agent a_i is $s_i = [x_i - u_1, x_i + u_i]$. For two agents, a_i and a_j, their opinion segments overlaps if and only if $h_{ij} = \min(x_i + u_i, x_j + u_i) - \max(x_i - u_i, x_j - u_i) > 0$, where h_{ij} is called an opinion overlaps. If the overlap is strictly positive, then the non-overlapping width (based on agent a_i) is:

$$2u_i - h_{ij}. \tag{1}$$

then the agreement is the overlap minus the non-overlap:

$$h_{ij} - (2u_i - h_{ij}) = 2 \cdot (h_{ij} - u_i). \tag{2}$$

then the relative agreement of agent a_j (towards agent a_i) is defined by the following equation:

$$\frac{2 \cdot (h_{ij} - u_i)}{2 \cdot u_i} = \frac{h_{ij}}{u_i} - 1. \tag{3}$$

When two agents meet, one of the agents, say a_j, is randomly sampled to be a passive (receptive) agent, while the other one, say agent a_i, is considered to be the active agent. In the classical relative agreement model, all individuals updating their behavior follow a single rule. Therefore, the initial opinion and uncertainty of the individuals may determine the final opinion state of the whole population. However, once some employees in the minority publicly express their strong attitude of non-conformist, such single opinion updating rule cannot fully reflect the reality, because the informational symmetry among the individuals is broken. In reality, the confidence of the common minority will be enhanced when they make some decisions, because they no longer have to worry about their opinions clashing with others. Meanwhile, because the public non-conformists have expressed their strong dissentient attitude publicly, they will receive attractive force from their companion and repulsive force from counter workers. Therefore, the homogeneous updating rule can not depict the scenario completely.

This paper classify the updating rules for individual opinion and uncertainty into three categories according to the type of interacting agent: 1) rule for interactions between common individuals based on the classical opinion updating rule; 2) rule for public non-conformists; and 3) rule for minority when they interact with public non-conformists. Figure 1 shows these updating rules between an active agent and a receptive agent coming from different types of individuals, where the active agent is on the left and the receptive agent in on the right. The receptive agent (on the right) chooses a suitable rule to update its opinion and uncertainty according to the identity of itself and that of the active agent. More specifically, common individuals (except for when interacting with public non-conformist) update their opinions according to rule 1; Receptive individuals who are public dissenters update their opinions according to rule 2; And common minority update their opinions according to rule 3 when they interact with public non-conformist. Below we describe these three types of rules in detail.

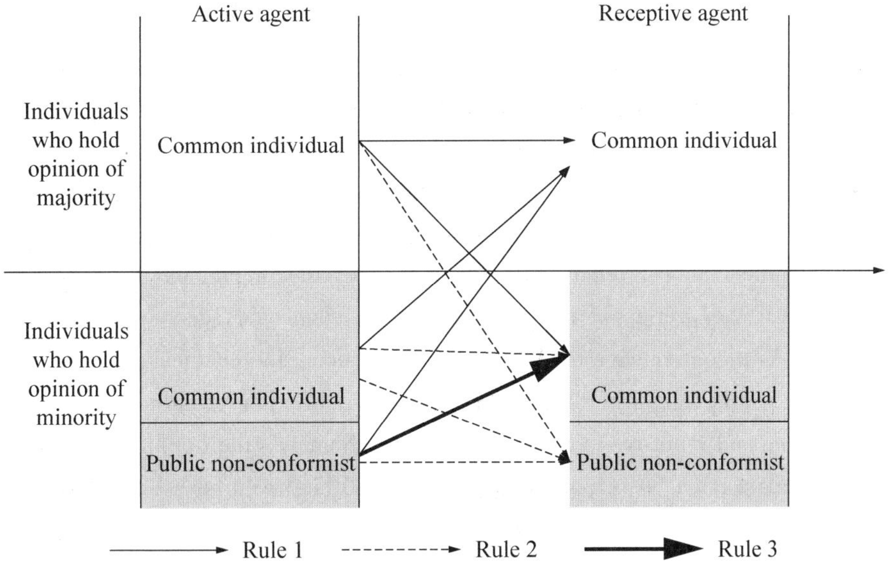

Figure 1 The opinion updating rules for different types of individuals, the three different lines represent different opinion updating rules, and they link different types of individuals respectively

3.1 Rule 1: updating rule for common interaction

The opinion and behavior updating rule for common individuals is based on the Deffuant-

Weisbuch model, a classical continuous opinion relative agreement model, proposed in [1, 38]. Behavior dynamics based on classical relative agreement model is described as follows. If $h_{ij} > u_i$, then the behavior and uncertainty of the passive agent a_j are updated according to Eq. 4 and Eq. 5:

$$x_j = x_j + \mu\left(\frac{h_{ij}}{u_i} - 1\right)(x_i - x_j), \tag{4}$$

$$u_j = u_j + \mu\left(\frac{h_{ij}}{u_i} - 1\right)(u_i - u_j). \tag{5}$$

where μ is a parameter of interacting intensity and $\mu \in \left[0, \frac{1}{2}\right]$. If $h_{ij} \leqslant u_i$, there is no influence of a_i on a_j.

The main features of this relative agreement model are[1]: 1) During interactions, agents not only influence each other's behavior but also each other's uncertainties. 2) The influence is not symmetric when the agents have different uncertainties; "confident" agents (low uncertainty) are more influential. 3) The influence (the modification of x_j and u_j) varies continuously when x_i, u_i, x_j and u_j vary continuously.

3.2 Rule 2: updating rule for public non-conformists

Public non-conformist agents represent the individuals from the target firm who publicly express their strong dissentient attitude. We assume that the public non-conformists are more confident, i. e., their uncertainty is lower. This assumption can be justified by the fact that people who have extreme attitude tend to be more convinced by themselves. On the contrary, people who have moderate initial attitude often express a lack of knowledge (and uncertainty).[39]

Note that in the classical relative agreement model, the interaction between agents takes place if and only if the overlap of opinion segments of connected agents is sufficiently large, i. e., $h_{ij} > u_i$. As a consequence of the imposed restriction, the classical model does not allow any disagreement. However, a key characteristic of the public non-conformists is that they have both attractive force and repulsive force simultaneously. Namely, their opinion will be persuaded by their companions when $h_{ij} > u_i$, and their opinion will be driven further apart when $h_{ij} \leqslant u_i$. This repulsive mechanism is not considered in the classical model. In this work, we modify the classical model to consider both the attractive force and repulsive force among individual interactions, making a reference to.[40,41] The modified model breaks the symmetry of the updating scale. Specifically, opinions of two interacting agents can diverge when the overlap of opinion segments is less than an opinion uncertainty of the active agent. When $h_{ij} > u_i$, there will be a attractive force for public dissenters to approve the opinion of active agent. Because the public dissenters are extreme, the attractive force is smaller than that in rule 1. When $h_{ij} < u_i$, there will be a small repulsive force for public dissenters to deviate more from the opinion of active agent. In order to meet the scenario above, the new updating rule for the behavior and uncertainty of a public non-conformist agent a_j is as follows:

$$x_j = x_j + \mu\left(\frac{h_{ij}}{2u_i}\right)\left(\frac{h_{ij}}{u_i} - 1\right)(x_i - x_j), \tag{6}$$

$$u_j = u_j + \mu\left(\frac{h_{ij}}{2u_i}\right)\left(\frac{h_{ij}}{u_i} - 1\right)(u_i - u_j). \tag{7}$$

where active agent a_i can be a minority agent or a majority agent. The scaling factor $\frac{h_{ij}}{2u_i}$ decreases the repulsive force of opinions, because the range of $\left(\frac{h_{ij}}{2u_i}\right)\left(\frac{h_{ij}}{u_i} - 1\right)$ is $[-0.125, 1]$ and the curve of $\left(\frac{h_{ij}}{2u_i}\right)\left(\frac{h_{ij}}{u_i} - 1\right)$ is under the curve of $\left(\frac{h_{ij}}{u_i} - 1\right)$ (as shown in Figure 2 later). In addition, we relax the restriction $h_{ij} > u_i$ of the classical RA model by allowing negative values for the relative agreement $\left(\frac{h_{ij}}{2u_i}\right)\left(\frac{h_{ij}}{u_i} - 1\right)$ when $0 < h_{ij} < u_i$. This is because $\left(\frac{h_{ij}}{2u_i}\right)\left(\frac{h_{ij}}{u_i} - 1\right)$ is smaller than zero when $0 < h_{ij} < u_i$, so their opinions will depart from each other according to Eq. 6 and Eq. 7. There is no modification of opinions and uncertainties when $h_{ij} < 0$.

3.3 Rule 3: updating rule for common minority when they interact with non-conformist

According to the concept of pluralistic ignorance, those who disagree (or who are hesitant to agree) with mainstream views on specific issues may mistakenly perceive themselves as the only non-conformists in a group. They either choose or feel compelled to publicly proclaim allegiance to group opinions because they don't know how many others also disagree with the mainstream view. However, in cases where employees of the minority interact with the public non-conformists, the pluralistic ignorance will disappear. Their opinions will be changed by a larger extent because the public non-conformists enhance their confidence. This is illustrated in Figure 2, as the thin line (which represents the updating rule 3) is above the others.

Specifically, suppose that agent a_j is a common minority agent and agent a_i is a public non-conformist agent. When $h_{ij} < u_i$, they will not change their opinion and uncertainty according to the bounded confidence assumption. When $h_{ij} < u_i$, the updating rule for the opinion and the uncertainty for agent a_j is as follows:

$$x_j = x_j + \mu\sin\left[\frac{\pi}{2}\left(\frac{h_{ij}}{u_i} - 1\right)\right](x_i - x_j), \tag{8}$$

$$u_j = u_j + \mu\sin\left[\frac{\pi}{2}\left(\frac{h_{ij}}{u_i} - 1\right)\right](u_i - u_j). \tag{9}$$

Figure 2 shows the updating function of the three rules, where the horizontal axe represents the value of $\frac{h_{ij}}{u_i}$, and the vertical axe represents the function value of updating scales for the three rules. In the figure, the thick line represents the updating scale of rule 1, the dotted line represents the updating scale of rule 2, and the thin line represents updating scale of the rule 3.

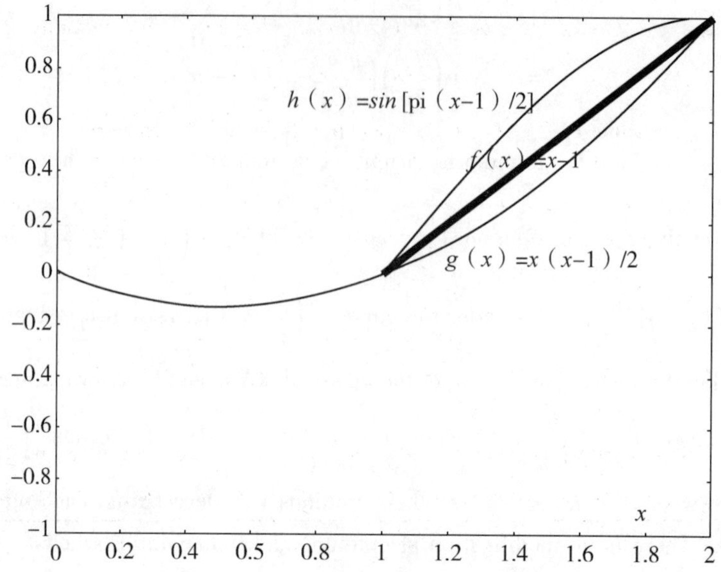

Figure 2　The updating function of the rules

4　Simulation Results

We carry out simulation experiments based on the proposed model. Initialization of the simulation system is as follows. The default population size is represented by a 15 * 15 cellular automata. Each individual belongs to one of the three different groups: employees from the acquiring firm, employees from the target firm and public non-conformist agents (from the target firm). Tichy[42] and Schweiger[43] show that scale of the target firms is inversely proportional to the acquiring performance, so we set the population size of the target firm as 30%-40% of the population size of acquiring firm in order to exclude the influence of non-cultural factors. Meanwhile, we set the population size of public non-conformists relatively large in order to promote the reversal probability and to have more opportunity to analyze the reversing process. The default parameters of simulations are summarized in Table 1. In the microscopic level, we refer to literature[9] and define the initial distribution of group opinion and uncertainty as uniform distribution, as shown in Table 2. Note that the default simulation settings shown in Table 1 and Table 2 are used throughout this paper unless explicitly specified otherwise. In addition, we suppose that the firms have both formed their own norm before acquisition. More specifically, the opinions of the employees from the acquiring firm are all positive and the opinions of the employees from the target firm are all negative. At each step, every agent will select one of its neighbors to do the update. The opinion of the receptive agent is updated according to Eq. 4, Eq. 6 or Eq. 8 based on its type. The simulation goes on until the organization reaches consensus or at most 100 steps are passed. All simulations are averaged over 1000 runs, and the simulation system is developed on the platform of net logo.[44] Figure 3 shows the GUI of the simulation model, where triangles represent majority employees, circles represent common minority employees, and stars represent public non-conformists. Red represents its opinion is positive and green represents its opinion is negative.

Table 1 The default settings for simulation parameters

Parameter	Value
Neighbors type	Moore
Maximum simulation steps	100
Total population size	default value = 15 * 15
Intensity of interactions, μ	default value = 0. 4
Population size of majority	default value = 165
Population size of minority	default value = 60
Population size of public non-conformist	default value = 15

Table 2 The default settings for different types' of agent

Type of agents		Aattribute	Value
Majority (Employees from Acquiring firm)		x	Uniform (0, 1)
		u	Uniform (0. 5, 1)
Minority (Employees from Target firm)	common minority	x	Uniform (-1, 0)
		u	Uniform (0. 5, 1)
	public non-conformist	x	Uniform (-1, 0)
		u	Uniform (0, 0. 5)

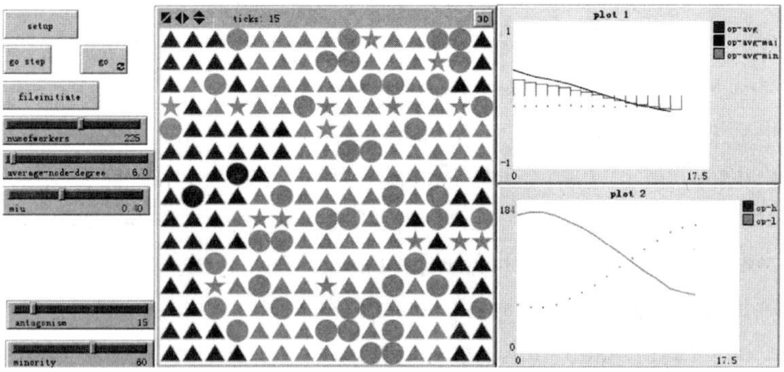

Figure 3 The GUI of the simulation model

4.1 The evolving process of opinion and uncertainty of the whole population

Repeated simulation experiments show that there is a probability that the minority can reverse the whole population's opinion successfully. Figures 4, 5, 6, 7 display the evolving process of population size of each opinion and uncertainty. Although there are several possible results of acculturation, the whole population will all form two groups holding opposite opinions shortly after M&A.

Figure 4 shows that the opinions of the whole population formed two groups holding positive opinion and negative opinion respectively when time is about 10. But with the continuous interaction among employees, the positive opinions are gradually assimilated by the negative opinions, and the uncertainties of the individuals decrease to low level. Figure 4 also shows that, when the opinions of the majority are reversed by the minority, the absolute values of final opinions are small and the average value of opinions is negative. In other words, the opinions of the two groups influence each other mutually and form a compromised cultural norm. Figure 5 shows the uncertainty aspect of this process. As can be seen, the final uncertainties of the whole population are mostly close to zero, which means that the opinions of the whole population have reached a consensus and will be difficult to change. After the M&A of Robust and Danone, the new company formed two groups which were called "people of new robust" and "people of original robust" respectively. The employees from Danone gradually accepted norm of Robust to some extent afterwards and formed a compromised norm. However, the new company adopted the organizational structure of original Danone and abandoned the business process of original Robust completely. Thus, the new Robust have loosen its leading position in drinking market so far.

Figure 6 shows that the opinions of the whole population also formed two group when time is about 10. However, with the continuous interaction among employees, no group is changed by the other group. Figure 7 shows that the uncertainties of the individuals tightly cohere in their group respectively. Although the uncertainty of the majority is relative large, their large population size still makes them hold a dominant position. Although the population size of the minority is small, their uncertainties are close to zero. Because of this, the two groups stand opposite to each other. For example, because most of the employees from DAZHONG were afraid of repulsed by the GOME, they held together with each other to fight against employees and managers from GOME shortly after the acquisition. This phenomenon that makes business procedures difficult to advance took place in many stores.

When opinions of the majority are reversed, one interesting research question concerns the speed for a society to reach consensus.[45] By means of sensitive analysis of the parameters, simulation experiments show that intensity of interaction (μ) is a key factor that determines the speed of opinion reversing. Figures 8 and 9 display the evolving process of public opinion and the uncertainty when μ is 0.1. Figure 10 displays the relationship between the speed of opinion

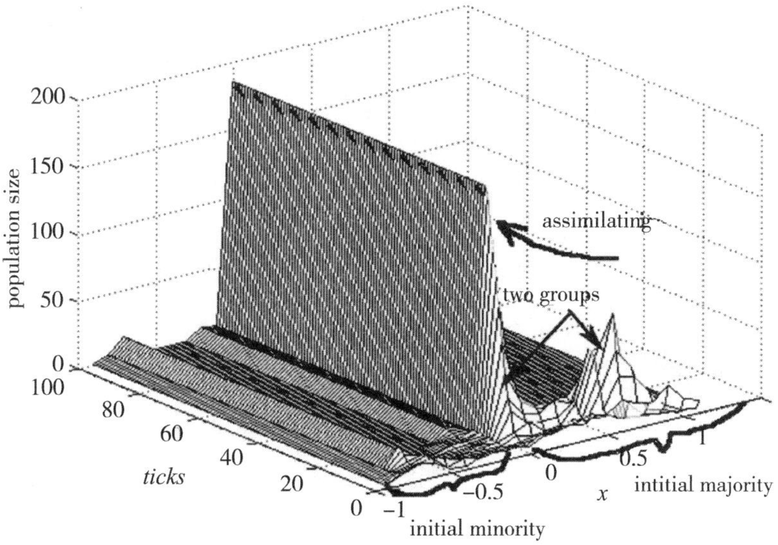

Figure 4 The evolving process of population size of each opinion (x) when the norm of the majority is reversed

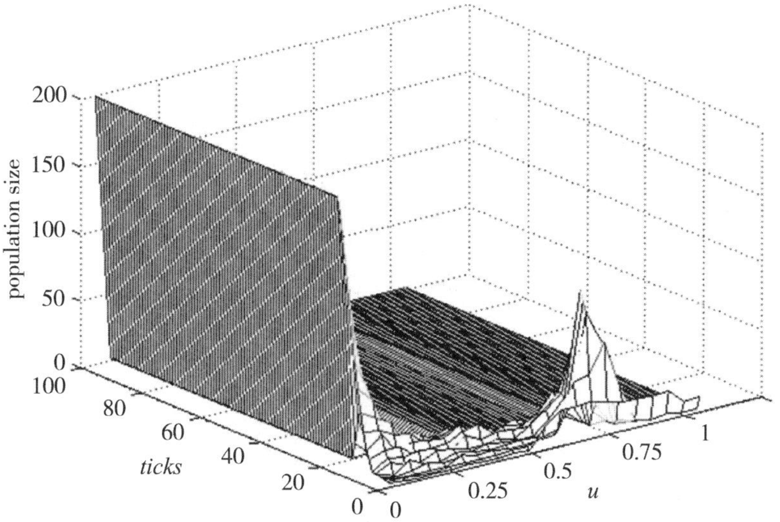

Figure 5 The evolving process of population size of each uncertainty (u) when the norm of the majority is reversed

reversing and the value of μ. From the figures we can conclude that the effect of agent interactions decreases as the intensity of interaction μ decreases. Therefore, employees need to interact more frequently in order to reach a consensus when μ is small. For example, soon after the acquisition, plasticity of the new recruited of GOME is stronger than the common employees, because they have not accept any company's norm. Therefore, the new recruited will accept the norm of GOME soon after training.

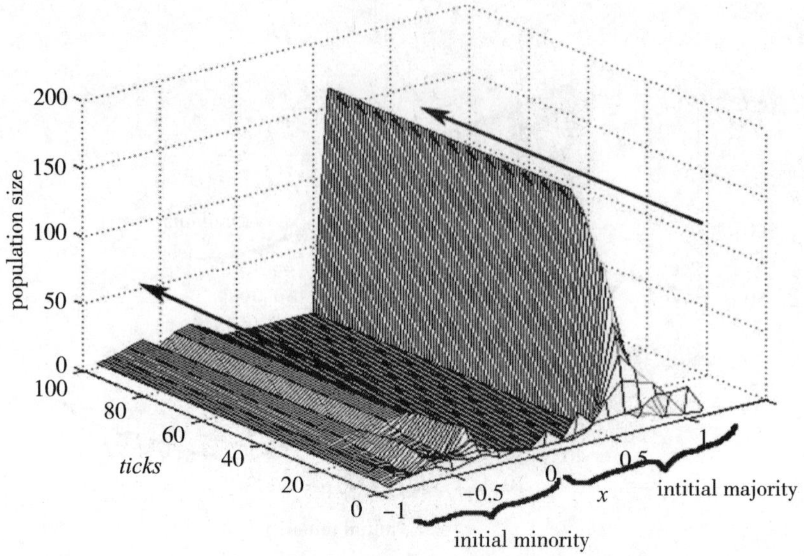

Figure 6 Evolving process of population size of each opinion (x) when the norm of the majority is not reversed

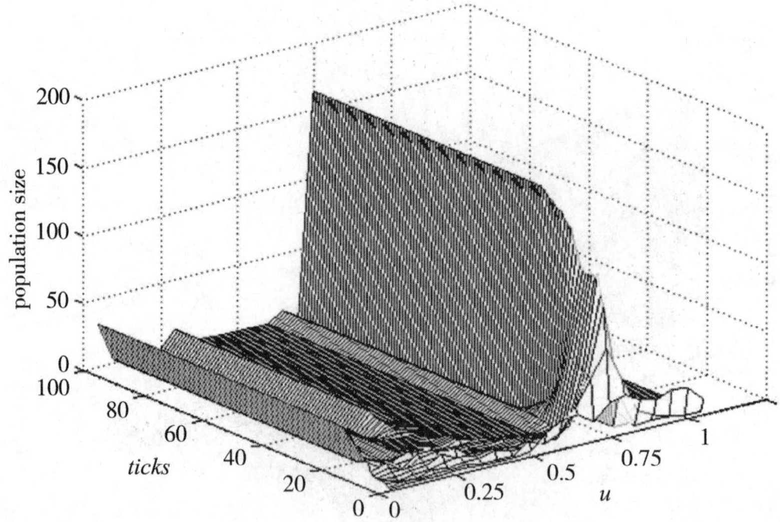

Figure 7 Evolving process of population size of each uncertainty (u) when the norm of the majority is not reversed

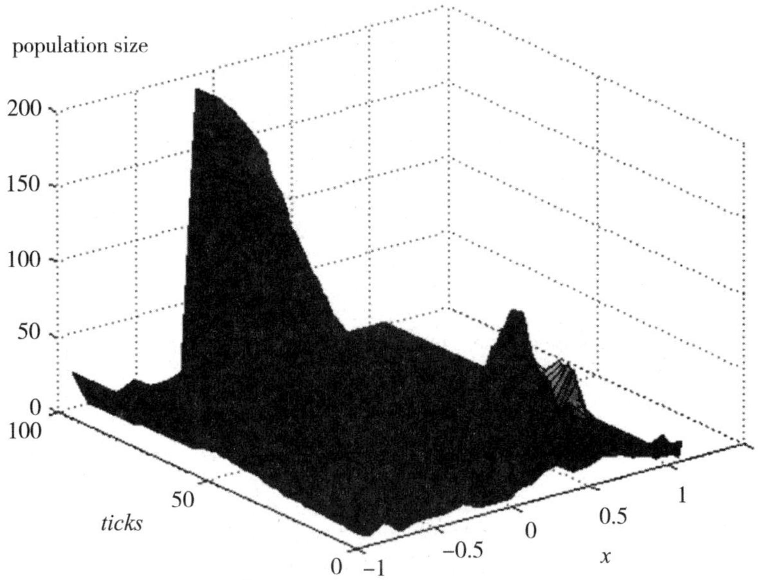

Figure 8 The evolving process of population size of each opinion (x) when $\mu = 0.1$

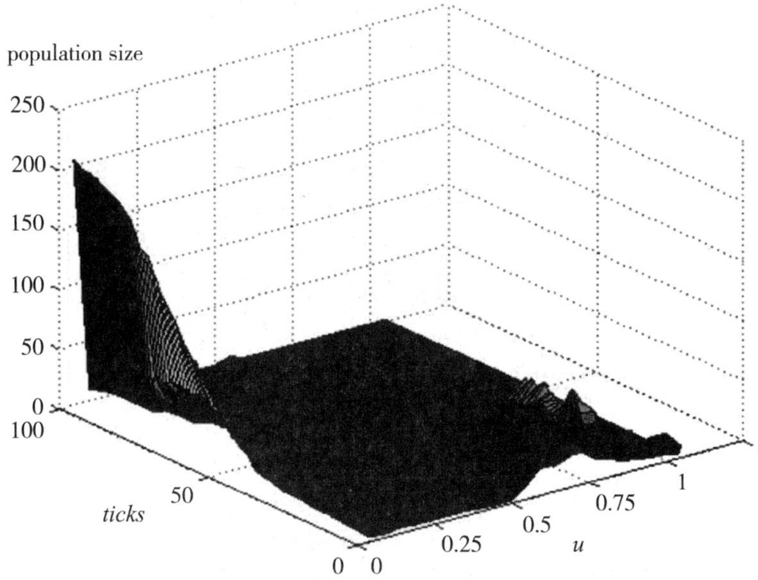

Figure 9 The evolving process of population size of each uncertainty (u) when $\mu = 0.1$

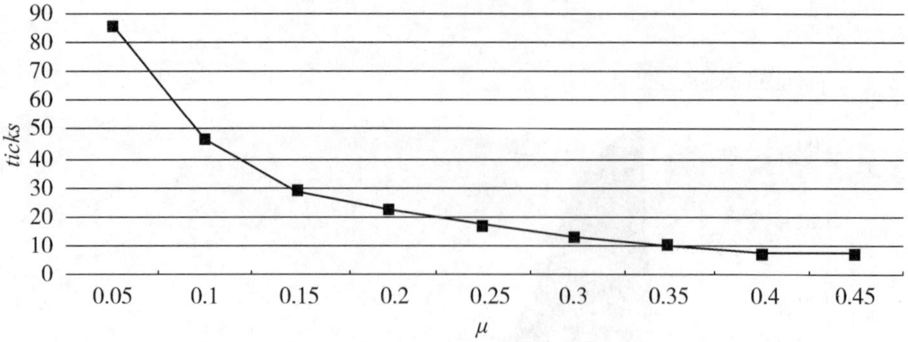

Figure 10　Impact of μ on opinion reversal speed

4.2　Initial opinion and uncertainty of employees from the target firm

According to general knowledge, we tend to believe that the more extreme the opinion of the minority is, the more likely the opinion of majority is reversed; and the individuals that are certain about their opinion are more influential than uncertain individuals. Are such the facts? In order to confirm these hypotheses, we adjust the initial distribution of x and u to analyze the simulation results.

Figure 11 shows the relationship between initial opinion overlap segment and the probability of opinion reversing. The opinion distribution of the acquiring firm is Uniform (0, 1). The mean value of opinion distribution in the left seven settings decreases gradually; the variance of opinion distribution in the right five settings decreases. Therefore, the overlap segment of initial opinion between the acquiring firm and the target firm increases continuously in the left settings and decreases in the right settings. Simulation experiments show that with the increase of initial opinion overlap segment between the acquiring firm and the target firm, the reversal probability increases. This is contrary to our hypothesis. This is because when the absolute value of initial opinion of the target firm is large and cohesive, there is no segment overlaps between opinions of the two groups. Therefore, although their attitudes are strong, they lose opportunity to change the opinion of the acquiring firm. In reality, two strangers may feel disappointed and their interacting probability is relatively low if they do not have common interest. However, if two strangers both like playing basketball, they may chat with each other and thus reach a consensus about some topics. As an example of this phenomenon, Guangzhou Automobile acquired PEUGEOT that is a France Company in 1985. Employees from Guangzhou Automobile were euphemistic and seldom expressed their dissatisfaction about the work. However, employees from PEUGEOT often expressed their dissatisfaction publicly directly. The two groups can not change the norm of each other. Therefore, French looked like the leading men, which was not benefit for management in the scenario at that time. Guangzhou Automobile had loosed 1.5 billion totally before August of 1997. Therefore PEUGEOT withdrew capital in October of 1998, and then the M&A broke up.

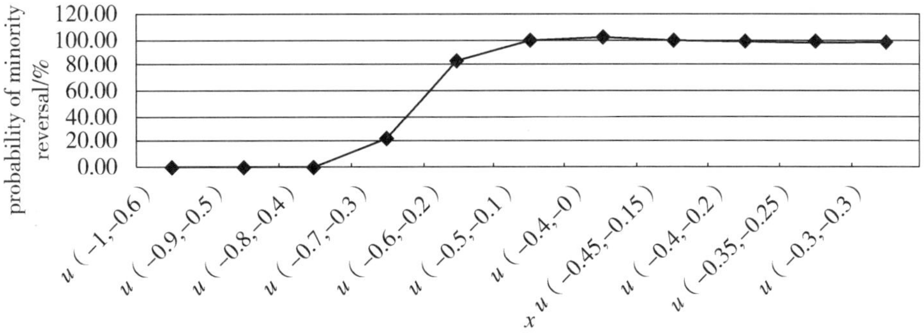

Figure 11　Impact of initial x of minority on reversal probability, the 7 points on the left depict the increasing of initial opinion (x) distribution and the 5 points on the right depict the cohesion of the initial opinion (x) distribution

Figure 12 shows the relationship between initial uncertainty of public non-conformists and the reversal probability. As can be seen, with the decrease of initial uncertainty of minority, the reversal probability gradually increases. This is consistent with our hypothesis.

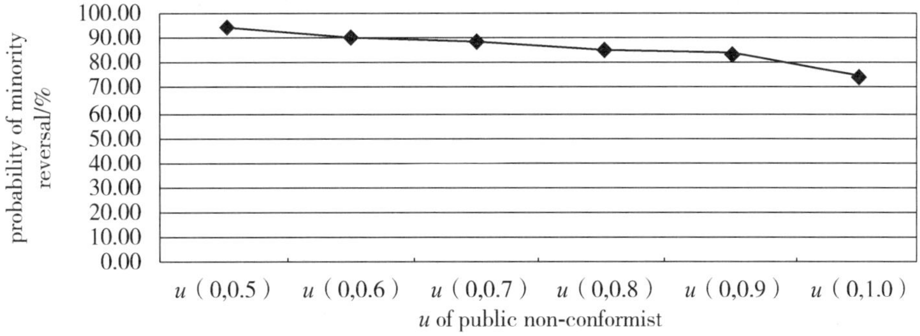

Figure 12　Impact of uncertainty of the public non-conformists on the reversal probability

4.3　Population size of public non-conformist and minority

Opinion fragmentation, polarization and consensus have been observed in the mixed model at different proportions of each groups, depending on the value of initial opinion tolerance of agents.[41] This section focuses on the relationship between the population size of the public non-conformists and the reversal probability. We carried out a set of simulation experiments by varying the population size of public non-conformists and the population size of minority, and show the simulation results in Figure 13 and Figure 14. Figure 13 shows that, the reversal probability is almost zero when the population size of public non-conformists is zero. And the reversal probability quickly rises to 80% when the population size of public non-conformists increases to 8. However, when the population size of public non-conformists increases further, the reversal probability will increases slowly. Therefore, when the population size of public non-conformists reaches above 8, the reversal probability is no longer sensitive to the population size of public non-conformists.

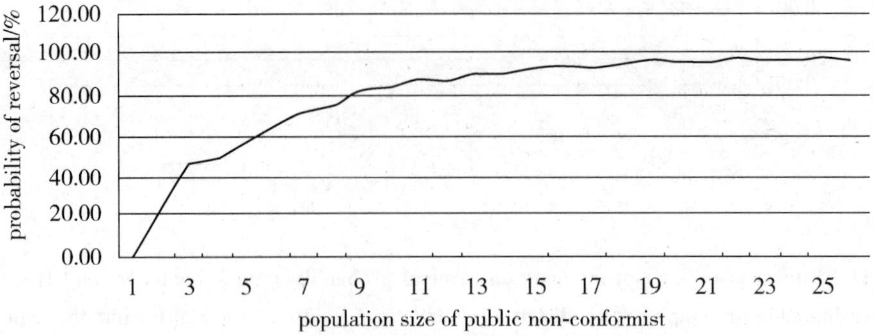

Figure 13 Impact of population size of public non-conformists on reversal probability

Figure 14 shows the relationship between population size of minority and the reversal probability. The reversal probability will continue to increase with the increasing of population size of minority. However, the increasing speed is slow. The reversal probability is close to 80% when the population size of minority is 15, and the reversal probability is about 95% when the population size of minority is 90. As a real example to show the impacts of population size of minority, in the development history of GOME, besides the Yolo and DAZHONG Electronics, the Jintaiyang, Zhongshang Electronics and Heitiane etc. are also acquired by GOME. However, their employees accept the cultural norm of GOME quickly because population size of the target firm is relatively small.

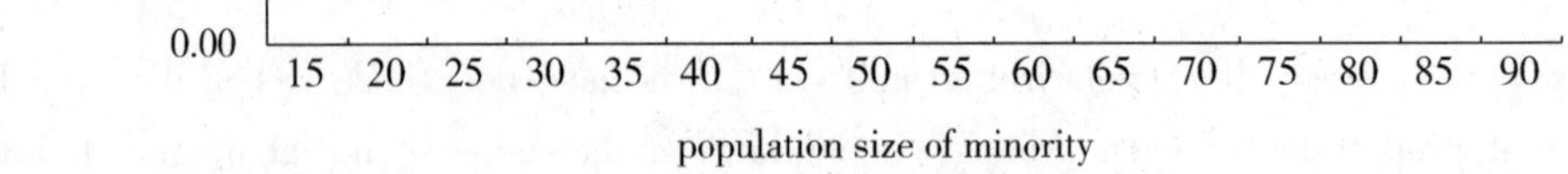

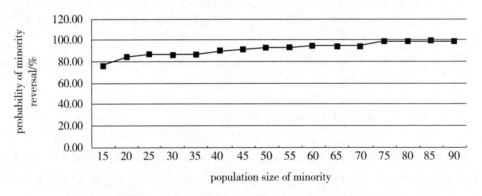

Figure 14 Impact of population size of minority on reversal probability

4.4 Cohesion of the local community

From the above analysis, we can see that the acculturation result in most settings is not static but stochastic to some extent. Employees from different firms will work together after acquisition. Therefore, organizational structure and social networks will change greatly. What is the relationship between the reversal probability and network structure after acquisition?

It is obvious that the opinion of the individuals in the tightly cohesive community may strongly differ from that of the whole population. The cohesion of the community regarding the overall structure depicts how strong the ties between members of a social group are and how homogeneous their properties are. We suppose that the cohesion inside a community influences the strength of the community. This may lead to more frequent interaction, and make individuals in the community have more opportunity to spread their opinion to others. In order to analyze the influence of network structure, we build a random network whose average nodal degree is 6. The new firm is described as a graph whose nodes represent the individuals and the edges represent their social relation. In order to compare results with different network structure, we increase the nodal degree of minority community and majority community respectively, so that the average nodal degree of local community reaches a special value and the average nodal degree of the rest remains 6. Figure 15 shows three sample of networks in the simulation model. The left figure shows the base network where average nodal degree is 6; the middle figure shows the network where the nodal degree of the majority is enhanced; and the right figure shows the network where the nodal degree of the minority is enhanced. The different shapes and colors of the nodes represent the different types of agents as explained in Figure 3.

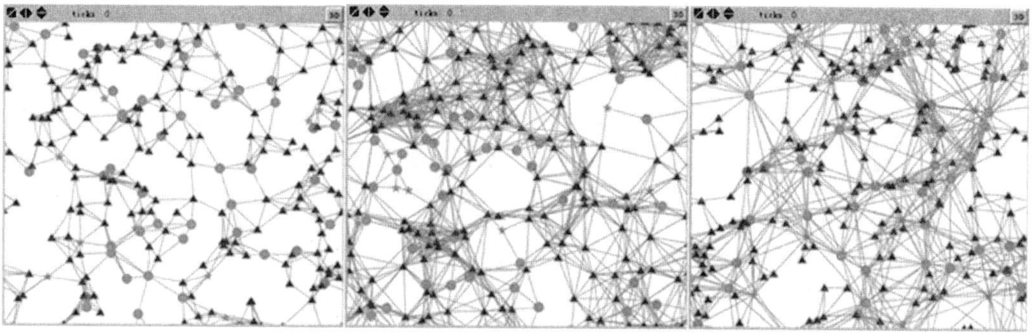

Figure 15 The network of the simulation, the average nodal degree of the left one is 6; in the middle one, the local average nodal degree among majority is 15, the number of total links is 1078; in the right one, the local average nodal degree among the minority is 15, the number of total links is 1551

Consider a network with N nodes, numbered from 1 to N and joined in pairs randomly by $\frac{NK}{2}$ edges, where K is the average degree of the network. Suppose the first M nodes ($M \leqslant N/2$) construct a community, hence the community takes a small proportion of the population. To enhance the cohesion of the community, we add edges randomly into the sub graph until the average degree of sub graph reaches R. The sub graph is a graph whose nodes and edges form subsets of the nodes and edges of a given graph. In order to make the average degree of sub graph reach R, it can be calculated that $\frac{1}{2}M(R - K\frac{M-1}{N-1})$ edges are needed to be added in average, as the average degree of the sub graph is $K\frac{M-1}{N-1}$ before any edges have been added. Hence, we can construct the topology of the model in the following two steps:

(1) Construct a N-nodes random graph with the average degree to be K.

(2) Add edges into the sub graph composed by the first M nodes.

It is worth noting that, after the two-step construction, the average degree of the nodes outside the community is still K, while the average degree of the nodes inside is neither K nor R, but $K\dfrac{N-M}{N-1}+R$.

Figure 16 shows the relationship between the local average nodal degree of minority and the reversal probability. The reversal probability is 85. 39% when the average nodal degree of local community is default value. And the reversal probability increases slowly when the local average nodal degree of the minority is larger than 7. However, although the local average nodal degree of the minority increases to 35, the reversal probability is still 87. 94%.

Figure 17 shows the fluctuation process of reversal probability when the local average nodal degree of majority increases. The reversal probability is decreasing with the increase of local average nodal degree of majority. However, the reversal probability will be not sensitive to the local average nodal degree once the local average nodal degree is larger than 30.

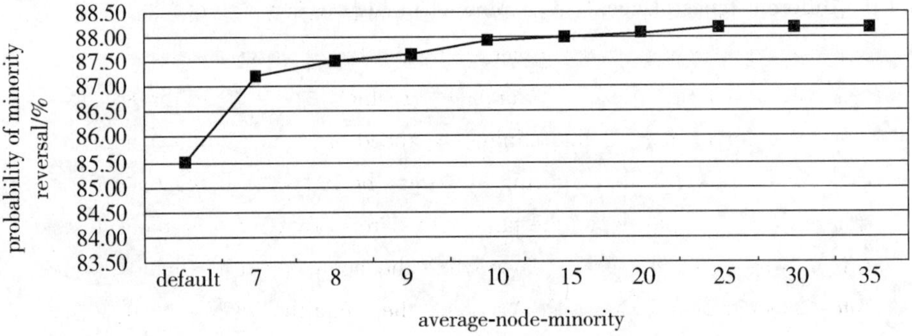

Figure 16 Impact of local average nodal degree among minority on reversal probability

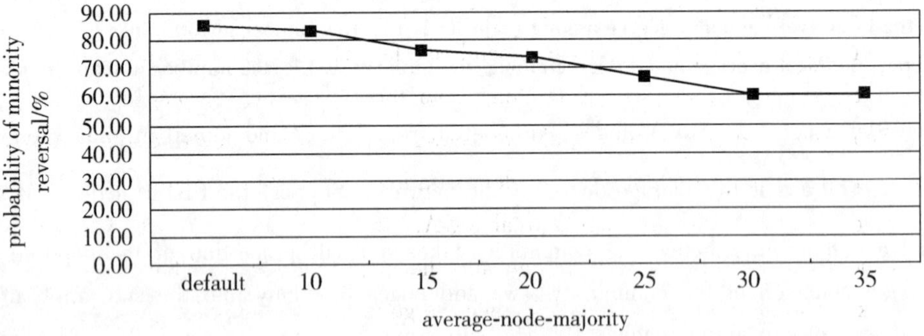

Figure 17 Impact of local average nodal degree among majority on reversal probability

Overall, the local average nodal degree can influence the reversal probability significantly. The reversal probability is increasing with the increase of local average nodal degree of minority. And the reversal probability is decreasing with the increase of local average nodal degree of majority. However, the reversal probability is no longer sensitive to the local nodal degree when the local average nodal degree reaches a special value. As an example, the employees from DAZHONG Electronics keep in tight touch with each other and adhere to their original norm soon after the acquisition. For this reason, they can maintain their own interests and original opinion successfully.

5 Discussion

In this research, a heterogeneous relative agreement model was proposed to study the influence of public non-conformists on norm reversion after M&A. Through simulation experiments, we can conclude that:

(1) Shortly after the merger and acquisition, the individuals will cohere in their own groups which hold two different cultural norms respectively. This time is a key period that determines the future of the new firm. Lack of proper guidance will lead to the conflict of the cultural norm or the cultural norm of the acquiring firm assimilated by the target firms.

(2) Managers need to inculcate the public dissenters timely once there are several employees expressing their non-conformist behavior publicly. When the cultural norm of the acquiring firm displays a trend of being reversed by the target firm, the acquiring firm needs to guide the parameter μ as far as possible. Parameter μ which represents the intensity of interaction is one of the most important factors determining the speed of group norm evolving.

(3) The cultural norm of the acquiring firms may be in risk of being reversed by the target firm if the opinions of the employees in the target firms are similar to the opinions of the employees in the acquiring firms to some extent. Therefore, the acquiring firm should take the cultural difference into consideration before M&A. And the acquiring firms need to enhance the connectivity of the social network among the employees from the acquiring firm and weaken the connectivity of the network among the employees from the target firms.

Note that an acquiring company might actually value the norms of the target company. It might want the target company to retain independence following its previous successful norms or it might want its bureaucracy to learn something from that of the target company. These are all routine phenomenon in reality. Just as all we know, modes of acculturation after M&A include integration, assimilation, separation and deculturation. And these results are all possible. Norm reversion is a rare phenomenon in real M&A. But once it occurs, the original external balance of the acquiring firm will be broken and the acquiring firm will have to adapt its most kinds of work. Therefore the acquiring firms need to guide the acculturation process after M&A to prevent norm reversion.

Therefore, how should the acquiring firm do in each step of the acquiring process to avoid norm reversion? We suggest some strategies of containment from three steps.

STEP 1, before the acquiring activity. Choosing a target firm is one of the most important things for the acquiring firm before the acquiring activity. When the norm segment between the acquiring firm and the target firm is small, the norm of the acquiring firm can assimilate the norm of the target firm and the norm of the acquiring firm can be reversed by the target firm. But when the norm segment is too large, the mode of acculturation will be separation.

STEP 2, early stage after M&A. Early stage is the key period to prevent norm reversion after M&A. The individuals' opinions and behavior will cohere in their own group in the early stage after M&A. When the acquiring firms expect the modes of acculturation being integration, assimilation and not being reversed, they need to enhance the networks of the employees from the acquiring firm and weaken the networks of the employees from the acquired firm. Meanwhile, propagation and cultural education are also required.

STEP 3, when public dissenters appearing. Once several public dissenters from the acquired firm appear, the acquiring firm need to try best to prevent the increase of population size of the public dissenters because large population size of public dissenters is one of the important factor that leads to norm reversion. Furthermore, the acquiring firms need to decrease the intensity of interaction as far as possible because intensity of interaction is one of the key factors that determine the reversing speed. The approaches include promoting the attitudinal immune and the individual commitment through propagation and education. Therefore, the acquiring firm will have more time to deal with the situation.

6 Conclusion

In the process of merger and acquisition, acculturation of different cultural norm is a key factor that determines whether the merger and acquisition will be successful. Once there are some cultural norm conflict between the acquiring firms and the target firms, the satisfaction and organization commitment of the employees will decline, and performance of the enterprise will also decline. Therefore, how to guide the acculturation after M&A and how to decline the risk of cultural norm reversing are both important aspects that need the manager's attention. This study improves the classical relative agreement model. The new proposed model defines different opinion and uncertainty updating rules for majority, minority and public non-conformists respectively. In the new model, there is not only attractive influence but repulsive influence among the individuals. And the pluralistic ignorance of the individuals from the target firm will disappear in this scenario. This new model overcomes the shortcomings of the classical relative agreement bounded confidence model based on which final organizational norm mainly depends on initial opinion and uncertainty. A series of simulation experiments are carried out to demonstrate the new model and to provide helpful suggestions for M&A.

Meantime, some more complex phenomena were not considered in this research. For example, we would like to study the effect of public non-conformists when two groups of public non-conformists with opposing opinion compete with each other. In our study, the social networks are static and the agents are chosen randomly. More interesting scenarios would include situations that some specific agents locate on specific nodes, e. g. the hubs in a social network, and that social networks evolve with the dynamic opinion.

Acknowledgement

The authors appreciate the helpful suggestions and comments of the editor and the anonymous referees. This work was supported by the National Natural Science Foundation of China (grant number 71071065 and number 71101059).

References

[1] Deffuant G, Amblard F, Weisbuch G, Faure T. How Can Extremism Prevail? A Study Based on the Relative Agreement Interaction Model [J]. Journal of Artificial Societies and Social Simulation, 2002, 5 (4).

[2] Björkman I, Stahl G K, Vaara E. Cultural Differences and Capability Transfer in Cross-Border Acquisitions: The Mediating Roles of Capability Complementarity, Absorptive Capacity, and Social Integration [J]. Journal of International Business Studies, 2007, 38 (4): 658-672.

[3] Shenkar O. Cultural Distance Revisited: Towards a More Rigorous Conceptualization and Measurement of Cultural Differences [J]. Journal of International Business Studies, 2001, 32 (3): 519-535.

[4] Cox Jr T. The Multicultural Organization [J]. The executive, 1991, 5 (2): 34-47.

[5] Walker A, Wooldridge M. Understanding the Emergence of Conventions in Multi-Agent Systems [M]. MIT Press, 1995: 384-389.

[6] López F L Y, Luck M, d'Inverno M. A Normative Framework for Agent-Based Systems [J]. Computational & Mathematical Organization Theory, 2006, 12 (2/3): 227-250.

[7] Horne C. Explaining Norm Enforcement [J]. Rationality and Society, 2007, 19 (2): 139-170.

[8] Helbing D, Johansson A. Cooperation, Norms, and Revolutions: A Unified Game-Theoretical Approach [J]. PloS One, 2010, 5 (10): 1-26.

[9] Huang C Y, Tzou P J, Sun C T. Collective Opinion and Attitude Dynamics Dependency on Informational and Normative Social Influences [J]. Simulation, 2011, 87 (10): 875-892.

[10] Nahavandi A, Malekzadeh A R. Acculturation in Mergers and Acquisitions [J]. International Executive, 1988, 30 (1): 10-12.

[11] Cartwright S, Cooper C L. The Role of Culture Compatibility in Successful Organizational Marriage [J]. The Academy of Management Executive (1993-2005), 1993, 7 (2): 57-70.

[12] Castellano C, Fortunato S, Loreto V. Statistical Physics of Social Dynamics [J]. Reviews of Modern Physics, 2009, 81 (2): 591.

[13] Kacperski K, Holyst J A. Phase Transitions as a Persistent Feature of Groups with Leaders in Models of Opinion Formation [J]. Physica A: Statistical Mechanics and Its Applications, 2000, 287 (3): 631-643.

[14] Latané B, Nowak A. Self-Organizing Social Systems: Necessary and Sufficient Conditions for the Emergence of Clustering, Consolidation, and Continuing Diversity [J]. Progress in communication sciences, 1997, 1 (13): 43-74.

[15] Krause U. A Discrete Nonlinear and Non-Autonomous Model of Consensus Formation [J]. Communications in Difference Equations, 2000, 7 (1): 227-236.

[16] Dittmer J C. Consensus Formation under Bounded Confidence [J]. Nonlinear Analysis-Theory Methods and Applications, 2001, 47 (7): 4615-4622.

[17] Groeber P, Schweitzer F, Press K. How Groups Can Foster Consensus: The Case of Local Cultures [J]. Journal of Artificial Societes and Social Simulationsn, 2009, 12 (2).

[18] Franks D W, Noble J, Kaufmann P, Stagl S. Extremism Propagation in Social Networks with Hubs [J]. Adaptive Behavior, 2008, 16 (4): 264-274.

[19] Galam S. Minority Opinion Spreading in Random Geometry [J]. The European Physical Journal B-Condensed Matter and

Complex Systems, 2002, 25 (4): 403 -406.

[20] Galam S. Heterogeneous Beliefs, Segregation, and Extremism in the Making of Public Opinions [J]. Physical Review E, 2005, 71 (4): 46 -123.

[21] Pajot S, Galam S. Coexistence of Opposite Global Social Feelings: The Case of Percolation Driven Insecurity [J]. International Journal of Modern Physics C, 2002, 13 (10): 1375 -1386.

[22] Friedman M, Friedman R. Tyranny of the Status Quo [M]. Diego: Harcourt Brace Jovanovich, 1984.

[23] Moscovici S. Silent Majorities and Loud Minorities [J]. Communication Yearbook, 1991, 14: 298 -308.

[24] Rogers E M. Diffusion of Innovations [M]. New York: The Free Press, 1995.

[25] Wood W. Attitude Change: Persuasion and Social Influence [J]. Annual Review of Psychology, 2000, 51 (1): 539 -570.

[26] Christakis N A, Fowler J H. The Spread of Obesity in a Large Social Network over 32 Years [J]. New England Journal of Medicine, 2007, 357 (4): 370 -379.

[27] Centola D, Macy M. Complex Contagions and the Weakness of Long Tiesl [J]. American Journal of Sociology, 2007, 113 (3): 702 -734.

[28] Granovetter M S. The Strength of Weak Ties [J]. American Journal of Sociology, 1973, 78 (2): 1360 -1380.

[29] Watts D J. Small Worlds: The Dynamics of Networks between Order and Randomness [M]. Princeton: Princeton University Press, 2003.

[30] Watts D J, Strogatz S H. Collective Dynamics of "Small-World" Networks [J]. Nature, 1998, 393 (2): 440 -442.

[31] Centola D, Eguíluz V M, Macy M W. Cascade Dynamics of Complex Propagation [J]. Physica A: Statistical Mechanics and Its Applications, 2007, 374 (1): 449 -456.

[32] Christakis N A, Fowler J H. The Collective Dynamics of Smoking in a Large Social Network [J]. New England Journal of Medicine, 2008, 358 (21): 2249 -2258.

[33] Wikopedia. Niche [OL] [2014 -11 -23]. http://En. Wikipedia. Org/Wiki/Niche.

[34] Anderson C. The Long Tail: Why the Future of Business Is Selling Less of More [M]. New York: Hyperion Books, 2008.

[35] Huang G, Cao J, Wang G, Qu Y. The Strength of the Minority [J]. Physica A: Statistical Mechanics and Its Applications, 2008, 387 (18): 4665 -4672.

[36] Wander J, Amblard F. Uniformity, Bipolarization and Pluriformity Captured as Generic Stylized Behavior with an Agent-Based Simulation Model of Attitude Change [J]. Computational & Mathematical Organization Theory, 2004, 10 (4): 295 -303.

[37] Salzarulo L. A Continuous Opinion Dynamics Model Based on the Principle of Meta-Contrast [J]. Journal of Artificial Societies and Social Simulation, 2006, 9 (1): 13.

[38] Deffuant G, Neau D, Amblard F, Weisbuch G. Mixing Beliefs among Interacting Agents [J]. Advances in Complex Systems, 2000, 3 (4): 87 -98.

[39] Windrum P, Fagiolo G, Moneta A. Empirical Validation of Agent-Based Models: Alternatives and Prospects [J]. Journal of Artificial Societies and Social Simulation, 2007, 10 (2): 8.

[40] Hales D, Rouchier J, Edmonds B. Model-to-Model Analysis [J]. Journal of Artificial Societies and Social Simulation, 2003, 6 (4): 5.

[41] Kurmyshev E, Juárez H A, González-Silva R A. Dynamics of Bounded Confidence Opinion in Heterogeneous Social Networks: Concord against Partial Antagonism [J]. Physica A: Statistical Mechanics and Its Applications, 2011, 390 (16): 2945 -2955.

[42] Tichy G. What Do We Know about Success and Failure of Mergers? [J]. Journal of Industry, Competition and Trade, 2001, 4 (1): 347 -394.

[43] Schweiger D M, Very P. Creating Value through Merger and Acquisition Integration [J]. Advances inmergers and Acquisitions, 2003, 1 (2): 1 -26.

[44] Wilensky U. Netlogo [OL]. http://ccl. northwestern. edu/netlogo, 1999.

[45] Delgado J. Emergence of Social Conventions in Complex Networks [J]. Artificial intelligence, 2002, 141 (1): 171 -185.

教师简介：

陈永生，男，中山大学历史学学士，中国人民大学管理学硕士、管理学博士。1983 年起任教于中山大学资讯管理学院，教授、博士生导师。现任中山大学大数据研究院院长、中山大学信息安全与电子文件研究院执行院长，历任中山大学信息管理系教研室主任、副系主任、系主任。主讲“档案学理论与历史”、“档案学论著述评与档案学方法论研究”、“政府信息公开与现行文件开放利用研究”、“档案事业发展调查分析”、“政府信息与档案管理”、“档案学概论”等课程。主要研究方向为档案学基础理论、档案现代化管理、电子政务与电子文件管理、信息资源整合与档案数字化、政府信息管理、信息安全与保密管理。主持科研项目 20 余项，发表学术论文 160 余篇，获各级教学和科研奖励 20 余项。兼任教育部档案学教学指导委员会委员、中国档案学会常务理事、广东省档案学会副理事长、广东省档案专家委员会主任、广东省党委系统信息化工作专家小组副组长、广东省实施大数据战略专家委员会专家、广东省保密科技专家委员会委员、广东省政府文史馆文史信息化研究院院长、广东省委办公厅档案信息化顾问、广东省政府办公厅政府信息化顾问、中山大学档案馆顾问。联系方式：isscys@ mail. sysu. edu. cn。

所选论文《政府信息资源趋利性整合共享及其应对策略》原载于《档案学研究》2014 年第 4 期

政府信息资源趋利性整合共享及其应对策略

陈永生，聂二辉①

摘　要：趋利性是政府信息资源整合共享中的重要特征，表现为部门间的横向政府信息资源趋利性整合共享、层级间的纵向政府信息资源趋利性整合共享、整合多利政府信息资源内部共享以及整合少利或无利政府信息资源内外共享。在信息时代，公众对政府信息资源的要求趋向于公开化、透明化、个性化，这与政府信息资源整合共享中所表现的趋利性是相背离的。在政府信息资源的趋利性整合共享中，涉及主体——政府、客体——政府信息资源以及受众——利用者，应对政府信息资源趋利性整合共享，可从它所涉及的主客体以及受众两个层面寻找策略。

关键词：政府信息资源；趋利性；整合共享

① 聂二辉，中山大学资讯管理学院档案学研究生。

The Profitable Integration and Sharing of the Government Information Resources and Its Coping Strategies

Yongsheng Chen, Erhui Nie

Abstract: Profit is an important feature of the integration and sharing of the government information resources. This concludes profitable integration and sharing of the government information resources between horizontal departments and between vertical departments, integrate the government information resources with much profit to share internally, integrate the government information resources with little profit or nothing to share internally and externally. The profitable integration and sharing of the government information resources is related to the subject—government, object—the government, information resources, and audience—the user. It is important and necessary to devise strategies to deal with this problem from the aspect of subject, object and audience.
Keywords: Government information resources; Profit; Integration and sharing

1 引　言

在全社会的信息资源所有者中，政府是内容丰富、质量优化的信息资源最大拥有者。随着公众从政府传统服务的附加服务对象[1]逐渐成为政府公共信息服务体系的中心[2]，公众的信息需求越来越为紧迫和多样化，公众对政府信息资源整合共享的数量和质量越来越难以满意。政府作为公共行政的主体，其存在的基本价值在于维护和发展社会公共利益。[3]但由于政府的双重属性，它作为市场的主体之一[4]，且按照布坎南的公共选择理论，政府主体都是有其自身追求的“经济人”，他们的行为都毫无例外地以其自身追求的最大化为目标，政府的这种“经济人”角色，具备自身的利益诉求，其行为具有趋利性的一面。政府信息资源的整合共享作为政府行为的一种，自然而然也具有趋利性的一面。

政府信息资源趋利性整合共享可以说是一种普遍现象，它基于政府的角度，在使自身利益最大化的前提下去满足公众对信息资源的需求，而此种需求是难于满足的，这实际上是对公共利益的一种侵犯。探讨政府信息资源趋利性整合共享的内涵及现状，提出较为可行的应对策略，对于满足公众的信息需求，促进信息社会的发展和进步具有至关重要的作用。

2 政府信息资源趋利性整合共享

政府信息资源趋利性整合共享是指政府在整合共享源于政府的信息资源时，以政府利益为导向，以满足自身客观需要为目标，虽一定程度上实现公共利益，但最终的落脚点还是政府自身。它主要表现为：①部门间的横向政府信息资源趋利性整合共享；②层级间的纵向政府信息资源趋利性整合共享；③整合多利政府信息资源内部共享，整合少利或无利政府信息资源内外共享。

2.1 部门间的横向政府信息资源趋利性整合共享

在我国，政府根据管理社会事务的需要分成若干职能部门，各部门具有一定的政治权威，它可以搜集与本部门相关的经济信息、科技信息等，作为部门所有的基本资源，甚至是垄断资源。[5]这是政府职能部门自利的一种表现形式，属于政府自利的一部分。[6]它所强调的是政府部门的局部利益，而非面向大众的公共利益。

部门间横向政府信息资源趋利性整合共享的实质是政府信息资源有限的整合共享，这种有限是站在公共利益的角度上来讲的，其主要特点是政府部门整合“部门私有化”的信息资源时，设定共享权限，形成事实上的资源“部门私有”格局，从而导致“信息孤岛”和“信息壁垒”现象频发，甚至“信息寻租”的违法案件也屡见不鲜。在现有的政府部门间信息资源共享阻碍性因素的研究方面，国内多数学者认为要实现共享，技术已经不是主要问题，需要去解决传统官僚体制下形成的政府部门壁垒、利益分配等问题。达沃斯（Sharon S. Dawes）指出，政府部门信息共享既存在收益也存在风险，排除掉既有的技术困难不讲，组织性障碍（组织的自身利益和部门专业技术分析框架）和政治性障碍（对部门决策的外部控制、部门的自由裁量权和项目的重要性）同样是部门间信息共享的阻碍因素。[7]

原则上讲，任何档案都有特定的用户，不提供任何人利用的档案是无意义的，没有存在的必要。[8]政府信息资源也同样如此，只是在趋利性整合共享的情境下，这种特定用户只限定在了政府部门内部，无疑这种方式是不利于满足部门之间以及公众的利用需求的。无利用或少利用，就无法充分突显政府信息资源的价值；没有充分突显政府信息资源的价值，其存在的必要性就值得质疑。

2.2 层级间的纵向政府信息资源趋利性整合共享

层级间的纵向政府信息资源整合共享的趋利性主要表现在两方面：

（1）内向型的政府信息资源管理。冯惠玲在《政府信息资源管理》[9]中强调透过政府业已建设的网络基础设施整合和共享信息资源使信息技术优势最大化，实现不同层级政府之间信息资源的共享。虽然网络环境下政府信息资源的整合共享已经取得了一定成绩，但由于层级间纵向政府信息资源整合共享的趋利性，政府信息服务的对象以政府机关为中心，以本机关及政府系统内部的共享为原则，强调上下级输入的信息应用于本机关的决策。这是一种“肥水不流外人田”的思维，虽然强调“为我所用”，但利益主体却始终是本机关、本部门。

（2）下级行政机关相对于上级行政机关具备信息优势。行政隶属关系适用于上下级行政机关，下级行政机关服从上级行政机关的领导，上级行政机关对下级行政机关拥有绝对权威。理论上讲，应该是上级行政机关更具备信息优势，但由于下级行政机关是行政信息的形成者和具体执行者，在报送什么、报送多少、什么时候报送、采用什么方式报送等诸多问题的处置上，下级机关拥有实际的信息制发权、优先处置权和主动权。[10]这就使得信息瞒报、信息失真现象层出不穷，行政机关自下而上的信息优势递减是层级间政府信息资源趋利性整合共享的主要特点。

2.3 整合多利政府信息资源内部共享，整合少利或无利政府信息资源内外共享

政府利益的价值取向是具有利己性的[11]，所谓“多利”、“少利”、“无利”政府信息资源是基于这一层面来阐释的。借鉴陈庆云、曾军荣[12]所描述的政府利益，多利政府信息资源即能够切实保障政府部门及其成员的基本利益、满足其角色利益甚至是获取失常利益的那一部分信息资源，此种政府信息资源往往也与公众具有极为密切和重要的关系；少利政府信息资源是指较少满足政府部门及其成员的基本利益、角色利益，基本不具备失常利益的那一部分信息资源，但这并不意味着对公众也少利；无利政府信息资源并非绝对意义上的“无利”，只是就政府部门及其成员而言，整合共享的成本远远大于收益，政府层面上的利益微乎其微，但需要指出的是这不意味着对公众的利益也是微乎其微，这是此种政府信息资源得以存在未被销毁的缘由所在。

政府信息资源的整合存在着多种基于不同技术的理论模型，如电子政务、知识管理、集成管理和主题地图等，都是随着社会发展而相应产生的。这些模型无论是对多利政府信息资源的整合，还是少利或无利政府信息资源的整合都具有极大的应用价值。但是在具体的操作层面，资源整合技术更倾向于也更有可能应用在多利政府信息资源的整合中，这与政府的利己性是分不开的。

政府信息资源的共享包括对内和对外两个层面。前者侧重于利用政府机关内部网在本机关内各组织机构之间开展信息共享与服务，其目标是通过有效的信息沟通，提高本部门各组织机构的行政运作效率；后者侧重于利用政府专用网、办公信息数据库和外部网在政府内部不同专业系统、不同组织系统之间开展的信息共享与信息处理服务，其具体目标是提高整个政府系统的信息服务能力，增强政府透明度。[13]但在具体的现实中，多利政府信息资源在对内共享中基本可以达到其目标，甚至少利或无利政府信息资源也能在对内共享过程中产生积极影响。而对外共享，也是社会共享，多利政府信息资源往往没有少利或者无利政府信息资源表现得好，不是指其价值方面，而是可获取方面。政府部门因为少利或无利而失去了整合共享政府信息资源的动力，或者在强大舆论压力下不得不整合部分少利或无利政府信息资源进行社会共享，但这远远不能满足公众的正常需求。

政府信息资源整合解决的是化分散为集中、化无序为有序的问题，为接下来的资源共享提供前提和基础；政府信息资源的共享则是指强化政府信息资源的可获知性和可获取性，使社会公众与组织公平地拥有对政府各类信息资源的获取权利和获取条件。但在现实中的政府信息资源整合共享过程中，多利政府信息资源更受政府部门青睐，也更易采用先进整合技术，充分发挥内部共享的功效。而少利或无利政府信息资源虽然名义上更有可能对外共享，但获取条件却不尽如人意，导致社会共享效果不明显，公众也多不满意；少利或无利政府信息资源即便对外共享了，也是迟缓于对内共享的。

《中华人民共和国政府信息公开条例》中规定，行政机关对符合下列基本要求之一的政府信息应当主动公开：①涉及公民、法人或者其他组织切身利益的；②需要社会公众

广泛知晓或者参与的；③反映本行政机关机构设置、职能、办事程序等情况的。这些基本涵盖了多利、少利或无利政府信息资源，某种程度上讲，它们被政府部门已经整合或正在整合，并且已经内部共享或准备内部共享。但在面向社会共享时却困难重重，如一些大学生向政府部门申请信息公开却屡遭拒绝，申请公开1.99亿客票系统相关招标信息，多延迟回复或被告知“申请的信息不存在”等。

3 政府信息资源趋利性整合共享的应对策略

在政府信息资源的趋利性整合共享中，涉及三个要素：①主体——政府；②客体——政府信息资源；③受众——政府信息资源的利用者，它既可划分为个人和组织，也可由政府内部和外部利用者组成。三者之间的关系如图1：客体来源于主体，受众利用客体，同时受制于主体。这三个要素贯穿政府信息资源整合共享的全过程，主体提供客体给受众使用，并设定权限，限制受众的利用。这种情形下，主体掌握着政府信息资源整合共享的话事权，它可以决定整合什么、共享什么，也可以决定谁来利用、利用多少。

应对政府信息资源趋利性整合共享，可从它所涉及的主客体以及受众两个层面寻找策略。

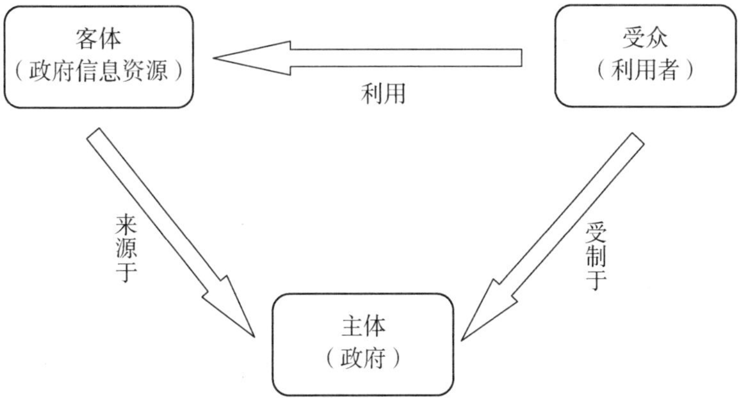

图1　政府信息资源整合与共享涉及主体相互关系

3.1 主客体层面的应对策略

部门间、层级间政府信息资源的趋利性整合共享归根结底是政府利益所致，而这种利益是建立在政府信息资源的基础上的。解决部门间、层级间政府信息资源趋利性整合共享的问题，首先要理清多利、少利和无利政府信息资源的社会价值，即提供一种解决方案，它既能满足社会公众的信息需求，又能实现保证政府部门及其成员的基本利益、满足其角色利益，但要打击失常利益的目标。若政府利益合法、合理的部分得以满足，那多利政府信息资源内部共享以及少利或无利政府信息资源由内部共享延伸至社会共享的情形也会得到改观。

政府信息资源因其内容不同、种类不同，以致所蕴含的社会价值高低不一。本文根据政府利己性的特点将政府信息资源划分为多利政府信息资源、少利政府信息资源和无利政府信息资源，但“多利”、“少利”和“无利”并非一定与“高社会价值”、“低社会价值”相对应。图2中，政府信息资源共分为六种类型，即A型、A′型、B型、B′型、C型和C′型。A型表示高社会价值的多利政府信息资源，A′型表示低社会价值的多利政府信息资源，B型表示高社会价值的少利政府信息资源，B′型表示低社会价值的少利政府信息资源，C型表示高社会价值的无利政府信息资源，C′型表示低社会价值的无利政府信息资源。

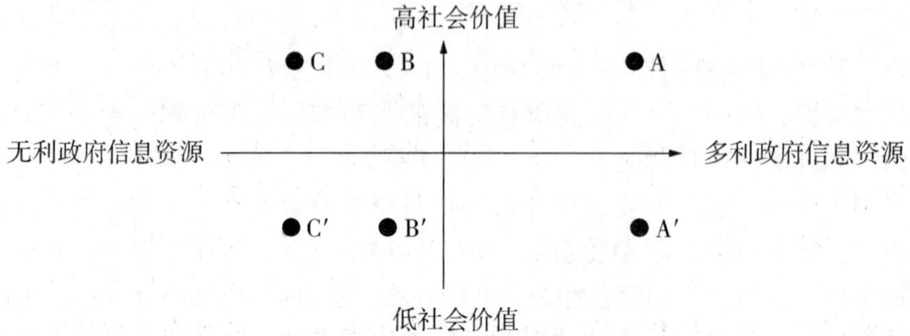

图2　政府信息资源共享类型划分

政府在信息资源的整合共享中，更倾向于A型和A′型，这是由其自身的趋利性所决定的。但从社会价值的角度——最大化满足公众的信息需求，政府理应优先整合共享A型、B型以及C型。达成这一目标，政府整合共享信息资源的理念要以公众需求为导向替代以政府利益为基础，将最大化实现社会价值为己任。

政府理念的转变能够一定程度上解决政府信息资源趋利性整合共享的问题，除此之外，参考公共物品理论，笔者提出另一应对策略（图3）。对于A型，因其“多利”，政府能够在利益的驱动下优先整合，并首先实现内部共享。再加上其高社会价值，外部共享成为必然的发展趋势和最终选择。A′型的社会价值低，但其多利的特点突出，这就使

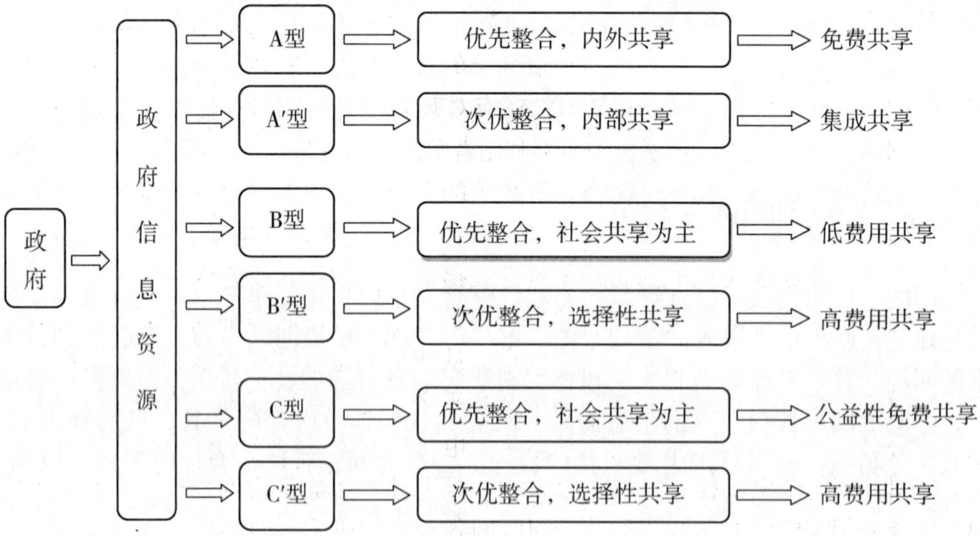

图3　政府信息资源趋利性整合应对策略

得政府具有了整合共享的动力，也正因如此，A′型最适宜内部共享。而要使 A′型得到最大化的利用，各政府部门需在共同战略目标的指引下，将信息资源、信息技术等相关要素整合在一起，形成优势互补，最终达到虚拟联盟状态，而各部门可以从这个虚拟的优势联盟中获取自身需要的信息资源。[14] 即实现 A′型的集成共享，从而更好地实现本部门的职能。B 型因其“少利”，政府缺乏足够的动力去整合共享，但它具有高社会价值，在公众的生活中起着至关重要的作用，所以政府优先整合共享 B 型以满足公众的信息需求是获取民众支持的良好选择。但为了能够保障政府有足够的动力去优先整合共享，采取一种低费用的有偿共享方式，保证政府部门及其成员的基本利益和角色利益显得尤为重要。B′型因具有较少的政府利益，与其他多利的类型相比只能次优整合，但又因为它具备一定的社会价值，所以在整合的基础上采取选择性共享能够满足特定人群的信息需求，同时收取高额费用，以弥补在整合共享中付出的成本。C 型与 B 型类似，在高社会价值下应当优先整合以满足公众的信息需求，但因其微乎其微的政府利益，内部共享所产生的价值远远不及社会共享，但社会共享一般是建立在内部共享的基础上的。此外，C 型应当采取一种公益性免费共享的方式向社会提供利用，这能够体现政府的公共服务职能和为人民服务的理念。C′型与 B′型在政府利益的多少上不同，即整合共享的驱动力不同之外，其他基本一致，同样采取一种高收费共享的方式提供给特定人群以满足其信息需求。

3.2 受众层面的应对策略

事物的发展是由内外因共同作用的结果。应对政府信息资源的趋利性整合共享，主客体层面的解决策略属于内因的一部分，而从受众——政府信息资源的利用者层面提出的解决方法则属于外因。政府信息资源的利用者根据不同的标准可以划分不同类别，在本文中，将利用者划分为政府内部利用者和外部利用者，与内部共享和社会共享相对应。

倒逼机制原本是一个经济学术语，但在当前社会转型期，它频繁地出现在日常生活和社会语境中，并在可持续社会发展中对社会矛盾和困境呈现了策略性的重要突破。[15] 倒逼机制具有传导路径的逆向性特点，表现为对信息源的决策产生约束性影响的逆向传导过程；它也具有鲜明的负反馈特性，从信号源的视角来看，它感受到的就是负反馈装置对它产生的来自外部的压力和约束力。[16] 在应对政府信息资源趋利性整合共享这一问题时，引入倒逼机制，从内部利用者和外部利用者分别进行阐述。

第一，政府内部利用者在行使法律所赋予的职权时，往往需要各方面的信息资源辅助决策，但“信息孤岛”、“信息壁垒”等横行，这严重影响了决策的科学性、针对性、实时性等。为了能够最大化地利用信息资源，提高行政效率，政府内部利用者必然会进行申诉，寻求获取其他部门所整合的信息资源，这是一种政府内部式的倒逼，有利于解决部门间、层级间信息资源趋利性整合共享，从而最大化地实现内部共享。如中山市电子档案馆模式，它在党政内网上建立一个共享平台，统一数据标准，档案馆建立一个电子文件中心，每个行政机构建立电子档案室，电子档案室与电子文件中心相连。电子文件中心逻辑控制每个电子档案室的电子文件，只要获得形成机构的授权，其他机关的人员就可以查询相应的政府信息。这样，同级的各个行政机构之间的信息资源就得到大范围的整合，提高了查询利用效率。

第二，信息社会下，我国公民的信息素养得以不断提升，“政府公开什么民众就看什么”的时代正逐渐远去，“民众想看什么就找政府获取什么”的时代正在到来。特别是在《中华人民共和国政府信息公开条例》公布以后，对于A型、B型和C型政府信息资源，公众更为迫切地促使政府提供获取条件。政府信息资源的趋利性整合共享，将在公民的倒逼之下得到改善，并最大化地实现社会共享。

4 结　　语

尽管政府完全为了人民利益而不具备一点私利是对政府利益的片面理解，但孟德斯鸠提出的“有权力的人们使用权力一直到遇有界限的地方才休止”警示我们政府利益某种程度上可以无限延伸。这样，从横向部门间、纵向层级间、内外部共享信息资源等方面探讨政府信息资源整合共享中的趋利性现象，将政府的这种趋利行为呈现在公众面前，以期形成信息时代下的社会监督。

在我们的社会和经济生活中，信息是不可分割且极具价值的资源，它能够为信息所有者和利用者带来经济利益。[17]这是信息时代的典型特征，也是公众呼吁政府信息资源公开化、透明化甚至个性化服务的动力之源。因而，积极应对政府信息资源趋利性整合共享，切实保障社会公民的信息获取权，充分发挥政府信息资源的价值，实现公共利益的最大化，以促进整个社会的发展进步和繁荣昌盛。

参考文献

[1] 周毅. 基于信息权利保护的政府信息资源规划研究［J］. 情报资料工作，2010（3）：45－49.
[2] 周林兴，仲雪珊. 以公众需求为导向的档案信息资源规划探讨［J］. 档案学通讯，2012（5）：45－48.
[3] 彭姝. 政府行为的目标——对政府行为的利益取向分析［J］. 内蒙古农业大学学报：社会科学版，2005（4）：307－310.
[4] 何秀玲，孔祥利. 论政府的趋利行为及其规范［J］. 理论探讨，2011（5）：36－39.
[5] 樊博. 跨部门政府信息资源共享的推进体制、机制和方法［J］. 上海交通大学学报：哲学社会科学版，2008（2）：13－20.
[6] 金太军. 政府的自利性及其控制［J］. 江海学刊，2002（2）：106－112.
[7] Dawes S S. Interagency Information Sharing：Expected Benefits，Manageable Risks［J］. Journal of Policy Analysis and Management，1996（3）：377－394.
[8] 张照余. 网络共享中档案信息的内容划控与权限控制研究［J］. 档案学通讯，2009（2）：62－65.
[9] 冯惠玲. 政府信息资源管理［M］. 北京：中国人民大学出版社，2006：178.
[10] 杨霞. 行政层级监督中信息不对称问题及其治理对策分析［C］//“构建和谐社会与深化行政管理体制改革”研讨会暨中国行政管理学会2007年年会论文集. 2007：1076－1083.
[11] 刘国玲. 政府利益的双重价值取向研究［J］. 经营管理者，2011（12）：4.
[12] 陈庆云，曾军荣. 论公共管理中的政府利益［J］. 中国行政管理，2005（8）：19－22.
[13] 何振. 政府信息资源共享的制约因素分析［J］. 中国科技论坛，2007（12）：84－88.
[14] 阎严. 政府信息资源集成共享中的利益驱动效应研究［D］. 成都：电子科技大学，2007.
[15] 张炜. 倒逼机制：作为实践逻辑的似真推理［J］. 中南大学学报：社会科学版，2012（3）：59－62.
[16] 吴翔阳. 倒逼机制：企业创新动力的政府作为［J］. 国家行政学院学报，2008（6）：51－54.
[17] Taylor W J，Marshall S，Amiri S. The E-Volution of the i-Society in the Delivery of E-Government［J］. AI & Society，2010（3）：359－368.

教师简介：

黄广琴，女，湘潭大学历史学学士、中国人民大学档案学教师进修班进修结业。1997 年起任教于中山大学资讯管理学院，副教授，硕士生导师。主讲“档案管理学”、“档案文献编纂学”等本科生课程，以及“档案信息资源研究”等研究生课程。研究方向包括档案管理学、档案信息资源开发与利用。参与档案利用方式改革与档案利用原理化问题研究、档案专业的改造与电子政务课程建设等科研项目。兼任广东省档案学会学术委员会委员。联系方式：isshgq@ mail. sysu. edu. cn。

所选论文《档案保护信息整合的认识与实践》原载于《档案学通讯》2010 年第 3 期

档案保护信息整合的认识与实践*

黄广琴，瞿楠香①，颜川梅②

摘　要：本文以界定档案保护信息及其整合概念为前提，通过对整合发展的趋势及需求的分析，说明对档案保护信息的整合的必要性及意义。通过对档案保护信息整合实践的介绍，探讨制约我国档案保护信息整合的因素及提出如何整合档案保护信息的几点建议。
关键词：档案保护信息；整合；系统；网站

The Understanding and Practicing of Protecting Information Integration on Archives

Guangqin Huang，Nanxiang Qu，Chuanmei Yan

Abstract：This paper is based on the definition of protecting information integration. It explains the necessity and significance of protecting information integration through the analysis of its growing tend and demand. Meanwhile this paper discusses the reasons that condition the integration of archival protecting information and provides some advices on how to intergrat archival protecting information.
Keywords：Archival protective information；Integration；System；Website

我国传统档案保护的理论与实践虽然历史久远，但在保护信息的记录、管理与整合共享方面还是一个尚待开发的新领域，在网络化程度愈来愈高及保护信息国际之间、行

* 本文系珠海市哲学社会科学规划课题“基于非技术视角的档案遗产保护管理研究”（课题批准号：200950）成果之一。

① 瞿楠香，华南理工大学档案馆主任科员。

② 颜川梅，广州市设计院主任科员。

业之间合作与交流日趋频繁的背景下，对档案保护信息的整合显得十分重要。同时，国内档案保护实践开始从技术层面转向管理层面，更加强调保护管理的科学性与合理性，开始认识到分散的保护信息阻碍系统内部的信息管理及系统内外的信息交流，不利于机构的保护决策、保护规划与保护管理活动的顺利执行，因此，对档案保护信息的整合也十分必要。本文试图从理论与实践角度开展对该问题的研究，以起到抛砖引玉的作用。

1 关于档案保护信息整合

对“档案保护信息”和“档案保护信息整合”两个概念的界定是本文研究的基础与起点。国内对档案保护信息及其整合的探讨刚刚起步，最早对档案保护信息概念加以界定的是周耀林教授，根据其在《档案文献遗产保护理论与实践》[1]357-359中的相关论述，可以认为档案保护信息是来源于各个机构和个人的、以保护各种形式的档案为目的的内容、知识的总汇。他还认为保护信息具有分散性、无序性、非对称性、稀缺性等特征，保护实践的共通性要求将处于分散状态的保护信息有效整合起来，以加强共享合作，减少重复工作和研究的可能性，等等。

综合国内外相关文献，我们认为档案保护信息有广义和狭义之分。广义上，凡是与档案保护相关的信息都是档案保护信息，包括与保护相关的机构、人物、业务、设备、方法、技术、项目、理论研究、新闻报道等，“欧洲存取地图”和“保护在线”就是立足于整合广义保护信息的网站。狭义上，特指在馆藏保护管理过程中所形成的信息，如馆藏档案的价值、材料、构成，对馆藏环境的跟踪记录，对已用保护技术的记录，或单个保护项目所产生的数据等，它与国外的“conservation documentation（保护记录）”一一对应。档案保护信息整合则是通过某种机制或标准，集成、描述、链接不同类型、不同来源、不同载体的档案保护信息，使相对独立的档案保护信息实体之间产生联系，实现保护信息资源全方位整合和一步到位的获取。整合后的信息呈现出集中有序、有机关联和便于获取等特征。

2 档案保护信息整合的趋势与需求分析

2006 年 4 月 27 日在美国纽约召开的“保护记录现况”研讨会一致认为[2]：保护信息整合共享是保护记录管理的最大价值所在，它有利于同行之间的合作与交流，有助于更加准确地解读文化遗产，能有效促进学术研究与保护实践的纵深发展。随着国内档案保护实践开始从技术层面转向管理层面，更加强调保护管理的科学性与合理性，无论是保护调查评估的实施，还是保护政策与规划的制定，都建立在对保护信息的分析基础之上，分散的保护信息阻碍了系统内部的信息管理和系统内外的信息交流，不利于机构的保护决策、保护规划与保护管理活动的顺利执行，因此档案保护信息整合是一种必然趋势，它可以有效满足以下三种需求。

2.1 档案保护管理实践的需求

档案保护管理是贯穿于馆藏档案整个生命周期的工作，根据管理流程与工作所需，档案可能处于不同部门的干预状态之下。刚接收进馆的档案流向加工整理部门，由其进行消毒、整理、编目等工作；送进库房的档案则由保管部门负责，确保其处在一个良好的库房环境中；一旦档案发生病变，则需由技术部门对其进行保护，如修裱、缩微、数字化等；当公众需要利用档案时，档案又被调出供公众使用。因此档案保护管理过程中所形成的数据是分散的，这些分散的数据只有整合起来才能更好地阐释档案，更加详细地说明档案的来龙去脉。

2.2 文化遗产保护行业交流与共享信息的需求

档案保护系统不是一个封闭的系统，它必须同外界进行广泛的信息交流与技术合作。图书馆、档案馆和博物馆都有馆藏，且藏品载体存在共性，随着记录技术的变化，加强对各种载体藏品的保护管理是三者面临的共同课题。在保护信息的全球共享要求越来越强烈、趋势也越来越明显的背景下，构建一个交流合作与成果共享的平台，将图书、博物、档案保护相关的信息、技术、科研成果、保护技术人员资料、保护组织、保护教育机构等信息整合在一起，为各个领域的保护工作者们提供交流与合作的便利，可以发挥保护信息资源整合的聚合效应。

2.3 大众获取便捷性、权威性、有效性的需求

大众对档案保护信息的需求是多种多样的。如新闻记者要根据保护信息写一篇新闻，学者需要根据档案保护数据做研究，学生需要保护信息来验证所学保护知识，私人收藏者想知道保护机构和专家的联系方式或购买保护设备，等等。由于普通大众对档案保护信息筛选与鉴别能力缺乏专业性，所以根据用户需求，建立起保护信息整合平台，建立档案保护专业甚至是专家鉴别机制，才能保证大众及时、便捷地进行档案保护信息的采集，从而保证获取档案保护信息的权威性和有效性。

3 档案保护信息整合的实践

档案保护信息整合分为三个发展阶段，即数据整合、信息整合和知识整合。[3]其中，数据整合集中表现为保护记录系统的建设上，信息、知识整合主要基于 Web 服务平台。现阶段，系统和门户网站建设成为保护信息整合实践的两大焦点。

3.1 系统建设

2008 年，Andrew W. Mellon Foundation 的博物馆与艺术品保护项目对世界范围内的保护从业者做过一次网上调查。[4]206 个保护从业者对此做出了反馈，分别代表了 15 个国家 156 个机构的保护管理实践。每个机构都有两三种主要馆藏，大部分是书和文件、物品和雕塑、绘画。调查结果表明：馆藏管理系统和其他商业与非商业系统已经逐步应用于保护信息的记录与管理，这些信息包括检查文件、治疗报告、分析结果、辅助图片等。

保护记录系统大致分为嵌入式和独立式两大类。其中，嵌入式模块使用比较广泛，调查数据显示，62%的使用馆藏管理系统的机构都在该系统中嵌入了保护模块，如英国大英博物馆和美国波士顿美术品博物馆。独立式记录系统更专业、灵活，更能满足保护者的需求，这需要开发独立的数据库和系统，该保护记录系统与馆藏管理系统可以进行数据交互，或者将保护记录系统链接到馆藏系统，采用这种模式的典型机构有美国费城艺术博物馆和哈佛大学艺术博物馆施特劳斯保护中心。

值得注意的是，我国在保护信息的记录、管理与整合共享方面还没有引起业内足够的重视。在信息化潮流的带动下，有很多单位启用了档案管理信息系统。但是诸多档案管理系统在研发时都没有将档案保护信息管理作为一个功能模块，虽然在管理系统的著录字段中出现了某些与保护相关的字段，但这些字段只是零散地折射了档案保护信息，并不能满足整个保护过程的记录所需，更不用说数据分析、制定保护规划、生成保护报告和管理保护记录等功能了。这种状况在信息时代已显得不合时宜。

3.2 网站建设

从网络调查中发现，国内外在网站建设上同样存在差异。在国外，虽然能真正摆脱自身性质的束缚与立足于保护信息整合的视角来构建网站的机构并不多，但却有很多注重提供文化遗产保护信息的机构，如文化遗产管理机构、保护机构、专业协会、教学科研机构、政府组织和国际组织等。根据其所提供信息的详略程度，可以将其分为粗粒度和细粒度两种整合模式，如欧洲存取地图和保护在线；根据表现形式，可以将其分为日历型、搜索界面型、浏览界面型、地图型，典型代表分别为保护大事记、文化遗产搜索引擎、保护在线、欧洲存取地图；根据整合主题及定位的不同，可将其分为学术型和综合型，典型代表分别为保护信息网络引文库和保护在线。

我国档案保护还尚未建立专门的门户网站，各级档案网站也很少设置档案保护专栏，保护信息分散于新闻、业内动态、公共服务、业务指导、资料库、工作信息等栏目。网站建设主体以企业和政府居多，缺乏档案保护专业组织和关注档案保护的非营利性组织，个人参与度不高。此外，档案保护信息在遗产保护信息整合平台中处于边缘化状态。我国文化遗产保护分散在各个专业领域，随着遗产热潮的兴起，博物馆界的文物保护有走向“文化遗产保护”的趋势，而由于体制的原因，它又不可能是完整意义上的文化遗产保护，于是造成这样的现象：博物馆界的很多与保护相关的网站都以“文化遗产保护”命名，而其所能提供的档案保护信息是少之又少，有的甚至将档案、图书等文献遗产保护信息遗忘。

4 我国档案保护信息整合所面临的困难

档案保护整合体系由实施主体、保护信息、整合技术三大部分组成，同时还受制于环境。因此，实施主体、保护信息、整合技术、驱动机制便成为制约档案保护信息整合实践发展的四个必要因素。人们对信息资源管理的科学认识与实践水平，都与特定历史时期的信息技术发展水平息息相关，但整合技术并不是当前我国档案保护信息整合所面临的难题。当前信息资源的整合技术多种多样，如分布式构建技术、互操作技术、知识组织技术、知识处理技术、基于组件的软件技术、网格技术和语义 Web 技术等，这些技术能应用于不同层次、不同类型的档案保护信息整合上。调研报告《数字技术和保护记录管理》显示：信息技术已经被广泛地应用到国外保护信息的记录、管理与整合领域。[4]我国所处的状态是管理的发展速度跟不上技术进步的节奏，因此，处于管理层面的保护信息、实施主体和驱动机制等因素才是真正制约我国档案保护信息整合的关键所在。

4.1 保护信息尚未得到应有的重视

周耀林教授在《档案文献遗产保护与实践》一书中指出：档案保护信息的研究普遍欠缺，近 10 年来几乎没有这方面的研究成果。[1]355这种评价的确反映了我国档案保护信息研究的现状与程度，究其原因，这多与我国档案保护记录管理的实践息息相关。我国档案保护信息的记录以纸和笔手工记录居多，多是记录温度、湿度等常规数据，还缺乏科学记录档案保护信息的程序与步骤，或者有记录但却没有合理的记录管理方案，实践上的粗放必然导致人们认识上的疏忽与理论研究的欠缺。该状况反射在互联网这种对信息极度敏感的虚拟空间中，便呈现出档案保护信息数量少、质量差、分散、无序等状态。档案界非常重视对档案信息资源管理的研究，但对保护这些档案信息资源过程中所形成的信息还缺乏应有的关注。

4.2 潜在的实施主体缺位

世界各主要文化遗产大国多将保护信息整合视为一门独立的学问，并以学术的眼光去关注出现在文化遗产管理、保护、研究、开发等各个环节所产生的信息的记录、管理与整合问题。这些国家通常会有多所科研院所、大专院校参与到保护信息的调查、研究、保护、教学及资料搜集等工作中来，因此学术科研机构成为保护信息整合的实践主体。我国在目前档案保护管理体制下，档案行政管理机构、馆藏管理机构、档案保护教育机构、科研机构、档案保护相关的协会是档案保护信息整合潜在的实施主体，其整合的侧重点可以各有不同。但根据笔者的调查，这类机构在档案保护信息的发布上并不是很活跃。具体表现为：没有档案保护信息的门户网站，这明显落后于国内的博物馆界和图书馆界；档案保护信息的发布机构以企业和馆藏机构居多，数量和质量都不高，如企业多限于广告的发布，馆藏管理机构或行政管理机构多重复书本常识；科研教育机构和协会组织很少主动发布档案保护相关信息；等等。

4.3 驱动机制因需求的紧迫性不够而停滞

驱动机制是推动档案保护信息整合实践发展的动力，一切发展中的事物没有动力就意味着停滞、萎缩或死亡。无论是系统建设还是网站建设，都需要驱动机制来确保整合持续、有效、健康地发展。按照事物发展变化的一般规律，外因是变化的条件，内因是变化的根据，即事物发展变化的根本原因。我们认为阻碍我国档案保护信息整合实践发展的内因是需求的紧迫性不够，主要原因：一方面是由于我国传统档案保护理论研究上对档案保护信息的忽视。传统档案保护管理实践中习惯实施的粗放性管理模式，导致这样的需求难以挖掘出来。另一方面是现实中的档案保护信息整合仅仅依靠单个行政机构或馆藏机构的摸索难以实现。特别是档案部门，受其资源分配局限的影响，其投入保护的人力、物力和财力本来就不足，由其单方面进行档案保护信息的整合的确是困难之举，因而也就会影响到其整合档案保护信息主动性的发挥。但是，信息整合毕竟是一种发展趋势。在这种趋势之下，目前需要从理论上探寻档案保护信息整合新的切入点，从而达到驱动档案保护信息的整合机制建立的目的。国外的一些做法就值得借鉴，如多数保护记录系统和网站的建立并不全是源自档案管理实践中需求的紧迫性，而是在科研项目的推动下逐步建立发展开来的，项目研究往往成为保护信息整合的驱动机制。有些研究项目就是以“保护信息整合”为研究方向，其研究成果便是一个完整的保护信息整合网站，欧洲存取地图和保护在线都是项目驱动的典型代表。

5 档案保护信息整合的几点建议

5.1 重视档案保护信息，将保护记录纳入档案保护的常规工作中

《中国文物古迹保护准则》[5]认为：记录档案是文物古迹价值的载体，是评估遗产价值的依据、制定保护规划的参考资料、设计保护方案的依据、日常管理事务的证据，真实、详细的记录文件在传递历史信息方面与实物遗存具有同等重要的地位，所以提出保护的每一个程序都应当编制详细的档案。“巧妇难为无米之炊”，信息整合与共享的前提是要有“货”，如果档案保护信息没有质量和数量的保证，我们谈整合也就失去了它应有的意义。因此当务之急是建立记录机制，将保护记录作为档案保护管理的常规工作确定下来，纳入保护者的职责范围之类，提升档案保护者的记录意识与记录技能。例如美国保护协会在《保护实践指南和道德规范》[6]中规定：保护专家有义务记录保护检查、取样、研究、处理所产生的数据，确保它们的精确、完整和永久留存。

5.2 开发档案保护记录与管理的系统

档案保护记录系统大致可以分为独立式和嵌入式两大类，主要用于记录和管理档案保护及保护研究活动所产生的所有信息，包括检查文件、治疗报告、分析结果、辅助图片等。档案保护记录系统模式的选择应该根据实际而定。从国外文化遗产保护管理的实践来看，嵌入式应用比较广泛，综合考虑档案的价值、材料、结构与数量，以及人力、物力和财力的投入，我们认为采取在档案管理系统中嵌入保护字段或者保护模块的做法更加符合我国实际。模式选定后，值得我们进一步思考的还有很多问题，如：嵌入哪些字段？添加哪些功能？流程如何构建？如何构建该系统的原则？如何实现设计灵活、录入功能强大、技术支持强硬等功能？此外，还必须有持续的资金投入和人员支持，等等。成功的档案保护信息记录与管理系统不仅对保护者和保护部门有用，而且还能广泛地影

响保护实践、科学研究及大众对保护的理解。

5.3 建立定位明确的档案保护信息整合的门户网站

门户网站是根据一定的需求，采用一定的技术和标准，将某一领域的重要资源及其资源间的有机关联集成，并提供相应的检索与服务的整合平台。保护信息包罗万象，门户网站的定位决定了其信息的筛选机制。目前信息整合的门户网站大致分为学科信息门户、企业信息门户、政府信息门户三种类型。由于文化遗产保护多为政府和科研机构主导，项目经费多靠政府拨款和基金资助，因此，信息门户也以学科信息门户和政府信息门户为主。学科信息门户应收集与档案保护教学、科研相关的信息，包括书本、期刊文章、学术论文、技术报告、学术会议、工作室、项目信息、科研成果、教学科研机构信息、学科信息等；政府信息门户应关注保护行政和实践相关的信息，包括法规、标准、指南、机构、专家、馆藏保护动态、会议、协会活动、产品、设备等。门户网站建设成熟后，逐步向知识整合靠近，通过一定的技术手段，通过本体、主题图等知识组织体系，组成一个有效获取档案保护知识的网络，从而实现信息整合向知识整合的跨越。

参考文献

[1] 周耀林. 档案文献遗产保护理论与实践 [M]. 武汉：武汉大学出版社，2008.

[2] Rudenstine A Z, Whalen T P. Conservation Documentation in Digital Form: A Dialogue about the Issues [EB/OL]. [2009-04-15]. http://www.getty.edu/conservation/publications/newsletters/21_2/news_in_cons.html.

[3] 马文峰，杜小勇. 数字资源整合理论、方法与应用 [M]. 北京：北京图书馆出版社，2007: 53-55.

[4] Green D, Mustalish R. Digital Technologies and the Management of Conservation Documentation [EB/OL]. [2009-06-15]. http://mac.mellon.org/Mellon%20Conservation%20Survey.pdf.

[5] 国际古迹遗址理事会中国国家委员会. 中国文物古迹保护准则 [EB/OL]. [2009-06-15]. http://www.getty.edu/conservation/publications/pdf_publications/china_prin_1chinese.pdf.

[6] The American Institute for Conservation of Historic and Artistic Works. Code of Ethics and Guidelines for Practice [EB/OL]. [2009-07-15]. http://aic.stanford.edu/about/coredocs/coe/index.html.

教师简介：

张锡田，男，湘潭大学史学学士，中国人民大学历史学硕士。1990 起任教于中山大学资讯管理学院，副教授，硕士生导师。2005 年在中国人民大学信息资源管理学院做访问学者。主讲“机关文件管理与保密”、“档案法学”等本科生课程，以及“现代文件管理研究”等研究生课程。主要研究方向为档案和文件管理、档案法学和档案历史。主持科研项目 5 项，发表学术论文 30 余篇。联系方式：isszxt@ mail. sysu. edu. cn。

所选论文《论个人信息的非技术性保护》原载于《档案学研究》2013 年第 3 期

论个人信息的非技术性保护

张锡田，范晓蔚①

摘　要：人类进入信息社会以后，社会对信息的依赖性加强，无论是政府还是各种商业组织都开始对个人信息进行大规模收集和处理，个人信息管理特别是保护出现了较多问题。如这些年社会上兜售房主信息、股民信息、车主信息、患者信息的现象已成泛滥之势，没节制的“人肉搜索”更让世人胆颤心惊，对个人信息及其当事人的相关权利造成了严重伤害。因此，从非技术的层面深入思考个人信息管理，从而促进对个人信息的合理有效保护，不得不引起我们的重视与关注。

关键词：个人信息；非技术性；保护

The Study of the Non-Technical Protection of Personal Information

Xitian Zhang, Xiaowei Fan

Abstract: Accessing to the information society, it's enhanced that the dependency of human society on information. Either the government or a variety of commercial or ganizations have begun to carry out large-scale collection and processing of personal information, there are more problems in personal information management, especially the protection. Selling information, such as homeowner, social investors, the owners, patient informations, has become a flood. Non-restraint " human flesh search" has alarmed the world, and caused serious injury to personal information and their clients. Therefore, how to think deeply from the non-technical level of personal information management, so as to promote the rational and effective protection of personal information, which we have to pay attention to.

Keywords: Personal information; Non-technical protection; Protection

① 范晓蔚，广发银行。

1 个人信息的基本含义

个人信息，即每个自然人的信息。它是关于某一特定个人的所有相关信息记录的总和，是每个公民从出生到死亡的方方面面的信息集合。基于各国法律体系、历史传统及语言习惯的差异，个人信息的表述与界定也不尽相同。美国、加拿大、澳大利亚等国家与地区主要使用个人隐私这个说法，强调个人信息的私隐性，而欧盟及其成员国更习惯将个人信息表述为个人数据（资料）。在我国，人们已经较为习惯个人信息这个概念。《中华人民共和国个人信息保护法（专家建议稿）》将个人信息界定为："指个人姓名、住址、出生日期、身份证号码、医疗记录、人事记录、照片等单独或与其他信息对照可以识别特定的个人的信息。"[1]

不管如何表述与界定，个人信息始终是特定个人的所有相关的信息，始终是与政府、社会组织及公民个人相关联。因此，属于政府信息范畴的个人信息，政府与个人当事人同为个人信息的主体，对个人信息享有权利承担义务。相对说来，作为个人信息的当事人，对其个人信息享有相应的信息权利，即对与个人有关的各类信息在收集、存储、处理、利用等过程中所享有的信息控制权，并排除他人侵害行为的权利，主要包括信息支配权，信息知情权，信息订正、删除或停止使用权，信息利用权、隐私权以及请求救济权等。[2]所以，个人信息的当事人可以说是个人信息的权利主体。与之相对应的政府，对个人信息的实体享有所有权，对个人信息负有形成、处理、管理等基本职责，因此，相应可称之为个人信息的义务主体。

个人信息作为特定个人的信息集合，具有双重属性、自然人属性、可识别性、特定目的性、动态性、多样性、隐私性、保密性等特点，其外延广、内容丰富，具体可划分为基本信息（如姓名、性别、年龄、出生日期等、健康医疗信息）、家庭婚姻信息、教育工作信息、经济财产信息、社会活动信息等种类。在我国，属于政府信息范畴的个人信息，归档后又通称之为档案或公共档案，如人事档案、病历档案、婚姻档案、个人信用档案、户籍档案等，均是一种比较专门的个人信息。因此，从概念来说，个人信息与档案有很密切的关系。可以说，个人信息是档案大家族中的一个特殊类型，它与档案在外延上有许多的重合之处。

2 目前我国个人信息保护存在的主要问题

2.1 信息失真

个人信息管理与保护，首先面临信息本身的真实性与准确性要求。这个问题，目前并不容忽视。媒体曝光较多的，如当发生医疗纠纷时，院方或当事医生为推脱责任，往往篡改、伪造病历，而学历及其他证照、票据造假更是屡见不鲜，以至社会上形成了所谓专门的产业链。例如，2009 年 6 月，某团市委原副书记王某，因其所有的身份、年龄、履历、档案均涉嫌造假，最终，被认定为"造假骗官"并已移送司法机关。[3]人事文件造假并非个别现象，有些甚至疯狂到"只有性别是真的"的地步。信息失真到底到了一个什么程度，尽管我们无法估算出结果，但就原因而言，应该是多方面的。当事人的造假和管理者篡改、伪造、变造以及管理中的失误等都将直接或间接地造成个人信息内容失真，而其带来的多方面的危害性，更是不言而喻的。

2.2 当事人知情权缺失

个人信息管理与保护，一个基本点就是要让当事人享有知情权。现实中，更多的情形是当事人不能查询利用自己的个人信息。长期以来，干部人事档案奉行“任何个人不得查看”的规定，房地产权属文件也不提供当事人直接查考。直到2002年，随着《医疗事故技术鉴定暂行办法》的修订，记载个人身体与健康状况的病历，才让当事人享有知情权，允许患者本人及其家属查询复制。当事人个人信息知情权的缺失，是一个较为长期与普遍的现象。例如，大学生陈某，自从2001年离开上海××公司后，就再也没有找到工作。造成这一切的原因，是那个他永远看不到的档案袋里神秘的“处分”决定。[4]个人信息的不知情，不仅伤害到当事人的信息权利，更造成了个人信息的严重不对称。

2.3 个人信息的不当使用

利益的驱动，管理的不严谨，往往造成个人信息使用不当。其主要表现为骗用、盗用、滥用、伪造使用，非法买卖个人信息以及擅自扩大个人信息使用范围等。信息社会，有人为了网络走红，甚至不惜他人与公共利益，在网上公开自己的隐私信息；无节制的人肉搜索，几乎能使个人信息的不当使用达到一种接近可怕的程度。例如，为了使女儿冒名顶替上大学，王某肆无忌惮伪造、盗用其他考生的个人信息。[5]如此不当使用他人的个人信息，从其行为主体来说，可以是个人信息的当事人的不当使用，也可以是本人之外的第三者，或者相关管理部门。但其典型之恶劣，也难以再出其右，最后害己伤人。

2.4 个人信息的非法买卖

作为一种较为特别的信息资源，个人信息不仅具现实效用，而且还有很高的社会与经济价值，对其需求可谓方方面面、形形色色。但是，由于其特有的隐私性，个人信息的利用又受到诸多限制。因此现实生活中，非法买卖并由此牟利甚至诈骗等不当行为愈演愈烈。例如，某市工商局档案室工作人员刘某非法泄露企业信息及股东信息，并在网上明码标价出售公司股东的身份证号、手机号、住址等个人信息，以获得非法收入。[6]打开网络，我们几乎随处看到有考生信息、孕妇信息、名人电话、车主业主资料的叫卖。

2.5 个人信息的泄密

个人信息，通常应对本人公开，对第三者限制公开。现实生活中存在的诸如个人信息的买卖牟利等，不仅是个人信息的不当使用，也属于个人信息的泄密行为。据某报报道，某县某女小丽（化名）遭到该县原党委书记强奸，案发后，小丽到该地市区公安分局刑警一中队报案。在询问笔录中，她详细描述了被强奸的整个过程。之后不久，这份笔录却出现在县城的街道、广场的电线杆上，被挂在树上、扔在地上，甚至还出现在了互联网上。[7]毫无疑问，个人信息的泄密将对当事人的信息权利和人身造成了重大的双重伤害。

2.6 个人信息当事人自我保护意识不强

市场经济条件下，个人信息的保护更需要有积极的自我意识。随着社会发展，尽管我们的权利与保护意识有了大的提升，但是，整体上还是不够。例如，2010 年春运首次实行火车票实名制，许多乘客出站后就随手丢弃自己实名制的车票。在随机采访的 12 位乘客中，有 9 人丢弃车票时并没想到“信息可能被利用”，3 人则表示“无所谓”。[8]随手丢弃已经使用过的实名火车票，虽然算不上什么大事情，但这样大的比例，足以小中见大，说明目前我们个人信息的自我保护意识淡薄之严重。

3 个人信息保护的非技术性对策

3.1 完善法律规范

首先，创制专门的个人信息保护法。目前，我们尚未颁布专门的系统的关于个人信息保护的法律，个人信息的法律保护处在一个零散状态。尽管社会对个人信息保护的立法呼声很高，2005 年也曾搞过一个个人信息保护法的专家建议稿，但个人信息保护的立法至今却没了音讯。没有专门系统的针对个人信息的立法，个人信息的权利与义务得不到调整，个人信息的有效保护根本无从谈起。

其次，完善档案立法中的个人信息保护。个人信息归档保存之后，就成为通常意义上的档案。因此，档案法在很大程度上所调整的，是个人信息法律关系。目前，我们有《中华人民共和国档案法》（以下简称《档案法》）及《中华人民共和国档案法实施办法》，也有较为系统的诸如《干部档案工作条例》、《各级国家档案馆馆藏档案解密和划分控制使用范围暂行规定》等专门性和地方性档案规范。但就其内容来说，个人信息的有效管理与保护还很不到位。公民个人信息的知情权、隐私权、修订请求权等几乎少有体现。例如人事记录的知情权，所有档案立法中，唯有青岛、哈尔滨等极少数地区新制定的《职工档案管理暂行办法》，规定职工凭有效身份证件可以查阅本人的人事档案信息。[9]因而档案立法中，要加强对个人信息的保护立法，特别是要完善个人信息的收集归档、内容真实性鉴定与保护、保密性管理及开放利用等相关规定。

最后，个人信息保护各相关立法的配套与协调。个人信息几乎涉及每个部门和领域，各部门各专业的立法，均应对相关个人信息及其保护作出相应的专门规定，从而形成个人信息保护的法律配套协调体系。与此同时，还要特别加强个人信息的刑罚保护，对个人信息犯罪实施有效打击。在这方面，我们看到了可喜的进步。2009 年，最高人民法院、最高人民检察院出台《关于执行〈中华人民共和国刑法〉确定罪名的补充规定（四)》，首次确定了出售、非法提供公民个人信息罪与非法获取公民个人信息罪这两个罪名，为个人信息的保护提供了重要的法律依据。[10]

3.2 建立全面有效的管理制度

3.2.1 集中统一管理制度

作为政府信息范畴的个人信息，必须确定归档范围，依规定对其实体实施归档，由档案部门集中统一管理。对此，《档案法》第十条规定：“对国家规定的应当立卷归档的材料，必须按照规定，定期向本单位档案机构或者档案工作人员移交，集中管理，任何个人不得据为己有。”第十一条规定“机关、团体、企业事业单位和其他组织必须按照国家规定，定期向档案馆移交档案。”个人信息的集中统一管理，不仅是其作为一种特别的公共资源的需要，同时也有利于个人信息的安全与保护。

3.2.2 审核鉴定制度

审核鉴定，主要包括两方面内容：一是个人信息的公开审核鉴定，从而将其区分为公开与不公开的两大类别，以便分类管理；二是在个人信息的收集归档过程中，对其内容的真实、准确与完整性进行审核把关，或者依权利主体的请求，对相关个人信息进行鉴定修正。建立与健全审核鉴定制度，不仅能有效保证个人信息的质量，而且对个人信息安全与隐私保护，以及促进个人信息的开发利用均有重要意义。

3.2.3 使用制度

个人信息的使用制度，应该包括三方面内容：第一，个人信息对当事人公开。当事人可以不受限制地直接查看本人的个人信息，这是保障与实现当事人个人信息相关权利的前提基础。第二，使用限制与利用许可。涉及个人隐私或其他不宜公开的个人信息，对当事人以外的第三者限制公开，控制使用。但如果当事人同意与许可，这种限制与控制解除。《各级国家档案馆馆藏档案解密和划分控制使用范围的暂行规定》第七条指出：“涉及公民隐私的……档案，应当控制使用。”《中华人民共和国政府信息公开条例》（以下简称《政府信息公开条例》）第二十三条也规定：“行政机关认为申请公开的政府信息涉及……个人隐私，公开后可能损害第三方合法权益的，应当书面征求第三方的意见；第三方不同意公开的，不得公开。”“行政机关不得公开涉及……个人隐私的政府信息。但是，经权利人同意公开……可以予以公开。”第三，个人信息的形成机关与组织，对所形成的个人信息，应当在职权范围里符合规定目的地使用。非经权利主体的同意，或者法律授权，不得进行超出目的的披露与公开。个人信息的使用，可以说事关个人信息保护之根本，必须建立健全相关的制度。

3.2.4 封闭期制度

封闭期制度，是指对不宜向社会公开与提供利用的个人信息，划定一定的封闭期予以封闭，限制其使用的一项管理制度。封闭期制度在档案管理中使用得较为成熟。《档案法》第十九条规定：“国家档案馆保管的档案，一般应当自形成之日起满三十年向社会开放。经济、科学、技术、文化等类档案向社会开放的期限，可以少于三十年，涉及国家安全或者重大利益以及其他到期不宜开放的档案向社会开放的期限，可以多于三十年，具体期限由国家档案、行政管理部门制定，报国务院批准施行。”国外对涉及个人隐私的信息记录，其封闭期的规定则更为详细，如法国《档案法》规定可供自由查阅的公共档案的期限为：“一、个人医疗文件，从产生之日算起满150年；二、人事案卷，从产生之日算起满120年；三、与司法事务有关的文件，包括特赦裁定书、公证人的文件原本和目录，以及户籍和公民状况登记册，从文件产生或案卷完成之日算起满100年；四、凡涉及个人情况，如私人和家庭生活方面的文件，以及一般由公共事业部门调查来的有关私人情况和行为的材料，从普查和调查之日算起满100年；五、处理与私人生活有关的诉讼案的文件……，从产生之日算起满60年。”[11]因此，对涉及隐私的个人信息，设置一定期限的封闭期，实施封闭期管理制度，不仅可行，而且还很有必要。它对于防止个人信息的泄密，保证个人信息的安全，有效保护个人隐私具有重要意义。

3.2.5 修订制度

修订制度，是针对个人信息的动态性、非固定不变性，对收集、保存的个人信息及时更新，保证其准确的一项动态制度。它对于保证个人信息的完整、准确，充分发挥其效用，具有重要作用。在国际社会，修订制度作为个人信息保护的一项基本制度而存在。如《德国联邦个人资料保护法》规定：“为了保护个人资料的内容完整与正确，本人有权利修改其个人资料以使个人资料在特定目的的范围内保持完整、正确及时性。”[11]虽然我国《档案法》没有涉及个人信息修改方面的规定，但《政府信息公开条例》第二十五条规定：“公民、法人或者其他组织有证据证明行政机关提供的与其自身相关的政府信息记录不准确的，有权要求该行政机关予以更正。该行政机关无权更正的，应当转送有权更正的行政机关处理，并告知申请人。”因此，一方面，包括档案机构在内的相关管理部门，对已保存的个人信息，要通过修订制度使之得到及时更新，确保其准确与完整；另一方面，信息当事人应充分行使信息修正权利，对不完整或与事实不符的个人信息，主动修正。另外，个人信息的修订应采取合适的方式，妥善处理好个人信息的修订与档案原始性的关系。

3.3 提升社会的个人信息保护意识

个人信息的保护意识对个人信息的有效保护具有极其重要的作用。目前，社会的个人信息保护意识，从管理者到个人信息的当事人都不太强。前面我们所总结的个人信息管理中存在的诸多问题，不少都直接或间接反映出社会的个人信息保护意识不容乐观这一现状。因此，必须全面提升社会的个人信息保护意识。一方面，强化个人信息管理者的职业素养。通过培训、考核、有效的监管等一系列方式，提高他们对个人信息及其保护重要性的认识，使他们具有良好的职业操守和职业精神。另一方面，提升权利主体的个人信息自我保护意识。加大个人信息保护宣传指引的力度，通过典型案例，使公民个人在自觉与不自觉之中了解个人信息，认识到个人信息保护的重要意义，懂得通过法律途径来维护自身的个人信息权利与安全，从而有意识加入到个人信息保护的行列，积极主动参与个人信息的管理与保护。个人信息保护意识的整体提升，必然优化个人信息保护的社会环境，形成良好的个人信息保护氛围，有力推进个人信息管理与保护的向前发展。

3.4 更新个人信息保护理念

传统管理中，对个人信息的保护通常奉行对本人公开对第三者限制公开的原则。也就是说，个人隐私与信息非经本人同意，或者非公共利益的需要，往往限制公开与使用。现在的问题是，网络的便利加速了个人信息自由流动，而个人信息完全不被他人收集、利用，事实上已经不可避免。网络个人信息的经营，包括身份证查询、名片网、黑名单网、人肉搜索等，已经发展成为并非个别的现象。如此情形底下，对个人信息的管理与保护有必要进行理论上的重新审视。也就是说在保护个人信息的同时，要平衡信息的自由流动和个人信息保护，积极引导个人信息的合理利用。目前，我国台湾地区“立法院”修正并通过了《个人数据保护法》，在相当程度上给予“人肉搜索”合法化地位。[12] 对于人肉搜索合法化，目前尽管还有很多争议，但这一尝试至少说明，面对网络环境，个人信息的管理与保护必须要有新的思考。

3.5 创新个人信息的管理机制

个人信息的当事人，作为信息的所有者和权利主体，对个人的信息享有相应的支配与控制等权利。从这个意义来说，个人信息的当事人可以也应该是个人信息的管理者之一，有效地参与对个人信息的管理。一方面，充分利用自身对信息内容了解的优势，协助相关部门对个人信息展开必要的鉴定与修正工作；另一方面，参与个人信息的利用管理，对个人信息是否公开与提供利用，提出意见。《政府信息公开条例》第二十三规定：“行政机关不得公开涉及……个人隐私的政府信息。但是，经权利人同意公开……可以予以公开。”“行政机关认为申请公开的政府信息涉及……个人隐私，公开后可能损害第三方合法权益的，应当书面征求第三方的意见；第三方不同意公开的，不得公开。”《档案法》第二十一条也规定：“向档案馆移交、捐赠、寄存档案的单位和个人，……可对其档案中不宜向社会开放的部分提出限制利用的意见，档案馆应当维护他们的合法权益。”此外，个人信息的当事人对个人信息的收集与保管予以直接监管。在我国，长期以来个人信息权利并未得到很好的落实，政府信息范畴的个人信息的管理也大多与当事人没多大关系。可以说，个人信息的当事人作为管理者参与个人信息的管理，理论上还是个新问题，实践中具体如何操作，真正构建与形成一种有效的管理机制，还有待进一步探索。

4 结　语

个人信息的保护，是时代赋予我们的一项紧迫而又神圣的使命，它直接关系着个人的权利与社会的和谐与稳定。个人信息的保护，更是一项涉及政府、社会、管理者、当事人，以及立法与制度、体制与技术的庞大而复杂的系统工程，需要我们从理论到实践的不懈努力与探索。

参考文献

[1] 周汉华. 个人信息保护前沿问题研究［M］. 北京：法律出版社，2006.

[2] 周汉华. 中华人民共和国个人信息保护法（专家建议稿）及立法研究报告［M］. 北京：法律出版社，2006.

[3] 石家庄市“造假书记”王亚丽的升官图［EB/OL］. http://leaders.people.com.cn/GB/11060194.html.

[4] 陈磊档案事件［EB/OL］. http://weilaiwansui.blog.hexun.com/62179457_d.html.

[5] 罗彩霞事件调查结果公布 王佳俊之父被批准逮捕［EB/OL］. http://news.sohu.com/20090603/n264300998.shtml.

[6] 非法贩卖个人信息背后：一条个人信息能卖6万元［EB/OL］. http://henan.people.com.cn/news/2012/04/27/612943.html.

[7] 强奸案笔录外泄侮辱不只一人?［EB/OL］. http://news.163.com/10/0521/02/6763KL2F00014AED.html.

[8] 废弃火车票泄露个人信息［EB/OL］. http://news.qq.com/a/20100223/002001.htm.

[9] 关于印发《青岛市职工档案管理暂行办法》的通知［EB/OL］. http://www.qdda.gov.cn/front/laoqingdao/previes.jsp?ID=12538473772961219001&subjuctid=12259385048122112001.

[10] 黄丽勤. 我国《刑法》对档案保护的新进展——论非法提供个人信息罪与非法获取个人信息罪［J］. 档案与建设，2009（6）：12-14.

[11] 外国档案法规选编［M］. 北京：档案出版社. 1983.

[12]“人肉搜索”在台湾［EB/OL］.［2010-5-26］. http://news.163.com/special/00012Q9L/renroutaiwan.html.

教师简介：

陈方，男，中山大学图书馆学大专生、华南师范大学文学硕士。1992 年起任教于中山大学资讯管理学院，副教授，硕士生导师。主讲“公务文书写作”、“中国政治制度”、“古代公文概论”等本科生课程，以及“中国古代档案文化研究”、“中国古代文书研究”等研究生课程。研究方向包括：公务文书概论、公务文书写作、古代公文概论、中国政治制度。研究方向为：文史教学与研究。著有《庄子注译》、《广东历史人物辞典》等，发表过中国古代文学、目录学史、文书档案史有关论文数十篇。联系方式：Chfang55@163. com。

论《汉书》载文述史的史纂范式

陈　方

摘　要：《汉书》沿承《史记》采文述史范式，“探篹前记，缀辑所闻”，构成专取经世政务之文直叙史实的史纂范式，约有五点：一是重大性，即以重大文本展现重大事件和重大策略；二是重要性，即所载之文牵涉当时重要决策和重要政举；三是连续性，即以官书档案揭示政体沿革和事态发展；四是互动性，即通过文本间性构成动态互叙和互文相足；五是对比性，即合传或跨传所载各篇具有辑序和对比叙述性质。综之，“文赡事详”庶可概括《汉书》载文述史的史纂范式。

关键词：《汉书》；载文述史；史纂范式

Depicting History According to Public and Private Records：A Paradigm of History Compilation of *Han Shu*（Former Han Dynastic History）

Fang Chen

Abstract：Adopting the paradigm of depicting history according to public and private records in *Shi Ji*（Historical Records），historical facts were extracted from records of government affairs and experience affairs of human life in *Han Shu*（Former Han Dynastic History）. The way of description included following features：1）Revealing momentous events or strategies from significant records；2）Selecting records about important measures or decisions；3）Describing history trend of political system and affairs according to public records；4）Comparing and corroborating related records；5）For context contrasting purpose，putting pieces of writing about several persons in one chapter or dividing pieces of one person into several parts. In short，full materials with accurate facts is the striking feature of the writing paradigm in *Han Shu*.

Keywords：*Han Shu*（Former Han Dynastic History）；Public and private records；Paradigm of history

作为首部断代史，班固的《汉书》一直是后世正史编纂的橅范。它的典范性固然来自司马迁《史记》创立的纪传体史例，其实还来自《史记》创下的载文述史之史纂范式，而后者往往得不到应有的强调。

《史记》编纂首先扎根于丰赡广博的史料，司马迁采摭《尚书》、《春秋》、《左氏》、《国语》、《世本》、《战国策》、各国史记、《楚汉春秋》、牒记历谱、功令官书等史籍档案，依据古代史官秉笔直书的史纂传统，遵守原文，直录旧文，援档入史，载文述史，构成文直事核的实录范式。对此，《汉书》作者十分认同。班彪称“其涉猎者广博，贯穿经传，驰骋古今”[1]，班固谓其“错综群言，古今是经”[2]4257，正表明《汉书》对采文述史范式的遵循。

就身份条件而论，与司马迁任职太史令一样，班固在编撰《汉书》的20多年间，一直身任兰台令史，非常了解和掌握官书公文、图册条例等国家秘档，况且兰台令史一职本身就是掌管官书公文起草归档的（《汉官仪》曰：“兰台令史六人，秩百石，掌书劾奏。”[3]）。身份与资料相应具备，班固故能“探篹前记，缀辑所闻，以述《汉书》”[2]4235。诚如明人陈文烛所言：“受诏于永平中，为郎，典秘书，优游兰台，尽发其石渠、天禄之藏。太初以后，建初以前，上下二百余年，积思二十余载，创藏山之秘宝，肇刊石之遐贯。文赡而事详，可谓比董狐、史马之良，而兼长卿、子云之丽矣。”[4]

《史》《汉》并称，历代轩轾。或以《史》简《汉》繁，或以《史》文《汉》质，或以《汉》袭《史》文，或以《汉》多《史》好。各持好恶，论胜纷纭。清人赵翼独具只眼，拈取载文述史作论：“晋张辅论《史》、《汉》优劣，谓司马迁叙三千年事，惟五十余万言；班固叙二百年事，乃八十余万言。以此分两人之高下，然有不可以是为定评者。盖迁喜叙事，至于经术之文，干济之策，多不收入，故其文简；固则于文字有关于学问、有系于政务者，必一一载之，此其所以卷帙多也。今以《汉书》各传与《史记》比对，多有《史记》所无而《汉书》增载者，皆系经世有用之文，则不得以繁冗议之也。”[5]从载文述史之史纂范式去把握《汉书》对《史记》的因创关系，庶可见出是继承而非抄袭，是创新而非因循。《史记》据文叙事，直录原文，或穿插官书公文于叙述之中，或缀合臣奏君诏来阐发事态，这在《汉书》都得以延续；《史记》出于叙述合乎时宜，或将《尚书》、《左传》等笔削迻译，或将谱牒世系等编成书表，这在《汉书》都有了改动。《史记》讲求行文流畅，专注辞章之言，多选富丽之句，而《汉书》侧重直叙史实，专取政务之言，多选经世之文；《史记》本以引文过繁有碍叙事，征引之处时作剪裁，而《汉书》留心经世国策，关乎国运之文必载，文义系于全局，一有删削即生偏颇，因此多存全文。

兹从载文述史把握《汉书》的史纂范式，可有五点。

一曰重大性。《汉书》所载制定国是、治国方略之文，皆具重大性质，像各帝纪中制策，各传记中诏书，无不揭示重大事项。各时期重大历史事件，无不通过这些重大文本展现出来。像约法三章。《高帝纪》载，高祖元年十月，刘邦进军霸上，秦王子婴系皇帝玺来降，刘邦于是西入咸阳。十一月召集各县豪强，约法三章：“杀人者死，伤人及盗抵罪。”宣布“馀悉除去秦法。吏民皆按堵如故”。并使人与秦吏到各县乡邑告谕。新章法预示了新时代的来临。又像平定诸吕。《外戚传》和《高后纪》载，吕后把持天下八年，临终遗嘱告诫吕产吕禄：“高祖与大臣约，非刘氏王者天下共击之，今王吕氏，大臣不平。我即崩，恐其为变，必据兵卫宫，慎毋送丧，为人所制。”吕后崩后，太尉周勃、丞相陈平、朱虚侯刘章等起兵解除吕禄吕产军印，行令军中曰：“为吕氏右袒，为刘氏左袒。”军皆左袒，遂夺军权。又像吴楚七国之乱。《荆燕吴传》留下吴王刘濞通报各诸侯王反书全文和汉景帝讨伐诏令。反书明骂晁错而实指景帝，“不以诸侯人君礼遇刘氏骨肉，绝先帝功臣，进任奸人，欲危社稷”。称吴国精兵钱粮可恃，并部署各王军事战略，订立封赏。而景帝诏令针锋相对，指斥“吴王濞背德反义”，窜同诸王“约从谋反，为逆无道”，明令“击反虏者，深入多杀为功，斩首捕虏比三百石以上者皆杀，无有所置。敢有议诏及不如诏者，皆要斩”。一场血腥杀戮跃然纸上。再像王莽篡政。仅《王莽传》上，以连串官文书，见证王莽从拜大司马，充三公位，封安汉公，至摄天子位，加九命锡，称假皇帝，直到践天子位。诏奏络绎，篡谋连贯。

重大性的另一面是指《汉书》所载之文揭示治国执政的重大策略，乃当时政治、文化、军事、外交活动指引。例如《西南夷两粤朝鲜传》载汉文帝赐南粤王赵佗玺书，反映出汉初安抚四夷的外交路线。文帝放下架子，低调致意：“皇帝谨问南粤王，甚苦心劳意。朕，高皇帝侧室之子，弃外奉北藩于代，道里辽远，壅蔽朴愚，未尝致书”。人性化地陈述分裂战争给人民带来灾难，通报已派人问候赵佗家乡真定的亲属，修治其祖坟。令人“尤觉陈义委曲，命辞恳到者，盖书中能尽褒劝警饬之意也”[6]。并命陆贾奉书再度使粤，果令赵佗诚惶诚恐，当即下令国中曰：“汉皇帝贤天子。自今以来，去帝制黄屋左纛。”又回书一通，称“老夫死骨不腐，改号不敢为帝矣”！人们或可从这些信件中去领略“文景之治”一斑。还有汉朝匈奴外交关系。议和时期如《匈奴传》载汉文帝前六年及后二年，匈奴单于与汉文帝两番互馈国书，订立和约，达成“匈奴无入塞，汉无出塞，犯今约者杀之，可以久亲”之共识。征战时期如《武帝纪》载武帝六年，匈奴入上谷，杀掠吏民。武帝遣车骑将军卫青出上谷，诏曰：“夷狄无义，所从来久。间者匈奴数寇边境，故遣将抚师”云云。武帝尊儒是中国专制统治方略的重大转折，对后世政治思想文化产生深远影响。《武帝纪》元光元年五月发布的《策贤良诏》显得尤为重要。在文治武功大盛之际，武帝标榜夙兴夜寐以求“上参尧舜，下配三王”，乃诏天下贤良认证他的功德：“贤良明于古今王事之体，受策察问，咸以书对，著之于篇，朕亲览焉。”于是董仲舒、公孙弘等出焉。此诏引出大儒，大儒对策尊儒，于是儒术一统天下千年焉。

二曰重要性。《汉书》所载尽是经术之文、干济之策，即是当时重要决策和重要提案。这些都是班固精心挑选的，他每提及：“掇其切于世事者著于传”[7]，“掇其切当世施朝廷者著于篇”[8]2526，可见所选绝非无补空言。这些篇目清人赵翼列举过：“《贾谊传》、《治安策》，皆有关治道，经事综物，兼切于当日时势，文帝亦多用其言。《晁错传》载其教太子一疏，言兵事一疏，募民徙塞下等疏，《贤良策》一道，皆有关世事国计。《路温舒传》载《尚德缓刑疏》，《贾山传》载其《至言》。《邹阳传》载其讽谏吴王濞邪谋一书。《枚乘传》载其谏吴王谋逆一书。《韩安国传》载其与王恢论伐匈奴事，恢主用兵，安国主和亲，反复辩论，凡十余番，皆边疆大计。《公孙宏传》载其《贤良策》，并待诏时上书一道，帝答诏一道。以上皆《史记》无而《汉书》特载之者。其武帝以后诸传，亦多载有用章疏。”[5]这些经世有用的重要文本，展现出西汉一代英明君主大开言路，有识之士踊跃献猷的励精图治风貌。唐代柳宗元曾盛称：“当文帝时，始得贾生明儒术，武帝尤好焉。而公孙弘、董仲舒、司马迁、相如之徒作，风雅益盛，敷施天下，自天子至公卿大夫士庶人咸通焉。于是宣于诏策，达于奏议，讽于辞赋，传于歌谣，由高帝讫于哀、平，王莽之诛，四方之文章盖烂然矣。史臣班孟坚修其书，拔其尤者，充于简册，则二百三十年间，列辟之达道，名臣之大范，贤能之志业，黔黎之风美列焉。”[9]此中尤以贾谊《陈政事疏》和董仲舒“天人三策”为翘楚。前篇陈述国家长治久安之策，重点加强统一政权和抵抗外来侵扰，提出“众建诸侯而少其力”，消减诸侯王的封地和权力；坚决抗击匈奴贵族的侵扰，“必系单于之颈而制其命”。后篇论证“圣人法天而立道”法则，规范封建大一统的统治秩序，揭橥“推明孔氏，抑黜百家”[8]2525，终为汉武帝采纳，形成二千年儒学正统局面。毋怪史学家钱穆迳称：“董仲舒天人三策，与贾谊政事疏，两篇大文，奠定了西汉一代政治之规模。”[10]

重要性的另一面是指《汉书》所载之文牵涉重要政举措施，或文出政举，或文行法定。《刑法志》载汉文帝即位十三年，齐太仓令淳于公获罪当刑，其少女缇萦乃随父至长安，上书天子，痛惜人一旦坐刑，即不可复生，更无由改过。“妾愿没入为官婢，以赎父刑罪，使得自新。”书奏天子，天子怜悲其意，遂下令曰：“夫刑至断支体，刻肌肤，终身不息，何其刑之痛而不德也！岂称为民父母之意哉？其除肉刑，有以易之；及令罪人各以轻重，不亡逃，有年而免。具为令。”引出废除肉刑和从轻论处。接着，又引出丞相张苍、御史大夫冯敬奏言建议将肉刑改为城旦舂，并按罪人服役年数递减，至免为庶人。得到文帝批准。这些系列文书揭示了法律的产生形成。又如，有的文书记录了汉武帝崇儒的政举措施。《武帝纪》记元朔五年六月发布诏书曰：“盖闻导民以礼，风之以乐，今礼坏乐崩，朕甚闵焉。故详延天下方闻之士，咸荐诸朝。其令礼官劝学，讲议洽闻，举遗兴礼，以为天下先，太常其议予博士弟子，崇乡党之化，以厉贤材焉。”于是，作为学官丞相的公孙弘立刻草章请示，全文载《儒林传》，建议由太常从各地择优为博士官置弟子五十人，从中再择优异者充任郎中史官之属。得到武帝批准。这些文书及其文化措施则是独尊儒术的具体化了。

三曰连续性。《汉书》叙述典章制度，善于将官书档案按专题排列，依朝代顺序铺叙，让国家政制沿革及历史事态发展清晰可见。《韦玄成传》有大篇幅围绕罢毁郡国宗庙一事，从元帝朝贡禹始，经韦玄成、匡衡，至哀帝朝孔光、王舜、刘歆，终平帝朝王莽，罗列历朝重臣奏议和天子诏书，展示或毁或复之经过。《礼乐志》有围绕制定礼仪一事，从高祖时叔孙通始，经文帝朝贾谊，武帝朝董仲舒，宣帝朝王吉，到成帝朝刘向，连篇建树，逐步完备，不过，都以种种原因“其议遂寝”，“其事又废”。那么，这些礼仪蓝图就更显可贵了。在《食货志》，围绕农业问题，留下了贾谊《论积贮疏》、晁错《论贵粟疏》等名篇；在《沟洫志》，围绕水利问题，留下了历朝专家开发渠灌的建议；在《郊祀志》，通篇留下了制、诏、言、议之类的历史档案。总之，有了《汉书》这么“略存大纲，以统旧文”[2]4236，才有了今天这些历史的真实记忆。

连续性的另一面是围绕焦点问题，公文叠架而出，连篇累牍，决策相与定制，连续争持。《韩安国传》载武帝即位不久，匈奴来请和亲。对匈奴是战是和，在大行王恢与御史大夫韩安国之间展开持久激烈争论。王恢主战，认为“汉与匈奴和亲，率不过数岁即背约。不如勿许，举兵击之”。韩安国主和，认为“汉数千里争利，则人马罢，虏以全制其敝，势必危殆。臣故以为不如和亲”。到第二年，和战之争更趋激烈，王、韩各执己见，各陈利害，文锋犀利，词义刚健，实为战国纵横遗风。武帝终从王恢之议，引出北逐匈奴之大举。又如《王嘉传》及《董贤传》，因哀帝每欲封宠臣董贤，丞相王嘉冒死抗争，连篇上封事言，力陈封了董贤则大失众心，致使海内引领而议。然而，每封书上，哀帝即下诏照封，卒之册封董贤为三公，“贤繇是权与人主侔矣”。而王嘉终遭没收相印，系狱而死。试取王嘉封事与哀帝册文排列，不啻天地正气荡涤旮旯猥亵。

四曰互动性。《汉书》直接通过公文档案的文本间性，构成动态互叙。如以奏诏对答，建构君臣互动，推述事态进展。这种互叙法创自司马迁，在《史记·淮南王刘长列传》中，通过连串丞相张苍等大臣的奏议和汉文帝的制批，相互对答，议定刘长罪谳和发落结局。这在《汉书》有了很好的承续。如《赵充国传》，赵充国以七十余岁高龄，镇守西塞重郡金城，抗拒羌人侵扰。酒泉各郡皆请示出击，天子下发文书咨询充国意见，充国以为劳师袭远，非为上计，还以“捬循和辑”为是。天子不听，以书敕让充国，令“将军急装”参战。充国又上书陈兵利害，主张对众羌严惩首恶，分化联盟，得到玺书报从。不久，又得进军玺书，敦促迅速破羌。而实际粮谷不济，于是充国遂上屯田奏，计明屯田之利。天子批复“即如将军之计”，但问“虏当何时伏诛”？充国上状详述不出兵屯田十二便，天子批答可行，却忧心日久众羌重聚兵力。充国再奏，分析众羌精兵现处饥冻，支羌羸弱，而“屯田内有亡费之利，外有守御之备”，势必逼虏不战自破，天子于是批准“将军计善”。如是往复，不仅商讨君臣战略，亦复叙述汉羌关系。其他如《李广传》叙李广拜为右北平太守，私斩霸陵尉，上书自陈谢罪。回诏不予追咎，反加勉励。《石庆传》叙石庆身为丞相，面对二百多万流民安置关头，上书请求辞位。汉武帝回诏责难这种不负责任行为。

互动性的另一面是用不同文本叙同一事情，采用互文相足之法，收取事态互动之功。互见法也是司马迁纪传体例，当同一历史事件涉及不同事主，叙述势必散落各传，构成各传之间互文互叙，司马迁以“语在某某传”记识。班固袭互见法模式于文本间性，以文本互文完成叙事。汉武帝孙昌邑王刘贺因行淫乱被废，其罪案是由奏本定谳的。《霍光传》记昌邑王被召殿上听诏，大将军霍光与群臣联名奏王，尚书令宣读奏书，历数昌邑王典丧（昭帝崩）废礼谊，使从官略女子载衣车，引内昌邑从官驺宰官奴二百余人，常与居禁闼内敖戏，与宫人淫乱。立为太子时，擅改皇朝礼仪礼器，不奉祖宗庙祠，受玺仅二十七日，持节诏诸官署征发，凡千一百二十七事。云云。是为废前罪状。《武五子传》记霍光改立武帝曾孙为宣帝，宣帝密遣山阳太守张敞刺探昌邑王废居状况。张敞条奏报告：故昌邑王仍居旧宫，宫中奴婢一百八十三人。宫门紧闭，不纳外人。故王今年二十六七，衣服言语举止已呈白痴迹象。云云。是为废后现状。将二传二奏对接，构成互文相足，展现昌邑王废前废后之完整状况。

五曰对比性。《汉书》中凡合传者，皆有性质相同之处，并具隐然对比之意。合传中所载文书，自然亦具对比性。关于汉武帝元狩六年夏四月乙巳同日册封三王，立皇子刘闳为齐王，刘旦为燕王，刘胥为广陵王，《史记·三王世家》以欣赏品味排列三封册书，称“文辞烂然，甚可观也”。然于三王之事并无一词。宣帝时褚少孙续《太史公书》，看出三策“各因子才力智能，及土地之刚柔，人民之轻重，为作策以申戒之”的写作特色，并补叙三王策后史实。至班固撰《武五子传》，刻意将三策分开，一策之下即叙一王之事，映衬策文意愿与三王表现之龃龉，既对比三策，又对比三王，使叙述寓意更深一层。《封齐王策》戒“悉尔心，允执其中，天禄永终”，结果齐王八年而亡，无子国除；《封燕王策》戒“悉尔心，毋作怨，毋作棐德”，结果燕王每因不得立为太子而作怨不已，遂与宗室中山哀王子刘长、齐孝王孙刘泽等谋反，事败没被治罪，再度伙窜其姊盖长公主、左将军上官桀父子，谋划诛杀霍光，废帝自立，最终落得“以绶自绞”；《封广陵王策》戒“悉尔心，祗祗兢兢，乃惠乃顺，毋桐好逸，毋迩宵人，惟法惟则”！结果广陵王却“好倡乐逸游”，“动作无法度”，终日觊觎帝位，招迎女巫祝诅，同样落得“以绶自绞”。

对比性的另一面是跨传对比。同传中之文事对比往往明比，而跨传间之文事对比往往暗比，须牵连而得之。试取《外戚恩泽侯表》中外戚誓词：“非刘氏不王，若有亡功非上所置而侯者，天下共诛之”。《高五王传》中赵幽王刘友歌词：“诸吕用事兮，刘氏微；迫胁王侯兮，彊授我妃。我妃既妒兮，诬我以恶；谗女乱国兮，上曾不寤。我无忠臣兮，何故弃国？自快中野兮，苍天与直！于嗟不可悔兮，宁早自贼！为王饿死兮，谁者怜之？吕氏绝理兮，托天报仇！”《外戚传》中吕后遗嘱（上文已引）诸文并观，再联系诸吕擅政举止，个中微意，不言而喻。

纵观《汉书》，载文述史堪与断代述史、纪传述史为鼎足而三的史纂范式。其帝纪基本用诏书串联纪事；列传则缀合诏奏信息交流叙述；八表则采集“臧诸宗庙，副在有司”[11]的列侯功籍和谱牒档案制作而成；十志更是征引赡富，《食货志》多记疏议，《沟洫志》全系奏言，《天文志》通篇占辞，《郊祀志》满载制诏，而《律历志》、《艺文志》等亦自旧文纂成。《汉书》征引繁富，至有“孟坚所掇拾以成一代之书者，不过历朝之诏令，诸臣之奏疏尔”[4]之讥；或者多引少述，只引不述，如《徐乐传》、《严安传》惟载上书一篇，别无它事，至有“述时务则谨辞章而略事实”（傅玄语）[12]、“唯上录言，罕逢载事”（刘知几语）[12]之议。然则，通过以上对《汉书》载文述史范式的剖析，更能体会范晔《后汉书·班固传论》所谓“赡而不秽，详而有体”最为笃论，“文赡事详”也正概括了《汉书》载文述史的史纂范式。

参考文献

[1] 班固．司马迁传［M］//班固．汉书．北京：中华书局，1962：2737.
[2] 班固．叙传［M］//班固．汉书．北京：中华书局，1962.
[3] 范晔．班彪列传［M］．范晔．后汉书．北京：中华书局，1965：1334.
[4] 郑鹤声．史汉研究［M］．上海：商务印书馆，1930.
[5] 赵翼．二十二史札记［M］．北京：中华书局，2001：30.
[6] 吴讷．文章辨体序说［M］．北京：人民文学出版社，1962：34.
[7] 班固．贾谊传［M］//班固．汉书．北京：中华书局，1962：2265.
[8] 班固．董仲舒传［M］//班固．汉书．北京：中华书局，1962.
[9] 柳宗元．柳宗直西汉文类序［M］//柳宗元集．北京：中华书局，1979：577.
[10] 钱穆．国史大纲［M］．上海：国立编译馆，1940：101.
[11] 班固．高惠高后文功臣表［M］//班固．汉书．北京：中华书局，1962：527.
[12] 浦起龙．史通通释［M］．上海：商务印书馆，1935.

教师简介：

聂勇浩，男，中山大学管理学学士、硕士、博士。2003 年起任教于中山大学资讯管理学院，副教授，硕士生导师。主讲"管理学原理"、"行政管理"等本科生课程，以及"图书情报调查研究法"、"实践领域案例分析"等研究生课程。研究领域为政府信息管理及档案公共服务，重点关注公益信息服务的机制创新以及档案馆如何更好地为社会公众服务。主持包括国家社会科学基金项目、教育部人文社会科学研究项目在内的纵向项目 4 项，以前三名成员参与省部级项目 3 项。在《档案学研究》、《图书情报知识》、《中国行政管理》、《社会科学》、《中国人民大学学报》、《中山大学学报》等刊物发表论文 20 多篇。曾获广东省 2008—2009 年度哲学社会科学优秀成果奖（论文类）三等奖（排名第二）、中山大学 2008 年青年教师授课竞赛三等奖及 2014 年青年教师授课竞赛优秀奖。2002 年在香港中文大学访学。是广东省高等学校"千百十工程"第八批培养对象（校级）。联系方式：issnyh@ mail. sysu. edu. cn。

民生档案远程协同服务机制研究

——以上海市为例

聂勇浩，郭煜晗①

摘　要：档案如何在信息时代服务民生？上海市开展的民生档案远程协同服务提供了一个典型案例。通过实地访谈、观察和收集相关的文本资料，论文从技术、管理、政策三个层面分析归纳了远程协同服务得以实现的关键条件。其中，技术层面的关键条件包括建设档案馆之间的业务协同信息平台，将民生档案服务融入政务平台以及实现民生档案信息的标准化；管理层面的关键条件包括合理协调档案馆和社区联动的人员分工，提供民生档案社区一站式查询，明确民生档案利用的审批归属权，以及在档案证明上加盖电子印章和实体图章来确保管理流程的畅通；最后，政策层面的关键条件涉及将民生档案远程协同服务纳入政府信息化战略中，以及借助政府权威自上而下推动服务的开展。

关键词：民生档案；远程服务；协同服务

Constructing the Long-Distance Collaborative Service of Livelihood Archives in the Information Era：A Case Study of Shanghai

Yonghao Nie，Yuhan Guo

Abstract：How Could archives contribute to make the livelihood of people better in the information age? The long-

① 郭煜晗，中国人民大学信息资源管理学院档案学专业硕士研究生。

distance collaborative service of livelihood archives in Shanghai gives an example. On the basis of interview, observation and documents, this paper attempts to conclude the key elements for its success in the perspectives of technology, management and policies. In the aspect of technology, the first step is building the information platform among archives, the second is combining the livelihood archives with e-government to achieve the collaboration of archives, community agencies and governments, and the third is carrying out the information standardization to ensure the sharing of data. In terms of management, the key elements include coordinating the staffs between the archives and communities, setting up the one-stop queries, defining the approval rights and affixing double seals to ensure the authority of the transcripts. As for the policies, these elements are getting the service into the information strategy and promoting the enterprise with the help of governments' authority.

Keywords: Livelihood archives; Long-distance service; Collaborative service

1 研究问题及文献综述

2008 年第十六届国际档案大会上，国家档案局局长杨冬权提出服务民生是我国档案服务方向的新选择。[1]2011 年民生档案被列为五大类基本档案之一[2]，在民生服务中的地位也越来越重要。然而，我国民生档案工作面临着管理主体分散、信息化技术应用程度低的困境[3]，这使得公众查阅、利用档案都颇费周折。如何充分利用先进信息技术，以及有效实现档案保管部门和政务服务部门之间的协同，无疑是推动档案更好地服务民生的重要课题。上海市档案部门于 2010 年开始实施的“就地查询、跨馆出证、馆社联动、全市通办”的民生档案远程协同服务机制就是一个有益的探索。因为其发展较快，协同服务的方式多样，处于国内探索和发展的前沿，所以研究者选择上海市的服务模式作为研究对象，通过实地调研和访谈，首先介绍这一机制的动因以及发展历程，然后具体分析该机制得以实施的技术基础、管理流程和政策支持这三个关键条件，最后对其进行总结和展望。

现有学者们普遍认为民生档案远程协同服务是档案利用者可以在就近的档案馆或社区事务服务中心查阅档案，同时可以当场获得档案证明并办理相关事务。如李广都认为远程协同服务是档案利用者可在就近首访的档案馆或街道社区事务受理服务中心通过网络查询自己所需要的档案，包括跨区域保存的档案，并可当场获得档案部门出具的档案证明。[4]张林华等认为远程服务是公众可以在家门口的社区事务受理服务中心查阅档案并拿到所需档案证明，同时又可凭档案证明在中心办理一站式服务的相关事务。[5]

关于实施模式的研究主要来源于档案实践工作者的实施案例和经验总结，概括起来主要有馆际协同、馆社协同和馆室协同三种模式。如长春市[6]、济南市[7]、天津市[8]等地档案馆总结了其开展的馆际协同服务，包括馆际的民生档案资源整合、协同查档和出证。浙江省档案局报道了嘉兴市进行的馆室协同服务，档案馆与市民政局及婚姻登记中心组成数据中心联络小组，使婚姻登记档案查询形成协同利用的服务体系。[9]上海市档案馆介绍了其民生档案服务的“三联动”：一是通过跨馆查询获得档案证明的馆际联动；二是可在所属区域的街道社区事务受理服务中心办理查档出证的馆社联动；三是向涉民部门办事中心延伸，使民生档案查询、补证、办事一步到位的馆室联动。[10]国外目前主要是利用信息网络技术提供档案远程服务，如法国的档案馆通过邮寄、电话、传真、网络提供档案信息，档案部门还积极将档案信息化建设纳入电子政府建设中[11]；美国建成了档案信息导航系统，可以联网查询全国的档案馆藏信息；英国档案馆依托各地的档案信息咨询窗口免费为英国公民提供档案信息，包括各类特色档案库信息，来满足社会公众的利用需求[12]。

在协同服务的困难方面，总结起来主要有三点。首先，民生档案种类繁多、涉及面广、分布分散，如陈玉萍认为民生档案的保存地点比较分散，给民生档案的信息资源整合带来不便[13]；其次，民生档案社会共享度低，如苏州档案局指出不少涉民档案信息开放程度不高、共享度不够给协同利用带来极大的不便[14]；最后，管理部门多、保管条件参差使得民生档案在管理上有一定特殊性，如欧阳琳、彭海艳认为民生档案的内容、建档标准、数据格式、归档范围、保管期限、管理方式都没有统一的标准，民生档案工作不规范，严重影响民生档案的协同利用效果[15]。

在实现条件和因素上，目前学者认为应该包括三个关键条件。一是要搭建协同服务技术平台，如李广都提出要建立一站式检索系统实现档案库资源联网，为社会公众提供民生档案异地利用、就地出证的便捷化服务。[4]邓羽提出要构建档案局主导，立档单位协同运作，共建共享的档案资源数据库平台和互动交流平台以共促发展。[16]张卫东通过对服务主体、服务受众、资源体系、服务手段等因素的分析，指出民生档案服务民生的模式是一个需要政府、档案部门、普通民众多组织共同参与、各种资源全面覆盖、多种手段全面实施的综合系统。[17]二是要整合民生档案资源，如罗夏钻提出要最大限度地把涉民部门的档案信息资源整合起来，建立覆盖人民群众的民生档案资源体系，真正发挥出民生档案的价值。[18]三是要获得政府的支持，如崔穗旭认为要加强民生档案信息体系建设，需要完善的电子政务技术条件和政府基层机构的职能转变。[19]

总结以上研究观点，目前关于民生档案远程协同服务的研究在实践层面上主要是来自档案实践部门的纪实报道和经验介绍；相比较之下，理论方面的研究迟滞于实践方面的研究，虽然在内容、实现条件、面临的问题等方面有所探讨，但对于其运行的理念、要素、模式等深入探究较少。综合来看，有关研究还处于起步阶段，在理论和规律方面的研究还有待增加。

目前远程协同服务对于民生档案而言还是一种比较新的服务模式，现有文献多是实践部门对具体案例进行经验介绍，档案学界对于这一课题进行系统深入研究的论文数量很少。因此，研究者于2015年2月5—6日对上海市普陀区档案馆和长寿社区进行实地调研，通过访谈和观察的方法了解上海市民生档案远程协同服务的实施情况，获得了相关的一手资料，并收集了相关的文本资料，对上海的服务模式进行系统的分析和总结，归纳出远程协同服务实施的关键条件，使其具有较强的实践指导性和普适性，从而更好地开展民生档案服务。

2 上海市民生档案远程协同服务的动因和历程

上海市的民生档案远程协同服务所采用的是多层次的社区网络服务模式，公众可以在家门口的社区事务受理服务中心查阅档案并获取所需档案证明，同时又可凭档案证明在该中心一站式办理相关事务。在这一服务背后，是档案馆、基层办事机构（街道办、乡镇、社区）以及形成涉民档案的政府部门三者之间的协同。[4]这一机制将市、区、社区三级的民生档案信息互联起来，借助信息化手段构建远程便民服务平台，实现全市通办。下面先对该机制的动因和发展历程做介绍。

2.1 民生档案远程协同服务的动因

2.1.1 满足民生档案利用需求

随着工资改革、知青退休返城、动迁安置、申请经适房、廉租房等一系列民生政策的出台，居民办理这些相关事项都需要民生档案作为凭证，因此社会公众对于婚姻证明、计划生育等民生档案的利用需求不断增加。近几年上海市普通市民在档案利用人数中所占比重越来越大，总体呈上升趋势，超过总利用人数的20%，这也相应带动了利用需求方面的变化。公民因涉及个人切身利益问题利用档案的情况不断增多，尤其是以知情和个人维权为目的查阅民生档案的数量明显上升，占查阅总量的近30%。同时利用对象也呈现复杂化趋势，有专家学者，有普通百姓，也有老年人、残疾人等弱势群体。由于行政区划调整、个人情况变动等原因，利用者往往需要来回奔波于各档案馆之间，查阅利用档案成为难事。档案利用主体及其利用目的的转变，反映出民生档案利用需求不断增加的社会现状。[5]

民生档案信息作为落实民生政策的基础，档案馆、社区事务受理服务中心和涉民部门之间的协同服务为档案服务民生提供了便利的条件，使得普通群众尤其是弱势群体能够就近查档，就近取件。[17]这充分顺应了社会日益增长的民生档案查阅利用需求。

2.1.2 提升民生档案管理层次

民生档案远程协同服务对于档案馆自身来说是对现有民生档案服务方式的一个创新举措，在档案资源整合、服务方式以及资金方面都有利于提升档案馆民生档案的管理层次。

远程协同服务可以改善档案资源条块分割、分布分散、管理混乱、重复建设的局面，为进一步丰富馆藏、改善馆藏结构、向社会提供利用创造条件；改进目前档案馆提供民生档案服务的方式，拓宽共建共享的渠道，建立民生档案馆际、馆社、馆室协同的平台，便于公众查询利用民生档案，满足民生信息需求。此外，远程协同服务还可以为各立档单位提供从事科学研究、学术研究的平台和良好的服务，更重要的是能够给予各立档单位政策和资金方面的支持，为其提供激励创新的机制。[20]

2.2 民生档案远程协同服务机制发展历程

2.2.1 馆际协同阶段

2010年9月，上海市档案馆和14个区县档案馆签订了承诺书，启动了以“就地查询、跨馆出证”为特征的馆际联动机制，利用者在档案馆查询民生档案信息而所需档案在另一档案馆时，可用跨馆联动的方式进行调阅和出证，形成了“前台（首访档案馆）预检、后台（档案保管地档案馆）审批、依法出证、统一用印”的管理网络。2011年通过电话和传真实现了跨馆出证全市覆盖。目前上海市的馆际联动主要是市辖区、县的各级综合档案馆之间的联动，馆际协同打破了各个档案馆之间信息资源孤立的围墙，实行查档就地受理、全市协同的档案馆大协作。

2.2.2 全区通办阶段

2010年3月杨浦区档案馆在延吉新村街道社区事务受理服务中心首开全国第一家馆社联动试点，7月正式运行；徐汇区档案馆通过区政务外网在三个月内将查档出证服务覆盖到区内13个街镇，2010年9月率先实现了全区通办；其他区也陆续跟进，纷纷将查档服务点延伸到老百姓家门口的社区事务受理服务中心。2012年年底馆社协同已经覆盖上海市208个社区，惠及全市2300多万市民。[10]全区通办阶段主要开展馆社联动，利用者可在所属区域的街道和社区事务受理服务中心查询和办理馆藏档案的调阅和出证。查询档案的方式从电话传真发展到计算机联网查询。

各个区县档案馆从民生意识出发，对居民利用率较高的婚姻登记、计划生育、知青上山下乡、知青返城和知青子女返沪等五类档案进行远程协同服务，并随着公众利用需求的变化不断调整服务内容，又先后新增了再生育子女审批档案、工伤认定档案和学籍档案，从而不断满足普通民众的民生档案利用需求。

2.2.3 全市通办阶段

2012年12月20日，民生档案远程服务平台全市通办的开通仪式在普陀区的长寿路街道办事处举行，标志着只要是在婚姻登记、计划生育、知青上山下乡、知青返城和知青子女返沪等五类档案范围内，群众可凭本人有效身份证件在就近受访的档案馆或街道社区事务受理服务中心查到有关档案信息并当场获得档案部门出具的档案证明，一次性把事情办完。

2014年通过档案馆与社区有关职能部门的多次协商和争取，民生档案社区查询项目最终落户上海市社区统一服务平台，这使得在社区事务受理服务中心查询民生档案成为了有正式户口的常规受理项目。联席会议纳入了八种民生档案的查询服务，在原有五种档案的基础上新增了再生育子女审批档案、工伤认定档案和学籍档案。档案部门还将远程协同服务向各涉民部门的办事中心延伸，在馆社协同的基础上实行馆室协同，使民生档案查询、出证、办事一步到位。自全市通办开通至2014年11月，受惠群众已超过25700人次。下面将详细分析该机制的技术基础、管理流程和政策支持三个关键条件。

3 民生档案远程协同服务的技术基础

上海市民生档案远程协同服务机制实现的技术基础主要有三点：一是建设各区县档案馆馆际业务协同平台，二是融合民生档案查询与市政务平台，三是进行平台和系统的标准化建设。这三个技术条件是通过档案部门的民生档案远程服务平台和基于社区服务统一平台的民生档案社区查询项目来实现的。前者主要是实现馆际协同，后者在馆际协同的基础上增加了馆社协同以及档案馆与各涉民部门办事中心的馆室协同。

3.1 建设馆际业务协同信息平台

馆际协同主要是依托于民生档案远程服务平台来实施的。该平台由档案部门基于政务内网构建，可以使各区县档案馆进行民生档案的资源整合、在线接收和移交、查询利用等业务操作，从而实现馆际档案信息的共建共享。

在资源整合方面，档案馆根据公众的知识背景、利用目的、利用方式等特征，对馆藏档案信息资源进行整合，对接待人次的数量和查阅档案的内容进行分门别类的整合统计，重点是查阅数量大、利用率高的知青上山下乡、返城、子女回沪档案、婚姻档案、独生子女审批档案。同时加大全文数字化力度，优先完成民生档案的数字化。2012 年底已基本完成了婚姻登记、计划生育、知青上山下乡、知青返城和知青子女返沪等五类档案的数字化，共扫描条目 4000 万条，全文数据超过 1 亿页。档案馆将民生档案目录和全文数据库上传至该平台，为实现馆际协同提供基础和前提。

在在线接收和移交方面，上海市各区县档案馆会同人口计划生育、民政、社会保障、住房、土地等部门，加强对民生档案的建档指导和接收进馆工作，各区县档案馆可通过该平台接收、移交档案。政务网能够保证政务信息的安全性，可以满足档案馆之间的数据交换以及档案馆与各涉民部门之间民生档案数据的在线归档。

在查询利用方面，由于不同的民生档案是由不同的档案机构、政府部门保管的，所以利用方式、利用范围等需要相互授权，在授权范围内按照协议内容才能完成远程查档和数据传递。在此平台的相互授权和共享模式建设中，上海市各档案馆共同签署《民生档案利用便民服务公约》，相互授权利用民生档案专用数据库目录信息，以及经审批后利用档案全文和出具证明。因为档案目录信息是查档最基本的信息，在授权的同时也相互开放各自的档案目录信息以实现共享，上海的市属综合档案馆之间的档案目录均可以相互查询。[4]通过这种相互授权查询利用的方式来实现跨馆出证。

3.2 融合民生档案服务与政务平台

民生档案要真正服务民生，需要走出档案馆，与政务平台相融合。社区是如今城市管理和服务民众的一线，承担着众多的民生服务职能。因此上海市档案部门在实现馆际联动的基础上，打破在档案馆出证的壁垒，将民生档案查阅出证向各社区和涉民部门的办事中心延伸，实现馆社协同和馆室协同。从 2011 年起上海各个区先后通过各区的政务平台在社区事务受理服务中心开通民生档案查询出证服务，又进一步在民政局、房管局、人口和计划生育委员会等涉民部门设立受理点，实现全区通办。2014 年又将民生档案查询项目纳入上海市社区服务统一平台，将档案馆与全市各街道、乡镇的社区事务受理服务中心建立协同服务，实现民生档案社区查询，居民可以就近在社区事务受理服务中心办理事项时查询自己所要利用的各类民生档案信息，由全区通办实现全市通办。

上海市社区服务统一平台采用分层和模块化的设计，通过一门式服务器和多台虚拟机服务器提供条线综合业务支持，整合劳动、民政、医保等各条线资源，建立后台联盟，实现信息不但可以在本身的系统中流转，还能通过消息总线与其他系统实现交互，实现社区服务平台的一门式服务。[21]该平台主要为居民提供221项全市统一的标准事务受理服务，民生档案查询作为其中一条线业务，可以与劳动、社保、医保、民政、计生、工会等其他条线的业务合作，从而实现档案馆与其他涉民部门的馆室协同，借助信息化网络一站式为利用者提供查档结果，使档案服务民生与社区建设融为一体。

这一平台的操作包括社区事务前台受理、后台协同办理、办理过程查询三大部分(图1)。居民和社区前台属于前台统一受理，档案部门以及其他涉民部门属于后台协同办理，档案部门以及其他涉民部门的业务数据库和服务器通过专线系统和政务网集成于一门式虚拟机服务器。社区事务受理服务中心将居民的需求传递到一门式受理服务器，档案部门和涉民部门办理后，再通过一门式受理服务器将相关信息发送给社区事务受理服务中心。

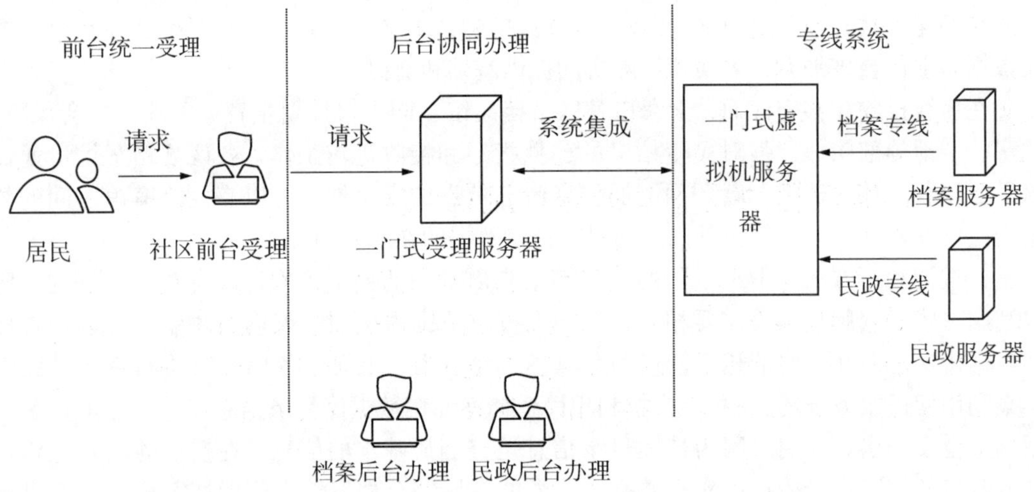

图1　上海市社区服务统一平台操作模式

上海市多位一体的社区服务统一平台不仅将市、区、社区三级的民生档案信息联系起来，实现全市通办，也将民生档案远程利用服务向社区和各涉民部门的办事中心延伸，使得民生档案查询、出证、办事都可在社区事务受理服务中心实现。

3.3　进行民生档案信息标准化建设

民生档案种类庞杂，数量多，动态性强，归属繁杂，管理标准不一，而民生档案远程协同服务又涉及了大量的数据信息、多个管理部门和众多工作人员。[22]基于民生档案这些特点，需要进行信息标准化建设，以保证各部门工作的统一。信息标准化建设包括信息技术、信息管理和信息服务的标准化建设[23]。上海市档案部门提出了“统一平台、统一流程、统一文本、统一印章”的四个统一要求来进行民生档案的信息标准化建设。

统一平台要求各区县档案馆使用统一的信息平台，即民生档案远程服务平台和社区统一服务平台。目前上海市各区县的档案馆基本都已采用上海市档案馆开发的民生档案远程服务网络平台及应用系统，档案部门提前规划档案的专门数据库，各种适用软件标准和数据采集标准、数据项做到统一性和协调性，由数据中心负责统一处理和备份数据，确保各个部门的软件和数据适用性的统一，不仅能节省成本，而且可以提高效率。2014年纳入上海市社区统一服务平台后，该平台提供基于属地化管理的统一的公共服务，采用统一的系统更新发布机制，以便于系统更新。

统一流程要求民生档案查询、审批、出证等流程的统一。上海市档案馆制定了统一的操作流程和办事告知，各区县档案馆的工作人员都要遵照统一的操作流程进行民生档案服务工作。档案馆也定期对社区事务受理服务中心的工作人员进行查档出证的培训来规范操作流程。

统一文本要求包括档案传输文本格式和证明文本格式的统一。上海市各区县档案馆之间、档案馆与社区之间相互传输的是经过全文数字化扫描的PDF格式的档案文件。此外，上海市档案馆也统一了档案证明的文本格式。

统一印章要求各受理点出证的盖章数目和样式统一。上海市档案局规定一份档案证明上加盖两个印章，保存地点的电子印章和受理地点的实体章。这代表着保存点和受理点同时证明该证明材料的真实性，同时档案局也争取了公安、民政部门对这种出具档案证明方式的认可，保证了档案证明的法律效力。

4　民生档案远程协同服务的管理流程

上海市档案部门不仅利用信息化手段为远程协同服务提供技术层面的支撑，也在管理层面上对馆社协同服务的人员分工以及民生档案查询、审批、出证的管理流程做出了统一规定，包括协调馆社联动的人员分工、建立民生档案一站式查询、明确民生档案利用审批归属权、加盖双章保证档案证明的法律效力等来确保民生档案服务在管理流程上的畅通。

4.1　协调馆社联动的人员分工

馆社协同的人员分工由档案馆与社区事务受理服务中心两个部门之间相互协调。由社区事务受理服务中心安排受理点的档案查询人员，在承担社区事务受理服务工作的同时，再兼职民生档案查询工作。委托档案馆给各个社区受理点的查档人员分配登录民生档案远程服务平台的特定ID号，以便掌握社区档案查询的动态。这样民生档案查询被分散到了各个社区，使居民能够在社区进行一站式地查档、出证和办事，而不用奔波于档案馆和社区之间。

此外，社区事务受理服务中心的查档人员要定期参加档案馆的培训，一般每年一次。档案馆主要培训社区工作人员如何使用民生档案远程服务平台以及针对不同的办理业务，应为居民查阅何种档案等。在培训过程中，档案馆会把受理量比较大、查档出证工作完成得较好的社区事务受理服务中心作为示范单位，让各中心的查档人员进行交流和学习。

4.2　提供民生档案一站式查询

居民在社区事务受理服务中心办理的很多事项，都需要民生档案作为证明材料。上海市将民生档案查询纳入社区统一服务平台后，居民就可以在社区事务受理服务中心办理业务的同时，查询与办理事项相关的档案资料，并且可以一站式查询到所有需要的民生档案。

在社区一站式查询中，首先由查询者填写申请单，工作人员通过服务平台把要查询的档案内容发给保管该档案的档案馆，如查询者的姓名、身份、查询档案的种类、内容等。档案馆从查询系统中收到社区发来的查询请求提示信息后，再由档案馆的工作人员查询档案数据库，并将经过全文数字化扫描的 PDF 档案文件通过系统传回社区，社区收到后确认无误就打印盖章，整个过程花费时间在 3～10 分钟。

图 2　社区一站式查询过程

这种与业务办理同时进行，一站式查询民生档案的方式，通过社区事务受理服务中心来连接起档案馆和居民，既满足了居民的查档需求，又完善了社区的一站式服务，同时还改变了档案馆提供民生档案的方式，能够使民生档案查询和出证快速便捷。

4.3　明确民生档案利用审批归属权

开展民生档案远程协同利用要明确档案利用审批的归属权问题。不同种类的民生档案的形成单位不同，保存部门也不尽相同，在协同服务中，受理单位很多不是档案保管单位，如民政局的婚姻收养登记中心。如果查档单位为外单位时，就必须明确档案利用审批权限的归属，来保证档案利用和出证的合法有效。因此上海市在远程协同服务的协调内容中明确保管档案的部门拥有审批归属权。无论档案利用申请由哪个受理点发出，必须经由保存该档案的部门进行审批，才能传递数据和出证。如果不同档案馆之间对某一民生档案审批的归属权发生异议时，应当交由双方共同的上一级档案部门指定审批归属权。如果是档案部门和其他政府部门发生归属权争议，应交由所在地的政府机构和档案部门共同协商后指定相关部门行使审批权。[4]

4.4　加盖双章保证法律效力

目前上海市的民生档案在远程打印出证时必须加盖两个印章，一个是保存档案的档案馆按照严密的电子签章技术出具的电子印章，另一个是受理点档案馆或其委托的社区事务受理服务中心的档案证明专用实体章。原保管单位的数字公章和原文传递中的加密技术，可以保证原文内容的真实性、有效性。档案证明加盖有效的公章后，可以追溯其源头和真实有效性。[4]

各个社区事务受理服务中心的档案证明专用章是由所委托的档案馆发放的，每个章都有编号，比如普陀区委托的曹阳社区中心的证明章是 1 号，长风社区中心的章是 2 号，以此类推。档案证明专用章一经使用，委托档案馆通过系统平台就知道是由哪个受理点盖的章，档案馆可以通过平台随时了解盖章状况。这样既能够体现档案保管方与利用方的关系，又能够确保利用者持有的查档证明所具有的合法性。

5 民生档案远程协同服务的政策支持

从馆际协同到馆社协同再到全市协同，这一步步的跨越都离不开政府政策的支持。上海市政府在民生档案远程协同服务的构建上给予了战略支持，将其纳入上海智慧城市的信息化战略中，在实施模式上借助政府权威，自上而下地来推动服务的开展。

5.1 纳入城市信息化建设战略

民生档案信息大多是政府部门形成的数据，馆际协同、馆社协同和全市协同又涉及海量民生档案数据的交换、共享和归档，这都需要依靠政务网和智慧城市建设中的网络设备才能完成。上海市政府将民生档案的协同利用服务纳入到了智慧城市的信息化战略当中，其所依托的技术平台，包括档案部门的民生档案远程服务平台以及社区服务统一平台，都是在政府的支持下构建运行的。

上海智慧城市建设的重要组成部分是智慧社区建设，智慧社区是利用信息化技术和手段整合各类服务资源，提供多种社区服务，这就需要充分发挥社区事务受理服务中心的作用。上海市民生档案协同服务的主要特征就是馆社协同，将社区事务受理服务中心作为最基层的民生档案查询受理机构，和各级档案馆、各涉民部门加强协作。2014 年上海市委办公厅、市政府办公厅在《关于加强和改进新形势下本市档案工作的实施意见》中明确要求将民生档案服务纳入社区事务受理服务中心服务范围，在此实施意见的指导下，社区标准化建设联席会议将民生档案社区查询列入了上海市社区服务统一平台，民生档案查询由区县档案馆的各自操作，成为纳入社区事务受理服务中心统建统管机制的服务项目，从而真正进驻社区服务，作为智慧社区和智慧城市建设的一部分来服务民生。

5.2 借助政府权威自上而下推动服务开展

在民生档案服务全市协同阶段，涉及更多的数据信息和管理部门，因此上海的协同机制采用自上而下的实施方式，借助政府权威，以上级部门推动为起点，以基层部门落实为归宿。由上海市档案馆统一部署，区县档案馆系统配合市档案馆，先选择部分区县档案馆进行试点以获取经验和优化方案，逐步攻克协同机制运行中面临的困难，包括如何进行远程操作，跨馆如何出具档案证明，如何保证法律效力，服务是否收费，查询门类如何约定等问题。上海市档案馆提出“同一平台、统一流程、统一文本、统一印章”的要求，先后研发了民生档案远程服务网络平台及应用系统，制定了规范的操作流程、办事告知及证书文本格式，统一档案证明专用章样式，统一开展工作人员业务培训，明确跨馆出证乃至异地出证均免收费用。

上海市政府办公厅还成立了社区事务受理服务中心标准化建设联席会议，对纳入社区事务受理服务中心的民生档案查询服务项目进行梳理，由市民政局和市经信委牵头保障受理服务中心标准化建设的技术措施，对民生档案查询项目进行升级改造，逐步完成与社区事务受理服务中心服务平台的接轨，这都为民生档案实现全市协同服务提供了政策支持。

6　结论与展望

综上所述，随着信息化的飞速发展，现有的民生档案服务已不能充分满足社会不断增加的民生档案利用需求，上海市档案部门从这一矛盾出发，树立民生意识和平等意识，顺应档案信息利用主体、利用需求的转变，关注弱势群体的档案信息权，开展民生档案远程协同服务，经历了馆际协同、全区通办和全市通办三个发展阶段，把握服务机制运行的关键条件来实现民生档案馆际协同、馆社协同和馆室协同（图3）。在技术基础上，建设档案馆馆际的协同信息平台，包括资源整合、在线接收和移交、查询利用服务等业务来实现馆际协同；将民生档案服务融合到政务平台来实现馆社协同和馆室协同；同时进行民生档案服务的信息标准化建设以实现共建共享。在人员分工和民生档案查询、审批、出证的管理流程方面，由档案馆和社区协调馆社联动的人员分工，建立民生档案一站式查询，明确民生档案利用审批归属权，加盖电子印章和实体图章保证档案证明的法律效力来确保民生档案服务在管理流程上的畅通；在政策支持上，政府将民生档案远程协同服务纳入到城市信息化的战略中，借助政府权威自上而下地来推动服务的开展，使其获得可靠的政策保障。

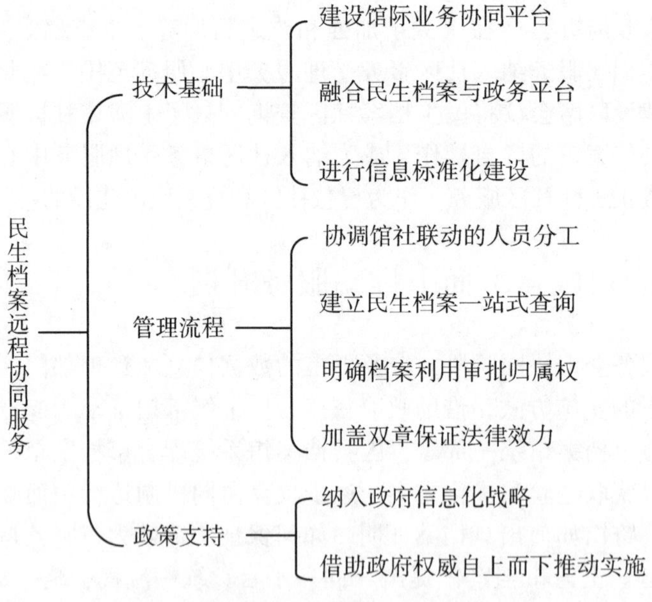

图3　民生档案远程协同服务关键条件

就研究的局限性而言，本研究属于个案研究，而远程协同服务的实施会受到各个地区的经济水平、科技水平、社会环境以及政策的影响。由于国内各地区经济、科技、社会发展不平衡，民生档案的管理、利用也参差不齐，因此从上海模式归纳出的远程协同服务方式和关键因素对于其他地区的适用性还需要具体问题具体分析。

此外，上海市从2010年开始实施此项服务，2014年12月刚刚纳入到社区服务统一平台，全市协同还处于起步阶段，存在的问题还未明显暴露出来，技术、管理、政策等关键因素需要进行时间检验，因此民生档案远程协同利用服务的开展和实施还需要进行历时的追踪和研究，不断完善，不断创新来更好地服务民生。

参考文献

[1] 杨冬权. 服务民生：中国档案服务方向的新选择 [N]. 中国档案报，2008-08-07 (1).

[2] 肖秋会，张欣. 基层档案馆民生档案工作现状、问题与对策研究 [J]. 档案学通讯，2014 (2)：96-100.

[3] 张林华，刘忻璇. 论民生档案资源建设及利用 [J]. 档案学通讯，2009 (5)：80-83.

[4] 李广都. 浅析民生档案远程利用服务的协调机制 [J]. 兰台世界，2014 (6)：24-25.

[5] 张林华，曹琳琳. "以公众为中心"的档案信息服务研究——以上海市民生档案远程服务机制的探索为例 [J]. 档案与建设，2014 (4)：8-11.

[6] 温娟莉，吕江燕. 创建民生档案信息区域共享服务平台——济南市开通民生档案远程共享服务 [J]. 中国档案，2013 (2)：28-29.

[7] 李际童. 十年磨一剑，创新铸辉煌：长春市档案局（馆）信息化建设十年回眸 [J]. 中国档案，2012 (9)：29-30.

[8] 丛为民. 天津市档案部门推出10项民生档案服务新举措 [N]. 中国档案报，2012-11-30 (1).

[9] 郑金月. 关注民生，服务民生——浙江省推进民生领域档案工作纪实 [J]，中国档案，2007 (8)：11-12.

[10] 张晶晶，姜龙飞. 融入智慧城市的档案服务——上海市民生档案远程协同服务机制建设纪实 [J]. 上海档案，2012 (7)：5-10.

[11] 江苏省档案考察团. 法国、意大利档案工作管窥 [J]. 档案与建设，2010 (4)：23-26.

[12] 陈灵. 基于数字环境的民生档案共享机制建设研究 [D]. 咸阳：西北农林科技大学，2013.

[13] 陈玉萍. 谈民生档案特点及管理体系建设 [J]. 北京档案，2009 (8)：39-40.

[14] 苏州档案局. 关注民生，服务和谐：探索民生档案工作机制 [J]. 档案与建设，2009 (4)：49-52.

[15] 欧阳琳，彭海艳. 两型社会建设中民生档案工作的问题与策略 [J]. 档案学研究，2010 (1)：22-26.

[16] 邓羽. 协同创新机制下的民生档案资源整合共享 [J]. 兰台世界，2014 (1)：15-16.

[17] 张卫东. 档案服务民生：理念与模式 [J]. 档案学通讯，2009 (5)：77-80.

[18] 罗夏钻. 我国民生档案协同服务机制构建探讨 [J]. 云南档案，2014 (2)：57-59.

[19] 崔穗旭. 民生档案信息如何实现社区查询——由上海市"民生档案远程协同服务机制"说开去 [J]. 中国档案，2012 (10)：68-69.

[20] Salamon L M. Partners in Public Service：Government-Nonprofit Relations in the Modern Welfare State [M]. Balttimore：Johns Hopkins University Press，1995：78.

[21] 上海一门式政务研发中心. 社区公共服务综合信息平台 [EB/OL]. [2015-3-16]. http：//www. shyms. org/ITSolution/ITSolutionsGov. aspx.

[22] 严永官. 论"民生档案" [J]. 档案管理，2009 (1)：21-24.

[23] 颜海. 电子政务信息资源共建共享研究综述 [J]. 情报杂志，2007 (8)：102-104，107.

教师简介：

李海涛，男，武汉大学管理学学士、管理学硕士、管理学博士。中山大学工商管理学院师资博士后。2011 年起任教于中山大学资讯管理学院，副教授，硕士生导师。主讲“电子文件与存取系统”、“公文写作”、“英文经典专业著作选读”、“电子文件管理” 等本科生课程，以及“阅读推广”等研究生课程。研究方向包括档案管理学、档案学基础理论、企业档案管理、电子政务、政府信息资源管理、电子文件管理、用户信息行为研究等。主持多项国家及省部级项目，在国内外权威、核心期刊发表论文 40 余篇。2016 年 2 月将访学美国威斯康辛大学密尔沃基分校信息科学学院。中国保密协会会员、广东省社会科学情报学会会员。联系方式：lihait8@ mail. sysu. edu. cn。

工程项目电子文件接收规范研究

李海涛，宋琳琳①，赖莉容②，高晶③

摘　要：本文在对国内外电子文件及工程项目电子文件接收规范研究现状分析的基础上，指出了工程项目电子文件接收规范的系统性、数量不足，且国际化程度较低。在对工程项目电子文件接收规范的研究意义阐明的基础上，从接收电子文件的格式、元数据、接口及基于 XML 数据封装包等维度探讨工程项目电子文件接收规范。

关键词：工程项目；电子文件；接收规范

Research on the Collection Specification for Electronic Record of Engineering Projects

Haitao Li，Linlin Song，Lirong Lai，Jing Gao

Abstract：Based on the analysis of collection specification at home and abroad in electronic records and electronic Records of engineering projects，it points out some problems related to the insufficient systems and numbers and lower international level in the national collection specification for electronic records of engineering projects. Firstly it analyzes the research meanings of collection specification for electronic records of engineering projects，and then it investigates the collection specification for electronic records of engineering projects from some angles such as format，metadata，interface and XML based data package.

Keywords：Engineering projects；Electronic record；Collection specification

---

① 宋琳琳，中山大学资讯管理学院，副教授，硕士生导师。
② 赖莉容，佛山市金的信档案咨询公司，档案馆员。
③ 高晶，广东省交通运输档案信息管理中心，高级工程师。

1 国内外研究现状

1.1 电子文件接收规范研究现状

目前，国外对于电子文件接收标准和实践研究领先并相对普及，主要具有以下几个方面：首先，国外注重完善电子文件接收管理机制。由于国外的信息科学技术较为普及，在构建电子文件管理系统对于电子文件接收标准、格式选择、存取利用等标准的外在机制铺设上，由政府主导，注重改革经济体制，力求经济体制与电子文件管理实践匹配，及时充分促进新信息技术应用到电子文件接收标准的完善之中，改造电子文件管理系统接收电子文件的业务流程。其次，形成了一套自上而下的电子文件及电子文件管理的术语体系及法制体系，具备了较为科学的电子文件管理系统的电子文件接收标准及管理法律、规范。由于国外电子文件管理实践较早，通过解决实践中的系列问题，逐步认识到统一界定电子文件内涵、外延，形成电子文件接收标准的重要意义，并在实践中制定并不断推动完善相关的系列法规、标准和规范。如在国际标准层面上，国际档案界已制定了规范电子文件管理的法规和标准《电子文件档案化管理指南》[1]；结合《电子文件档案化管理指南》及本国实际，澳大利亚国家档案馆制定了《电子文件管理政策》、《计算机证据法》[2]；英国国家档案馆制定了《电子文件鉴定办法》[3]等电子文件管理办法，明确了电子文件管理系统接收电子文件的元数据内容、保存格式及接收业务流程。最后，在利用电子文件管理系统接收电子文件的过程中，国外档案业界意识到开发专门软件、构建电子文件管理系统是实现接收电子文件并保证其完整、真实、可靠的有效途径。而与系统功能实现相关的接收电子文件标准、电子文件元数据封装及格式的规范直接影响到电子文件管理系统接收电子文件的质量及其长期存取与共享利用。国外电子文件接收、管理标准及配套管理系统建设往往同步展开。如为了应对数字时代的特性及公众不断增长的使用电子技术与政府沟通的要求，美国国家档案馆与档案局（NARA）在尝试新技术、保证电子文件接收质量，保障接收后的电子文件在电子文件管理系统各业务流程运转过程中的完整、真实、可靠性等方面开展多年探索。[4]

其中2005年启动的美国国家电子档案馆（ERA）系统项目是电子文件管理中系统建设及标准开发同步开展的典型案例，该项目对于联邦数字遗产保护的电子文件接收标准方案进行了探讨，并同步研发了能够接收、保存、利用任何类型数字遗产的电子档案管理系统。[5]

目前，国内对基于电子文件管理系统的电子文件接收标准或规范的研究和应用处于发展阶段。从上个世纪末开始，国家档案局和有关部门开始研究制定与电子文件接收相关的管理标准或规范，前后出台了《GB/T 17678.1—1999 CAD电子文件光盘存储、归档与档案管理要求　第一部分：电子文件归档与档案管理》、《GB/T 17678.2—1999 CAD电子文件光盘存储、归档与档案管理要求　第二部分：光盘信息组织结构》、《GB/T 18894—2002 电子文件归档与管理规范》、《GB/T 23286.1—2009 文献管理长期保存的电子文档文件格式　第一部分：PDF1.4（PDF/A-1）的使用》、《GB/Z 23283—2009 基于文件的电子信息的长期保存》等5个国家标准和《DA/T 31—2005 纸质档案数字化技术规范》、《DA/T 32—2005 公务电子邮件归档与管理规则》、《DA/T 38—2008 电子文件归档光盘技术要求和应用规范》、《DA/T 46—2009 文书类电子文件元数据方案》、《DA/T 47—2009 版式电子文件长期保存格式需求》、《DA/T 48—2009 基于 XML 的电子文件封装规范》等6个档案行业标准。[4]

1.2 工程项目电子文件接收规范研究现状

工程项目电子文件是电子文件资源的重要来源，它全面反映了工程建设的详细进展状况。对于工程质量评定、竣工管理和维护、新建工程的准备都具有重要的利用价值。随着各级各类档案部门对工程项目质量管理的重视，工程项目电子文件的管理绩效直接影响到工程项目质量。目前除了人工管理的纸质文件外，工程项目电子文件主要来源于在线办公等信息系统形成的大量电子文件。由于国内暂无工程项目电子文件及电子文件管理系统标准规范，工程项目档案接收实践中仍以接收纸质档案为主。部分已基于工程项目电子文件管理系统开展的电子文件接收实践中，存在着接收电子文件搜集不全面、整理不及时，部分接收电子文件未签字确认，查询利用电子文件过程繁琐等缺点。在对在线办公系统形成的大量电子文件的接收中也存在着电子签名有效认证等系列问题。此外，与工程项目电子文件管理匹配的信息系统，其设计核心应以全面、有效接收具有保存备考价值的电子文件并保证其真实、完整、可信为基础，凸显电子文件长期存取功能。尽管目前国内部分文档软件开发公司如用友、万维等已经开发出具有一定监控、追溯、验证及存取功能的电子文档接收及管理系统，但由于缺乏统一的接收电子文件的内容、格式及程序标准，使得现有工程项目电子文件管理系统多以市场用户的业务需求为主导，突出电子文件的查找利用功能，弱化甚至缺失接收入库后的电子文件长期存取功能。

综上可知，尽管我国已经出台了系列电子文件管理标准，但是指导工程项目电子文件接收及电子文件管理系统建设的国家、行业标准不多，且专指度及应用性不强。体现为：一是标准的系统性不足。由于缺乏统筹规划、组织协调，各个现有的电子文件管理标准之间难以衔接，甚至相互冲突，整个电子文件管理领域的标准结构散乱、未成体系。二是标准的数量不足。目前仍缺乏涉及电子文件接收管理等关键环节如接收电子文件内容、接收电子保存格式及电子文件数据迁移、电子文件封装等标准规范；缺乏音频、视频、网页等特殊电子文件长期存取格式标准。三是电子文件接收标准的国际化程度较低。主要体现为我国电子文件管理领域采纳国际相关电子文件接收、管理标准的比例偏低，而且我国自身的电子文件接收及管理标准在国际上的影响力较低。四是推广不够。在实际工作中，部分单位和电子文件管理软件、系统研发企业缺乏标准化意识。实践中，对于国家现有电子文件接收、管理标准没有充分的推广，在本机构工程项目电子文件接收及管理系统建设中一味地追求实际需求，忽视机构体系间相关电子文件长期存取格式标准、系统接口标准、电子文件元数据封装的格式标准及电子签名技术标准的统一。

电子文件是现代化的产物，没有标准化就没有现代化。从目前我国研究的现状看，对电子文件标准化这一重要课题的研究涉及还不多。因此，可以预见，随着电子文件管理的实践与理论的发展，对电子文件的标准化管理的力度将会进一步加大。毫无疑问，随着标准建设步伐的加快，我国电子文件管理将进入一个新的发展阶段。

2 工程项目电子文件接收规范的研究意义及应用说明

为保障进入工程项目电子文件管理系统的电子文件的真实性、完整性、有效性、可用性和合法性，并可系统有效地记录工程项目电子文件对管理过程，结合广东省交通厅工程项目电子文件管理系统构建及应用实践，我们对工程项目电子文件系统接收电子文件的格式和要求，电子文件元数据封装包及电子文件交换、长期保存和利用的有效形式的规范进行了探讨性研究。

规范研究拟面向工程建设项目、各类各级档案机构、机关、团体、企业事业单位和其他社会组织在电子文件管理方面进行系统研发和部署的人员及其他相关的研究开发群体。需要指出的是，我们在规范探讨中考虑到多种电子文件管理系统实现技术与语言的复杂性，未对具体实现的技术和语言做出规定，用户可根据业务实际与开发成本，自行选择所要采用的技术和语言，并对于规范中未做规定的接口可以根据业务需要进行扩充。

3 工程项目电子文件接收规范的主要内容

本节将从我们拟从接收电子文件的格式、元数据、接口及基于 XML 数据封装包等维度探讨工程项目电子文件接收规范。

3.1 接收电子文件的格式

3.1.1 PDF/A 格式

PDF（Portable Document Format 的简称，意为“便携式文件格式”）是由 Adobe 公司在 1993 年开发的一种电子文件格式。它的优点在于跨平台、能保留文件原有格式（Layout）、开放标准，能自由授权（Royalty-free）自由开发 PDF 兼容软件。因其准确、安全、高效和支持跨平台（包括硬件和软件平台）操作的显著特性，已在世界范围成为用户进行电子文档发布和存储以及数字化信息传播的理想文档格式，并在电子文件的发布与长期存储、数字化出版印刷等方面得到了广泛的应用。PDF/A 是一种 ISO 标准的 PDF 文件格式版本，用于电子文档的数字信息保存。它基于 Adobe 公司的 PDF 格式参考版本 1.4，在 2005 年 10 月 1 日发布的 ISO 标准 ISO 19005 - 1：2005 中被定义为：Document Management—Electronic document file format for long term preservation—Part 1：Use of PDF1.4（PDF/A-1）。PDF/A 实际上是专门针对电子文档长期保存而开发的 PDF 的一个子集。

3.1.2 PDF/A 格式特点及其在工程项目电子文件接收存储中的应用

（1）开放标准。2007 年 12 月，PDF 被国际标准组织（ISO）批准为 ISO 32000 国际标准。ISO 32000 开放标准可确保保存的 PDF 文件的完整性和寿命。而长期保存的版式电子文件格式要求必须格式开放透明，有公开发表的相应标准和技术规范，有与产品无关的技术专家组和标准化组支持该格式，可以免费获得阅读工具等。PDF 格式完全符合上述要求。

（2）可信。如今 PDF 已经成为众多政府和行业协会规定的标准，包括联合国教科文组织和美国、德国、英国、巴西等国政府在内的 2400 多个政府机构已将 PDF 作为电子文件交流的标准格式。

（3）多平台兼容。PDF 格式是与平台无关的文件格式，因而 PDF 文档几乎可在任何平台上查看并与之交互，包括 Windows、Mac OS 和移动平台，后者包括 AndroidTM 和适合 iPhone 和 iPad 的 iOS 系统下跨平台使用，只要安装了浏览软件，用户就可以在不同环境下原版原式地读取 PDF 文件。同时，PDF 是可以嵌入字体的。因为 PDF 格式与平台、字体的无关性，就避免了文件因长期保存或因存取原因而需要进行转换，这自然就减少了文件数据丢失的风险，也利于文件的长期保存、读取和便于资源共享。

（4）丰富的文件完整性。PDF 与原始文件一样，并保留所有源文件信息，即使将文本、绘图、视频、音频、3D 地图、彩色图形、照片和业务逻辑合并在单个文件或 PDF 包中也是如此。

（5）可搜索。当您需要在 PDF 中查找特定单词或短语时，使用光学字符识别（OCR）技术搜索文本和元数据（包括已转换的扫描文本）很简单。

（6）广泛采用。全球有数千家供应商提供基于 PDF 的解决方案、增效工具和其他工具，以及专门针对 PDF 的培训和咨询。

（7）安全可靠。PDF 支持数字签名和验签。通过对 PDF 文档进行数字签名以及加盖时间戳，可以保证文档的真实性、完整性和有效性。

（8）国家标准。2009 年 9 月 1 日，作为电子文档长期保存格式的 PDF/Archive（PDF/A）经中国国家标准化管理委员会批准，已成为正式的中华人民共和国国家标准（GB），标准号为 GB/T 23286.1—2009。

综上，从目前来看，在众多的电子文件格式中，PDF/A 格式是最符合电子文件长期保存格式需求的电子文件格式。因此，规范中我们认为工程项目电子文件由业务系统进入电子文件管理系统前，凡是能转换为 PDF/A 格式的电子文件必须转换为 PDF/A 格式，并经过有效的数字签名，确保其真实性、完整性和有效性。[6]

3.2 工程项目电子文件元数据标准的构建

工程项目电子文件元数据是描述工程项目电子文件背景、内容、结构及其整个管理过程并可为计算机及其网络系统自动辨析、分解、提取和分析归纳的数据。它既可用于保障相关工程项目电子文件的真实性、完整性、一致性、关联性和长期有效性，又可帮助对分布式网络环境下的工程项目电子文件进行有效的集成管理和协助提供集成服务，是构建工程项目数字档案馆信息组织体系必不可少的工具。因此，为了维护工程项目电子文件与其元数据的完整性，并保障两者之间的可靠联系，对于进入工程项目电子文件管理系统的电子文件元数据应全面且具有规范性与普适性。在结合《电子文件管理元数据规范》[7] 及工程项目电子文件管理实践的基础上，我们规范了工程项目电子文件的元数据。

3.2.1 构建的原则

在工程项目电子文件元数据标准构建中，我们主要以文件运动理论作为指导，遵循一致性、可扩展性、稳定性、互操作、开放性原则。其中一致性原则体现为元数据内容设计中尽量与国际、国家及行业标准相一致，以保障信息组织的一致性。可扩展性原则强调保留工程项目电子文件元数据元素的空间，并为未来的复用、细化、嵌接、修改、扩展现有元数据提供空间余地。构建中注意遵循稳定性原则，对于基本、共同、必需的元数据内容定义为一个核心元数据集，以保证工程项目电子文件管理的应用需求。同时构建中兼顾互操作原则，即在工程项目各组织机构系统间实现互操作能力支持，慎重选择元素语义，准确定义元数据元素结构。为适用不同工程项目的多种信息来源和种类，内容构建上还遵循开放性原则。

3.2.2 工程项目电子文件元数据内容

遵循以上原则并结合交通建设项目电子文件管理的实践经验，我们设计了交通建设项目电子文件元数据，从内容上看主要由元数据名称及其代码构成，其中代码由各元数据名称各字拼音首字母组成，包含了电子文件管理过程中的项目、单位、标段及文件来源系统编码体系及文件 ID、标题、原始名称、形成时间、摘要等构成。具体如表 1 所示。

表 1　交通建设项目电子文件元数据

编码	元数据	编码	元数据
XMBM	项目编码	BDBM	标段编码
DWBM	单位编码	SystemCode	文件来源系统编码
FileID	文件 ID	FileTitle	文件标题
FileName	文件原始名称（包括扩展名）	FileDate	文件形成时间
FileSHA1	文件 SHA1 值（用作签名原文，非 PDF 必需）	FileSignedData	文件 SHA1 签名值（非 PDF 必需）
FileSummary	文件摘要		

3.3 应用接口规范

信息技术的高速发展，给交通建设项目电子文件长期保存带来巨大障碍。信息技术范式转换如数字信息呈现方式和查询接口的不同造成电子文件信息传输不畅，信息流失；信息技术多样性和多种软硬电子文档管理系统存在，也会导致系统不兼容及异种结构的电子文件存在。因此，与其他业务管理软件进行电子文件交换时须遵循应用接口规范。结合电子文件管理元数据规范和交通建设项目的电子文件及电子文件管理业务流程和实践，我们设计包含响应数据包格式、返回码定义、接口细则在内的交通建设项目电子文件管理系统应用接口规范。其中响应数据包格式规范：响应数据包的格式为 XML 格式，输出内容为 UTF－8 编码格式。XML 输出形式如下：

```
<?xml version = "1.0" encoding = "UTF - 8"? >
<msginfo >
<parameters >
<parameter name = "returnCode" >0 </parameter >
    <parameter name = "returnMessage" > </parameter >
</parameters >
</msginfo >
```

并针对接口调用过程中可能会返回的代码，作出定义，具体如表2所示。

表2 返回定义码

return Code	return Message	return Code	return Message
0	成功	104	签名无效
1	未知错误	105	参数过多
2	后端服务暂时不可用	106	参数签名算法未被支持
3	接口不被支持	200	没有权限访问数据
4	应用对接口的调用请求数达到上限	301	必选参数格式错误
5	调用端的IP未被授权	302	提交字符串长度不合法
100	参数无效或缺失	303	无效的用户信息
101	访问key无效	404	应用不存在
103	SessionID参数无效或已过期	999	其他出错信息

对于与系统接口的相关细则如获取项目名称列表、获取项目标段、获取单位列表、上传文件接口等做了具体规定。

3.3.1 获取项目名称列表

采用接口原型为public String getProject（String key，String projName），其功能主要是获取建设项目编码列表。其相关参数如表3、表4所示。

表3 获取建设项目名称的相关参数

参数名	类型	描述
key	String	访问key
projName	String	建设项目名称（关键字）

表4 获取返回值的相关参数

返回值	类型	描述
XML	String	包含返回码和数据集

返回 XML 示例：


```
<?xml version="1.0" encoding="UTF-8"?>
<msginfo>
<parameters>
<parameter name="returnCode">0</parameter>
    <parameter name="returnMessage"></parameter>
</parameters>
<rowsets>
    <rowset label="建设项目信息" name="epm/ProjInfo">
        <row >
            <proj_id>31600</proj_id>
            <proj_name>梅州市梅县至大埔高速公路梅县三角至大埔三河段</proj_name>
        </row>
        <row >
            <proj_id>32200</proj_id>
            <proj_name>乐昌至广州高速公路樟市至花东段</proj_name>
        </row>
    </rowset>
</rowsets>
</msginfo>
```


3.3.2 获取项目标段

接口原型为 public String getProjPact（String key，String projID），其功能设计为获取建设项目合同段编码列表。相关参数及返回值如表 5、表 6 所示。

表 5　获取建设项目编码的相关参数

参数名	类型	描述
key	String	访问 key
projID	String	建设项目编码

表 6　获取建设项目编码的返回值

返回值	类型	描述
XML	String	包含返回码和数据集

返回 XML 示例：

```
<?xml version = "1.0" encoding = "UTF - 8"? >
    < msginfo >
    < parameters >
    < parameter name = "returnCode" >0 </parameter >
        < parameter name = "returnMessage" > </parameter >
    </parameters >
    < rowsets >
        < rowset label = "建设项目合同段信息" name = "epm/ProjPactInfo" >
            < row  >
                < pact_id >31601 </pact_id >
                < pact_name >梅大高速 TJ01 合同段 </pact_name >
            </row >
            < row  >
                < pact_id >31602 </pact_id >
                < pact_name >梅大高速 TJ02 合同段 </pact_name >
            </row >
        </rowset >
    </rowsets >
    </msginfo >
```

3.3.3 获取单位列表

接口原型为 public String getUnit（String key，String unitName），其功能是获取单位编码列表。获取单位名称及返回值参数如表 7、表 8 所示。

表 7　获取单位名称相关参数

参数名	类型	描述
key	String	访问 key
unitName	String	单位名称（关键字）

表 8　获取建设项目编码的返回值

返回值	类型	描述
XML	String	包含返回码和数据集

返回 XML 示例：

```
    <?xml version = "1.0" encoding = "UTF - 8"? >
    < msginfo >
    < parameters >
```

```
<parameter name="returnCode">0</parameter>
    <parameter name="returnMessage"></parameter>
</parameters>
<rowsets>
    <rowset label="单位信息" name="epm/UnitInfo">
        <row >
            <unit_id>24543</unit_id>
            <unit_name>XX 高速公路有限公司</unit_name>
        </row>
        <row >
            <unit_id>24672</unit_id>
            <unit_name>XX 高速 JL01 总监办</unit_name>
        </row>
    </rowset>
</rowsets>
</msginfo>
```


3.3.4 上传文件接口

接口原型为 public String uploadFile (String key, byte [ ] file, String xml)，其功能为上传电子文件及其元数据到电子文件管理系统。相关参数如表 9 所示。

表 9 上传文件接口相关参数

参数名	类型	描述
key	String	访问 key
file	byte [ ]	要上传的电子文件的字节流
xml	String	要上传的电子文件元数据 xml 封装包

XML 封装包示例：


```
<?xml version="1.0" encoding="UTF-8"?>
<msginfo>
<parameters>
<parameter name="proj_id">31600</parameter>
    <parameter name="pact_id">31601</parameter>
<parameter name="unit_id">24543</parameter>
    <parameter name="SystemCode">1</parameter>
<parameter name="FileID">03E624E1-6965-42BF-9205-F5902D041B2B</parameter>
    <parameter name="FileTitle">文件标题</parameter>
<parameter name="FileName">文件原始名称(包括扩展名)</parameter>
<parameter name="FileDate">2013-01-01 09:30:06</parameter>
```

< parameter name = " FileSHA1 " > CC9C86C1874A7C9E9C0B449ACDFD29BA98C2F573 </ parameter >
< parameter name = " FileSignedData " > MIIFgQYJKoZIhvcNAQcCoIIFcjCCBW4CAQExCTAHBgUrDg
MCGjATBgkqhkiG9w0BBwGgBgQEn1OHZaCCA/gwggP0MIIC3KADAgECAhBKKcIF9pjU0V6NQK4K/Ukk
MA0GCSqGSIb3DQEBBQUAMIGRMQswCQYDVQQGEwJDTjEOMAwGA1UEChMFTkVUQ0ExNTAzBgNVBAs
TLENsYXNzQiBUZXN0aW5nIGFuZCBFdmFsdWF0aW9uIE9yZ2FuaXphdGlvbkNBMTswOQYDVQQDEzJORV
RDQSBDbGFzc0IgVGVzdGluZyBhbmQgRXZhbHVhdGlvbiBPcmdhbml6YXRpb25DQTAeFw0xMzExMTIxNjAw
MDBaFw0xNDExMTMxNTU5NTlaMHIxCzAJBgNVBAYTAkNOMRIwEAYDVQQIEwlHdWFuZ2RvbmcxKTAn
BgNVBAceIF5/Xd5eAl5/Xd5ZJ5BTUxcAMQAzADhT9wA3AC0AOGl8MREwDwYDVQQKHgh3AVOFbUuL1
TERMA8GA1UEAx4IdwFThW1Li9UwgZ8wDQYJKoZIhvcNAQEBBQADgY0AMIGJAoGBANgko4N4sLtzp6InI3
G1esTC7o/rrx1tHW9rlffQCNNxGvmb6XqIHvakLtOH6AwpBu4dHBhdMrgICbCULee/yxuOh4z4lZPyLpvGqJw
KtvbrH5dRDPw7xdT3AAWeFzmXgnA9NNOOsDf/2A9WcKFAdsoxMPPSwOA/eH5Q0bNoO6kfAgMBAAGjgek
wgeYwHwYDVR0jBBgwFoAUSApq/8tqfApKiey + Y5ixwA0YCH4wHQYDVR0OBBYEFKCO0lYDRHyi1srXkb
KOtTlybZxoMEMGA1UdIAQ8MDowOAYKKwYBBAGBkkgFATAqMCgGCCsGAQUFBwIBFhxodHRwOi8vY2xh
c3NidGVzdGNhLmNwcy5uZXQvMAwGA1UdEwEB/wQCMAAwDgYDVR0PAQH/BAQDAgbAMEEGA1UdHw
Q6MDgwNqA0oDKGMGh0dHA6Ly9jbGFzc2FjYTEuY25jYS5uZXQvY3JsL09yZ2FuaXphdGlvbkNBLmNybDAN
BgkqhkiG9w0BAQUFAAOCAQEAhEDgrm9rxqZ2w15TbKzYZxXQN/kAIYz4ZamQYj + DHNqwkWcBvL7zoN0
LzZuZ4j/HMYLA5eSR4PY9Ch06o9 + bWgSZMEG6B63h28rpCDfjmPSwGVPyTR7D2tixDv9Zjp40uXayDzoxIT
of8Xu6cll05vWyVnaZ5nG5014QdxZBS/LqXhEJ2bFOOXpQ + /SzfY0MlHsdDYHZvci72WSjA6tWYZf5XTRdVh
Qz0muJQ4SnDXkwrUXqMUrEhf2U79te9Jh9mg5ItCL8aUbhX + cCuJzYZPpV4DR4x2pUux2LW/R98KB7Dgqd
X + CObvap7s0A48PZdWwmQM9Q5hkhiIf2T9KfQzGCAUswggFHAgEBMIGmMIGRMQswCQYDVQQGEwJD
TjEOMAwGA1UEChMFTkVUQ0ExNTAzBgNVBAsTLENsYXNzQiBUZXN0aW5nIGFuZCBFdmFsdWF0aW9uIE
9yZ2FuaXphdGlvbkNBMTswOQYDVQQDEzJORVRDQSBDbGFzc0IgVGVzdGluZyBhbmQgRXZhbHVhdGlvbiB
Pcmdhbml6YXRpb25DQQIQSinCBfaY1NFejUCuCv1JJDAHBgUrDgMCGjANBgkqhkiG9w0BAQEFAASBgAtnd
AdRL57WWH5fu + FnuZjOumIAheoNoR0Xc782heS7QamyhUK + kQaD6KTjXfOpzpyvXEpCw0ClR7gz81OT
1bq4g9Y0EKWdbq2lioSxAjpn1D7u2EoeQK2xfYEYx2LQXdHIYeMgz1Y9RRGtkB0rzAbSrS + PbZRocmXXavA/
YALB </parameter >
</parameters >
</msginfo >

其中 XML 标签说明如表 10 所示，其返回值参数类型及示例如表 11 所示。

表 10　上传文件接口相关参数

标签名	是否必填	描述
key	String	访问 key
file	byte [ ]	要上传的电子文件的字节流
xml	String	要上传的电子文件元数据 xml 封装包

表 11　上传文件接口返回值相关参数

返回值	类型	描述
XML	String	返回码

返回 XML 示例：

```
< ?xml version = "1. 0" encoding = "UTF - 8"? >
< msginfo >
< parameters >
< parameter name = "returnCode" >0 < /parameter >
    < parameter name = "returnMessage" > < /parameter >
< /parameters >
< /msginfo >
```

3.4 XML 技术要求

基于 XML 的工程项目电子文件封装的信息组织结构应该符合 ISO 14721：2003 定义的档案信息包（AIP）模型，遵从 XML 的规范。其中 EEP 文件必须是遵从 GB/T 18793—2002 的格式良好的 XML 文件。EEP 文件必须由 XML 声明开始，声明形式如下：< ?xml version = "1. 0" encoding = " UTF - 8" standalone = " no" ? >。声明的具体要求应包含如下内容：

——version 属性值必须是" 1. 0" ；

——encoding 属性值必须是" UTF - 8" ；

——standalone 属性可以缺省，若定义该属性，值必须是" no" 。

XML 命名空间。EEP 文件中应包括如下命名空间：xmlns = http://www. dyna. org. cn。而在 XML 元素的值域上，本规范规定枚举值的，表示已穷尽枚举，不应扩展；本规范没有规定枚举值的，可由用户结合实际扩展定义。

4 电子签名技术要求

在电子签名形式上，交通建设项目电子文件管理系统规范中应指明电子文件元数据封装包中的电子签名指数字签名。并采用强制电子签名形式，要求规范没有规定电子文件元数据封装时必须使用电子签名。在电子签名方法上，采取对签名对象进行签名时，被电子签名的部分从电子文件元数据封装包中“ <签名对象>” 的第一个字符“ <” 开始至“ </签名对象>” 的最后一个字符“ >” 结束。

对被签名数据的要求上，强调数据被签名时应满足以下要求：①被签名的数据必须采用 Unicode 字符集或在签名前转换为 Unicode 字符集；②所有签名数据中的空白字符必须被删除。空白字符包括 tab （0x0009）、回车（0x000D）、换行（0x000A）和空格（0x0020）；③Unicode 字符的 UTF - 8 编码二进制流用于签名和验证。签名结果的编码要求采用 Base64 进行编码。数字签名中使用的证书要求满足：①所有证书必须是 X. 509 证书；②不能用加密的形式表示证书；③签名人的私钥不能包含在封装包中；④证书应采用 Base64 进行编码。对于电子签名的验证，当验证一个电子签名时其一系列证书必须全部验证。

参考文献

[1] ICA Committee on Electronic Records. Guide for Managing Electronic Records from an Archival Perspective, 1997 [OL]. [2015-06-12]. http://www.ica.org.

[2] 刘国伟. 澳大利亚电子文件管理标准体系研究 [J]. 浙江档案, 2008 (2): 37.

[3] 段荣婷. 国际电子文件置标理论与应用研究综述 [J]. 浙江档案, 2011 (8): 36-38.

[4] 安小米. 电子文件管理标准建设的国际经验及借鉴研究 [J]. 电子政务, 2010 (6): 31.

[5] 顾玉程. 美国电子文件档案馆 (ERA) 建设状况 [J]. 中国档案, 2013 (11): 54-55.

[6] PDF/A Facts—An Introduction to the Standard [OL]. [2015-06-22]. http://www.pdfa.org/2013/02/pdfa-facts/.

[7] 电子文件管理元数据规范 [EB/OL]. [2015-06-21]. http://eakmrc.hubu.edu.cn/newscontent.aspx?articleid=1127.

教师简介：

韦景竹，女，毕业于武汉大学信息管理学院，管理学博士。现任中山大学资讯管理学院院长助理、工会主席、硕士生导师。主讲“信息描述”、“知识产权”、“信息管理概论”、“信息伦理与政策”、“信息资源管理/信息资源管理原理及案例”等课程。2008 年入选广东省高等学校“千百十工程”培养对象，2009 年入选第三届广东省宣传思想战线优秀人才“十百千工程”培养对象。研究方向包括公共文化建设、信息资源知识产权管理、网络学术信息组织、政府信息管理、信息政策与信息法律等。主持国家社会科学基金重大课题子课题一项，国家社会科学基金两项，省部级项目 6 项，校级项目 2 项，横向项目若干项。出版专著 3 本，独著被遴选入中山大学学术丛书。在国内外重要学术期刊、报纸和国际会议上发表学术论文 40 余篇。荣获广东省哲学社会科学优秀成果奖一等奖（第一作者），荣获其他省部级奖项 2 项，校级奖励 2 项。任中国社会科学情报学会常务理事、副秘书长，广东社会科学情报学会常务理事、副秘书长，中国法学会信息法学研究会会员，广东省科学技术情报学会理事，广东图书馆学会学术研究委员会委员，从化政府专家库成员，武汉大学知识产权高级研究中心兼职研究人员，《图书情报工作》特邀审稿专家、《图书馆论坛》审稿专家等。在多个国际和全国性学术会议上任中方主席、执行主席、主持人、组织委员会委员、程序委员会委员等。联系方式：weijzhu@ mail. sysu. edu. cn。

中美 LIS 学院课程设置比较研究

韦景竹，何燕华①，刘颉颃②

摘　要：采用网站调查法、文献调查法、比较分析法，调查分析了中美各十所大学图书情报专业的课程设置情况，从核心课程、选修课程、技术课程、实践课程等角度进行比较，并总结了中美两国图书情报专业课程设置的各自特点与不同点，以期为我国图书情报教育提供参考。

关键词：图书情报学；课程设置；信息教育

A Comparative Study of Library and Information Science Curriculum between China and America

Jingzhu Wei, Yanhua He, Xiehang Liu

Abstract: Using website survey method and Literature survey method, this paper investigates and analyses library and information science curriculum of ten universities in both China and America. The paper is to compare and summarize difference and characteristics of library and information science curriculum between China and

① 何燕华，中山大学资讯管理学院 2009 级硕士研究生。

② 刘颉颃，中山大学资讯管理学院 2009 级硕士研究生。

America, and provide experience for domestic library and information science education.
Keywords: Library and information science; Curriculum; LIS education.

信息环境的变化使图书情报学教育面临不断发展与完善的机遇与挑战。优化课程设置、完善课程体系，对提高图书情报学教育水平具有重大意义。本文采用调查法与比较法，选取美国图书情报专业排名前十的大学以及中国十所重点高校，以网站调查为主，并结合文献调查分析法，比较、总结中美两国图书情报学课程设置的异同，以期为我国图书情报学教育发展提供借鉴。

1　美国图书情报专业课程设置

根据2010年《美国新闻与世界报道》（*U. S. News & World Report*）的排名[1]，美国图书情报专业排名前十的学校依次是伊利诺伊大学、北卡罗来纳大学教堂山分校（以下简称北卡大学）、雪城大学、华盛顿大学西雅图分校、密歇根大学安娜堡分校、罗格斯新泽西州立大学新伯朗士威校区、印第安纳大学伯明顿分校、德州大学奥斯汀分校（以下分别简称华盛顿大学、密歇根大学、罗格斯大学、印第安纳大学、德州大学）、德雷塞尔大学、西蒙斯学院。

1.1　不同学校课程设置情况的比较

1.1.1　核心课程

上述十所大学图书情报专业的核心课程设置都较重视管理、信息组织、信息服务、职业与技术等方面。其中，10所大学都开设了管理类方面的课程（含信息机构管理与资源管理），8所大学开设了信息组织方面的课程，8所大学开设了信息服务方面的课程（含参考咨询、用户服务等），4所大学开设了信息职业方面的课程。此外，10所大学中除德州大学奥斯汀分校外，都开设了信息技术方面的核心课程，既包括基础技术类课程，如信息架构、信息工具、信息系统基础等，也有与图书馆紧密相关的技术类课程，如数字图书馆、图书馆与信息技术、信息处理基础，还开设了网络信息技术方面的课程，以顺应图书馆与信息行业的发展对网络技术的要求（表1）。

表1　美国排名前十信息学院核心课程设置情况

学校	核心课程
伊利诺伊大学	信息组织与获取，图书馆、信息与社会，参考咨询与信息服务，图书馆及信息机构的管理，编目与分类Ⅰ，网络系统导论，图书情报科学信息处理基础
北卡大学	文献组织，信息资源与服务，资源选择与评价，人类信息交互，研究方法，信息职业的管理，学位论文，信息工具

续表 1

学校	核心课程
雪城大学	信息和信息环境，图书馆和信息职业概论，参考咨询与信息素质服务，图书馆规划、营销与评估，信息资源：组织和存取，管理理论与信息职业，通讯与信息政策纵览
华盛顿大学	生命周期理论，信息行为，信息资源、服务和馆藏，信息与资源的组织，社会环境下的信息，信息职业指导与培训策略，研究方法，信息机构的管理，4 个学分的技术课程（信息检索，XML，数据库设计，网络系统管理）
密歇根大学	社会系统中的信息：收集、流动与处理，语境咨询与项目管理，网络化计算机运作：信息存储、交流及处理
罗格斯大学	用户信息行为，信息组织、检索原理，图书馆与信息代理的信息技术，图书馆与信息中心管理，信息专业知识架构
印地安纳大学	参考咨询，馆藏发展与管理，信息资源展示与管理，编目，图书馆管理，大学图书馆管理，公共图书馆管理，学校媒体，研究导论，信息系统评估，资源与服务评估
	情报学导论，信息架构，数据库设计，人机交互，组织情报学，编程需求，系统分析和设计，基于电脑的信息工具
德州大学	情报学导论，用户服务与分析，信息组织与获取，信息服务与信息组织中的管理，情报学研究导论
德雷塞尔大学	信息职业的社会内容，信息用户与服务，信息获取与信息资源，档案学基础，信息系统基础与展望，数字图书馆，管理信息组织，组织中的知识财产管理，数字图书馆技术，信息架构，图书馆自动化，馆藏管理，信息专家角色教育
西蒙斯学院	信息服务评价，管理学原理，参考咨询/信息服务，信息组织，信息专业技术

1.1.2 选修课程

上述十所大学的选修课程涉及面广，课程较为细化。总的来说，十所大学选修课程都非常重视信息组织、资源、服务、管理、技术方面，所占的比例也相对较高。其中，8所大学开设了信息组织与检索相关选修课程。信息资源类相关课程，除印地安纳大学外，其他 9 所大学都较为细化，细分为政府信息、企业信息、法律信息、医学信息、健康信息、人文社会科学信息等；而信息服务相关课程更以特定对象作划分，如特定用户的信息服务、讲故事、儿童文献、青少年服务等课程；管理学相关的课程，主要包括图书馆管理（人力资源、财务管理等）、项目管理与评估、服务与组织的营销等方面。选修课中的技术类相关课程相对核心课程而言，内容更具体深入，主要集中在数据库、网页设计、信息系统、人机交互、信息检索等方面（表 2）。

表 2　美国排名前十信息学院选修课程设置情况

学校	课程方向的设置	课程示例（仅列举部分）
伊利诺伊大学	信息组织与知识表达	信息资源表示及组织，网络结构与信息构建，知识表达及形式本体论等
	信息资源、利用及用户	信息利用及信息用户，健康信息资源与服务，政府信息等
	信息系统	系统分析与管理，信息存储与检索，搜索引擎与信息检索系统等
	历史、经济、政策	图书史，全球化通讯及信息政治经济学，信息政策等
	管理与评价	特殊馆藏管理，人力资源管理，信息服务营销，评价项目与服务等
	青少年文学及服务	青少年文学与资源，讲故事，面向青少年的智识自由与图书馆服务等
北卡大学	高校图书馆	特定用户的信息服务，教学与艺术人生研讨会，人文社会科学信息等
	公共图书馆的青少年服务	讲故事，青年用户服务的管理，公共图书馆研讨会，儿童文学表演等
	信息与文献组织	信息检索，数据库Ⅱ：中级数据库，元数据构建与应用，文档挖掘等
	参考咨询	企业信息，健康科学信息，音乐图书馆，用户视角的信息系统与服务等
	学校媒体	学校图书馆媒体中心，信息伦理，课程问题与学校馆员等
	专门图书馆与知识管理	专门图书馆与知识管理，企业信息，法律图书馆与法律信息等
雪城大学	服务与资源	法律信息资源与服务，生物医学信息，讲故事，信息职业战略与技能指引
	组织、检索与获取	基于网络服务的信息构建，数据挖掘，知识管理，编目，分类与主题描述理论
	信息系统设计、实施与管理	信息系统分析，网络环境下的信息安全，电子商务，通讯与网络管理技术
华盛顿大学	信息组织	编目与分类，信息与资源组织专题研讨，索引与文摘等
	信息系统	信息系统设计，信息检索系统，信息系统、结构与检索等
	资源和服务	信息资源、服务与收集专题研讨，企业信息资源，健康科学信息需求等
	儿童、青少年、成年	讲故事，少年文献的评价与利用，公共图书馆的青年用户服务等
	学校图书馆、资源与服务	信息素质，图书馆的计划与营销，图书情报学专题研讨等

续表 2

学校	课程方向的设置	课程示例（仅列举部分）
密歇根大学	信息表达、组织和检索	信息检索之人机交互，数据库应用设计，网页存档，信息检索，信息资源组织
	文献知识：内容和收集	儿童与青少年媒体，图书与印刷品历史，信息素质，数字化与保存等
	信息需求、利用和环境	信息查找行为，非营利图书馆与信息服务的管理，职业实习，社区信息利用等
罗格斯大学	人机交互	界面设计，信息媒体与课程，儿童与青少年服务，用户教育等
	信息组织	元数据等
	信息获取	馆藏发展与管理，手稿与档案，政府信息资源，竞争情报，儿童读物等
	信息系统	信息可视化与展示，多媒体产品，数据库设计与管理，管理信息系统等
	管理学	图书馆与信息组织的财务管理，教育媒体中心管理，媒体中心管理等
	信息与社会	儿童文学的历史，成人阅读兴趣，图书文档印本记录及电子环境历史等
印地安纳大学	图书馆学	图书馆服务与信息服务实习，图书信息学专题研究，本体等
	情报学	网络技术与管理，定向研究，图书信息学研修班，图书信息学专题研究等
德州大学	信息管理	信息服务与组织的管理，信息项目评价，社会中的信息，信息营销等
	信息组织与信息系统	信息检索与评价，图书馆技术的规划与管理，知识管理系统，编目与元数据等
	资源和服务	馆藏管理，信息服务：理论、技术与主题，网络信息，信息素养等
	专业信息资源	儿童读物，电子资源与服务，儿童资料，青少年资料，法律信息资源等
	资源保藏与文献修复	文献修复和实习，可持续的数字化保存，电子记录长期保存相关问题等
德雷塞尔大学	档案学与文献保护	档案学，档案评价，数字化保藏等
	信息系统	知识库系统，实用数据库技术，人机交互，信息检索系统等
	信息服务	公共图书馆服务，组织中的信息服务，数字参考咨询服务等
	专业信息资源	健康信息，特藏，社会科学资源，商业资源，法律研究等
	信息组织	元数据与资源描述，编目与分类，内容表达等

续表2

学校	课程方向的设置	课程示例（仅列举部分）
西蒙斯学院	信息技术与系统	信息检索，数字图书馆，多媒体技术与信息管理，网页开发和信息架构等
	信息服务	用户教育，青少年图书馆服务，讲故事，数字信息服务，弱势群体服务等
	档案学	档案方法与服务导论，档案获取与利用，档案与手稿评估等
	专业信息资源与服务	儿童信息资源，商业信息源和服务，医学图书馆事业，儿童文学等
	信息与社会	社会信息学，信息政策相关问题，口述历史，信息自由和审查制度等

1.1.3 专业社会实践课程

形式上，这些学校的专业社会实践课多以顶点课程、实习等形式出现，且必须完成一定的学分，实习日志、实习报告及论文等是大多数实习课程必需的。内容上，有的偏重于学校图书馆的工作实践，如西蒙斯学院的实习课程分为幼儿园到高中（preK-12）、幼儿园到初中（preK-8）阶段的图书馆工作等；有的结合本学院自身特色，提供专业实习课程，如德州大学在文献保护、馆藏修复等方面提供实习项目；有的偏重信息服务方面，如德雷塞尔大学的实习课程集中在组织中的信息服务、信息系统管理、竞争情报方面，密歇根大学则提供循证医疗健康信息的实习。华盛顿大学的实践课程分为两部分，一是作为必修课的毕业前实习，要求在图书馆或相关信息机构实习100～200个小时；二是选修的指导性实习，提供图书馆、档案馆的实习，包含参考咨询、数据库开发、网页设计、青少年服务等工作，成为该校iSchool最受欢迎课程之一。

1.1.4 技术课程

技术类课程主要涉及信息系统与信息管理这一类。其中，数字图书馆、信息检索系统、系统分析与管理、管理信息系统、人机交互、数据库等是技术类核心课程，而文本挖掘、信息可视化、知识管理、网络技术与分布式计算等课程的设置紧跟图书情报领域信息技术发展的最新动向。其中，雪城大学图书情报学、印地安纳大学情报学开设的技术类课程体系完备、内容较为先进。技术类课程的设置往往针对不同的背景与需求，提供具有层次区分的课程内容。如德雷塞尔大学为数字图书馆方向的学生提供高级数据库管理、数字图书馆技术等选修课程。

1.1.5 特色课程

除较为核心、普遍的课程外，一些学校在课程设置上体现了独有的特色。

（1）学科内特色课程。特色课程如非洲书目（伊利诺伊大学）、东南亚书目（西蒙斯学院）、音乐书目（密歇根大学）等，希望学生了解各种书目并掌握检索特定地域或专门领域信息资源的技巧；伊利诺伊大学的词库建设课程，要求学生学会自建词库，掌握词库建设的理论与实践；艺术与视觉信息管理（北卡大学）、从查理大帝到古腾堡的中世纪手稿（西蒙斯学院）等课程，重视特殊信息资源的管理；少数民族地区之信息查找行为（华盛顿大学）、弱势群体服务的问题与对策（西蒙斯学院）等，关注特殊群体的信息服务问题；德州大学奥斯汀分校开设企业档案课以及专门讲授如何寻求信息研究资助的课程。

（2）跨学科课程。十所大学中，大部分学校开设了跨学科的课程，如全球化通讯及信息政治经济学、信息经济学、美国通讯史、财政管理、图书情报学的法律问题（伊利诺伊大学），法律研究（华盛顿大学）、口述历史（西蒙斯学院）、图书馆建筑与空间设计（西蒙斯学院），体现了图书情报学与其他学科的交叉渗透，北卡还推荐学生选修一门本校商学院或政务学院的课程。

（3）职业环境与指导课。一些大学着重培养学生的职业意识，开设了职业环境与指导方面的课程，如，信息职业中的种族与性别、信息职业的社会公平（伊利诺伊大学）、图书馆和信息职业概论（雪城大学）、信息职业指导与培训策略（华盛顿大学）、信息职业的社会内容（德雷塞尔大学）。

2 美国图书情报专业课程设置比较和特点

2.1 相同课程之比较

不同学校的课程设置各不相同，而对于同一门课程，不同学校的理解与安排也不尽相同。同一门课程在某个学校被设为核心课程，而在另一些学校可能为选修课，其选修的前提与课程内容也可能存在差异。例如，数字图书馆课在德雷塞尔大学为核心课程，而在雪城大学为选修课；编目与分类课，在伊利诺伊大学为核心课程，而在华盛顿大学与德雷塞尔大学都为选修课，选修前提各不相同，前者要求已修信息与资源组织及信息生命周期理论课，后者要求已选修信息获取与信息资源且成绩至少达到 C。课程内容上，雪城大学的数字图书馆课程着重使学生掌握数字图书馆的信息表达、检索机制及数字图书馆的社会政治环境，德雷塞尔大学则关注数字图书馆的历史发展与趋势、数字化保存与保护以及用户界面设计等内容；编目与分类课程，在伊利诺伊大学与华盛顿大学是介绍基本理论、标准和实践，这两所大学还开设编目与分类Ⅱ或高级编目与分类，深入讲授更为复杂的编目与分类，着重介绍如何对各种类型资源进行编目与分类，而德雷塞尔大学却没有专门讲授这方面内容。

2.2 特点总结

2.2.1 课程细分程度高

如多数大学对信息资源的讲授细分为人文社科信息资源、法律信息资源、生物信息资源、健康信息资源、政府信息资源、商业信息资源等，如此细化的课程适应了信息相关职业对不同专业领域知识的需求，有利于培养更为专业更具竞争力的图书情报人才。有人提出“图书馆员好像什么都知道一点，但对特定领域又知之甚少”[2]，馆员仅具备单一专业背景难以满足用户多元化的需求，不利于提供优质服务，也可能使图书馆花费大量经费购买的各学科纸本资源及电子数据库闲置。

2.2.2 重视信息管理与信息技术课程

十所大学都开设了信息管理与信息技术课程，皆居于核心课程之列，且占课程总量的比例较高，如雪城大学开设的技术类课程占全部课程的1/3之多。纵观这十所大学开设此类课程的情况，可以看出，信息管理学作为一门研究信息与人复杂而紧密关系的学科，希望通过技术类课程，从人或组织的角度关注信息技术，如北卡开设的用户界面设计、用户视角的信息系统与服务，雪城大学开设的自然语言处理，罗格斯大学开设的以用户为中心的信息服务与系统的设计等课程，这些课程还体现出对信息技术之于信息创造、传播、存取、管理等方面影响的关注。

2.2.3 注重用户相关的课程

十所大学均开设用户相关课程，主要包括以下三个方面：①用户信息行为。如华盛顿大学开设的少数民族语言地区的信息查找行为课，罗格斯大学开设的用户信息行为课。②用户研究与分析。如德州大学开设的用户研究与用户服务与分析，德雷塞尔大学开设的信息用户与服务，北卡大学开设的特定用户的信息服务等课程。③针对不同用户的信息资源与服务。十所大学都开设了此类课程，旨在将信息资源与服务按用户需求细分。

2.2.4 学院定位在一定程度上影响课程体系的构建

从调研来看，各信息学院的自我定位和对图书情报专业的理解直接影响到课程体系的建设。以下以伊利诺伊大学与雪城大学为例说明。

伊利诺伊大学信息学院的使命被定义为："引领科学、社会、文化、商业等领域信息认识与利用上的变革，改变人类日常生活。"目标是培养学生对专业基础、原理、观念、职业等方面的理论知识与实践技能，使学生学会预测社会与技术的变化并推动信息职业的变革、锻炼专业研究批判性思维以及掌握信息服务的发展与评价。[3]据此，该院设置了六个课程方向，其"预测社会与技术的变革"的培养目标引领了"历史、经济、政策"等课程方向的设置，"管理与评价"方面课程的设置则受到"掌握信息服务的发展与评价"培养目标的影响。

雪城大学信息学院的使命定位是"用信息扩展人类能力"，认为学院的竞争力在于提供计算机科学、管理、信息科学课程及相关项目的教学科研，并基于用户及用户信息需求整合信息及信息技术。[4]受此影响，该院目前共开设了23门技术类课程，占64门课程总数的34%，形成了偏重技术并拥有技术优势的课程体系。

3 中美课程设置比较及结论

为掌握国内图书情报专业课程设置的整体情况，笔者选取了国内不同地区"211工程"学校共十所，包括武汉大学、北京大学、中山大学、南京大学、南开大学、浙江大学、四川大学、东北师范大学、华东师范大学、华南师范大学，对这些高校图书情报专业本科与硕士课程进行了调查。限于篇幅，本文省略了对这十所高校图书情报专业课程设置调研结果的整体性描述，而将部分调研结果分散使用在比较分析的过程中。

美国大学的图书馆学专业不开设本科层次教育，硕士教育大多整合了图书馆学与情报学专业，只有个别学校分别开设。在教学内容上，尝试突破以“图书馆”为对象的局限，突出以信息为中心的导向，关注图书情报学的内在本质联系，整合教学内容。[5]我国图书馆学与情报学专业为独立开设，且这两个专业都包含本科与硕士层次的教育。以下将从核心课程、选修课程、技术课程、实践课程、职业指导课程等方面比较中美图书情报专业的课程设置。

3.1 核心课程

在美国十所大学图书情报专业的核心课程中，信息组织、信息服务、技术、管理与职业指导等方面课程占了很大比重。我国在 2003 年的湘潭会议上确定了 7 门图书馆学专业本科核心课程：图书馆学基础、信息组织、信息描述、信息资源共享、信息存储与检索、数字图书馆、目录学概论。[6]这 7 门课程也是本次调查的国内高校图书馆学本科核心课程中比较集中的课程。可以看出，中美在核心课程的设置方面有一定的重合。我国图书馆学本科教育技术与职业方面的核心课程比例较小，硕士核心课程更多侧重研究性，注重培养专业研究型人才，而美国的相关课程教育则关注培养应用型人才。有研究人员指出，图书情报专业核心课程应由反映图书情报专业与职业本质特征的不同课程组成，而这些课程既包括理论知识，又涉及专业技能。[7]应根据学科发展和社会环境的变化，构建实用而科学的核心课程体系，使课程在反映学科本质的同时，既体现学科传统，也紧跟学科和社会发展的前沿。

3.2 选修课程

美国十所大学图书情报专业的选修课具有数目多、范围广、注重技术与实践、学科交叉性强、细化深入等特点，学生的自主选择空间较大，有助于构建满足学生意愿与需求的知识结构。此外，这些大学的选修课程大多分方向而设，如信息组织、资源与服务等方向，在每个方向下开设若干相关课程，可帮助学生增强对学科体系和课程间联系的认识。与此同时，课程细分程度高使课程具有较强的针对性与实用性，有利于培养竞争力较强的应用性信息人才。我国图书情报专业的选修课程数目也较多，但体现学科交叉的课程少，且无清晰划分课程模块，课程内容的深度与广度存在局限。研究人员指出，图书馆工作中对情报学、通讯学知识的需求越来越大，图书情报专业课程应体现出图书馆学、情报学和通讯学科的交叉。[8]根据调研结果，我们认为，应对专业选修课程体系加以改革，细化课程设置，强化课程间的联系，注重课程的整体性和实用性。同时开设与职业需求相关的学科交叉课程，以培养较高综合素质、较强竞争力的信息人才。

3.3 技术课程

无论在美国还是在中国，技术类课程都属于图书情报学科的核心课程，一些大学对毕业生的调查结果也显示图书情报学科的教育需更多地侧重信息技术。[9]相比较而言，美国大学开设的技术类课程注重先进技术及理念在图书情报领域的应用与发展，国内开设的课程更为关注技术的基础应用及发展趋势；美国同行通过选修课、高级课程等方式开设内容深浅不同的课程，在完备性与层次化方面优于国内高校。国内多数高校开设的技术类课程略显单一，同时需要在技术的功能实现与用户需求之间寻找更好的切合点。正如有学者所指出的那样，使我们的学生既懂技术又懂管理，形成专业的核心能力。[10]

3.4 实践课程

在瑞典实施的一项关于图书情报教育的调研中提出，图书馆学的实践应该存在于更广泛的社会背景之中，需提高学生理解与分析学科环境的能力。[11]专业社会实践课程就是为帮助学生理解认识该职业的社会角色，并了解该角色是如何受到社会变革的影响。中美高校信息学院都较重视学生的社会实践能力，要求提交实习日志、实习报告等以检验效果。国内高校近几年对学生的社会实践重视度增加，但社会实践课程内容普遍趋同，在具体操作上略显粗糙。美国高校多在顶点课程的框架下组织专业实践课程，形式多样，内容细分程度较高，更注重与相关公司或信息机构合作进行实习基地建设，如雪城大学通过设立由国内外公司组成的咨询理事会，不断加强与有关公司的合作，保证学生的实践机会。[12]而这方面国内也需加强。

3.5 职业指导课程

美国大学注重开设与图书馆或信息职业相关的职业指导课程，如职业环境、职业规划、职业管理、职业培训策略、职业内容等方面的课程，且大多被列为核心课程。相比而言，一方面，我国高校图书情报专业提供的职业指导课针对性不够，如就业指导课、职业规划与领导能力等课程，多为适用于所有专业的通用而笼统的指导，缺少针对图书情报行业的专门职业指导；另一方面，国内很多高校的职业指导课程仅在高年级开设，这就使学生无充足时间做职业规划和准备，也无法排解学生可能产生的专业抗拒情绪。

4 尾论和研究展望

虽然笔者花费了大量时间和精力对中美各10所高校信息学院的课程设置进行了调研、整理和总结、比较，并引用了相关文献进行印证，但我们也认识到，本研究存在明显不足：首先，课程内容问题。课程名称及课程描述虽有助于对该课程内容进行初步判断并作为比较的基础，但由于客观原因笔者并不能深入地知晓被调研课程的具体内容和讲授深浅程度，在未来的研究中需增加访谈法和现场观察法以弥补该不足。其次，课程名称问题。由于跨语言障碍及相关专业知识的局限，本研究中美国高校的课程名称及相关译文的准确性也可能存在欠缺。最后，国内高校选择的典型性问题。笔者的选择标准主要有两个：一是否是“211 工程”的高校，本研究选择的高校全部在“211 工程”高校之列；二是不同地区，本文在参考了国内相关大学图书情报档专业排名的同时，强调了所选高校所在的区域不同。这两个标准可能会使国内高校的选择在代表性上有所不足。

本研究基于中美图书情报专业课程设置调研进行总结、比较，并以此为基础进行了简单评价。但我们同时认为，从课程设置本身评价课程体系并不是科学的。本文没有涉及评价课程体系的标准和原则，而评价标准和原则亦受到诸多因素的制约，如已毕业学生、雇主、用人单位的反馈、在读学生及家长的期望、社会环境的要求等。有文献强调图书情报学院明显需要清楚他们的新生、在读生的职业期待和毕业生所在的岗位，惟其如此，才能提供一流的课程，也才能最大化地提升他们的技能以胜任其工作。[13]另有文献指出，发展和健全学科课程体系，在设置课程之前充分了解用户的需求非常重要。[14]图书馆学情报学应理论联系实际，并要在实践中反思。[15]有研究人员认为由于图书情报本身是一个多学科组成的专业领域，所以讨论其核心课程就像讨论生命的意义一样徒劳无功。[11]更进一步而言，只有好的课程体系也不一定能促进学科的发展，还应注意全面评估影响和制约学科发展的其他因素。[16]而这些将是未来的研究重点。

参考文献

[1] Library and Information Studies Programs [EB/OL]. [2010-05-08]. http://www.usnewsuniversitydirectory.com/graduate-schools/library-information-studies.aspx.

[2] Wilson K, Train B. The Future of Business Information Services and Schools Library Services [EB/OL]. [2010-08-08]. http://www.sheffield.ac.uk/content/1/c6/07/01/24/CPLIS%20-%20The%20Future%20of%20Business%20Information%20Services.pdf.

[3] University of Illinois at Urbana-Champaign. Master of Science Degree [EB/OL]. [2010-05-10]. http://www.lis.illinois.edu/academics/programs/ms.

[4] Syracuse University. About the School [EB/OL]. [2010-05-16]. http://ischool.syr.edu/about/.

[5] 肖希明，卢娅. 论图书馆学情报学教育的整合 [J]. 图书情报工作，2009（5）：7-10.

[6] 潘燕桃. 中国大陆图书馆学教育发展现状及社会需求调查 [J]. 中国图书馆报，2009（6）：29-40.

[7] Audunson R. LIS and the Creation of a European Educational Space [J]. Journal of Librarianship and Information Science, 2005 (4): 71-174.

[8] Larsen L R. Libraries Need iSchool [J]. Library Journal, 2007 (10): 11.

[9] Bravo B R. Library and Information Science Graduates from Spain: Professional Training and Workforce Entry Profiles [EB/OL]. (2005-06-08) [2010-08-02].

[10] 挑战与机遇，传承与创新：数字时代图书馆学情报学教育展望——第二届中美数字时代图书馆学情报学教育国际研讨会访谈之一 [J]. 图书情报知识，2006（6）：6.

[11] Audunson R. Library and Information Science Education: Is There a Nordic Perspective [EB/OL]. [2010-08-02]. http://archive.ifla.org/IV/ifla71/papers/061e-Audunson.pdf.

[12] Tampone K. New Dean Outlines iSchool Relationship with Business [J]. The Central New York Business Journal, 2008 (7).

[13] Weech T L, Konieczny A M. Alternative Careers for Graduates of LIS Schools: The North American Perspective—An Analysis ofthe Literature [J]. Journal of Librarianship and Information Science, 2007, 39: 67-78.

[14] Tedd L A. The What? and How? of Education and Training for Information Professionals in a Changing World: Some Experiences from Wales, Slovakia and the Asia-Pacific Region [J]. Journal of Information Science, 2003, 29 (1): 76-86.

[15] Edwards P M. Theories-in-Use and Reflection-in-Action: Core Principles for LIS Education [J]. Journal of Education for Library & Information Science, 2010, 51 (1): 18-29.

[16] Johnson I M. Education for Librarianship and Information Studies: Fit for Purpose? [J]. Information Development, 2009, 25 (3): 175-177.

教师简介：

王乐球，男，1994 年毕业于浙江大学，获硕士学位。2001 年起任教于中山大学资讯管理学院。主讲“Java 语言”、“程序设计”等课程。研究方向包括信息管理、电子商务、数据库应用。联系方式：wangleqiu@ 21cn. com。

所选论文《构建高校“程序设计基础”微课程的探索》拟发表于《软件导刊》2015 年第 10 期或第 11 期

构建高校“程序设计基础”微课程的探索*

王乐球

摘　要： 微课程是一种基于信息技术的新型教学资源和教学模式，构建高校“程序设计基础”微课程可以实现课程教学的灵活性，启发学生对程序设计知识和技能的主动探索。本文介绍微课程的概念和发展背景、构建“程序设计基础”微课程的意义，进行“程序设计基础”微课程的架构设计和微课的脚本设计、微课的拍摄与录制。“程序设计基础”微课程的构建，有利于推动高校师资团队的建设和专业建设，有利于提高高校计算机类专业人才培养质量。

关键词： 微课程；微课；教学模式；程序设计基础

The Exploration of Building Micro-Course of “Basis of Program Design” in Colleges

Leqiu Wang

Abstract: The micro-course is a new kind of teaching resource and model based on information technology. Building the micro-course of program design in college can achieve the flexibility of teaching and enlighten students to explore programming knowledge and skills initiatively. This paper introduces the concept of micro-course and development background, the importance of building program designing micro-course. Furthermore, it designs the frame and script of the program design micro-course, as well as recording of the micro-course. Building the micro-course of program design is beneficial not only to promoting the development of teachers team construction, but also to the quality of computer professional training in colleges.

Keywords: Micro-Course; Micro-Class; Teaching model; The basis of program design

* 该文系国家中小科技型企业创新基金“基于 BIM/BLM 的同望工程决算管理系统”、广东省中小科技型企业创新基金“Listener 客服数据分析及运营辅助决策系统”成果之一。

1 引　言

随着微课程的兴起、高等教育信息化的深度应用和智能移动终端的逐渐普及，越来越多的高校一线教师尝试在教育教学中应用微课程。“程序设计基础”课程作为一门重要的高校计算机类专业技能基础课程，是一门实践性较强的课程，该课程对引导计算机类专业学生进行专业学习和对学生的程序设计逻辑思维培养起着非常重要的作用。构建高校“程序设计基础”微课程可以实现课程教学的灵活性，将启发学生对程序设计知识和技能的主动探索，必将引起深刻的课堂教学模式变革。

2 微课程

微课程（micro-course）是运用构建主义方法，以在线学习或移动学习为手段，具有完整的课程设计、开发、实施、评价等教学设计环节的课程教学模式。微课程概念于2008 年率先由美国新墨西哥州圣胡安学院的高级教师戴维·彭罗斯提出，是针对某专题的系列教学内容和教学活动的总和，课程教学载体是时长约 10 分钟的教学视频。微课程的“微”体现在时间、内容、资源容量，对专业学科的抽象知识点、需要复杂设备的实验操作和疑难问题等教学内容具有重要意义。目前在国内外微课程受到越来越多的研究者关注，成为一种课程建设的新趋势。[1]

2.1 微课与微课程

“微课”是“微型教学视频课例”的简称，而“微课程”是“微课”的高级阶段或发展趋势。

2.2 翻转课堂与微课程

翻转课堂（“Flipped Classroom”或“Inverted Classroom”）是指重新调整课堂内外的时间，将学习的决定权从教师转移给学生的一种教学模式。在翻转课堂教学模式下，课堂内学生更专注于“项目导向，任务驱动”的学习，师生共同研究解决课程任务问题，使学生获得更深入的理解和更熟练的实操。课程涉及的知识和技能，学生在课前完成课程内容的自主学习，学生可进行随时随地学习，学习途径有观看课程视频、听播客、阅读电子参考书、与别的同学在网络上进行学习讨论、在网上查阅课程参考材料等，学生自主规划学习内容、学习节奏；教师不再用课堂时间讲授课程知识和技能，在课堂时间更多地与学生交流，采用实操演示法、讨论协作法来引导学生进行更深入的学习，课堂教学演变为师生交流、生生间互动的学习，以达到更好的教育效果。翻转课堂是一种大教育运动模式，在本质上它与探究性学习、混合式学习等教学方法在内涵定义上有相似之处，是为了实现“以学生为本”的教学目标，提高学生的参与度，使学生学习更加主动和灵活。[2]

翻转课堂是一种基于微课程资源的新型教学模式，将微课程与翻转课堂有机结合，在课前学生利用微课程资源进行自主学习，在课堂上教师解答学生疑问、测试学生自学效果、指导学生学习实践，在课后学生利用微课程资源进行复习巩固、作业练习。

2.3 微课程的特点

微课程具有六项特点：①视频时间较短，一个“微课”教学视频时长控制在5～15分钟，不宜超过15分钟；②教学内容较少，“微课”的教学内容知识点单一、主题突出、问题聚焦，主要是针对教学中某个学科知识点（如教学中的重点难点、疑点内容）的教学，或是课堂中某教学环节的教与学活动；③资源容量小，一个“微课”视频及配套资源的总容量一般为几十MB，视频格式一般支持在线播放的流媒体格式（如.rm、.wmv、.flv等）；④资源组成“情景化”，微课程以“微课”视频为主线进行课程教学设计，微课视频、多媒体素材、课件、教师课后教学反思等相关教学资源完整构成“微课资源包”；⑤微课程内容具体，一个微课程研究的问题来源于教育教学具体实践中的具体问题，或是教学反思，或是重点强调，或是难点突破，或是学习策略、教学方法、教育教学观点等，呈现具体性、真实性等特点；⑥传播方式多样，可使用手机传播、网上下载传播、微博讨论等多种形式进行传播。

3 开发“程序设计基础”微课程的意义

“程序设计基础”课程是一门重要的计算机类专业技能基础课程，它是一门高校培养学生程序设计逻辑和思维的入门课程。通过本课程的学习，可以培养学生程序设计的理念，促使学生使用计算机程序解决现实世界中业务逻辑的问题，使学生学会程序设计的基本方法。该门课程是一门理实一体化课程，在第一学期开设，其前导课程没有特别要求，后续课程是“面向对象的程序设计基础”，包括C#和Java两种语言方向，任选其一。软件技术专业的课程体系结构如图1所示。

3.1 对教师的意义

对于高校教师，进行“程序设计基础”微课程的建设，学习先进的微课程理念，进行微课程的总体设计，应用计算机技术和多媒体技术等进行微课视频制作，将先进的微课程教学模式应用于“程序设计基础”课程，这将促进教师专业发展与信息化教学手段应用，促使教师对课程教学进行总体设计、内容更新和反思总结，革新传统的课程教学教研方式，进行课程改革和探索新型的课程教学模式。这将提高教师的教学能力，提高教师课程建设能力，成为教师专业成长的重要途径。

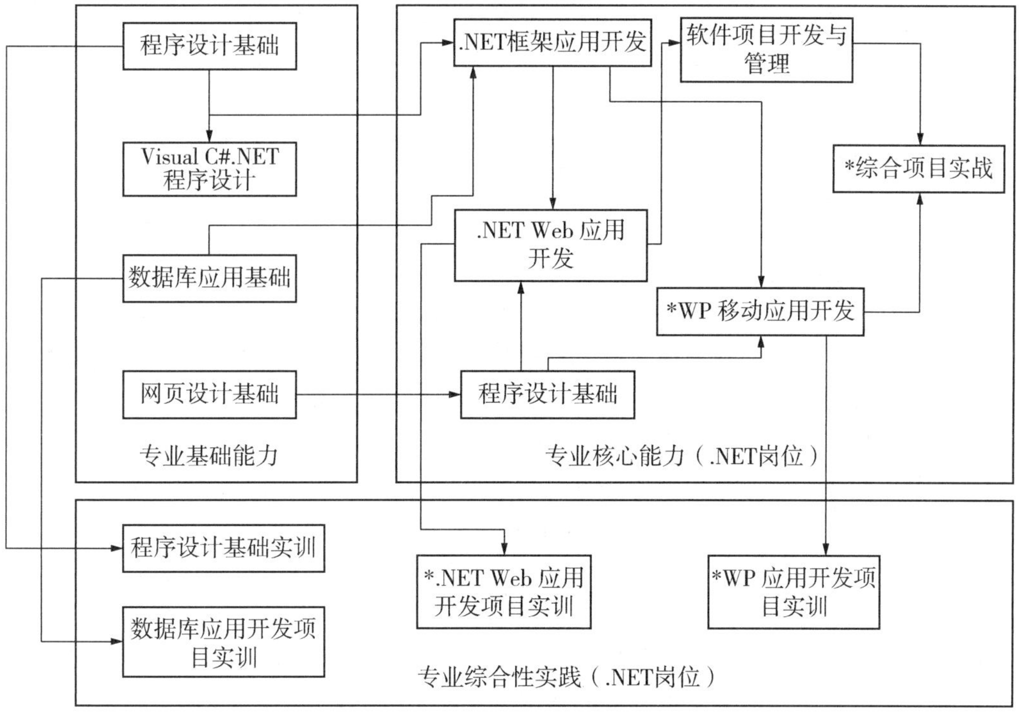

图 1　软件技术专业 .NET 方向的课程体系结构

3.2　对学生的意义

对于高校学生，在进入大学学习的初期，通过"程序设计基础"微课程的应用，"程序设计基础"课程的学习由"以教师为主"改变为"以学生为主"，课程教学由教师单方向的讲授改变为师生共同探索和实践，学生根据自己原有的知识架构主动与外界环境进行交互、探索、发现，这有利于激发学生专业学习兴趣，增强学生程序设计和程序开发实践能力，培养自学能力和主动学习的动力，为计算机类专业课程的学习打下良好基础，从而提高计算机类专业学生培养质量。

4　"程序设计基础"微课程的设计

首先确定微课程设计原则，然后进行微课程设计。"程序设计基础"微课程的设计过程为：微课程架构设计、微课程教学方案设计、微课程制作、微课程存储、微课程发布、微课程评价。[3]

4.1　微课程设计原则

（1）微课程总体设计原则。微课程改变传统教学中师生角色，实现"以学生为主"

的学习。这需要对课程教学时间重新规划，教师细分教学知识点和实操技能，围绕知识点和实操技能进行微教案设计、微练习设计及微课件制作，设计微教学活动和完成微视频的拍摄和制作，在课前引导学生进行自主学习，在课后教师进行微教学反思，整理形成微课程资源并上传到网络教学平台。

（2）微课程选题设计原则。首先对课程进行知识点和实操技能目标进行分解，分解的最小单元应该满足每节微课需具备的容量和学习时间，微课教学单元的教学目的要明确。然后选取教学环节中某一知识点、专题、实验活动作为选题，针对教学中的常见、典型、有代表性的问题或内容进行设计。选题尽量“小而精”，具备独立性、示范性、代表性，应针对教学过程中的重点、难点问题。

（3）教学内容设计原则。微课程是日常教学内容的提炼，与传统课堂相比，微课的时间要精简。每次微课的教学内容应严谨充实，无科学性、政策性错误，能理论联系实际，反映社会和学科发展。

（4）教学组织设计原则。教学组织与编排要符合学生的认知规律；教学过程主线清晰，重点突出，逻辑性强，明了易懂；注重突出学生的主体性以及教与学活动有机结合。教学组织应按照提出问题、分析问题、解决问题的思路进行设计。一是吸引学生进入课题内容。或者从以前的基本教学内容引入课题，或者抛出一个题目引入课题。可采取提出问题的形式进入课题，或以一个故事引入主题，切入方法要新颖、具有吸引力，能够让学生马上产生浓厚的兴趣，吸引他们的眼球。需要注意的是课程导入要与微课的教学内容关联紧凑、和谐统一。二是课程内容讲授思路要清晰。在微课程的讲授过程中，突出重点内容，展现核心知识点，围绕一条知识或实操技能主线进行展开讲解。三是课后总结要高度提炼。课后小结是一节微课的精髓所在，总结一节课的核心内容、重点、难点，可以使学生掌握本节课的知识点内容。

（5）技术规范设计原则。①微课视频：时长 5 ～ 15 分钟，力争简明易懂；视频图像清晰稳定、构图合理、声音清楚，主要教学内容有字幕提示等；视频片头应显示微课标题、作者、单位。②多媒体教学课件：配合视频讲授使用的主要教学课件为 PPT 格式。③教学方案设计表内应注明微课讲课内容所属学科、专业、课程及适用对象等信息。

4.2　微课程架构设计

“程序设计基础”课程的微课程学习架构按照总分关系，依次为微课群、微课模块、微课、微课素材。“程序设计基础”课程设计了 5 个微课群：程序语言的集成环境、程序的基本数据结构、程序语言的控制结构、程序的复杂数据结构、程序的算法。其中，“程序语言的控制结构”微课群设计了 4 个微课模块：顺序结构、选择结构、循环结构、函数应用；“程序的复杂数据结构”微课群设计了 4 个微课模块：数组应用、结构体、指针应用、文件应用。“循环结构”微课模块设计了 5 个微课：微课 1 while 循环—打印抽奖号码、微课 2 do-while 循环—模拟抽奖、微课 3 for 循环—韩信点兵、微课 4 循环嵌套—打印吉祥图案、微课 5 循环综合应用—猜牌游戏拓展，每个微课都包括若干微课素材，如微视频、微课件、微反思等。即课程由多个微课程群组成（一个微课程群课可看作一个学习情景），每个微课程由多个微课模块组成（一个微课模块可看作一个学习单元），每个微课模块包含若干微课，每个微课包含若干微课素材。每个微课一般不可再分，可称为微课程元。"程序设计基础"课程的微课程设计架构如图 2 所示。

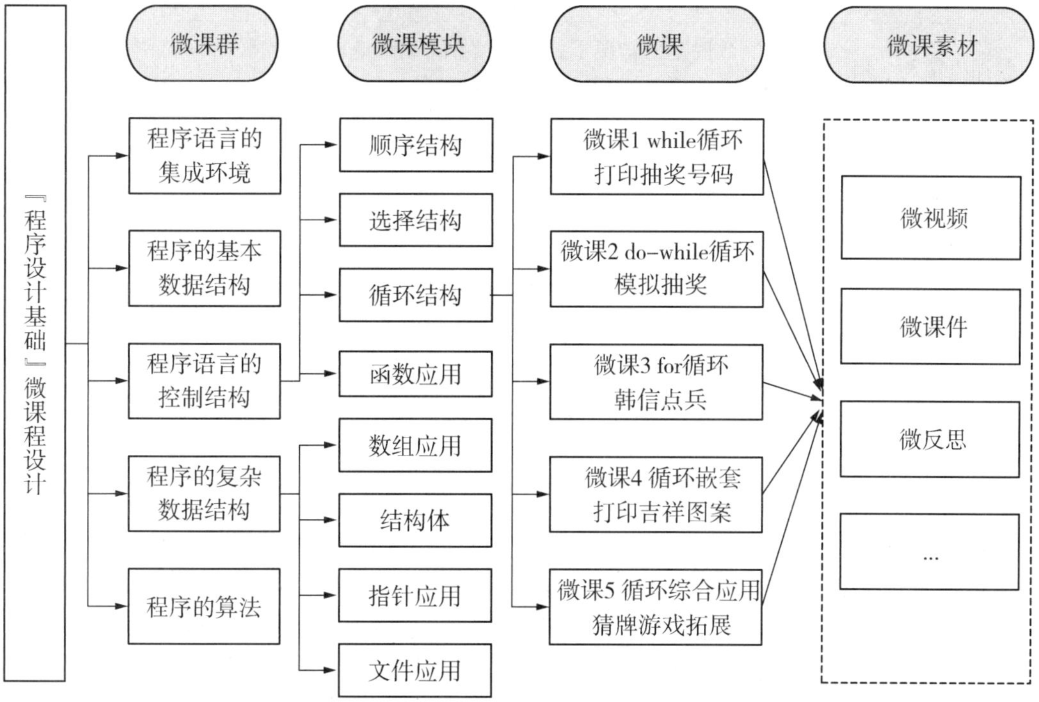

图 2　程序设计基础课程的微课程设计架构

4.3　微课程教学方案设计

每次微课的教学方案设计主要包括七方面内容：教学目的、教学重点、教学难点、导入环节设计、教学过程设计、思考问题和素材准备。例如，"for 循环"微课的教学方案设计示例如表 1 所示。

表 1　"for 循环"微课的教学方案设计实例

微课名称	for 循环
所属课程名称	程序设计基础
先修知识	程序设计语言的集成环境、基本数据类型、变量与常量、顺序结构、选择结构
课程类型	□讲授型□讨论型■演示型□练习型□表演型□自主学习型
授课对象	计算机相关专业一年级或者计算机软件开发爱好者

续表 1

微课名称	for 循环			
设计思路	教学过程设计			
	内容	画面	声音	时间
课程导入	在循环次数确定的情况下，一般使用什么循环语句呢?	使用 do while 实现循环控制	讲解 do while 循环语句的注意事项	1 分钟
内容讲授	提出新任务和学习目标	PPT 播放	讲解任务	1 分钟
	分析任务	PPT 播放	讲解算法、程序流程图	2 分钟
	for 语句的语法结构	PPT 播放	讲解语法、执行过程和应用场景	2 分钟
	编程完成任务	平台上编程	演示编程操作过程，进行程序说明	3 分钟
	break 语句与 continue 语句	平台上编程	讲解韩信点兵的拓展任务和实现	3 分钟
技能实训题目布置	布置实训题目	PPT 播放	讲解 3 个实训题目	1 分钟
总结	总结 for 循环语句	PPT 播放	总结本次课程	1 分钟

5 微课程制作

微课的拍摄与录制是微课程制作的重要环节，包括微课情景的拍摄或者微课实操演示过程的录制。“程序设计基础”微课的制作综合采用两种制作方法：教师真人出境拍摄和录屏软件录制电脑实操演示。制作的主要步骤如下：①微课设计。进行详细的微课教学设计。②拍摄和录制。用两台摄像机从前后两个方向拍摄展现课程的教学过程，用录屏软件录制电脑屏幕的实操演示过程。课程内容讲解语音清晰，有必要的黑板板书，邀请学生参与，完成部分教学情景的再现，课堂教学拍摄要保证画面清晰、准确、稳定。③视频文件和录制文件后期处理。如增加片头、片尾和字幕，用视频编辑软件对录制视频进行适当的后期编辑和美化，对视频文件和录制文件、实操演示操作与讲解进行同步处理等。

设备配置。拍摄视频的设备有：两个带三角架的数码摄像机，一个麦克风；录制电脑屏幕的设备配置：一台多媒体电脑、录屏软件 Camtasia Studio（也可使用屏幕录像专家）、PPT 课件。

微课程视频制作技术标准。视频制作使用标清制式，视频压缩推荐采用 H. 264 编码方式，码流率为 1 Mbps，封装格式使用 MP4，录制操作演示的电脑屏幕分辨率为 1024 × 768，视频时间控制在 15 分钟以内。

6 结　语

积极吸收国内外微课程的优点，构建高校“程序设计基础”微课程，探索适合具有区域特色的计算机类专业人才培养模式，有利于满足我国社会对高层次信息技术应用型技能型人才培养的迫切需求。“程序设计基础”微课程的构建使我们对微课程的认识更加深入，对应用微课程进行课程改革和人才培养模式改革有更深入的体会，这将有利推动高校师资团队的建设和专业建设，有利于提高高校计算机类专业人才培养质量。

参考文献

[1] 李娇娇，汤才梅，陈倩. 微课程的设计与制作及其发展趋势 [J]. 软件导刊，2014 (3)：61－62.
[2] 黄建军，郭绍青. 论微课程的设计与开发 [J]. 现代教育技术，2013 (10)：31－35.
[3] 梁乐明，等. 微课程设计模式研究——基于国内外微课程的对比分析 [J]. 开放教育研究 . 2013 (2)：65－73.

教师简介：

杜育松，男。2010 年 7 月—2012 年 5 月在中山大学信息科学与技术学院从事博士后研究工作。2012 年起任教于中山大学资讯管理学院（国家保密学院），讲师。主讲“计算机网络”、“信息安全”、“密码学理论与技术”、“保密技术应用”等课程，研究方向为密码学，主要研究兴趣是密码学布尔函数和格基公钥密码。目前，已发表受 SCI 或 EI 检索的学术论文 15 篇以上，主持国家自然科学基金（青年项目）和广东省科技计划项目各 1 项，参与在研的国家级科研项目 3 项。联系方式：duyusong@ mail. sysu. edu. cn。

所选论文《椭圆曲线离散对数的不动点》原载于《密码学报》2014 年第 1 期

椭圆曲线离散对数的不动点*

杜育松，张方国①

摘　要： 椭圆曲线离散对数问题在密码领域有着重要的应用。本文将模素数 p 的离散对数的不动点问题推广到有限域上椭圆曲线离散对数的不动点问题。对于有限域 F_p 上的任意椭圆曲线 $E(\mathrm{F}_p)$，证明了当 p 足够大时，以大概率存在一点 $Q=(x,y)\in E(\mathrm{F}_p)$ 使得 $\log_P Q = x$，即 $Q = x\cdot P$，其中 $\log_P$ 被看成以点 $P\in E(\mathrm{F}_p)$ 为底的离散对数，且点 P 满足 $\mathrm{ord}(P)=n$，而 x 被看成在区间 $[0,\ n-1]\cap[0,\ p-1]$ 上的整数。

关键词：　椭圆曲线；有限域；离散对数；不动点

Fixed Points for Elliptic Curve Discrete Logarithms

Yusong Du，Fangyuan Zhang

Abstract：Elliptic curve discrete logarithm problem（ECDLP）has very important applications in cryptography. Extending the fixed point problem for the discrete logarithm modulo prime p，we study the fixed point problem for discrete logarithms on elliptic curves over finite fields. For any elliptic curve $E(\mathrm{F}_p)$，we show that when p is sufficiently large there exists，with a high probability，a point $Q=(x,y)\in E(\mathrm{F}_p)$ such that $\log_P Q = x$，i. e.，$Q = x\cdot P$，where $\log_P$ is considered as the discrete logarithm function to the base $P\in E(\mathrm{F}_p)$ with $\mathrm{ord}(P)=n$ and x is also regarded as an integer in the interval $[0,\ n-1]\cap[0,\ p-1]$.

Keywords：Elliptic curve；Finite filed；Discrete logarithm；Fixed point

---

* 该文系国家自然科学基金项目（61309028，61379154，U1135001）成果。

① 张方国，中山大学信息科学与技术学院教授，博士生导师。

1 引　言

考虑群 Z/p 或 F_p^*，其中 p 是素数。它是一个阶为 $p-1$ 的循环群。假设 g 是这一群的生成元，也即 p 的一个本原根。以 g 为底模 p 离散对数的不动点是 $x \in F_p^*$（或者看成区间 $[1, p-1]$ 上的整数）使得 $g^x \equiv x \pmod p$，记为 $\log_g x = x$。

Brizolis 曾给出猜想[1]认为，对于每一个素数 $p>3$ 存在一个本原根 g 和一个区间 $[1, p-1]$ 上的整数 x 满足 $\log_g x = x$。Brizolis 已经注意到，如果有一个 p 的本原根 x 满足 $\gcd(x, p-1)=1$，那么利用 x 模 $p-1$ 的乘法逆 y 就可以得到 $g = x^y$ 也是 p 的一个本原根，并且

$$g^x \equiv x^{xy} \equiv x \bmod p,$$

也就是说，找到了一个不动点问题的解。这一条件也被称为不动点问题的 Brizolis 性质。张文鹏和 Cobeli 等分别证明了 Brizolis 性质对所有足够大的素数成立。[2,3] Levin 等证明 Brizolis 性质对每一个大于 3 的素数成立，即对素数 $p>3$ 存在一个 p 的本原根 $x \in [1, p-1]$ 与 $p-1$ 互素。[4]

离散对数问题也可以定义在有限域上的椭圆曲线中，即椭圆曲线离散对数问题（Elliptic Curve Discrete Logarithm Problem，ECDLP）。ECDLP 不仅是一个重要的数论问题，在现代密码学中也起到非常重要的作用。[5-7]

鉴于有限域上椭圆曲线离散对数问题的重要性，在这篇文章中，我们将扩展模 p 离散对数的不动点问题，考虑有限域上椭圆曲线的离散对数的不动点问题，并概率证明奇数特征有限域上的椭圆曲线离散对数不动点的存在性。

在结论的证明过程中，利用到素数计数函数 $\pi(x)$（不超过 x 的素数个数）的 Chebyshev 不等式[8,9]，以及有限域上带多项式观点的（扩展的）Polya-Vinogradov 不等式[10]。

文章组织如下：第二节给出一些预备知识，然后讨论有限域上椭圆曲线离散对数的不动点以及相应的 Brizolis 性质。第三节是预备工作，包括三个引理。第四节给出主要结论及证明，并指出结论对任意大阶数奇特征的有限域也成立。

2 预备知识

设 F_p 是一个含有 q 个元素的有限域。由 Weierstrass 方程确定的曲线

$$y^2 + a_1 xy + a_3 y = x^3 + a_2 x^2 + a_4 x + a_6,$$

加上无穷远点 ∞ 被称为有限域 F_p 上的椭圆曲线，记为 $E(F_q)$，其中 $a_1, \cdots, a_6 \in F_q$ 为常数，即

$$E(F_q) = \{\infty\} \cup \{(x,y) \in F_q \times F_q \mid y^2 + a_1 xy + a_3 y = x^3 + a_2 x^2 + a_4 x + a_6, a_i \in F_q\}。$$

如果有限域 F_q 的特征不是 2，那么曲线方程可以写成

$$y_1^2 = x^3 + a_2' x^2 + a_4' x + a_6'。\tag{1}$$

其中 $y_1 = y + a_1 x/2 + a_3/2$ 且 a_2'，a_4'，a_6'为常数。如果有限域 F_q 的特征既不是 2 也不是 3，那么曲线方程可以写成

$$y_1^2 = x_1^3 + Ax_1 + B。$$

其中 $x_1 = x + a_2'/3$ 且 A、B 为常数。

给定椭圆曲线 $E(\mathrm{F}_q)$ 上点的加法运算，椭圆曲线 $E(\mathrm{F}_q)$ 构成一个加法阿贝尔群，并以无穷远点为群单位元。[7,11] 这个群要不然是一个循环群，要不然就是两个循环群的直积。由 Hasse 定理可知，$E(\mathrm{F}_q)$ 上有理点的个数 $\#E(\mathrm{F}_q) = N$ 满足 $q+1-2\sqrt{q} \leqslant N \leqslant q+1+2\sqrt{q}$。

设 $P \in E(\mathrm{F}_q)$ 且 $<P>$ 是由点 P 生成的加法子群。如果点 $Q \in <P>$，则存在某一整数 t 满足 $t \cdot P = Q$。找到这样的整数 t 被称为椭圆曲线离散对数问题（ECDLP）。假设点 P 的阶 $\mathrm{ord}(P) = n$，那么 t 实际上是模 n 的剩余类。与一般对数记号类似，可以把椭圆曲线离散对数记为

$$\log_P Q \equiv t \bmod n。$$

记 $E(\mathrm{F}_q)$ 为 F_p 上的一条椭圆曲线。在文章以后的内容中，总是令 p 是素数而 n 为正整数且满足 $n \mid N$。F_p 上椭圆曲线离散对数的不动点问题可以定义如下。

定义 1（椭圆曲线离散对数的不动点） 设 $P \in E(\mathrm{F}_q)$ 且 $\mathrm{ord}(P) = n$。$<P> \subseteq E(\mathrm{F}_q)$ 上离散对数 $\log_P$ 的一个不动点是一个满足 $\log_P Q = x$ 的点 $Q = (x, y) \in <P>$，也即 $x \cdot P = Q$，其中 x 被看成区间 $[0, n-1] \cap [0, p-1]$ 上的一个整数。

在定义 1 中，特别地，如果 $\mathrm{ord}(P) = \#E(\mathrm{F}_p) = N$，即 $E(\mathrm{F}_p)$ 是一个循环群，且 P 为生成元，则称 $Q = (x, y) \in <P> = E(\mathrm{F}_q)$ 是 $E(\mathrm{F}_q)$ 上离散对数的一个不动点。

回忆在第一节中提到的模 p 离散对数不动点的 Brizolis 性质。它可以类似地推广到 F_p 上椭圆曲线离散对数的不动点上来。如果 $\mathrm{ord}(Q) = n$ 且 $\gcd(x,n) = 1$，那么利用 $y = x^{-1} \cdot \bmod n$ 和 $P = (x^{-1} \bmod n) \cdot Q$，可以得到 P 是 $<P> = <Q> \subseteq E(\mathrm{F}_q)$ 的一个生成元，且 $x \cdot P = xy \cdot Q = Q$，也就是说，找到了 $\log_P$ 的一个不动点。这样就有了 F_p 上椭圆曲线离散对数不动点的 Brizolis 性质。

引理 1（椭圆曲线离散对数不动点的 Brizolis 性质） 如果 $\mathrm{ord}(Q) = n$，$\gcd(x, n) = 1$ 并且 $P = (x^{-1} \bmod n) \cdot Q$，那么 $Q = (x, y) \in E(\mathrm{F}_q)$ 是 $<P> \subseteq E(\mathrm{F}_q)$ 上离散对数 $\log_P$ 的不动点。

如果 n 是素数且 $x \neq n$，则 $\gcd(x, n) = 1$。因此，在引理 1 中，如果 $\mathrm{ord}(Q) = n$ 是一个素数且 Euler 函数 $\varphi(n) \geqslant 3$，那么在 $E(\mathrm{F}_p)$ 上总是存在阶为 n 的一个点满足其 x 坐标的值与 n 互素。由此可得如下结论。

推论 1 设 $P \in E(\mathrm{F}_q)$。如果 $n \geqslant 5$ 是素数，那么对于 $<P> \subseteq E(\mathrm{F}_q)$ 上的离散对数 $\log_P$ 存在一个不动点 $Q = (x, y) \in <P>$ 使得 $\mathrm{ord}(\mathrm{Q}) = \mathrm{n}$ 且 $P = (x^{-1} \bmod n) \cdot Q$。

在引理 1 的基础上，为了找到 $E(\mathrm{F}_q)$ 中阶为 n 的某一子群上离散对数不动点问题的一个解，需要找到一个阶为 n 的点 $Q = (x, y) \in E(\mathrm{F}_q)$ 满足 $\gcd(x, n) = 1$。

3 预备工作

在这一节中，为了确定 $E(\mathrm{F}_q)$ 上使得其 x 坐标与某一固定整数 n 互素的点的个数下界，将证明三个引理作为文章的预备工作。在下一节中，将给出 n 恰好为 $E(\mathrm{F}_q)$ 上某一点的阶的概率下界，主要结论将由此产生。

引理 2 设整数 N 满足 $p+1-2\sqrt{p} \leqslant N \leqslant p+1+2\sqrt{p}$，$\omega(N)$ 为 N 的不同素因子的个

数。那么有$\lim\limits_{p\to\infty}(k/\log_2 p)=0$，其中$k=\max_N\omega(N)$。

证明： 若$\max_N\omega(N)=k$，则$\log_2 p\geqslant\log(\prod_{i=1}^{k}p_i)$，其中$p_i$是第$i$个素数。根据素数计数函数$\pi(x)$的Chebyshev不等式[8,9]，可以验证第$i$个素数$p_i(i\geqslant 2)$满足$p_i>(1/6\cdot\ln 2)\cdot i\ln i$。因此有

$$\prod_{i=1}^{k}p_i=2\prod_{i=2}^{k}p_i>2\left(\frac{1}{6}\right)^{k-1}\cdot(\log_2 2\cdot\log_2 3\cdots\log_2 k)\cdot k!。$$

于是

$$\log_2(\prod_{i=1}^{k}p_i)>1+\log_2\left(\frac{1}{6}\right)^{k-1}+\sum_{i=2}^{k}\log_2\log_2 i+\log_2 k!。$$

再根据Stirling估计$\ln k!=k\ln k-k+O(\log_2 k)$，可得

$$\begin{aligned}\log_2(\prod_{i=1}^{k}p_i)&=\log_2\left(\frac{1}{6}\right)^{k-1}+\sum_{i=2}^{k}\log_2\log_2 i+\log_2 e\cdot(k\ln k-k)+O(\log_2 k)\\&=\log_2 e\cdot k\cdot(\ln k-1-\ln 6)+\sum_{i=2}^{k}\log_2\log_2 i+O(\log_2 k)\\&>\log_2 e\cdot k\cdot(\ln k-1-\ln 6)+O(\log_2 k)。\end{aligned}$$

所以

$$\log_2 p>\log_2 e\cdot k\cdot(\ln k-1-\ln 6)+O(\log_2 k)。$$

这样

$$\frac{\log_2 p}{k}>\log_2 e\cdot\ln k+O(1),$$

即$\lim\limits_{p\to\infty}(k/\log_2 p)=\lim\limits_{k\to\infty}(k/\log_2 p)=0$。

如果$\#E(\mathrm{F}_p)=N$，由引理2可知$\omega(N)$的增长速度小于素数p长度的增长速度。这一趋势如表1所示。

表1　$\omega(N)$的增长速度

$\log_2 p$	k	$k\cdot\ln k\cdot\log_2 e$
160	31	147
256	44	233
512	76	467
1024	132	921
1536	183	1357

此外，当p和$\max_N\omega(N)=k$充分大时，$k\cdot\ln k\cdot\log_2 e$可以被看成关于$\log_2 p$下界的一个粗糙估计。

在文章以后的内容中，我们令$\varepsilon(k)=\prod^{k}(1-1/p_i)$且$p_i$是第$i$个素数。

推论2　设$\#E(\mathrm{F}_p)=N$且$\max_N\omega(N)=k$。如果k趋向于正无穷，那么$\varepsilon(k)\cdot N$趋向于正无穷。

证明：因为 $N \approx p$，所以 $\varepsilon(k) \cdot N >> p/2^k$，而当 k 趋向于正无穷时 $\varepsilon(k) = \prod_{i=1}^{k}\left(1-\frac{1}{p_i}\right) >> \left(\frac{1}{2}\right)^k$。因此由引理 2 可得$\lim_{p\to\infty}(2^k/p)=0$，即当 k 趋向于正无穷时 $\varepsilon(k) \cdot N >> p/2^k$ 趋向于正无穷。

由推论 2 可知 $\varepsilon(k)$ 的递减速度远小于 N 的递增速度。由此可知 F_p 中与固定整数 $n(n|N)$ 互素的元素个数（或者看成区间上的［0，$p-1$］整数）可以足够的大。

引理 3　设整数 N 和 n 满足 $p+1-2\sqrt{p} \leqslant N \leqslant p+1+2\sqrt{p}$ 和 $n|N$，如果 $\omega(N)=k$，那么

$$\sum_{\substack{x=0\\ \gcd(x,\,n)=1}}^{p-1} 1 > N\cdot\varepsilon(k) - 2\sqrt{p} - 2,$$

并且 $\varphi(n)/N \geqslant \frac{n\cdot\varepsilon(k)}{N}$。

证明：N 的 k 个不同的素因子可以记为 $p_{s_1} < p_{s_2} < \cdots < p_{s_k}$，其中 p_{s_1} 是 N 的最小素因子。由 $n|N$ 可以推出

$$\frac{\varphi(n)}{N} \geqslant \frac{n}{N}\left(1-\frac{1}{p_{s_1}}\right)\left(1-\frac{1}{p_{s_2}}\right)\cdots\left(1-\frac{1}{p_{s_k}}\right) \geqslant \frac{n\cdot\varepsilon(k)}{N}。$$

因为 $p+1-2\sqrt{p} \leqslant N \leqslant p+1+2\sqrt{p}$ 且

$$\begin{aligned}\sum_{\substack{x=1\\ \gcd(x,\,N)=1}}^{N} 1 = \varphi(N) &= N\left(1-\frac{1}{p_{s_1}}\right)\left(1-\frac{1}{p_{s_2}}\right)\cdots\left(1-\frac{1}{p_{s_k}}\right)\\ &\geqslant N\left(1-\frac{1}{p_1}\right)\left(1-\frac{1}{p_2}\right)\cdots\left(1-\frac{1}{p_k}\right)\\ &\geqslant n\cdot\varepsilon(k),\end{aligned}$$

所以有

$$\sum_{\substack{x=0\\ \gcd(x,\,N)=1}}^{p-1} 1 = \sum_{\substack{x=1\\ \gcd(x,\,N)=1}}^{p-1} 1 \geqslant \sum_{\substack{x=1\\ \gcd(x,\,N)=1}}^{N-2\sqrt{p}-2} 1 > \left(\sum_{\substack{x=1\\ \gcd(x,\,N)=1}}^{N} 1\right) - 2\sqrt{p} - 2。$$

注意到对于 $n \mid N$ 有

$$\sum_{\substack{x=0\\ \gcd(x,\,n)=1}}^{p-1} 1 \geqslant \sum_{\substack{x=0\\ \gcd(x,\,N)=1}}^{p-1} 1,$$

因此

$$\sum_{\substack{x=0\\ \gcd(x,\,n)=1}}^{p-1} 1 > N\cdot\varepsilon(k) - 2\sqrt{p} - 2。$$

引理被证明。

对于 $F_p(p>3)$ 上的一条椭圆曲线 $y^2=x^3+Ax+B$ 和 F_p 上的二次乘法特征 $\eta(\cdot)$，众所周知，如果 $\eta(x^3+Ax+B)=1$，那么 $x\in F_p$ 是曲线上某一有理点的 x 坐标。

引理 4　设 $\#E(F_p)=N$，$P\in E(F_p)$ 且 $\mathrm{ord}(P)=n$。如果 $\omega(N)=k$，则

$$\left|\sum_{\substack{x=0\\ \gcd(x,\,n)=1}}^{p-1} \eta(x^3+Ax+B)\right| \leqslant 3\cdot 2^k\sqrt{p}\log_2 p。$$

其中 $\eta(x)$ 是 F_p 上的二次乘法特征。

证明： 设 $f(x)=x^3+Ax+B$ 是 F_p 上的一条椭圆曲线。对于 Moebius 函数 $\mu(\cdot)$，如果 $\gcd(x,n)=1$，则 $\sum_{d\mid\gcd(x,n)}\mu(d)$ 为 1，否则为 0。引理中的特征和满足

$$\left|\sum_{\substack{x=0\\ \gcd(x,n)=1}}^{p-1}\eta(x^3+Ax+B)\right| = \left|\sum_{x=0}^{p-1}\sum_{d\mid\gcd(x,n)}\mu(d)\cdot\eta[f(x)]\right|$$

$$= \left|\sum_{x=0}^{p-1}\sum_{d\mid\gcd(x,n')}\mu(d)\cdot\eta[f(x)]\right|$$

$$= \left|\sum_{d\mid n'}\mu(d)\cdot\sum_{0\leqslant x\leqslant d\frac{p-1}{d}t}\eta[f(dx)]\right|。$$

其中 n' 是 n 的最大无平方因子（quare-free factor）。对于任意代数次数不为 2 的方幂的多项式 $g(x)\in F_p[x]$，根据有限域 F_p 上的 Polya-Vinogradov 不等式[10]，当 $1\leqslant k\leqslant p$ 时有下面的不等式成立：

$$\left|\sum_{x=0}^{k-1}\eta[g(x)]\right| \leqslant \deg(g)\cdot\sqrt{p}\log_2 p。$$

结合 $n\mid N$，又得到

$$\left|\sum_{\substack{x=0\\ \gcd(x,n)=1}}^{p-1}\eta(x^3+Ax+B)\right| \leqslant \sum_{d\mid n'}|\mu(d)|\cdot\left|\sum_{0\leqslant x\leqslant d\frac{p-1}{d}t}\eta[f(dx)]\right|$$

$$= 2^{\omega(n')}\cdot\left|\sum_{0\leqslant x\leqslant d\frac{p-1}{d}t}\eta[f(dx)]\right|$$

$$\leqslant 3\cdot 2^{\omega(n')}\sqrt{p}\log_2 p$$

$$\leqslant 3\cdot 2^{k}\sqrt{p}\log_2 p。$$

引理被证明。

4 不动点的存在性证明

定理 1（椭圆曲线离散对数不动点的存在性） 设 $P\in E(F_p)$，$\#E(F_p)=N$ 并且 $\mathrm{ord}(P)=n\mid N$。当 p 足够大时，对于常数 $c(0\leqslant c\leqslant 1/2)$，如果 $N/n=O(p^c)$，那么以大概率存在 $<P>\subseteq E(F_p)$ 上离散对数 $\log_P$ 的一个不动点 Q 满足 $P=(x^{-1}\bmod n)\cdot Q$。

证明： 记 F_p 上的椭圆曲线 $y^2=f(x)=x^3+Ax+B$ 为 E。用 S 表示 $E(F_p)$ 上其 x 坐标的值与 n 互素的所有点组成的集合。集合 S 的元素个数 $\#S$ 不小于

$$\sum_{\substack{x=0\\ \gcd(x,n)=1}}^{p-1}\frac{1+\eta[f(x)]}{2} = \frac{1}{2}\sum_{\substack{x=0\\ \gcd(x,n)=1}}^{p-1}1+\frac{1}{2}\sum_{\substack{x=0\\ \gcd(x,n)=1}}^{p-1}\eta[f(x)],$$

其中 $\eta(x)$ 是 F_p 上的二次乘法特征。设 $k=\omega(N)$ 是 N 的不同素因子的个数。根据引理 3 和引理 4，可得

$$\#S > \frac{N\cdot\varepsilon(k)}{2} - \sqrt{p} - 1 - 3\cdot 2^{k-1}\sqrt{p}\log_2 p = \frac{N\cdot\varepsilon(k)}{2} - O(2^k\sqrt{p}\log_2 p)。$$

$E(\mathrm{F}_p)$ 上任意一点其阶为 n 的概率不小于 $\varphi(n)/N$ 。因此，阶为 n 的点 $Q=(x,y)$ 满足 $\gcd(x,n)=1$ 的概率不小于

$$1-\left[1-\frac{\varphi(n)}{N}\right]^{\#S} \geqslant 1-\left[1-\frac{n\varepsilon(k)}{N}\right]^{\#S}。$$

于是，由引理 1 可知至少以概率

$$\theta = 1-\left[1-\frac{n\varepsilon(k)}{N}\right]^{\#S}$$

存在离散对数 $\log_P$ 的一个不动点 $Q=(x,y)\in\langle P\rangle$ 。当 p 趋向于正无穷时 $N\approx p$ 且 $\varepsilon(k) \gg (1/2)^k$ ，因此由引理 2，可得

$$\frac{N\cdot\varepsilon(k)}{2^k\sqrt{p}\log_2 p} \gg \frac{\sqrt{p}}{2^{2k}\log_2 p} \to +\infty。$$

这样，如果 p 足够大则 $\#S$ 也可以足够大。对于常数 $0\leqslant c\leqslant 1/2$ ，如果 $N/n = O(p^c)$ ，那么 $\frac{N}{n\cdot\varepsilon(k)} \gg 2^k\sqrt{p}$ 。这就表明，当 p 趋向于正无穷时，

$$\#S - \frac{N}{n\cdot\varepsilon(k)} > \frac{N\cdot\varepsilon(k)}{2} - O(2^k\sqrt{p}\log_2 p) \to +\infty。$$

因此

$$\begin{aligned}\lim_{p\to\infty}(1-\theta) &= \lim_{p\to\infty}\left[1-\frac{n\cdot\varepsilon(k)}{N}\right]^{\#S}\\ &= \lim_{p\to\infty}\left[1-\frac{n\cdot\varepsilon(k)}{N}\right]^{\frac{N}{n\cdot\varepsilon(k)}+\#S-\frac{N}{n\cdot\varepsilon(k)}}\\ &= \lim_{p\to\infty}\left(\frac{1}{e}\right)^{\#S-\frac{N}{n\cdot\varepsilon(k)}},\end{aligned}$$

且

$$\lim_{p\to\infty}\theta = 1-\lim_{p\to\infty}\left(\frac{1}{e}\right)^{\#S-\frac{N}{n\cdot\varepsilon(k)}} = 1。$$

所以，对于常数 $0\leqslant c\leqslant 1/2$，如果 $N/n = O(p^c)$ ，那么至少以概率 θ 存在 $\langle P\rangle \subseteq E(\mathrm{F}_p)$ 上离散对数 $\log_P$ 的一个不动点 $Q=(x,y)\in\langle P\rangle$ 满足 $P=(x^{-1}\bmod n)\cdot Q$ 。这里 θ 满足 $\lim\limits_{p\to\infty}\theta = 1$ 。

定理 1 表明如果素数 p 和阶数 n 足够大，那么以大概率存在 $\langle P\rangle \subseteq E(\mathrm{F}_p)$ 上离散对数 $\log_P$ 的一个不动点。然而，由定理 1 也可以看出，对于 $E(\mathrm{F}_p)$ 上某些小阶数的子群，即使素数 p 较大时不动点存在的概率也可能比较小。

使用定理 1 中的符号，如果 $E(\mathrm{F}_p)$ 是循环群，则 $n=N$。于是

$$\lim_{p\to\infty}\theta = 1-\lim_{p\to\infty}[1-\varepsilon(k)]^{\#S} = 1。$$

如果 $E(\mathrm{F}_p)$ 不是循环群，则它一定是两个循环群的直积，并且其中一个的阶大于 $\sqrt{N}$。这意味着，当 p 足够大时，总是以大概率存在点 $Q\in E(\mathrm{F}_p)$ 且 $\mathrm{ord}(Q)\geqslant\sqrt{N}\approx\sqrt{p}$ ，满足 Brizolis 条件。因此，有以下推论成立。

推论3 设$P \in E(\mathrm{F}_p)$。如果p足够大，那么以大概率存在$<P>\subseteq E(\mathrm{F}_p)$上离散对数$\log_P$的一个不动点$Q$满足$P=(x^{-1}\mathrm{mod}\ n)\cdot Q$。

定理2 假设$E(\mathrm{F}_p)$是循环群。令$\#E(\mathrm{F}_p)=N$。记$k=\omega(N)$是N的不同素因子的个数。如果$\left[\frac{3}{2}\varepsilon(k)-1\right]\geqslant\left(\frac{1}{2}\right)^{\mathrm{O}(k)}$，那么当$p$足够大时一定存在$<P>\subseteq E(\mathrm{F}_p)$上离散对数$\log_P$的一个不动点$Q$满足$P=(x^{-1}\mathrm{mod}\ n)\cdot Q$。

证明： 使用定理1中的符号，记$\#S$为$E(\mathrm{F}_p)$上满足其x坐标的值与n互素的点的个数。于是根据引理3和引理4，可得

$$\#S>\frac{N\cdot\varepsilon(k)}{2}-\mathrm{O}(2^k\sqrt{p}\log_2 p)。$$

$E(\mathrm{F}_p)$上有$\varphi(N)$个点的阶为N，因此，$E(\mathrm{F}_p)$上阶为N且其x坐标的值与n互素的点的个数是

$$\begin{aligned}\#S-[N-\varphi(N)]&=\frac{N\cdot\varepsilon(k)}{2}-\mathrm{O}(2^k\sqrt{p}\log_2 p)+\varphi(N)-N\\&>\left[\frac{3}{2}\varepsilon(k)-1\right]N-\mathrm{O}(2^k\sqrt{p}\log_2 p)。\end{aligned}$$

因为$\left[\frac{3}{2}\varepsilon(k)-1\right]\geqslant\left(\frac{1}{2}\right)^{\mathrm{O}(k)}$，所以，当$p$趋向于正无穷时，有

$$\frac{\left[\frac{3}{2}\varepsilon(k)-1\right]N}{2^k\sqrt{p}\log_2 p}>\frac{\sqrt{p}}{2^{\mathrm{O}(k)}\log_2 p}\rightarrow+\infty。$$

再根据引理1即可推出结论。

定理2表明当$E(\mathrm{F}_p)$是循环群时，如果素数p和N的所有素因子足够大，那么一定存在$E(\mathrm{F}_p)$上离散对数的一个不动点。

现在来考虑一般有限域上离散对数的不动点问题。记F_q是阶为$q=p^s$、特征为素数p的有限域。选择F_q的一组基$\{\beta_1,\beta_2,\cdots,\beta_s\}$。$\mathrm{F}_q$中的每一个元素$x\in\mathrm{F}_q$可以写成$x=x\beta_1+x_2\beta_2+\cdots+x_s\beta_s$，其中对于$1\leqslant i\leqslant s$有$x_i\in\mathrm{F}_p$。这样可以建立$\mathrm{F}_p$和整数区间$[0,q-1]$的一一对应，即把

$$x=x\beta_1+x_2\beta_2+\cdots+x_s\beta_s\in\mathrm{F}_q$$

等同于p进制整数$x=\sum_{i=0}^{s}x_ip^i\in[0,q-1]$，其中$x_i$和以前一样被看成区间$[0,p-1]$中的整数。给定$\mathrm{F}_q$的一组基$\{\beta_1,\beta_2,\cdots,\beta_s\}$，$\mathrm{F}_q$上离散对数的不动点问题可以类似地定义如下。

定义2（一般有限域上椭圆曲线离散对数的不动点） 设$P\in E(\mathrm{F}_q)$且$\mathrm{ord}(P)=n$。$<P>\subseteq E(\mathrm{F}_q)$上离散对数$\log_P$的一个不动点是满足$x\cdot P=Q$的一点$Q=(x,y)\in<P>$，其中$x=x\beta_1+x_2\beta_2+\cdots+x_s\beta_s\in\mathrm{F}_q$也被看成区间$[0,n-1]\cap[0,q-1]$中的$p$进制整数$x=\sum_{i=0}^{s}x_ip^i$。

当F_q上的元素x被看成区间$[0,n-1]\cap[0,q-1]$中的p进制整数时，可以定义

$\gcd(x,n)=1$。这样，Brizolis 性质对于 F_q 上椭圆曲线离散对数的不动点也是有意义的。为了找到 $E(\mathrm{F}_p)$ 中某个 n 阶子群上不动点问题的解，需要找到 n 阶点 $Q=(x,y)\in E(\mathrm{F}_q)$ 满足 $\gcd(x,n)=1$。

不难看出，引理 2 和引理 3 对于 F_q 上的椭圆曲线离散对数也类似地成立。

引理 5 设整数 N 满足 $q+1-2\sqrt{q}\leqslant N\leqslant q+1+2\sqrt{q}$。$\omega(N)$ 是 N 的不同素因子的个数。那么 $\lim\limits_{p\to\infty}(k/\log_2 q)=0$，其中 $k=\max_N\omega(N)$。

引理 6 设整数 N 和 n 满足 $q+1-2\sqrt{q}\leqslant N\leqslant q+1+2\sqrt{q}$ 和 $n\mid N$。如果 $\omega(N)=k$，那么

$$\sum_{\substack{x=0\\ \gcd(x,n)=1}}^{q-1}1>N\cdot\varepsilon(k)-2\sqrt{q}-2,\qquad \text{且}\quad \frac{\varphi(n)}{N}\geqslant\frac{n\cdot\varepsilon(k)}{N}。$$

当域的特征 $p\neq 2$ 时，对于多项式 $g(x)\in\mathrm{F}_q[x]$，如果其代数次数不为 2 的方幂，并且在 F_q 的分裂域上拥有 m 个不同零点，那么根据 F_q 上扩展的 Polya-Vinogradov 不等式[10]，有不等式

$$\left|\sum_{x=0}^{k-1}\eta[g(x)]\right|<m\sqrt{q}(1+\log_2 q)$$

成立，其中 $1\leqslant k\leqslant q$。设 $f(x)=x^3+a_2'x^2+a_4'x+a_6'\in\mathrm{F}_q$，其中 a_2',a_4',a_6' 如等式（1）所定义。显然，$f(x)$ 的代数次数不为 2 的方幂，且在 F_q 的分裂域内有 3 个零点。因此有与引理 4 类似的结论成立。

引理 7 设 $\#E(\mathrm{F}_q)=N$，$P\in E(\mathrm{F}_q)$ 并且 $\mathrm{ord}(P)=n$。如果 $\omega(N)=k$，那么

$$\left|\sum_{\substack{x=0\\ \gcd(x,n)=1}}^{q-1}\eta(x^3+a_2'x^2+a_4'x+a_6')\right|\leqslant 3\cdot 2^k\sqrt{q}(1+\log_2 q)。$$

其中 $\eta(x)$ 是 F_q 上的二次乘法特征，且 a_2',a_4',a_6' 如等式（1）所定义。

由上述三个引理，根据定理 1 的思想，可以推出如果有限域的阶足够大且特征为奇数，则对于其上的任意椭圆曲线以大概率存在阶为 n 的点 Q 是 $<P>\subseteq E(\mathrm{F}_q)$ 上离散对数 $\log_P$ 的不动点满足 $P=(x^{-1}\bmod n)\cdot Q$。

5 结　论

本文推广了模素数 p 离散对数的不动点问题。主要研究了椭圆曲线 $E(\mathrm{F}_q)$ 上 n 阶子群中离散对数的不动点问题。证明了如果 p 和 n 足够大，对于 F_p 上的任意椭圆曲线，以大概率存在阶为 n 的点 Q 是 $<P>\subseteq E(\mathrm{F}_q)$ 上离散对数 $\log_P$ 的不动点满足 $P=(x^{-1}\cdot\bmod n)\cdot Q$。对于特征为奇数的一般有限域，这一结果可以类似地被证明成立。对于特征为偶数的有限域，这一结果不能类似地证明。因为在这种情况下没有引理 4 的结论。但是，我们仍然相信这种情况下不动点也是存在的。

参考文献

[1] Guy R K. Unsolved Problems in Number Theory [M]. Berlin: Springer, 1984.

[2] 张文鹏. 关于 Brizolis 的一个问题 [J]. 纯粹数学与应用数学, 1995, 29 (4): 1 -3.

[3] Cobeli C, Zaharescu A. An Exponential Congruence with Solutions in Primitive Roots. Rev. Roumaine Math [J]. Pures Appl, 1999, 44: 15 -22.

[4] Levin M, Pomerance C, Soundararajan K. Fixed Points for Discrete Logarithms [M]. Lecture Notes in Computer Science, 2010, 6197: 6 -15.

[5] Miller V S. Use of Elliptic Curves in Cryptography [C] // Williams H C. CRYPTO'85, Lecture Notes in Computer Science: 218. Berlin: Springer, 1986: 417 -426.

[6] Koblitz N. Elliptic Curve Cryptosystems [J]. Mathematics of Computation, 1987, 48 (177): 203 -209.

[7] Washington L C. Elliptic Curves: Number Theory and Cryptography. Second Edition [M]. Boca Raton: Chapman and Hall/CRC, 2008.

[8] Apostol T M. Introduction to Analytic Number Theory [M]. Berlin: Springer, 1998.

[9] Nair M. On Chebyshev-Type Inequalities for Primes [J]. The American Mathematical Monthly, 1982, 89 (2): 126 -129.

[10] Winterhof A. Some Estimates for Character Sums and Applications [J]. Designs, Codes and Cryptography, 2001, 22 (2): 123 -131.

[11] Silverman J H. The Arithmetic of Elliptic Curves. Second Edition [M]. Berlin: Springer, 2009.

教师简介：

余维杰，男，中山大学工学学士、工学博士。2014 年起任教于中山大学资讯管理学院，讲师。主讲“智能信息处理”等本科课程。主要研究方向包括计算智能、建模优化与智能信息处理等。参与国家级科研项目 5 项，已发表学术论文 9 篇。联系方式：yuweijie6@mail. sysu. edu. cn。

Differential Evolution with Two-Level Parameter Adaptation

Weijie Yu , Meie Shen①, Weineng Chen②, Zhihui Zhan③, Yuejiao Gong④, Ying Lin⑤, Ou Liu⑥, Jun Zhang⑦

Abstract: The performance of differential evolution (DE) largely depends on its mutation strategy and control parameters. In this paper, we propose an adaptive DE (ADE) algorithm with a new mutation strategy DE/lbest/1 and a two-level adaptive parameter control scheme. The DE/lbest/1 strategy is a variant of the greedy DE/best/1 strategy. However, the population is mutated under the guide of multiple locally best individuals in DE/lbest/1 instead of one globally best individual in DE/best/1. This strategy is beneficial to the balance between fast convergence and population diversity. The two-level adaptive parameter control scheme is implemented mainly in two steps. In the first step, the population-level parameters F_p and CR_p for the whole population are adaptively controlled according to the optimization states, namely, the exploration state and the exploitation state in each generation. These optimization states are estimated by measuring the population distribution. Then, the individual-level parameters F_i and CR_i for each individual are generated by adjusting the population-level parameters. The adjustment is based on considering the individual's fitness value and its distance from the globally best individual. This way, the parameters can be adapted to not only the overall state of the population but also the characteristics of different individuals. The performance of the proposed ADE is evaluated on a suite of benchmark functions. Experimental results show that ADE generally outperforms four state-of-the-art DE variants on different kinds of optimization problems. The effects of ADE components, parameter properties of ADE, search behavior of ADE, and parameter sensitivity of ADE are also studied. Finally, we investigate the capability of ADE for solving three real-world optimization problems.

---

① Meie Shen, an Associate Professor with the School of Computer Science, Beijing Information Science and Technology University, Beijing, China.

② Weineng Chen, a Lecturer with the Department of Computer Science, Sun Yat-Sen University, Guangzhou, China.

③ Zhihui Zhan, a Bachelor and Ph. D. from the Department of Computer Science, Sun Yat-Sen University, Guangzhou, China.

④ Yuejiao Gong, a Ph. D. in Computer Science from Sun Yat-Sen University, Guangzhou, China.

⑤ Ying Lin, a Lecturer with the Department of Psychology, Sun Yat-Sen University, Guangzhou, China.

⑥ Ou Liu, an Assistant Professor with the School of Accounting and Finance, Hong Kong Polytechnic University, Hung Hom, Hong Kong.

⑦ Jun Zhang, a Cheung Kong Professor with the Department of Computer Science, Sun Yat-Sen University, Guangzhou, China.

Keywords: Adaptive parameter control; Differential evolution (DE); Global optimization

1 Introduction

Differential evolution (DE), first proposed by Storn and Price[1,2], is a simple and efficient evolutionary algorithm (EA) for global optimization. It has been successfully applied to a variety of numerical optimization problems[3-9] and real-world applications such as signal processing[10], robotic system control[11], and wireless sensor networks[12]. Theoretical studies on DE such as convergence analysis[13] and population-dynamics analysis[14] have also been conducted by some recent work.

A classic DE algorithm involves three general evolutionary operators, i. e. mutation, crossover, and selection, which are associated with certain control parameters. The values of the parameters greatly influence the convergence speed and population diversity. Therefore, how to choose an appropriate parameter setting to improve the performance of the algorithm has become a significant and promising research topic in DE.

A large amount of research work has been conducted to analyze the effects of these control parameters and suggest suitable parameter settings.[2,15,16] However, optimal parameter settings *ad hoc* to a specific problem are often based on a *priori* or empirical knowledge, and there exists no single value being good for all types of problems. For example, a small crossover probability *CR* is suitable for separable functions while a large one is effective for non-separable function.[17] Thus, lots of studies have been undertaken on parameter control for improved DE, where parameters are automatically adjusted at runtime.

In the literature, the works on parameter control can be mainly classified into two kinds of strategies. The first one is population-level parameter control and the second one is individual-level parameter control.

In the earlier works of parameter control for DE, the control parameters are usually applied at a population level. All individuals in the population are associated with the same parameter values. Two kinds of information can be used to adjust the parameter values for the whole population. The first kind is some deterministic factors such as generation number or fitness evaluations number.[18] Parameter control based on such factors is easy to implement but may be not effective enough since it does not utilize any search feedback information from the evolution. The second kind is some form of feedback derived from the search process which can be in one of different evolutionary states. Examples of this feedback information are the relative fitness values over individuals[19-20] and population diversity[21-22].

In recent years, more researchers apply the adaptive control parameters at an individual level.[23-30] Each individual maintains its own set of parameters which are adapted during the optimization process. Most of these adaptive approaches are based on the idea that the parameters which can lead to good individuals should be propagated throughout the population. There are various methods for adaptively updating the parameter values for each individual among these approaches. The related works will be reviewed in Section Ⅱ-B of this paper.

It can be seen that most existing methods for parameter adaptation only take the population-level strategy or individual-level strategy into consideration. By themselves, however, the population-level and the individual-level parameter adaptations can make use of only one aspect of the evolutionary process information, that is, the state of the whole population or the characteristics of single individual. For the use of only population-level strategy, some deterministic factors or feedback information from the population are utilized to control parameter values. Nevertheless, since all the individuals share the same population-level parameters without diversity, the diversity of population search behavior may also be in sufficient. For the use of only individual-level strategy, each individual is associated with its own parameters which are controlled based on individual characteristics instead of the overall population information. Therefore, this kind of strategy cannot quickly adjust the parameters to adapt to different optimization states.

How to utilize both of the two kinds of evolutionary process information to design a more efficient parameter adaptation strategy is still a challenging and significant task. So far as we know, in the literature, there is no reported work on combining both population-level and individual-level parameter control. In this paper, we propose a novel two-level adaptive parameter control scheme, which is an extension of our previous work[31], utilizing both population and individual information to provide a more comprehensive description of the evolutionary process. Thus, the proposed scheme can tackle the limitations of using only population-level or individual-level strategy. In this scheme, the parameters of the algorithm are adaptively controlled at two levels. At the population level, the population-level parameters shared by the whole population are first controlled. In each generation, the population-level parameters are updated according to different optimization states which are estimated by measuring the population distribution. In order to fit the characteristics of different individuals, the individual-level parameter control is then performed. The individual-level parameters assigned to each individual are generated by further adjusting the population-level parameters. The adjustment is based on considering the individual's fitness value and its distance from the best individual. Consequently, the two-level parameter adaptation scheme can provide adaptive parameters more effectively. Through population-level control, the proposed scheme is able to quickly adjust parameters to match the overall population state. Moreover, the resulting parameters can be further fine-turned to adapt to the characteristics of different individuals through individual-level control.

This two-level adaptive parameter control scheme is applied to DE with a new mutation strategy called DE/lbest/1, which is a variant of the classic DE/best/1. In traditional DE, DE/best/1 utilizes the globally best solution to guide the mutation, and can thus converge very fast on simple unimodal problems. However, such a greedy strategy may suffer from premature convergence when it deals with complex multimodal problems. By contrast, in the DE/lbest/1 mutation strategy, the population is attracted by multiple locally best solutions instead of a single globally best solution. Therefore, our proposed mutation strategy is helpful for balancing the exploration and exploitation abilities of the algorithm. Although there exist DE mutation strategies like DE/current-to-*p*best/1 in JADE[26] utilizing multiple good solutions, our DE/lbest/1 differs from those strategies in the following major aspects.

1) The population of DE/lbest/1 is divided into a predefined number of non-overlapping groups, whose number and members are kept unchanged at runtime.

2) In DE/lbest/1, multiple locally best solutions are selected from different groups of solutions, each of which is mutated under the guide of its respective locally best solution.

Since DE/lbest/1 utilizes the locally best solution which only directly attracts the individuals in the same group with it, the entire population is in fact attracted by multiple good solutions chosen from different groups. Therefore, it is less likely for DE/lbest/1 that the entire population is attracted to a specific region in the search space, and the problem of premature convergence can be better alleviated for DE/lbest/1.

Combining the DE/lbest/1 strategy with two-level adaptive parameter control, we develop a novel adaptive DE algorithm (ADE), the robustness and efficiency of which are further enhanced. The proposed ADE is tested on different types of benchmark functions and three real-world optimization problems. The performance of ADE compares favorably with four state-of-the-art DE variants.

The remainder of this paper is organized as follows. Section Ⅱ reviews the DE algorithm and the related works on parameter control methods and variants of mutation strategies for DE. Section Ⅲ describes the proposed ADE algorithm in detail, including the DE/lbest/1 mutation strategy, the two-level parameter control scheme, and the runtime complexity of ADE. In Section Ⅳ, the ADE algorithm is compared with four state-of-the-art DE variants on a suite of benchmark functions and three real-world optimization problems. The experimental results are also discussed. In addition, the effects of ADE components, parameter properties of ADE, search behavior of ADE, and parameter sensitivity of ADE are studied in this section. Finally, Section Ⅴ draws the conclusions.

2 DE Algorithm and Related Works

2.1 Differential evolution (DE) algorithm

DE is a population-based stochastic algorithm designed for global numerical optimization. Similar to other EAs, DE searches for a global optimum in the search space with a population of vectors $\{\mathbf{x}_i^g = [x_{i,1}^g, x_{i,2}^g, \cdots, x_{i,D}^g], i = 1, 2, \cdots, NP\}$, where g denotes the current generation, D is the dimension of the search space, and NP is the population size. In generation $g = 0$, the jth component of the ith vector can be initialized as

$$x_{i,j}^{0} = x_{\min,j} + \mathrm{rand}(0,1) \cdot (x_{\max,j} - x_{\min,j}). \tag{1}$$

where rand (0, 1) is a uniform random number on the interval [0, 1], and $x_{\min,j}$, $x_{\max,j}$ are the prescribed minimum and maximum bounds of the jth dimension, respectively. After initialization, DE enters an evolutionary process which includes mutation, crossover, and selection operations.

Mutation: In each generation g, the mutation operation is applied to each individual $\mathbf{x}_i^g$ (also called the target vector) to create its corresponding mutant vector $\mathbf{v}_i^g$. The five frequently used mutation strategies are listed as follows:

"DE/rand/1":

$$\mathbf{v}_i^g = \mathbf{x}_{r_1}^g + F \cdot (\mathbf{x}_{r_2}^g - \mathbf{x}_{r_3}^g); \tag{2}$$

"DE/current-to-best/1":

$$\mathbf{v}_i^g = \mathbf{x}_i^g + F \cdot (\mathbf{x}_{\text{best}}^g - \mathbf{x}_i^g) + F \cdot (\mathbf{x}_{r_1}^g - \mathbf{x}_{r_2}^g); \tag{3}$$

"DE/best/1":

$$\mathbf{v}_i^g = \mathbf{x}_{\text{best}}^g + F \cdot (\mathbf{x}_{r_1}^g - \mathbf{x}_{r_2}^g); \tag{4}$$

"DE/best/2":

$$\mathbf{v}_i^g = \mathbf{x}_{\text{best}}^g + F \cdot (\mathbf{x}_{r_1}^g - \mathbf{x}_{r_2}^g) + F \cdot (\mathbf{x}_{r_3}^g - \mathbf{x}_{r_4}^g); \tag{5}$$

"DE/rand/2":

$$\mathbf{v}_i^g = \mathbf{x}_{r_1}^g + F \cdot (\mathbf{x}_{r_2}^g - \mathbf{x}_{r_3}^g) + F \cdot (\mathbf{x}_{r_4}^g - \mathbf{x}_{r_5}^g). \tag{6}$$

It can be seen that the mutant vector $\mathbf{v}_i^g$ is generated by combing a base vector with one or two scaled difference vectors. In the above equations, the indices r_1, r_2, r_3, r_4, and r_5 are distinct integers randomly selected from [1, 2, ⋯, NP], and are all different from the index i. $\mathbf{x}_{\text{best}}^g$ is the vector with the best fitness value in the current generation. The factor F is a positive control parameter for weighting the difference vectors.

Crossover: In order to enhance population diversity, a crossover operation exchanges some components of the mutant vector $\mathbf{v}_i^g$ with the target vector $\mathbf{x}_i^g$ to generate a trial vector $\mathbf{u}_i^g$. The process can be expressed as

$$u_{i,j}^g = \begin{cases} v_{i,j}^g, & \text{if } \mathrm{rand}(0,1) \leqslant CR \text{ or } j = j_{\text{rand}} \\ x_{i,j}^g, & \text{otherwise} \end{cases}. \tag{7}$$

where rand (0, 1) is a uniformly distributed random number as before. j_{rand} is an integer randomly generated from the range [1, D], which is used to ensure that the trial vector has at least one component different from the target vector. The crossover probability CR is another control parameter, which determines the fraction of vector components inherited from the mutant vector.

Selection: To decide whether the target or the trial vector can survive to the next generation, the selection operation is finally performed. For a minimization problem, the vector with the lower objective function value enters the next generation, which can be expressed as follows:

$$\mathbf{x}_i^{g+1} = \begin{cases} \mathbf{u}_i^g, & \text{if } f(\mathbf{u}_i^g) \leqslant f(\mathbf{x}_i^g) \\ \mathbf{x}_i^g, & \text{otherwise} \end{cases}. \tag{8}$$

where $f(x)$ is the objective function for the minimization problem.

2.2 Parameter control methods for DE

Control parameters in DE have significant effects on the performance of the algorithm.[9,16] However, there is no fixed parameter setting that can achieve the best performance for all types of problems. Therefore, various parameter control methods have been proposed for DE to dynamically adjust the parameter values. These methods are capable of enhancing the robustness and efficiency of DE algorithm. In this paper, we classify the parameter control methods into two categories as follows.

2.2.1 Population-level parameter control

All individuals in the population share the same parameter values which are controlled based on some deterministic rules or feedback information from the DE search process. Deterministic rules change the parameter values without exploiting any information from the evolution. In [18], Das *et al.* proposed two schemes to control the scale factor F for DE. The first one decreases the value of F based on a linear rule, and the second one generates the value of F in a random way. Since the linear rule in the first scheme is based on both the current number and the predefined maximum number of generations, it is actually determined before running the algorithm.

By using some form of feedback from the DE search process, parameter control strategies dynamically adjust the parameter values which can adapt to different evolutionary states. In [19], the value of the parameter F is adaptively adjusted based on the minimum and maximum fitness values over the individuals in each generation. In [20], a fuzzy logic control approach was proposed to adapt the DE parameters F and CR. The fuzzy controllers incorporate the relative fitness values and individuals of the successive generations as their inputs, and the outputs are the values of F and CR. Zaharie[21] proposed a method of adapting the parameters of DE guided by the population diversity evolution. Based on the same idea, Zaharie and Petcu[22] further developed an adaptive Pareto DE for multi-objective optimization problems.

2.2.2 Individual-level parameter control

In this form of adaptation, each individual in the population maintains its own set of parameter values, which are optimized through the evolutionary process. Brest *et al.*[24] introduced a self-adaptive approach for the control parameters F and CR. In each generation, new F_i and CR_i for each individual are randomly generated in their respective ranges with probabilities τ_1 and τ_2, respectively. Qin *et al.*[25] proposed a self-adaptive DE (SaDE) algorithm, in which the trial vector generation strategies as well as the control parameters F and CR are self-adapted by learning from the previous experiences. Zhang and Sanderson[26] introduced a new adaptive DE algorithm called JADE. The control parameters for each individual in JADE are updated based on their historical record of success. In [27], JADE is further combined with a strategy adaptation mechanism. Wang *et al.*[28] proposed a composite DE (CoDE), which uses three trial vector generation strategies and three control parameter settings of F and CR. In each generation, each individual randomly combines these strategies and parameters to generate trial vectors. More recently, Zhong and Zhang[29] self-adapted the values of F and CR of DE for the subpixel mapping problem.

2.2 Variants of DE mutation strategies

Besides the five most frequently used mutation strategies mentioned in Section Ⅱ-A, a lot of other variants have been proposed to further improve the performance of DE. To make the performance of DE rotationally invariant, Price[32] proposed a new mutation strategy named DE/current-to-rand/1. In [3], Price *et al.* proposed the DE/rand/1/either-oralgorithm, where the trial vectors that are either pure mutants or pure recombinant soccur with probabilities p_F and $1 - p_F$, respectively. Fan and Lampinen[33] proposed a trigonometric mutation to increase the convergence speed of DE. Kaelo and Ali[34] proposed a hybrid mutation operator which uses the attraction-repulsion technique of an electromagnetism-like algorithm. More recently, Wang *et al.*[35] proposed a parameter-free Gaussian mutation strategy which uses Gaussian sampling method to generate mutated individuals. This Gaussian mutation strategy was further hybridized with the classic DE/best/1 to balance the global search ability and convergencerate.

In order to balance the exploration and exploitation capabilities of DE, many researchers designed variants of some greedy mutation strategies.[26,36,37] These variants utilize the information of multiple good solutions instead of the best solution in the entire population. For example, DE/current-to-*p*best/1 in JADE[26] chooses any of the top *p*% solutions from the entire population to play the role of the single global best solution. Das *et al.*[36] proposed a local mutation model for DE/current-to-best/1, in which the best solution so far is chosen from a small neighborhood. The local mutation model is further combined with the global mutation model by a weight factor. In [37], Islam *et al.* also proposed a variant of DE/current-to-best/1 which utilizes the best solution of a dynamic group of randomly selected solutions from the current population.

Besides developing new DE mutation strategies, some researchers investigated DE mutation frameworks which can be applied to different DE variants. For example, Epitropakis *et al.*[38] proposed a mutation framework in which the probability of selecting an individual to become a parentis inversely proportional to its distance from the individualundergoing mutation. In [39], Gong and Cai proposeda kind of ranking-based mutation framework, where some of the parents in the mutation operatorare proportionally selected according to their rankings in the current population. In [40], Cai and Wang proposed a DE mutation framework which exploits the neighborhood and direction information of the population.

3 Adaptive DE Algorithm

In this section, we propose a new adaptive DE algorithm (ADE). The ADE is characterized by a new mutation strategy called DE/lbest/1 and a two-level adaptive parameter control scheme. The DE/lbest/1 mutation strategy helps to balance the fast convergence and population diversity of the proposed algorithm. In the adaptive parameter control process, the optimization state is first estimated, and then the population-level parameter values F_p and CR_p are adjusted for the whole population. Finally, the individual-level parameter values F_i and CR_i for each individual are generated based on the values of F_p and CR_p. Figure 1 illustrates the flowchart of the proposed ADE algorithm, and Figure 2 shows the process of the two-level adaptive parameter control scheme.

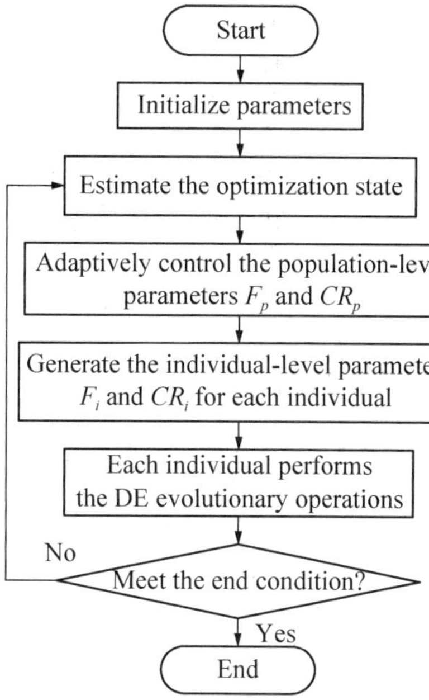

Figure 1 Flowchart of the proposed ADE algorithm

3.1 DE/lbest/1 mutation strategy

For global numerical optimization, the experimental studies in [41] indicate that the DE/best/1 with binomial crossover is the most competitive approach among eight DE variants. DE/best/1 generates a mutant vector by combining the best vector with a scaled difference vector. Here the "best" indicates the vector with the best fitness value in the entire population. This way, all the vectors are guided by the same best solution information during the evolutionary search process. Such a greedy strategy is helpful for improving exploitation, which means the ability of a search algorithm to quickly converge to a near-optimum. Nevertheless, due to the exploitative tendency, the population may lose its diversity too early and reduce its exploration ability to search new regions of the search space. Thus, individuals of the population are more likely to be trapped in some local optima, especially when solving complex multimodal problems.

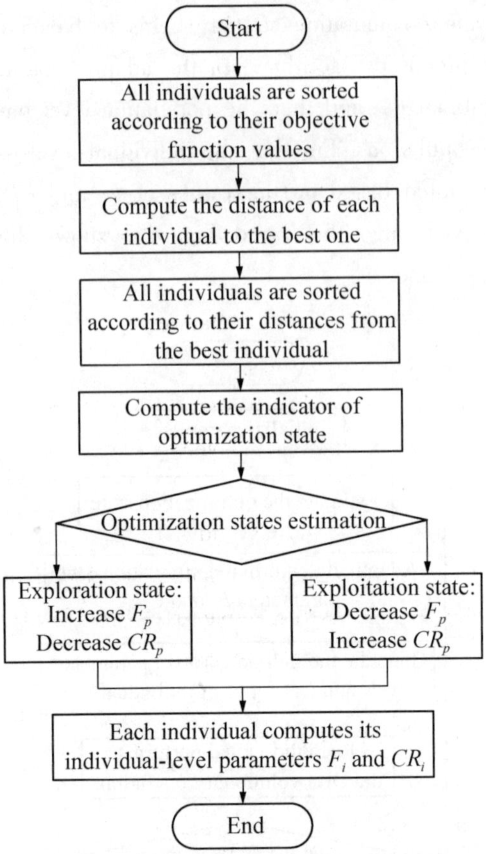

Figure 2　Flowchart of the adaptive parameter control process

In order to cope with the problem of early loss of diversity and promote the exploration ability, we propose a new mutation strategy called DE/lbest/1.

In the proposed strategy, the entire population is divided into a predefined number of non-overlapping groups simply based on the vector indices. Each group contains the same number of vectors. Since the vector indices are sorted randomly during initialization, the population is randomly divided into equal-size groups in fact. Note that the number of groups and group members are kept unchanged during the algorithm's execution. As mentioned earlier, a mutant vector in DE/best/1 is generated by combining a globally best vector with a scaled difference vector. In DE/lbest/1, the best vector is selected from the group to which the target vector belongs instead of the entire population. Therefore, the individuals of each group are attracted by the best vector of their own group, and the entire population is indeed guided by several locally best vectors instead of a single globally best vector. Such an approach thus benefits from a balance between fast convergence and population diversity. On the other hand, the difference vector involved in the mutation strategy can be generated not only by two vectors from the same group, but also by two vectors from different groups (i. e. the entire population). According to the above description, the DE/lbest/1 mutation strategy can be expressed as follows:

$$\mathbf{v}_i^g = \mathbf{x}_{\text{lbest}_i}^g + F \cdot (\mathbf{x}_{r_1}^g - \mathbf{x}_{r_2}^g). \tag{9}$$

where the subscript lbest_i denotes the best vector in the group with respect to target vector i, and r_1, r_2 are the difference vector indices that are indistinct integers randomly selected from $[1, 2, \dots, NP]$ and are also different from i.

In the neighborhood-based local and global mutation models proposed for DE (DEGL)[36], also the local mutation model considers the vector index based onmultiple groups of solutions to improve the exploration ability of DE. Our DE/lbest/1 differs from DEGL in the following major aspects.

1) DEGL employs both local and global mutation models, while our DE/lbest/1 utilizes only local mutation model (locally best solutions).

2) The local mutation model of DEGL considers the vector index based overlapping groups of solutions, while our DE/lbest/1 considers the vector index based non-overlapping groups of solutions.

3) For DEGL, the locally best solution and two other solutions involved in the local mutation model are chosen from the same group of solutions. Differently, for DE/lbest/1, only the locally best solution is chosen from its respective group, while two other solutions are chosen from the entire population (may be from different groups).

3.2 Optimization state estimation

In order to formulate an approach to optimization state estimation for DE, the population distribution characteristics are first described. At the early stage of evolution, the population distribution is relatively dispersive, since individuals are scattered in the searching space to explore different promising regions. As the optimization progresses, the population will gradually converge, and finally cluster around a global or local optimum at the later stage. Due to the variation, the information of population distribution can be used to estimate the optimization state in the DE algorithm. In the following paragraphs, we describe how to measure the population distribution and how to use the distribution information to estimate the optimization state.

In the procedure of optimization state estimation, all individuals are first sorted according to both their fitness values and their distances from the best individual. Further, the relationship between these two sorting orders can be used to measure the population distribution. The detailed steps are as follows.

Step 1): In the beginning of each generation, the fitness values of all the individuals are sorted in a descending order (from the best to the worst). Suppose that the ranking of the fitness value of individual i is denoted as f_i, where $i = 1, 2, \dots, NP$.

Step 2): Compute the Euclideandistancesfrom the best individual to the other individuals. Then, these distances are sorted in an ascending order (from the nearest to the farthest). Suppose that the ranking of the distance of individual i is denoted as d_i, where $i = 1, 2, \dots, NP$.

Step 3): After obtaining the two rankings f_i and d_i for each individual i, compute the indicator of the optimization state (*IOS*) so as to estimate the current optimization state:

$$IOS = \sum_{i=1}^{NP} |f_i - d_i|. \tag{10}$$

If the two rankings for each individual are exactly the same (i. e. , $f_i = d_i$ for each i), then the better individuals are also closer to the best individual, and *IOS* has its minimum value:

$$IOS_{\min} = \sum_{r=1}^{NP} |r - r| = 0. \tag{11}$$

On the contrary, if the two rankings for each individual are just the opposite (i. e. , $f_i + d_i = NP + 1$ for each i), then the better individuals are also farther from the best individual, and *IOS* has its maximum value:

$$IOS_{\max} = \begin{cases} \dfrac{NP \cdot NP}{2}, & \text{if } NP \text{ is even} \\ \dfrac{(NP+1) \cdot (NP-1)}{2}, & \text{if } NP \text{ is odd} \end{cases}. \tag{12}$$

Step 4): The value of *IOS* is normalized by the difference between the values of $IOS_{\max}$ and $IOS_{\min}$ as

$$\overline{IOS} = \frac{IOS - IOS_{\min}}{IOS_{\max} - IOS_{\min}}. \tag{13}$$

where $\overline{IOS}$ is the normalized value of *IOS*, ranging from 0 to 1.

Step 5): Perform the estimation of the optimization state. According to the value of $\overline{IOS}$, we formally define the exploration and exploitation states based on (14):

$$\Phi = \begin{cases} S_1, & \text{if } \mathrm{rand}(0,1) < \overline{IOS} \\ S_2, & \text{otherwise} \end{cases}, \tag{14}$$

where Φ is the estimated optimization state, S_1 and S_2 represent the exploration state and exploitation state, respectively, and rand(0, 1) is a uniform random number within [0, 1].

Exploration State: If rand(0, 1) is smaller than the value of $\overline{IOS}$, the optimization state is estimated to be exploration state. That is, the optimization process has a probability of $\overline{IOS}$ to be classified into exploration state.

Exploitation State: If rand(0, 1) is not smaller than the value of $\overline{IOS}$, the optimization state is estimated to be exploration state. That is, the optimization process has a probability of $(1 - \overline{IOS})$ to be classified into exploitation state.

The definitions of exploration and exploitation states are based on the following considerations. Note that the definitions are based on considering the population set of the current generation. When the value of $\overline{IOS}$ is large, the differences between the two rankings f_i and d_i are obvious. A large $\overline{IOS}$ can be caused by two cases. Forone case, there exist many good individuals far away from the best individual, which means that the population is exploring different promising regions. For another case, there exist many bad individuals close to the best, which indicates that the region around the best may be not the most promising one in the search space, because only a few good individuals have located there. Even if these bad individuals are close to the global optimum locating in a very narrow steep niche, there exist other better individuals which are farther from the optimum. These better individuals should be exploring other regions in the search space, or they would be closer to the optimum. In other words, only some but not most individuals have converged to the region round the global optimum. For both cases, the optimization process is more likely to be in the exploration state, for the population is indeed exploring different regions in this particular generation. This is also true if the population of previous generation favors more exploration (larger value of $\overline{IOS}$). Since the current and previous sets of populations are both exploring different regions in the search space, it is reasonable to individually estimate each as exploration state (although to different degree). On the contrary, when the value of $\overline{IOS}$ is small, most of the good individuals have converged around the best individual, and thus the optimization process has a large probability to be in the exploitation state.

3.3 Two-level adaptive parameter control scheme

Our proposed adaptive parameter control scheme is a two-level adaptation strategy that includes two steps to adjust the parameters. In the first step, the population-level parameter values F_p and CR_p for the whole population are adaptively controlled. The control method is based on the optimization states which can be estimated by the approach described above. Based on the population-level parameter values F_p and CR_p, the individual-level parameter values F_i and CR_i for each individual are further computed in the second step. Since both the population and individual information are utilized in the control, the parameter values can be adapted to the characteristics of both population and individual.

Before describing the detail of the control scheme, we first briefly discuss the effects of the parameters F and CR. According to (9), the control parameter F is used to scale the difference vector. Using a large value of F generates a mutant vector largely different from the base vector chosen from the population, and thus helps maintain the population diversity. In contrast, a small value of F is more likely to facilitate convergence. According to (7), CR is the probability that a vector component will be inherited from the mutant vector. In our proposed mutation strategy, a mutant vector is generated by the guide of a locally best vector. Therefore, a large value of CR causes the newly generated vectors to converge around the locally best vectors, whereas a small value of CR makes the whole population more diverse.

Based on the above considerations, the strategies for adjusting the population-level parameter values F_p and CR_p in different optimization states are defined as follows.

Exploration State—Increasing F_p and Decreasing CR_p: In the exploration state, in order to explore more promising regions, it is better to increase the value of F_p. Conversely, the value of CR_p should be decreased so that the newly generated vectors will not crowd around some locally best vectors.

Exploitation State—Decreasing F_p *and Increasing* CR_p: In the exploitation state, an appropriate way to accelerate convergence is to decrease the value of F_p. Meanwhile, increasing the value of CR_p can help exploitation around some promising vectors.

Based on the above strategies, the values of F_p and CR_p can be adjusted adaptively according to the current estimated optimization state Φ. The adjustment is based on the values of F_p and CR_p of the previous generation, as shown in (15) and (16):

$$F_p^g = \begin{cases} F_p^{g-1} + c_F \cdot \Delta F_p, & \text{if } \Phi = S_1 \\ F_p^{g-1} - c_F \cdot \Delta F_p, & \text{if } \Phi = S_2 \end{cases}, \tag{15}$$

$$CR_p^g = \begin{cases} CR_p^{g-1} - c_{CR} \cdot \Delta CR_p, & \text{if } \Phi = S_1 \\ CR_p^{g-1} + c_{CR} \cdot \Delta CR_p, & \text{if } \Phi = S_2 \end{cases}. \tag{16}$$

where

$$\Delta F_p, \Delta CR_p = \begin{cases} \dfrac{IOS - IOS_{\min}}{IOS_{\max} - IOS_{\min}}, & \text{if } \Phi = S_1 \\ \dfrac{IOS_{\max} - IOS}{IOS_{\max} - IOS_{\min}}, & \text{if } \Phi = S_2 \end{cases}. \tag{17}$$

Obviously, the values of ΔF_p and ΔCR_p are clamped in the range of [0, 1]. The coefficients c_F and c_{CR} are used to control the adjustment steps $c_F \cdot \Delta F_p$ and $c_{CR} \cdot \Delta CR_p$, respectively. In order to shrink the adjustment steps smaller than 10% of the value ranges of F and CR (i. e. 0.1), we set c_F and c_{CR} as 0. 1 and 0. 05 empirically. According to (17), the adjustment step is also related to the value of IOS. The values of F_p and CR_p are both clamped in the range of [0, 1].

After obtaining the population-level parameter values F_p and CR_p for the whole population, the individual-level parameter values F_i and CR_i are generated for each individual i according to their rankings of fitness values and the distances from the best individual. It is implemented by adjusting the values of F_p and CR_p of the current generation:

$$F_i^g = \begin{cases} F_p^g + \Delta F_i, & \text{if}(f_i > \frac{NP}{2}) \wedge (d_i > \frac{NP}{2}) \\ F_p^g - \Delta F_i, & \text{if}(f_i < \frac{NP}{2}) \wedge (d_i < \frac{NP}{2}) \\ F_p^g, & \text{otherwise} \end{cases}, \tag{18}$$

$$CR_i^g = \begin{cases} CR_p^g - \Delta CR_i, & \text{if}(f_i > \frac{NP}{2}) \wedge (d_i > \frac{NP}{2}) \\ CR_p^g + \Delta CR_i, & \text{if}(f_i < \frac{NP}{2}) \wedge (d_i < \frac{NP}{2}) \\ CR_p^g, & \text{otherwise} \end{cases}. \tag{19}$$

where

$$\Delta F_i, \Delta CR_i = \begin{cases} \dfrac{(f_i + d_i) - NP}{2NP}, & \text{if}(f_i > \frac{NP}{2}) \wedge (d_i > \frac{NP}{2}) \\ \dfrac{NP - (f_i + d_i)}{2NP}, & \text{if}(f_i < \frac{NP}{2}) \wedge (d_i < \frac{NP}{2}) \end{cases}. \tag{20}$$

In these adaptive strategies for the individual-level parameters, we can see that if individual i has a low fitness value and is far from the best individual, a large F_i and a small CR_i can help it to explore new promising regions of the search space. In this case, F_i and CR_i should be generated by increasing F_p and decreasing CR_p, respectively. In contrast, if individual i has a high fitness value and is near the best individual, a small F_i and a large CR_i would allow it to do more exploitation around its current position. Thus, F_i and CR_i should be generated by decreasing F_p and increasing CR_p, respectively. Based on the above considerations, only the individuals with both rankings either high or low will adjust the parameter values accordingly, while the rest of individuals utilize only the population-level parameters. In this implementation, the rankings above or below half of the population size are considered as high or low, respectively. The values of F_i and CR_i are also clamped in the range of $[0, 1]$.

3.4 Runtime complexity of ADE

The runtime complexity of a classic DE algorithm is $O(NP \cdot D \cdot G_{max})$ [36], where G_{max} is the maximum number of generations. ADE differs from the classic DE mainly in the DE/lbest/1 mutation strategy and the two-level parameter adaptation.

For the DE/lbest/1, the runtime complexity of finding the locally best vector in each group depends on comparing the fitness value with that of the locally best vector. Note that the locally best fitness value should be upgraded for each target vector in the respective group if it is replaced by the newly generated trial vector. In the worst possible case, when the trial vector always replaces the target vector, the overall runtime complexity is $O(NP \cdot D \cdot G_{max})$.

For the population-level adaptation, we need to sort all the vectors based on their fitness values and their distances to the best vector respectively in the beginning of each generation. The runtime complexity of computing the distances for all the vectors is $O(NP \cdot D)$ since we use Euclidean distance. By utilizing the heap sort algorithm, the sorting procedure can be completed in $O(NP \cdot \log_2 NP)$ time. For the individual-level adaptation, each vector needs to compare their rankings against $\frac{NP}{2}$ (see (18) and (19)), and the number of additional comparisons is $O(NP)$. Hence, over G_{max} generations, the overall runtime complexity of the two-level parameter adaptation is $O(\max(NP \cdot D \cdot G_{max}, NP \cdot \log_2 NP \cdot G_{max}))$.

Considering both DE/lbest/1 and two-level parameter adaptation, the runtime complexity of ADE is $O(\max(NP \cdot D \cdot G_{max}, NP \cdot \log_2 NP \cdot G_{max}))$. If $D \geqslant \log_2 NP$, the asymptotic order of complexity for ADE remains $O(NP \cdot D \cdot G_{max})$. This condition is usually satisfied when D is relatively high. In this case, ADE does not impose any serious burden on the runtime complexity.

4 Experimental Results

4.1 Benchmark functions and experimental setup

In this section, experiments are carried out to evaluate the performance of the proposed ADE. We use 33 benchmark functions chosen from [42] and [43]. Functions $f_1 - f_{22}$ are summarized in Table 1[42]. A detailed description of functions $f_{23} - f_{33}$ can be found in [43]. These functions can be classified into four groups. The first six functions $f_1 - f_6$ are unimodal functions. These functions can be used to test the convergence speed of the algorithms. The next six functions $f_7 - f_{12}$ are multimodal functions where the number of local optima increases exponentially with the problem dimension. The next ten functions $f_{13} - f_{22}$ are low-dimensional multimodal functions with a few local optima. The algorithms' global search ability to escape from local optima can be verified by these multimodal functions. The last eleven functions $f_{23} - f_{33}$ are hybrid composition functions taken from the CEC 2005 competition ($F_{15} - F_{25}$)[43], each of which is composed of 10 sub-functions. Obviously, the functions in the fourth group are much more complex and make our test suite more comprehensive and convincing.

Table 1 Benchmark functions[42, 43]

Name	Test function	D	S	$f_{\min}$
Sphere	$f_1(x) = \sum_{i=1}^{D} x_i^2$	30, 100	$[-100, 100]^D$	0
Schewefel 2. 22	$f_2(x) = \sum_{i=1}^{D} \lvert x_i \rvert + \prod_{i=1}^{D} \lvert x_i \rvert$	30, 100	$[-10, 10]^D$	0
Schewefel 1. 2	$f_3(x) = \sum_{i=1}^{D} (\sum_{j=1}^{i} x_j)^2$	30, 100	$[-100, 100]^D$	0
Rosenbrock	$f_4(x) = \sum_{i=1}^{D-1} [100(x_{i+1} - x_i^2)^2 + (x_i - 1)^2]$	30, 100	$[-30, 30]^D$	0
Step	$f_5(x) = \sum_{i=1}^{D} \lvert x_i + 0.5 \rvert^2$	30, 100	$[-100, 100]^D$	0
Noisy Quaric	$f_6(x) = \sum_{i=1}^{D} i x_i^4 + random[0,1)$	30, 100	$[-1.28, 1.28]^D$	0
Schewefel 2. 26	$f_7(x) = \sum_{i=1}^{D} - x_i \sin(\sqrt{\lvert x_i \rvert})$	30, 100	$[-500, 500]^D$	-12569. 5 for $D=30$
Rastrigin	$f_8(x) = \sum_{i=1}^{D} [x_i^2 - 10\cos(2\pi x_i) + 10]$	30, 100	$[-5.12, 5.12]^D$	0
Ackley	$f_9(x) = -20\exp(-0.2\sqrt{\frac{1}{D}\sum_{i=1}^{D} x_i^2}) - \exp(\frac{1}{D}\sum_{i=1}^{D}\cos 2\pi x_i) + 20 + e$	30, 100	$[-32, 32]^D$	0

Continue Table 1

Name	Test function	D	S	$f_{\min}$
Griewank	$f_{10}(x) = \frac{1}{4000}\sum_{i=1}^{D} x_i^2 - \prod_{i=1}^{D}\cos(\frac{x_i}{\sqrt{i}}) + 1$	30, 100	$[-600, 600]^D$	0
Penalized	$f_{11}(x) = \frac{\pi}{D}\{10\sin^2(\pi y_i) + \sum_{i=1}^{D-1}(y_i - 1)^2 \times [1 + 10\sin^2(\pi y_{i+1})] + (y_D - 1)^2\} + \sum_{i=1}^{D} u(x_i, 10, 100, 4)$	30, 100	$[-50, 50]^D$	0
	$f_{12}(x) = 0.1\{\sin^2(3\pi x_1) + \sum_{i=1}^{D-1}(x_i - 1)^2 \times [1 + \sin2(3\pi x_{i+1})] + (x_D - 1)^2[1 + \sin^2(2\pi x_D)]\} + \sum_{i=1}^{D} u(x_i, 5, 100, 4)$	30, 100	$[-50, 50]^D$	0
Foxholes	$f_{13}(x) = \{1/500 + \sum_{j=1}^{25}[j + \sum_{i=1}^{2}(x_i - a_{ij})^6]^{-1}\}^{-1}$	2	$[-65.536, 65.536]^D$	1
Kowalik	$f_{14}(x) = \sum_{i=1}^{11}[a_i - x_1(b^2 + b_i x_2)/(b_i^2 + b_i x_3 + x_4)]^2$	4	$[-5, 5]^D$	0.0003075
Six-hump Camel-back	$f_{15}(x) = 4x_1^2 - 2.1x_1^2 + 3^{-1}x_1^6 + x_1x_2 - 4x_2^2 + 4x_2^4$	2	$[-5, 5]^D$	-1.0316285
Branin	$f_{16}(x) = (x_2 - 5.1/4\pi^2 \cdot x_1^2 + 5/\pi \cdot x_1 - 6)^2 + 10(1 - 1/8\pi)\cos x_1 + 10$	2	$[-5, 10] \times [0, 15]$	0.397887
Goldstein-price	$f_{17}(x) = [1 + (x_1 + x_2 + 1)^2(19 - 14x_1 + 3x_1^2 - 14x_2 + 6x_1x_2 + 3x_2^2)] \times [30 + (2x_1 - 3x_2)^2 \times (18 - 32x_1 + 12x_1^2 + 48x_2 - 36x_1x_2 + 27x_2^2)]$	2	$[-2, 2]^D$	3.00000
Hartman	$f_{18}(x) = -\sum_{i=1}^{4} c_i \exp[-\sum_{j=1}^{4} a_{ij}(x_j - p_{ij})^2]$	4	$[0, 1]^D$	-3.86278
	$f_{19}(x) = -\sum_{i=1}^{4} c_i \exp[-\sum_{j=1}^{6} a_{ij}(x_j - p_{ij})^2]$	6	$[0, 1]^D$	-3.32237
Shekel's	$f_{20}(x) = -\sum_{i=1}^{5}[(x - a_i)(x - a_i)^T + c_i]^{-1}$	4	$[0, 10]^D$	-10.1532
	$f_{21}(x) = -\sum_{i=1}^{7}[(x - a_i)(x - a_i)^T + c_i]^{-1}$	4	$[0, 10]^D$	-10.4029
	$f_{22}(x) = -\sum_{i=1}^{10}[(x - a_i)(x - a_i)^T + c_i]^{-1}$	4	$[0, 10]^D$	-10.5364

Continue Table 1

Name	Test function	D	S	f_{min}
Hybrid composition functions	$f_{23}-f_{33}$: $F_{15}-F_{25}$ from the IEEE CEC 2005 special session and competition[43]	30	given in[43]	given in[43]

The population size NP of ADE is set to 50 and 200 for problems with $D \leqslant 30$ and $D = 100$, respectively. The population of ADE is divided into 10 groups. The initial values of F_p and CR_p of ADE are both set as 0.5. Each experiment is run 25 times independently and the results are averaged. In addition, we make use of the Wilcoxon's rank sum test[44] at $\alpha = 0.05$ to evaluate the statistical significance of theresults.

4.2 Comparison with existing state-of-the-art DE variants

We compare ADE with four state-of-the-art DE variants, i.e., CoDE[28], JADE[26], jDE[24], and SaDE[25] on all test functions with 30 dimensions (except the low-dimensional functions $f_{13}-f_{22}$). All these algorithms use some strategies to adaptively control the parameters F and CR. The other parameters of the four algorithms are set according to their original papers.

4.2.1 Unimodal functions

The mean and standard deviation of the results for 25 independent runs on $f_1 - f_6$ are presented in Table 2. Each algorithm is run for the number of fitness evaluations indicated in the FEs column of the table[42]. For clarity, the results of the best algorithms are marked in boldface. According to the results, it can be seen that ADE, JADE, and SaDE perform better than CoDE and jDE on these functions in general. This is because the former three algorithms use greedy mutation strategies to some degree. The relatively low accuracy results of CoDE and jDE should be due to their more diverse mutation strategies. It is interesting to note that CoDE achieves the best results on f_4, which is a unimodal function for $D \leqslant 3$, but may become multimodal when the dimension is high. [45]

Table 2 Comparison between ADE and four state-of-the-art DE variants on unimodal functions

Fun.	FEs	ADE Mean (Std Dev)	CoDE Mean (Std Dev)	JADE Mean (Std Dev)	jDE Mean (Std Dev)	SaDE Mean (Std Dev)
f_1	150000	1.49E-70 (3.95E-70)	4.85E-25† (6.07E-25)	2.19E-57† (1.10E-56)	4.67E-31† (5.08E-31)	5.02E-65† (5.96E-65)
f_2	200000	3.21E-51 (6.57E-51)	2.98E-19† (1.77E-19)	1.07E-27† (5.32E-27)	1.22E-25† (1.24E-25)	6.28E-46† (6.09E-46)
f_3	500000	8.13E-27 (2.60E-26)	8.40E-05† (8.25E-05)	3.55E-99† (1.68E-98)	1.71E-14† (5.81E-14)	3.22E-28† (1.03E-28)

Continue Table 2

Fun.	FEs	ADE Mean (Std Dev)	CoDE Mean (Std Dev)	JADE Mean (Std Dev)	jDE Mean (Std Dev)	SaDE Mean (Std Dev)
f_4	2000000	2.28E-29 (3.84E-29)	0.00E+00† (0.00E+00)	3.19E-01† (1.10E+00)	3.19E-01† (1.08E+00)	3.19E-01† (1.10E+00)
f_5	150000	0.00E+00 (0.00E+00)	0.00E+00 (0.00E+00)	0.00E+00 (0.00E+00)	0.00E+00 (0.00E+00)	0.00E+00 (0.00E+00)
f_6	300000	2.88E-03 (1.17E-03)	3.62E-03† (1.22E-03)	5.94E-04† (2.43E-04)	3.40E-03† (7.71E-04)	1.34E-03† (4.43E-04)

† The difference between the results of ADE and the corresponding algorithm is signficant at $\alpha = 0.05$ by Wilcoxon's rank sum test.

In order to compare the reliability and search speed of different algorithms, Table 3 summarizes the success rates at which acceptable solutions are found over 25 runs and the number of FEs required to find the acceptable solutions. A solution is considered acceptable if it is obtained with sufficient accuracy: 1E-10. The ranks in the table are evaluated based onthe descending order of the success rates and ties are broken by the ascending order of FEs. From Table 3, we find that all the algorithms perform with a high reliability on most of the unimodal functions. In particular, the proposed ADE algorithm is able to find acceptable solutions with 100% success rate on all the functions. On the other hand, only CoDE and ADE always obtain the near-global optimum for f_4, while JADE, jDE, and SaDE sometimes fail to locate the acceptable solutions. However, CoDE totally fails to reach acceptable solutions for f_3. From the aspect of search speed, JADE, SaDE, and ADE use a smaller number of FEs than CoDE and jDE do to reach acceptable results on average. Overall, ADE performs the best on most functions in this group.

Table 3 Success rate and search speed comparisons on unimodal functions

Fun.	Acceptable accuracy		ADE	CoDE	JADE	jDE	SaDE
f_1	1E-10	SR	100	100	100	100	100
		FEs	2.89E+04	7.58E+04	3.42E+04	6.41E+04	3.18E+04
		rank	1	5	3	4	2
f_2	1E-10	SR	100	100	100	100	100
		FEs	4.60E+04	1.18E+05	6.35E+04	9.07E+04	5.13E+04
		rank	1	5	3	4	2
f_3	1E-10	SR	100	0	100	100	100
		FEs	2.30E+05	N/A	7.74E+04	3.98E+05	2.15E+05
		rank	3	5	1	4	2

Continue Table 3

Fun.	Acceptable accuracy		ADE	CoDE	JADE	jDE	SaDE
f_4	1E − 10	SR	100	100	92	92	92
		FEs	2. 73E + 05	4. 98E + 05	9. 96E + 04	6. 76E + 05	3. 18E + 05
		rank	1	2	3	5	4
f_5	1E − 10	SR	100	100	100	100	100
		FEs	1. 12E + 02	2. 14E + 02	1. 00E + 02	2. 10E + 02	9. 20E + 01
		rank	3	5	2	4	1
f_6	1E − 10	SR	100	100	100	100	100
		FEs	7. 76E + 04	1. 18E + 05	3. 06E + 04	1. 04E + 05	3. 61E + 04
		rank	3	5	1	4	2
avg_rank			2	4. 5	2. 2	4. 2	2. 2

4. 2. 2 Multimodal functions with many local optima

Table 4 compares the five DE variants on the multimodal functions with many local optima. It can be seen that ADE, CoDE, and jDE are capable of reaching near-global optima on all the six functions. These three algorithms obtain the same best results on f_7, f_8, and f_{10}, but CoDE and jDE get higher accuracy than ADE on f_9, while ADE outperforms CoDE and jDE on f_{11} and f_{12}. On the other hand, JADE and SaDE perform the best on f_9, f_{11}, and f_{12}, but they are sometimes trapped in local optima on f_{10} and f_8, respectively. These results indicate that ADE manages to avoid premature convergence and also find solutions with high accuracy on multimodal functions with a lot of local optima.

Table 4 Comparison between ADE and four state-of-the-art DE variants on multimodal functions with many local optima

Fun.	FEs	ADE Mean (Std Dev)	CoDE Mean (Std Dev)	JADE Mean (Std Dev)	jDE Mean (Std Dev)	SaDE Mean (Std Dev)
f_7	900000	− 12569. 49 (1. 82E − 12)	− 12569. 49 (1. 86E − 12)	− 12564. 75 (2. 37E + 01)	− 12569. 49 (7. 28E − 12)	− 12550. 54† (4. 43E + 01)
f_8	500000	0. 00E + 00 (0. 00E + 00)	0. 00E + 00 (0. 00E + 00)	0. 00E + 00 (0. 00E + 00)	0. 00E + 00 (0. 00E + 00)	1. 63E + 00† (1. 37E + 00)
f_9	200000	5. 99E − 15 (1. 77E − 15)	4. 14E − 15† (0. 00E + 00)	4. 14E − 15† (0. 00E + 00)	4. 28E − 15† (6. 96E − 16)	4. 14E − 15† (0. 00E + 00)
f_{10}	200000	0. 00E + 00 (0. 00E + 00)	0. 00E + 00 (0. 00E + 00)	3. 94E − 04† (1. 97E − 03)	0. 00E + 00 (0. 00E + 00)	0. 00E + 00 (0. 00E + 00)

Continue Table 4

Fun.	FEs	ADE Mean (Std Dev)	CoDE Mean (Std Dev)	JADE Mean (Std Dev)	jDE Mean (Std Dev)	SaDE Mean (Std Dev)
f_{11}	150000	1.57E-32 (2.74E-48)	2.31E-26† (2.73E-26)	1.57E-32 (2.79E-48)	3.79E-32† (1.91E-32)	1.57E-32 (2.79E-48)
f_{12}	150000	1.35E-32 (5.47E-48)	1.91E-25† (2.51E-25)	1.35E-32 (5.59E-48)	2.17E-31† (2.41E-31)	1.35E-32 (5.59E-48)

† The difference between the results of ADE and the corresponding algorithm is signficant at $\alpha = 0.05$ by Wilcoxon's rank sum test.

The reliability and search speed of different DE variants are further compared and reported in Table 5. The acceptable accuracy is set as -10000 for f_7 and 1E-10 for all others. The results show that all six functions are optimized by ADE, CoDE, and jDE with 100% success rates. Moreover, the proposed ADE reaches the acceptable solutions with a smaller number of FEs than CoDE and jDE. Although JADE and SaDE converge faster than ADE on some functions, their reliability is relatively low, as reflected by their success rates on f_{10} and f_8, respectively. Overall, the ADE also exhibits very competitive performance on multimodal functions with a lot of local optima. Not only does it benefit from fast convergence but also high algorithm reliability which may stem from the two-level adaptive parameter control scheme.

Table 5 Success rate and search speed comparisons on multimodal functions with many local optima

Fun.	Acceptable accuracy		ADE	CoDE	JADE	jDE	SaDE
f_7	-10000	SR	100	100	100	100	100
		FEs	2.42E+04	2.43E+04	2.21E+04	3.36E+04	3.95E+04
		rank	2	3	1	4	5
f_8	1E-10	SR	100	100	100	100	28
		FEs	1.74E+05	1.97E+05	1.45E+05	1.23E+05	1.60E+05
		rank	3	4	2	1	5
f_9	1E-10	SR	100	100	100	100	100
		FEs	4.93E+04	1.22E+05	5.52E+04	1.10E+05	5.14E+04
		rank	1	5	3	4	2
f_{10}	1E-10	SR	100	100	96	100	100
		FEs	5.84E+04	9.03E+04	3.73E+04	6.79E+04	3.53E+04
		rank	2	4	5	3	1
f_{11}	1E-10	SR	100	100	100	100	100
		FEs	5.53E+04	6.90E+04	3.39E+04	5.92E+04	2.91E+04
		rank	3	5	2	4	1

Continue Table 5

Fun.	Acceptable accuracy		ADE	CoDE	JADE	jDE	SaDE
f_{12}	1E-10	SR	100	100	100	100	100
		FEs	3.93E+04	7.28E+04	3.59E+04	6.32E+04	3.11E+04
		rank	3	5	2	4	1
avg_rank			2.3	4.3	2.5	3.3	2.5

4.2.3 Multimodal functions with a few local optima

For multimodal functions with a few local optima, we run the algorithms for a small number of FEs to find out whether they can locate the global optimum quickly. The experimental results are tabulated in Table 6. We find that ADE and SaDE are the best among the five DE variants for this group of functions. They are able to find the global optimum within the predefined maximum number of FEs for all the functions. CoDE, JADE, and jDE perform worse than ADE and SaDE on one or more functions, e.g., f_{14}, f_{19}, and f_{20}. Overall, the performance of different algorithms is similar on most of functions in this group, and we skip the comparison of success rate and number of FEs. ADE remains the best one among these algorithms.

Table 6 Comparison between ADE and four state-of-the-art DE variants on multimodal functions with a few local optima

Fun.	FEs	ADE Mean (Std Dev)	CoDE Mean (Std Dev)	JADE Mean (Std Dev)	jDE Mean (Std Dev)	SaDE Mean (Std Dev)
f_{13}	20000	0.998004 (0.00E+00)	0.998004 (0.00E+00)	0.998004 (1.36E-16)	0.998004 (0.00E+00)	0.998004 (0.00E+00)
f_{14}	20000	0.0003075 (4.03E-13)	0.0003075 (2.56E-08)	0.0011099† (4.01E-03)	0.0003544† (1.82E-04)	0.0003075 (1.02E-12)
f_{15}	20000	-1.0316285 (4.44E-16)	-1.0316285 (4.53E-16)	-1.0316285 (2.82E-14)	-1.0316285 (4.44E-16)	-1.0316285 (4.53E-16)
f_{16}	20000	0.397887 (0.00E+00)	0.397887 (0.00E+00)	0.397887 (7.73E-11)	0.397887 (0.00E+00)	0.397887 (0.00E+00)
f_{17}	20000	3.000000 (1.78E-15)	3.000000 (1.81E-15)	3.000000 (1.50E-15)	3.000000 (1.35E-15)	3.000000 (1.81E-15)
f_{18}	20000	-3.86274 (8.33E-16)	-3.86274 (8.65E-16)	-3.86274 (9.06E-16)	-3.86274 (8.88E-16)	-3.86274 (8.21E-16)
f_{19}	20000	-3.321995 (1.26E-15)	-3.302972 (4.45E-02)	-3.288704† (5.45E-02)	-3.307725† (3.86E-02)	-3.321995 (1.84E-09)

Continue Table 6

Fun.	FEs	ADE Mean (Std Dev)	CoDE Mean (Std Dev)	JADE Mean (Std Dev)	jDE Mean (Std Dev)	SaDE Mean (Std Dev)
f_{20}	20000	-10.1532 (4.19E-15)	-10.1532 (3.80E-15)	-9.9511 (1.01E+00)	-10.1532 (4.74E-11)	-10.1532 (4.93E-15)
f_{21}	20000	-10.4029 (4.11E-15)	-10.4029 (3.52E-15)	-10.4029 (6.36E-10)	-10.4029 (3.47E-14)	-10.4029 (3.46E-15)
f_{22}	20000	-10.5364 (2.71E-15)	-10.5364 (2.46E-15)	-10.5364 (1.16E-10)	-10.5364 (2.11E-14)	-10.5364 (3.40E-15)

† The difference between the results of ADE and the corresponding algorithm is signficant at $\alpha = 0.05$ by Wilcoxon's rank sum test.

4.2.4 Hybrid composition functions

All of the functions in this group are non-separable, rotated, and multimodal functions with a huge number of local optima. Such functions appear to be the most difficult class of problems for most optimization algorithms. The experimental results are shown in Table 7 and Table 8. It can be noted that no DE variant is able to obtain a near-global optimum on any function. Overall, ADE achieves better results on more functions. It performs better than CoDE, JADE, jDE, and SaDE on five, seven, eight, and eight functions, respectively. Conversely, CoDE, JADE, and jDE surpass ADE on three, one, and two functions, respectively. SaDE cannot outperform ADE on any functions in this group.

Table 7 Comparison between ADE and four state-of-the-art DE variants on hybrid composition functions

Fun.	FEs	ADE Mean (Std Dev)	CoDE Mean (Std Dev)	JADE Mean (Std Dev)	jDE Mean (Std Dev)	SaDE Mean (Std Dev)
f_{23}	300000	1.80E+02 (1.31E+02)	4.16E+02† (6.25E+01)	3.88E+02† (6.52E+01)	3.28E+02† (1.08E+02)	3.88E+02† (5.15E+01)
f_{24}	300000	1.20E+02 (3.27E+01)	7.95E+01† (6.97E+01)	1.20E+02 (1.41E+02)	8.97E+01† (6.40E+01)	1.32E+02 (2.13E+01)
f_{25}	300000	1.27E+02 (2.92E+01)	7.86E+01† (7.68E+01)	1.56E+02 (1.39E+02)	1.42E+02 (3.12E+01)	1.71E+02† (1.95E+01)
f_{26}	300000	8.58E+02 (1.08E+02)	9.05E+02† (1.27E+00)	9.04E+02† (7.30E-01)	9.04E+02† (8.16E-01)	8.76E+02 (5.26E+01)
f_{27}	300000	8.70E+02 (5.75E+01)	9.04E+02† (6.11E-01)	9.04E+02† (1.05E+00)	9.04E+02† (3.92E-01)	8.73E+02 (5.47E+01)

Continue Table 7

Fun.	FEs	ADE Mean (Std Dev)	CoDE Mean (Std Dev)	JADE Mean (Std Dev)	jDE Mean (Std Dev)	SaDE Mean (Std Dev)
f_{28}	300000	8.65E+02 (5.76E+01)	9.04E+02† (1.06E+00)	9.04E+02† (9.69E−01)	9.04E+02† (9.71E−01)	8.75E+02 (5.18E+01)
f_{29}	300000	5.00E+02 (1.31E−13)	5.00E+02 (9.85E−14)	5.00E+02 (1.89E−13)	5.00E+02 (1.62E−13)	5.12E+02 (5.88E+01)
f_{30}	300000	9.25E+02 (1.22E+01)	8.55E+02† (2.28E+01)	8.56E+02† (2.24E+01)	8.62E+02† (2.09E+01)	9.25E+02 (1.29E+01)
f_{31}	300000	5.34E+02 (5.45E−03)	5.34E+02 (4.09E−04)	5.50E+02 (7.89E+01)	5.40E+02 (2.96E+01)	5.34E+02 (5.99E−03)
f_{32}	300000	2.00E+02 (1.56E−12)	2.00E+02 (2.90E−14)	2.00E+02 (2.84E−14)	8.60E+02† (2.88E+02)	2.00E+02 (2.84E−14)
f_{33}	300000	2.10E+02 (4.10E−01)	2.11E+02† (7.32E−01)	2.11E+02† (5.88E−01)	2.11E+02† (6.47E−01)	2.12E+02† (1.25E+00)

† The difference between the results of ADE and the corresponding algorithm is signficant at $\alpha = 0.05$ by Wilcoxon's rank sum test.

Table 8 Success rate and search speed comparisons on hybrid composition functions

Fun.	Acceptable accuracy		ADE	CoDE	JADE	jDE	SaDE
f_{23}	2E+02	SR	40	4	0	40	4
		FEs	3.86E+04	5.05E+04	N/A	7.46E+04	5.41E+04
		rank	1	3	5	2	4
f_{24}	2E+02	SR	100	96	80	96	96
		FEs	1.94E+04	3.11E+04	3.32E+04	4.94E+04	5.11E+04
		rank	1	2	5	3	4
f_{25}	2E+02	SR	100	96	80	92	92
		FEs	5.49E+04	5.82E+04	1.06E+04	9.89E+04	1.44E+05
		rank	1	2	5	3	4
f_{26}	1E+03	SR	100	100	100	100	100
		FEs	4.30E+03	4.41E+03	2.03E+03	4.50E+03	4.80E+03
		rank	2	3	1	4	5
f_{27}	1E+03	SR	100	100	100	100	100
		FEs	4.30E+03	4.32E+03	2.08E+03	4.55E+03	4.65E+03
		rank	2	3	1	4	5

Continue Table 8

Fun.	Acceptable accuracy		ADE	CoDE	JADE	jDE	SaDE
f_{28}	1E+03	SR	100	100	100	100	100
		FEs	4.25E+03	4.41E+03	2.06E+03	4.82E+03	4.65E+03
		rank	2	3	1	5	4
f_{29}	1E+03	SR	100	100	100	100	28
		FEs	3.70E+03	4.95E+03	2.88E+03	7.74E+03	4.25E+03
		rank	2	4	1	5	3
f_{30}	1E+03	SR	100	100	100	100	100
		FEs	2.49E+04	1.04E+04	5.70E+03	1.21E+04	1.53E+04
		rank	5	2	1	3	4
f_{31}	1E+03	SR	100	100	100	100	100
		FEs	3.85E+03	5.22E+03	2.94E+03	7.91E+03	4.40E+03
		rank	2	4	1	5	3
f_{32}	5E+02	SR	100	100	100	16	100
		FEs	5.65E+03	8.46E+03	4.73E+03	1.36E+04	5.70E+03
		rank	2	4	1	5	3
f_{33}	5E+02	SR	100	100	100	100	100
		FEs	4.35E+03	6.63E+03	3.47E+03	8.51E+03	5.00E+03
		rank	2	4	1	5	3
avg_rank			2	3.1	2.1	4.0	3.8

In terms of reliability, ADE achieves 100% success rates on all these functions except f_{23}, while the other algorithms yield relatively low success rates on three or four functions. In terms of search speed, JADE converges fastest on most functions and ADE is the second fastest. ADE still obtains the smallest value of average rank on this group of functions. Although the average rank of JADE is very close to that of ADE, the former performs the worst in terms of reliability on three functions.

The convergence curves of CoDE, JADE, jDE, SaDE, and ADE are plotted in Figure 3 for some selected benchmark functions.

4.3 Scalability of ADE

In order to demonstrate the scalability of ADE, we further compare the performance of the five DE variants on $f_1 - f_{12}$ with $D = 100$. Table 9 reports the mean and standard deviation of the results. For most unimodal functions, the performance of ADE, JADE, and SaDE remains significantly superior to that of CoDE and jDE. One may note that the performance of

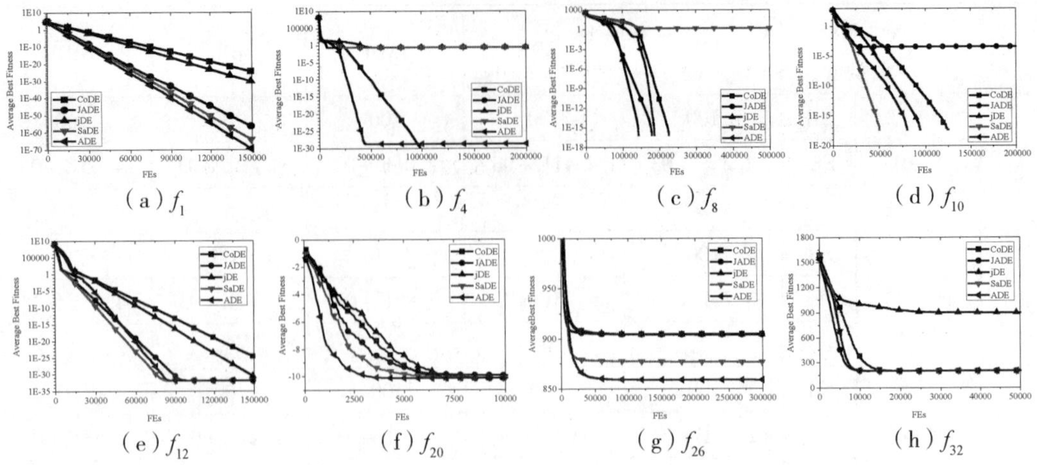

Figure 3 Comparison of convergence performance between ADE and four state-of-the-art DE variants on eight benchmark functions

CoDEdeterorateswith the increase of dimension for f_4, where CoDE achieves the best results for $D=30$. For the multimodal functions, we can observe that the algorithms obtain similar rankings as on $30D$ functions. Overall, ADE, CoDE, and jDE present better global search ability than JADE and SaDE. ADE outperforms all other algorithms on f_7, f_8, and f_{12}.

Table 9 Comparison between ADE and four state-of-the-art DE variants on 100*D* functions

Fun.	FEs	ADE Mean (Std Dev)	CoDE Mean (Std Dev)	JADE Mean (Std Dev)	jDE Mean (Std Dev)	SaDE Mean (Std Dev)
f_1	1000000	3.80E−100 (7.01E−100)	1.01E−72† (8.70E−73)	5.06E−76† (6.63E−76)	3.14E−22† (2.98E−22)	1.84E−137† (3.32E−137)
f_2	1000000	6.57E−47 (3.17E−46)	1.10E−40† (8.11E−41)	5.17E−42† (7.91E−42)	1.93E−13† (4.41E−14)	1.19E−83† (2.78E−83)
f_3	1000000	3.92E−03 (2.47E−03)	9.29E+02† (3.01E+02)	9.99E−09† (1.05E−08)	3.68E+02† (1.14E+02)	2.27E−02† (2.07E−02)
f_4	1000000	2.98E+00 (6.45E+00)	6.27E+01† (3.06E+01)	5.25E+00† (6.69E+00)	9.56E+01† (1.91E+01)	7.10E+01† (3.75E+01)
f_5	1000000	0.00E+00 (0.00E+00)	0.00E+00 (0.00E+00)	0.00E+00 (0.00E+00)	0.00E+00 (0.00E+00)	0.00E+00 (0.00E+00)
f_6	1000000	3.31E−02 (7.27E−03)	1.25E−02† (3.60E−03)	1.88E−03† (4.08E−04)	1.98E−02† (2.50E−03)	1.27E−02† (2.45E−03)
f_7	1000000	−41898.29 (1.95E−11)	−41893.55 (2.37E+01)	−41879.02† (5.46E+00)	−41897.95† (5.16E−01)	−39555.56† (5.43E+02)

Continue Table 9

Fun.	FEs	ADE Mean (Std Dev)	CoDE Mean (Std Dev)	JADE Mean (Std Dev)	jDE Mean (Std Dev)	SaDE Mean (Std Dev)
f_8	1000000	6.37E−01 (1.97E+00)	1.04E+01† (3.25E+00)	7.53E+00† (6.72E−01)	1.99E+00† (1.81E+00)	3.65E+01† (5.23E+00)
f_9	1000000	2.72E+00 (4.89E−01)	4.85E−15† (1.45E−15)	1.14E−14† (1.25E−15)	5.97E−12† (2.65E−12)	1.56E+00† (2.81E−01)
f_{10}	1000000	1.28E−03 (3.49E−03)	3.94E−04 (1.97E−03)	1.28E−03 (3.56E−03)	0.00E+00 (0.00E+00)	9.04E−03† (1.59E−02)
f_{11}	1000000	3.12E−02 (6.95E−02)	4.71E−33† (1.40E−48)	4.61E−02† (8.58E−02)	1.05E−22 (5.83E−23)	2.49E−02 (3.70E−02)
f_{12}	1000000	1.75E−32 (4.65E−33)	4.39E−04† (2.20E−03)	4.39E−04† (2.20E−03)	1.06E−21† (6.40E−22)	6.14E−01† (1.23E+00)

† The difference between the results of ADE and the corresponding algorithm is signficant at $\alpha = 0.05$ by Wilcoxon's rank sum test.

Reliability and search speed comparisons are shown in Table 10. ADE and JADE yield 100% success rates on all test functions, while CoDE, jDE, and SaDE achieve relatively low success rates on two, two, and three functions, respectively. From the aspect of search speed, SaDE converges fastest on most functions, followed by ADE. CoDE and JADE exhibit similar convergence performance while jDE converges slowest in general. These results demonstrate that ADE remains good at striking a balance between reliability and search speed when the dimension increases to 100.

Table 10 Success rate and search speed comparisons on 100*D* functions

Fun.	Acceptable accuracy		ADE	CoDE	JADE	jDE	SaDE
f_1	1E−10	SR	100	100	100	100	100
		FEs	1.41E+05	1.96E+05	2.01E+05	5.76E+05	1.02E+05
		rank	2	3	4	5	1
f_2	1E−10	SR	100	100	100	100	100
		FEs	2.66E+05	2.96E+05	3.08E+05	8.24E+05	1.43E+05
		rank	2	3	4	5	1
f_3	1E+02	SR	100	0	100	0	100
		FEs	2.74E+05	N/A	1.83E+05	N/A	2.81E+05
		rank	2	5	1	4	3

Continue Table 10

Fun.	Acceptable accuracy		ADE	CoDE	JADE	jDE	SaDE
f_4	1E + 02	SR	100	84	100	88	68
		FEs	4. 68E + 05	4. 14E + 05	5. 13E + 05	8. 40E + 05	6. 43E + 05
		rank	1	3	2	4	5
f_5	1E − 10	SR	100	100	100	100	100
		FEs	5. 40E + 04	5. 93E + 04	5. 37E + 04	1. 94E + 05	2. 03E + 05
		rank	2	3	1	4	5
f_6	1E + 00	SR	100	100	100	100	100
		FEs	1. 96E + 04	2. 33E + 04	2. 06E + 04	9. 64E + 04	6. 73E + 03
		rank	2	4	3	5	1
f_7	− 40000	SR	100	100	100	100	28
		FEs	3. 79E + 05	3. 65E + 05	6. 97E + 05	7. 58E + 05	2. 40E + 05
		rank	2	1	3	4	5
f_8	1E + 02	SR	100	100	100	100	100
		FEs	2. 72E + 05	5. 54E + 05	5. 04E + 05	4. 67E + 05	2. 00E + 05
		rank	2	5	4	3	1
f_9	1E + 01	SR	100	100	100	100	100
		FEs	7. 80E + 03	1. 62E + 04	1. 74E + 04	9. 88E + 04	4. 71E + 03
		rank	2	3	4	5	1
f_{10}	1E + 00	SR	100	100	100	100	100
		FEs	4. 02E + 04	5. 67E + 04	6. 48E + 04	1. 83E + 05	2. 55E + 04
		rank	2	3	4	5	1
f_{11}	1E + 00	SR	100	100	100	100	100
		FEs	2. 58E + 05	5. 63E + 04	2. 83E + 05	2. 01E + 05	3. 00E + 04
		rank	4	2	5	3	1
f_{12}	1E + 00	SR	100	100	100	100	80
		FEs	2. 28E + 05	6. 74E + 04	1. 68E + 05	2. 30E + 05	1. 59E + 05
		rank	3	1	2	4	5
avg_rank			2. 2	3. 0	3. 1	4. 3	2. 5

4. 4 Effects of ADE components

Two main components of ADE are the DE/lbest/1 mutation strategy and the two-level parameter adaptation. First, we compare DE using DE/best/1 and DE using DE/lbest/1 to reveal the effectiveness of the DE/lbest/1 mutation strategy. They use the same parameter setting of $NP = 50$, $F = 0.5$ and $CR = 0.5$. The population of DE/lbest/1 is divided into 10 groups. The results on $f_1 - f_{12}$ with $D = 30$ are shown in Table 11. We can observe that DE/best/1 can find very high accuracy solutions on simple unimodal functions $f_1 - f_3$, but it fails to locate the near-global optima on most multimodal functions. The proposed DE/lbest/1 is helpful for balancing the performance between unimodal and multimodal functions. It can find the near-global optimum on most multimodal functions while still being able to converge quickly on unimodal functions. The strengths of the DE/lbest/1 are further demonstrated by comparing with DE/current-to-*p*best/1 in JADE ($F = 0.5$, $CR = 0.5$), which also utilizes multiple good solutions. The results of DE/current-to-*p*best/1 on $f_1 - f_{12}$ can be found in the last column of Table 11. We can observe that the overall performance of DE/lbest/1 is better than that of DE/current-to-*p*best/1. In fact, DE/lbest/1 performs better than or at least the same as DE/current-to-*p*best/1 on nine out of the twelve test functions, while DE/current-to-*p*best/1 beats DE/lbest/1 on three test functions.

Table 11 Effect of DE/lbest/1 mutation strategy

Fun.	FEs	DE/lbest/1 ($CR = 0.5$) Mean (Std Dev)	DE/best/1 ($CR = 0.5$) Mean (Std Dev)	DE/current-to-*p*best/1 Mean (Std Dev)
f_1	150000	8.04E-70 (5.08E-31)	6.17E-173 (0.00E+00)	1.33E-67 (6.25E-68)
f_2	200000	5.01E-47 (4.58E-47)	1.22E-122 (4.88E-122)	1.78E-44 (5.22E-45)
f_3	500000	1.19E-03 (9.23E-04)	2.55E-35 (7.12E-35)	2.92E-15 (2.89E-15)
f_4	2000000	4.78E-01 (1.30E+00)	7.97E-01 (1.59E+00)	1.78E+01 (1.68E+00)
f_5	150000	0.00E+00 (0.00E+00)	3.92E+00 (5.99E+00)	0.00E+00 (0.00E+00)
f_6	300000	1.75E-03 (5.80E-04)	2.85E-03 (1.69E-03)	8.82E-04 (2.31E-04)
f_7	900000	-11599.82 (4.83E+02)	-10600.99 (4.89E+02)	-11958.34 (2.21E+02)
f_8	500000	2.44E+01 (5.91E+00)	3.18E+02 (9.83E+00)	6.17E+01 (5.24E+00)
f_9	200000	4.14E-15 (0.00E+00)	1.10E+00 (8.98E-01)	4.14E-15 (0.00E+00)
f_{10}	200000	0.00E+00 (0.00E+00)	2.77E-02 (5.89E-02)	2.96E-04 (1.48E-03)
f_{11}	150000	1.09E-21 (5.33E-21)	5.05E-01 (1.38E+00)	4.15E-03 (2.07E-02)
f_{12}	150000	1.35E-32 (5.47E-48)	2.94E-01 (7.68E-01)	1.35E-32 (5.47E-48)

In order to investigate the effect of the population-level parameter control, we consider ADE without parameter control (i. e. DE/lbest/1) and ADE with population-level control only (denoted as ADE-p only). Three DE/lbest/1 algorithms with different parameter settings are compared with ADE-p only on $f_1 - f_{12}$. All of them set F to 0.5 as suggested in most of the literature[2,16], and set CR to 0.1, 0.5, and 0.9 respectively. The experimental results averaged over 25 runs are listed in the last four columns of Table 12. Although DE/lbest/1 performs better than DE/best/1, the performance of DE/lbest/1 is still sensitive to the parameter settings. The DE/lbest/1 ($CR = 0.1$) is able to find the near-global optimum on most of the multimodal functions, but it performs the worst on the unimodal functions. In contrast, DE/lbest/1 ($CR = 0.9$) obtains the most accurate results on the unimodal functions $f_1 - f_3$, but it suffers from frequent premature convergence on all the multimodal functions. The performance of ADE-p only is less dependent on the optimization problems. Not only can it get relatively high accuracy solutions on the unimodal functions, but also it is able to preserve premature convergence on most multimodal functions. These results demonstrate that the population-level parameter control strategy is helpful for improving robustness of the algorithm.

Table 12 Effect of two-level parameter adaptation

Fun.	FEs	ADE Mean (Std Dev)	ADE-ponly Mean (Std Dev)	DE/lbest/1 ($CR = 0.1$) Mean (Std Dev)	DE/lbest/1 ($CR = 0.5$) Mean (Std Dev)	DE/lbest/1 ($CR = 0.9$) Mean (Std Dev)
f_1	150000	1.49E-70 (3.95E-70)	1.46E-65 (3.60E-65)	5.83E-42 (3.62E-42)	8.04E-70 (5.08E-31)	1.21E-74 (3.21E-74)
f_2	200000	3.21E-51 (6.57E-51)	1.34E-49 (6.12E-49)	3.03E-31 (1.15E-31)	5.01E-47 (4.58E-47)	8.66E-61 (2.63E-60)
f_3	500000	8.13E-27 (2.60E-26)	5.05E-28 (2.23E-27)	4.53E+01 (1.55E+01)	1.19E-03 (9.23E-04)	3.71E-57 (1.57E-56)
f_4	2000000	2.28E-29 (3.84E-29)	6.38E-01 (1.46E+00)	1.76E+01 (5.45E+00)	4.78E-01 (1.30E+00)	1.75E+00 (1.98E+00)
f_5	150000	0.00E+00 (0.00E+00)	0.00E+00 (0.00E+00)	0.00E+00 (0.00E+00)	0.00E+00 (0.00E+00)	2.00E+00 (2.73E+00)
f_6	300000	2.88E-03 (1.17E-03)	3.09E-03 (1.49E-03)	4.89E-03 (1.01E-03)	1.75E-03 (5.80E-04)	6.51E-03 (2.59E-03)
f_7	900000	-12569.49 (1.82E-12)	-12569.49 (1.82E-12)	-12569.49 (1.82E-12)	-11599.82 (4.83E+02)	-6942.89 (3.89E+02)
f_8	500000	0.00E+00 (0.00E+00)	7.16E-01 (9.13E-01)	7.96E-01 (7.45E-01)	2.44E+01 (5.91E+00)	9.01E+01 (1.16E+01)
f_9	200000	5.99E-15 (1.77E-15)	5.06E-01 (6.50E-01)	8.69E-15 (1.60E-15)	4.14E-15 (0.00E+00)	1.40E+00 (6.95E-01)
f_{10}	200000	0.00E+00 (0.00E+00)	0.00E+00 (0.00E+00)	0.00E+00 (0.00E+00)	0.00E+00 (0.00E+00)	7.88E-03 (1.93E-02)
f_{11}	150000	1.57E-32 (2.74E-48)	1.74E-32 (5.21E-33)	1.64E-32 (3.79E-33)	1.09E-21 (5.33E-21)	8.07E-01 (1.38E+00)
f_{12}	150000	1.35E-32 (5.47E-48)	1.38E-32 (1.02E-33)	1.35E-32 (5.47E-48)	1.35E-32 (5.47E-48)	6.61E-02 (3.13E-01)

The effect of individual-level parameter control can be verified by a comparison between ADE and ADE-p only. The results can be found in the first two columns of Table 12. One can observe that the ADE achieves solutions with slightly higher accuracy than ADE-p only on the unimodal functions. Moreover, ADE also has better global search ability to escape from local optima on the multimodal functions f_8 and f_9. The better performance of ADE should be due to the diversified parameter values brought by the individual-level parameter control.

4.5 Properties of F and CR of ADE

From the experimental results in Table 12, we observe that DE/lbest/1 performs better on $f_1 - f_3$ when it is assigned a smaller value of CR, while a larger value of CR is more beneficial to f_7, f_8, and f_{10}. Therefore, we can further analyze the property of CR value in ADE on these six functions to further check the effectiveness of parameter adaptation. We divide the range of population-level parameter CR_p [0, 1] into ten intervals with equal lengths. In each generation, the value of CR_p is recorded. After a run of the ADE algorithm on a certain function, we compute the count of the CR_p value within each interval. Figure 4 shows these counts on each test function. For the unimodal functions $f_1 - f_3$, we find that the counts of CR_p keep increasing as the value of CR_p increases. On the contrary, for the multimodal functions f_7, f_8, and f_{10}, the counts of CR_p decrease in general with the value of CR_p, as we expected.

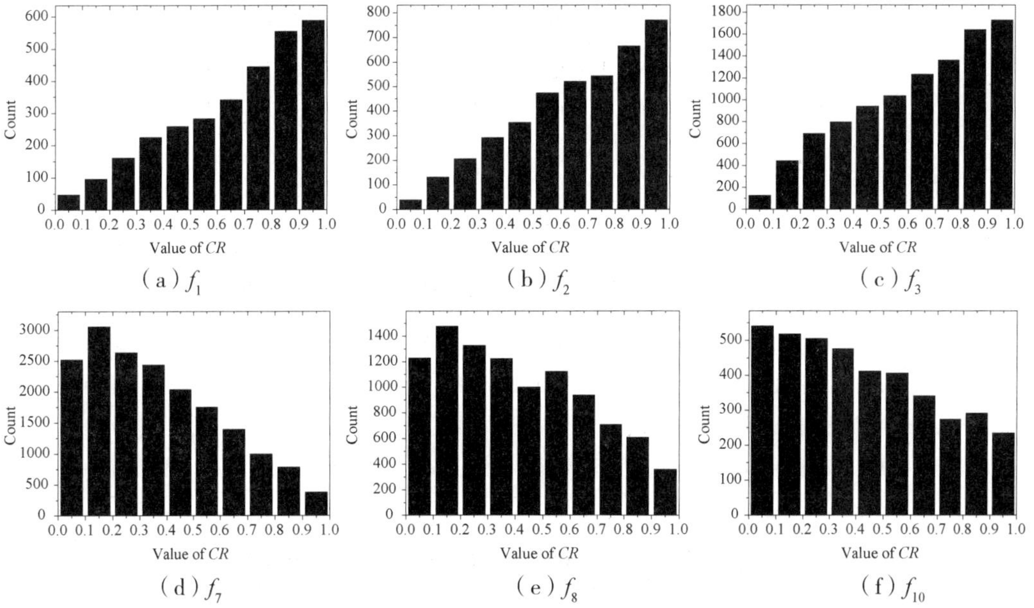

(a) f_1 (b) f_2 (c) f_3

(d) f_7 (e) f_8 (f) f_{10}

Figure 4 Counts of different *CR* values during the evolutionary process of ADE on six benchmark functions

In addition, we show the corresponding results of F_p in Figure 5. It can be seen that F_p exhibits an opposite property of CR_p. Relatively small values of F_p are beneficial to finding solutions with high accuracy for unimodal functions. Conversely, relatively large values of F_p can help alleviating premature convergence for multimodal functions. Based on the above observation, it can be concluded that ADE can adapt the parameter effectively to meet the needs of differentoptimization problems.

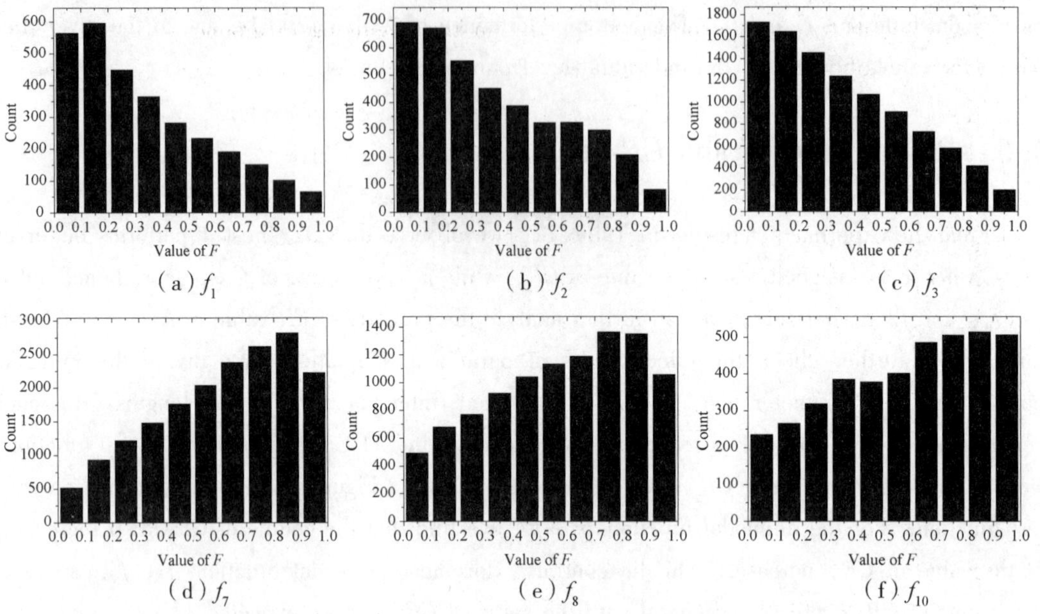

Figure 5 Counts of different F values during the evolutionary process of ADE on six benchmark functions

4.6 Search behavior of ADE

The search behavior of ADE is compared with that of DE/lbest/1 ($F=0.5$, $CR=0.9$) on three unimodal functions f_1-f_3 and three multimodal functions f_7-f_9. Figure 6 and Figure 7 illustrate the results of DE/lbest/1 and ADE, respectively, based on the data of a typical run. In the figures, the X-axis represents the number of generations and the Y-axis represents the cumulative counts of optimization states (i.e., exploration state and exploitation state) the algorithm has been in. The search behavior of algorithm can be analyzed by comparing these two cumulative counts during the evolution. According to Figure 6, the cumulative count of the exploitation states is larger than that of the exploration states throughout the evolutionary process on both unimodal and multimodal functions. This is because DE/lbest/1 utilizes a greedy mutation strategy to some degree without parameter adaptation. The population is attracted by some locally best individuals, and thus the exploitation state always dominates the exploration state. Such a search behavior is good for unimodal functions but it may lead to premature convergence for complex multimodal functions. According to Figure 7, the search behavior of ADE on unimodal functions is similar to that of DE/lbest/1. The curve of the exploitation state is always beyond that of the exploration state. Furthermore, the gap between these two curves is larger than that of Figure 6, which is beneficial to obtaining solutions with higher accuracy for unimodal functions. However, the search behavior of ADE is quite different from that of DE/lbest/1 on the three multimodal functions. The cumulative count of exploitation states is not always larger than that of the exploration states, but they dominate each other alternately during the evolutionary process. We take f_9 for example. The cumulative count of exploitation states increases faster than that of exploration states from the beginning to around 1500 generation. After that, this trend changes to the opposite, i. e. the exploration states begins to dominate the exploitation states. Finally, the cumulative count of exploration states overtakes that of exploitation states in around 3000 generation. For multimodal functions, it is important for the algorithm to keep exploring new regions of the search space and hence being trapped in local optima can be avoided. The ADE performs such a search behavior as we expected due to the parameter adaptation, which adjusts the parameters to suitable values that allow the algorithm to perform more explorative behavior.

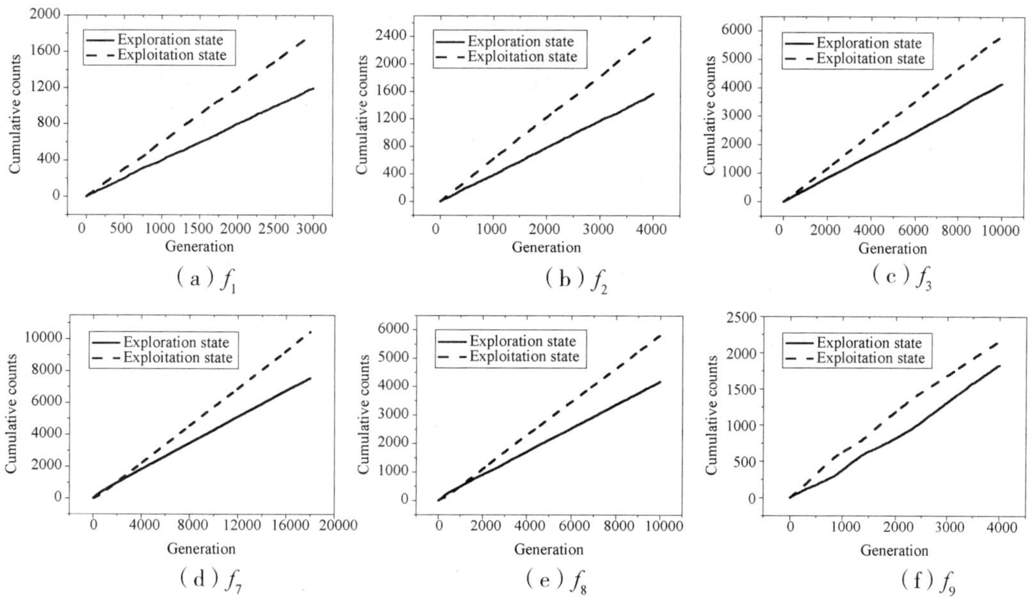

Figure 6 Cumulative counts of exploration and exploitation states derived from DE/lbest/1 versus the number of generations on six benchmark functions

4.7 Sensitivities to population parameters

As mentioned in Section Ⅲ-A, the mutation strategy of ADE is designed to achieve a better balance between exploration and exploitation. The best vector involved in mutation is selected from its respective group of vectors. Thus, the performance of ADE maybe sensitive to the selected population size and the number of groups the population divided into. If the population size is large and the number of groups is small, which means the best vector is selected from a large group of individuals, the mutation strategy would be relatively greedy. On the contrary, if

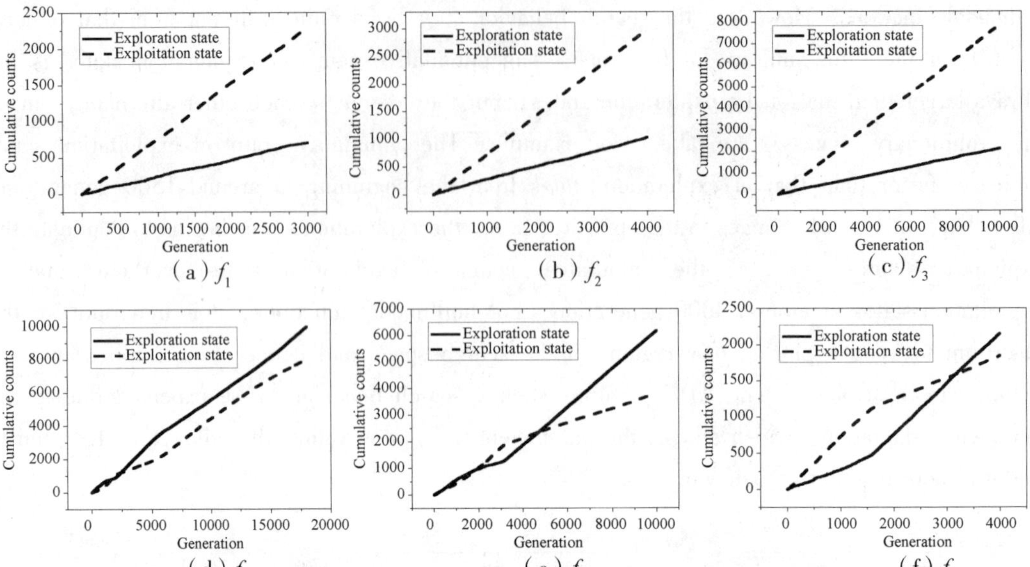

(a) f_1 (b) f_2 (c) f_3 (d) f_7 (e) f_8 (f) f_9

Figure 7 Cumulative counts of exploration and exploitation states derived from ADE versus the number of generations on six benchmark functions

the best vector is selected from a small group of individuals and the number of groups is large, then the mutation strategy becomes relatively diverse. In order to investigate the sensitivity of ADE to the combination of the population size and the number of groups, we compare ADE with different values of these two parameters. The ADE algorithm with a population size of 50 and 10 groups, for example, is denoted as ADE – p50g10. Table 13 reports the experimental results on $f_1 - f_{12}$ with $D = 30$. In general, for the simple unimodal functions like $f_1 - f_3$, using a smaller population size and a smaller number of groups is more helpful to get solutions with high accuracy. However, such a setting suffers from frequent premature convergence on multimodal functions. On the contrary, for multimodal functions, using a larger population size and a larger number of groups is better for maintaining diversity and preventing premature convergence. In addition, it can be observed that when the number of groups is set to 10, the performance of ADE is not so sensitive to the population size. Overall, a population size of 50 and dividing the population into 10 groups is a suitable combination to balance the performance on both unimodal and multimodal functions.

Table 13 ADE with different population parameterss

Fun.	FEs	ADE – p50g10 Mean (Std Dev)	ADE – p100g10 Mean (Std Dev)	ADE – p50g5 Mean (Std Dev)	ADE – p100g5 Mean (Std Dev)
f_1	150000	1.49E – 70 (3.95E – 70)	1.40E – 55 (2.68E – 55)	6.66E – 99 (1.63E – 98)	1.01E – 80 (3.80E – 80)
f_2	200000	3.21E – 51 (6.57E – 51)	4.68E – 39 (5.65E – 39)	8.61E – 80 (1.61E – 79)	4.78E – 60 (1.45E – 59)

Continue Table 13

Fun.	FEs	ADE - p50g10 Mean (Std Dev)	ADE - p100g10 Mean (Std Dev)	ADE - p50g5 Mean (Std Dev)	ADE - p100g5 Mean (Std Dev)
f_3	500000	8.13E-27 (2.60E-26)	3.04E-22 (4.99E-22)	5.20E-37 (1.74E-36)	6.93E-31 (1.72E-30)
f_4	2000000	2.28E-29 (3.84E-29)	1.59E-01 (7.81E-01)	6.38E-01 (1.46E+00)	1.12E+00 (1.79E+00)
f_5	150000	0.00E+00 (0.00E+00)	0.00E+00 (0.00E+00)	1.60E+00 (1.96E+00)	1.28E+00 (3.94E+00)
f_6	300000	2.88E-03 (1.17E-03)	2.88E-03 (1.13E-03)	4.69E-03 (2.23E-03)	2.86E-03 (9.38E-04)
f_7	900000	-12569.49 (1.82E-12)	-12569.49 (1.82E-12)	-12440.78 (1.71E+02)	-12526.85 (8.12E+01)
f_8	500000	0.00E+00 (0.00E+00)	0.00E+00 (0.00E+00)	2.55E+00 (1.59E+00)	1.95E+00 (1.90E+00)
f_9	200000	5.99E-15 (1.77E-15)	4.71E-15 (1.30E-15)	1.34E+00 (1.18E+00)	2.37E-01 (5.94E-01)
f_{10}	200000	0.00E+00 (0.00E+00)	0.00E+00 (0.00E+00)	1.00E-02 (1.58E-02)	6.39E-03 (1.19E-02)
f_{11}	150000	1.57E-32 (2.74E-48)	1.57E-32 (2.74E-48)	3.32E-02 (1.24E-01)	3.74E-02 (1.64E-01)
f_{12}	150000	1.35E-32 (5.47E-48)	1.35E-32 (5.47E-48)	8.79E-04 (2.98E-03)	1.43E-32 (2.15E-33)

4.8 Results on real-world optimization problems

The performance of the ADE is further tested on three real-world optimization problems from the IEEE CEC 2011 competition.[46] The three test problems are Parameter Estimation for Frequency-Modulated Sound Waves (P1), Lennard-Jones Potential Problem (P2), and Bifunctional Catalyst Blend Optimal Control Problem (P3). More details of these problems can be found in [46].

Table 14 compares the mean and standard deviation of the final results over 25 runs of the five DE variants. The algorithms are executed for 50000, 100000, and 150000 FEs respectively on all the problems. From Table 14, it can be noted that ADE remains a competitive approach among the five DE variants. In the case of problem P1, ADE significantly outperforms the other four DE variants. JADE performs the best on problem P2 and ADE is the second best. For problem P3, all the five DE variants present similar results without significant difference. These observations demonstrate that the proposed ADE has some potential for solving real-world optimization problems.

Table 14 Comparison between ADE and four state-of-the-art DE variants on three real-world optimization problems

Problem	FEs	ADE	CoDE	JADE	jDE	SaDE
		Mean (Std Dev)	Mean (Std Dev)	Mean (Std Dev)	Mean (Std Dev)	Mean (Std Dev)
P1	50000	8.19E-02 (1.87E-01)	1.18E+00† (3.25E+00)	3.56E+00† (3.53E+00)	1.10E+01† (3.79E+00)	9.57E+00† (5.32E+00)
	100000	1.36E-03 (5.18E-03)	9.46E-01† (3.28E+00)	7.02E-01† (9.36E-01)	3.09E+00† (2.56E+00)	6.49E-01† (3.73E+00)
	150000	4.12E-04 (1.76E-03)	8.13E-01† (2.82E+00)	5.11E-01† (1.71E+00)	2.60E-01† (6.38E-01)	4.92E-01† (2.46E+00)
P2	50000	-1.55E+01 (2.34E+00)	-1.16E+01† (1.12E+00)	-1.86E+01† (1.06E+00)	-1.33E+01† (1.89E+00)	-1.05E+01† (7.92E-01)
	100000	-1.90E+01 (2.50E+00)	-1.48E+01† (1.20E+00)	-2.22E+01† (9.42E-01)	-1.75E+01† (1.45E+00)	-1.29E+01† (1.14E+00)
	150000	-2.20E+01 (1.99E+00)	-1.85E+01† (2.79E+00)	-2.39E+01† (7.25E-01)	-1.98E+01† (1.08E+00)	-1.43E+01† (1.06E+00)
P3	50000	1.15E-05 (1.26E-19)	1.15E-05 (2.38E-19)	1.15E-05 (1.64E-19)	1.15E-05 (2.17E-19)	1.15E-05 (1.46E-19)
	100000	1.15E-05 (1.46E-19)	1.15E-05 (2.49E-19)	1.15E-05 (1.84E-19)	1.15E-05 (1.34E-19)	1.15E-05 (2.70E-19)
	150000	1.15E-05 (1.24E-19)	1.15E-05 (1.45E-19)	1.15E-05 (1.47E-19)	1.15E-05 (1.32E-19)	1.15E-05 (2.38E-19)

† The difference between the results of ADE and the corresponding algorithm is signficant at $\alpha = 0.05$ by Wilcoxon's rank sum test.

4.9 Discussion

To improve the efficiency and robustness of DE, we propose a greedy mutation strategy DE/lbest/1 and a two-level parameter adaptation scheme for DE. Experiments are extensively conducted on 33 benchmark functions and three real-world optimization problems. From the experimental results, the strengths and weaknesses of the proposed ADE can be summarized as follows.

1) In the case of unimodal functions, the overall performance of ADE is similar to that of JADE and SaDE, but better than CoDE and jDE. However, ADE is beaten by the classic DE/

best/1 on three simple unimodal functions due to the high greediness degree of the latter. Importantly, only ADE can achieve 100% success rates on all these functions.

2) In the cases of multimodal functions and hybrid composition functions, ADE, JADE, and SaDE converge faster than CoDE and jDE in general. CoDE and jDE are more robust than JADE and SaDE in some cases since the formers utilize more diverse mutation strategies. Note that ADE still shows the most reliable performance in all cases in spite of its greedy DE/lbest/1 mutation strategy. Also, ADE achieves the best final accuracy results on most of these functions.

3) The ranks of ADE in the success rates and search speed comparison tables may be close to that of its competitor in some instances. For example, the average ranks of ADE and JADE are 2 and 2. 1 respectively in Table 8. It is found that the small average rank of JADE largely stems from its fast search speed on most functions in this group. On the other hand, in the case of ADE both algorithm reliability (indicated by success rate) and search speed contribute to the small average rank. A close inspection of Table 8 indicates that JADE converges fastest for the optimization of functions $f_{26}-f_{33}$. ADE is beaten by JADE on these functions but still converges second fastest. However, JADE shows the worst performance in terms of reliability on the other three functions $f_{23}-f_{25}$. On the contrary, ADE achieves the highest success rates on all test functions. Moreover, when the problem dimension increases to 100, the difference between the average rank of ADE and that of JADE becomes more obvious. The advantage of ADE is that it benefits from fast convergence without sacrificing its robustness.

4) Regarding the results of real-world problems, a close inspection of Table 14 reveals that ADE is the only one that may provide consistent good performance on all test problems. Although ADE is beaten by JADE on problem P2, it is still the second best among the five DE variants. Conversely, CoDE, jDE, and SaDE show relatively poor or fair performance on both problems P1 and P2. Even for JADE which is the best on problem P2, it performs the second worst on problem P1 in terms of final accuracy. Since the problem characteristics are usually not known *a priori* when solving real-world problems, it should be a good choice to use an algorithm like ADE which is expected to perform favorably on problems with various characteristics.

5) Overall, by combining the DE/lbest/1 mutation strategy with the two-level parameter adaptation scheme, ADE is efficient in terms of solution quality and search speed, while maintaining the algorithm reliability at a high level.

5 Conclusion

In this paper, a new DE variant called ADE has been proposed. The ADE algorithm is characterized by a novel mutation strategy DE/lbest/1 and an adaptive parameter control strategy. The DE/lbest/1 strategy utilizes the information of several locally best solutions instead of the single globally best solution used in the classic DE/best/1. Such a mutation strategy is helpful for balancing the fast convergence and population diversity of the algorithm. Two levels of parameters, i. e. , population-level and individual-level parameters, have been introduced into the parameter adaptation scheme of ADE. The population-level parameters are first controlled based on an optimization state estimation. Then, the individual-level parameters for each individual are generated by adjusting the population-level parameters, according to the individual fitness rank and its distance rank from the best individual.

We have tested ADE on a suite of benchmark functions and three real-world optimization problems. The results show that ADE exhibits appropriate search behavior for both unimodal and multimodal problems. The performance of ADE is compared with four state-of-the-art DE variants, i. e. CoDE, JADE, jDE, and SaDE. It can be concluded that ADE performs better than, or at least comparably to the other DE variants in terms of solution quality, convergence speed, and algorithm reliability. However, ADE cannot perform the best for all kinds of optimization problems. For example, the DE/best/1 obtains solutions with higher accuracy than ADE on three simple unimodal problems due to the greediness of DE/best/1, which can be observed from Table 11. ADE only can achieve a balanced performance for different kinds of optimization problems. In addition, the effects of ADE components, parameter properties of ADE, and parameter sensitivity of ADE have been studied.

For future work, we will extend the ADE algorithm to solving other complex optimization problems such as multi-objective and dynamic optimization problems, etc. In addition, we can regard the proposed two-level parameter adaptation strategy as a general two-level parameter control framework and apply it to other EAs.

Acknowledgment

The authors would like to thank the associate editor, the anonymous reviewers, and Prof. Y. -H. Shi for their valuable comments and suggestions on this paper.

References

[1] Storn R, Price K. Differential Evolution—A Simple and Efficient Adaptive Scheme for Global Optimization Over Continuous Spaces [J]. Journal of Global Optimization, 1995, 11 (4): 341 -359.

[2] Storn R, Price K. Differential Evolution—A Simple and Efficient Heuristic for Global Optimization over Continuous Spaces [J]. Journal of Global Optimization, 1997, 11 (4): 341 -359.

[3] Price K, Storn R, Lampinen J. Differential Evolution: A Practical Approach to Global Optimization [M]. Berlin: Springer Science & Business Media, 2006.

[4] Das S, Suganthan P N. Differential Evolution: A Survey of the State-of-the-Art [J]. Evolutionary Computation, IEEE Transactions on, 2011, 15 (1): 4 -31.

[5] Zhao S Z, Suganthan P N, Das S. Self-Adaptive Differential Evolution with Multi-Trajectory Search for Large-Scale Optimization [J]. Soft Computing, 2011, 15 (11): 2175 -2185.

[6] Halder U, Das S, Maity D. A Cluster-Based Differential Evolution Algorithm with External Archive for Optimization in Dynamic Environments [J]. Cybernetics, IEEE Transactions on, 2013, 43 (3): 881 -897.

[7] Wang Y, Cai Z. Combining Multiobjective Optimization with Differential Evolution to Solve Constrained Optimization Problems [J]. Evolutionary Computation, IEEE Transactions on, 2012, 16 (1): 117 -134.

[8] Qu B Y, Suganthan P N, Liang J J. Differential Evolution with Neighborhood Mutation for Multimodal Optimization [J].

Evolutionary Computation, IEEE Transactions on, 2012, 16 (5): 601 -614.

[9] Basak A, Das S, Tan K C. Multimodal Optimization Using a Biobjective Differential Evolution Algorithm Enhanced with Mean Distance-Based Selection [J]. Evolutionary Computation, IEEE Transactions on, 2013, 17 (5): 666 -685.

[10] Storn R. Differential Evolution Design of an IIR-Filter [C] // Evolutionary Computation. Proceedings of IEEE International Conference on, IEEE, 1996: 268 -273.

[11] Joshi R, Sanderson A C. Minimal Representation Multisensor Fusion Using Differential Evolution [J]. Systems, Man and Cybernetics, Part A: Systems and Humans, IEEE Transactions on, 1999, 29 (1): 63 -76.

[12] Sengupta S, Das S, Nasir M, et al. An Evolutionary Multi-Objective Sleep-Scheduling Scheme for Differentiated Coverage in Wireless Sensor Networks [J]. Systems, Man, and Cybernetics, Part C: Applications and Reviews, IEEE Transactions on, 2012, 42 (6): 1093 -1102.

[13] Ghosh S, Das S, Vasilakos A V, et al. On Convergence of Differential Evolution over a Class of Continuous Functions with Unique Global Optimum [J]. Systems, Man, and Cybernetics, Part B: Cybernetics, IEEE Transactions on, 2012, 42 (1): 107 -124.

[14] Dasgupta S, Das S, Biswas A, et al. On Stability and Convergence of the Population-Dynamics in Differential Evolution [J]. Ai Communications, 2009, 22 (1): 1.

[15] Gämperle R, Müller S D, Koumoutsakos P. A Parameter Study for Differential Evolution [J]. Advances in Intelligent Systems, Fuzzy Systems, Evolutionary Computation, 2002, 10: 293 -298.

[16] Ronkkonen J, Kukkonen S, Price K V. Real-Parameter Optimization with Differential Evolution [C] // Proc IEEE CEC, 2005, 1: 506 -513.

[17] Sutton A M, Lunacek M, Whitley L D. Differential Evolution and Non-Separability: Using Selective Pressure to Focus Search [C] // Proceedings of the 9th Annual Conference on Genetic and Evolutionary Computation. ACM, 2007: 1428 -1435.

[18] Das S, Konar A, Chakraborty U K. Two Improved Differential Evolution Schemes for Faster Global Search [C] // Proceedings of the 7th Annual Conference on Genetic and Evolutionary Computation. ACM, 2005: 991 -998.

[19] Ali M M, Törn A. Population Set-Based Global Optimization Algorithms: Some Modifications and Numerical Studies [J]. Computers & Operations Research, 2004, 31 (10): 1703 -1725.

[20] Liu J, Lampinen J. A Fuzzy Adaptive Differential Evolution Algorithm [J]. Soft Computing, 2005, 9 (6): 448 -462.

[21] Zaharie D. Control of Population Diversity and Adaptation in Differential Evolution Algorithms [C] //Proc of MENDEL, 2003, 9: 41 -46.

[22] Zaharie D, Petcu D. Adaptive Pareto Differential Evolution and Its Parallelization [M] // Parallel Processing and Applied Mathematics. Springer Berlin Heidelberg, 2004: 261 -268.

[23] Teo J. Exploring Dynamic Self-Adaptive Populations in Differential Evolution [J]. Soft Computing, 2006, 10 (8): 673 -686.

[24] Brest J, Greiner S, Boškovié B, et al. Self-Adapting Control Parameters in Differential Evolution: A Comparative Study on Numerical Benchmark Problems [J]. Evolutionary Computation, IEEE Transactions on, 2006, 10 (6): 646 -657.

[25] Qin A K, Huang V L, Suganthan P N. Differential Evolution Algorithm with Strategy Adaptation for Global Numerical Optimization [J]. Evolutionary Computation, IEEE Transactions on, 2009, 13 (2): 398 -417.

[26] Zhang J, Sanderson A C. JADE: Adaptive Differential Evolution with Optional External Archive [J]. Evolutionary Computation, IEEE Transactions on, 2009, 13 (5): 945 -958.

[27] Gong W, Cai Z, Ling C X, et al. Enhanced Differential Evolution with Adaptive Strategies for Numerical Optimization [J]. Systems, Man, and Cybernetics, Part B: Cybernetics, IEEE Transactions on, 2011, 41 (2): 397 -413.

[28] Wang Y, Cai Z, Zhang Q. Differential Evolution with Composite Trial Vector Generation Strategies and Control Parameters [J]. Evolutionary Computation, IEEE Transactions on, 2011, 15 (1): 55 -66.

[29] Zhong Y, Zhang L. Remote Sensing Image Subpixel Mapping Based on Adaptive Differential Evolution [J]. Systems, Man, and Cybernetics, Part B: Cybernetics, IEEE Transactions on, 2012, 42 (5): 1306 -1329.

[30] Ghosh A, Das S, Chowdhury A, et al. An Improved Differential Evolution Algorithm with Fitness-Based Adaptation of the Control Parameters [J]. Information Sciences, 2011, 181 (18): 3749 - 3765.

[31] Yu W, Zhang J. Adaptive Differential Evolution with Optimization State Estimation [C] //Proceedings of the 14th Annual Conference on Genetic and Evolutionary Computation. ACM, 2012: 1285 - 1292.

[32] Price K V. An Introduction to Differential Evolution [C] //New Ideas in Optimization. McGraw-Hill Ltd, UK, 1999: 79 - 108.

[33] Fan H Y, Lampinen J. A Trigonometric Mutation Operation to Differential Evolution [J]. Journal of Global Optimization, 2003, 27 (1): 105 - 129.

[34] Kaelo P, Ali M M. Differential Evolution Algorithms Using Hybrid Mutation [J]. Computational Optimization and Applications, 2007, 37 (2): 231 - 246.

[35] Wang H, Rahnamayan S, Sun H, et al. Gaussian Bare-Bones Differential Evolution [J]. Cybernetics, IEEE Transactions on, 2013, 43 (2): 634 - 647.

[36] Das S, Abraham A, Chakraborty U K, et al. Differential Evolution Using a Neighborhood-Based Mutation Operator [J]. Evolutionary Computation, IEEE Transactions on, 2009, 13 (3): 526 - 553.

[37] Islam S M, Das S, Ghosh S, et al. An Adaptive Differential Evolution Algorithm with Novel Mutation and Crossover Strategies for Global Numerical Optimization [J]. Systems, Man, and Cybernetics, Part B: Cybernetics, IEEE Transactions on, 2012, 42 (2): 482 - 500.

[38] Epitropakis M G, Tasoulis D K, Pavlidis N G, et al. Enhancing Differential Evolution Utilizing Proximity-Based Mutation Operators [J]. Evolutionary Computation, IEEE Transactions on, 2011, 15 (1): 99 - 119.

[39] Gong W, Cai Z. Differential Evolution with Ranking-Based Mutation Operators [J]. Cybernetics, IEEE Transactions on, 2013, 43 (6): 2066 - 2081.

[40] Cai Y, Wang J. Differential Evolution with Neighborhood and Direction Information for Numerical Optimization [J]. Cybernetics, IEEE Transactions on, 2013, 43 (6): 2202 - 2215.

[41] Mezura-Montes E, Velázquez-Reyes J, Coello C A. A Comparative Study of Differential Evolution Variants for Global Optimization [C] //Proceedings of the 8th Annual Conference on Genetic and Evolutionary Computation. ACM, 2006: 485 - 492.

[42] Yao X, Liu Y, Lin G. Evolutionary Programming Made Faster [J]. Evolutionary Computation, IEEE Transactions on, 1999, 3 (2): 82 - 102.

[43] Suganthan P N, Hansen N, Liang J J, et al. Problem Definitions and Evaluation Criteria for the CEC 2005 Special Session on Real-Parameter Optimization [R]. Kan GAL Report, 2005.

[44] Derrac J, García S, Molina D, et al. A Practical Tutorial on the Use of Nonparametric Statistical Tests as a Methodology for Comparing Evolutionary and Swarm Intelligence Algorithms [J]. Swarm and Evolutionary Computation, 2011, 1 (1): 3 - 18.

[45] Shang Y W, Qiu Y H. A Note on the Extended Rosenbrock Function [J]. Evolutionary Computation, 2006, 14 (1): 119 - 126.

[46] Das S, Suganthan P N. Problem Definitions and Evaluation Criteria for CEC 2011 Competition on Testing Evolutionary Algorithms on Real World Optimization Problems [R]. Jadavpur University, Nanyang Technological University, Kolkata, 2010.